SELF-UNDERSTANDING AND LIFEWORLD

SELF-UNDERSTANDING AND LIFEWORLD

BASIC TRAITS OF A PHENOMENOLOGICAL HERMENEUTICS

HANS-HELMUTH GANDER

TRANSLATED BY
RYAN DRAKE AND JOSHUA RAYMAN

INDIANA UNIVERSITY PRESS

This book is a publication of

Indiana University Press
Office of Scholarly Publishing
Herman B Wells Library 350
1320 East 10th Street
Bloomington, Indiana 47405 USA
iupress.indiana.edu

Published in German as Hans-Helmuth Gander, *Selbstverständnis und Lebenswelt*
© 2001 by Vittorio Klostermann GmbH, Frankfurt am Main
English translation © 2017 by Indiana University Press

The paper used in this publication meets the minimum requirements of
the American National Standard for Information Sciences—Permanence
of Paper for Printed Library Materials, ANSI Z39.48–1992.

Manufactured in the United States of America

Library of Congress Cataloging-in-Publication Data

Names: Gander, Hans-Helmuth, 1954- author.
Title: Self-understanding and lifeworld : basic traits of a
    phenomenological hermeneutics / Hans-Helmuth Gander ;
    translated by Ryan Drake and Joshua Rayman.
Other titles: Selbstverst?andnis und Lebenswelt. English
Description: 1st [edition]. | Bloomington : Indiana University Press, 2017. | Series:
    Studies in Continental thought | Includes bibliographical references and index.
Identifiers: LCCN 2017013831 (print) | LCCN 2017030883 (ebook) | ISBN
    9780253026071 (e-book) | ISBN 9780253025555 (cloth : alk. paper)
Subjects: LCSH: Husserl, Edmund, 1859-1938. | Heidegger, Martin, 1889-1976. |
    Hermeneutics—History. | Phenomenology—History. | Life—History.
Classification: LCC B3279.H94 (ebook) | LCC B3279.
    H94 G3613 2017 (print) | DDC 193—dc23
LC record available at https://lccn.loc.gov/2017013831

1 2 3 4 5   22 21 20 19 18 17

It is a rule of life that we can and must learn from all people. There are serious things in life that we can pick up from charlatans and bandits; there are philosophical insights that make fools of us; there are lessons in consistency and adherence to law that surface by chance and originate from chance. Everything lies resolved in all things.

Fernando Pessoa

Work in philosophy—in many ways like work in architecture—is actually more like work on oneself. On one's own perception. On how one sees things. (And what one demands from them).

Ludwig Wittgenstein

Only he who understands this art of existing, treating in his acting the particular thing apprehended as the utterly unique and being just as clear about the finitude of his acting, only he understands finite existence and can hope to complete something in it.

Martin Heidegger

CONTENTS

INTRODUCTION

PART ONE

IN THE NETWORK OF TEXTS: TOWARD THE PERSPECTIVE CHARACTER OF UNDERSTANDING

PART TWO

I AND WORLD: THE QUESTION CONCERNING
THE GROUND OF PHILOSOPHY

CHAPTER ONE

On the Search for the Certainty of the 'I'

CHAPTER TWO

*On Life in Lifeworlds: Critical Considerations of Husserl's
Phenomenology of the Lifeworld*

PART THREE

SELF-UNDERSTANDING AND THE HISTORICAL WORLD:
BASIC TRAITS OF A HERMENEUTICAL ONTOLOGY
OF FACTICITY

CHAPTER ONE

*The Hermeneutical Turn: Heidegger's Critical Dialogue with
Husserlian Phenomenology*

TRANSLATORS' INTRODUCTION

In *Self-Understanding and Lifeworld: Basic Traits of a Phenomenological Hermeneutics*, Hans-Helmuth Gander's Gadamerian orientation leads him to think seriously about what is typically ignored or neglected in the current state of phenomenology, namely, our hermeneutic experience of reading. Phenomenological inquiry is most often directed to our experience of the world, to sense experiences, to questions of reality and knowledge, and to a lesser extent to thinking and understanding. But when we, as philosophers trained in or engaged with the continental tradition, are steeped so heavily in the reading of texts, this experience of reading demands its own proper explication as an interpretive mode of letting the phenomena show themselves in themselves as they are, in Heidegger's terminology. Gander's text is an attempt to develop a phenomenological hermeneutics out of an examination of reading. He locates Heidegger's turn from Husserl, which he dates back almost a decade prior to *Being and Time,* in precisely this turn to hermeneutics. In Gander's hands, the pursuit of a phenomenological hermeneutics constitutes an attempt to uncover the prior or "fore-" structure of the interpretation of sense or meaning in every act of reading. From this complex forestructure (for which Gander identifies three constitutive parts) that enables human experience, he goes on to uncover the hermeneutical problems hitherto foreclosed by the dominant model of the Cartesian subject, whereby the nature of the 'I' cannot be distinguished rigorously from the world. World, for Gander, is lifeworld. But this position differs from that of Husserl, since the self cannot be abstracted from this lifeworld and it involves the hermeneutical exposition of the prior relations of the self within the lifeworld. The concepts that Gander articulates from this mode of analysis involve experience, particularly the experience of wonder, seen through the lens of the hermeneutics of facticity. The task of setting forth self and world is never to be separated from a lifeworldly self-understanding that is historical and that involves the significance of the self-world. For this reason, while drawing so much from Heidegger, Gander nonetheless faults his work for failing to engage as critically with its own time as did the work of Kant, Kierkegaard, Nietzsche, and others. Thus, where Heidegger places the task of the destruction of the history of ontology very early in *Being and Time* (§ 6), Gander closes with this task of phenomenological destruction of the tradition (historical critique) as something essentially focused on the enlightenment of the present, such that the historical character of human existence entails that we not close our eyes to the significance of what is unfolding before them.

In this project the reader is rewarded by Gander's sustained and idiosyncratic focus on the early Heidegger, which in his thinking is not a means of once again reducing Heidegger's work entirely to the status of mere preparatory drafts, revisions, and stages on the way to the "mature" thought of *Being and Time,* but rather a body of work considered in its own right. In particular, Gander shows us that we must go all the way back to Heidegger's 1919 lectures in order to grasp the appearance and development of what he terms "phenomenological hermeneutics," which to no small degree sets out and guides the collection of considerations that compose the philosophical heart of Gander's study.

While Heidegger enjoys a privileged position in this study, a primary virtue of Gander's text is that it sets its sights on locating and bridging the differences within the phenomenological-hermeneutical triad of Edmund Husserl, Martin Heidegger, and Hans-Georg Gadamer. In so doing, Gander seeks to constitute something novel, forging a unique synthesis of their work wherein underlying and overlapping difficulties can be brought to light and overcome. And as head of the Husserl Archive at Freiburg University and a former editor of Heidegger's *Gesamtausgabe* (during which time he was able to conduct numerous conversations with Gadamer), he undertakes this project from a distinct position of expert knowledge of the textual traditions in which these thinkers are involved. Indeed, his exceptionally thorough footnotes regarding German scholarly treatments of the subject will be immensely valuable for an English-speaking audience unfamiliar with so much of this very careful work.

Just as valuable, as we hope to demonstrate through our translation, is the form of Gander's composition itself, the specific expressive language that he has developed in order to carry out a through phenomenological hermeneutics. To take a single example, he writes:

Hermeneutisch betrachtet handelt es sich um die Anerkennung der in der verstehend auslegend erfahrenen Differenz der Bedeutlichsamkeiten sich ereignenden Pluralität des in sich von Grund auf pluralisierten Lebenswelt—als Durchdringungszusammenhanges der so genannten Sorgenswelten, wobei die

> *Erfahrung auf die Offenheit des in sich je schon Differentiellseins von Leben und Welt verweist.*

> Taken hermeneutically, it is a matter of the recognition of the manifest plurality appropriating itself within the interpretively and understandingly experienced difference of significance, a plurality of fundamentally varied lifeworldly contexts as interpenetrating contexts in what [Heidegger] calls worlds of care, whereby experience refers to the openness within the always already differential being of life and world in itself.

Here there is a gap of eleven words between recognition and that of which it is the recognition (plurality). The plurality is itself *in* the act of *Ereignis* of an eventlike appropriation of itself that involves retreating ten words, a combined action of understanding and interpreting, or more literally "laying out" (setting elements apart from one another for the sake of analysis and contextualization, as opposed to a more customary notion of interpretation—saying what something is intended to mean in a particular context), a difference of the plural significances and meanings, a difference that is itself experienced. And Gander will go on in this same sentence to articulate how the plurality is grounded and related to lifeworld, interpenetrated in context, and related to worlds of care, such that experience, he argues, refers itself to the self-differentiating openness between life and world. In this one sentence, then, he wants to argue that hermeneutics regards an entire set of operations as occurring simultaneously in our experience, involving plurality and difference, openness (*Dasein*), life and the lifeworld, conscious recognition, meaning or significance, and interpenetrating contexts. The difficulty of translating and reading Gander derives, then, not merely from a way of using language that is inordinately complicated, but more deeply from using language to convey the interpenetration of so many different operations all at once in our act of experiencing-understanding-interpreting.

It might be said that contemporary German academic prose represents an intensification of Kantian form and style, with the added armor of hundreds of footnotes. While Kant's work remains legendary in Germany for the staggering length of his sentence-paragraphs and the difficulty of identifying his multiple pronominal referents, today's German academics can be said to surpass him in nearly every measure of difficulty (not to say profundity, rigor, or justifiable influence). Gander's work is as difficult to translate as it is not merely because it is a substantial book (some 360 pages long in its German version) on substantial subjects, its language interlarded with Heideggerian and Gadamerian references, nor because the tiny print of its footnotes so often crowds out all but a line or two of the main text on any particular page. It is rather that Gander packs so much into every set of modifications of every noun that to translate him into English requires that in every sentence one advance swiftly to the end to pick up the verb, only to walk back nearly every step of seized territory, halting at each station along the way to reverse the direction of the varied modifiers, gerundival phrases, and portmanteau words. Each of Gander's sentences is a world unto itself, albeit a highly referential one, carrying with it all of its presuppositions and relationships and entrusting precious little to neighboring sentences or paragraphs. Thus, to present an English version of Gander that adopted the stylistic forms of American academic usage, according to which each sentence should involve a single thought or *sententia*, rather than the most serious, austere version of rococo embellishment around a central theme, would have amounted to a counterfeit, a brazen act of cultural appropriation and transformation. It simply would not be Gander. This text, then, is our effort to set Hans-Helmuth Gander before the English-speaking reader as authentically as we are able, precisely as this German academic phenomenon. Of course, it has been impossible to capture his layered and manifold intentions precisely, because the dense thicket of variants on a few generic German root words by which Gander constitutes his thinking of a hermeneutical phenomenology proves resistant even to the most intrepid English translator. While English is a richly specific language with its vast reservoir of vocabulary, far exceeding any other, it simply cannot match the general or multivocal character of the German language.

To an English speaker, German seems to require that the same word signify many different meanings, whether by itself or with the aid of various directional or locative prefixes. But the possibility must also be considered that each term is not in fact signifying many different meanings at all, that the German contains a broader, more general—or to an English speaker, indeterminate—meaning. That is, to choose one of the dozen or more English translations of just one of these basic forms or their variants is to impose a particularity on it that simply does not exist in German. Whether texts can be composed with such terms and in such a way as to make it possible to know more clearly what the author's intentions were, the fact is that the options for English translation often entail particular choices and thoughts completely absent from the German. For this reason, we have tried as much as possible, pursuant to sense, to select and consistently retain the literal or cognate translation of Gander's countless variants of words like *weisen, halten,* and *sehen.* Among other choices, we have attempted to retain the distinction between *Sinn* and *Bedeutung,* sense and meaning, where possible; we have retranslated all of the German texts quoted by Gander, retaining only some of the best known and most inescapable terms from Macquarrie-Robinson's fundamental translation of *Being and Time;* and finally, we have in a few cases here and there committed as it were the crimes of departing from strict and literal adherence to Gander's vocabulary and phrasing for the sake of clarity and flow.

R. D. & J. R.

PREFACE

> *To what extent are you the same person you were at ten years, fifteen years old—and so on? And as an embryo, a fetus—?*
>
> *Paul Valéry*

> *Living means being an other.*
>
> *Fernando Pessoa*

Augustine's famous question—"What is time?"—with respect to which he professes to be in the condition of an intelligible unintelligibility [*verständigen Unverständigkeit*], could have as an answer precisely this knowing ignorance, if the question concerning human being itself is asked: "If nobody asks me about it, I know it; if I want to explain it to a questioner, I don't know it."[1]

Attempts to solve this riddle have not been lacking in the long history of thought—because it sits so uncomfortably in its perplexity, and not only for philosophers. From different directions and approaches, one has assumed the disquieting question of just who we are and how we are in the world. The present investigation seizes the hermeneutical-phenomenological track from these manifold philosophical access points and develops from here its paths of thought. That this leads its reflections above all into an interpretive dispute with Husserl and in particular the early work of Heidegger is due to the prehistory of this treatise.

At the time in which I edited Heidegger's lecture course *Grundprobleme der Phänomenologie* from the winter semester 1919–1920, it became more and more clear to me that Heidegger's restructuring of phenomenology into a *hermeneutical phenomenology of the lifeworld* during his first creative period in Freiburg concealed within itself an untapped potential. It therefore seems to me appropriate, in the present discourse concerning the philosophical task of human self-understanding, to be able to deliver a productive contribution to the conception of a worked-out philosophy of

---

1. Augustine, *Confessions*, trans. Joseph Bernhart (Munich: Verlag Kösel, 1966), 629.

the situation in the midst of newly self-forming orders of our experience of reality.

The preponderance of Heidegger research—fascinated by the pregnant effects of the fundamental-ontological project of *Being and Time*—investigates his early work genealogically, with a view to possible preliminary steps and persisting chains of motives that prefigure Heidegger's first major work. Next to these studies there are renowned interpretations by Günter Figal, Jean Grondin, and Manfred Riedel, which from the beginning accorded a relatively high value to Heidegger's early work in its own right, and also underlined this outside their writings in various conversations. It may be that these authors have been sensitized to this insight in their own respective ways through their intimate associations with Hans-Georg Gadamer, who, as a witness to the Heideggerian beginning, never grew tired of praising those early years for the originality of their contribution to thinking. Conversations with Hans-Georg Gadamer, which I could carry on at the time of my editorship, lastingly reinforced my insight into the relevance of Heidegger's early work for present philosophical fundamental questions of hermeneutics.

After the edition that I supervised was published in 1993 as volume 58 of Heidegger's *Gesamtausgabe,* I began that summer with the conception and development of the present investigation. In April of 1994, at the invitation of Ingeborg Schüßler, I was able to present the first results of my research in the framework of a lecture at the University of Lausanne. The resulting offer to collaborate with Hans Rainer Sepp in 1995 on the volume *Metamorphose der Phänomenologie* (Freiburg and Munich 1999) gave me the occasion to grapple anew with the relation between Heidegger and Husserl. Finally, a colloquium arranged by Dominique Janicaud in Nice in May of 1996 offered me the opportunity to set into discussion the questions I had labored over in the interim.

In the winter semester of 1997/98 the treatise was submitted to the committee of the philosophy department at Albert-Ludwigs University in Freiburg, and accepted as my written *Habilitation.* The present book offers a revised version of this work. The attentive, careful, and fair mode of treatment at each stage after the inception of the *Habilitation* process awakens good recollections of this time of newly orienting my academic existence, and allows me to honestly thank all of my colleagues who participated in the process. In particular I would like to say thanks to Ute Guzzoni, Günter Schnitzler and especially Friedrich-Wilhelm Hermann, who in numerous conversations has accompanied me critically in this project from its beginnings.

It can be assumed that every book and even any writing that owes its origin (beyond the author's identification of the starting point of the theme and its realization) to the pragmatic end of passing some formal qualification induces the author from time to time, if problematic sections threaten to become overcomplex, to seek out interlocutors who help to clarify the relevant connections in constructive ways. Having friends who as a matter of course do not refuse such service is what I call luck. And in this sense I heartily thank Hans-Ulrich Baumgarten, Mathias Mayer, and in particular Michael Kober for their readiness, at differing points in my undertaking, to engage my inquiry critically and competently. Inasmuch as a project may demand friendly aid in other ways, I would also like to heartily thank Joachim Blank, Maria Borcsa, Monika Fludernik, Sabine Karl, and finally, Andreas and Beatrice Graf von Kornis.

For their assistance with proofreading the manuscript, my thanks go to Katharina Held, Tanja Zeeb, and Rayk Meckel. In addition, I thank Jochen Bojanowski, Rayk Meckel, and Tanja Zeeb for putting together the index.

I would like to dedicate this book to the memory of Jürgen von Kempski. Whoever knows his writings knows that he has trodden other philosophical paths than the one I am embarking upon here. At the same time, there are good reasons for me to want to commemorate him in this way. Beyond familial bonds and personal affection, through him I have learned to value great scholars and resolute independent thinkers. His philosophical acumen and flair remain a model for me—the breadth and depth of his range of interests have impressed me just as much as his openness to different forms of inquiry, insofar as the latter knew to ground themselves independently following his challenge "Let me know more precisely!"

Lisbon, Spring 2001

SELF-UNDERSTANDING AND LIFEWORLD

INTRODUCTION

The position between strangeness and familiarity that the tradition holds for us is "the between" between historically intended, deteriorated objectivity and belonging to a tradition. In this between is the true place of hermeneutics.

Hans-Georg Gadamer

We never fully realize ourselves. We are two abysses—a well that stares up into the heavens.

Fernando Pessoa

§ 1. Exposition of the Connection between Selfhood, Lifeworld, and History

"Actually abiding philosophy can only become the true philosophy of its time, i.e., is powerful [*mächtig*] over its time."[1] With this reflection, in which Martin Heidegger expresses a maxim of his thinking, he binds himself to a tradition within which Aristotle as much as Augustine, Kant, Hegel, Kierkegaard, or Nietzsche can be named. They all found themselves challenged in their thinking by the questions of their time to a type of critical contemporaneity, which sought to posit a diagnosis of their respective historical situations with the means of philosophy. Even if the boundaries are fluid and overstepping them appears unavoidable, it must be recognized that this must not simply be equated with that moral dimension of the responsibility of intellectuals in their time that has found as it were its

---

1. Martin Heidegger to Adolfe Grimme, Prussian Minister of Culture, May 10, 1930, in Martin Heidegger and Elisabeth Blochmann, *Briefwechsel 1918–1969*, ed. Joachim Wolfgang Storck. (Marbach: Deutsche Schillergesellschaft, 1989), 144. Heidegger accounted for his declining a post offered at the University of Berlin.

overlapping and persistent warning signs in Emile Zola's "J'accuse." Since *as a philosopher* one wishes to strive for insight into one's own time and—insofar as one is ready to admit for the first time a type of singularity—to occupy a position *in the name of philosophy,* then that does not mean simply to let oneself immediately and in the foreground be involved in daily affairs, that philosophy can engage in the position, for example, of concrete political decision making in the manner of an omnipotent knowing. Painful experiences have been frankly proverbial in this connection since the days of Plato! In the aforementioned *as* of philosophy, there is indicated instead a *reflexive distancing* that understands itself as an experience of something like knowledge of reality *sui generis.* Of course, any analysis is bound to produce a wealth of varying conclusions depending upon philosophical points of departure and their corresponding hermeneutical frameworks. In setting the task that will be handled in the following investigation, the early Heidegger delivers a fitting phrase when he offers up his solution to this question of a *"Hermeneutics of the Situation."*[2]

The ontological dimension, which thoroughly feels the lack of this problematization, can also be traditionally focused on both concepts, *subjectivity* and *history.* In these concepts [*Begriffen*] the grounding concept [*Grundkonzept*] of classical modern philosophy appears to be called up at the same time, which has its binding and leading task in the question of the *realization of reason in history.* But with the onset of the so-called collapse of an idealistic philosophy of history after Hegel's death, the theme 'history' has not even been settled, as is well known. Indeed, in really different endeavors, the problem of history has immediately come back much strengthened as a center of attention. Thus, massive attacks against any form of speculative philosophy and accordingly all metaphysics were formulated, for example, in the name of history and science.[3] In the historicism of the second half of the nineteenth century[4]—in whose path his-

---

2. Heidegger, *Ontologie (Hermeneutik der Faktizität), Gesamtausgabe 63,* 29 (emphasis added). Henceforth, volumes from Heidegger's *Gesamtausgabe* will be designated as *GA* followed by the volume number.

3. Herbert Schnädelbach provides a succinct, incisive overview of this movement in *Philosophie in Deutschland 1831–1933* (Frankfurt: Suhrkamp, 1983), 49–87. A more thorough account can be found in his *Geschichtsphilosophie nach Hegel: Die Probleme des Historicismus* (Freiburg: Alber, 1974).

4. "Historicism," which is here invoked merely as a catchword, in reality comprises an extraordinarily complex and difficult conglomeration of questions and problems, in particular with regard to the theoretical self-determination of historical science (*Geschichtswissenschaft*).

torical knowledge in the historical and human sciences institutionalized itself—a reflexive mode of observation of history developed, for which Wilhelm Dilthey furnished the methodological principle in *The Concept of Understanding*, in order to discover its lawfulness as universally valid in the consciousness of the relativity of all historical actuality, without being able to dispense with the logical-scientific and epistemological problem of sufficient grounding.[5] Despite being burdened by this methodological insufficiency, the fundamental insight remains of effective-historical, eminent significance—that the human being has the proper element of its existence [*Dasein*] in history and it is the privileged object for a self-mediating knowledge of human beings about itself. In Dilthey, this [historical knowledge], regarded philosophically, gains its most pregnant expression, which can be grasped thoroughly as the signature of historicism; it also finds expression, among others, in the historian Johan Gustav Droysen's thesis that "history [is] the becoming conscious and consciousness of humanity of itself"[6]

In this elevation of history to a principle,[7] however, the relation of 'human-history' remains ontologically more or less in the dark. And even *Lebensphilosophie*, which, to use a formulation of Nietzsche's, tests history for its advantages and disadvantages for life, determines the connection, seen ontologically, of history and subjectivity as finally inadequate. This insecurity about the ontological role and function of history for and in human life, regarded merely *hermeneutically*, nevertheless forms an encouraging, thoroughly creative unrest in itself, which ever again sets free a first push into different perspectives and temporal distances like a sort of *Leitmotif* in the philosophical discussion of the twentieth century. In all anticipation, were one to look for the traditional connection of history and subjectivity—whose bond is that which one is accustomed to think of as unity in the concept 'human being,' for instance, 'human life'—according to a significant feature it permits, to adequately conceptualize hermeneutically under the conditions of present thinking, one finds oneself assigned

---

Cf. Annette Wittkau-Horgby, *Historicismus: Zur Geschichte des Begriffs und des Problems* (Göttingen: Vandenhoeck and Ruprecht, 1992).

5. Cf., Hans-Helmuth Gander, *Positivismus als Metaphysik: Voraussetzungen und Grundstrukturen von Diltheys Grundlegung der Geisteswissenschaften* (Freiburg: Alber, 1988).

6. Johan Gustav Droysen, *Historik: Vorlesungen über Enzyklopädie und Methodologie der Geschichte*, ed. Rudolf Hübner (Munich: Oldenbourg, 1971), 357.

7. Cf. Walter Schulz, *Philosophie in der veränderten Welt* (Pfullingen: Neske, 1972), 471.

to a state of affairs marked as decisive for hermeneutic philosophy of the twentieth century. What is meant is that the question of history now is no longer considered primarily of methodological and scientific-theoretical interest for knowledge, but rather that history itself proves eminently, as Max Müller stresses, to be a "problem of the mode of being of human beings and the structure of the human world,"[8] which determines itself conceptually as lifeworld [*Lebenswelt*].

In its ontological application according to common judgment, this new determination of the problem of history connects itself to the fundamental insight into the constitution of being of human beings as being-in-the-world, as Heidegger's novel philosophical approach both formulates and makes possible. In this unfolding, *historicity* exhibits itself as the *existential structure* of human beings. As the following investigations will show, an appropriate grasp of the problematic of this approach requires that we revert to Heidegger's early work as it formed itself in all essential respects after the First World War in his *Dozentenvorlesungen* between 1919 and 1923. Here it is of decisive significance that the human self is historicized; that is, it can no longer be identified as an ahistorical transcendental ego, but rather is conceived as *a historical self in the current of history*. This becomes sufficiently graspable only in a hermeneutic interpretation, insofar as the philosophical question of the connection of self and history takes shape as what the early Heidegger calls "'historical' cognition [*Erkennen*] in the radical sense."[9] This exposes the conditions under which the human self-conception has formed, which indicates the different cultural and historical possibilities in the key term 'image of the human' [*Menschenbild*].

This philosophical problem, as it is traditionally understood, asks after the unity of the human self, and thus after what it means, as an individual ego in the current of its life history, to be an identity; identical, that is, in the midst of manifold configurations of meaning. Throughout its long tradition this identity is frequently associated with the representation of an essential kernel, a substance, that maintains itself through change and against which any alteration appears merely incidental. More recently,

---

8. Max Müller, *Erfahrung und Geschichte: Grundzüge einer Philosophie der Freiheit als tranzendentale Erfahrung* (Freiburg: Alber, 1971), 223.

9. Heidegger, *Phänomenologische Interpretationen zu Aristoteles (Anzeige der hermeneutischen Situation)*. In *Dilthey-Jahrbuch für Philosophie und Geschichte der Geisteswissenschaften*, ed. Hans Ulrich Lessing (Göttingen: Vandenhoeck and Ruprecht, 1989), 6:249 (hereafter *Phänomenologische Interpretationen zu Aristoteles*).

however, since Nietzsche and within the intellectual history of his writing, the assumption of something like an identity, like a subject as identical being, has come into question. Philosophical thinking that aims at selfhood from a post-Nietzschean starting point turns out to be rather that which moves in a multitude of plays of sense (*Sinnspielen*).[10] These plays of sense—which do not only diverge from or cut across one another in their regeneration but also often enough oppose one another in abrupt qualitative shifts—testify to a differing self-understanding for the individual 'I' that accords with varying alternatives of meaning.[11]

The initial suggestion here is that human identity, while acting as a universal unifying category, "dynamizes" itself, as it were, and gives way to a multiplicity of aspects in its varying relations, so that instead of a homogenous, static concept of the ego (such as we find in Descartes's foundation of understanding self and world), we can henceforth only discuss the ego in the diversity of its facets by applied perspective. The structure of the ego shown to be fragmentary means—along with the accompanying insight into the finitude of the human—that the ego is no longer a subject in the substantial sense and therefore no longer able to be construed from the Cartesian perspective that deems only objects to be its correlates.[12] This is, however, neither a deficiency nor a loss, but in fact proves to be advanta-

10. The possible resonance here with Wittgenstein's famous concept of a language game is valid insofar as language games clarify the meaning of an expression through the determination of its use, and therefore are constitutively based upon practical relations; there is an agreement of expedience such that within language games linguistic and nonlinguistic activities prove to be intertwined, where we find that "the speaking of a language is a part of an activity or a form of life" (Ludwig Wittgenstein, *Philosophische Untersuchungen*, §23, in *Werkausgabe* [Frankfurt: Suhrkamp 1984], 1:250).

11. Bernhard Waldenfels correctly notes, however, that where multiplicity is *simplistically* opposed to unity, thinking remains "'reactive thinking' [and therefore] still [stands] on the ground of that which it strives to subvert" ("Schatten der Aufklärung. Zur französischen Philosophie im 20. Jahrhundert," in *Deutsch-Französische Gedankengänge* [Frankfurt: Suhrkamp, 1995], 20). In this sense, plurality, as manifoldness for example, is incomprehensible in the connection mentioned above. It is thus not a mere reversal of unity, but rather gestures toward the possibility—also inaugurated by Waldenfels—of a "recasting of subjectivity and rationality" (ibid.) in which hermeneutical-phenomenological methods of *Destruktion* can be used to unearth transformational potential (*Transformationspotential*) within traditional possibilities and utilized wherever necessary.

12. Regarding the question of how the modern concept of the subject, in the sense of subjectivity, comes into being out of the initial 'formal-apophantic category' of the *subjectum*, see Heidegger, *Die Grundprobleme der Phänomenologie*, ed. Friedrich Wilhelm von Herrmann, in *GA* (Frankfurt: Klostermann, 1975) 24:178ff.

geous for us, as a task that grounds and determines our existence, namely a task of having to identify incessantly from within oneself.

Accordingly, *self-projection* [*Selbstentwurf*] *as self-identification* is that process in which the ego acts no more from out of a self-certainty, but rather proximity and distance constantly intersect, overlap, or displace [*ablösen*] each other. In this fluctuating play, the human experiences himself as underway toward the traces of a progressive-anticipatory self-confirmation, which is just as manifoldly as necessarily intertwined in the historical world. The *human being as self-understanding* in its sense-making projects must unravel this to-and-fro as its *lifeworld*. Therein the lifeworld shows itself in its manifoldness to be determined by an equiprimordial, reciprocal grasping of individual options of meaning, social mechanisms and structures of power, and orders, which predispose life-forms both traditionally and culturally in their symbolic structures of meaning.

We can shed a bit of light on this connection by turning our attention to ourselves and reflecting upon the fact that each of us is what we are only through what we have become. In so doing, it is to be noted in the first place that personal biography takes shape in the netting, as it were, of cultural-historical webs that, as spheres of influence, constitutively mark out possibilities of self-perception in advance. Therefore, the dichotomy of outer (the public space of history) and inner (private biography) proves to be insufficient from the outset.[13] I am who I am as always already an integral and constitutive component of the external, insofar as in my experience of myself I am the focus wherein history unfolds its effects—indeed, its possibility of being—and thus, however, decidedly shape my self-relation at the same time. Georg Picht astutely notes that there, where history is

13. Seen thus, the ego always already has, as Wilhelm Vossenkuhl emphasizes, a "social identity." Vossenkuhl vividly demonstrates the relevance of the social dimension for self-imputation by taking up Tom Wolfe's *The Bonfire of the Vanities*; the life of the dramatically overrated hero Sherman McCoy goes out of control through an unforeseeable turn of events, such that in what ensues the personal and social aspects of his descent increasingly intertwine. Since the private no longer permits retreat, it does not form any reserves of integrity, which is why "the inner or inwardness cannot be the refuge of my identity" (Wilhelm Vossenkuhl, "Eigenes 'Ich.' Ein Essay über die menschliche Identität," in *Eigenes Leben: Ausflüge in die unbekannte Gessellschaft, in der wir leben*, ed. Ulrich Beck, Wilhelm Vossenkuhl, and Ulf Erdmann Ziegler (C.H. Beck: Munich, 1995), 209. In its identity the ego thus reveals itself to be socially constituted and is from that position, as reference to Hegel shows, dependent upon the recognition of another. As socially constituted to an extent, a person's self-determination is carried out necessarily in pathways that sketch it out historically in its contents and forms for the recognition that is to be gained. Seen thus, "identity [is] not subjectivist, but rather transsubjective" (ibid., 215).

misunderstood, it is inevitable that we cannot also rightly understand ourselves, since our "association with ourselves and our intimates would then
be deformed by false theories about history."[14] Formulated as a thesis, this
means that history does not refer to a sphere of construction that exists
aloof from or external to us. Following Picht, "History is not something to
be studied as a given, independently of ourselves."[15]

We live (experience) history as our own life history, but not in such
a way that we autonomously have it at our disposal. Much more is it the
case that our self-understanding is effected by our life history: "We do not
[have] our biography; our biography has us."[16] To this extent, we are nothing other than our life history, always already situated "lifeworldly" in its
sense of relation as well as that of fulfillment. *The historical lifeworld therefore shows itself to be that horizon from which we encounter ourselves.* Admittedly, this takes place implicitly for the most part, because we require no
explicit knowledge of the situatedness of our existence in order to master
a concrete life situation—indeed, as little as we require knowledge of lin-
guistics in order to be able to speak. Nonetheless, it belongs to the possibilities of our existence to articulate, in the sense of disclosing structures
as the *task of a phenomenological hermeneutics,* what remains implicit in the
execution of a practiced, factical life.

§ 2. Conception and Outline of the Treatise with an Excursus on the Paratextual Functions of Remarks

In the task of a structural analysis that I have thus far posited, the concept
of structure [*Struktur*] denotes that hermeneutic categorical (and therein
from the outset already historicized) sense that Merleau-Ponty also had

---

14. Georg Picht, *Geschichte und Gegenwart* (Stuttgart: Klett-Cotta, 1993), 5. Picht illustrates
this point by reference to competing ideologies regarding, for example, child rearing, sexual
practices or even political worldviews in order to draw out the fact that in their basic conception—concretely codetermined by our contemporary practices—they are thereby supported by
a preconception of history. As a theory of history, this preconception itself has taken the shape,
among other things, of a current historical condition, and precisely in this dislocation becomes
ideology.

15. Ibid., 6f.

16. Ibid., 6.

in view in his determination of the concept of structure.[17] As far as the historically variable and subtle relational context is to be thought with the concept of structure so grasped, *structure as sense* intends no fixing of a final or originary sense, and thus may not be bound up with something invariant, intransient, or eternal.[18] Structures do have, however, a *relational constancy.* That is, they denote something that one can return to qua sense order as a principle of organization, as it were of elements, whether these are just texts or life situations. They describe that which can be *understood methodologically* and they also denote the contribution of understanding in their exhibition.

The understanding of sense methodologically and epistemically presupposes for hermeneutical activity—and this grounds the point of departure for the subsequent investigation—an *ontological* preunderstanding of the object of sense, which is disclosed cognitively in the explicit cognition and determination of something as formed as such and such. In order to carry out this determination as accurately as possible, hermeneutic thinking must prove to be a perspectival, dynamic, and in this sense, one might say, *lateral* thinking through the necessary adaptation to its respective content and the inclusion of its fundamental conditions of finitude and historicity. Insofar as it orients itself in its implementation in the how of the givenness of its object, such thinking can be marked as *phenomenological.* In this formal scope philosophical hermeneutics no longer defines itself in its traditional sense as the doctrine of understanding and interpreting texts. In its intended contributions to understanding, it also includes the realm of actions and human works, and insofar as it posits understanding therein as a fundamental existential, as it does explicitly in Heidegger and Gadamer, the human being in its being-in-the-world is itself the outstanding theme of hermeneutical reflections.

So regarded, "actual life and history [are] the guiding threads or better the *guiding experience* for phenomenological investigation."[19] The early

---

17. Cf. Maurice Merleau-Ponty, "Von Mauss zu Claude Levi-Strauss," in *Leibhaftige Vernunft. Spuren von Merleau-Pontys Denken,* ed. Alexandre Métraux and Bernhard Waldenfels (Munich: Wilhelm Fink 1986), 17.

18. Structure, as Merleau-Ponty emphasizes, does not, in principle, possess the ontological status of a Platonic idea, insofar as "the same traits of physiognomy can assume a different sense according to the system in which they are found" (ibid).

19. Heidegger, *Grundprobleme der Phänomenologie (1919/20),* ed. Hans-Helmuth Gander, in *GA* (Frankfurt: Klostermann, 1993), 58:252. Thus, the much-discussed universality of hermeneutics would be determined from this point by the performative sense of its knowledge, in the

Heidegger thereby widely extended the narrative arc of his thematic approach. But with the implied programmatic link to the field of hermeneutic philosophy of life in Dilthey's sense on the one side, and to Husserl's methodological approach on the other, he let the marks of orientation become visible, giving a sense of direction to his proper way. In place of a simple synthesis, it sufficed for Heidegger in the passage through the basic ideas of phenomenology and philosophy of life to relate both to one another conceptually in productive ways under the critical comprehension of the metaphysical tradition that itself finds something pathbreaking and new set in the way for the subsequent history of hermeneutics: what Heidegger called up at the beginning of his path of thought under the key word of a "phenomenology as originary science of life" (*Phänomenologie als Ursprungswissenschaft vom Leben*). The structural and functional character of this program—which Heidegger addresses in a note to § 15 of *Being and Time* in signifying the early phase of his thinking as a *hermeneutics of facticity*—stands at the center of the following investigations.

An adequate hermeneutical, systematic interpretation of this early work remains a desideratum. Admittedly, in Heidegger studies, this early phase has been given thorough attention in recent years.[20] By and large, such investigations are geared toward developmental aspects of his work

---

sense of an elevated claim to conclusive finding of success, much more than through its field of work, which knows no "terra incognita," which must necessarily remain withdrawn from a *"hermeneutical curiosity."* To characterize this hermeneutical position here as curiosity may indicate that any suspicion regarding an irresolvable sense of dominance or even omnipotence in the claim to validity of hermeneutical knowledge is precluded from the outset. Rather, hermeneutic curiosity signals an openness that implies a transdisciplinary interest (with respect, for example, to scientific discourse) wherein—according to hermeneutic-philosophical consciousness—clearly apportioned roles and tasks can be concretely transported into an interdisciplinary discussion. Here, the boundaries of each discipline are not suspended, yet access to phenomena is to be expanded through the respective lens of each.

20. See, e.g., Claudius Strube, *Zur Vorgeschichte der hermeneutischen Phänomenologie* (Würzburg: Königshausen and Neumann, 1993); Theodor Kisiel, *The Genesis of Heidegger's Being and Time* (Berkeley: University of California Press, 1993); John van Buren, *The Young Heidegger: Rumor of the Hidden King* (Bloomington: Indiana University Press, 1994); Rolf Buchholz, *Was heißt Intentionalität? Eine Studie zum Frühwerk Martin Heideggers* (Essen: Die Blaue Eule 1995); Georg Imdahl, *Das Leben verstehen: Heideggers formal anzeigende Hermeneutik in den frühen Freiburger Vorlesungen (1919 bis 1923)* (Würzburg: Königshausen and Neumann, 1997); Gerhard Ruff, *Am Ursprung der Zeit: Studie zu Martin Heideggers phänomenologischem Zugang zur christlichen Religion in den ersten "Freiburger Vorlesungen"* (Berlin: Duncker and Humblot, 1997); Peter von Ruckteschell, *Die Intentionalität im frühen Denken Martin Heideggers: Von der Urwissenschaft zur Fundamentalontologie* (Freiburg: Universität Freiburg im Breisgau, 1999).

such as his use of gerunds. Their guiding insight consists primarily in discussing the question of the formation of Heidegger's approach to thinking, in his early lecture courses, with regard to the grounding program of a fundamental ontology unfolded in *Being and Time* in its preliminary steps and early forms. The rank of this way of positing the problem is not under scrutiny here. Without a doubt it is of interest with regard to looking at the beginnings of his path toward becoming a modern classicist as he has inscribed himself into the history of twentieth-century thought with and since *Being and Time*. However, the developmental approach to *Being and Time*'s prehistory also conceals a gradual perspectival narrowing arising out of its preliminary determinations, insofar as it tends to dissect the textual space of the early work in accordance with its own interpretive guidelines and to level it off from the viewpoint of its intended results.

No understanding, however, is free of directives that guide its execution as a form of preunderstanding brought to the text. The directives that unfold their effect in the present treatise determine themselves from out of the hermeneutic situation of the present expressed in the opening paragraphs, a situation whose discourse on self- and world understanding cannot itself be unfolded today under anything other than postmetaphysical conditions. In the process, Nietzsche's insight into the "soul as subject-multiplicity"[21] in particular counts among the decisive impulses of discourse in the exhibition of the internally plural structure of human self-understanding. And yet Nietzsche perceived himself as an echo of that which Montaigne, around the beginning of modernity, already glimpsed with a sensible trace at the ground of his ever-concentric searching, questioning exploration of the ego as self as *"autant de difference de nous à nous mesmes, que de nous à autruy."*[22] Thus, rediscovering Montaigne as a thinker of the plural, differing composition of human life within Nietzsche's effective-

<hr>

21. Friedrich Nietzsche, *Jenseits von Gut und Böse*, in *Werke: Kritische Gesamtausgabe* (hereafter *KGW*), ed., Giorgio Colli and Mazzino Montinari, div. 6, vol. 2 (Berlin: Walter de Gruyter, 1968), 21. In this sense, Nietzsche asks at another point, "The assumption of *a subject* is perhaps not necessary; perhaps it is permitted just as well to assume a plurality of subjects whose interplay and strife lie at the base of our thinking and of our consciousness in general?" *Nachgelassene Fragmente: August—September 1885.* in *KGW*, div. 7, vol. 3 (Berlin: Walter de Gruyter, 1974), 382. For Nietzsche, what follows from this is the "hypothesis," formulated as a fundamental assumption, of "the subject as multiplicity" (ibid.), and combined therewith, "the abiding ephemerality and fleetingness of the subject" (ibid.).

22. Michel de Montaigne, *Essais*, 2:1, in *Oeuvres completes*. ed. Albert Thibaudet and Maurice Rat (Paris: Gallimard, 1962), 321.

historical scope may serve to illustrate a certain fact: that, in light of the present experience of manifold tectonic shifts within the orderly system of our lifeworld concerning the question of self-understanding in effective historical consciousness, the activation of diachronic voices can manifest a remarkable potential for posing answers. The question of the possibility of such asynchronous synchronicity contours the horizon within which Heidegger's early work can be discussed *retrospectively* in the sense of a historical hermeneutics.

As will be shown, the *hermeneutics of situation* unfolded in the early work, which transformatively extrapolates the Kantian idea of a "world-concept of philosophy," offers up possibilities—precisely in connection with the network of philosophical questioning expressed above—for building bridges from Heidegger's own answers to current philosophical positions like those evoked by the names Gadamer, Ricoeur, Foucault, Rorty, or Taylor. Insofar as these positions demand on their side a hermeneutical clarification of human self-relation, in striving for a philosophy of the situation in the sense of a '*historical ontology of ourselves,*'[23] to use Foucault's term, reference to the early Heidegger promises new and productive approaches to the solution of the problem of interpretation. However, it is therefore necessary first to open our view to the potential of this early hermeneutics by a systematic, directed discussion of its domain of thought. And just that is the aim of the following investigation.

Heidegger's phenomenology gains its entry point and its beginning as a primordial science of life [*Ursprungswissenschaft des Lebens*] in the *hermeneutical transformation* of the Husserlian conception of a phenomenology of consciousness. In the process, the self for Heidegger is no longer grasped from the beginning as an ego-consciousness. His considerations find their point of departure in reflection on the general crisis of consciousness as it is articulated at the beginning of the twentieth century in, among other places, the signs of *Lebensphilosophie*. A chance for a positive overcoming of this crisis—historically as well as systematically—offers itself for Heidegger in the exhibition of self-projection's constitutive reference back to the *facticity* on which it is founded.

In our detailed analysis, the hermeneutical turn of phenomenology is treated in chapter 1 of part 3, in order to investigate from that vantage point

---

23. Michel Foucault, "Was ist Aufklärung?" in *Ethos der Moderne: Foucaults Kritik der Aufklärung,* ed. Eva Erdmann, Rainer Forst, and Axel Honneth (Frankfurt: Campus, 1990), 48.

the program of Heidegger's hermeneutics of facticity in its fundamental moves and central aspects. This structural ontological analysis will show that Heidegger's hermeneutics of historical, factical life in the project of a "phenomenology of the historical lifeworld" (§§ 31–33) is developed as a "hermeneutics of the self" (§§ 34–37). In chapter 3, this form of hermeneutics leads to an answer to the question of humanity's relation to its history as an "organon of understanding life" with regard to its "self-world significance" (*Selbstweltbedeutsamkeit*) (§§ 38–40), which comprehends the thematic relation of self-understanding and lifeworld as a *correlative explication*.

As with every interpretation of a work, the present study unfolds from out of a situational context that today no longer corresponds essentially to the original Heideggerian one, and the latter therefore may never be reproduced exactly in an interpretation. This can be transmitted only in the manifold shadings of the perspective imprinted from his texts, which is never to be picked up completely in its presuppositions and with regard to the temporal condition therein mediated. For the practice of interpretation, this means nothing other than taking seriously the Heideggerian insight into the radical finitude of the human constitution, which also places interpretation, binding itself in general to the *principle of authenticity,* under the measure of the aptly named 'hermeneutics of finitude' in its claims to validity as we find it formulated in central pieces of Gadamer's hermeneutical epistemology.

The implications to be drawn from this principle become visible in the course of the present study to the extent that it ensures, in effective-historical consciousness of hermeneutical necessity, that we locate in advance the question of our understanding of self-and-world within the *space of its effective history* for the interpretive examination of the Heideggerian position. That means to investigate more closely, in regard to the phenomenological tradition, the problem of self and world as it has been passed down since Descartes, with his turn to the subject as leading paradigm of modern philosophy. That is the task of part 2. The discussion of the tradition established by Descartes and Husserl (which lays down as affirmatively as possible the final foundation of all knowing of the world considered in the onset of a finally assured subjectivity), which is carried out in both chapters of this part, opens a view into its effective historical [*wirkungsgeschichtlich*] and significant background.

Chapter 1 of part 2 begins with the explication of that transition which, in the course of one's life, marks the point of entry into the philosophical attitude as a reflexive relation of oneself to oneself *as a self*. This attitude has traditionally been made precise in the concepts of *wonder* and *doubt*, and as this philosophical view, is still only what it is in the constitutive reference back to the lifeworld. This reference stands, and can show itself from out of its latency—even in its concealment—as consequential in general for the development of modern philosophy, which Descartes's own entry point signals with the turn to subjectivity and the positioning bound up with it, of the 'I' between self-possession and forfeiture of world. With Descartes's opening of the modern theory of subjectivity, what has been passed down is closed off, roughly in the tradition of Augustine's establishing possibilities of letting step into view the relation of tension between 'I' and world, now seen phenomenally more openly and appropriately in the direction of the problematic of the lifeworld.

In chapter 2 the lifeworld as theme of Husserlian phenomenology becomes the proper object of a critical discussion. It is thereby shown in the context of the question concerning self-understanding that the transcendental-phenomenological approach to consciousness, and the unity of the lifeworld bound up with it, falls short as a sort of 'transcendental singular' opposed to the demands of a plural dispersal of lifeworldly undertakings. For that reason, this second chapter sees itself as guided from the outset by the insight of treating the theme of the lifeworld by means of *hermeneutical phenomenological destruction* for the sake of the positive exhibition of being-in-the-world as the primary self-relation. Accordingly, it becomes clear why the Husserlian conception does not suffice to give a phenomenally adequate answer to the problem of history in relation to historicity in the framework of hermeneutical reflections on the self-understanding of human beings in the world. Against the backdrop of this path of seeing, part 2 also fulfills the function of a necessary transition to the positive exposition of the hermeneutical question concerning the connection of *self-understanding and lifeworld*, as it takes shape in Heidegger's project of a hermeneutics of facticity.

Observed as effective-historical, this worked-out conception appears after the First World War in the space of Heidegger's texts as they have become accessible since the mid-1980s. The 'nonsimultaneous simultaneity' addressed above would not have made itself present to us without this sense of the text as a space of experience. The eminent meaning of the text for hermeneutical understanding, "materialized memory," as Günter Figal names it,[24] in which experience and history are embedded, forms in the text's lifeworldly contextualization a problem of the highest significance for the question concerning the self. In part 1 this problem in the sense of the question of self- and world understanding is traced in hermeneutical excursuses. The path to the I's hermeneutical self-investigation is blazed with a view to its contextualization in the discussion of the *question of the reading and writing of texts*. This seems perfectly obvious, insofar as from the beginning it has been primary texts in which hermeneutics has known the privileged object of its activity. However, this part does not work out the relation of text and sense activity in the traditional understanding of a hermeneutics of text. Rather, it seeks to show that and how texts themselves can unfold themselves as *crystallizations of human self- and world understanding*.

From this posing of the question, it becomes clear in which ways the texts each bring into play their meaning both as part of and within us in the process of self-formation. This process is reserved in advance in an occurrence of transmission from which, as history, we seek to wrest away selections of meaning in understanding appropriation for our own self-understanding. Insofar as we read these traces so that we ourselves can get on track, we write ourselves into the discussion with texts themselves in this occurrence of transmission and thereby inscribe ourselves on it. Yet we do so without ever being able to exercise, with any substantial degree of certainty, a comprehensible awareness of this event as a decipherable totality of sense.

Texts as *historical objectivations of life* offer a grasp on them to readers and writers as a constitutive condition of composing meaning, as well as unique access to the perspectival angle of refraction of *interpretation* as the fundamental pattern of all knowledge, as Nietzsche formulates it; this interpretation is itself illuminated only perspectivally and in the relation back to its historically factical, relational bondedness to a situation. In other words, the hermeneutical situation is in equal measures an angle of incidence and an angle of reflection for the self-unfolding power of the

---

24. Günter Figal, *Der Sinn des Verstehens: Beiträge zur Hermeneutischen Philosophie* (Stuttgart: Reclam, 1996), 18.

text in the field of tension that comprises self- and world understanding, which, however, is not simply mirrored by them in its situatedness, but rather is above all historically constituted with them in advance as a situation directly through the texts. Texts in this sense open reflection into what is proper and foreign and therein at the same time open the possibility for experiencing them in self-projections as border crossers at the narrow edge of understanding between self-possession and self-forfeiture. Insofar as the singular knows itself as interwoven in a network of relations, the *philosophical question concerning the self* thereby becomes *the question of self-understanding in the historical world* with regard to the essential structure of the historicity of human beings.

Excursus: Toward a Paratextual Function of Remarks

For our present study—which, in the form of a text itself, is bound precisely by this insight—the contextuality of our experience of self means that our course of thinking only achieves its desired analytic clarity in unfurling the different strands of this problem once we take into account (including what lies in the margins, wherein a text's own course of thought necessarily sets out and breaks off) the extent to which it attaches weight to those referential relations that coalesce in the text as well as those which push beyond it.

One way that these margins can be incorporated by a reckoning on the side of the author is mirrored in the way that the present text handles what one usually calls *remarks*. Remarks, which can signify forewords and afterwords, blurbs, titles, dedications, proverbs, appendices, and so on, are what with Gérard Genette we call *paratexts*,[25] or, as the case may be, paratextual addenda enmeshed within the body of a text. Such elements can be grasped in a formal respect as "expressions of differing length (a single word suffices), each relating to a more or less determinate segment of a text and arranged in such a way that it refers to that segment or is situated on its periphery."[26] In view of a given text, the handling of partial, local, concretely related remarks deformalizes itself in three respects:

25. See Gérard Genette, *Paratexte: Das Buch vom Beiwerk des Buches* (Frankfurt: Campus, 1992).
26. Ibid., 304f.

1. In the first respect, it trades in the usual evidence of quotations or other sources, which are selectively and precisely determined in relation to their text, and therefore remain without independent meaning.

2. In a further type of application the remarks constitute a textual space in which scholarly opinions are reported and discussed. While they are drawn from beyond the point of view of the author, they adhere closely to the thoughts detailed in the body of the text. It is significant, however, that this part of the text concerns discussions whose interlocutors are *not* selected as willing participants in the manner of bringing in expert testimony. As well, the discussion of research in no way raises the claim, wherever possible, to a complete overview. Strictly speaking, one may not speak of the "beyond" of an overview at all, insofar as this concept could imply accepting an elevated standpoint over the author, and even this is not the case. On the contrary, what is the case is that it becomes particularly evident where the horizon of tradition opens itself to reflection with a view to the matter for discussion. Therein are collected for the author all of those voices that, whenever we so wish, offer their counsel and conclusions, functioning as partners in reflection and serving as markers along the path of literary forms of expression. Accordingly, we can indeed never be sure that we could have done everything conceivable to collaborate in our role as a responsible participant in our discourse, but every new look at the matter, every new voice stretches a new network of referential possibilities onto it. That this in no way reflects a shortcoming on the author's part can be easily demonstrated once we see the development of the phenomenological-hermeneutical approach. On the contrary, this approach directs itself explicitly against the notion of self-isolation in thinking, because we in no way become an isolated ego even in solitary meditation.

As thinking things we are, observed hermeneutically, always already inscribed—and write ourselves—into historically situated discourses, which transcend and even transform us as communally shared within them. This means that, with a view to our discussion of remarks, the voices of other authors displace one's own course of thinking, and in this displacement, engender a certain productive tension. Such tension is generated whenever one's own position is forced to self-critically reorient itself in rejecting other positions. Yet this tension becomes creative even where the author's perspective occasionally (perhaps in some cases where it comes up hard against the limits of one's own account) overwrites itself in a reflexively designated agreement, as it were, in written remarks. As always, with this discussion, the path of thought situates itself at the same time in the extended, effective-historical network concerning it, that is, in the matter thematized. This becomes apparent of necessity only when the respective scholarly positions, with desired conciseness yet in sufficient measure, are allowed to have their say. Accordingly, in regard to this second usage a considerable distantiality—and thus, autonomy—is accorded to footnotes in distinction from the main text.

3. The third way that the remarks in the present text should be understood functionally is not unlike what we intend by *excursuses*. Like the glosses in manuscripts of the Middle Ages or the marginalia of the sixteenth century, these remarks tend toward commentary upon given segments of a text. They can also, however, act as stepping stones between a concrete phase within a course of thought and positions already established, those still to come, those as yet unelaborated, or those that touch obliquely yet meaningfully upon the issue at hand. Metaphorically speaking, these remarks venture, from the banks of the river of thought, a view out beyond the embankment. What prospect therein shows itself to the interpreting look does not mean to let the path of thought unravel arbitrarily in its pursuit. What opens itself, rather, as an opportunity in these excursuses is the possibility of casting an additional illuminating light on the borders of the problem at issue. Thus, the "direct path" sought in the main text is enriched in such remarks with a complexity that, observed from outside, may appear to hinder direct access to the problem occasionally, but for that reason equally cannot be simply neglected, because they lend to the text a *depth of focus* in a type of *synthesizing interpretative style as a second discursive level*. Here it is a matter, to borrow a motif from Genette, of "changes in register that thereby contribute to mitigating the well-known and occasionally disagreeable linearity of discourse. Registers . . . of intensity, nuances in terms of critical reading that eventually double back upon themselves, or to put it paradoxically: the main issue as manifest within a remark."[27] In such sorts of remarks, the text bifurcates itself as it were, that is, its potential for meaning [*Sinnpotential*] branches off in under- and overtones.

These modulations of an adequate conception of constitutive foundational possibilities of our processes of self-understanding are to be taken as attending to those individual voices that address us from the historical field of effects to which we always already belong, and which themselves frequently enough hold only at the margins and—who knows how often—also lie under the threshold of the simple known and conscious level of audibility. Since we can only listen from the hither side of this threshold—which in our thinking always manifests itself in advance as (pre) knowing—from a hermeneutic perspective this involves the task of making audible that discourse on the other side, in its tones and pitch, through that reflexive labor which, under the guidance of a given question, we call effective-historical consciousness. It is to this discourse that we bind ourselves as participants, and in which we are, in turn, bound.

27. Ibid., 312.

What is thereby introduced to the voice in the conversation of a text is *selection,* and even in relation to that which we ourselves perceive in us, there is no complete knowledge to be disclosed. All totality of sense lies beyond our possibilities, and thus we can refer only to plausibility in regard to the claim of the validity of our illumination of the relation of sense. The fact that by 'plausibility' we mean a hermeneutically motivated justification in the form of requisite argumentation—a justification that cannot make any claim to truth, either in general or of any special order—has precisely to do with the fact that regarding it is requisite when accurately assessing problems confronting us historically that their initial reflexive elucidation generally requires consciousness to break with, as Gadamer emphasizes, the "univocity of the 'thus and not otherwise'"[28] which in turn becomes a "venture into the possibility of 'thus *or* otherwise.'"[29] This 'thus or otherwise' may be associated just as little with arbitrariness or caprice as the aforementioned notion of choice, but rather occurs *under the methodological direction of the hermeneutically executing conditions of understanding,* in which the phenomenological character of the hermeneutical procedure proves itself.

What has been called the fact of the imperative of choice is intertwined with the consciousness that whatever we say has at some point already been said or, to put it more carefully, could have been said. Echoing Robert Musil, let it be said that our sense of what is real is always already undercut by our sense of what is possible. That is, real possibilities are only such as to have become real—and in this sense, realized—possibilities, and as such are by birth contingent and relational. The present study takes up its tracks and traces them in order to investigate in the network of texts the hermeneutical problem of self-understanding as a basic existentiell phenomenon. But the *hermeneutical situation of interpretation* itself thereby becomes an object of a metahermeneutical reflection in the course of understanding: to seek to understand *how* we can understand. To come upon the trace of the mystery so indicated does not require that we finally in fact solve it or even do away with it. For in relation to the possibility of its philosophical knowledge, mutatis mutandis, Diotima's misgiving—leveled against Plato himself—may finally prove true, namely that at the threshold of complete

---

28. Hans-Georg Gadamer, *Philosophische Begegnungen.* in *Gesammelte Werke* (hereafter *GW*) (Tübingen: Mohr-Siebeck 1995), 10:440.
   29. Ibid.

insight human knowledge may afford from out of itself only a Socratic openness as readiness for experience of one's own limits, and bound up with that also necessarily one's own failure, which turned the conscious renunciation of the final illumination of sense into a positive means. What remains is the task of lifting the fog of understanding to such a point that the identity that imprints itself upon human individuality becomes structurally comprehensible, in and as difference in its ontologically constitutive function for human relations of self and world as displayed through historicity.

PART ONE

IN THE NETWORK OF TEXTS:
TOWARD THE PERSPECTIVE CHARACTER
OF UNDERSTANDING

In writing the point is not to manifest or exalt the act of writing, nor is it to pin a subject in language; it is rather a question of creating a space into which the writing subject constantly disappears.

Michel Foucault

Every point of view is the apex of an inverted pyramid, whose base is indeterminable.

Fernando Pessoa

§ 3. Inception and Beginning:
Toward a Forestructure of Understanding

One is to write one's first sentence in such a way that the reader will want, without fail, to read the second sentence. So reads the advice that William Faulkner imparted to anyone who wishes to embark on the adventure of writing a text. Truthfully, this is no easy demand to fulfill, especially if one considers that—regarded from outside—at first something entirely arbitrary belongs to every beginning. And if it is adequate to satisfy the Faulknerian precept, it thus remains that such a beginning in every case possesses something compelling or seductive, though not compulsory in the strict sense.

Whether or not the starting point of a text can be justified is only to be decided through reading. For the reader whose own presuppositions the text can never divine, there stands its conclusion, which perhaps and in the best case with further development aids the decision whether or not the reader grants plausibility, indeed, the force of conviction, to the thoughts developed in the text by the author. In the question of reader recognition, a text or its author, seen correctly, may not finally be able to claim as much, insofar as concerns texts, as the so-called Holy Books or legal texts claim the force of the authoritative validity ascribed to them from their consent, indeed obedience. By contrast, for texts without such status and even those that one usually calls philosophical, the demand for consent falls away in advance. It develops itself or fails to develop on the reader's side to the degree of his readiness to enter into discussion with what is there.

What is there presents itself as *text*—taking text quite conventionally as that corresponding to the particular form of notation of a determinate written language[1]—even if it is there as an image in the intended form of a complete totality of sense, and is thereby equally included in a *network* of subtextual and extratextual presuppositions which at most are no longer visible in the text itself. What is there has, observed more precisely, always already a type of prehistory. Thus, what we are concerned with is not at all a specific problem about texts; rather, it characterizes something that applies to everyone within the limits of possible human experience and which at the same time identifies the text itself as a part of the human realm of experience whose *objectivations* can be made accessible to us.

Martin Heidegger, among others, calls our attention to that which proximally can be addressed as sub- and extratextual prehistory in his first Hölderlin lecture (winter semester 1934/35), where he devotes his thinking to the entry point and the path of his discussions, differentiating *inception*

---

1. It should be pointed out that a text consists of sentences, and every sentence in itself already follows a determinate system of rules, such that its clarification necessitates a linguistic or philological analysis. So uncontroversial is this that the path indicated is not contested in the following reflections on the question of the text. The orientation adopted here in the text takes the sentence in view only insofar as it is always already included in the context of other sentences with its referential sense, the referential connection which is in the form of a text as totality of sense and rules the particular sentence in its referential sense as this whole. However, from this perspective the sentence itself functions as a type of text that should not be observed as isolated, but much more finds acceptance only now in connection with the currently interesting question of referential relations that it refers beyond itself to the context for disclosing the structures of sense, i.e., hermeneutically. In this understanding of a text there still resonates underground the original Middle High German meaning of the word, which corresponds to the text as a textile or woven mesh, derived from the Latin *textus*.

[*Anfang*] from *beginning* [*Beginn*] and clarifying this difference in an every-day experience: "A new weather pattern, for example, begins [*beginnt*] with a storm, but its inception [*Anfang*] is the advance effect of the full transformation of the air ratios."[2] Beyond the phenomenally relevant level of this example, Heidegger indicates this difference such that the beginning "is that with which something rises up, the inception that out of which something springs forth."[3]

Under Heidegger's interpretation of inception as an ontologically originary occurrence that is inaccessible to us, it remains unseen in this lecture whether the perceived historical approach to being already indicated can form a corresponding transformation of the ancient metaphysical thought of *arche,* that is, of *principium,* which, taken as a supreme foundation, has supplied the ground of philosophy as first science since the Greeks. It is more important at this point, however, that the emphasis on inaccessibility to be sounded out within this difference—which now means the supra- and impersonal difference—between inception and beginning, is positively capable of delimiting, in the connection between author, text, and reader, the attempt to confine the causal derivation and deduction of a text out of personal motives to the problem of beginning, which itself now no longer appears as what is first in the sense of what lacks presuppositions.

In this sense, the differentiation of Heidegger's difference, seen structurally, is enlightening in relation to the beginning, "as soon as it is left behind, it disappears into the progress of the occurrence,"[4] while the inception "on the other hand, first comes to appearance in occurring, and is only fully there at its end."[5] If one suppresses the possible problem lying in the textured relation of inception and end, namely, that of always thinking an inverted teleology, which in fact Heidegger sees, for example, in the inceptual promise of metaphysics completing itself in Nietzsche, it still remains as an essential characteristic of this difference that the inception must not be thought as a discrete occurrence, but rather as a process seen as always already and still occurring and therefore not to be grasped.

2. Heidegger, *Hölderlins Hymnen "Germanien" und "Der Rhein,"* ed. Susanne Ziegler (Frankfurt: Klostermann, 1980), GA 39:3.
  3. Ibid.
  4. Ibid.
  5. Ibid.

With a view to this procedural character, every binding [*Festlegung*] of an occurrence to an inception point as original point connotes a construction. As such, in the intention of methodological clarifications of the matter, this binding fixes possible and perhaps even necessary points of approach and reference as full of sense, but must always again posit them under the reservation that it is provisional and therefore never capable of being made absolute.

In the *inception,* which displaces the beginning from itself and in contrast is not to be outstripped, it is a matter of discerning in the connection of interest between author, text, and reader the general and factical disposition out of which a text and its beginning—that is, the stipulated course of thought—achieve a form in which they can be read and received. In this form it comes to light why, for example, precisely this issue is to be approached and examined from this and not another perspective.

With a view to this particular philosophical attitude, Fichte famously and emphatically laid out the much-cited confession: "What one chooses for a philosophy depends on what one is as a human being: because a philosophical system is not dead furniture, which one could cast aside or take up at one's pleasure, but rather it is animated by the soul of the human being who has it."[6] Günter Patzig rather laconically replied to this charged Fichtean pathos when he remarked in addition that one does not simply choose a philosophy, "but rather one grows gradually into philosophical conceptions. Also in those who sincerely philosophize, the influence of philosophic thoughts and arguments upon the development of their personality may actually be more important for what is illuminating and what seems significant to them than the influence of their individual temperament."[7] Of course, the personal inclinations respected by Patzig are not trivial to our interests and claim a not inconsiderable part of the development of our standpoint.[8] But these inclinations themselves can be taken seriously

6. Johann Gottlieb Fichte, "Erste Einleitung in die Wissenschaftslehre" (=Versuch einer neuen Darstellung der Wissenschaftslehre). In *Werke,* ed. Fritz Medicus (Leipzig: Fritz Eckardt, 1911), 3:18.

7. Günther Patzig, *Tatsachen, Normen, Sätze: Aufsätze und Vorträge* (Stuttgart: Reclam, 1980), 3.

8. Patzig begins the book mentioned above with an autobiographical introduction whose sense he grounds by the notion that the understanding of determinate texts can be thoroughly enhanced when the reader is oriented to the author's biographical development.

only if they have gained their acuity in self-testing and from taking the influence of factors as they are predesignated in a serious measure by the academic milieu in which one gains one's scientific experiences.

What in this sense plays a part in influences of the most various sort upon the formation of our ideas and our judgment can be apprehended hermeneutically as the *forestructure of understanding*. In this phrase, understanding does not only mean a way of bringing about knowledge in the foregrasping of still closer approximation, but rather the existential basic structure of our self- and world relation in which all understanding accordant with knowledge and interpretation is founded. Hermeneutics in this sense thus does not aspire to be a doctrine of method as much and at first as it designates a self-enlightenment of the understanding, which assumes the form of an interpretation [*Interpretation*], a laying out [*Auslegung*] of which Heidegger stresses that it is "not the taking notice of what is understood, but rather the working out of the possibilities projected in understanding."[9]

This working out is not proximally theoretical-conceptual. It can become so, and if it takes up the question of the human existentially, as in Heidegger's work, this laying out [*Auslegung*] becomes a hermeneutics of facticity, as is to be seen. More fundamental than the conceptual laying out is the pretheoretical way of being of this laying out in which the human being itself constantly moves. Even in what we assume to be the activity of simple looking, we register what is seen *as* something. This 'as' can be called the *hermeneutical 'as'* in distinction from the apophantic 'as' of the expression. It "composes the structure of explicitness; it constitutes the laying out,"[10] which stands under three conditions of implementation in which the tripartite forestructure of pretheoretical and theoretical laying out [*Auslegung*] takes shape.

In this, the *forehaving [Vorhabe]*, which also could be called *pregivenness [Vorgabe]*, designates that which must already be pregiven to laying out, although not yet expressly, in order to fulfill itself. The laying out holding itself in this pregivenness is thereby led by a determinate insight that has it in view as *foresight,* about which what is understood and still

<hr>

9. Heidegger, *Sein und Zeit*, ed. Friedrich-Wilhelm von Hermann (Frankfurt: Klostermann, 1977), *GA* 2, 197; cf. ibid., 308.

10. Ibid., 198.

shrouded is to be unconcealed in laying out. Thus, the foresight guides laying out as a prior sight of the particular concrete being laid out of the given in forehaving. Insofar as laying out holds itself in advance in a mode of language in which it addresses and conceives what is being laid out, it is determined as a third moment of the forestructure through the anticipation [*Vorgriff*] that is a preconception [*Vorbegriff*]. All three structural moments together compose the *preunderstanding* that constitutes the *hermeneutical situation*. Insofar as all laying out holds to the preunderstanding in a necessary dependence, in order to make this explicit a circular structure can be formed therein, which is referred to as the *hermeneutical circle*. This signifies a movement in whose completion understanding differentiates and clarifies itself.

It is important to see with regard to this preunderstanding that it is, following Heidegger, the "mode of being of particular beings," which guides laying out [*Auslegung*] in the formation of its conceptuality, so that methodology and ontology may already show themselves as constitutively intertwined in this approach.[11] Hans-Georg Gadamer grasps this prestructure of the understanding as a constitutive basic condition of all processes of understanding accordant with knowledge in the concept of *prejudgment* [*Vorurteil*]. After its discrediting by the Enlightenment, which as a consequence of its ahistorical ideal of reason tied the objectivity of knowledge

---

11. In the sense of a broad anticipatory indication, we should call attention to a difficulty here. It shows itself in the fact that, as Heidegger shapes this foreunderstanding in *Sein und Zeit* it is at the least not quite clear whether it, seen ontologically, does not still finally possess in its transcendental function of constituting the hermeneutical situation a transcendental status in the classical sense. In other words, the impression arises that the status is inferred from the function. But with this account the question remains obscured in favor of the sense of validity, here addressed as function, a) how this forestructure forms itself factically and genetically, and is therein bound up with b) how in this formation the dynamic, historically advancing transformation can be thought together. From the insight that the ontic variance grounds itself in the ontological structure of historicity, facticity and historicity, which do not mean simply the particular concrete, ontic transformations, entail that a transcendental ahistorical fixing of the forestructure in general is fundamentally problematic.

Formulated as a question, to be considered more closely in the context of the early Heidegger's outline for a program of a hermeneutic of facticity, we would ask: Does not the alignment (*Gleichschaltung*) of transcendental function and ontological status at the very least appear, if only implicitly, problematic where an account of the function of forestructure is not considered within historically defined parameters? Does not the adoption of the more or less transcendental-hermeneutic forestructure as a situation's constitutive condition presuppose a historical "coming-to-be-subject" (*Subjektwerdung*) of the human, insofar as this emergence must have already, among other things, revealed language to be the fundamental occurrence in human Dasein as a condition of self-understanding?

to its lack of prejudgment, the latter now may again be rehabilitated in the careful distinction of legitimate and illegitimate prejudgments.[12]

Individual presuppositions, however they account for the process of socialization, belong accordingly to the genetic dispositions of a text. As a thought profile, it develops ways of seeing that, unwilling to stand only in the realm of the 'null values'[13] designated thus by Schleiermacher, raise a claim to validity, or rather, suppose it, which must redeem itself intersubjectively in a discursively enacted bond, admittedly not looking at the question whether this claim to validity can or cannot establish itself philosophically in a final grounding.[14]

12. See Gadamer, *Wahrheit und Methode*, in *Gesammelte Werke* (hereafter GW) vol. 1 (Tübingen: Mohr Siebeck, 1986), esp. 281–290. Along with this rehabilitation as recognition of the forestructure of understanding goes the fact that these foremeanings (*Vormeinungen*) must necessarily be made transparent as presuppositions of self-clarification, yet relinquishing any hope for their complete elimination, much the way in which Francis Bacon considered them to be indispensable for scientific knowledge in his doctrine of the idols. Bacon thoroughly recognized—and this is a decisive step on the way toward the critique of knowledge (*Erkenntniskritik*), which thereby reflects what is to be known in its claim to validity with an eye to the conditions and procedures of the act of knowing—that the human spirit is determined in its nature proximally and essentially through prejudices (see Francis Bacon, *Neues Organon*, ed. and trans. Wolfgang Krohn (Hamburg: Meiner, 1990, Aph. 38–62, spec. 39–44).

13. "What has null value holds interest neither as an action, nor as meaning for language," and is in this sense determined through "relative nullity of content [*Inhaltsnichtigkeit*]" Friedrich Schleiermacher, *Hermeneutik und Kritik*, ed. Manfred Frank (Frankfurt: Suhrkamp, 1977), 82, 83. How such "talk about the weather" [*Wettergespräche*, i.e., small talk] is to be grasped in the frame of the hermeneutics conceived by Schleiermacher, in terms of its capability and need to be laid out with regard to the place value within everyday self-understanding in the being with one another of those speaking, is not going to be discussed in the given connection. Here it is only indicated in order to set talk apart from the problematic content of texts, which cannot redeem its claim to validity by trivial ways of giving consent.

14. Even if, as in the work of Ulrich Wienbruch (*Das bewußte Erleben: Ein systematischer Entwurf* (Würzburg: Königshausen & Neumann, 1993), the task is fixed of conceiving philosophy systematically as the "attempt at an ultimate grounding" (18)—and admittedly through the fact that "conscious experience [is] an absolute given" (21), i.e., "the fact: I consciously experience something as foundational" (20), is shown and revealed in its structural manifoldness—this attempt at an ultimate grounding remains constitutively determined by an experience of contingency that makes one conscious as such, insofar as "he who philosophizes [may] not gauge in such a way that he expects himself to be capable of naming or even elucidating all of the conditions of his enactment. For to these conditions belongs also the circumstance that each always takes place in a particular, shifting attitude (*Einstellung*), as well as in an historical situation and in a particular language. . . . Consequently, every attempt to know the necessary presuppositions of those things as one comes across them is inconclusive. Philosophical reflection, like conscious experience in all of its other particularities, does not permit its task to be solved in such a way that one achieves a complete conclusion" (139).

§ 4. Approaching the Question of Interpretation:
On the Relation of "Author-Text-Reader"

However, with the reference to the claim of validity raised within and by philosophical texts, we may be at the same time prevented from a possible misunderstanding that could be assumed with regard to the genetic disposition of the text, namely that the task is dictated to the reader of a text for its *interpretation,* that is, that the task is to reconstruct the meaning behind the text in the sense of striving for comprehension of the author's individuality. This task signifies what the traditional hermeneutics of a Schleiermacher or Dilthey has classified as "psychological understanding," and authors like E. D. Hirsch or Emilio Betti still argue within their tradition. And even if psychological components of understanding appear to be weakened in favor of a more linguistic orientation, as in the work of Hans Ineichen, the truth of the interpretation of a text, in the traditional sense, is still throughout constitutively bound to the fact that it primarily comprises "the sense *intended* by the author."[15] In contrast, Gadamer has provided evidence that in interpretation it is not a matter of a tripartite relation of text-reader-author, but rather a *two-party relation* between text and reader. For the primacy of authorial intention imposed by tradition, he reserves a still useful, though ultimately "reduced task."[16] For the intra-subjective intention of the author, according to its status, which can certainly seek to rule the understanding of a text normatively, is itself only to disclose from out of the present text so that it is *the text itself;* the response directed intersubjectively according to its intention unfolds to the reader as the "sense movement of understanding and interpreting [*Auslegens*]."[17]

For a reading of texts oriented exclusively to the immanence of the work, it would nonetheless not be about the word spoken, insofar as for a pure interpretation immanent to the work there neither is nor can be a presumed total exhaustion of meaning on the basis of a—likewise necessarily assumed—enclosed textual structure, as is shown not merely with regard

---

15. Hans Ineichen, *Philosophische Hermeneutik* (Freiburg: Alber, 1991), 40.

16. Gadamer, *Wahrheit und Methode,* 378. On this point see Dieter Teichert, *Erfahrung, Erinnerung, Erkenntnis: Untersuchungen zum Wahrheitsbegriff der Hermeneutik Gadamers* (Stuttgart: Metzler, 1991), esp. 127–131; see also Hans-Helmuth Gander, "Die Geschichtlichkeit des Verstehens. Zu Gadamers Theorie der hermeneutischen Erfahrung," *Filozofia* 48 (1993), esp. 284f.

17. Gadamer, *Wahrheit und Methode,* 272.

to the elusive, intrasubjective authorial intention for a final determination and conclusive indication of the sense. This does not, however, constitute the only mode of a detectable withdrawal in the process of understanding texts. Rather, the disposition of a text remains constitutively determined through still further forms of withdrawal. They show themselves, among others, in the fact that, seen genetically, the text forms itself in the reflex of its obvious, situationally relevant, as well as latent influences; final clarity about the inclusions in a text cannot be imposed by the author, nor complete enlightenment upon the reader. It becomes clear that this must not immediately be perceived as a shortcoming, given that one would consider it, at least in scientific and philosophical texts in accordance with established notions, actually irrelevant to wish to spell out these *situating* presuppositions. For the binding force of the theses set out in a text leaves directly out of view the questions in their intersubjective claim to validity according to the conditions of their emergence, such that even then, if it suffices more or less precisely to enlighten the situational conditions, their use appears rather secondary with regard to the expressive capacity and force of scientific or philosophical theses of the text.

What thus constitutively withdraws itself in and from a text is, as it were, flanked by a further withdrawal of the text never to be outstripped by the reader. What is meant is that a text is never congruent with the conditions under which it is received as a text by its reader, to whose presuppositions it belongs, that the text appears in his own life-worldly situation, indeed is interwoven in it and remains irrevocably with the reader and as a read text, belongs to his knowledge, irrespective of how the reader takes the meaning of the text.

§ 5. On the Relation of Writing and Reading to Self-Formation

The relationship between author, text, and reader is not an equation in the sense that seamlessly communicates intentions of the author to the reader about and as a text. A text thus does not determine itself only by the intentions bound up with the author, nor exhaust itself in the effects bound up with them, which the author wants to achieve with them and then even achieves in fact. And this is not merely because the author himself never emerges monocausally as the source of creation; he also presents a type of medium, through which the text itself as it were produces itself as surface with a deep structure. To speak with Gadamer, the text is "a phase in the fulfillment of an occurrence of understanding."[18] This occurrence of understanding encompasses the *implicit as well as explicit* self-understanding of human beings in the world—whether author or reader. From this point, therefore, the questions of the understanding of a text explained here can be legitimated in the horizon of a philosophical labor on the hermeneutics of self-understanding as prereflections, particularly as philosophical and scientific work gains access to canonical problems of textual interpretation [*Auslegung*].

Observed in relation to the text, the reader forms a type of *interface* for the effects of texts, which in turn underlie manifold differentiations on the side of the reader. For in the process of reading, reactivated and relativized effects of all other effective-historical, meaningful texts cross and overlie the present reading of the text at hand, namely as incorporations of which we are presently aware, or aware of as something we had previously forgotten, or even as things of which we are simply no longer conscious, which, in the collective potential of their possible effects form the reader's distinctive "point of view."[19] Texts let themselves be grasped as *objectivations of historical life,* as Wilhelm Dilthey formulates it,[20] which on their side for-

18. Gadamer, *Text und Interpretation,* in *GW,* vol. 2 (Tübingen: Mohr Siebeck, 1986), 345.

19. Wolfgang Iser rigorously investigates the meaning of what is read for the structure of a text from the perspective of his theory of effects. The structure of a text is determined for him in the "directive to be (*Anweisung zu sein*)." Insofar as these directives must be taken up in order to constitute the reality of a text, the question arises for Iser, in connection with the constitution of texts, of the role and function of the reader, a kind of reading that he develops in detail in his "Phänomenologie des Lesens." Through the model of an "interaction between text and reader" Iser seeks purchase, in connection with his "theory of aesthetic effects," for the insight that interpretation necessarily includes reflection upon its own guiding assumptions and interests. See Wolfgang Iser, *Der Akt des Lesens: Theorie ästhetischer Wirkung* (Munich: Fink, 1976), esp. chaps. 3 and 4. Cf. Iser, *Die Appellstruktur der Texte: Unbestimmtheit als Wirkungsbedingung literarischer Prosa* (Konstanz: Universitätsverlag, 1970).

20. This is in reference to the later Dilthey, who in fact never really leaves the track of psychological understanding, but in opposition to looking at introspection as more and more indispensable for an understanding of life, "[lets] the conception of the structure of mental life [rest] upon the interpretation of works in which the context of mental life comes to full expression." Wilhelm Dilthey, *Die Abgrenzung der Geisteswissenschaften,* in *Gesammelte Schriften* (hereafter *GS*), ed. Bernhard Groethuysen (Göttingen: Vandenhoeck & Ruprecht, 1973), 7:322). Thus Dilthey can differentiate between the psychological and the hermeneutical dimension, whose interpretive insight is not just that, for example, "there are inner events in the poet, but rather a connection created in them, yet indissoluble from them" (*Der Aufbau der geschichtlichen Welt in den Geisteswissenschaften,* ed. Bernard Groethuysen (Göttingen: Vandenhoeck &

matively effect the self-understanding. That means that texts are not given to us objectively like other objects of perception. They are not primary objects in opposition to a knowing subject. In turning to them, they speak to us in that they work [*wirken*] in us—i.e., they work us [*bewirken*] and make us work [*erwirken*] as that which addresses and concerns us in this claim and so co-forms our self- and world experience. "*Se comprendre, c'est se comprendre devant le texte et recevoir de lui les conditions d'un soi autre que le moi qui vient à la lecture.*"[21] In a certain formulaic pointedness, it can therefore be said that we not only have but also are what we read and have read. *Every sentence read belongs to us, encamps and is stored within us.*

The organic process of ingestion can lead erroneously from talk oriented to 'reading as digestion' to 'what is read as what is to be digested,' insofar as excretion belongs to digestion, which as a type of detoxification of the body possesses a hygienic unburdening function. With reading, on the contrary, if one wants to maintain such corporeal analogies, it is more like heavy metals or other environmental toxins emerging in our environment, which are taken up into the chain of necessary survival behaviors somehow, without the real possibility of warding them off and ridding ourselves of them. Naturally, reading should not be associated with this comparison as a phenomenon of sickness; it is only to make clear that the relation to texts cannot be grasped as something incidental to a substantially conceived (and therefore dictatorial) reading and writing subject. Texts embed themselves within us, albeit for an indeterminate time, and

---

Ruprecht, 1973), *GS* 7:85), which is as a "mental formation of a structure and lawfulness proper to it" (ibid.) and in this sense presents as text an objectivation of life.

21. Paul Ricoeur, *Du texte à l'action: Essais d'herméneutique II.* (Paris: Éditions de Seuil, 1986, 31. With this basic insight, Ricoeur describes the principle of the textual hermeneutics that he developed in the 1970s. The fact that reading is an "initiator whose magical key opens the door to spaces in the depth of ourselves, into which we would not have otherwise been able to penetrate," numbers among the essential insights that Marcel Proust firmly emphasizes in his essay *Journées de lecture* (*Tage des Lesens: Drei Essays* [Frankfurt: Suhrkamp, 1995], 36). To refer to the long and rich history of reflection on reading in relation to Proust, there is suggested an obvious proximity to Ricoeur's basic insight, because in his essay Proust succeeds, with richness of allusion and on manifold levels, in unfolding the tableau of interweavings, overlaps, and counterreflections of reading and living in the leading voice of his lifelong search for self-assurance. However, this does not nourish itself from out of the Cartesian hope for an Archimedean point of full self-possession, but rather knows that it remains at all times in the many-faceted process of progressive approximations, carried out in an experiential space that opens and holds itself according to its coordinates in the span of self-location and the constant possibility of again losing oneself.

they unfold their effects ultimately unaccountably as a part of, and within, us. They are thus meaningful for our *self-formation*.[22]

§ 6. The Text as a Connection of Sense in the Horizon of the Occurrence of Tradition as Effective History

What we can sketch out for the role of the reader in the meshwork of a text applies also to the author, who in similar fashion is not only himself a reader, but also in writing weaves himself into a net of relations whose threads he no longer holds authoritatively in his hands, and can only at best still lull himself into illusions. In the writing of texts, the author articulates himself, to speak with Gadamer, always at the same time as *effective-historical consciousness*, which opens contingent options for the immanent

22. This connection displays itself forcefully precisely where, instead of free self-formation, a subjugation of the individual is demanded under totalitarian orders whose claim to power is cemented through repressive techniques, i.e., the "means of censorship" belonging to those in prominent positions from time immemorial. The study of respective *Indices librorum prohibitorum* opens the interesting possibility of conceiving the history of a culture from the *perspective of denied knowledge*.

An important aspect of such analysis consists in investigating the constitution of an order as the inception of regulations by means of the asymmetry in scientific relations becoming visible at its indices as relations of power. Thus in correlation with the prohibition that the political—in particular, the moral—order wishes to maintain, against the free development of one's judgment, it disciplines the knowledge of the members of a society through exclusion; the censors guarantee the emerging order for their part in their self-determination *as* censors in an original constitutive transgression, whereby, in suspending the prohibition of reading for themselves, they retain that instrument of power (knowledge) that a diagnostic consciousness illuminates as the dangerous potential of texts, namely the tendency toward destabilization therein regarding their own ruling interests.

Against this, not only the governed, but also those censors freed from censure must be ideologically immunized—and this comes about in that by means of an ingeniously reasoned system of reciprocal controls, a proportionate ownership of power is signaled, whereby as a price of the knowledge bound up with this power, public silence with regard to it is established. In so doing, despite the pretension to truth that it claims from its own position of alleged superior insight, this force of self-immunization does not believe itself a match for the power of temptations against those values held to be binding by the regime in which the latter are anchored, so that for the purposes of stabilizing ruling interests, an immunization of others through prohibition—thus, through ignorance—must be instituted. Texts can even, as Plato already knew in the *Phaidros* (274e), when he lets Theuth and Ammon discuss the uses of writing as *pharmakon,* function either as cure or poison, depending upon their attitude and application. Plato, *Phaidros*, in *Werke,* vol. 5, ed. Gunther Eigler (Darmstadt: Wissenschaftliche Buchgesellschaft, 1981).

formation of sense in the production of a text, and admittedly within an *occurrence of tradition* designated by divergent bonds with traditional lines as well as by breaks with tradition, which itself for the most part hands down what is composed in texts once again as linguistic.

The quasi-dialogical situation, grasped as the relation of the tradition to the reader and author mediated in texts and thus linguistically, and also insinuated by Gadamer as well,[23] should not be overpromoted with a view to the dialogical. For it is ultimately and essentially in this relation "that understanding of the tradition does not understand the passed down [*überlieferten*] text as the expression of the life of a Thou, but rather as a content of sense detached from all bonds to those intending meaning, an I and Thou."[24] Seen thus, the reconstruction of an author's opinion from out of the text that it transcends is neither meaningful nor possible, according to Gadamer. And thus Bernhard Waldenfels rightly refers to the fact that Gadamer himself approaches "those textual theories that let the author disappear behind or into the text."[25] Those thought to be in this camp would be Merleau-Ponty, Derrida, Levinas, or Foucault, insofar as the removal named by Gadamer breaks open the immediate dialogical model of conversation or, taken strictly, even undercuts it.

Indeed, this feature in Gadamer is not always easily understood due to a certain haziness in his train of thought, especially in that he continually determines the relation to the text as a dialectic, the logic of the question and answer as and within the model of conversation.[26] Despite occasional

---

23. "Tradition is not simply an occurrence that one knows through experience and learns to master, but is rather *language (Sprache)*; that is, it speaks from out of itself like a Thou. A Thou is not an object, but instead relates itself to one" (Gadamer, *Wahrheit und Methode*, 363–364).

24. Ibid., 364.

25. Bernhard Waldenfels, *Antwortregister* (Frankfurt: Suhrkamp, 1994), 124. Within the framework of his conception of a responsive rationality that circulates around that "*to which* we answer . . . without it transforming itself into *something* that can be answered" (15), Waldenfels has undertaken to open the path, in far-reaching analyses of the relation of question and answer, to a different questioning "that leaves ignorance its due place" (ibid.), and thus lets the answer appear as "the type and way in which we enter into the alien, without sublating it out through appropriation" (ibid.).

26. Cf. Waldenfels, who, in his answers in *Antwortregister* to the 'hermeneutical priority of the question' postulated in Gadamer's textual model, has clarified the question-answer relation that can be a little vexing here in a transparent schematization close to Gadamer, as follows: "(I) The text poses a question (Q_1) to the interpreter, (a) wherein the text itself gives an answer to a question (Q_2); (II) The interpreter gives an answer (A_1) to (Q_1), (a) wherein he reconstructs (Q_2), (b) in that he himself (Q_2) questions and seeks to give to (Q_2) his own answers

vacillations in expression, for Gadamer it must be maintained as a core principle that even when the text poses the question, the text is not hypostatized into a subject sui generis, as in the tradition passed down within it. Rather, "the question that the text poses to us [means] that understanding itself always already involves the task of historical self-mediation of the present with tradition,"[27] and thus only attains itself as a question from out of the effective relation that the text unfolds on the side of the reader.

Addressed as *effective history* with Gadamer, the occurrence of tradition essentially can never open itself entirely as an encompassing horizon, but only partially. As an encompassing horizon, tradition is not itself to be enclosed within a text, but rather the text for its part is an integral constituent of this occurrence of tradition. It is so in that even through the (in principle) infinite possibility of rereading—through which it does not only make itself present but can always become originarily present again—it is not finally a privileged site from which the horizon discloses itself from itself, if always only partially; the horizon is that with a view to the text from which and within which the play of sense determines itself as the text's direction of sense. To secure the horizon of the question of the interpretation thus signified, formulated with an eye to the text, is indispensable for the understanding of a text. This capacity of disclosing the horizon of the text can thereby never indeed be ultimately codified, insofar as it also holds other answers ready beyond the answers that are accessible to the person disclosing them in the transformation of perspectives of access. "Insofar as the sense of a sentence is relative to the question for which it is an answer, however, that means it necessarily goes beyond what is said in itself."[28] According to Gadamer, this means that the horizon of the question within which understanding moves is always already retained in the encompassing horizon of effective history, which the text itself does not contain but only opens up.

Effective history does not thus simply mean reception history, but instead signifies as a hermeneutical principle the basic comportment— that in all that ever seeks to understand historical knowing, it fulfills it-

---

(A2)" (125), so that as a whole, a chiasm is formed: "the text questions, in that it answers—the interpreter answers, and in that he questions" (126—cf. 125–133).

27. *Wahrheit und Methode*, 379.

28. Ibid., 375.

self within the effective power of history.[29] This does not become clear to knowledge itself with final evidence. Thus, it lies in the effective historical consciousness as a task of hermeneutics to enlighten the historical situatedness of understanding in its conditions of execution and to reflect upon the finitude of the claim to understanding therein coposited at the same time. It goes along with this that this partial opening up of the horizon of effective history for its course admits no immanent options and suppositions of sense as acceptable that rise above or transcend the governing totality of sense within the occurrence of tradition. Observed as a totality, the process of effective history is with a view to a final analysis indifferent to any given meaning.[30]

The horizon always already transcending effective historical consciousness may therefore not be hypostatized roughly in the sense of idealistic rational history, which, for example, in Fichte, Hegel, or Schelling is oriented teleologically toward the actualization of reason in history. The sense horizon intended here may not be grasped in general as a homogeneous, closed unity that takes shape a priori and necessarily as if it were a kind of continuum or continuity. Instead, in the horizon to which we refer, an always already discontinuous plurality of a manifold of sense that never itself becomes transparent as totality is to be uncovered, in whose net thoroughly particular and contingent lines of development can and indeed are admittedly thoroughly bound up. In its demonstration, we can uncover the respective situating of our self, if only by disavowal, with the identical knowing-acting being in the world. But addressed as an *encompassing* horizon, it obeys the principle, insofar as it is still permitted to speak of it, as it were of a sort of "random number generator." That means that a collective sense of history extending beyond the contingent and plural provinces of meaning, and as it were guiding and founding them within its unity, is not to be formed from the perspective of the finite and thus human possibility of knowing.

---

29. We cannot today, for example, turn to Kant's thinking without at the same time attesting to its effects. That Kant's thinking is today still a central constituent of a philosophical curriculum attests not to an affectionate, antiquated sense on the part of philosophers, but rather reflects historical consciousness as borne by, and itself as a bearer of, Kant's meaningfulness for our contemporary age.

30. An indication of this, for example, is that a conjecture of sense that transcends the immanence of history and the world more or less in accordance with the Christian plan of creation has lost the authoritative, ordering function once central for the lifeworld and social life, and only still preserves its worth and bindingness in the social rank of an upright private bearing.

§ 7. In the Governing Network of Discourse

In a borrowing from Nietzsche's term and concept [*Begriff und Konzept*] of genealogy, which he characterizes as "real history" or "historical sense,"[31] Michel Foucault speaks about the fact that "the world of actual history [knows] only a single realm in which there is neither providence nor a final cause, but only [and here Foucault cites Nietzsche] 'those iron hands of necessity which shake the dice-box of chance.' This chance is not to be understood as a mere drawing of lots, but rather as the constantly renewed risk of the will to power, which counters every chance occurrence with another, still stronger chance."[32] According to Foucault, for the formation of a "true historical sense," it is necessary to know "that we live without originary fixed points and coordinates among innumerable lost events [*Ereignisse*]."[33] Seen in this way, the text shows itself to be an objectivation of this meaningful [*Sinn-*] and thus historical relation of reference, which, as a world within a text, preserves a new particular structuring of sense, objectivating itself in and through its respective text.

Proceeding from Foucault, this is not to be understood as if an order of an originarily founded wholeness of sense, closed in itself, could be projected in this referential connection and discovered or reproduced. Were this the case, according to Foucault, there would have to be an origin in the sense of a sovereign subjectivity from which this foundation of sense would ensue. With a view to the question of the possibilities of ordering sense, Foucault confirms for one that there are "fundamental codes of a culture—those governing its language, its perceptual schemas, its forms of exchange, its techniques, its values, the hierarchy of its practices—[that] establish for every human from the beginning the empirical orders with which he will be dealing and in which he will be at home."[34]

---

31. Nietzsche, *Jenseits von Gut und Böse,*. 163. Cf. section 7 of the preface to the *Genealogie der Moral*, in *KGW*, vol. 6 part 2, 266f.

32. Michel Foucault, *Nietzsche, die Genealogie, die Historie*, in *Von der Subversion des Wissens*, ed. Walter Seitter (Munich: Hanser, 1974), 83–109. The citation of Nietzsche to which Foucault refers is found in *Morgenröthe* 2:130, in *KGW* vol. 6, part 1, eds. Giorgio Colli and Mazzino Montinari (Berlin: Walter de Gruyter, 1971), 120; Nietzsche also recalls the context in *Genealogie der Moral* 2:12, 329–332.

33. Foucault, *Nietzsche*, 99.

34. Foucault, *Die Ordnung der Dinge: Eine Archäologie der Humanwissenschaften* (Frankfurt: Suhrkamp, 1993), 22.

Alongside this empirical level, there is further the reflective knowledge of the sciences and philosophy, which accordingly asks why there is an order, what its law is, and from what principles it justifies itself. In addition, however, according to Foucault, "in every culture, between the use of what one might call the ordering codes and reflections upon order itself, there is the pure experience of order and of its modes of being."[35] This "'middle'-region"[36] depends upon this experience, as that "certain mute order" that "is given in things as their inner law, the hidden network that determines the way they confront one another, and also that which has no existence except in the grid created by a glance, an examination, a language."[37]

What is thus decisive for Foucault is the irreducible fact "that *there is* order."[38] It has its form in that which the concept of discourse grasps, into which what is here called a text is integrated as an occurrence of language. The concept of *discourse* is specified in three senses: "First, the general region of all expressions, then individualizable groups of expressions, and finally, regulated practice that chronicles a certain number of expressions."[39] Expression as a nonisolatable and yet elementary moment of discourse is not to be grasped in Foucault in the sense of that which is determined logically as a proposition, grammatically as a sentence, or analytically as a speech act.[40]

Seen thus, no unifying structural criteria can be found for expression, insofar as it is not to be conceived in general as a unity. Rather it presents a function, about which Foucault notes that it "crosses a region of structures and possible unities and allows these to appear with concrete content in time and space."[41] In this sense, following Waldenfels, *énoncés* can be translated more correctly as "utterance" [*Äußerung(sgehalt)*][42] than as

35. Ibid., 24.
36. Ibid., 23.
37. Ibid., 22.
38. Ibid., 23.
39. Foucault, *Archäologie des Wissens* (Frankfurt: Suhrkamp, 1986), 116. Under the concept of archaeology, Foucault intends a nonsubjective philosophical epistemology or theory of knowledge, which affords an analysis of historical connections in which concrete structures form human experience.
40. Cf. in this connection ibid., 117–127.
41. Ibid., 126f.
42. Waldenfels, "Michel Foucault: Ordnung in Diskursen," in *Spiele der Wahrheit: Michel Foucaults Denken,* ed. François Ewald and Bernhard Waldenfels (Frankfurt: Suhrkamp, 1991), 285.

"expression," [*Aussage*] insofar, that is, as it concerns the "analysis of the discursive field, to grasp the 'expression' in the narrowness and particularity of its appropriative event; to determine the conditions of its existence, to fix its limits most exactly, to establish its correlations with other expressions with which it is bound up, to show which other forms of utterance it excludes."[43] Discourse is thus formulated in expressions, or seen more exactly, as "a host of expressions that belong to one and the same system of formation."[44] In this sense, Foucault can also then speak of a "clinical discourse," a "psychiatric discourse," an "economic discourse," and so on.

What then takes shape as an ensemble of expressions departs in Foucault's work from traditional determinations such as subject and object, transforming them in the varying functions of expression.[45] Describing an expression thus means "defining the conditions under which a given function has been effective in having given existence to a series of signs (in which this series is not necessarily structured either grammatically or logically)."[46] The expression is thus for Foucault an "existence-function proper to signs and starting from which one can decide, through analysis or intuition, whether they 'produce a sense' or not, in accordance with which rule they assume a sequence or collocation, that of which they are a sign and through what mode of action (oral or written) they are generated

---

43. Foucault, *Archäologie des Wissens*, 43. "One could formulate the typical question for such an analysis in the following way: what sort of strange existence is it that comes to light in what is said—and nowhere else?" (Ibid.). From this point, however, it is shown "that discourses do not merely underlie determinate orders, but rather that orders evolve and embody themselves in discourses" (Waldenfels, "Ordnung in Diskursen," 283). Seen in this way, Axel Honneth's attempt to separate 'order *of* discourse' sharply from 'order *in* discourse' (*Kritik der Macht: Reflexionsstufen einer kritischen Gesellschaftstheorie.* [Frankfurt: Suhrkamp, 1989), 163) shows itself as problematic. And then, it is not possible in Foucault's texts to critically note his unclear fluctuation between the positions of a "semiological structuralism" (ibid., 139) and a "linguistically revitalized philosophy of life" (ibid., 163). In contrast, Waldenfels stresses in connection with Merleau-Ponty—and thereby matches Foucault's own intention—the interposition of 'linguistic appropriative events' "*between* system of rules and stream of life" ("Ordnung in Diskursen," 295).

44. Foucault, *Archäologie des Wissens*, 156.

45. Discourse is not the "manifestation of a thinking, knowing, articulating subject; on the contrary, it is a matter of a collectivity wherein the dispersion of the subject and its discontinuity with itself can be determined. It is a space of outer expressiveness (*Äußerlichkeit*) in which a network of differing sites unfolds . . . In the same way, one must now recognize that when it is a matter of defining the system of expressions, it is achieved neither through recourse to a transcendental subject nor to a psychological subjectivity" (ibid., 82).

46. Ibid., 158.

through their (oral or written) formulation."[47] More significant therein is the fact that expressions know neither intentions, nor addressees, but rather have their discursive order exclusively in the positivity of what is said, which precisely opens therein a space of the play of possibilities for what is sayable, and thus regarded, what is thinkable.[48]

In the absence of intention and addressees of expressions, it comes to light that they may not themselves be grasped as outer expression of a subjective willing, but rather as organizing themselves as it were in and as discursive order itself in the anonymity of the 'one says' or 'it speaks.' In this anonymity of saying, of the text's speaking, which Foucault also thinks in the concept of the outer (*extériorité*),[49] there is no speaker, no more authorial subject, i.e. there is naturally factically this I, but it is without relevance for the sense of validity of discourse.[50] Following the words of Beckett, "What does it matter who speaks, someone said, what does it matter who speaks," Foucault formulates his credo as "one of the fundamental ethical principles of contemporary writing.[51] It has to do with a principle that, in the sense of an immanent rule, "does not signify writing as a result, but

47. Ibid., 126. On the expressive function see ibid., 128–153.

48. "To describe a crowd of expressions not as the closed and overfull totality of a meaning, but as a dismembered figure, full of gaps; to describe a crowd of expressions not as in relation to the inwardness of an intention, a thought or a subject, but rather according to the dispersion of an outwardness; to describe a crowd of expressions not in order to find again within the moment or the trace of the origin, but rather the specific forms of a clustering; it certainly does not mean the bringing forth of an interpretation, the discovery of a founding, the exposure of grounding acts. It also does not mean the decision of a rationality or the hasty course of a teleology, but rather the establishing of that which I would like to signify as a *positivity*" (ibid., 182).

49. Cf. ibid., 175–177.

50. "It would surely be absurd to deny the existence of a writing and inventing individual. But I think that—at least since a particular epoch—the individual that goes about writing a text out of which perhaps a work is produced claims the function of the author. What it writes and what it does not write . . . this entire differentiated game is prescribed by the author-function, which it takes over from its epoch or on its part, modifies. And if it overturns the traditional picture that one has of an author, it thus creates a new author-position by which it lends its work a new, still hazy profile in everything that it ever says." Foucault, *Die Ordnung des Diskurses.* (Frankfurt: Ullstein, 1977), 20f.

51. Foucault, *Was ist ein Autor?* in *Schriften zur Literatur*, ed. Daniel Defert and François Ewald (Frankfurt: Suhrkamp, 1988), 11. See also Foucault's self-characterization in *Archäologie des Wissens*: "Probably more than one person writes like I do and has no longer, in the end, a face. One does not ask me who I am, and one does not tell me that I should remain as I am: this is a moral of legal status; it dominates our papers. It is supposed to set us free when it is a matter of writing" (30).

rather dominates it as a practice"[52] and thus grasps writing as a self-related "play of signs [*Zeichenspiel*],"[53] that is not determined through its interiority. In the play of signs it is not so much the meaningful content as the essence of meaning that is of importance, which at the same time means that the "regularity of writing is always again experimented upon from its limits."[54] "Writing develops like a game that is compelled to overstep its own rules and thus to step beyond them."[55] What a text thus achieves is the "opening of a space in which the writing subject continually disappears."[56] In place of the author's individuality, Foucault sets the "singularity of his absence."[57]

Foucault's thinking does not remain at the position, here severely abbreviated, which in being variously termed archaeological has caused him to be classified among the structuralists, whom, however, he increasingly resisted, despite having welcomed this categorization through his means

52. Foucault, *Was ist ein Autor?* 11.

53. Ibid.

54. Ibid.

55. Ibid. Jacques Derrida also refers to the character of play in writing in *Grammatologie* (Frankfurt: Suhrkamp, 1994), 17.

56. Foucault, *Was ist ein Autor?* 11.

57. Ibid., 12. From this point, and in a certain proximity to Maurice Blanchot, Foucault emphasizes "the kinship of writing with death" (ibid., 11), insofar as both attest to an absence that cannot be recovered by the understanding. According to Foucault the millennia-long relation that undertook around the time of the Greek epic to eternalize the immortality of the mortal heroes, or as in Scheherazade's stories in *The Thousand and One Nights*, motivated by the wish to forestall death, has now inverted itself. In that period storytelling and writing were determined by averting death in its transformation into the immortality of the works. Over against this it is the case today that, as Foucault stresses in reference to Flaubert, Proust, and Kafka, the work has preserved the right "to kill, to be the murderer of its author" (ibid., 12), that is, "the relation of writing to death exteriorizes itself . . . in the obliteration of the writing subject's individual traits" (ibid.).

The oft-cited and manifoldly misunderstood talk of "the disappearance of human beings"—that is, of human beings as an epistemological category of the late eighteenth century—whose most famous formulation ("the human being disappears like a face in the sand on the beach") is found at the end of *The Order of Things* (462; cf. Foucault, *L'homme est-il mort?* in *Dits et écrits*. ed. Daniel Defert and François Ewald [Paris: Gallimard, 1994] 1:540–544) and to which Foucault's thought has since been reduced as a mere formula, here has its factual ground and finds in the posing of the problem that now interests us its fitting coinage in Foucault's thesis of the work and fullness of that which makes history possible, the "murmur of a language that speaks *by itself* and continually of itself, without a speaking subject and without an interlocutor, crushed unto itself . . . and without being noticed returns into the silence from which it had never freed itself" (Foucault, *Wahnsinn und Gesellschaft* [Frankfurt: Suhrkamp, 1993], 12. On this point, see the critical defenses of this position in Derrida, "Cogito und die Geschichte des Wahnsinns," in *Die Schrift und die Differenz*, 53–101 [Frankfurt: Suhrkamp, 1985], 59).

of argument and formulation. The difficulties in which Foucault involves himself lie in short in the fact that he shows that archaeology itself resorts to the role of the disengaged observer,[58] which shows that discourses obey rules that are constitutive for the production of their subjects and objects and which is to describe empirically the possibility and task of archeology as the positivity of discursive practices. On the other hand, in this "descriptive self-definition" a simultaneously contradictory theory is implied, which now as well explains the production of discursive practices, indeed is to be able to rule them, through which however the rules that the discourse grasps descriptively transform, in their formulation, into existential conditions of this discursive ordering. A prescription thus comes from out of the description. It is thereby shown that the role of the disengaged observer does not bear the weight that Foucault assigns to archaeology and seeks to undergird, that he leaves out truth and meaning as criteria of the strictness of discursive analysis in order to dedicate himself entirely to the positivity of expression. The claim bound up with it to an alleged standpoint for the analysis of as it were 'neutral outside' is thus in any case untenable, insofar as the analysis of discourse must adhere equally in its execution within and outside that which it thematizes.

One can grasp this problem hermeneutically in such a way that Foucault as an archaeologist is unable to avoid operating implicitly with a "preunderstanding" and a "horizon," even though he decidedly rejects these hermeneutic structures for his analysis of discourse. Underhandedly, however, they still have their effect, insofar as Foucault grants, for example, that the discursive formations rest in a foundation, which as "the universal system of the formation and transformation of expressions,"[59] determines itself terminologically as *archive* and can never be described in its totality and delineated in its actuality, or in this sense, objectivated. Instead, it determines us continuously and beneath the surface as a *vis a tergo*, so to speak, because "it [is] impossible for us to describe our own archive,

---

58. Jürgen Habermas calls attention, albeit in a rather abbreviated and simplistic manner, to the way in which Foucault constitutes a starting point for communication theory in *Der philosophische Diskurs der Moderne: Zwölf Vorlesungen* (Frankfurt: Suhrkamp, 1988), 290f., 325f.). Hubert Dreyfus and Paul Rabinow show the way in which those difficulties that ultimately drove Foucault himself away from this stance in his thinking can be properly depicted in their study, *Michel Foucault: Jenseits von Strukturalismus und Hermeneutik* (Weinheim: Beltz, 1994), 105–127.

59. Foucault, *Archäologie des Wissens*, 188 (emphasis deleted).

since we speak within its rules."[60] That means, hermeneutically and speaking analogically according to the matter at hand, that effective-historical consciousness does not encompass effective history as a whole, but much more always already underlies it. What can be grasped with effective history or the archive also goes for the total cultural horizon, which is transcendent in its relation to the subject as it is grasped, analogically in Gadamer and Foucault, as refusal of the possibility of grasping history theoretically as a totality of sense. *For human self-understanding history opens itself as that originary and therein ever-withdrawn space of presence inside which relations of sense and indication find themselves, but cannot still be derived from an origin, nor projected to a final goal.*

What comes to light here is the insight into the finitude of the knowing subject, which, as Foucault shows, manifests itself at the same time as *historical*. We also find difficulties enmeshed in this approach, insofar as the constitutive finitude and historicity of human experience—conceived as archaeology in the analysis of contexts of experience and experiential structures—is not tied to any ultimately ahistorical-positivistic claim as with structuralist approaches, a claim that for its part cannot be settled on the basis of the constitutive condition of the subject. Just as little is the interpreting subject to be silenced as presupposition of discursive analysis. That means that the renunciation of the author-I as explanatory ground of the constituting discursive order in the text itself has *not* already suspended or quite discredited the question concerning the self once and for all.[61]

Foucault's own shift toward the question of the constitution of a self, which he defines as care of the self, comes to be, as a hermeneutic that investigates the diverse technologies of the self, a central concern of his later, existentially inspired thinking. And it is precisely at this point, in the context of an "aesthetics of existence" worked out as the notion of a self-

60. Ibid., 189.

61. To formulate an indicator of the problem, one can pose the question whether, in Foucault's renunciation, his rejection of the situatedness of a text in terms of the traditional tripartite relation of author-text-reader in favor of the emphasis on the anonymity of discourse into which one inscribes oneself, or rather, is always already inscribed, anything can have an effect with respect to discursive orders. That is, what can be presented in relation to the weight of anonymity for the day-to-day living of the individual and its communal formations in their ground as an existential structure of human being? With a view to this relation to self-formation, it would be apt here to recall Heidegger's analyses from the famous 'They' chapter of *Being and Time.*

determined life, that a new role is developed for literature beyond its function within the discursive constellations of power of the moderns, a role that leads to an analysis of writing as a practice of self-discovery and, in light of ancient techniques of selfhood, to investigate writing historically.

In the given connection, it is simply to be noted that the space of the play of possibility of the sayable, which determines itself in discourse and as an occurrence of language, thus also determines itself in the text in such a way that it constantly defers its limits in themselves without, as Foucault stresses, the ability to possess 'originary fixed points' or 'coordinates.' For that reason, it emphatically indicates that in the realm of the knowable accessible to us, there never is *the,* but rather only *an* order. Yet there is an order within and it must also be in and for the processes of self-understanding of humans. Such discursive orders form themselves roughly in art and science, but also in and as socially regulated institutions.

It is decisive that these orders constitute themselves without being posited by a subject in a kind of 'act of creation.' It is therefore necessary, according to Foucault, for a sufficient analysis of these orders of discourse that they are determined from an archaeological as well as a genealogical perspective, which brings these orders to light in their historical emergence, that is, in their sense of possibility [Möglichkeitssinn]. It is from this point, and in a conscious allusion to Nietzsche, that the problem is reflected in its genesis with an eye toward the constellation of power and relations of power effecting it, as the embodiment of those orders that exempt themselves from art and the sciences, among others. It is to be noted here that there is no instituting individual master subject. It is also the case that the above-mentioned principle of anonymity as it were pushes and comes to power, which thus constitutes discourse as a complex referential connection, itself becoming manifest in its contingent orders and in self-organizing expressions in Foucault's sense. Within its relations of reference, what can be said in the domain of this order comes to be determined, but also has effects beyond the sayable out of what, in irrecoverable events, is unsaid. It is precisely here that that historical network is extracted in its plural tension, which in the renunciation of that sense of unity and origin as discontinuous structured historical horizon is to interpret the task of hermeneutical analysis in the contingent options of sense, and is present approximately in the form of textual objectivation; hermeneutical analysis, like the text itself, can produce itself only *within* the horizon as a partial opening of the horizon.

§ 8. The Sense-Creating Potential of Texts: The Modification of the World

Retained in this equally complex and discontinuous structured horizon, the text accordingly reproduces the pregivenness of the world—understood as sense—neither simply nor in parts, with regard to the question of the connection of the occurrence of the text, in that the text produces contingent self-formation, i.e., a social-historical referential connection, which also can be grasped in the term *lifeworld,* and admittedly in the sense of its use, which is to be still more closely determined in the early Heidegger (see § 31). The text—and herein lies its potential for sense creating—*modifies* in each case what itself becomes visible in and through it as the effective-historically conditioned *(con)text of the world.* In this sense, Wolfgang Iser states as well that a text is "a reformulation of already formulated reality, though which something comes into the world that previously was not in it."[62]

The text orders itself in the sense of a relatively autonomous—given that it is only to be thought in relation to its situatedness—creation of sense as the possible answer to a problem sketched out in advance in a previous occurrence, in a context understood as a subjective act, corresponding at one time with the intention of the author and at another in accordance with the intentions of his recipients. But both intentions cannot be compatible in the last sense, because the intentions of the author can be taken up and interpreted on the side of the reader only in the form of their textualization, and this even only according to one's own disposition of knowing. What the author wants to say to us, we experience thus from within the autonomously functioning text, or otherwise not at all. And even the possible deferred oral explanation produced by the author as self-interpretation, taken strictly, is yet another text of its own.[63]

Accordingly, it must be borne in mind that the text's connection of sense is not to be composed as something constant in itself, but rather re-

---

62. Iser, *Der Akt des Lesens,* 8.

63. A commentary text stands in a dependent position with respect to the original and may appear to that extent ancillary, given that a commentary holding itself in a constitutive connection to the antecedent text has its special function through the fact that it discloses the text's potential as yet in need of interpretation on the reader's part, which can serve as evidence either for the weakness, that is, the lack of clarity of what is written, or for its level of difficulty. From whichever motive, in a commentary on their own work authors encounter their text as interpreters, which means that they switch, strictly speaking, over to the side of the recipient.

mains exposed to perpetual dislocations and deferrals. This condition corresponds to what Gadamer has highlighted as the constitutive hermeneutical experience proper to us, insofar as it means, as experience of history, that "we stand within an occurrence without knowing how it happens to us and only grasp in hindsight what has happened,"[64] whereby even "history must be written anew from every new present."[65]

In these *deferrals of sense* appropriating themselves within texts on the ground of historical experience, which allow understanding to appear as a constantly self-renewing interpreting, one could, with a view to the textual connection, believe in a proximity to the manifold, varied, programmatic thesis of Jacques Derrida on the infinite play of linguistic signs, which constantly produces other new texts and aspires to withdraw from a traditionally conceived concept of interpretation, which aims to decipher the truth of a revealed originary sense. For Derrida, the approach to limitless play, with its positive connotations, and to the order of signs generated from it, eludes from the start any basic determination according to truth and origin.

In light of Derrida's notion and the "affirmation . . . of *genetic* indeterminacy"[66] bound up with it, which involves the demand to defer the "*seminal* adventure of the trace (*l'aventure séminale de la trace*),"[67] that intends at the same time an interruption of the unity of a text's meaning and thus of the bindingness of meaning, it should also be noted from the vantage point of the Gadamerian approach—which Derrida prematurely charges with the tendency toward determination—that interpretation, hermeneutically considered, must always forego an original or final meaning. Hence, we must consider the experience of history as the experience of those texts situated historically within it, whose interpretation becomes the unending task of ongoing restructured renewal in the face of the effective potential lying therein, as a result of which every age gives rise to "its own Goethe."

With Derrida in mind, and with regard to the "question, that decides about the rank and range of hermeneutics as about the objections of their

---

64. Gadamer, *Text und Interpretation*, 333.

65. Ibid.

66. Derrida, "Die Struktur, das Zeichen und das Spiel im Diskurs der Wissenschaften vom Menschen," in *Die Schrift und die Differenz*, 441.

67. Ibid.

opponents,"[68] it is therefore right to clarify at the outset whether interpretation "is an *imposition* of sense and not a *finding* of sense."[69] If one attempts to follow Gadamer's (admittedly not always sharply clarified) reflections on interpretation as a finding of sense, then that in no way means that finding, as is assumed from the Derridean perspective, would be equated with deciphering an originary truth. Indeed, on the contrary, finding does not mean decoupling the bond of the assumption of sense from the text, but rather recognizing it as a basis of the assumption of sense—a sense that can never be exhausted. It cannot be so, because the text never says everything, but rather essentially contains an excess of meaning [*Sinnüberschuß*],[70] insofar as the text is not a pregiven object in the historical context as a self-transforming horizon, but rather must be seen, qua an objectivated structure of sense, as just "a phase in the execution of an occurrence of understanding."[71] This execution demands to be interrogated anew according to the historical transformation in order to be able to be exposed

68. Gadamer, *Text und Interpretation*, 340. With regard to the concept of hermeneutics, it is to be manifestly conceded, indeed emphasized, that there is no one single hermeneutic, and where it is spoken of in this way today, it is often to be found in the words of its critics, who— whether they be Jacques Derrida or Karl-Otto Apel—form their own straw man of hermeneutics that allows them to easily rebuff the hermeneutical approach for their own purposes. Yet hermeneutics for their own purposes is not the proper hermeneutical view of the problems that they respectively attempt to negotiate.

Against such sweeping and unitary concepts one must point out that entirely different and even antagonistic positions are traded under the concept of hermeneutics. Names like Schleiermacher, Droysen, Dilthey and Heidegger, as well as Gadamer, Ricoeur, and Donald Davidson, themselves indicate in this starkly abbreviated selection an extraordinarily broad spectrum within which this label is applicable. And even when such positions are accepted that in their own self-description are not taken expressly as hermeneutical, yet can be identified as in fact akin to hermeneutics—as is the case with Spinoza's critique of the Bible, and with Freud, Marx, and Nietzsche—allowances are made for more distant positions that break new ground in their discussion with hermeneutics, as is demonstrated in the cases of Habermas, Rorty, Foucault and Vattimo: then it is easily understood when self-identified hermeneuticists like Jean Grondin (see *Einführung in die Hermeneutik* [Darmstadt: Wissenschaftliche Buchgesellschaft, 1991], 21) attest to the concept of an "enormous haziness" and opponents in the meantime are able to speak of one's own communicable "hermeneutical sickness" (Herbert Schnädelbach, "Morbus Hermeneuticus: Thesen Über eine Philosophische Krankheit," in *Vernunft und Geschichte: Vorträge und Abhandlungen* 279–284 [Frankfurt: Suhrkamp, 1987], 279. See Grondin's reply: "Ist die Hermeneutik eine Krankheit? Antwort auf Herbert Schnädelbach," in *Zeitschrift für Philosophische Forschung* 45 [1991], 430–438).

69. Gadamer, *Text und Interpretation*, 339f.

70. Cf. Günter Figal's study, "Vom Schweigen der Texte," in *Für eine Philosophie von Freiheit und Streit: Politik-Ästhetik-Metaphysik* (Stuttgart: Metzler, 1994), 7–19.

71. Gadamer, *Text und Intepretation*, 345.

to its possible (but not static and originary) fixed sense as the articulation that issues *hic et nunc* from the text from under the reader's corresponding effective-historical conditions for reflecting. Thus, it is always necessary to hold in view what H. R. Jauss described as the "*hermeneutical difference between the former and the present understanding of a work.*"[72]

This difference in which, following Gadamer, the problem of temporal distantiation (*Zeitenabstand*) reveals itself, comes into greater focus when the question posed in the text is, on the readers' part, no longer their own, no longer concerns them, whereby pathways to misunderstanding open up over and against the text. In such a case, the hermeneutical interpretation under consideration, bearing in mind hermeneutical difference, itself poses the task of the "reconstruction of the question of which a given text is an answer."[73] For this task, Gadamer unequivocally declares that such a reconstruction cannot be grasped "as a pure achievement of historical methodology."[74] This also does not mean that 'psychological understanding' is capable of gaining access, as it were, to the space of hermeneutical

72. Hans Robert Jauss, *Literaturgeschichte als Provokation* (Frankfurt: Suhrkamp, 1970), 183. The "hermeneutical difference" evinces itself, among other places, with the historical change in conditions of reading as well as of writing the degree to which the bindingness of a text's meaning can modify itself, and this modification can be understood from the perspective of a validity claim that takes itself to be authoritative as a relativization of the text's meaning. One can thus see in Jauss's favored basic principle an "aesthetic hermeneutics that gives priority to the question of the interpreter, whereby the answer to a text is newly developed time and again" (*Ästhetische Erfahrung und literarische Hermeneutik* [Frankfurt: Suhrkamp, 1991], 398).

The extent to which the position of the reader determines the relation to the text—the relation which at the same time, however, is rivaled by the effective history of the text—can be seen by the fact that a person who believes in Christ can read the Bible as a binding reference for action in leading his own life, and at the same time a historian of religion can consult it in comparison with the Koran or the Torah as an object for the investigation of possible interdependencies; or, further, one can, as an atheist, challenge the notion of revealed content as truth content.

That such changes in attitude toward a book that was formerly protected as authoritative, and to that extent sacred, can be carried out today without fear of penalty is itself in turn a possibility that, roughly put, has only opened through the historical process of modern secularization. In the wake of this opening I, as a reader or interpreter who comport myself in one of the attitudes toward the Bible mentioned above, always already experience myself as shaped by the effective history of this secularization as my lifeworldly horizon, which I can neither transcend nor produce, but in which I am held, exceeding and conditioning me. In regard to this process of secularization, see Hans Blumenberg's expansive study, *Die Legitimität der Neuzeit: Erneute Ausgabe* (Frankfurt: Suhrkamp, 1988).

73. Gadamer, *Wahrheit und Methode*, 379.

74. Ibid.

interpretation itself. Rather, this reconstruction carries itself out as a hermeneutical task corresponding to that which Waldenfels noted in dependence on the phenomenological, taken as "*hermeneutical epoché.*"[75] What he has in mind by this is that all validity claims, and thus the truth content of the text's expression, are suspended in advance in order to take hold of the question formulated in the text as a problem that poses itself; that is, to reconstruct the "sense" of the discourse prior to its interpretative evaluation.

With regard to Gadamer's 'dialectic of question and answer' applied to the understanding of texts as 'the logic of the question,' as he calls it, that means as an operative principle: "one can only understand a text if one has understood the question to which it is an answer."[76] But this is only possible under an adequate consideration of the hermeneutical difference as the task posed therein of reconstruction, to communicate the *historical horizon* of the text. At the same time, however, as a point of reference in reconstruction this is already exceeded, and precisely in the direction of the horizon that encompasses us as questioners and therein as addressees of the word of tradition. It is in this being-addressed, this being-struck, that Gadamer discerns the "truth of effective-historical consciousness,"[77] which as historically experienced and experiencing consciousness is open to the experience of history, and which Gadamer describes in its manner of execution as the "fusion of horizons of understanding mediating between text and interpreter."[78]

Bound to this concept of horizon that is so central to Gadamer's work as a whole is what is carried out in the prejudicial character of understanding. For the progressive self-formation of the horizon of the present has its impetus in the fact that all assumptions—in the sense of the forestructure of understanding—that determine us must be investigated and monitored in a sustained process, to which belongs the task of reflecting upon these assumptions as factically situated within the event of tradition. In other words, the horizon of the present can in no way take shape of itself, without the past. Gadamer famously characterizes this horizonal context of occurrence by the notion of a fusion of horizons (*Horizontverschmelzung*).

75. Waldenfels, *Antwortregister*, 131.
76. Gadamer, *Wahrheit und Methode*, 376.
77. Ibid., 383.
78. Ibid.

What is meant with this much-criticized and misunderstood term can be illustrated in the phenomenon of tradition. For in the persistence of traditions such a fusion already occurs continually, insofar as therein "the old and new always again [grow] together into a vital significance, without one expressly setting itself apart from the other."[79] In spite of this insightful grounding of the use of the concept of fusion, Gadamer poses an objection to himself, asking why, instead of horizonal fusion we do not simply speak "of the formation of a horizon that pushes back its limits into the depths of tradition."[80] Such a designation, as one can interpret the self-objection, still abetted the misunderstanding of finally assuming in the concept of fusion an acceptance of a synthesis of the primarily partial horizons existing for themselves.

Against this notion of fusion that follows normal linguistic usage, Gadamer stresses that the methodologically selected and applied term 'horizonal fusion' responds *in advance* to the achievement of that understanding which already reflects upon itself *as* hermeneutical consciousness and therein sees posed in front of the scientific task the relation of tension, which is experienced in the encounter with tradition between it and the present, "not to be discovered in naive comparison, but rather to be unfolded consciously."[81] Thus, what belongs to the hermeneutical understanding necessarily is "the project of a historical horizon, which distinguishes itself from the horizon of the present."[82] As already seen, however, this project is itself only, as Gadamer stresses, "a momentary phase in the process of understanding and does not rigidify itself in the self-alienation of a past consciousness, but rather is outstripped by the proper horizon of understanding of the present."[83] But this is nothing other than the event of the fusion of the horizon, "which completes at the same time this suspension with the project of the historical horizon,"[84] and this precisely in the sense of an applied achievement (cf. § 38). For the hermeneutical understanding arrives essentially, according to Gadamer, at the "controlled completion of

79. Ibid., 311.
80. Ibid.
81. Ibid.
82. Ibid.
83. Ibid., 312.
84. Ibid.

such fusion,"[85] which is itself the achievement of effective-historical consciousness.

If the context of the lifeworld—in which a text *inscribes* itself and which it at the same time therein also *modifies*—is brought into play as connection of the past and present individual and historical-social referential relations under the key word *effective history*, that does not mean that effective history is to be thereby converted into the function of a world or universal history.[86] Rather, effective history actualizes itself particularly and at the same time plurally in the manifold histories into which history, insofar as one wants to use this collective singular, is always already broken up,[87] thus constituting itself at the same time as manifoldness of discourses. In such discourse one can, on the one side, like Michel Foucault, know the rule-governed praxis of the forms of knowledge arising from it.

85. Ibid.

86. We should concede that it remains undecided whether and to what extent Gadamer's effective history is conceived, alongside the notion of the occurrence of tradition and in light of the tradition determined therein, primarily as a continuity that potentially keeps aspects of discontinuity underexposed. Nevertheless, the occurrence of tradition does not permit of being hypostatized in this way. For determining effective history as world or universal history means nothing other than translating Gadamer's hard-won hermeneutical insights back into a historical conception of history and simply equating the one with the other.

The historical notion of history departs from the position of idealist philosophy of history, and thereby from the belief in the progress of reason as the self-unfolding of spirit in the course of history. But in its perspective of the individual as historically solitary and concrete, it adheres to a connection of history grounded on continuity, whether founded as world history of God as in Leopold von Ranke, or as cultural history borne by historical consciousness as in Jacob Burckhardt, or as universal history grounded back on life in its social-historical reality, as in Wilhelm Dilthey. For more on these points, see Leopold von Ranke, *Über die Epochen der neueren Geschichte* (Darmstadt: Wissenschaftliche Buchgesellschaft, 1965); Jacob Burckhardt, *Weltgeschichtliche Betrachtungen* (Stuttgart: Alfred Kröner, 1978); Dilthey, *Der Aufbau der geschichtlichen Welt*, 79–188; see also Schnädelbach, *Geschichtsphilosophie nach Hegel: Die Probleme des Historismus* (Freiburg: Alber, 1974), 34–76; Karl Löwith, *Weltgeschichte und Heilgeschehen: Die theologischen Voraussetzungen der Geschichtsphilosophie*, in *Sämtliche Schriften*, vol. 2, ed. Klaus Stichweh (Stuttgart: Metzler, 1983), 30–42; Franz Joseph Wetz, *Lebenswelt und Weltall: Hermeneutik der unabweislichen Fragen* (Stuttgart: Campus, 1994), 92–96; Thomas Gil, *Kritik der Geschichtsphilosophie: L. von Rankes, J. Burckhardts und H. Freyers Problematisierung der klassischen Geschichtsphilosophie* (Stuttgart: M & P, 1993), 47–204.

87. Within the phenomenological milieu, the Husserl scholar Wilhelm Schapp has developed his *Philosophie der Geschichten* (Frankfurt: Rautenberg, 1981), which undertakes, in opposition to the conception of a single universal or world history, to show that history only happens in narratives (*Geschichten*) in which a person is enmeshed, as Schapp meticulously portrays it in his book *In Geschichten verstrickt (Zum Sein von Mensch und Ding)*, (Frankfurt: Klostermann, 1985). See Hermann Lübbe, *Bewußtsein in Geschichten: Studien zur Phänomenologie der Subjektivität; Mach-Husserl-Schapp-Wittgenstein* (Freiburg: Rombach, 1972), esp. 98–114.

On the other side, one has to accentuate, with Paul Ricoeur, language practice in this structuring discourse as histories, and admittedly in distinction from a code, or from a closed system of linguistic signs.

§ 9. Excursus on the Metaphor of the "Book of the World"

If texts take shape as discourse in this sense, where possible, they also formulate and inscribe themselves in the horizon of the effective-historical, actualized, intersected and extended occurrence of tradition, then talk of the text here should not awaken the association that this horizon, appearing as it were like a "supertext," resuscitates the old metaphor of the *book of the world*. As Hans Blumenberg has thoroughly shown in *The Legibility of the World*, this metaphor of the world book, in its use as an expression of a longing for the possession of sense [*Sinnbesitzverlangens*], is bound to the assumption of a totality of sense spelled out in the ordering of the world or of nature.

Blumenberg traces in detail the establishment as well as the stages of the utilization throughout history of the metaphor of the book of the world, in their progressive and regressive moments alike, and shows that only with Christianity and its "collective singularity of the holy book"[88] does the book gain ascendancy as a "metaphor of a totality,"[89] whether in relation to nature or to history, which thus becomes conceived as salvation history. Decisive here is the notion that the word, in distinction from Greek thought (that as *logos* in the Christian doctrine of creation is conceived as the beginning in God and consequently creation itself, as Blumenberg notes by way of Hugo of Saint Victor) appears as a book written by the hand of God, whereby its legibility is at the same time warranted as a task directed to understanding and interpreting.[90]

With regard to the question of authority at the beginning of modernity, the legibility of the world persists as a fundamental conviction where the

---

88. Blumenberg, *Die Lesbarkeit der Welt* (Frankfurt: Suhrkamp, 1981), 23.

89. Ibid.

90. Ibid., 52. Augustine (*Über den Wortlaut der Genesis*, trans. Carl Johann Perl, vol. 2 [Paderborn: Ferdinand Schöningh, 1961–1964]) was in this sense the first to establish a two-book theorem with God as the author. See on this point Heribert Maria Nobis. "Buch der Natur," in *Historisches Wörterbuch der Philosophie*, ed. Joachim Ritter (Basel: Schwabe, 1971), 1:957ff.; Helmut K. Kohlenberger, "Buch der Schöpfung," in *Historisches Worterbuch*, 959f.

'book of nature' gains dominance in the transition from the book of Revelation with the rise of the modern natural sciences. It is written, according to Galileo, in the spirit of mathematics, through which nature gradually becomes scientific in progress and harmony with the process of secularization, and the totality of sense of the world and natural order invested in the foundation of the metaphor of the world book is lost. The word, which held sway for reading the book of the world, disappears in favor of the formalizations and formulas of the mathematized natural sciences.

The Romantics forcefully struggled against this tendency, striving to decipher the book of nature by means of the language of poetry. Blumenberg argues in particular, relying on the work of Novalis, that the romantic search for a book of nature disclosed by means of poetry, which hopes thereby to win back the order of the world as totality of sense, can no longer base itself on an unproven, originary trust in an inherently meaningful world. The suspicion remains that an indifferent nature behind this desired order could ultimately manifest itself as a mask of a self-projected, poetic dream of romantic consciousness opposed to all claims to sense.[91]

In the successors to the Romantics, there is shown what Blumenberg discovers in interpretations of Flaubert, Mallarmé, and Valéry as an ineluctable finding: the "blank book of the world."[92] With a view to the course of the history of metaphors about the world as a book, the world appears at first as an annunciation of God's creation to his created beings, on account of which "the loss of this function [must] then leave behind the empty gesture of meaning, the world as a book about nothing."[93] But with

91. The unreasonable demand made of humans, often bound up with this, of recognizing one's life as meaningful for oneself and yet as indifferent for the world, is taken up by Franz Joseph Wetz as a point of departure for his "hermeneutics of the scientific worldview," which raises the "scientifically apprehended reality of the natural world to the level of fundamental reality" (*Lebenswelt und Weltall*, 15) and consequently represents as his own basic position, in decided proximity to Blumenberg's "absolutism of reality," an "absolutism of the world," which concerns itself "with a methodological concluding interpretation concordant in its content with naturalism, but proceeding hermeneutically" (ibid., 18), whose central thesis consists in recognizing the physical universe as fully groundless and aimless in itself and without any higher sense present at hand. But for Wetz, this recognition is not equivalent to the despair of a nihilism; rather, taking the view that the human being is capable of accepting himself as "ultimately nothing more than an absolutely evanescent particle around an organic material that looks out for itself" (ibid., 19), he can learn to positively mark off the framework of the indispensable orientations of sense for himself and his form of life on this side of the illusions of religion and metaphysics.

92. Blumenberg, *Die Lesbarkeit der Welt*, 300.

93. Ibid., 304.

this, the use of the metaphor of the book of the world as a totality of sense becomes questionable in general—even if it no longer contains hyperbolic modifications of metaphysical horizons of totality, which Blumenberg sees to an extent in the psychoanalytic 'reading of dreams'[94] or the deciphering of the genetic code[95] in fact without the fulfillment of expectations aligned to the totality of sense corresponding or being able to correspond to psychoanalytic or genetic readings.

Keeping this in view, the talk of the text in its relation to the world invoked in the present reflections—and this is what we are attempting to make clear through this excursus guided by Blumenberg—does not just reconstitute speech about the 'book of the world.' For in the hermeneutical talk about the text, against this programmatic history in its most comprehensive extension as objectivation for thinking plurally in itself it is objected that for the text the renunciation of the originary and final inner orientations is just as constitutive as for something like the unified totality of sense. As we have seen, the text, as a "phase in the execution of the occurrence of understanding," is an immanent structure of meaning with its own bindingness, and is so always and only in being traced out by effective-historically actualized or actualizable perspectives, so that this bindingness itself is only what it is in the force field (*Kraftfeld*) of all of those histories and developments the echoes of which have taken on a new voice in this or that text. It becomes perceptible in the understanding appropriation that forms itself only in connection to tradition, with which it has to relate its standpoint. This standpoint projects the perspective of the horizon of the present. This horizon of the present is the hermeneutical situation determined by assumptions [*Vormeinungen*].

§ 10. In the Network of Tradition: On Understanding as an Incursion into the Current of Texts

The understanding appropriation of texts is part of the occurrence of tradition comprehending them, on account of which Gadamer can stress that the understanding is "*not to be thought of so much as an action of subjectivity, but rather as an incursion into an occurrence of tradition* in which past and

---

94. Ibid., 337–371.
95. Ibid., 372–409.

present constantly mediate one another."[96] Since tradition passes itself down in texts and can address itself in the sense of the historical force field (therefore as a textual current or even textual field),[97] the self-completing understanding as an incursion into the current of the text conceives the understanding in itself, as already indicated, as itself determined by the subterranean effect of past texts. And that means, as will be shown, that it above all finds itself, even invents itself, in the sense of the self-understanding inserted hermeneutically within the occurrence of tradition.

In this incursion into the occurrence of tradition, however, there may not be seen a self-incorporation of the tradition of whatever type, in which the tradition transformed itself therein into the same form accessible to us. Contrary to Waldenfels's critique,[98] if only implicit, against Gadamer in connection with Derrida, it must instead be seen that for understanding, the passive moment of an inaccessible "always-already-being-immersed" plays a leading role, taking place prior to an active appropriation.

Instead of speaking of understanding as incursion, one could also speak of it as a type of *inscription,* which, in that it inscribes itself into something, leaves behind its traces, such that in so doing it is determined within the proper present as from that which has been and includes itself in advance as an occurrence of tradition. Thus, this inscription completes itself at the same time also as a search for traces. Yet in consequence, this is shown as inscription or incursion into a grasping understanding as some-

---

96. Gadamer, *Wahrheit und Methode,* 295.

97. If the text is addressed with a view to understanding as a "phase in the occurrence of understanding," so that a conversational model imposed by Gadamer, with the limitation noted above (§ 6), also proves its relevance here, then Waldenfels's structuring of a field of discourse, taken up in the context of his own investigations of "placing and displacing of the question and answer in the field of discourse" (*Antwortregister,* 270) is also fruitful for an analysis of the current or field of texts. Waldenfels determines the discursive field in its temporal, spatial, and social moments as an "embodiment of that which is *said with, heard with,* and *understood with* in a discourse" (ibid., 271), and in this sense as an "environment that encompasses discourse" (ibid.). Accordingly, three aspects are differentiated in the field of discourse: *context,* that is, "the linguistic (and practical) references . . . that are respectively expressed" (ibid.); *situation,* "which comprises all extra-linguistic (and extra-practical) circumstances in which something is said and understood" (ibid.); and *background,* "which comprises everything that was once said and which can be said again in appropriate circumstances" (ibid.). With respect to discourse, context, situation and background are, as should be easily seen from what has been detailed, distinguished as structural moments of a text and are indeed also already thematized, so that now in particular what Waldenfels calls background experiences a certain weight whenever the question of understanding qua incursion into the occurrence of tradition takes center stage.

98. See Waldenfels, *Antwortregister,* 556.

thing successive in relation to that which as tradition is still prior to all explicit relating to tradition at first as an open field of possibilities, and admittedly in reflection on the proper and alien. The proper completes itself in inscription as incursion into that which in its ground as a passing down is always already also far withdrawn, remains alien, and whose traces take up the incursion as inscription into themselves without thereby destroying the alien in the proper, so that the proper thus always remains to an extent alien. Even the historical occurrence of tradition is not finally determinable, which means that it is always more than that which can be recognized as a trace of this tradition in the form of established lines of tradition.

Of significance here is that this incursion into the connection of tradition determined as and through the text includes not only the appropriated texts read, that is, understood. Insofar as the tradition constitutes itself through and within the effect of texts—whether fixed through writing or orally repeated—every individual interwoven therein exists in and of himself only as the relations of tradition transcending him and preceding him, which means, seen as effective-historical, that one shows oneself to be determined by more than the texts that have become appropriated de facto. In other words, the human self- and world understanding underlies and forms itself from out of the force field of the particular historical-cultural tradition and therefore as it were as the tradition's co-constitutive memory and passed-down texts, which transcend in their effect the degree of understanding appropriation in the particular readings.[99]

If one pays attention, it is possible to clarify that where individual self-persuasion forms itself through reading in the exchange with texts, this always occurs against a background of established convictions, which already coeffect in this process of formation, without one's necessarily being

---

99. Within the discourse of the cultural sciences in recent years investigation has crystallized around the themes of 'recollection' and 'memory,' which Jan Assmann suspects signify the construction of a new paradigm of the cultural sciences, to which his own studies would then also be a contribution (*Das kulturelle Gedächtnis: Schrift, Erinnerung und politische Identität in frühen Hochkulturen,* 2nd ed. [Munich: C.H. Beck, 1997]). It bears notice that this dovetails with tendencies and studies that have been taking shape under the heading of a *"mémoire collective"* since the mid-twentieth century in the work of Maurice Halbwachs of the Bergson school (see *Das kollektive Gedächtnis* [Stuttgart: Fischer, 1967]).

The potential, reflecting its own groundwork, and thus metahermeneutical, which could directly spring from even such cultural-scientific analyses through the insights into the hermeneutical principle of effective history and effective historical consciousness, remains to this point quite underutilized, in spite of the indisputable gains for the meaning of hermeneutics in the philosophical and scientific discourses of recent years.

aware of their formative force. The question of the autonomous formation of judgment or even the enlightened postulate of thinking for oneself restricts itself from thence to a relational and historically effected autonomy, which cannot really cast off the conditions of its historical genesis, but rather has the limits and possibilities of its self-development in the situatedness of its approach.[100]

Europeans, for example, are so culturally stamped by Christianity and even by the effective history of Judeo-Christian texts that those who today

100. In order to avoid misunderstandings, it ought to be indicated that this restriction in no way subverts the postulate of a Horatian '*Sapere aude!*' or even Kant's demand for the courageous employment of one's own understanding, in the sense that the tradition exists as a constructed authority that is to be accepted without question or complaint. It is precisely the historically relational character indicated in hermeneutical reflection of the autonomous use of reason that no longer has an unquestionable basis, in regard to thinking for oneself, in the authority of tradition. Authority, in its regulative function, is not, however, thereby disavowed, much less removed.

It has its irrevocable sense and preserves itself in daily life, for example, in the regulation of street traffic or in the teacher-student relationship. But even here authorities must make themselves insightful [*einsichtig*] in their claims, that is, to prove themselves through competence, in order to count as authority and not as arbitrary (see Max Weber, *Wirtschaft und Gesellschaft* [Tübingen: Mohr Siebeck, 1976]; Joseph M. Bochenski, *Autorität, Freiheit, Glaube* [Munich: Philosophia, 1988]). With regard to philosophy, that means bracketing naive adoptions of educational authority and critiquing them in their claims to validity, whereby such examination must include a self-explication and self-monitoring with regard to its own claims.

In the context of this problematic, Gadamer's formulation of a "rehabilitation of authority and tradition" (*Wahrheit und Methode*, 281–290) at the end of the 1960s triggered a well-known debate documented in the collected volume *Hermeneutik und Ideologiekritik*, ed. Karl-Otto Apel (Frankfurt: Suhrkamp, 1971). Jürgen Habermas in particular posed the thesis that Gadamer short-circuited tradition and authority as a countermaneuver to the Enlightenment's postulate of reason, which is a misrepresentation, since for Gadamer the question of authority is, qua acquired competency, bound up affirmatively with reason. Also, without going deeper into this debate, the more so as these respective positions have been further developed and sharpened in the meantime (see Gadamer, *Zwischen Phänomenologie und Dialektik* in *GW* vol. 2, esp. 21ff.; see also Grondin, *Einführung in die Philosophische Hermeneutik*. [Darmstadt: Wissenschaftliche Buchgesellschaft, 1991] 166–173), the reproach made time and again against Gadamer—that consistency is lacking in his use of concepts—is itself enlightening.

Within certain limits, this reproach is justified. Yet it should be noted that for Gadamer it is not simply a matter of providing a precise specification of the circumscribed field of a concept, such that once established, it persists as a fixed terminological constant. Admittedly, Gadamer operates with an excessive mistrust of the formulation of terminology, since he suspects such methods in general of the tendency of all too quickly objectivating, which is to say, phenomenally abbreviating. More important than this rather dismissive stance—in fact, positively decisive—is the fact that Gadamer's formation of concepts, not unlike that of Hegel, is determined through the context of a given question. His conceptual indexing thus determines its respective phenomena in order to "broaden, in concentric circles, the unity of comprehended meaning" (*Wahrheit und Methode*, 296), which primarily describes an open, unending process.

command hardly any or even no express knowledge of the Bible are carried in their self-understanding by Christian background convictions, which make them into a perceptible echo, to a certain degree, of the effect of this textual current. What testifies more to a broken relation to the text as such a kind of echo in ignorance and half-knowing can be transformed in scientific appropriation into something explicit, as we find in contemporary readings. But even this textual relation as explication is itself carried again by background convictions in the type and mode of its explicitness, which for example in the form of the existentiell, credibly determined connection to the text shapes the relation to it and thereby forms the space of encounter of the effect in the text.

As a further example of this constitutive antecedent interweaving within the network of tradition, we can point to the notion that today we can only regard works of representational art with "postimpressionist eyes" as it were, regardless of our wishes.[101] And since in effective history what was once innovative, which comes forth in art from the point of view of established habits of seeing as at most a scandal, over time erodes these forms of habituation to finally become a collective general aesthetic standard. This standard then implicitly and without question influences the shaping of our capacity of judgment. Hermeneutical efforts, perhaps even as well as historical analysis, are required in order to allow a work to be grasped from the point of view of its aesthetic as well as its historical conditions of emergence, as for example, is necessary when one visits the Museé d'Orsay in Paris and encounters Manet's great scandal, *Le Déjeuner sur l'Herbe*. By this means the as it were archeological and genetically constitutive layers of our present aesthetic consciousness are exposed in our being able to see and conceive of what was once morally offensive, but aesthetically innovative. The formerly innovative, which has formed our habits of vision the more it decisively becomes our own, becomes all the more strange as what was revolutionary in its innovative advance that conditioned our seeing. But therein it can become clear that it has a most prob-

---

101. See Gottfried Boehm, who demonstrates in his study "Zur Hermeneutik der Abstraktion" (in *Verstehen und Geschehen: Jahresgabe der Martin-Heidegger-Gesellschaft* [n.p.: Martin-Heidegger-Gesellschaft,1990], 13–25) how, by means of that process of abstraction constitutive for painting in the twentieth century and proceeding from Monet and stressing Kandinsky's role, through the formal, that is, the stylistic, new forms in painting—primarily through "the drawing out of pure pictorial elements" (23)—"new equivalents of reality" were created, which as such have in general changed our mode of perception.

lematic relationship with that which is considered self-evident [*Selbstver-ständliches*] or even natural, insofar as the self-evident always shows itself to be the result of *historically conditioned self-understanding*. And in general the question whether there is something like the natural and accordingly human nature, understood as constancy of sense, must at the very least be able to be meaningfully posed with regard to its historical constitutedness.

Turning our view to effective-historical philosophical thinking shows that that which is called metaphysics—if one is ready to accept this term in Heidegger's sense as the program of Western European philosophy—belongs to us historically and culturally as our own horizon and therein still always conceals to a large extent the possible scope of our thinking, and admittedly of the philosophical as much as the extraphilosophical.[102] Now, however much philosophical texts, in their conceptual language, may not be generally understood and are regarded as difficult to access, however much their concrete literature appears tied to the presuppositions of a correspondingly trained and educated understanding, considered from the standpoint of effective history the so-called metaphysical ideas and basic principles occupy, on the contrary, a far less exclusive status. For these have long since found their way into cultural, that is, among others, political, aesthetic, and ethical principles so that they can, at least relative

---

102. For example, we can detect a metaphysically established body of thought in those trivial lyrics that sing of a "freedom above the clouds" or the like, if only in the mode of deprivation. In such demonstrations one must, however, exercise great care. That is, one must attend to the relational contexts in which metaphysically handed-down linguistic expressions are applied. Such concepts as 'freedom' or 'being free' will have to be categorically and differentially determined in accordance with their usage within a concrete context if one wants to avoid abstruseness or, to speak with Gilbert Ryle, to be guilty of a category mistake. Precisely here, as Michael Kober (*Gewißheit als Norm: Wittgensteins erkenntnistheoretische Untersuchungen in Über Gewißheit* [Berlin: Walter de Gruyter, 1993], 32–35) has shown in connection with Eike von Savigny (*Die Philosophie der normalen Sprache: Eine kritische Einführung in die 'ordinary language philosophy'*, rev. ed. [Frankfurt: Suhrkamp, 1993], 323–363), in recourse to the normal use of an expression, one must differentiate between the differing functions in which this use is intended in order to ask "what actually is to be achieved in 'returning a word from its metaphysical-philosophical usage back to its normal usage'" (Kober, *Gewißheit als Norm*, 32).

And even when one positively adopts the table of precepts and prohibitions of analytical modes of clarification in ordinary-language philosophy, there remains the gnawing fundamental doubt whether so-called everyday language as a 'natural basis' may present a corrective to philosophically formulated problems, precisely because the naturalness of everyday language is shaped through *historical* and thus also metaphysical modes of tradition. Accordingly, there is no "philosophy free" natural or original employment of concepts. This of course in no way undercuts the need for a critical reflection on the linguistic employment of expressions in order to be able to differentiate between meaningful and meaningless philosophical problems.

to the realm of Westernized culture, be granted a universal meaningfulness, and perhaps are still most vital where they unconsciously influence, as so to speak "cryptoprejudices," formations of opinion in their historical origin.[103]

Such cultural principles can only be brought to light, however, when they are subject to their own comprehensibly interpreted efforts to illuminate critically their self-givenness (*Selbstgegebenheit*) with those validity claims tied to them in their historical conditionedness. Whether a possibility is already opened therein for overcoming or getting over that which is called metaphysics, in a positive constructive critique by means of a self-enlightenment of the decisive directions for its development, remains to be seen. In any case, every attempt at an overcoming, be it carried out in substantive attacks or *sine studio et ira*, ultimately proves itself to be dependent upon that which is to be overcome. Seen thus, there can be no situation of access to a tabula rasa, and where, as in Descartes's *Meditations*, something is feigned as methodologically sensible, one would of necessity be forced to ask in discussion with this methodological fiction whether it can be maintained in its intended sense and if so, what the price is for this sort of basic assumption. Just as little can one reasonably assume a thinking ab ovo as a point of departure, since no one ever actually turns back to an origin.[104]

One is precisely not, and never can be, in the situation of a "blank slate," but is rather more like that of litmus paper, which in the discussion of a given text experiences its reactions to the latter in that it engages the occurrence of tradition, weaves itself into the network bound in the texts,

---

103. How far these Western European basic principles of metaphysics have asserted themselves around the globe through declarations of human rights, techniques, or the idea of democracy and what this means for the problematic of non-European, tendential, or Europeanized cultures of the Americas or for the inherent character of strongly maintained Asian cultures, has been fruitfully discussed in studies undertaken by Gadamer ("Europa und die Oikoumene," in Hans-Helmuth Gander, ed. *Europa und die Philosophie* [Frankfurt: Klostermann, 1993], 67–86) and Klaus Held ("Europa und die interkulturelle Verständigung: Ein Entwurf im Anschluß an Heideggers Phänomenologie der Grundstimmungen," ibid., 87–103), among others.

104. In this sense Georg Picht emphasizes that "philosophy today can no longer understand itself as the path of the spirit to its eternal origin" (*Geschichte und Gegenwart*, 4). Seen thus it is also no longer possible, in Hegel's sense, that philosophy might know the *logos* "as it is in its eternal essence before the creation of nature and a finite spirit" (Georg Wilhelm Friedrich Hegel, *Wissenschaft der Logik I*, in *Werke*, ed. Eva Moldenhauer and Karl Markus Michel [Frankfurt: Suhrkamp, 1974], 5:44).

and thus actualizes—and modifies itself in the process—its effective potential in the interface of its reading.[105]

Metaphysics proves itself in accordance with this explication as a *vis a tergo*, that is not to be put behind it but to be illuminated where necessary in its apparent as well as its hidden traditions. In thereby illuminating the traditions, it is important to envision, aside from making present the strands of tradition determined by continuity, what this traditional current carries along with it in the way of underground and discontinuous dead ends

105. This effective historical relation becomes intuitive with regard to its actualization in effective historical consciousness when one considers the history of theatrical and operatic production. This shows itself particularly impressively in the displacement of the title character in the German-language reception of Shakespeare's *Merchant of Venice*. This example is particularly appropriate, because with the task of the actual staging of the text itself the present ontological and aesthetically significant question concerning the historical situation as hermeneutical space of experience of the production inevitably plays a role in the process of its realization.

This can be glimpsed in Fritz Kortner's famous interpretation of Shylock from 1969, which, in the literality of the script as background mood—subtly prompted in the space of the play as enmeshed in the consciousness of the audience—the historical experience of the Holocaust enters as if written on the wall in the mode of a palimpsest. Shylock's demand for justice rises in its aporia to a tragic conflict of innocent guilt—or guilty innocence—which in his person bears (suffers) [(er)trägt] the fate of a people. Thereby, however, comedy is transformed at the same time into tragedy, wherein Kortner's Shylock advances to become a spiritual relative of Lear.

Peter Zadek's 1990 Viennese production of the *Merchant* again individualizes these figures, having them operate in a rather secular world of money, which at the same time only mitigates in a certain sense the religious dimension of meaning over against Otto Schenk's production. From his own actual perception of the social reality of the 1980s, Zadek opens up a space within the piece for the possibility of showing the individuals involved as participants in an economically driven society in which at the same time, as a parable of gender relations, the cunning of women arises in a response to the discourse of "gender history" on the impotent [or unconscious, *ohnmächtige*] power of men. In this way, the piece regains its comic side, which the reception had determined up to the time of Max Reinhardt, and thereby situated *The Merchant of Venice* in the company of *As You Like It*.

But in the effective current of the text, Zadek's Shylock neither negates Kortner's reading nor supersedes it, but rather answers it, in that he perceives the text in the possibilities for its realization that gain their authenticity in the effective historical consciousness of its own situation as its realization, but in which the unalienable history of the Jews in the twentieth century belongs.

Accordingly, the question of how the *Merchant of Venice* can be produced is answered in light of the fact that the thoroughly resonant Elizabethan anti-Semitic ressentiment, typical of its time, is no longer made decisively into a constituent of the appraisal that formerly implicated its audience in an unspoken complicity with social prejudices. Insofar as this causes a production to fail today, effective historical consciousness answers as well where in the undertone of the play comedy dominates, at one with the voices of the victims.

and breaks.[106] That is, that one must question whether linearly maintained developments do not denote rather perspectival abbreviations, precisely from the point of view of contemplating consciousness, which seeks in the labyrinth of contexts of reference—and thus in the world—to pursue its Ariadne's threads, already taking the paths and passages tied to them for the whole, since it is unable to see directly its own blind spot.

§ 11. On the Interpretive Character of Knowledge in the Wake of the Historicity of Understanding

If in connection with the question of the understanding of texts the conversation repeatedly turned to the *principle of effective history* so central in Gadamer's thinking, it should in no way be inferred that effective history should thereby be implemented as a supplementary methodological instrument to the end of a "better" textual interpretation. Effective history, Gadamer rightly stresses, is no "new independent ancillary discipline of the human sciences"[107] that would allow a higher measure of exactitude for the interpretation of texts with regard to their intentional indication. Because the horizon of interpretation of the text, in the sense of effective history, proves itself open in principle and therefore irretrievable, the request to fix the text in such a way that it presents itself as a possible object of exact explanation is already invalid from the outset.[108]

106. Umberto Eco formulates this point programmatically: "Discontinuity is, in the sciences as well as in the connections of daily life, the category of our time: modern western culture has finally dissipated the classical concepts of continuity, universal laws, causal relations, and predictability of phenomena: it has, in short, renounced developing universal formulae that pose a claim to determine the wholeness of the world in simple and ultimate terms. New categories have gained entry into modern languages: ambiguity, uncertainty, possibility, probability" (Umberto Eco, *Das offene Kunstwerk* [Frankfurt: Suhrkamp, 1973], 214).

107. Gadamer, *Wahrheit und Methode*, 306.

108. Here it is to be maintained that the hermeneutical critique of the methodological ideal of exactness in human scientific knowledge, modeled by Gadamer and Heidegger and since become standard, is not something of an insight of resignation, arising from a "need to keep oneself modest," as was expressed by Wolfgang Stegmüller, among others, insofar as understanding, in the logic of expression, proves itself insufficient, for which reason it could be accorded solely a heuristic function in the form of empathy (see Stegmüller, "Walther von der Vogelweides Lied von der Traumliebe und Quasar 3 C 273," in *Rationale Rekonstruktion von Wissenschaft und ihrem Wandel* [Stuttgart: Reclam, 1979], 27–86).

But on the other hand, hermeneutical critique in no way intends a regression back to Schleiermacher's divinatory principle of understanding. Where it is a matter of critiquing

As we have seen, effective history functions as a *fundamental principle* in the framework of hermeneutics. This becomes evident if one considers that in explicit and thus hermeneutical consciousness corresponding to its reflective structure, the chance opens itself in as it were privileged ways for the self-understanding of human beings, that one learns to understand oneself better and admittedly through that one knows that every understanding, equally whether it is conscious explicitly as execution or not, preserves itself in the trace of effective history and consequently functions as its irrefutable echo, strengthening the effect therein. The historicity of understanding put so pointedly here reveals hermeneutical consciousness as that which cannot reflect its way out of this process in a pre- or transhistorical position of absolute reason. Instead, effective-historical consciousness, as we have seen, determines itself through the effect of effective history, but in such a way that *as itself hermeneutical,* it possesses an explicit knowing of itself as *finite* through and through.

Accordingly, hermeneutical consciousness, as actively interpreting and thus reflecting, is in the position to demonstrate, on the one hand, that and how all knowing unfolds from out of historical pregivenness, which equally reshapes and exceeds knowing. In the interminability thereby constitutively coposited as imperfectability of knowing, on the other side, the hermeneutical understanding reflects itself—as with all knowing in general—under the condition of finitude and in correspondence with the basic existential structure of human being (stressed from Schleiermacher on but first exhibited by Heidegger), the *circularity of understanding,* as that which Gadamer calls "the interactive play of the movement of tradition and the movement of the interpreter."[109]

This interactive play is in itself an open process, that is, one that cannot be confirmed in its point of departure in the sense of a result that can be fixed, but rather as constantly outstripping itself and therefore always also outrunning itself and provisional. For as the text-reader relation has shown in connection with the discussions on the factical disposition, the movement of tradition addressed here is no objectively reckonable pregivenness, no fixed point from which an interpretive thread could be

---

this ideal of exactness, it is rather to avoid false standards, and thus to realize a phenomenally identifiable adequacy to the object, wherein the mode of access is undogmatized, which occurs when the methodological processes of an advancing critical self-reflection are undertaken, which itself measured the relevant phenomena of interpretation.

109. Gadamer, *Wahrheit und Methode,* 298.

unspooled with regard to its testimony. Rather, it is always already code-termined as self-showing phenomenon in the mode of its self-showing, co-constituted through the countermovement of interpreting as that of the letting-encounter (*Betreffenlassens*) particular to its forms of presentation.

In this ability to let oneself encounter the space of possibility first open for that which becomes visible in the current of the occurrence of tradition to effective-historical consciousness, so that for understanding—in the sense of incursion, self-inscription into the occurrence of tradition—it only becomes possible to explicitly unlock the tradition as such precisely within the particular perspective opened to it of an interpreting cognition. As knowing, I stand in relation to the that which is known, not in the position of a "neutral counterpart," but rather I am implicated therein. This *self-implication* is a condition of the possibility of my knowing, but at the same time also of its limit. For that reason, every claim to an ahistorical being-known in itself of the particular object of knowledge itself leads *ad absurdum*. For if I am the limit, then I am able only within the drawing of the limit, which is inscribed for me in my existence and which is always historical, to know the appearing in the mode of its emergence.

One can therefore establish as a fundamental insight for hermeneutics as a theory of the process of understanding that knowing, as Nietzsche has already shown, possesses an *interpreting character;* the knowing of something as historical understanding is always already *interpretation,* notwithstanding whether its intentional relation to the particular *interpretandum* to be coposited has gone unseen.[110] But then as Nietzsche manifoldly stresses, "the *value of the world* [lies] in our interpretation,"[111] whereby "interpretations up to this point are perspectival estimates through which we are able to preserve ourselves . . . in life"[112] and whose inner dynamic in itself demands the process of life, "that every *elevation of human beings* brings with it the overcoming of narrower interpretations [and thus] every attained strengthening and expansion of power serves new perspectives

110. This constitutive basic principle of a hermeneutical theory of cognition can be applied mutatis mutandis as a kind of common denominator to the differing positions of Dilthey and his school just as much as the existential-hermeneutical approach taken by Heidegger. And here we can include as well the hermeneutics of Gadamer indebted to Heidegger, as also the hermeneutics of Paul Ricoeur.

111. Nietzsche, *Nachgelassene Fragmente: Herbst 1885—Herbst 1887,* in *KGW*, div. 8, vol. 1. (Berlin: Walter de Gruyter, 1974), 112.

112. Ibid.

and means believing in new horizons."[113] Seen from this point, Nietzsche turns vehemently against the positivistic belief in the facts given objectively in themselves: "No, there are no mere facts, only interpretations."[114] So it is with Nietzsche, as Paul Ricoeur stresses—as one of the first to make Nietzsche relevant for hermeneutical discourse—that "all of philosophy [becomes] interpretation,"[115] since he "derived from philology its concept of *indication, interpretation* [*Deutung, Auslegung*] in order to introduce them into philosophy."[116] In this way, the exegetical concept of interpretation seen by traditional hermeneutics is extended to the method of philosophy in general.

As Ricoeur stresses, a new determination of that which is called representation is associated with this elaboration. For the central problem according to Kant—whether and how objective validity comes to subjective representation—now recedes and will likewise also leave the enclosure of Platonic philosophy determined by truth and knowledge, insofar as a possibility appears, through Nietzsche's insight into the interpretative character of knowing, of replacing the problem of knowledge so radically that the central question neither turns around truth and falsehood in an epistemological sense, nor handles the lie in a moral sense. In the center instead, now stands illusion.[117]

Already by 1873, Nietzsche had put forth: "Truths are illusions of which we have forgotten that they are such."[118] Nietzsche thereby completes his leave-taking from the old "opposition of a true and an apparent world," in opposition to which he maintains "there is only one world, and this is . . . without sense. . . . Such a created world is the true world."[119] All

113. Ibid.

114. Ibid., 323.

115. Paul Ricoeur, *Die Interpretation: Ein Versuch über Freud* (Frankfurt: Suhrkamp, 1993), 38. On the question of Nietzsche and hermeneutics, see Johann N. Hoffman, *Wahrheit, Perspektive, Interpretation: Nietzsche und die philosophische Hermeneutik* (Berlin: Walter de Gruyter, 1994).

116. Ricoeur, *Die Interpretation*, 38.

117. See ibid., 39.

118. Nietzsche, *Über Wahrheit und Lüge im aussermoralischen Sinne*, in *KGW* div. 3, vol. 2 (Berlin: Walter de Gruyter, 1973), 374f.

119. Nietzsche, *Nachgelassene Fragmente: Herbst 1887–März 1888*, in *KGW* div. 8, vol. 2 (Berlin: Walter de Gruyter, 1970), 435. In another place, it reads: "there is no 'other,' no 'true,' no essential being . . . the opposition between seeming world and the true world reduces itself to the opposition of 'world' and 'nothing'" (*Nachgelassene Fragmente: Anfang 1888–Anfang Januar 1889*, in *KGW* div. 8, vol. 3 [Berlin: Walter de Gruyter, 1972], 163), whereby the character of

eschatological expectations are therefore deceptive in themselves. For Nietzsche, it is simply the case that the "destruction of an illusion does not produce a truth, but rather only a further piece of ignorance."[120] Therein also exists the "negative . . . character of 'truth'—as removal of an error, an illusion,"[121] but which therefore does not idly run on skeptically, because the "existence of illusion [means] an incitement to life."[122] "We need the lie . . . in order to live. . . . That the lie is necessary in order to live, this fact itself still belongs to this horrible and questionable character of existence. . . ."[123]

The hermeneutical task that grows from out of that means the unmasking of the lie as deciphering of illusions, by which Nietzsche registers soberly that "it [is] naive to believe that we could ever come out of this sea of illusions."[124] Seen in this way, it testifies to an "infinitely naive belief" to be of the opinion that it is sufficient "not to let illusions themselves be master,"[125] even if this is "the intellectual imperative, the command of science."[126] In order to come away from this naiveté and profile the question of knowledge in a positive sense, the only valid intellectual imperative according to Nietzsche, instead of the removal of illusions, aims much more at knowing them as such in general. In order to unmask them without the claim to a final sense of elucidation, we are in need, according to Nietzsche, of an *art of mistrust*,"[127] in which it is shown positively that there are no facts and no factual states, but only interpretations.[128]

For the possibility of knowing the world means that it has "no sense behind itself, but rather innumerable senses. 'Perspectivism.' It is our

semblance is for Nietzsche the perspectival, and thus the apparent world is a world "regarded, ordered, and selected in terms of values" (162), and insofar as the "entire determined valuing" (163) is itself the perspective, there remains no world apart from this, "when one properly accounts for the perspectival" (ibid.).

120. Nietzsche, *Nachgelassene Fragmente: Herbst 1884–Herbst 1885*, in *KGW* div. 7, vol. 3 (Berlin: Walter de Gruyter, 1974), 206.

121. Nietzsche, *Nachgelassene Fragmente: Frühjahr-Herbst 1884*, in *KGW* div. 7, vol. 2 (Berlin: Walter de Gruyter, 1974), 54.

122. Ibid.

123. Nietzsche, *Nachgelassene Fragmente: Herbst 1887–März 1888*, in *KGW* div. 8, vol. 2 (Berlin: Walter de Gruyter, 1970), 435.

124. Ibid.

125. Nietzsche, *Nachgelassene Fragmente: Herbst 1869–Herbst 1872*, in *KGW* div. 3, vol. 3 (Berlin: Walter de Gruyter, 1978), 106.

126. Ibid.

127. Nietzsche, *Nachgelassene Fragmente: Herbst 1884–Herbst 1885*, in *KGW* div. 7, vol. 3, 207.

128. See Nietzsche, *Nachgelassene Fragmente. Herbst 1885—Herbst 1887*, in *KGW* div. 8, vol. 1, 323.

needs which map out the world: our drives and their for and against. Every drive is a type of longing for mastery; each has its perspective, which it would like to force upon all other drives as the norm."[129] Seen in this way, the world that concerns and involves us is false for Nietzsche; it is no "factual state, but rather a poetic invention and rounding out of a meager sum of observations; it is 'in flux,' as something becoming, as an ever-new, deferring falsity, which never nears truth: for—there is no 'truth.'"[130] And there is also no universally valid metaphysical foundation from which truth could authenticate itself. This fundamental insight for him reveals that signature, which Nietzsche earlier cast as a conspicuous feature of the age in the famous formula: "God is dead!"[131]

§ 12. Parenthesis on the Discourse of Metaphysics "As Such" as a Problem of an Epochal Revaluation in View of a Signature of the Present

What appears as a profound insight in Nietzsche's thesis of the death of God is, as Manfred Frank formulates it, the "becoming-doubtful of 'metaphysics' as a socially effective creator of justification and giver of sense."[132] Properly grasping this insight, however, requires, with regard to the ailing—and as we have implied in the context of the present considerations

129. Ibid.

130. Ibid., 112.

131. Nietzsche, *Die fröhliche Wissenschaft*, in *KGW* div. 5, vol. 2 (Berlin: Walter de Gruyter, 1973), 159.

132. Manfred Frank, *Conditio Moderna: Essays, Reden, Programm* (Leipzig: Reclam, 1993), 9. Here it is a matter only of observing this relevant paradigm shift of history of philosophy, specific to the epochs, which concerns not the sense of existence, but rather the sense of validity of the content, and is also intended by Nietzsche when he stresses: "The greatest recent event—that 'God is dead'—that has come to pass for the faith in a Christian God unworthy of belief, has already begun to cast its first shadows across Europe" (Nietzsche, *Die fröhliche Wissenschaft*, 255).

Nevertheless this does not mean that henceforth no personal convictions of faith are possible. The individual religious experience of the promise of deliverance remains undisturbed in Nietzsche's formulation for the context of a given problem, yet it is, as Heidegger notes, "not the effecting-effective principle of that which is now occurring. The supersensible foundation of the supersensible world, thought as the effective reality of everything real, has become unreal. This is the metaphysical sense of the metaphysical thought saying 'God is dead'" (Heidegger, "Nietzsches Wort 'Gott ist tot' Holzwege," in *GA*, ed. Friedrich-Wilhelm von Herrmann [Frankfurt: Klostermann, 1977], 5:254).

generalized—form of discourse, a certain measure of caution, not least since with the questionability of its universal claim to validity, metaphysics is not already abandoned as well. In general, there is no *single* metaphysics. What is so named is so thoroughly complex, historical, and far-reaching that it appears not unproblematic to want to succinctly short-circuit the millennia of history simply by means of the definite article.

In the field of the historical and epochal revaluation, regardless of specific discipline, the pronounced use of the definite article marks as a rule an argumentatively conditioned, and in this sense aim-defined, *rational construction*. This usage need not be transparent as such on the side of the individual historian; perhaps it does not always want to give itself to knowing as a construction; in any case, regarded philosophically, it must not be taken or served sight unseen in its claim in the sense of a model that has been passed down. Nevertheless, such a construction is not to be avoided—and that in no way signifies a flaw; it has much more decisively something to do with the *interpreting character of human knowing* demonstrated by Nietzsche, and thus with the in-itself-perspectival self- and world understanding of humans. According to Nietzsche, "there is no event in itself. What occurs is selected from a group of appearances and comprehended by an interpreting being."[133]

Accordingly, when one works with such a unification as "metaphysics" [*'der' Metaphysik*] and with a concomitant narrowing of the spatially occurring projection of sense qua totalization, one ought to be clear that it concerns an operative application of the concept of metaphysics and involves if anything only a heuristic principle with regard to which it then must be claimed that the schema under which this unification—in the sense of a model conception—is executed is methodologically exposed, by means of which determinate positions can qualify as metaphysics.[134] It is

---

133. Nietzsche, *Nachgelassene Fragmente: Herbst 1885–Herbst 1887*, in *KGW* div. 8, vol. 1, 34.

134. Heidegger's conception of the *ontological difference* offers such a schema, by means of which the history of thinking can be analyzed by way of a leading thread that allows the philosophical positions to be bound not just linearly as a history of development, but rather as a history of a problem. The history so described by Heidegger is one that unfolds primarily in the mode of errors and distortions, whereby it becomes possible to fix various degrees of convergence as well as failure with regard to ontological difference at different times, and not in a fixed chronology. Accordingly, the history of philosophy is projected by Heidegger under the insight of the question of the ontological difference for its future possibilities as a self-transforming constellation of nearness and distance, in which, for example, Heraclitus measured in the *potential* of the phenomenally appropriate comprehension of being seems more *pregnant* in

important that even where one indicates the presupposition under which the unifying determination stands and offers its insights up for scrutiny as working hypotheses, it is only at the level of the highest assumption of plausibility—no matter, ultimately, the insight into the principally irremediable fact of its construction—that any claim to absolute bindingness of this particular way of reading is open to deconstruction. Following the view that Husserl strikes in the *Crisis of the European Sciences and Transcendental Phenomenology,* which has indeed here been turned against him, there is only one unique *worldview* for humans, but no overview and not even such a view from which history, always finitely constructed qua interpreted occurrence, could transform itself into law or a set of lawful results. This is also turned against Husserl insofar as he, to anticipate (cf. § 24), seeks to transcend this fact of a finite worldview in the transcendental reduction aimed at a final valid universal ground, which is determined as pure subjectivity and thereby develops a thematization of history as in itself teleologically related to this final ground.

As we have stressed, it counts among Nietzsche's central insights that our knowing is interpretation. This fundamental thought is profiled against the background of both his existentiell experience and the thinker's suffering experience of the death of God, which in relation to human beings means in essence the loss of the transcendental creation of sense. With the loss of the sense- and value-holder of his own essence, the human

---

effect than, e.g., Descartes, whose approach to the ontological difference in its error has equally been more historically *powerful* in effect, insofar as he has decisively stamped the development of the modern picture of the world.

Other contemporary schemata can be named—without wanting to enter into a comparison—that allow the history of philosophy to be designated as a field of investigation, such as the thought of *reason,* in which, for example, Habermas, with reference to Gadamer and Schadewaldt, recognizes the "basic philosophical theme" par excellence, since "philosophy has strived from its beginning to explain the world as a whole, the unity in the manifoldness of appearances, with principles that are to be discovered through reason" (*Theorie des kommunikativen Handelns* [Frankfurt: Suhrkamp, 1988] 1:15).

Further, it would certainly be a worthwhile task to investigate more thoroughly whether and which points of continuity and difference are present that thinkers as different as Emmanuel Levinas (see *Totalität und Unendlichkeit: Versuch über die Exteriorität* [Freiburg: Alber, 1987) and Foucault (see, e.g., *Überwachen und Strafen: Die Geburt des Gefängnisses* [Frankfurt: Suhrkamp, 1976]) see, in their own ways, the thought of the traditional primacy of reason as constitutively bound with that of *power,* and who have found precisely therein a possibility of schematization that enables a view for them through the development of philosophical traditions of discourse up to the present, and accordingly moves the idea of totality (and totalization) back into the center.

being is assigned to carry out his self-understanding, in that he projects his creation of sense from himself and to himself.

It belongs, as it may now be preliminarily indicated, to the finite constitution of humans that the world itself is capable of opening the projective paths of the possibilities of their being in the world only in certain facets of perspective refractions, on account of which the self- and world interpretations not only constantly overhaul but renew themselves synchronically and diachronically. Even more, the perspectival view of the world as ourselves means that the project of something like personal identity in the middle of one's ever-changing, interwoven relations—both different in themselves and heterogeneous—itself is carried out in the shadow of its irretrievability, from which, if we can put it this way, one undertakes an abbreviation of existence akin to that of Schlemihl.[135]

If the perspective character of the human self- and world relation cannot be carried over into a universally valid, identical thinking, as was inaugurated in the idealist philosophy of identity, the generalizing and totalizing view of the history of this relation and thus of metaphysics in itself is from the outset already problematic at the very least. However, that still does not mean that metaphysics has finally played itself out. For on the contrary, it evinces—as the present investigation has already indicated and will again confirm—the metaphysical thinking handed down in manifold ways as yet a quite vibrant and forceful *vis a tergo*, even where from early positivism onwards, metaphysics was declared dead in various rites of burial. Now the dead live all the longer, as is widely acknowledged, and therefore it is correct to assert: it is not metaphysics that is directly at an end, but rather what has come to an end after a process of deprivation— and Nietzsche's formula addresses—namely, the universal bindingness of the commanding claim to validity of a cultural and not only philosophical, metaphysical, tradition-forming principle of unity, which anchored the *omnitudo realitatis* in a *summum ens* as the idea of God, from which the world came as his creation *ex nihilo* and consequently the human being as *ens creatum* was legitimated and normalized in its order and essence a priori.[136]

---

135. Adalbert von Chamisso's character Schlemihl sold his shadow to the devil at the cost of his place among other human beings.

136. That there should be an end with respect to this metaphysical principle as a general epistemologically relevant (or for that matter morally binding) basis of legitimation, and likewise with its legitimate and illegitimate progeny (whether they are called "absolute reason"

or however one might put it), is—and this is by no means recent—a broadly accepted platitude over which varying philosophical temperaments and opposed, incompatible positions continue to struggle. The fact that the mere mention of contemporary representatives such as Derrida or Habermas, Vattimo or Rorty, MacIntyre or Ernst Tugendhat immediately and with good cause evokes the reproach of unreliable delimitations, if not the suspicion of outright personal preference, reflects in particular that the critique of metaphysics in the form of a fundamental doubt of God as a universal source of legitimation of human claims did not only come to articulation with Nietzsche. His is rather only one particularly influential voice in a choir of criticism that moves like a guiding thread through the thought of the modern period, precisely as a process of secularization and—in this sense—the emancipation of reason.

One need only think, for example, of the diversely developed deistic conceptions of a "natural religion" in opposition to revealed religion, in the vein of Jean Bodin or Herbert of Cherbury, who shows himself in his *De veritate* (1624) to be, as Ernst Cassirer notes (*Descartes: Lehre-Persönlichkeit-Wirkung* [Hamburg: Meiner, 1995], 9–38), "a Cartesian *avant la lettre*." Here it would be fruitful to mention the great debates over natural rights during the Enlightenment that, bound up with figures such as Hugo Grotius or Samuel von Pufendorf against the scholastic doctrines of natural rights following Thomas Aquinas, no longer adopt the order of creation as a basis of rights, according to which the principles of a *lex aeterna* are reflected as *lex naturalis* through the *lumen naturale*. Against the latter, rationally identifiable rights in their binding character were decoupled from such theological dogmatics, which means that in the doctrines of natural rights of the Enlightenment, right is now grounded solely in the sources of reason, precisely with the claim that it applies even in case of the nonexistence of God or a disregard of the legal order. (See Cassirer, "Vom Wesen und Werden des Naturrechts," *Zeitschrift für Rechtsphilosophie* [1932–1934], 6:1–27).

In connection with this problematic it is necessary to take into account the broad current of a morally and religiously unlimiting *critique of religion* bound up with the Enlightenment and with, among others, names like Bayle, Voltaire, Diderot, and La Mettrie. Here Kant famously set the decisive cut, in proving the possibility of a theoretical knowledge of God as inaccessible and thereby binding the question of God for the subsequent time with the question of practical reason as a standard.

With the visibility of history arising as a central theme of the nineteenth century, the critique of religion also became a main theme of philosophical reflection. Names like Ludwig Feuerbach, Karl Marx, Max Stirner, and Sigmund Freud stand for this development. If one has these historical relationships before one's eyes, Nietzsche's turn away from the idea of God as a ground of legitimation is held in a network of tradition bound in very different strands, with which Heidegger, in his treatise "Nietzsches Wort 'Gott ist tot'" (*GA* 5, 209–267), also affiliates, under particular other signs, Hegel and Pascal as further thinkers among whom the thought of the death of God already announced flashes up (ibid., 214).

Yet even as early as the proof for the existence of God undertaken in Descartes's Third Meditation—which Husserl, among others, believes has to be recognized as merely a testimony dictated by the circumstances of the age—we find portrayed in the fact that it is undertaken as a *"cogitatio-analytic* proof for the existence of God" (von Herrmann, "Husserl und Descartes," in *Perspektiven der Philosophie. Neues Jahrbuch* 23 [1997], 59), a disempowerment, in the traditional manner of such proofs, of the formerly highest, universally valid principle of justification. Since, in the foundation of knowledge as the productive positing of reality proceeding from the fundamental insight into the cogito, the principles of being are reflected as the principles of knowledge, a profound shift takes place away from the thought of analogy—so important for scholasticism—in which human knowledge, in its directedness toward God, knows itself through an attestation to its productive capacity precisely by means of analogy with God.

But the apocalypse did not follow the falling away of the theocentric order, which in its self-legitimation through the self-manifesting God made human beings first into true knowers through the *assumption* of the message. The verification of thinking fell much more, if one can say so, from heaven directly to earth. Thinking thereby ever again stumbled in the 'learning of the self-conscious path,' tangled up in theoretical, skeptical, or positivistic aporias, and found itself once again in a deep hole. Distinct from that of the Platonic cave, for the hermeneutically oriented philosopher whose task it was to free oneself again from such unfortunate conditions, there did not shine at the far end of the darkness the timeless sun of reason. Before that philosopher [Thales] could get a foothold again on the way toward the light in the well shaft, it was the ears, rather, that were subject to the echo of the spiteful laughter of the maidservant.

The case of philosophy—whether now as fall or as the particular matter to be handled—is from the beginning a public matter, a *res publica*. And therefore one ought to be on guard against wanting to leave lifeworldly relations dreamily (spinning) out of view. Not that the maid's derision in itself signals a superiority in circumspect behavior, but certainly it points to the fact that ultimately the marketplace, this original and bustling location of philosophers, is still a right vicious terrain in its publicness for stargazing and shining lanterns in broad daylight.

If one remains mindful of the existentiell "grip on reality" of philosophy in the everyday, it is certainly not so false if philosophers in philosophizing always again make present the ridicule of the Thracian maid,[137] conscious of being irritated by that and accepting in this sense as it were the thorn in their own flesh, so that displaced, they are ready in (productive) unrest to place in question their own action. Not that they should compare themselves now to the ways of seeing of sound human understanding— under which Hegel formerly understands "the local and temporary restric-

---

In acknowledging these factors, we in no way disavow the radicality and originality of Nietzsche's thesis, which culminates with powerful effect in the diagnosis of mounting nihilism as the "'inner logic' of Western history" (Heidegger, "*Nietzsches Wort 'Gott ist tot,'*" 223) and with the death of God abandons at once the idea of a universally valid truth guaranteed through a supersensuous realm of ideals.

137. Hans Blumenberg offers a spiritual and theoretic-historical journey tracing the clash, carried out repeatedly over the centuries, between the Milesian world-spectator and reality in *Das Lachen der Thrakerin: Eine Urgeschichte der Theorie* (Frankfurt: Suhrkamp, 1987).

tion of a type of human beings"[138]—seamlessly and unconditionedly, for that means to efface the difference, as if philosophy could practice everyday business or even science itself. Even here there holds sway a "bright difference,"[139] rather analogously to what Heidegger stresses with regard to the proper law of philosophy in distinction to poetry.

The provocation of the laughter of the Thracian maid and all her sisters in spirit beyond the millennia challenges philosophers positively in the context of life as referential connection, which the world is, in which the philosophical and natural attitude is encountered, to account for the difference that triggers such laughter as a fracture in the relation to reality, in the sense of a point of departure for philosophical questioning. This fragment, however, divides not just two absolutely separated worlds from one another, but even marks a *change of perspective on reality*.

This change includes in itself no "higher valuation" of the philosophical over against the nonphilosophical attitude. The philosophical perspective as such in ontological formal indication is abstinent in the face of such ultimately morally motivated qualifications.In this sense, the "world of philosophy" is also not equivalent to Sarastro's holy halls. On the contrary, the philosophical view signifies proximately only a difference in attitude toward reality, value-neutral in itself, which however can lead to self-enlightenment worth consideration for other life-practical or even scientific attitudes with regard to content and methodology.

Founded in concrete execution of existence, the philosophical attitude distinguishes itself from the extraphilosophical and prephilosophical attitudes proximally and at first through a specific reflexivity. It intends, as will be seen in the next chapter, in the theoretical effect of astonishment and in its corresponding doubt, a will to knowledge, which concretizes itself in its content specifically with regard to the particular philosophical posing of the question as ontological, logical, ethical, aesthetic, and so on.

138. Hegel, *Einleitung: Über das Wesen der philosophischen Kritik*, in *Werke* (Frankfurt: Suhrkamp, 1974), 2:182.

139. Heidegger, "Das Wesen der Sprache," in *Unterwegs zur Sprache*, ed. Friedrich-Wilhelm von Herrmann, GA (Frankfurt: Klostermann, 1985), 12:185. Heidegger characterizes this difference from poetry more closely as 'delicate' [*zart*], because philosophy and poetry are determined in their relation to one another through an essential kinship of proximity. And as this difference holds sway over poetry, as will still be seen, as does the difference of philosophy to all other regions of life in general, it as such may not be simply leapt over brightly, that is, clearly in the sense of a 'common sense' position.

§ §13. *Critical Remarks on the Concept of an Absolute Reason*

What remains is to pursue the business of a critique, which, in the self-illumination of its own conditions—that which has been called the hermeneutical situation—brings to light the network of historical relations even in its fissures and disparate developments, which is concrete as *life-world,* the underlying ground of our self- and world understanding. Implied therein is the renunciation of an assumed final enlightenment of the sense of our existence, as it is effected by positing an absolute reason. For the assumption of the idea of such an absolutely posited reason already transcends the space of possibilities of human existence. Thus, since Kant, the usual rational-metaphysical approach in, e.g., Fichte or Hegel, with its difference between absolute "I" or absolute spirit and the empirical subject in its ontological status takes the world and accordingly the historical subject as something empirical and as corresponding to this approach of a "doubling of the subject" as posited by absolute subjectivity or grounded in it. Absolute and as such *ahistorical* subjectivity moves thereby into the function of an originally constituting agency, in relation to which we appear, qua empirical subject, as its sober mind, but which as such is again part of this absolute subjectivity or reason.

Yet even where, in Husserl, subjectivity no longer functions transcendentally-phenomenologically as world ground, but rather only within the framework of its transcendental constitutive attainment as a type of ground of validity for our knowledge, reason remains an absolute, in the sense of a "transcendental-phenomenological subjectivity . . . with its constitutive life-consciousness and its transcendental power."[140] It is then, for Husserl, to be differentiated clearly from "the psychological or psychophysical subjectivity,"[141] which count for him (under the title of the 'human soul') as the 'person and community of persons' with their psychic experiences, understood in the psychological sense of the "constituents of the objective world."[142] This psychophysical subjectivity shows itself therefore only as something founded, i.e., "my psyche, the psychophysical-world of conscious life is not identical with my transcendental ego, in

---

140. Husserl, *Formale und transzendentale Logik: Versuch einer Kritik der logischen Vernunft,* ed. Paul Janssen (The Hague: Martinus Nijhoff, 1974), 17:259 (emphasis deleted).
141. Ibid. (emphasis deleted).
142. Ibid.

which the world constitutes itself for me with all its physical and psychical aspects."[143] Transcendental subjectivity is and remains for him the "originary site of all objective formations of sense and validations of being."[144]

On this ground and from it, Husserl turns to psychophysical subjectivity in the midst of the objective world: "We . . . are human beings ourselves, European human beings; we have ourselves become historical; as historians, we ourselves engender world history and world knowledge of every sense, a historical form in the motivation of the European history in which we stand. The world that is for us is itself a historical image of us; we ourselves according to our being are a historical image."[145] This descriptive summation of our situational relatedness as culturally-historically determined human beings is for him only the outer skin or surface of human existence, which he believes has to penetrate for itself down to a final level of sense and validity in a transcendental-phenomenological unrest, as it were. For Husserl, the decisive question poses itself therefore: "What is the nonrelative presupposed in this relativity?"[146] His answer is: "Subjectivity as transcendental."[147] As the true inner a priori kernel wholly in the sense of the tradition of transcendental idealism, transcendental subjectivity is essentially distinct from its empirical expression, and in this sense, is regarded unchangeably as absolute reason in its structure.

If one can speak of reason in connection with the reflections set out here, it is precisely not absolute and in this sense nonrelative. For as *historical, finite reason,* it is referred for its self- and world knowledge to that which it conditions, under whose conditions it forms itself historically and, addressed as history, reason cannot afford to a people a perspective in which an accessible totality of meaning might be secured. With Gadamer it can therefore be said: "In truth history does not belong to us, but rather we belong to it. Long before we understand ourselves in recollection, we understand ourselves in self-evident ways in the family, society, and state, in which we live. The focus of subjectivity is a distorting mirror. The self-

143. Ibid., 245.
144. Husserl, *Die Krisis der europäischen Wissenschaften und die transzendentale Phänomenologie,* ed. Walter Biemel, in *Husserliana: Edmund Husserl—Gesammelte Werke* (The Hague: Martinus Nijhoff 1976), 6:102 (emphasis deleted).
145. Ibid., 313.
146. Ibid.
147. Ibid.

reflection of the individual is only a flicker in the closed circuit of historical life."[148]

For the goal of a hermeneutical investigation of presuppositions and structures of the constitution of something like the human self-and-world relation, the question of the *connection between self-formation and history* therefore poses itself as the preeminent problem. It is therefore necessary from the beginning to stave off a possible misunderstanding. That is to say, one could assume that in such a connection, history would ultimately be reprivatized in something like the type of approach that suggests itself in certain positions in Dilthey, when autobiography, as foundation of hermeneutical reflection, is taken up as a point of entry to history and the self. In contrast, it must be noted that in such a departure what is contained in the problem is thereby falsified, because this analysis intends to go into the central approach of Dilthey's philosophizing in the internalizing of lived experience [*Erlebnisses*] with the individual lived experience of a psychological as quasi-transcendental point of departure. In truth, however, this also shows itself as always already conditioned in the stream of tradition and determined by those untraceable prior historical presuppositions that structure the proper reality of individual lived experience and therein also the possibility of self-experience [*Selbsterfahrungsmöglichkeit*]. Knowledge of the connection of self and history must therefore choose a path that conceives something like individuality in its constitution through an enlightenment of self-formation as having become historical, and admittedly in recourse to the *historicity* of human being as an existential constituent of its possibility of self-experience, which as the horizon of the sense disclosure of all self-projections of its space of reality has in it what is regarded philosophically as the *problem of the lifeworld*.

148. Gadamer, *Wahrheit und Methode*, 281.

PART TWO

I AND WORLD:
THE QUESTION CONCERNING THE
GROUND OF PHILOSOPHY

Philosophy is only itself when it foreswears the ease of a world with a unique entry as well as the ease of a world with more entrances, all of which are accessible to the philosopher. Like the natural human, it tarries there, where the passage from one's own self into the world and toward others occurs, where the paths cross.

Maurice Merleau-Ponty

Does anyone know the limits of his soul, such that he could say: I am I?

Fernando Pessoa

PART TWO

CHAPTER ONE

ON THE SEARCH FOR THE CERTAINTY OF THE 'I'

*§ 14. Toward the Task of a Hermeneutical
Interpretation of the Concept and Its Relation to
Everyday Experience: An Approximation*

In order to disclose the problem area of self-understanding in a more far-reaching way, in the following the ground that founds and bears all knowing, and presents in the concept of the *lifeworld* one of the central challenges for philosophical thinking, is shown. According to Kant's famous formula, philosophical thinking—and in this sense, philosophy—is "*rational knowledge from concepts*."[1] From a hermeneutical perspective it is to be noted, however, that the philosophical analysis of concepts to follow is defined by what Manfred Riedel calls "the aim of clarifying the contents of experience and sense, which are already laid out prior to all philosophical tasks in the cultural universe: in the form of religion, art, poetry, economics and politics."[2] In this projection of aims there is included, as it were, a methodological apriori, which Dilthey also forcefully stresses, namely, that "reality itself . . . in the final instance is not logically elucidated, but rather [can] only be understood."[3]

In the workings of meshing relations, which are first brought to light in reflexive consciousness as partial functions of an originally integrated experience of a connection of life determined plurally in itself, the philosopher always already finds himself displaced. The field of reality thereby

---

1. Immanuel Kant, *Kritik der Reinen Vernunft* ed. Raymund Schmidt (Hamburg: Meiner, 1976), A713/B741.

2. Manfred Riedel, *Norm und Werturteil: Grundprobleme der Ethik* (Stuttgart: Reclam, 1979), 126.

3. Wilhelm Dilthey, "Der Fortgang über Kant," in *Weltanschauungslehre, GS*, ed. Bernhard Groethuysen (Göttingen: Vandenhoeck & Ruprecht, 1991), 8:174.

opens its relations of tension to him in the language that he speaks, in the meaning of its concepts, which themselves are set out in historical and contextual fluctuations and deferrals and so apportion its conceptual-analytic task to specific philosophical reflection as the *hermeneutical interpretation of concepts.* It can rightly be indicated that in the framework of such an approach, the conceptual analysis is "only an instrument of philosophical action. It is not ... itself the end, but rather the means to clarify that which the language that we speak always already co-knows of experiences and indications of sense."[4]

4. Riedel, *Norm und Werturteil,* 125. The eminent significance of language is indisputable for philosophical hermeneutics, and famously means, for one of its most formative representatives, Hans-Georg Gadamer, that, in connection with Heidegger, language, in which self and world are antecedently disclosed and therein communicated to one another, yields that universal horizon that makes possible an ontological turn [*Wende*] of hermeneutics to the leading thread of language, indeed even necessitates it. In general it can reasonably be established that in view of historical development and the present situation to which it is tied, language has become not merely one, but rather *the* central theme, with the paradigm shift from consciousness to language in twentieth-century philosophy.

Above and beyond philosophy itself the paradigmatic meaning that stems from the crisis of consciousness shows itself strikingly, for example, in the reform movements in theology, as in the demythologizing program of Rudolf Bultmann. In a more generalizing cultural-historical perspective, this *crisis of language* proves to be *symptomatic of a crisis of self-understanding of modern human beings in the world,* as it was also already diagnosed by Nietzsche precisely in its advent. A testimony from poetry that this crisis has lent a concise, effective-historical, meaningful expression is Hugo von Hofmannsthal's famous "Chandos-Letter." Roughly put, this universal crisis of modern consciousness as a crisis of language can also be perceived by further traces, such as the upheaval in music with the development of technical composition in the direction of the sequentially interrelated twelve-tone system, or as in Fauvism, the dissolution of the canon of color and form through abstraction.

Naturally, these events and structures cannot be fixed and precisely dated in a strict and narrow sense. Neither are they "fallen from the sky"; precursors and antecedent stages can be found here and there. Manet, in including the materiality of the canvas into its exhibition, thus making the bearer of the image aesthetically conscious, counts just as much for that as all impressionism in general. And in the case of poetry one can cite, among others, Hölderlin, Büchner, or Kleist. But precisely for these latter it is such that after a long existence, eked out, often enough, on the margins, the full significance of their work unfolds, effective-historically, only in the experience of the crisis at the turn of the twentieth century, in order thenceforth to become recognized as "contemporaries out of the past," who consequently chart the horizontal lines of the present and who, in a productive echo of voices, no longer go unheard.

From this vantage it can easily be seen how Heidegger's famous coinage of the term "*Gewesenheit*" is thoroughly appropriate for the temporal horizon customarily referred to as the past, despite its unwieldiness next to the usual course of speaking. Marcel Proust (*Tage des Lesens,* 22) had already distinguished, against what he called the "cruel time" of the indicative imperfect "that portrays to us life at one and the same time as something ephemeral and passive," narrative time, the preference of the perfect, which allows for the "solace of activity" (ibid.) and thus visibly opens up the continuing effects of occurrences in the present.

The fundamental relation to the situatedness of human beings in practical life coposited therein means that a philosophical hermeneutics, i.e. hermeneutical philosophy, finds its basis or must gain its connection in the view to everyday experience.[5] But that does not occur so that it emerges

---

In view of the "crisis of language," Georg Büchner's *Woyzeck* appears in its speechlessness like sketches by Samuel Beckett, like a neighbor across the corner, and one can also draw connective strands from Kleist to Kafka or from the later Hölderlin to Celan. And in the long progression of Francis Bacon's studies of Velázquez's *Portrait of Pope Innocent X*, there can be found in a pictorial act of unmasking behind the façade, where everything Nietzschean, as it were, yet only appears as an interpretation of interpretations, correspondences with Dostoevsky's Grand Inquisitor. The announcement of the death of God here finds an existentiell correspondence, which as Bacon's answer to Velázquez therein at the same time sharpens the view of the beholder regarding the ambiguity [*Doppelbödigkeit*] of the Spaniard's pictorial inventions. Michel Foucault finds his way here from a completely different perspective when he interprets Velázquez's "Las Meninas" in the famous opening passage from *The Order of Things*, and shows how the space of representation of representations opened up in this painting remains governed by an "essential emptiness."

This effective meshwork becomes particularly intuitive when one turns in diachronic observation to the history of production in the realm of theater and opera, because here one is under the demands of a work whose consistency proves itself to be a bearer of meaning of historical processes, which themselves carry within them that potential for historical reflection that preserves its expression in the production.

5. In the use of the concepts "philosophical hermeneutics" and "hermeneutic philosophy," the points of crossover are generally fluid. O. F. Bollnow is an exception here. He distinguishes both to the effect that "philosophical hermeneutics" is to be "the elevation of the method developed in the philological and historical sciences to a higher philosophical consciousness" ("Festrede zu Wilhelm Diltheys 150. Geburtstag," in *Dilthey-Jahrbuch* [1984], 2:49). On the other hand, "hermeneutic philosophy" designates "the striving of philosophy for a hermeneutic method as a whole, and thus the interpretation of life-worldly reality" (ibid., 49).

As illuminating as this distinction appears at first glance, it nonetheless conceals within it further questions, insofar as, for example, hermeneutic philosophy is determined here through an unclear understanding on its part of the lifeworld. If anything, the de facto widely prevalent lack of unity in this term's application speaks against a strict division of these concepts. For example, Otto Pöggeler uses the term 'hermeneutic philosophy' more or less continuously, yet in the respect and with a view to the posing of questions, which for Gadamer, Ricoeur, or Riedel—and the list could be extended—is covered by the concept of a philosophical hermeneutics, whereby in all cases the term is accounted for by means of the concept of philosophic hermeneutics (or, respectively, hermeneutic philosophy) in a displacement of the tradition of ontological universalizing of the concept of understanding as a bridge to modern hermeneutics. Seen thus, it promises, in my opinion, a strict terminological codification, problems of practicability notwithstanding, yet at the present time, it offers very little assistance in orientation.

Within the present investigation there consists a pragmatic preference in favor of philosophical, specifically phenomenological, hermeneutics. This is not to say, however, that further endeavors at terminological clarity would not be useful; in the long run such could prove fruitful. Above all, then, in a metahermeneutical sense these can prove to be helpful, if thereby the demarcations between contemporary and traditional theories of understanding can be more clearly marked out. In this connection see Gunter Scholtz, "Was ist und seit wann gibt es 'hermeneutische Philosophie?'" in *Dilthey-Jahrbuch* (1992–1993), 8:93–119.

as hermeneutical reflection only as ontic-existentiell in the everyday and its performances. Rather, these experiences, insofar as they are the subject of philosophical contemplation, are transformed and consequently, as Hans Ineichen stresses, presented "in an argumentative connection withdrawn from the everyday, that is, in a theoretical connection."[6] Seen thus, a clearly marked dividing line exists, which nevertheless does not mean that the relation to the everyday in the broad sense of a pre- and extraphilosophical experience would be thereby effaced. On the contrary, this itself becomes an unceasing *movens* that productively and enduringly initiates philosophical contemplation, and inscribes it as a *constituens* simply as distinct from indissoluble togetherness, which shows that, to use Heidegger's conceptual determination, an existential-hermeneutic mindfulness [*Besinnung*] is capable of developing itself only in reflection upon existentiell experiences. Thus, in this mindfulness something like philosophy takes its starting point. That means its intellectual hour of birth strikes when the unquestioningly active certainty of our enactment of existence—why and how it is always concrete even in the singular details—breaks open and enters into a *reflexive tension* in which the individual withdraws himself from carrying out actions and thus in pausing makes himself as the questioner into the theme of his questioning.

§ 15. Wonder and Doubt: On the Entry Point of Philosophical Reflection

If one looks around in the history of philosophy, one finds this state of affairs clearly depicted in large part in that classic opening passage of Descartes's *Meditations on First Philosophy*, in which the dialectical tension between a premeditative and meditative bearing generates that stimulating climate in which the philosophical question forces itself open, and thereby prepares the proper ground for a new founding of philosophy in self-consciousness. It belongs constitutively to the tension of premeditative and meditative bearing that the philosophizing 'I' never really can dispense with their interlocking.

This insight into the relation of philosophical reflection grounded in the lifeworld is, however, neither an originary invention of Descartes's, nor

6. Hans Ineichen, *Philosophische Hermeneutik* (Freiburg: Alber, 1991), 24.

does it find its conclusion in it, if one thinks, say, of Husserl's distinction between the natural and the phenomenological attitude. Nevertheless, with regard to Descartes one will have to ultimately declare it doubtful—in particular if one, looking ahead, takes into view the Heideggerian analyses of human being-in-the-world, to be discussed in the next section—whether his distinction between the meditative and premeditative bearing can consider the everyday experience of life-certainty, intended positively in the given connection, in its philosophical relevance as ground and basis to be phenomenally appropriate. For according to Descartes, in the tension of premeditative and meditative bearing, the philosophical attitude turns itself away from natural experience, and seeks to shut it off, because it ever again offers occasion for deception in relation to the certainty of knowledge for which one strives.

Only after the sought-after Archimedean point is found on the path of self-certainty in the ego cogito can there be success, according to Descartes, in adopting the natural attitude in the limits of its justified claims with regard to the concrete human performance of life again in its validation. In the beginning of his ontic self-experience as a meditating 'I,' it thereby remains binding for Descartes that the human being first can go on the way of philosophizing ineluctably from out of his situatedness in the world, if he experiences himself as in tension toward his inexpressible everyday self- and world relation.

Without wanting to anticipate at this point, that means that for Descartes the 'I' must necessarily withdraw methodologically from the regions and relations of the innerworldly entities under the stipulation of the certainty of knowledge striven for on the path of self-certainty, because only from the distance thus won is that sought *fundamentum inconcussum* to be found. As a meditating 'I,' it remains, seen ontologically, nevertheless equally part of this world, and has itself as pure ego therein, as Husserl stresses, "retrieved a little corner of the world."[7]

---

7. Husserl, *Cartesianische Mediationen*, in *Husserliana*, ed. Stephan Strasser (The Hague: Nijhoff, 1973), 1:63 (emphasis deleted). For Husserl, this state of affairs means a "failure of the transcendental turn [*Wendung*]" (ibid.) constitutive for Descartes, i.e., the mistaking of the sense of the transcendental subjectivity on account of which he also "does not traverse the entryway that leads into genuine transcendental philosophy" (ibid., 64). We will come back to the Cartesian "ambivalence" indicated by this state of affairs, but here we may take heed of it, because in the preview to the problematic of the lifeworld even this 'worldliness' or world-boundedness of the 'I' can positively contour the access of philosophical knowledge as the connection of astonishment and doubt.

In this connection, it is of no little significance that this philosophizing self-thematization is neither owed nor must owe itself either predominantly or exclusively to a rational construction. Rather, the rupture of our natural self-experience as the certainty-of-carrying-out, which makes possible the reflexive conspicuousness of ourselves to ourselves, is of a thoroughly *affective* nature. This finds itself already familiarly remarked where one sees the beginning of European philosophy usually designated as metaphysics grounded in θαυμάζειν, thus in *wonder,* according to the general type of reading of Plato and Aristotle.

"For this is just [Plato has Socrates say in the *Theaetetus*] the condition of a friend of wisdom, wonder (φιλοσόφου τοῦτο τὸ πάθος, τὸ θαυμάζειν); for there is no other beginning of philosophy (οὐ γὰρ ἄλλη ἀρχὴ φιλοσοφίας) than this."[8] A corresponding position is to be found in Aristotle's *Metaphysics*, in the second chapter of book 1, where he states, "For wonder (τὸ θαυμάζειν) was for human beings once, as it is now, the beginning of philosophy."[9]

In order to evade this conceptual daydreaming, in which numerous speculations into this legendary beginning of philosophy have been spun out over the centuries and have even grounded a "cult of θαυμάζειν,"[10] it

8. Plato, *Theaetetus*, 155d.

9. Aristotle, *Metaphysics*, 982b11.

10. Wolfgang Welsch, *Aisthesis: Grundzüge und Perspektiven der Aristotelischen Sinneslehre* (Stuttgart: Klett-Cotta, 1987), 159. On the problem of wonder in philosophy, see Stefan Matuschek, *Über das Staunen: Eine ideengeschichtliche Analyse* (Tübingen: Niemeyer, 1991), which investigates the history of wonder in the selection of its most effective junctures from antiquity up to the Enlightenment with regard to their epistemological and poetical forms of reception. Despite his otherwise prudent approach, Matuschek inclines in the direction of mere conceptual speculation by following Heidegger's far-reaching phenomenology of wonder (see *Grundfragen der Philosophie. Ausgewählte "Probleme" der "Logik,"* in *Gesamtausgabe*, ed. Friedrich-Wilhelm von Hermann (Frankfurt: Klostermann, 1984), 45:153–181), in which Heidegger unfolds wonder, within the framework of his approach, motivated by the history of being as the fundamental attitude of the "first beginning" that describes the history of Western metaphysics. Matuschek's unease with Heidegger's analysis is unjustified insofar as the independence and originality of his interpretation—which Heidegger himself always admits—is too hastily equated with philological inadequacy and inappropriateness.

Gadamer, who confesses often to have difficulties with Heidegger's textual interpretations "because he bends texts with violence to suit his own intentions" (*Heidegger und die Griechen*, in *GW* (Tübingen: Mohr Siebeck, 1995), 10:45), nevertheless admits—and here he may well be thinking, among other things, of the analysis of wonder—that in his eyes Heidegger was the greatest in "that he understood how to listen to *words* with regard to their secret provenance and their hidden presence ... and in so doing brought the background knowledge of the words to speech. That he knew how to lay open in general the multi-dimensionality of words and the inner gravitational force of the living usage of words and their conceptual simplifications, and requires only attention to the context in which the discourse on wonder as the beginning of philosophy stands in Plato and Aristotle. In short, in both cases the respective investigation aims at the determination of philosophical as theoretical knowledge. Accordingly, a *critical epistemic function* is appropriate to the affect of wonder here as there, that is to say, wonder is in itself already reflexive, a mode of initial consciousness of an ignorant knowing.[11]

---

to sharpen our sense for them, that seems to me in any case the abiding legacy that he left to us" (ibid. 44f.). On a debate with Heidegger's analysis of wonder concerning factual insight, see Klaus Held's study "Grundstimmung und Zeitkritik bei Heidegger," in *Zur philosophischen Aktualität Heideggers vol. 1: Philosophie und Politik,* ed. Dietrich Papenfuss and Otto Pöggeler (Frankfurt: Klostermann, 1991), 31–56, esp. 44–55.

11. Philosophical wonder is already distinguished by Plato and Aristotle from those other forms of wonder—which in the encounter with something new range from mere perplexity to active curiosity or even retreating dread—as they are, for example, themes in developmental psychology in regard to the socialization of early childhood behavior. Such phenomena can, however, be of thoroughly philosophic interest, perhaps as a question of the genesis and constitution of early childhood relations to self in the framework of the processes of self-perception. This can be investigated respectively in Merleau-Ponty and Lacan, among others.

A further form distinguished from philosophical wonder, yet equally philosophically relevant, has found its literary precursor in the logbook of Christopher Columbus, when he portrays the encounter with the indigenous population of America and thus delivers a significant testimony of that momentous event in which alien cultural groups encounter one another. It is not that we find here the hour of the birth of ethnology and cultural anthropology, but rather that it initiates the tableau—so significant for the period that followed—of the noble or evil savage, which raises the fundamental philosophical problem of the alien and the other as, for example in Husserl, the question of the "accessibility of the originally inaccessible" (*Cartesianische Meditationen,* 144), in the face of which the self-understanding and self-ascertainment of Western thinking undertake to secure what is proper to themselves in forms of exclusion and inclusion.

Decisive here, as Held has detailed from a phenomenological view in his study "Heimwelt, Fremdwelt, die eine Welt" (in *Perspektiven und Probleme der Husserlischen Phänomenologie,* ed. Ernst Wolfgang Orth [Freiburg: Alber, 1991], 309), is that the unfamiliar becomes the alien primarily through the respective alien context of apperception in which the other, in relation to himself and his behavior in the world, proves himself to be noticeably different from me, whereby the unanimity of the experience of the world between us is disrupted, and thus soon everything alien in the sense of the foreign is conceived as abnormal over and against our presupposed order-constituting normality.

On the problem of the alien and other in the tension with what is one's own, to which we will return in the context of the Heideggerian thematization of the lifeworld (§ 33), see also from a phenomenological perspective Bernhard Waldenfels, *Der Stachel des Fremden* (Frankfurt: Suhrkamp, 1990); *Topographie des Fremden: Studien zur Phänomenologie des Fremden* 1 (Frankfurt: Suhrkamp, 1997). With a greater regard to the history of ideas, the study by Hinrich Fink-Eitel, *Die Philosophie und die Wilden: Über die Bedeutung des Fremden für die europäische Geistesgeschichte* (Hamburg: Junius, 1994) offers an outline, historically as well as systematically rich in thought, of the problem of the alien in the cultural history of the past five

Looked at a bit more closely, Socrates praises Theaetetus for his capacity for philosophy because in connection with the question of whether and how perception can be knowledge, he does not evade the difficulties resulting from Protagoras's teaching—posed for him by Socrates in accordance with his mode of reading—but rather, in wonder over it, still withholds from Socrates his consent that it is correctly known. After Socrates has carried out a complicated play on the concept of identity in the art of sophistic eristic, Theaetetus answers the question whether he is still following it: "Truly, Socrates, by the gods, I wonder extraordinarily how this could be; sometimes when I truly look into it, it downright staggers me."[12] Bound to this thoroughly affectively tinged wonder as a reaction to that which is newly—irritatingly—encountered is at the same time an insecurity regarding what up to that point was deemed true, and thus a first reflexive consciousness in the sense of doubt as the germinating possibility of the "thus or otherwise" over and against what had up to that point been valid.

Hegel refers as well to the *fraternal relation between wonder and doubt,* which for Plato shows itself in the beginning of philosophizing, when he notes: "This confusion now has the effect of leading to contemplation; and this is Socrates' goal. . . . It is confusion [thus affective experience of wonder unified with a cognitively directed doubt], with which philosophy in general must begin and that it generates for itself; one must cast doubt on everything, one must give up all presuppositions, in order to win it back as engendered by the concept."[13] If we leave out of view for the moment the specific Hegelian content in the inflection of this thought, it thus remains, taken formally, in it as in Plato or even Descartes generally, possible to establish a clearly accentuated *knowledge-securing function* with regard

---

hundred years, without, however, penetrating further into the role of wonder as (in my thinking) that point of crystallization for the problem of the self- and world relation.

12. Plato, *Theaetetus,* 155c.

13. Hegel, *Vorlesungen über die Geschichte der Philosophie I,* in *Werke* (Frankfurt: Suhrkamp, 1975), 18:466. What clearly is reminiscent of Descartes in Hegel with the accentuation of the imposition of doubt, itself has a decisive demonstration also in Descartes with relation to the connection of knowledge and wonder. In the systematically consequential article 71 of his *Les Passions de l'Ame* (trans. Klaus Hammacher [Hamburg: Meiner, 1984], 110–111) in a resonance of Platonic and Aristotelian indications of philosophical cognition based in wonder, Descartes, for his part, displays an affective presupposition of cognition with wonderment (*admiration*).

to doubt as well as wonder. This also becomes graspable in the Aristotelian determination of the birth of philosophy from wonder cited above.

In the systematically presented opening chapter of the *Metaphysics* Aristotle's course of thought aims to give an adequate concept of a science of first principles and causes, which he designates as wisdom (σοφία). In this connection he outlines wonder in distinction from practical considerations of utility as the theoretical affect of philosophy, and in so doing constitutively links it to doubt concerning what is usually taken to be securely known.[14] As a consequence, it is evident that just as much as Cartesian doubt, Platonic and Aristotelian doubt is led by a *methodological intention;* that is, it possesses a *critical epistemic* function. It is accordingly not the wondering naive child's look that already gives birth to a mode of philosophizing from itself. Philosophically relevant wonder remains just as little within itself as methodologically directed Cartesian doubt, but instead drives out beyond itself to the epistemic security at that inner *telos* in which wonder and doubt sublate themselves in and by means of theory in the security of knowledge.

In the concept of theory brought in thus from the outset, the originary meaning of the word θεωρέιν resonates, whereby theory as a form of life (βίος), which later developed itself into the *vita contemplativa,* bears in itself the goal in distinction to *praxis* (πρᾶξις) and *poiesis* (ποίησις), and as contemplative knowing therein grounds the priority of *logos* over *ethos* and technology. Thereby—this now only as a critical preview—it is brought onto the path of that effective leap out of the pretheoretical lifeworld, as we see in Husserl. But it is now precisely, as Heidegger has shown, that fundamental state of affairs in whose reflection the self- and world relation first attains *self-disclosing* in the sense of philosophically reflected self-understanding. Reflection as philosophical activity, as Heidegger understands it, has in fact given up[15] the primacy of θεωρέιν, insofar, that is, as

14. "But whoever is in doubt and wonder about a thing believes himself not to know [*kennen*] it. . . . Therefore whenever they philosophized in order to escape ignorance, thus they sought knowledge evidently on account of knowing, not for any arbitrary use" (*Metaphysics,* 982b 17–21).

15. Thus, for Heidegger, for example, in the analysis of world-knowing in § 13 of *Sein und Zeit,* (ed.Friedrich-Wilhelm von Hermann [Frankfurt: Klostermann, 1977], GA 2, 80–84), extracting oneself from the caring access with the inner world of entities in the sense of the classical understanding of theory as a form of life still only has the status of a deficient mode.

it is "only a mode of self-*apprehension*, yet not the manner of a primary self-disclosing."[16]

When Heidegger nonetheless designates "the type and way in which the self is revealed to itself in factical Dasein"[17] applicable to the term 're-flection,' this is not because he grasps 'reflection' in the sense of its traditional meaning as a kind of self-observation turned back on itself. Rather, Heidegger fastens onto the meaning of 'reflection' familiar from optics, according to which it means "refracting against something, radiating back from there, i.e. showing itself from something in the reflection,"[18] and precisely this is the world, the world, however, as it shows itself, understood as meaningfulness.[19]

§ 16. Under the Spell of Certainty: Descartes's Self-Certainty of the 'I am' as a Hermeneutical Problem

The allusion to Heidegger is appropriate, beyond the terminologically illuminating clarification of the concept of reflection applied in the given connection, in directing attention to the possibility of now letting those tears and breaks become visible in the continuous spectrum opened by means of wonder and doubt as permanent agents of philosophical reflection, which contrast Greek thinking with Descartes's approach. Thereby at the same time that manifoldly apostrophized caesura comes into clarity as the dawn of an epoch that makes all thinking after Descartes, and not merely temporally, "post-Cartesian thinking," which is why, even where philosophical intention struggles against Descartes in its basic assumptions—as is the case in Heidegger and the hermeneutics growing out of the dialogue with him—the debate with Descartes has neither been nor can be abandoned.

The reason for this lies in the fact that within the meshwork of effective history, if again one accepts this picture, on the one hand, to one's credit,

---

16. Heidegger, *Die Grundprobleme der Phänomenologie GA* 24, 226.

17. Ibid.

18. Ibid.

19. "There lies together in the existence of Dasein something like an *anticipatory under-standing of world, significance.* . . . *World understanding* is . . . essentially *self-understanding*" (ibid., 420.)

the history of human self-understanding—whether in science, philosophy, or the everyday—experiences itself as stamped in its guiding themes over the centuries by the Cartesian paradigm of consciousness. But on the other hand, the losses and abbreviations of self-experiences in the phenomenal realm issued in the ledger must let the body, nature, or history themselves be perceived as an echo of Descartes, and yet only when other (non)solutions announce themselves against the Cartesian paradigm in new leading voices, whether initiated by Nietzsche, Freud, Dilthey, or whoever else yet.[20]

In this sense all philosophy is post-Cartesian, yet it is therefore also post-Platonic, post-Aristotelian, post-Kantian, or even more recently post-Nietzschean. This means that in the meshwork of options of thought and horizons ongoing superimpositions and transformations develop which exact an exposure of the historical levels of discourse from methodical understanding in the encounter with the tradition, which on its side as a controlled performance cannot absolve itself from its own hermeneutical prejudice and holds itself indissolubly in a productive relation of tension toward tradition. For the hermeneutic task, the presupposition inscribed as unalterable for it means, as Gadamer stresses, "not to cover this tension in naive assimilation, but rather to unfold it consciously."[21] Hence the "project of a historical horizon,"[22] which sets itself apart from the present horizon, is appropriate as a constitutive moment to the hermeneutical approach in its claim to knowledge.

However, the historical horizon is not to be chosen arbitrarily, but rather must itself be unfolded from the position of the matter to be treated, that is, from the historical processes of self-understanding that in a way find themselves initiated as binding for modernity with Descartes's turn to subjectivity, which still holds Husserl in its spell when he declares the approach to his transcendental phenomenology as neo-Cartesianism. This turn itself clarifies that which differentiates Greek from Cartesian think-

20. How the echo of Descartes can be perceived in the discourse of contemporary French philosophy from Sartre to Derrida is shown by Waldenfels's study "Metamorphosen des Cogito: Stichproben französischer Descartes-Lektüre," in *Descartes im Diskurs der Neuzeit*, ed. Walter Friedrich Niebel, Angelica Horn, and Herbert Schnädelbach (Frankfurt: Suhrkamp, 2000), 349–370.

21. Gadamer, *Wahrheit und Methode*, 311.

22. Ibid.

ing with regard to, say, the direction of the movement of philosophical reflection. In Platonic thinking, philosophical reflection, in short, endeavors to bind together human reason and in this sense to determine it as integral from its connection, seen ontologically, with the transsubjectively thought and cosmologically imposed unity and order of the whole. The task of a successful life for the individual grows out of this reflection in the participation won through rational insight into the integral and integrating unity of the cosmos as an originary supporting world structure.[23]

By contrast, the direction of the movement of the self-legitimation of knowledge in Descartes no longer tends outward in this sense. Rather, it turns inward and locates its principle in self-consciousness[24]—with the familiar consequence of the subject-object split, in which not only the world as an object for knowing is bound to the antecedent enlightenment of subjective conditions of knowledge for its being known. The subject is itself also thereby dissected in itself through this fundamental epistemological distinction, that is, ontologically split in the empirical, bodily 'I' and the 'I' of consciousness, so that as a consequence of this substance-dualistic assumption within the idealistic approaches of a philosophy of self-consciousness, empirical world- and self-knowledge is only on the basis of the extramundane and in this sense absolutely transcendental subjectivity contributing to it.

This oft-depicted *turn to subjectivity,* which appears in the family register of modern philosophy virtually as a birth record and, after Husserl's formulation, possesses its "ur-genius" in Descartes, means that thinking thus grounds itself in itself, and it is precisely for this reason that Hegel praises the Cartesian approach as the authentic beginning of autonomous philosophy.[25] Rightly, however, scholars such as Gerhart Schmidt have pointed out that it is not "'the I' [that is] the new reality, but rather the self-

<hr>

23. See Plato, *Timaeus,* 41b–43a.

24. On the genesis and analysis of the turn to inwardness constitutive of the formation of modern human self-understanding, see Charles Taylor's wide-ranging investigation in the history of ideas (*Quellen des Selbst: Die Entstehung der neuzeitlichen Identität* [Frankfurt: Suhrkamp, 1994], esp. part 2), which concentrates selectively on the "traces of connections between self- and moral representations" (9).

25. "Here, we can say, we are at home and can, like the sailor after a long journey on stormy seas, cry 'Land.'" Hegel, *Vorlesungen über die Geschichte der Philosophie III,* in *Werke* (Frankfurt: Suhrkamp, 1975), 20:120.

encounter of the I, the circumstance that I become for myself."[26] Tied to this, in short, as an essential aspect of the Cartesian strategy of grounding, is the application of *truth as certainty*. With it, a significant break is carried out in the period that followed, up to Husserl, namely that insofar as Descartes was successful in redeeming, on the path of the meditative certainty of the ego cogito and its modes of consciousness, the self-chosen claim of '*clara et distincta perceptio' from out of itself*, so that, with the methodically clear and distinctly regulated demonstration of self-consciousness as the power of knowledge, the truth now appears as something that can be produced by humans. The "fundamental positive meaning"[27] thereby bound to it, as is well known, is the experiential-as-epistemological foundation with regard to the constitution of the mathematical natural sciences; this foundation concerns Descartes himself at the threshold of modernity—at the price, as Heidegger stresses from out of his own approach, of a "narrowing of the posing of the question concerning reality,"[28] insofar as Des-

26. Gerhart Schmidt, *Aufklärung und Metaphysik: Die Neubegründung des Wissens durch Descartes* (Tübingen: De Gruyter, 1965), 71. As a possible indication of the way in which the 'I' is already an extensive theme prior to Descartes, yet was not necessarily such in the Cartesian sense of reflexive considerations, one can refer to Montaigne or more generally to the widely branched literary genre of autobiography. Yet not just here, but also in the pretheoretical region of everyday life practices one can find countless examples of making the self present, because an implicit knowledge of the self is itself borne within where everyone is directed or displayed customarily to oneself in the theoretical and practical access to things.

Franz Brentano conceives this self-consciousness that is tied to every act of consciousness as "inner perception" and grasps it in a readmission of an Aristotelian formulation from the *Metaphysics* (1074b36) as one that is directed "to itself only incidentally" (see Brentano, *Psychologie vom empirischen Standpunkt* [Hamburg: Meiner, 1973], 1:185), insofar as this figure of self-consciousness is not given in reflexive attention. The terminological difficulty arising here, that of the extent to which one can appropriately still speak of perception in this case, finds a solution independently of Brentano in Dilthey, who famously speaks of an inner being in relation to the modes in which self-consciousness carries itself out.

And even in the case, for example, when I reflect upon myself as a source of possible errors after a failed undertaking, I do not think of myself in such a way that the 'I' steps into view as the source of possible experience in general. Insofar as that occurs, however, explicitly in Descartes's epistemological approach, it is carried out from out of a reflexive attitude, which thus heralds for philosophical theory, as we will see, the turn towards self-consciousness as the metaphysics of subjectivity.

27. Heidegger, "Prolegomena zur Geschichte des Zeitbegriffs," in *Gesamtausgabe*, ed. Petra Jaeger (Frankfurt: Klostermann, 1979), 20:250.

28. Ibid.

cartes orients himself primarily to the concept of world as nature[29] in the context of the broadening of a "general theory of the reality of the world."[30]

The lynchpin for this approach of *certitudo* as certainty is the *certainty of the I*, which as Walter Schulz stresses, is "Descartes's greatest discovery."[31]

29. In this respect the individual's relation to reality opens itself in the relation of a *homo faber*, who reads the blueprints of a reality in which he invents and produces himself. As effective as this approach was in view of developing conceptions of scientific-technological reason—which then, to speak with a concept of the late Heidegger, conceives the object in its ontological constitution under the condition of utility and viability as *existence,* and thereby posits it completely in total availability—the "limits to growth," as the famous programmatic formulation of the Club of Rome reads, seem to have been reached in the intervening period, at least according to the general estimate of the global situation, and not merely in the ecological realm, thus requiring new answers.

Nevertheless, these answers can themselves only be developed out of the technological status quo of the risk society, as Ulrich Beck has called it in his eponymous book (*Risikogesellschaft: Auf dem Weg in eine andere Moderne* [Frankfurt: Suhrkamp, 1986]), and to begin with precisely in the form of a comprehensive self-critique as a critique of its determining paradigms. For Beck this means that beyond all romanticism and fantasies of escape this must be provided in a project of a theory of reflexive modernity that is open to the future, which does not leap beyond the presuppositions of the moderns, but rather reclaims them (see Beck, *Die Erfindung des Politischen: Zu einer Theorie reflexiver Modernisierung* [Frankfurt: Suhrkamp, 1993]; for a discussion of this conception, see Ulrich Beck, Anthony Giddens, and Scott Lash, *Reflexive Modernisierung: Eine Kontroverse* [Frankfurt: Suhrkamp, 1996]).

If anything, this project can only succeed in the approach of a changing self-relation that decisively destabilizes the foundations of traditional models of identity, in which it can no longer formulate, among other things, self-determination as the free will of calculating self-employment for itself, but rather, antecedent to the always already historically interpreted space of human self-understanding, reveals its constitutional conditions as the formatting of historical orders of discourse. In this sense, among other things, nature proves to be in no way a region of being independent of humanity, but instead is determined through the self-relation of humans that rules access to nature.

Seen from this vantage point the ecological crisis is in a decisive sense the crisis of a historical paradigm of a human self- and world relation that can only be surmounted insofar as access to nature is determined otherwise. Possibilities show themselves here, for example, in the tendency of a philosophy of nature as a hermeneutics of nature, as Riedel (see "Naturhermeneutik und Ethik im Denken Heideggers," *Heidegger Studies* [1989], 5:153–172) conceives it, in which the experience of nature and history is set back within the original horizon of *ethos* and *physis* as that connection of being that is only sufficiently illuminated in the interpretation of the relation of being that the appearance of the natural demonstrates as being-in-the-world in human beings themselves. Cf. Georg Picht's analyses of the foundational crisis of natural science as the challenge for a postmetaphysical cognition of nature, presented in *Der Begriff der Natur und seine Geschichte* (Stuttgart: Klett-Cotta, 1990.

30. Heidegger, "Prolegomena zur Geschichte des Zeitbegriffs," in *Gesamtausgabe*, ed. Petra Jaeger (Frankfurt: Klostermann, 1979), 20:250.

31. Walter Schulz, "Descartes und das Problem der Subjecktivität," in *Der gebrochene Weltbezug: Aufsätze zur Geschichte der Philosophie und zur Analyse der Gegenwart* (Pfullingen: Neske, 1994), 118. One can as little proceed back behind this discovery as go beyond it. And to the extent that in the present investigation the question of self-understanding in its historicity

He breaks through to the position in the Second Meditation, in the enactment of methodical doubt after its most explicit point emerges in a type of qualitative inversion—that after everything has been more than sufficiently considered, as Descartes says, it remains to be established "that the proposition, 'I am, I exist' (*pronuntiatum, ego sum, ego existo*), is necessarily true, as often as I say it or grasp it in my mind."[32] From this point Descartes famously clears the way, as Heidegger pregnantly formulates it, to "fundamental certainty [as] indubitably the always representable and represented *me cogitare = me esse*. That is the fundamental equivalence of all calculation by the self-securing representation. In this fundamental certainty the human is certain of the fact that he, as the one who sets-before [*Vor-stellende*] all setting-before [*Vor-stellens*] and thus as the realm of all representedness [*Vorgestelltheit*] as well as every certainty and truth, is securely posited, i.e., now *is*."[33]

The fundamental certainty of the 'I' spelled out in this way as self-consciousness does not yet gain its full unfolding in Descartes. It finds its general explication first in Kant's 'transcendental ego' as a 'consciousness in general.'[34] On the other hand, Descartes still conceives the ego primarily as "the 'I' of itself as the individuated person (*res cogitans* as *substantia*

---

is the proper theme, recourse to Descartes proves to be meaningful in the historical realization of the strands of the problem. Thereby it can be established with Hans-Peter Schütt that the "average image that we have of Cartesian philosophy [is] in each case a product of effective history" ("Descartes und die moderne Philosophie: Notizen zu einer epochalen Vaterschaft," in *Selbstverständnisse der Moderne:. Formationen der Philosophie, Politik, Theologie und Ökonomik*, ed. Günter Figal and Rolf-Peter Sieferle [Stuttgart: Metzler, 1991], 12). That a review of these effects amounts to the same as our coming analysis of Descartes regarding a fundamental critique of his conception of an ultimately ahistorical subject will hardly be wondered at after the previous chapter's conclusion, with its reference to the historicity of all understanding, and in addition will be further clarified philosophically from the explicit approach of a hermeneutics of facticity in the next chapter.

32. René Descartes, *Meditationes de Prima Philosophia*, trans. Gerhart Schmidt (Stuttgart:Reclam, 1986), 78–79.

33. Heidegger, "Die Zeit des Weltbildes," in *GA* 5:109. "That the ego is named in this fundamental equivalence of certainty and then in the actual *subjectum,* does not mean that the human is now egolike and egoistically determined. It says only this: to be a subject now becomes the distinguishing mark of the human as the thinking-representing being. The 'I' of the human is placed in the service of this *subjectum.* . . . The certainty is binding for every 'I' as such, i.e. as *subjectum*" (ibid.).

34. See Heidegger, "Überwindung der Metaphysik," in *Vorträge und Aufsätze* (Pfullingen: Neske, 1978), 71–100, 82. Heidegger thematizes the extent to which the Kantian problematic is presaged in Descartes, e.g., in *GA* 20, § 22.

finita)."[35] Indeed, for Descartes meditating reflection upon the 'I' is also already antecedently determined through the command of that as yet "veiled relation to I-ness as the certainty of itself and of what is represented. . . . Only out of this relation is the individual I capable of being experienced."[36]

In the context of his own reflections on "Ground and Abyss of Subjectivity in Descartes," which are integrated into the programmatic demonstration of the esoteric [*akroamatisch*] dimension of hermeneutics,[37] Manfred Riedel raises the notion that the development of modern thinking sketched out by Heidegger as the metaphysics of subjectivity has its origin and center in the insight that the "interpretation of the ego as ego-ity (*Egoität*) [rests] upon a change in the understanding of being,"[38] on account of which for Heidegger the subject belongs "not only to the world, but rather to the *history of being-in-the-world,* to the experience of the proper character of being of the 'I am,' that interprets itself in the categories of subject and object in the modern era."[39] Despite this significant discovery, according to Riedel Heidegger does not extract from it all of the necessary consequences for an understanding devoted to Descartes on his own terms, insofar as he gives preference in his rendering of Descartes to a way of reading the Cartesian approach with the assumption of ego-ness [*Ichheit*], or subjectivity, as the ultimate ground of a possible knowledge of self and of the world, a reading that, "in harmony with post-Kantian transcendental philosophy,"[40] overlooks something crucial.

In relation to this interpretation, generally accepted as appropriate, the critical question now poses itself for Riedel, by contrast, with a view to Descartes as the point of departure of such an assumption (the thesis of subjectivity as the ultimate ground), whether this accepted way of reading the position formulated in Descartes's *Principles of Philosophy* of the principle *cogito, ergo sum* is not too hastily universalized, and whether something thereby remains unobserved that is at least laid out in the *Meditations* as *another possibility* and that appears in the above-cited *pronuntiatum*, with-

35. Heidegger, *Überwindung der Metaphysik,* 82.

36. Ibid. "This ego-ness appears . . . in the form of the *certum,* the certainty that is nothing other than the securing of the represented for the representing" (ibid.).

37. Riedel, *Hören auf die Sprache: Die akroamatische Dimension der Hermeneutik* (Frankfurt: Suhrkamp, 1990), 17–49.

38. Ibid., 26.

39. Ibid. See also Heidegger, *GA* 24, §§ 13.

40. Riedel, *Hören auf die Sprache,* 32.

out Descartes having been able to grasp it in thinking. It eludes Descartes himself as soon as he transforms the *pronuntiatum* into the named principle.[41]

With a view to the meditating ego, Riedel's reflections at the same time open up an illuminating perspective on the proper dichotomy of the Cartesian imposition of the ego. His demonstrations show themselves to be determined at the start by the hermeneutical experience, formulated fundamentally by Gadamer in particular, that therein permits one to take up again the "leading threads of I-saying" and indicates according to its structure that language is in its essence conversation,[42] thus that all 'I'-speaking is always already therefore an *address* to another, to whom I declare myself as like and yet different from him.[43] The decisive point lies in the fact that the I-speaking does not make visible what it announces from out of itself, but rather lets it be heard.[44] This refers, however, to the fact "that the I at bottom is an *esoteric [akroamatisch] phenomenon.*"[45] determined in its mode of appearance through the constitutive "alternation

---

41. See ibid., 35, 47. According to Riedel that which is buried here neither succeeds in being revealed out of transcendental-philosophical optics, nor can it possibly be yielded from out of such positions as that of the late Heidegger or the late Wittgenstein. These thinkers guide Riedel here not only because he owes something essential to them for his own approach (see ibid., 25–29), but also because they as thinkers have together shaped the binding paradigm, today no longer able to be transcended philosophically, of the constitutive connection of language-thinking-world from out of their hermeneutical and analytical viewpoint, whereby Heidegger and Wittgenstein demonstrate a noteworthy convergence.

In short, this lies in the fact that famously in their late thinking it is for both language itself that thinks, i.e. speaks (compare, e.g., Heidegger, "Der Weg zur Sprache," in *GA* 12, 227–257 with Wittgenstein, *Philosophische Untersuchungen*, no. 329ff.). Therewith it cannot be maintained, however, that with this convergence itself a tendency toward congruence is also already apparent. What it depends upon, rather, is the circumstance bound to the evidence for this convergence, that both thinkers slipped off their path on "the leading-thread of I-saying" (*Hören auf die Sprache*, 28), which Riedel sees initiated and conditioned through the "great, yet . . . futile attempt meditatively to relinquish the transcendental ego, in any case to think in such a way as if no 'I' but rather 'it' thinks being" (ibid.).

42. See Gadamer, *Wahrheit und Methode*, 442–460.

43. See Riedel, *Hören auf die Sprache*, 29; Gadamer, *Wahrheit und Methode*, 384.

44. Cf. Riedel on the first of Husserl's *Logical Investigations* in the second volume, "Expression and Meaning," in particular § 26, where Husserl writes: "The word '*I*' does not have in itself the force to awaken directly the particular representation of the I that determines its meaning in discourse. It does not function like the word '*lion*' does, which makes it possible to call up on its own the representation of a lion. Rather, it communicates an indicative function, which calls out, as it were, to the listener: your opposite intends yourself." *Husserliana*, vol. 19:1, ed. Ursula Panzer (The Hague: Nijhoff, 1984), 88; see also Husserl's supplement, *Logische Untersuchungen*, vol. 6, §5 (*Husserliana*, vol. XIX/2, 556)

45. Riedel, *Hören auf die Sprache*, 29.

of speaking-hearing [as] the speculative originary relation of language, wherein each of us identifies himself as an individuated person."[46] In this process, it is decisive that the identification of the ego does not occur primarily and alone as a comportment of speaking to itself, but instead occurs "originally with respect to an alter ego, the relation to the other wherein it transcends the in-itself empty ego-relation."[47] This means that the identity of the ego gains its confirmation in thought, though it does not take shape in general without the relation to a 'thou' that is not to be thought personally or dialogically, but rather experienced as an other in distinction to the I. In other words, the identity of the I founds itself in and from out of its difference to the other.[48]

With a view to Descartes, this fundamental structure folded within, as it were, the basic relation of human identity, shows itself where he *ties the self-certification of the meditating I back to language* in the cited *pronuntiatum*. It is indeed not so that Descartes discovered language on its own in express application as the ground of this self-certification. Rather he sees himself forced into the approach of his posing of the question out of, as Riedel calls it, the "demand of the phenomena,"[49] to turn himself to language. Descartes must hold himself to this in order to be able to describe the path of methodological doubt, which he therefore designates as programmatic and appropriate in carrying out the *"in dubium revocare."* The path of revocation, rigorous in itself, leads him to that phenomenon which

46. Ibid.

47. Ibid.

48. It would be an interesting and worthwhile task to set the 'transcendental ur-relation' of self-constitution through the other, as we characterize it here, in connection with Emmanuel Levinas's ethical transcendentalism. This would also be valuable because Levinas himself, in reference to Descartes—in particular to the idea of God from the Third Meditation as a possibility of the experience of the infinite within the finite (Levinas, "Die Philosophie und die Idee des Unendlichen," in *Die Spur des Anderen* [Freiburg: Alber, 1987], 200)—no longer conceives the question (central for him) of the humanity of human beings from an antecedent clarification of the essence of human beings, which then first applies to the other in a second step. Instead, he formulates—roughly as in *Totalität und Unendlichkeit* (Freiburg: Alber, 1987)—the question of the human in a novel way, to the effect that in setting out from the relation of the human to the other for the question of the subject's autonomy, he now recognizes the social relation itself ontologically as world-constituting, and thus as what is primary in the sense of a primordial structure.

49. Riedel, *Hören auf die Sprache*, 37. Cf. ibid., 43.

can no longer be revoked, namely, toward the voice of doubting itself, toward the "*vox humana.*"[50]

What shows itself thus is the possibility, apparent but not yet grasped in Descartes, of establishing an identity of the meditating 'I' certified in itself, where the knowing of the self binds itself to linguistic performance in the phenomenally appropriate experience of human being-in-the-world. Insofar as it is always already dialogical as a mean and means of self-understanding in such I-discourse in the sense of the above-indicated difference, that is, it is installed as self-transcending, the ground of certainty of the 'I' remains from this point pervaded by, indeed contained in, a fundamental, because unsublatable, uncertainty. Insofar as the self-understanding is constitutively woven in the relation to the other of itself, the historical lifeworld opens itself up at the same time with the *alter ego* as that horizon of reality within which the question concerning the being-relation of the 'I am' can then also be posited.

This form of an implicit 'finite world' that thus at least appears to be preserved here in the meditating ego as possibility would now, through an explicit reflection upon language as the ground of self-certification, be capable of becoming a positive point of entry that indeed leads in another direction, the transcendental direction envisaged by Husserl that we have mentioned above. For in crossing the threshold Descartes could have already, on the path of self-reflection, at least indicated what Heidegger calls "the *sense of being of the 'sum,'*"[51] *as a problem.*[52] And admittedly this would have been possible precisely in that position where, in the qualitative reversal of the thought path with the *pronuntiatum*, self-certification completes itself in the formulation of the *ego sum,* which, illuminated as *ego existo,* certifies my egoic existence in the absolutely indubitable truth sought without the principle 'cogito, ergo sum' having to be deduced, at least not necessarily. Instead of this, the situating of the 'I' as a *question of linguistically grounded world-relatedness of the I am* would have had to be

---

50. Ibid., 42. Riedel thus emphasizes that the *pronunciatum* as *fundamentum inconcussum* "[must] more completely state: *I proclaim that I am and thus I am*" (ibid., 43).

51. Heidegger, *GA 2,* 33.

52. For this reason it cannot, however, be maintained that from Descartes's ontological approach an adequate understanding for this sense of being could be formulated in the sense of a differentiation of modes of being. That lies outside of the Cartesian perspective on being, insofar as for Descartes the differentiations of being, taken traditionally, can be fixed solely as distinctions in the realm of *essentia,* while *existentia* remain uniformly determined as being present at hand [*Vorhandensein*].

able to shape a positive possibility in Descartes for the phenomenally appropriate grasping of the meditative self.

Descartes famously undertakes the step toward the *principium,* and so sufficient attention cannot also be found for another phenomenon equiprimordially cogiven with the *pronuntiatum.* What is meant is the fact that the 'I am' experiences itself as linguistically determined at the same time as it is in time, i.e., *temporally* composed. That this lies thoroughly in the wide reach of the Cartesian train of thought shows itself also in that for Descartes the 'I am' certifies itself directly in its being as often as it expresses itself. Thus, after all innerworldly relations are shut off, so that the 'I' has made itself present in reflexive self-perception as pure *res dubitans,* its certification carries itself out in the horizon of an experience of time belonging to it—that is, the presence of itself in each of its current, respective performances.

As much as this can be taken as a further index for the hermeneutical meaningfulness of a Cartesian insight, for Descartes himself something rather disquieting lies prior, insofar as the 'I am' therein advises of the danger of not being sufficient for the self-posited claim to an unconditioned certainty. So regarded, the *pronuntiatum,* and thus the expressed and self-confirming proposition in expression, still does not yet have the axiomatic sharpness of the sought '*fundamentum inconcussum*' by its own status, which in the sense of an all-as-supratemporally valid axiomatic is inaugurated by Descartes from the beginning and in the double sense of the word as an '*absolutum.*' In consideration of this basic orientation, the Cartesian approach leads necessarily just as well from out of the sighting of the 'I' as a self-enactment determined through temporality as on the other hand also from out of language. In the latter sense, it leads to the decided exclusion of language from the act of knowing,[53] and this with the far-reaching consequence that the connection between reason and language, with notable exceptions such as Herder or Wilhelm von Humboldt, persists up to the threshold of the twentieth century without a more profound significance for philosophical reflection.

---

53. This becomes clear in Descartes's famous example of the beeswax in the Second Meditation, *Mediationes,* 89–95; see also *Principia Philosophiae,* §74 in *Oeuvres de Descartes* (Paris: Vrin 1996), 8:37. Cf. Riedel, *Hören auf die Sprache,* 44.

§ 17. The Ontological Positioning of the Cartesian Ego between Acquisition of the Self and Loss of the World

The methodological start of the *ego sum* as *ens certum* is that which drives Descartes into the monologue with doubt, which hyperbolically separates thinking of the self from everything worldly in well-known stages of the path of doubt.[54] By this means, as Gerhart Schmidt stresses, the "existentiell, freely chosen solitude of the one meditating [became] ontological solitude,"[55] in which the 'I' transposes itself into an epistemological postulate of certainty from out of a necessary worldlessness, motivated methodologically from it, of which Walter Schulz remarks that it is "an artificial construct."[56] Thus, the 'I' in Cartesian self-perception is a "pure formal point-like character [*Punktualität*]"[57] as simple consciousness of itself. In order not to end in methodological solipsism, it is necessary to break this up in itself, especially since Descartes explicitly recognizes one's own mundane existence holding itself in its natural relation to life.[58] Again and again, the *Meditations* clarifies this and unites therein the fact that the ontological *qua* egological isolation of the ego is itself hyperbolic in its methodological structure.

54. Under (or outside of) this methodological elevation of doubt, however, the doubt is not necessarily extinguished from a skeptical vantage point, as certain remarks of Descartes's seem to suggest. Rather, doubt, like wonder, holds itself in the productive insecurity of the above-indicated 'thus or otherwise.' And that means that of itself it characterizes, in the undecidedness of certainty and uncertainty, as we have seen, the originary ground of philosophical reflection and thereby sets, from what is doubted, the knowledge-intending 'I' into relation to the *intentum* from the outset, as much the ground of certainty as the uncertainty of its knowing.

55. Schmidt, *Aufklärung und Metaphysik*, 66.

56. Schulz, "Descartes und das Problem der Subjektivität," 117.

57. Ibid., 118 (emphasis deleted).

58. See the relevant passages at the beginning and end of the First and Second Meditations. See also Descartes's letter to Princess Elizabeth of June 28, 1643 (*Oeuvres de Descartes* 3:690–697). In Descartes's correspondence—conditioned by the circumstance that, with respect to the addressee, a more pedagogical matter in the intention of a self-explication often enough informs his writing—the resistance of the natural attitude to the substance-dualistic hypostasis more often becomes visible, and does not always thereby want it to appear as if it exclusively dealt with "opposites." The depth of the problematic of the Cartesian approach is directly marked out in the fact that he does not dogmatically fix his standpoint, but rather lets it be called forth through the sought or ensuing defense in the continuity thoroughly dominating his thinking in a way that understands how to make use of doubt productively toward itself with respect to his insights.

The relation of being as relation to entities as a whole is thus to be secured apodictically by the meditating 'I' under the epistemic standard of truth qua certainty, but not thereby disclosed. The methodologically conditioned *worldlessness of the subject* may not therefore be read in the direction of a subjective idealism à la Berkeley, but rather has its origin in the subject, uncertain with regard to the claim to truth of all knowledge of its world, which sees itself confronted from there with the problem of first securing itself a world in general.[59] Seen ontologically, however, Descartes's reflexively secured 'step into the world,' which he famously undertakes by means of the proof of the existence of God in the Third Meditation, never really overcomes this worldlessness. For the meditating 'I,' factically and finitely experiencing and knowing itself, discloses itself as an egological consciousness of itself as *substantia cogitans* in the world relation through its self-positioning and self-legitimating activity in opposition to a *substantia infinita* declared to be an innate idea, which therein becomes a mirror for the '*mens sive animus.*'

In short, this shows itself in the fact that in the activity of thinking determined no longer discursively but ultimately intuitively, the meditating 'I' detects the ideas in consciousness that have the source of their legitimation independently of and prior to all linguistic comprehension in the originary idea of God as that *idea innata,* which transcends in its reality that of my thinking 'I' eminenter and thus not only formally.[60] And having proved itself to be immanent to consciousness, in guaranteeing the existence and essence of the I as *res cogitans,* it communicates the return of the

59. Therewith, the question of the belief in the reality of an outer world is formulated as a classical problem from Descartes up through Dilthey, which, precisely because the world is here thought of as the outer world in opposition to the fact of consciousness, indicates for Heidegger, among others, an originary lapse regarding the phenomenon of the world (see *GA* 2, esp. §§ 21, 95–101; 43, 200–211). For even "when one wanted to appeal to the fact that the subject must presuppose, and also must always already do so unconsciously, that the 'outer world' is present at hand, the constructive taking up of an isolated subject nonetheless remains in play" (ibid., 273), and thus from this point "on the ground of what remains, of the isolated subject, the conjoinment with a 'world' is realized" (ibid., 274), which for Heidegger amounts to a "destruction of the originary phenomenon of being-in-the-world" (ibid.).

60. In this sense the divine *substantia infinita* itself is something represented from and within consciousness, yet in such a way that it "ascends, *as the enabling of an encompassing dimension of being,* out ahead of the ego and its *cogitare* and *cogitatum* alike, and thus necessarily expels out of itself, e.g. out of its egological immanence, the self-reflection and pure intuition of the reflecting ego" (Friedrich-Wilhelm von Hermann, *Husserl und die Meditationen des Descartes* [Frankfurt: Klostermann 1971], 20).

'I' in the world at the same time for Descartes. So regarded, the dualism of *substantia cogitans* and *substantia extensa* is framed and therein sustained by the *substantia infinita,* albeit determined as thinking.[61]

In the course of orienting toward the ego as the *ens certum* the second ontological proof of the existence of God (as it has been called since Kant) in the Fifth Meditation fixes the meaning of God as the paradigm for worldlessness, i.e., the independence from the world, of the *res cogitans* as ego-subject. Therein, *corporeality* at the same time becomes the other over against the mind, and that means conceiving the delimited and circumscribed principle of the *res extensa* in comparison to the divine understanding, which co-constitutes the *ens humanum* as such. Insofar as the human is thus not 'pure spirit' in the sense of a divine being, the task is now set in the Sixth Meditation for Descartes to think about the incorporation of human consciousness on its own in the recognition of the substantial difference between consciousness and body; seen thus, the meditating ego's path of self-ascertainment only here succeeds in reaching its goal, which in itself, however, formulates a clear hierarchy with respect to both substances. Insofar as the *res cogitans* possesses, in its indivisibility, a higher degree of dignity than the in-itself arbitrarily divisible *res extensa,* on the ground of its extendedness, consciousness cannot also depend upon matter. The *cogito* uncovering itself in the path of doubt, seen in this way, gains if not its being, then nonetheless the consciousness of itself and thus of its being from out of "the devaluation of all other things."[62]

With the "insight into the immateriality of one's own essence,"[63] an ontological hiatus is opened up in the realm of the material. It separates not merely I and world, but runs as a fissure through human existence itself, insofar as the human being in its composition as dual body-soul onto-

61. See ibid., 29. On the function of the idea of God as mediator between 'I' and world, see also Schulz, "Descartes und das Problem der Subjektivität," 119.; Ludger Oeing-Hanhoff, "Der Mensch in der Philosophie Descartes," in *Die Frage nach dem Menschen: Aufriß einer philosophischen Anthropologie,* ed. Heinrich Rombach (Freiburg: Alber, 1966), 375–409; Hans-Peter Schütt, "Kant, Cartesius und der 'sceptische Idealist,'" in *Descartes nachgedacht,* ed. Hans-Peter Schütt and Andreas Kemmerling (Frankfurt: Klostermann, 1996), 170–199; Konrad Cramer, "Descartes antwortet Caterus: Gedanken zu Descartes Neubegründung des ontologischen Gottesbeweises" *Descartes nachgedacht,* 123–169; Hermann Schrödter, "Der Gottesdanke in der Metaphysik des Ich als substantia cogitans," in *Descartes im Diskurs der Neuzeit,* ed. Walter Friedrich Niebel, Angelica Horn, and Herbert Schnädelbach (Frankfurt: Suhrkamp, 2000), 103–124.

62. Schmidt, *Aufklärung und Metaphysik,* 76.

63. Taylor, *Quellen des Selbst,* 266.

logical substance belongs with its body as innerworldly *res extensa*. Under the standard of the criterion of truth, that means for knowledge in relation to the properly bodily, "to separate the clear from the obscure, [for that] is to attend carefully to the fact that pain, color and similar properties are only then grasped clearly and distinctly if one looks merely at perceptions or thoughts,"[64] which means, takes perceptions and thoughts as contents of consciousness and refers them necessarily back to the intellectual principle of consciousness privileged for Descartes as the primary self-relation of human beings over against all others.

It would be a misunderstanding, however, to wish to attribute to Descartes himself an ascetic intention hostile to the body. On the contrary, for Descartes the issue is to arrive at a distinction—conceptually clear and in accordance with the philosophical criterion of truth—between two regions of being from out of the insight into the dual composition of the human, a composition that only ever appears to us phenomenally as a unity. It is to grasp appropriately their relation of belonging-together as well as that perspective, to clarify these, and from there to determine positively, in the sense of the requisite apodictic certainty, the *res extensa* experienced in itself as the physical body [*Leibkörper*].[65] In this sense Descartes emphasizes in the Sixth Meditation that my sensible perceptions are "lent [me] actually only by nature in order to show the mind what is conducive or harmful to the composite whose part it is, and for that they are clear and distinct enough. But I let them serve me as safe guiding threads in order to discern without anything further the bodies outside of us according to their essence."[66] But that first occurs, as we have seen, when the sensible perceptions are secured as phenomena of consciousness. One's own physical body is thereby ultimately transformed into the side of objects as itself part of the *res extensa*.

As a result, consciousness occupies an external perspective with regard to its own body, namely, the perspective of observation. From out of this perspective, the human body appears famously as an automaton.[67]

---

64. Descartes, *Principia Philosophiae*, 1:68. 33.

65. See also Descartes's discussions of substance dualism in his reply to Antoine Arnauld's objections in *Meditationen über die Grundlagen der Philosophie mit den sämtlichen Einwänden und Erwiderungen*. ed. Artur Buchenau (Hamburg: Meiner, 1972), 202–209.

66. Descartes, Sixth Meditation, *Meditationes* 199–201.

67. See Descartes, *Discours de la Méthode*. trans. and ed. Lüder Gäbe (Hamburg: Meiner, 1969), part 5, esp. 90. Among others, Klaus Hammacher ("Einige methodische Regeln Des-

cartes und das erfindende Denken," in *Zeitschrift für allgemein Wissenschaftstheorie IV* [1973], 203–223) has, as had Kurt Hübner ("Von der Intentionalität der modernen Technik," in *Sprache im technischen Zeitalter* [1968], 25:27–48) before him, noted that the model of the automaton was dismissed over the course of time as merely mechanistic, while in truth a cybernetic model is prefigured within it. For Descartes had—specifically in *Passions de l'Ame* and *La Description du Corps Humain* (in *Oeuvres de Descartes*, vol. 11)—assessed the human body as a system determined through self-regulation. Thereby, Descartes's achievements in physiology can be related to current theories in an exemplary way, theories which no longer explain bodily processes from the point of the autonomy of a general principle of life, but rather out of their physiological structures and subsystems.

Analogous to the animal organism, the human organism functions in Descartes's view as an independent circuit. Descartes's linkage of the circulatory and nervous systems in particular, which allows the bloodstream—and in this sense, the self-regulation of the body—to appear as an autonomous functional cycle, is thereby determined as a machine. This self-regulation has nothing to do, however, with the Platonic principle of the soul's self-movement (*Phaedrus* 245e, *Laws* 896a), but rather explains itself only from out of the shared physiological processes, which thus at the same time relate themselves back to the connection between body and soul, to the function—mediated by the alternating effects upon each other—that Descartes settles in the pineal gland, the epiphysis, as the organic "headquarters of the soul" (*Passions de l'Ame*, art. 32). Seen thus, in place of the heart as the traditional central organ of the life of feeling, he now articulates a correlation of heart and brain. The central control of the physical-chemical bodily processes assumed to be automatic is thus the responsibility of the brain (see ibid., art. 16).

In this "*interactionist* relationship" (Martin Carrier and Jürgen Mittelstraß, *Geist, Gehirn, Verhalten: Das Leib-Seele-Problem und die Philosophie der Psychologie* [Berlin: De Gruyter, 1989], 18) existing between thinking and bodily substance the hierarchy of substances is ontologically established at the same time with the dualism itself. For it is thoughts, and thus thinking, that make it possible to operate in a directed way in the functional connection of the human body, and in such a way that the so-called animal spirits (*esprits animaux*), as physiological substance-bearers of the *passions,* move in the outpouring from the pineal gland in the nervous system such that in the soul one desire emerges in correspondence with a passion, a desire that for its part, however, can (and for Descartes, must) in turn be rationally controlled on the side of the soul in the implementation of the will as an intelligible capacity for action.

This theorem of the pineal gland in particular very quickly attracted harsh criticism—see here, in the degree of its effects, particularly Spinoza (esp. the introduction to part 5 of his *Ethica*, ed. Konrad Blumenstock, in *Opera* [Darmstadt: Wissenschaftliche Buchgesellschaft, 1980], 2:504–511); see also Kant's shrewd pleas in *Träume eines Geistersehers, erläutert durch Träume der Metaphysik*, in *Gesammelte Schriften*, ed. Royal Prussian Academy of the Sciences [Berlin: Reimer (1902–1917) and De Gruyter (1918–), 2:324 (1912). In general, this privileged problem of the mind-body relation was counted over time among the markedly debated themes within the development of Cartesianism. Here, the positions to be considered are influxion-ism, occasionalism, and psychophysical parallelism (see Rainer Specht, *Commercium mentis et corporis: Über Kausalvorstellungen im Cartesianismus* [Stuttgart: Frommann-Holzboog, 1966]; see also Carrier and Mittelstrass, *Geist, Gehirn, Verhalten*, 20–29).

In a view of Descartes from a contemporary perspective, Walter Schulz sees his approach as an enduring positive asset, in that in contrast to materialist theories he does not simply resolve the mental into physiological processes and as well does not, on the other hand, spiritually exaggerate the bodily as idealistic metaphysics does (*Descartes und das Problem der Subjektivität*, 124). Wherever the debate has expanded in its historical course, one way

Nonetheless, this self-distancing initiated methodologically from knowledge's claim to certainty of its own bodily existence, ensuing from the perspective of consciousness, sublates the factical bondedness of human beings to the body, as little as bodily sensible self-experience is thereby shut off. In the Sixth Meditation Descartes emphasizes that "nature [teaches] me through sensations of pain, hunger, thirst, and so on that I am joined to my body not merely like a sailor to a ship, but that I am united with it in the innermost way, penetrate it, as it were, and form with it a unified whole."[68] The primary way in which sensuous self-experience appears in it and for it as content of consciousness with a view to self-consciousness determined as the *cogito*, is the feeling that Descartes designates as *passion* in connection to the Thomistic concept. In the passions, the feelings in the sense

---

or another Hammacher's characteristic hits upon it: "The persistent meaning of Descartes's individual-disciplinary model of thought—outstripped in content—consists thus in making us conscious of the methodological preliminary decisions of our scientific modes of observation" (introduction to *Passions de l'Ame*, 42).

The extent to which this possesses validity, in particular in the field of analytic philosophy, for the treatment of the mind-body problem is shown by Heiner Hastedt's study, *Das Leib-Seele-Problem: Zwischen Naturwissenschaft des Geistes und kultureller Eindimensionalität* (Hamburg 1989). which subjects scientistic and reductionistic tendencies to a comprehensive critique and thus shapes a new theory of emergence of the mental. With regard to analytic positions on the mind-body problem, see further Richard Rorty's investigation (*Der Spiegel der Natur: Eine Kritik der Philosophie* [Frankfurt: Suhrkamp, 1981]) whose aim is that of a critique of the idea of the mental as a self-contained dimension and of the paradigm erected therein of philosophy qua epistemology (44–84).

A particularly telling example of how extraordinarily powerful in effect Descartes's mechanistically designed position is can be found in the history of the reception of the discoverer of the circulatory system, William Harvey. On the basis of Descartes's integration of the Harveyean model into his own thought, Harvey's vitalist conception—originally intended and oriented to the teleological Aristotelian philosophy of nature—fell into oblivion, so that Harvey himself, mirrored through Descartes in his influence, is largely seen as the forefather of a physicalistically stamped medicine. Significantly, the study by Spaemann and Löw (*Die Frage Wozu? Geschichte und Wiederentdeckung des teleologischen Denkens* [Munich: Piper, 1985]), which investigates the ramifications of teleological thought in the tradition, leaves Harvey out in its aim of a rehabilitation of teleological phenomena, while treating Descartes's role in the process of its decline in great detail. In his dissertation on medical history, which illuminates Descartes's as yet unacknowledged role in the formation of modern medicine's image of the human, Thomas Fuchs investigates the extent to which Harvey's reception is carried out from its beginnings under Cartesian auspices, which thereafter led to the occlusion of Harvey's own intentions (*Die Mechanisierung des Herzens: Harvey und Descartes—Der vitale und der mechanische Aspekt des Kreislaufs* [Frankfurt: Suhrkamp, 1992]).

68. Descartes, Sixth Meditation, *Meditationes*, 195.

of affects express themselves, as Gerhart Schmidt puts it in an apparently paradoxical, yet striking, formulation as: "the corporeality of the soul."[69]

Thereby another, equally authentic possibility of self-experience, distinguished from pure intellectual self-apprehension, shows itself in which the self-relation manifests itself in feelings in distinction from self-consciousness as *"self-feeling."*[70] As earnestly as Descartes poses the problem of the affects, just as little does he admit uncertainty of the phenomenon into his basic position. This means that the treatment of the problems issuing from this one-sidedness proceeds in advance under the premise that the *'animalitas'* of human beings determines itself from the point of its *'rationalitas.'* Consequently for Descartes the 'passions' prove themselves in light of the traditional caveat of their pathological functions of disturbance as *perturbatio animi* with regard to their philosophical thematization, posited with the intention of demonstrating *ratio as principle of direction and control,* on account of which then the question of self-mastery stands at the center in the sense of rational access to the feelings in such a way that Descartes in the *Passions de l'Ame* can formulate his ethics as a doctrine of affects.[71]

Without more closely entering into these ways of posing the problem, we may in conclusion simply refer to a meaningful aspect of the Cartesian doctrine of the affects for the given context. In the rational analysis of the human life of feeling an order of six originary and simple basic affects is revealed by Descartes in light of his methodological construction. They possess in themselves again a hierarchizing tendency to the effect that for Descartes, *admiration* or wonder shows itself as the ground-laying *'passion*

---

69. Gerhart Schmidt, *Aufklärung und Metaphysik,* 151. What is thereby indicated is the rejection of those all-too-simple ascriptions that take on merely a 'purely mental [*geistige*] status,' in Descartes's approach to the emotions. See Dominik Perler, "Cartesianische Emotionen," in *Descartes Nachgedacht,* 51–79.

70. Gerhart Schmidt, *Aufklärung und Metaphysik,* 151

71. See Taylor, *Quellen des Selbst,* 269–287, who under the key phrase of "disengaged reason," motivated out of the "step from the usual body-dependent on the disengaged perspective" (ibid., 267), makes the Cartesian "ethic of rational control," that is, the "self-mastery of reason," into a theme of his investigation. On the control of the affects on the basis of a theory of psychophysical reciprocity, see also Wolfgang Röd, *Descartes: Die Genese des Cartesianischen Rationalismus* (Munich: Beck, 1995), 131–157. A look at the conception and placement of the 'provisional morality' in *Discours de la Méthode* already shows the extent to which the question of securing knowledge for Descartes is linked from the outset to the good life. Ernst Cassirer thus even maintains for Descartes a "primacy of the practical" (*Descartes: Lehre-Persönlichkeit-Wirkung* [Hamburg: Meiner, 1995], 33).

de l'ame' par excellence, in which its function shines through according to the ancient phenomenon of wonder introduced above (§15). Descartes determines wonder as "a sudden surprise of the soul (*subite surprise de l'ame*), which causes it to see itself brought to the point of regarding with attention (*attention*) the object, which appears to it as rare and extraordinary."[72] This attentiveness as an intellectual presupposition for methodologically guided knowledge is ever again demanded by Descartes in the *Meditations*, as elsewhere, and achieves its affective coloring in wonder.

Decisive for wonder is thus "that it neither has a good, nor an evil for an object, but rather has only the knowledge of the matter (*connaissance de la chose*), about which one wonders. It has for that reason no relation to the heart and blood, on which the complete wellness of the body depends, but rather only to the brain (*le cerveau*), in which both sense organs [that is, the sense of sight and hearing], which serve for such a knowledge, are found."[73] Thus wonder is exhibited as an *affective condition of knowledge,* which becomes therein *directive for methodological doubt,* and which initiates the philosophical attitude in the connection with wonder, as we have seen. It is to be noted in the affective side of thinking that—according to its ontological status—the affects themselves signify *a class of cogitationes.* And only in so far as they are *cogitationes,* which, founded in turn as affects themselves, are they in the primary class of ideas, and have a function relative to knowledge and thus truth.

This means, when one once more recalls the employment of θαυμάζειν in accordance with the reflections we have made, that wonder possesses an eminent e*pistemic-critical function;* that is, as a catalyzing moment it transports the process of philosophical knowing along its path. Yet the Cartesian wonderer is itself upon closer inspection hardly a Socratic friend of wisdom—whose paths, as the early Platonic dialogues in particular show, often enough even end on difficult terrain in aporias and lay open the anticipatory and defenseless character of human self- and world understanding as lacking a pathway and counsel. Cartesian admiration is above all a matter of a laboratory worker's approach to certainty, who determines the answer to the question concerning knowledge and its truth—corresponding to the antecedent lawfulness of inner, conscious self-apprehension—

---

72. Descartes, *Passions de l'Ame*, art. 70.
73. Ibid., art. 71.

whose constitutive elements always already apply as true for themselves.[74] That is, wonder may unfold itself only in attention as methodological doubt from out of an a priori secured indubitability of mental being as the immediate path to the *cogitatio* for itself.[75]

With a view to the metaphysical claim to grounding, the *principles of being* thus show themselves *as principles of knowledge*. From out of this point, Descartes then unfolds his hypostasis of substantialization of self-consciousness over against matter, which as a consequence—one thinks of Kant's famous critique in the Paralogisms of the *Critique of Pure Reason*—was repeatedly subjected to a penetrating critique without thereby touching upon the methodological and ontological primacy of consciousness in its self-enactment as thinking, which according to Descartes involves the demand for immediacy and certainty. "From this point on," as Rorty notes, "it stood open for philosophers to prefer to make the strictness of the mathematician or the mathematical physicist their own—or to explain the prevailing apparent strictness in these fields. . . . In place of life, science became the theme of philosophy and epistemology in its core."[76]

The ego stands at the center of all intention, and in this sense Descartes's philosophy is precisely an incessant striving after the *self-understanding of the human*, which takes itself to be the aim with the discovery of the *ego cogito*. Yet how does the ego stand in this case? In insisting that knowledge, if it is to be true, must be apodictically certain, the richness of immediacy in self-experience is narrowed to the criterion of a theoretical certainty. As Descartes attributes to alterity something unsettling, which, warranted by the immediacy of his experience, accrues to the 'I' precisely in its self-encounter where illusion, dream, or feeling put one in mind of the changeability, uncertainty, and even ambivalence of the human world and self-relation, which are excluded in the act of methodological distan-

74. "Now, whatever pertains to the ideas (*ad ideas attinet*), cannot thus actually be false when one considers them only for themselves (*si solae in se spectentur*) and not in relation to some other thing. . . . Even in the act of willing and in the affections as such (*in ipsa voluntate, vel affectibus*) I need not fear any error, for whenever I wish something evil, or even something impossible, it nonetheless remains true that I wish such things" (Descartes, Third Meditation, *Meditationes*, 105).

75. Descartes defines this context of immediacy and thinking when he states: "Under thinking I understand all that occurs within us such that we are immediately conscious of ourselves. Thus not merely understanding, willing, and imagining, but also perceiving belongs here to thinking" (*Prinzipien*, vol. 1, 9).

76. Rorty, *Der Spiegel der Natur*, 76.

tiation and disciplining, access to the question 'who am I?' above and beyond the experience '*that* I am,' remains barred.

Yet it is indicative of the strength of his problematic that, as in the *pronuntiatum* with '*existo*,' a genuine indication of the phenomenal asserts itself into his meditations, namely where, in the persisting obscurity regarding itself as the 'I' that is already ascertained in its *existentia*, the question of the 'who' of this 'I,' at the very least, appears.[77] But analogous to the first experience of the 'I am' and bound up with it in its innermost character, the '*quis*,' on the presupposition of the demand of certainty, is pushed aside and becomes '*quid*,' and thus it harmonizes with the tradition around the question of *essentia*, of essence as in itself unchanging substance: "*Sed quid igitur sum? Res cogitans.*"[78] This is Descartes's answer, which thereby seals the human 'I' intellectualistically in itself. In this hoped-for self-security the 'I,' nevertheless, becomes emptied of its relations to the natural as well as the historical world.

However, the loss of the world is, though consequential, ultimately only so *within* the Cartesian construction, which, when we consider it more precisely, is already capable, in its choice of epistemological methodological premises, of actualizing itself solely *within the weave of historical horizons* as an answer to the demands and questions posed of its own time. Naturally, this is not to say thereby that the Cartesian position arose in historical dependencies or could therein be worked out. For precisely through its answers regarding human self-experience and self-understanding it transcends the horizon out of which it grows, and thus makes merely reductive attempts at explanation impossible. With Descartes new horizons and options of sense open up historically that themselves cannot be reduced [*hinterschritten*] further.

Observed methodologically, every claim to a reconstruction of originary givennesses in the condition of the 'in itself' transforms itself from the outset into an impossible imposition. This reconstructed account of historical connections is profitable only in the relation to the particular, current (and thus always selective) context of analysis in which the sense for what has become historically and therein always in anticipation of our answers forms an attitude toward questioning that finds its basic form in

---

77. "*Nondum vero satis intelligo, quisnam sim ego ille, qui iam necessario sum.*" Descartes, Second Meditation, *Meditationes*, 78).

78. Ibid., 86.

the kinship of doubt and wonder. Through variance and flexibility, this kinship testifies, as it were, seismographically to its contemporaneity in 'untimely observation' and as a type of being can inform the *habitus* (perhaps the ἦθος, but at the least the ἕξις, if one admits the Aristotelian distinction) of philosophical practice.

With *wonder* it is accordingly signified that an entry point—in which a reflexive reversal determined methodologically, whatever the details— takes place that itself cannot be further grounded or derived as causally compelling, which lets the familiar appear as unfamiliar and strange. This enables a distancing from the inquiring vision, sparking at the same time a productive curiosity that in the course of the methodological suspension of the current preunderstanding creates a new basis for an adequate understanding in the matter. Such understanding still knows that everything with which one is acquainted, the familiar, fundamentally harbors unknown aspects within the multiplicity of its different facets. In this knowing, however, cognition [*Erkennen*] reflects itself hermeneutically as radically finite with regard to its possibilities.

At the same time, the scission that distinguishes the extraphilosophical from the philosophical self- and world relation is thereby marked out.[79] That the world of philosophy appears, in a famous phrase of Hegel's, from the point of view of sound human understanding as "an inverted world"[80] does not necessarily mean—as it does not ultimately mean in Hegel—that it rises above such understanding in the sense of an intended spiritual rank order, nor does this phrase necessarily commit one to the assumption of cleanly separating two possible realms of reality. For opposed to this is the fact that the relation of the philosopher to the experiences and contents of sense that precede him is constitutive for it and thus unsublatable. The

---

79. In the sense of a concretization of this distinction, one can refer, for example, to Gottfried Boehm's study, "Der erste Blick: Kunstwerk-Ästhetik-Philosophie," *Deutsche Zeitschrift für Philosophie*, 41 no. 1 (1993), 44–53, which thematizes a specific extraphilosophical—and yet nonetheless philosophically relevant—perspective upon the world. Boehm here exhibits certain parallels between the view of the art contemplator and the wonder of the philosopher, which lets him question the 'possible bridge' between art and philosophy that binds both in such a way that the "philosopher [encounters] the *beginning* of his own task in the artwork" (ibid., 53). In this task, as in art, it is not merely the whole that becomes the theme; rather an examination of the "presuppositions of one's own thinking and perception" (ibid.) is always already included in this thematization.

80. Hegel, "Einleitung: Über das Wesen der philosophischen Kritik überhaupt und ihr Verhältnis zum gegenwärtigen Zustand der Philosophie insbesondere," in *Werke* [Frankfurt: Suhrkamp 1975], 2:182.

world, as that reality in which we all live, first and foremost opens up an entry for the questions of the philosopher. In this sense, philosophy offers, to speak with Wilhelm Dilthey, a unique "interpretation of reality"[81]; indeed, it is "the science of the real."[82]

81. Dilthey, *Das Wesen der Philosophie*, ed. Georg Misch, in *GS* (Göttingen: Vandenhoeck & Ruprecht, 1974), 5:379.

82. Dilthey, *Grundgedanke meiner Philosophie*, ed. Bernhard Groethuysen, in *GS* (Göttingen: Vandenhoeck & Ruprecht, 1991), 8:172. In recollection of the manifoldly interwoven levels of understanding indicated in the first section with regard to the problematic of the text, and as a hint of what is to come, the question may be posed as to the extent to which it would be more meaningful to speak here of 'realities,' insofar as pluralization (in the sense of a historically occurring destabilization of what one is accustomed to grasp as reality, in the sense of a self-authenticating totality [of sense]) can correspond to the modern *condition humaine*. And is not philosophy thus able to encounter its present—in the modern consciousness, with its renunciation of the sort of Hegelian assumption of an all-encompassing systematic that determines its essence—only still as plural and therefore in the form of 'philosophies'?

For Dilthey this pluralization of the concept of philosophy harbored something disquieting, to which he nonetheless did not close himself off when he undertook the preliminary work on the idea of *a* systematic philosophy in which life was to attain to its own self-evaluation (see *Das Wesen der Philosophie*, ed. Georg Misch, in *GS*, 5:339–416). On the contrary, Nietzsche's experimental perspectivism celebrates just this plurality out of the insight into the "interpretative character of all occurrence" (*Nachgelassene Fragmente: Herbst 1885–Frühjahr 1886*, in *KGW* 8, 1, 34), for "there is no event [*Ereigniß*] in itself. What occurs is a group of appearances, *selected* and summarized by an interpreting being" (ibid.).

CHAPTER TWO

ON LIFE IN LIFEWORLDS:

CRITICAL CONSIDERATIONS OF HUSSERL'S

PHENOMENOLOGY OF THE LIFEWORLD

§ 18. The Concept of "Lifeworld" as an Indication of the Problem

The understanding of reality brought into our approach orients itself to
that which has long since become indigenous to philosophy in the concept
of the lifeworld.[1] If Gadamer's dictum applies, that a statement is "always

---

1. The theme and concept of the lifeworld are usually associated with the later thinking of
Edmund Husserl, in particular with his last text: *Die Krisis der europäischen Wissenschaften und
die transzendentale Phänomenologie*, ed. Walter Biemel, in *Husserliana* (The Hague: Nijhoff,
1976), GW 6. Yet this concept is found in Husserl even earlier, in the 1917–1918 "Beilage XIII"
of *Ideen zu einer reinen Phänomenologie und phänomenologischen Philosophie: Zweites Buch*, in
Husserliana, ed. Walter Biemel [The Hague: Nijhoff, 1952], 4:374ff). Iso Kern, in *Edmund Husserl: Darstellung seines Denkens*, ed. Rudolph Bernet, Iso Kern, and Eduard Marbach (Hamburg: Meiner, 1989), 199–208, cites further appearances of it in the as-yet-unpublished papers:
Manuscript D 13 I, p. 173 a; Manuscript A IV 22, p. 70.

Yet what is more, the publication of Heidegger's early Freiburg lectures has meanwhile
made it apparent that he already utilized the concept of the lifeworld from 1919 to 1923 for his
conception of a phenomenology as the originary science of life. But insofar as the manuscripts
of Heidegger's prewar lectures are no longer preserved and Husserl's posthumous papers have
not yet been made fully accessible, care must be exercised in any attribution of the initial use of
the term 'lifeworld.' At any rate, with respect to the formation of this concept, neither can lay
claim to original authorship.

For prior to these authors, Georg Simmel speaks of a lifeworld in the 1912 revised edition
of his text *Die Religion* (*Gesamtausgabe*, ed. Otthein Rammstedt [Frankfurt: Suhrkamp 1995],
10:46). With a broader cultural-philosophical intention, Rudolph Eucken makes use of the
concept in 1918 (*Mensch und Welt: Eine Philosophie des Lebens* [Leipzig: Quelle & Meyer 1920],
429) as does Hans Freyer in 1923 in *Theorie des Geistes: Eine Einleitung in die Kulturphilosophie*
(Darmstadt: Teubner/Wissenschaftliche Buchgesellschaft, 1966, 133). On the extraphenom-

111

an answer,"[2] the enormous resonance that this coinage has—in such a way that the concept after all became, without further ado, a part of our everyday and common language—offers a material indication of a constellation of problems in the air, as it were, and focusing itself in it as in a burning lens.[3]

---

enological prehistory of this concept with a view to possible lines of connection with Husserl's approach, see Ferdinand Fellmann, *Gelebte Philosophie in Deutschland: Denkformen der Lebensweltphänomenologie und der kritischen Theorie* (Freiburg: Alber, 1983), 120.

An even earlier source for the use of the term is found in Hugo von Hofmannstahl, who speaks of the lifeworld in his 1907 essay "Tausendundeine Nacht," in *Gesammelte Werke in Einzelausgaben: Prosa II,* ed. Herbert Steiner (Frankfurt: Fischer, 1951), 319. Hofmannsthal—a distant relative of Malvine Husserl—who accepted an invitation to visit the philosopher in Göttingen in 1906 (see Rudolph Hirsch, "Edmund Husserl und Hugo von Hofmannsthal: Eine Begegnung und ein Brief.,"in *Sprache und Politik,* ed. Carl Joachim Friedrich and Benno Reifenberg [Heidelberg: Schneider, 1968], 108–115), means by 'lifeworld' that spiritual-cultural milieu out of which the collected stories in *Tausendundeine Nacht* grew, as their natural ground.

In view of the prehistory of the concept, it is to be further noted that Husserl's demand for an analysis of the lifeworld has a significant formative influence in the empiricocritical program, formulated by Richard Avenarius, of a yet-to-be recovered 'natural concept of the world,' which Husserl himself uses with a terminological intention in, among other places, the 1910/11 lecture "Grundprobleme der Phänomenologie" (in *Zur Phänomenologie der Intersubjektivität. Texte aus dem Nachlaß. Erster Teil.* In *Husserliana,* Vol. XIII, ed. Iso Kern. The Hague, 1973, 125). Cf. Hermann Lübbe, "Positivismus und Phänomenologie. Mach und Husserl," in *Bewußtsein in Geschichten,* 33–62; Manfred Sommer, *Husserl und der frühe Positivismus.* (Frankfurt: Klostermann, 1985). On the varying meanings of the concept of lifeworld see also Gerd Brand, *Die Lebenswelt. Eine Philosophie des konkreten Apriori* (Berlin: De Gruyter, 1971); Ludwig Landgrebe, "Lebenswelt und Geschichtlichkeit des menschlichen Daseins," in *Phänomenologie und Marxismus,* Bd. 2, ed. Bernhard Waldenfels, J. Broekman, and Ante Pazanin. (Frankfurt: Suhrkamp, 1977), 2:13–58. Rüdiger Welter offers a detailed intellectual-historical study in *Der Begriff der Lebenswelt. Theorien vortheoretischer Erfahrungswelt* (Munich: Fink, 1986).

2. Gadamer, *Die phänomenologische Bewegung,* in *GW* (Tübingen: Siebeck, 1987), 3:123.

3. For the *equation,* widely assumed today, *of the lifeworld with the everyday,* it is, however, less appropriate to bring into play Husserl's *Krisis* here. Its origin is to be found instead, as Carl Friedrich Gethmann remarks in his preface to the collection *Lebenswelt und Wissenschaft: Studien zum Verhältnis von Phänomenologie und Wissenschaftstheorie* (Bonn: Bouvier, 1991), 8, in the way in which Alfred Schütz makes use of it within his conception of a phenomenological basis of the social sciences. It attempts, by its own admission, "to subject the posing of the problem and method of the 'interpretive sociology' grounded by Max Weber to a philosophical critique [that is, one definitively oriented to Husserl's phenomenology]," as Schütz emphasizes in his first letter to Husserl on April 26, 1932 (Husserl, *Briefwechsel,* ed. Karl Schuhmann. [Dordrecht: Springer, 1994], 4:481) enclosed as an accompaniment to his book *Der sinnhafte Aufbau der sozialen Welt: Eine Einleitung in die verstehende Soziologie* (Frankfurt: Suhrkamp, 1993).

In his study, Schütz endeavors to clarify the intersubjective structure of everyday conduct and its objectivations, precisely through a phenomenological analysis of the processes of meaning attribution with regard to human beings as bound up within the social everyday world. Here, as in the continuation of this approach (cf. the late work completed and edited by his student: Alfred Schütz and Thomas Luckmann, *Strukturen der Lebenswelt* 2 vols. [Frankfurt: Suhrkamp, 2 vols. 1994]), Schütz lays out a paradigm, relevant to contemporary sociology, with

The high "value of sympathy"[4] that the expression 'lifeworld' undoubtedly possesses, in particular in the environment of a strengthened, more technical-critical assessment of relations of social life of the human, assuming its place in the everyday, may not hide the fact that the multitude of the meanings bound up with it is subject to considerable variation and testifies to such a *fundamental ambiguity* of the concept.[5] Without looking

---

his transformation of a phenomenology of the lifeworld into a sociology of the everyday that carries out its analyses "under the conscious renunciation of the problematic of transcendental subjectivity and intersubjectivity . . . as [borrowing a phrase from Husserl] a constitutive phenomenology of the natural attitude" (*Der sinnhafte Aufbau*, 56).

Thus, in opposition to the transcendental-apriori ground-function of the lifeworld, a conception is given precedence that grasps the lifeworld *mundanely* as the phenomenal region of cultural-historical reality, "which the alert, normal adult, in the attitude of sound human understanding, finds as simply given" (*Strukturen der Lebenswelt*, 1:25) and which Husserl also thematizes as the 'concrete lifeworld,' yet does not set with this primary function, which "understood in its totality as the natural and social world [is] as much the setting as it is the destination" (ibid., 28; on Schütz's conception, see Richard Grathoff, *Milieu und Lebenswelt. Einführung in die phänomenologische Soziologie und die sozialphänomenologische Forschung.* [Frankfurt: Suhrkamp, 1989]).

Meanwhile this understanding of the lifeworld has expansively colored the pedagogical and ecological literature, among others, and within the debates outlined here, the 'lifeworld' has famously become a key methodological concept. As Manfred Sommer shows in his study "Der Alltagsbegriff in der Phänomenologie und seine gegenwärtige Rezeption in der Sozialwissenschaften" (in *Pädagogik und Alltag: Methoden und Ergebnisse alltagsorientierter Forschung in der Erziehungswissenschaft*, ed. Dieter Lenzen [Stuttgart: Klett-Cotta, 1980], 27–43), Heidegger's existential-hermeneutic approach is of central significance for the understanding of the lifeworld in the development of the social sciences. With a view to present philosophical discussions, Franz Joseph Wetz provides a summary overview of the varying notions of the concept of the lifeworld in *Lebenswelt und Weltall* (101–115), whereby Wetz betrays a preference for one conception in particular in the exchange with Jürgen Habermas's mature outline of the sociological paradigm of the lifeworld (*Theorie des kommunikativen Handelns*, vol. 2, chap. 6), which he accords a "prominent position" (*Lebenswelt und Weltall*, 112). Ferdinand Fellmann also investigates the Habermasian conception in comparison to Husserlian phenomenology of the lifeworld with respect to their sociohistorical background in *Gelebte Philosophie in Deutschland*.

4. Welter, *Der Begriff der Lebenswelt*, 78.

5. This makes it necessary to test the respective use of the concept of consistency in relation to Husserl's conception of the lifeworld precisely where it explicitly intends to identify itself with reference to Husserl. This should not mean that the relevant positions are thus to be treated along the lines of a 'true/false' criterion of value, since in Husserl's own usage, as Welter shows, "the expression 'lifeworld' [comes into] contact with all levels of the problems of Husserlian phenomenology: from the cultural anthropology of the human sciences to the . . . 'ontology of the lifeworld' . . . to transcendental phenomenology" (*Der Begriff der Lebenswelt*, 79, as well as its overall context from 77–87).

Within the framework of the present investigation it is not a matter of tightening up, in the details of its construction or in the path of its thought, the *"Krisis"* essay, especially since the "fractures in the construction of the 'Krisis'" noted by Landgrebe and others ("Lebenswelt

at particular possible accentuations and priorities it is ultimately the case, as Waldenfels remarks, that everyone who "today uses the word 'lifeworld' . . . does not only [speak] the language of Husserl, but also the language of a transitional time that reaches back to the threshold of our century."[6] The term "lifeworld" thereby manifestly clarifies and is thoroughly consistent with the matter that the world as cosmos or universe was an originary theme of philosophy from time immemorial,[7] but as a whole is now related to the notion of *life,* a notion which famously advanced as a central theme in all its variations in particular detail in the fin-de-siècle nineteenth century, which itself stood under the sign of a grounding crisis of the concept of reason and consciousness.[8]

In *Lebensphilosophie*—in Henri Bergson or particularly in Wilhelm Dilthey, just to mention two of the formative thinkers of the school, whose influence upon the development of phenomenology (one need only think of Schütz or Heidegger) should not be underestimated—the turn to the

---

und Geschichtlichkeit," 26, 31–45; see also Ulrich Claesges, "Zweideutigkeit in Husserls Lebensweltbegriff," in *Perspektiven transzendentalphänomenologischer Forschung,* ed. Ulrich Claesges and K. Held [The Hague: Nijhoff, 1972], 85–101), make a philological study of the text, true in its details, challenging work, not least on account of the fragmentary character of Husserl's work itself. In addition, it is worthwhile to refer to E. W. Orth's commentary (*Edmund Husserls "Krisis der europäischen Wissenschaften und die transzendentale Phänomenologie"* [Darmstadt: Wissenschaftliche Buchgesellschaft, 1999]), which offers an in-depth interpretation of Husserl's late work. For Orth's analysis is not to be left out of future treatment of the "Krisis," though its recent publication comes too late to be included in the present investigation. If, seen thus, it must remain here as a mere reference, this "fault" can be compensated by the fact that in the present investigation the passage through Husserl's philosophy of the lifeworld results in a preview of the analysis, unfolded in the third section, of the Heideggerian hermeneutical phenomenology of the lifeworld, which for its part remains outside of Orth's interests.

6. Bernhard Waldenfels, *In den Netzen der Lebenswelt* (Frankfurt: Suhrkamp, 1985), 7.

7. See, e.g., Klaus Held: *Heraklit, Parmenides und der Anfang von Philosophie und Wissenschaft: Eine phänomenologische Besinnung* (Berlin: De Gruyter, 1980). Held proceeds from the thesis that the totality of beings—and in this sense, the world—exhibits the oldest idea of philosophy. Held more closely investigates the consequences issuing from a phenomenological approach of a world-thematic in "Husserls neue Einführung in die Philosophie: Der Begriff der Lebenswelt," in *Lebenswelt und Wissenschaft,* 79–113; see further Held's study *Heimwelt, Fremdwelt, die eine Welt* (in *Perspektiven und Probleme der Husserlischen Phänomenologie,* edited by Ernst Wolfgang Orth, 305–337 [Freiburg: Alber, 1991]) and his "Heidegger und das Prinzip der Phänomenologie," in *Heidegger und die praktische Philosophie,* ed. Annemarie Gethmann-Siefert and Otto Pöggeler (Frankfurt: Suhrkamp, 1988), 111–139.

8. This being the case, it seems plausible that the term 'lifeworld' migrated from *Lebensphilosophie* to phenomenology, and as a result of this constellation in Heidegger's work—as we shall see—helped to motivate the transmutation of phenomenology into an originary science of life, and from here, into a hermeneutics of facticity.

subject, constitutive for modern philosophy, is thereby further upheld in the direction of an experiential "I" [*Erlebnis*-Ich], yet which as such reveals the claim of reason not, as suspected, in a turn to the irrational, but rather only makes its reasonableness sufficiently graspable precisely in the full concept of experience as the awareness of life. Dilthey's well-known basic principle runs: "thinking cannot go back behind life."[9] Dilthey thereby allocates to philosophy the task of uncovering the connection of life[10] in

9. Wilhelm Dilthey, *Die Geistige Welt. Einleitung in die Philosophie des Lebens, Vorrede*, in *GS*, 5:5. On Dilthey's point of entry into life, see Gander, *Positivismus als Metaphysik*, 161–200.

10. "This is the first issue, and as well the last, of philosophy in general" (ibid., 193). Correspondingly, the later Dilthey had reformulated what was for him the functioning 'principle of phenomenality, that is, of consciousness' (see *Breslauer Ausarbeitung*. In *GS*, ed. Helmut Johach and Frithof Rodi [Göttingen: Vandenhoeck & Ruprecht, 1982], 19:60) into what he took to be the more complete 'principle of experience' [*Erlebnissatz*] with regard to its universal validity (*Kategorien des Lebens*, in *GS*, 7:230). In just this approach Dilthey sees himself entirely in agreement with Husserl's phenomenological intentions, which is why he perceives the latter's polemic in the famous LOGOS essay "Philosophie als strenge Wissenschaft," ed. Wilhelm Szilasi (Frankfurt: Klostermann, 1965), wherein Husserl condemns Dilthey's position, from the point of view of his own project, as being at one with all *Weltanschauungsphilosophie* (ibid., 50–55)—as a 'test of strength' of their amicable relationship (see his letter from June 29, 1911 in Husserl, *Briefwechsel*, 7:47). Heidegger emphasizes the inappropriateness of the Husserlian critique as well in the winter-spring lecture of 1923/24 ("Einführung in die phänomenologische Forschung," *GA* 17, ed. Friedrich-Wilhelm von Hermann [Frankfurt: Klostermann, 1994], 91).

Though Husserl's detailed letter in response makes known his efforts at reaching an understanding, it indicates, despite his almost imploring tone: "Are we not basically of the same opinion in all of these things?" (*Briefwechsel*, 50.), right in the gesture of the question itself, a doubt not easily dispelled as to whether a true understanding is possible regarding the issue. Precisely this clearly audible skepticism in all estimation of Dilthey's contribution, which does not actually revoke the position of the LOGOS essay and at the most mitigates the acrimony in their personal connection, remains hidden to the Dilthey student Georg Misch in his efforts at mediating *Lebensphilosophie* and phenomenology when he sets, as it were, an exclamation point in place of a question mark regarding the above citation expressed by Husserl (see Georg Misch, "Lebensphilosophie und Phänomenologie: Eine Auseinandersetzung mit Heidegger," *Philosophischer Anzeiger* [1929], 3:438. See also Misch's letter to Husserl, August 9, 1929, in *Briefwechsel*, 7:278).

Even when Husserl emphasizes with respect to Dilthey that phenomenological theory, in the descriptive demonstration of the principles of knowledge, must, in correspondence with Dilthey's demand, hearken back to "inner life" (*Briefwechsel*, 49), and thus "first of all to the actual understanding of coming 'forms of life' in the reliving of inner motivations" (ibid.), the difference ultimately remains, on all accounts, decisive in any convergence. And this is the case because for Husserl the historical forms of life, as we will see more precisely below, must be transcended on the way to ideal valid unities, whereby the factically historical is devalued, since this only serves as an example "when we are directed to the *pure* ideal" (ibid.).

Dilthey himself had not concealed the difference in his own position relative to Husserl's and admits in his last letter to Husserl his difficulty "in penetrating into such a wholly other world of thought" (*Briefwechsel*, 52). The fact that in the time following their personal exchanges Husserl's estimation of Dilthey had yet again been modified in a certain sense—specifically through the formation of the approach of a genetic phenomenology—was something he

experience as the becoming aware of life through 'self-contemplation,'[11] behind the objectivism of the sciences.

That means, however, that life and thus the lifeworld is no longer regarded as something over against the subject, as it is presented in Descartes, and thus not as an objective sphere to be analyzed from the outside. For that reason, the structural and ontological clarification of the connection of life can only take place in the form of a self-contemplation or self-enlightenment, which, also inspired essentially by the Husserlian phenomenological approach, can first posit itself as a task for the later Dilthey and mutatis mutandis for Heidegger (when the Cartesian-inspired foundations of neo-Kantianism at the turn of the century had again become frangible, or at least problematic with regard to their sustainability), wherein the *epistemic-critical* moment of wonder and doubt reappears anew or is brought to bear in particular transformed ways.

§ 19. Husserl's Recourse to Θαυμάζειν as an "Irruption into the Theoretical Attitude"

In his Vienna "Crisis" lecture, Husserl himself refers to the Greek-European understanding of science (that is, for him, "spoken universally: philosophy as such"[12]), inaugurated by Plato and Aristotle, which has its origin

---

expressly confessed, and it was ultimately a matter of this displacement in emphasis according to which he was prepared to recognize in Dilthey a positive precursor (see *Phänomenologische Psychologie*, in *Husserliana*, ed. Walter Biemel. [The Hague: Nijhoff, 1968], 9:34, 354–364).

On the tensions of closeness and distance between the phenomenological and *lebensphilosophical* approaches, see among others, Guy van Kerckhoven, "Die Grundansätze von Husserls Konfrontation mit Dilthey im Lichte der geschichtlichen Selbstzeugnisse," in *Dilthey und der Wandel des Philosophiebegriffs seit dem 19. Jahrhundert: Studien zu Dilthey und Brentano, Mach, Nietzsche, Twardowski, Husserl, Heidegger,* ed. Ernst Wolfgang Orth (Freiburg: Alber, 1984), 134–160; Elisabeth Ströker, "Systematische Beziehungen der Husserlschen Philosophie zu Dilthey," in *Phänomenologische Studien* (Frankfurt: Klostermann, 1987), 160–186; Otto Friedrich Bollnow, "Dilthey und die Phänomenologie," in *Dilthey und die Philosophie der Gegenwart,* ed. Ernst Wolfgang Orth (Freiburg: Alber, 1985), 31–61; Thomas Seebohm, "Die Begründung der Hermeneutik Diltheys in Husserls transzendentaler Phänomenologie," in *Dilthey und die Philosophie der Gegenwart,* 97–124.

11. See Dilthey, *Was Philosophie sei,* in *GS,* vol. 8, esp. 192f.

12. Husserl, *Die Krisis des europäischen Menschentums und die Philosophie* (hereafter "Krisis-Lecture"), in *Krisis,* 329. Regarding Husserl's analysis of the beginning of philosophy and science, see Klaus Held, "Husserl und die Griechen," in *Profile der Phänomenologie. Zum 50. Todestag von Edmund Husserl,* ed. Ernst Wolfgang Orth (Freiburg: Alber, 1989), 137–176.

precisely in the knowledge-forming moment of Θαυμάζειν as the "irruption into the theoretical attitude."[13] In the "*epoché* of all practical interests"[14] as the deliberate foundational impulse of that "originary *theoria*,"[15] which in theoretical qua scientific-philosophical interest becomes "knowledge of the world out of a mere universal intuition,"[16] the experience of Θαυμάζειν is determined for Husserl decisively as a "modification of curiosity, that has its originary place in natural life"[17] and is conceived not just as a 'habitual vice,' but according to its essence is already itself "a modification, an interest that has relieved itself of the [directly realized] life interests [in their execution]."[18]

In wonder, as the modification here referred to, in which the pretheoretical bearing is changed into a theoretical one, the phenomenological bearing is nonetheless not yet intended. This becomes clear when it is noticed that the self-differentiation of the scientific-philosophical attitude initiated by the practical, pretheoretical interest in opposition to Θαυμάζειν—an attitude which, as will be seen, shapes the difference between δόξα and ἐπιστήμη—according to Husserl does not already thematize the world *as* world (that is, in its horizonal character), within which thematization the *how* of the appearance of objects can be elucidated as an achievement of phenomenological theory. Seen thus, the theoretical attitude, as is characteristic of the scientific and even the traditional philosophical bearing, is carried out on the ground of the inviolate (because unexpressed) belief in the world [*Weltglauben*] in view of the distinction between prescientific and scientific knowledge of objects, and indeed, as Klaus Held remarks, in a "competition of both of these ways of knowing

---

13. Husserl, *Krisis*-Lecture, 331.

14. Ibid., 332.

15. Ibid.

16. Ibid. In his study *Husserls Begriff der Lebenswelt*, Held indicates that Husserl establishes the motivation of the shift from the natural into the philosophical attitude precisely in wonder, notwithstanding an insufficient grasp of its affective character; indeed in the concept of vision [*Schau*] the moment of attunement in the erupting experience of the world in wonder is impelled to dim down, without its being able to do so, insofar as the "'observing,' world-opening attunement . . . bleeds into an emergent theoretical curiosity" (110; cf. 90 f.).

17. Husserl, *Krisis*-Lecture, 332.

18. Ibid. From this point, curiosity in Husserl, in its mediation of the immediate relatedness to its object, hits upon a form of interest that tends toward practical knowing as a pretheoretical bearing, one that is not in opposition to wonder, as in Heidegger—for whom curiosity, as a specific tendency of everyday existence, "[has] nothing to do with the wondering observing of beings, Θαυμάζειν" (*Sein und Zeit*, GA 2, 229).

for the validation of objects."[19] Therefore, in regard to the scientific attitude, as it appears in Husserl's perspective, Held speaks of a "second-order natural attitude,"[20] or rather, a "second natural attitude."[21] This indicates that for Husserl philosophy (brought onto its path in the basic pattern of experience established by the Greeks and determined by the displacement of the mythical interpretation of the world through the scientific-rational knowledge of the world) and science itself still uniformly hold themselves in an "unavoidable naiveté,"[22] whose most general title in Husserl reads "*objectivism.*"[23]

19. Held, *Husserls Begriff der Lebenswelt*, 95.

20. Ibid., 91. In a related sense Eugen Fink, in the context of reflections on a phenomenological critique of dogmatic positions within the framework of his exhibition of phenomenology, finds that "the thematic experiential bearing of our everyday life, as well as the theoretical practical experience of the positive sciences, as well as the cognitive attitude towards eidetic relations (for example, mathematics), as even the philosophical cognition of a priori forms of the world . . . are all determined equally in their essence as merely *internal differences* within the natural attitude" (Eugen Fink, "Die Phänomenologie Edmund Husserls in der gegenwärtigen Kritik," in *Studien zur Phänomenologie 1930–1939* [The Hague: Nijhoff, 1966], 152 [emphasis added]).

21. Held, *Husserls Begriff der Lebenswelt*, 100. Held's formulation implicitly refers to the fact that the natural attitude, as the everyday, takes shape under specific, concrete, historically conditioned circumstances. In view of the twentieth century, this means that for the everyday activity of life its configurations are determined with and by scientific technical standards, insofar as to the degree that technical-scientific innovations become self-evident, the everyday, as the natural, consciousness takes shape in accordance with this process. That this does not amount to a merely affirmative adoption and acceptance of scientific-technical developments not only becomes clear in Husserl's characterization of the present condition as a crisis, but can be seen widely throughout the twentieth century, as even a cursory look reflects a boom, through manifold and heterogeneous voices, in critiques of technology.

The approaches concerned here show themselves to be motivated, among other things, by the problem of alienation—as for example the tense relation of so-called natural necessities and their like under the conditions of the technicization of the everyday and its requirements. Thereby consciousness as well as the playing out of this emerging tension as possible divergences can give rise to thoroughly different inducements—for instance, a merely traditional discontent with new innovations, or even the rational insight, arising through technical sophistication, into the excessive demand for natural bases of life. Theoretical critique is thereby specifically evoked as well, as will become clear in the next section, through scientific-technological rationality's claim to truth itself. This is all, however, like bringing sand to the beach when one simply calls to mind the abundance of analyses making up the long-standing strands of a tradition that, alongside phenomenologically inspired positions varying in their critical potential, involves those of Horkheimer, Adorno and Habermas, or in another category, the critiques of Karl Jaspers, Hans Jonas, and Carl Friedrich von Weizsäcker.

22. Husserl, *Krisis*-Lecture, 339; see also *Krisis*, 144.

23. Husserl, *Krisis*-Lecture, 339.

§ 20. The Problem of Objectivism in the Tension Between Δόξα and Ἐπιστήμη

In the emergence of objectivism, according to Husserl, there is presaged that crisis which assumes its final hardened form in the development of the modern mathematized sciences and the technological domination of the world ascribed to them. Husserl accordingly recognizes the cause of this crisis in the claim raised on the side of ἐπιστήμη, to permit only the scientifically known to count as the 'true world,' while the natural view of the world of the "δόξα scorned"[24] by it is shunted to the level of mere everyday knowing in which the being of the mathematically structured world taken as true can only "manifest itself vaguely."[25]

Without going into further detail, it can be seen easily from what has been said that there is here a self-elevation of epistemic reason with its tendency toward delimitation and exclusion, which according to Husserl leads to the groundlessness of modern sciences; that is, it shuts off the relatedness to the environment relative to the subject in the process of the scientific method's gaining autonomy and thereby enacts an "attribution [*Unterschiebung*]," designating the essence of objectivism, "of the mathematically substructured world of idealities for the only real . . . experienced and experience-able world."[26] Husserl calls this "our everyday lifeworld."[27]

24. Husserl, *Krisis*, 158. On the relation of ἐπιστήμη and δόξα—which are frequently transliterated as "episteme" and "*doxa*" and can have alternative spellings—in Husserl's later work, see Werner Marx, "Vernunft und Lebenswelt" in *Vernunft und Welt: Zwischen Tradition und anderem Anfang* (The Hague: Nijhoff, 1970), 45–62; see also Walter Biemel, "Zur Bedeutung von Doxa und Episteme im Umkreis der Krisis-Thematik," in *Lebenswelt und Wissenschaft in der Philosophie Edmund Husserls*, ed.Elisabeth Ströker (Frankfurt: Klostermann, 1979), 10–22, and Bernhard Waldenfels, "Die verachtete Doxa. Husserl und die fortdauernde Krisis der abendländischen Vernunft," in *In den Netz der Lebenswelt*, 34.

25. Husserl, *Krisis*, 54.

26. Ibid., 49.

27. Ibid. On this complex, see Bernhard Rang's study, "Die bodenlose Wissenschaft. Husserls Kritik von Objektivismus und Technizismus in Mathematik und Naturwissenschaft," in *Profile der Phänomenologie*, ed. E. W. Orth (Freiburg: Alber, 1989), 88–136. With careful insight, Rang argues that for a sufficient evaluation of the Husserlian critique of science, discussed primarily in the secondary literature under the keyword 'critique of objectivism' [*Objektivismuskritik*], it is necessary to reconsider the problem of the technicization of knowledge—thematized by Husserl himself, yet widely overlooked in interpretation up to now—in its intimate connection with the mathematization of the natural sciences. In view of possible connections resulting from this in tasks posed by phenomenology and philosophy of science, Carl Friedrich Gethmann refers emphatically, in the foreword to *Lebenswelt und Wissenschaft*—which attempts a fruitful illumination of the relation between phenomenology and constructive theory

Seen thus, "lifeworld" is applied by Husserl in the context of his critique of science primarily in a mundane sense.

Therefore, it amounts to a *rehabilitation of δόξα* when with regard to the above diagnosis of objectivism and the technicism of the modern sciences, Husserl stipulates that they must be overcome to reinstitute the subject-relative in its originary authority. But that means that the subject-relative must be seen not as "an irrelevant passageway, but rather as the ultimately grounding theoretical-logical validation for all objective verification"[28] and thus functions as "an evidentiary source, a verifying source."[29] Seen in this light, δόξα, revalued once again by Husserl, attains at the same time the proper authority granted to it in advance,[30] namely, as Waldenfels stresses, "a *privilege* with regard to scientific insights, because it cedes the ground and foundation for all theoretical constructions; [and indeed] as source of the formation of sense."[31] By this means, in Husserl, after all, it becomes a "*remedy* against the crisis of the sciences [for] it equips it to re-embed an uprooted and vacuous rationality in the connection to life."[32]

The *prescientific* givenness of the lifeworld can be characterized, in view of the genesis of the sciences, from this point through "a threefold aspect"[33] that situates the scientific attitude within the dimension of the lifeworldly orientation of human self-relations. This is on the one side in its

---

of science (see Gethmann's own contribution, "Phänomenologie, Lebensphilosophie und Konstruktive Wissenschaftstheorie: Eine historische Skizze zur Vorgeschichte der Erlanger Schule," *Lebenswelt und Wissenschaft*, 28—to the fact that with Rang's study a "fundamental shift" (8) has been carried out on the part of phenomenology in the assessment of constructive theory of science.

28. Husserl, *Krisis*, 129.

29. Ibid.

30. "The retailer at the market has his market-truth; is it not in its relation a good truth and the best that can be useful to him? Is it thus a pseudotruth, since the scientist, in a different relativity, judging with different goals and ideas, seeks different truths with which one can accomplish much more, yet cannot offer precisely that which one needs at the market?" (Husserl, *Formale und transzendentale Logik*, 284).

31. Waldenfels, "Die verachtete Doxa," 39.

32. Ibid. In this connection Waldenfels refers (40) to the fact that this revaluation of δόξα possesses an ancient formative influence in Aristotle's determination of ἐμπειρία, which, as an independent form of human experience, is a kind of knowing equated, in its practical aspect, with a τέχνη, a grounded knowledge (see *Metaphysik* 981a12) and is superior with respect to abstract knowledge of principles (*Nicomachea*, 1141b16). On the return to δόξα, see also Rang, "Die bodenlose Wissenschaft," 125 ff.

33. Friedrich-Wilhelm von Herrmann, *Subjekt und Dasein: Interpretationen zu "Sein und Zeit"* (Frankfurt: Klostermann, 1985), 45. On the subsequent specification of the aspects, see ibid., 45.

details a *cultural-historical* aspect, insofar as the rise of the sciences is a relatively late-emerging phenomenon datable historically within the history of humanity. On the other side, there is an *individual-biographical* aspect of the decision for science, insofar as everyone yet holds themselves in a natural connection to life long before they themselves acquire scientific knowledge. The third aspect is *scientific-theoretical*. It refers to the fact that the consciously pregiven prescientific and extrascientific lifeworld is not only not sublated in the constitution of the scientific relation to the world, but is also necessarily coposited, insofar as it "remains presupposed for the carrying out of the scientific praxis in the sense that the scientist is constantly directed toward it and has recourse to it."[34] But that means that the objectivity claimed by the modern sciences with its objective apriori is necessarily referred back to a "*lifeworldly apriori*,"[35] which as universal still goes beyond the objectivistically intended elimination of concrete lifeworldly relations—so that, for example, even "mathematical evidence [possesses] its source of sense and right in lifeworldly evidence."[36] Decisive therein is the fact that this "backward reference [is] that of a founding of validity."[37]

In the demonstration of this "ground function of doxa,"[38] an outstanding position with regard to the intended management of the crisis is conferred upon the self-giving lifeworld in it as the natural ground of experience, a position that can inspire a sustained discourse that unites life, world, and science, and among the most varied authors, if one thinks of Alfred Schütz or Aron Gurwitsch. Husserl always emphasizes this function and meaning of the natural experience of the world,[39] expressly in a

34. Ibid., 46. See Husserl, *Krisis*, 107, 127, 132, 136, 139, 141, 460.

35. Husserl, *Krisis*, 143 (emphasis added). We should refer here, in light of what is to come, to the fact that with the a priori function of the lifeworld posed by Husserl, that decisive point appears at which the mundane meaning is undergirded by the ontological, which as such for Husserl opens the way ultimately for an intended phenomenological exposition of transcendental subjectivity.

36. Ibid.

37. Ibid. Jürgen Mittelstraß, in *Das lebensweltliche Apriori*, in Gethmann, ed., *Lebenswelt und Wissenschaft*, 114–142, latches onto the thesis formulated thereby—namely, that the form and construction of scientific knowledge can be brought to light only from out of the connection, which must be methodologically reconstituted, between the theoretical and pretheoretical (as the lifeworldly) orientation, whereby the latter functions as the primary presupposition—when he investigates the relevance of the lifeworldly apriori for the constructions of the sciences within more recent debates in the philosophy of science.

38. Biemel, "Doxa und Episteme in der 'Krisis,'" 18.

39. "If one were ever to return to the full originary concretion of the world, as it is experienced each moment in naive primordiality, and if one were never to forget this concretely

significant place for the given connection in "Experience and Judgment." This is additionally salient for Husserl himself to illuminate his stance in relation to the sustainability of the natural ground of experience as ground of knowledge in its ambivalence. Husserl here establishes his *"vindication of doxa,"*[40] with the insight "that this realm of doxa [is] just the realm of the latter originariness; exact knowledge goes back to the sensible, whose character as a mere method and not as a path of knowledge communicated of itself must be seen through."[41]

For Husserl, against potential expectations to the contrary, this rejection of the objectivistic self-misunderstanding of the sciences is "in no way [conjoined with] a devaluation of exact knowledge."[42] Rather, it concerns "an illumination of the path by which higher [i.e., scientific] evidences, and the concealed presuppositions on which they rest, are to be attained."[43] Thus these will neither be infringed upon in their dignity by Husserl with regard to content, nor does he doubt that "knowledge terminates in them,"[44] or that it is the path to knowledge in general "to ascend from *doxa* to *episteme.*"[45] The decisive thing, as the history of *episteme* as advancing development of its objectivistic self-misunderstanding teaches, lies solely in—and here it concerns Husserl—the fact that "the origin and proper authority of the lower levels may not be forgotten over the final aim."[46] Thereby, the constitutive tie between *doxa* and *episteme* consists in

---

intuitable world as an originary field in the act of methodological abstraction, then the aberrations of naturalistic psychology and the human sciences would not have been possible, one would never have been able to lapse into construing spirit as a mere causal annex of the material body or as a causal sequence paralleling that of physical materiality. One would never have been able to regard humans and animals as psychophysical machines or even as parallel double machines" (Husserl, *Phänomenologische Psychologie*, 55).

40. Husserl, *Erfahrung und Urteil: Untersuchungen zur Genealogie der Logik*, ed. Ludwig Landgrebe (Hamburg: Classen & Goverts, 1948), 44.

41. Ibid.

42. Ibid.

43. Ibid., 44

44. Ibid., 45.

45. Ibid.

46. Ibid. In consideration of this disclosure of the proper right of natural experience in its relevance to knowledge, the somewhat peculiar and apparently high estimation, on first glance, of empiricism for a transcendental-philosophical position, namely, that of Hume, can be explained upon closer investigation, in which Husserl credits empiricism with "the tendency toward a scientific discovery of the familiar, and yet scientifically unknown, everyday lifeworld" (*Krisis*, 448; on Hume, see ibid., 434).

the fact that the "world as lifeworld [has] the 'same' structures prescientifically [as] the objective sciences."[47]

Only from out of this likeness can the lifeworld lastingly function as substratum in such a way that "its manifold prelogical validations are constitutive for the logical, the theoretical truths."[48] Therefore, in the context of his reflections on the lifeworldly and objective nature of science, Paul Janssen indicates that only "at the ground of a certain structural equality between lifeworld and ideal scientific elementary concepts . . . the phenomenological derivation of objective science can be accomplished from out of the lifeworld."[49] Seen thus, the lifeworldly apriori functions, as Welter puts it, as "the final norm of critique for all factical science,"[50] insofar as "knowledge of the objective-scientific [world] 'is grounded' in the evidence of the lifeworld."[51]

If the notion were that Husserl's consequential revaluation of the natural life-experience is pervaded by an ambivalence, then it would be easily seen what is meant if one once again makes present the part of the text adduced for the relation of *doxa* and *episteme* from "Experience and Judgment." For in the recognition of the originary function of natural life experience the sought end is not yet reached for the scientifically minded Husserl by its mere demonstration. The discovery of the natural ground of experience evinces it precisely as a supporting layer, but as a 'lower stage' it is not yet the first fundament of human world- and self-understanding; thus the reduction to the prescientific lifeworld, as we shall see, is not yet the final reduction.[52] Accordingly, the discovery of the 'ground-function

47. Husserl, *Krisis*, 142.

48. Ibid., 127.

49. Paul Janssen, *Edmund Husserl: Einführung in seine Phänomenologie* (Freiburg: Alber 1976), 142.

50. Welter, *Der Begriff der Lebenswelt,* 99. See also Husserl's remarks on the apriority of the natural concept of the world in the lecture "Grundprobleme der Phänomenologie," in *Zur Phänomenologie der* Intersubjektivität, ed. Iso Kern (The Hague: Nijhoff, 1973) 1:135.

51. Husserl, *Krisis*, 133.

52. That means that in the face of the heterogeneity of forms of knowledge, Husserl, like a good Platonist, holds to a schema of classification of higher and lower degrees of knowledge. With admirable sharpness, yet for all that not altogether phenomenally to the point, in his lecture "Grundprobleme der Phänomenologie" (winter semester 1910/11), Husserl extensively treats the 'I of the natural attitude,' speaking of the fact that this as experience is the "natural one, insofar as it is exclusively that of animals and of pre-scientific humans" (120). Within a broad spectrum Husserl varyingly characterizes this determination of the natural throughout his writings as a pre-scientific, and therein also even tendentially an objectivistic, attitude. See, *Der Begriff der Lebenswelt,* 47–56.

of *doxa'* on Husserl's view cannot of itself be the desired access to the phenomenologically identified '*fundamentum inconcussum,*' as little as, given the demonstration of its objectivistic failings, the methodologically scientific *episteme* handed down is to be credited as the solution to the problems of knowledge posed by Descartes.

Therefore, for Husserl, the "matter cannot rest with the disclosure of the lifeworld as a theoretical theme (namely, that of objective science as self-intelligibility of the pregiven world)."[53] That means that he cannot, for his own part, stop at the demonstration of the legitimacy, even the privilege, of *doxa,* and this because the discovery of its grounding function could be carried out only from a reflexive approach, which has transcended in advance the constitutive naiveté of *doxa.*[54] Put otherwise, this means for Husserl that the discovery of the lifeworld carries itself out from out of a knowing that, in its intention to demonstrate the conditions of the possibility of scientific knowing, discovers *itself* on this side of the possible ways of knowledge for the sciences and everyday knowing as a possibility of a knowing sui generis, which in its transcendental structure affords a new advance for *episteme—phenomenology* as rigorous science.[55]

In this new *episteme* Husserl unites the demonstration of the proper right of *doxa* and its *devaluation.* For with a view to the development of a universal reason to be achieved out of the spirit of phenomenology, *doxa* is valid merely as a provisional stage, a prefiguration.[56] For Husserl, as the idea of a final end—in connection with Kant and according to his self-understanding, yet even a step beyond Kant, whom he charges with

<hr>

53. Husserl, *Krisis,* 463.

54. Waldenfels refers to the fact that Husserl's 'theory of the lifeworld and the everyday' therefore clearly distinguishes itself from a 'philosophy of common sense' and its putative immediate access and recourse to everyday experience and language (see "Die verachtete Doxa," 40).

55. Corresponding to this ideal, when Husserl programmatically specifies the direction of phenomenological research, is the necessity of breaking with the "notions of profundity" (*Philosophie als strenge Wissenschaft,* 69) traditionally vaunted as philosophical, e.g., the "matter of wisdom" (ibid.), and instead attending to "conceptual clarity and exactness [as] matters of rigorous theory" (ibid.), because it is only in this way that the "essential process of the new constitution of rigorous sciences" (ibid.) can be advanced, a constitution which for Husserl has its valid form in transcendental phenomenology.

56. See Waldenfels, "Die verachtete Doxa," 41.

leaping over the dimension of the lifeworld[57]—it is a matter of "a philosophy, which in contrast to prescientific and even scientific objectivism, goes back to *knowing subjectivity as the original site of all objective formations of sense and validations of being,* and it undertakes to understand the existing world as a form of sense and validity and to direct on track in this way *an essentially new type of scientificity and philosophy.*"[58]

Husserl never abandoned this transcendental-idealistic standpoint attained in *Ideas.*[59] As E. W. Orth has shown, Husserl's thematization, his reduction to the lifeworld, "is grasped in *Ideas* as a deepening of his determination of the natural attitude."[60] If Husserl initially thought that he had demonstrated the sphere of pure subjectivity, the pure life of consciousness in apodeictic certainty, by means of the exclusion of the general thesis of the natural attitude—and thus, the bracketing of the universal belief in being and, bound up with that, the exclusion of the worldly objects of knowledge—it thus becomes clear to him with the discovery of *horizonal intentionality* that the exclusion of the general thesis and its positings of reality itself still remain framed by letting belief in the world be valid.[61] Accordingly, the transcendental phenomenologist, in carrying

57. On the situation of his own approach in contrast to the Kantian transcendental-philosophical position, see also Husserl, *Erste Philosophie: Erster Teil; Kritische Ideengeschichte,* in *Husserliana,* ed. Rudolf Boehm (The Hague: Nijhoff, 1956), 8:381–395; see also *Krisis,* 101–104.

58. Husserl, *Krisis,* 102.

59. To this extent, the turn to the lifeworld signifies, in opposition to the thesis proposed by Ludwig Landgrebe, no such fundamentally new orientation, as is suggested in the title of his study, "Husserls Abschied vom Cartesianismus," in Ludwig Landgrebe, *Der Weg der Phänomenologie: Das Problem einer ursprünglichen Erfahrung* (Gütersloh: Mohn, 1963), 163–206. Ernst Wolfgang Orth's study, "Die unerfüllte Rolle Descartes in der Phänomenologie" (in *Descartes im Diskurs der Neuzeit,* ed. Wilhelm Friedrich Niebel, Angelica Horn, and Herbert Schnädelbach, 286–302) shows both that and why, for phenomenology, such a 'departure from Cartesianism' is to be conceived as premature.

60. Ernst Wolfgang Orth, "Phänomenologie der Vernunft zwischen Szientismus, Lebenswelt und Intersubjektivität," in *Profile der Phänomenologie,* 63–87. In much the same sense Gadamer had previously called attention to the continuity of Husserlian thought; see "Die phänomenologische Bewegung" (in *GW* 3:105–146) and "Die Wissenschaft von der Lebenswelt" (in *GW* 3:147–159); Klaus Held also emphasizes this continuity in "*Husserls Begriff der Lebenswelt,*" 79. Within the framework of his investigation of Husserl's philosophy of nature, Bernhard Rang refers, with a view to the "ground function of the intuitively given world of perception in our everyday life," to the proximity of the "*Krisis*" conception to that of the *Ideas* (Rang, *Husserls Phänomenologie der materiellen Natur* [Frankfurt: Klostermann, 1990], 395).

61. According to Husserl, this shows itself in the fact "that the entire daily life of the individual and of the community is related to a *typical homogeneousness of situations,* of the sort that each who enters into the situation has, as a normal human, *eo ipso* the *horizon of the situ-

out a reduction, is held back at the point of the pure life of consciousness as constitutive subjectivity in the antecedent universal world horizon, which encompasses the entirety of intentional life and, as this ground of the world, cannot cancel itself out. Therefore, numbered among Husserl's fundamental insights is "that every worldly givenness is a givenness in the how of a horizon, that in horizons, further horizons are implied, and after all everything as a worldly given carries with it the world horizon and only through that comes to consciousness as worldly."[62] In Husserl, this consciousness of the world is only grasped adequately, and with that, the crisis of the present world situation led to a possible overcoming, if it suffices to transform the development inaugurated with the Greek original foundation of θεωρία within the scientific and philosophical formation of theory into a "theory of actual science" projected from out of a transcendental phenomenological attitude.[63]

§ 21. Toward a Philosophical Thematization of Natural Life-in-the-World

In order to be able to appreciate this step in correspondence with its philosophical consequence, which, as will be seen, not only adumbrates the claim to a solution raised therein but at the same time also its failure, it is initially necessary to concern oneself a bit more intimately with the relation of prephilosophical life praxis and its philosophical thematization. For only where the self-evidence of the carrying out of life, which Husserl characterizes in its main feature as a "constant living in certainty of the world,"[64] becomes problematic, does the supporting ground first become

---

ation belonging to it in common. One can explicate this horizon *a posteriori*, but the *constituting horizonal intentionality*, through which the environment of daily life is in general a *world of experience*, is always antecedent to the interpretation of the one reflecting" (*Formale und transzendentale Logik*, 207). On horizonal consciousness, see also *Cartesianische Meditationen*, 84 and *Krisis*, 146, 152, 160 f., 165, 267

62. Husserl, *Krisis*, 267.

63. Husserl, *Krisis*-Lecture, 332. Ludwig Landgrebe thus characterizes the development traced in the "*Krisis*," in a critical history of ideas from Descartes to Kant, as a "struggle between objectivism and transcendental philosophy" to be conducted from Husserl onwards, which is positively decided only in its own transcendental-phenomenological conception ("Lebenswelt und Geschichtlichkeit," 24).

64. Husserl, *Krisis*, 145; see also appendix 4, in which Husserl highlights the "certainty of the world's being" as the presupposition of every epoché, so that the "general certainty of the

visible as *the lifeworld,* insofar as the disturbance bound up with the eruption of self-evidence reflexively catches itself in the phenomenological reflection on life and finally in a transcendental reduction.

That means, however, that for Husserl the lifeworld is not accessible for an immediately descriptive comprehension.[65] In the ontological status of *pregivenness* that he ascribes to it,[66] it only becomes possible to exhibit it by means of a phenomenological, methodological recollection. In the departure from the experience of the present crisis in the historical and critical inquiry back into the lifeworld, this lays bare the *foundation of sense* of that "which originally and yet still, intended as philosophy [i.e., that which is to be determined still more precisely in detail in its inner teleology], manifests a *final originary genuineness,* which once seen *apodeictically conquers* the will."[67] The Husserlian recollection thereby binds itself to the lifeworld, as Waldenfels stresses,[68] with a threefold intention.

First, the exhibition of the lifeworld aims, as we have seen, at a supporting foundation for the sciences, which are groundless in their objectivism. Second, this scientific basic position characteristic for Husserl is accompanied by the fact that with the lifeworld shown as subjective-relative in its constitution, as already indicated, the possibility of an access into transcendental phenomenology should be given. Third, in laying open transcendental subjectivity, this rational telos inscribed from it makes possible a "*historical total perspective,*"[69] which, as will be seen more precisely,

---

world" is assumed as the "functioning ground of validity upon which all ontological sense of every kind depends" (ibid., 400).

65. Elisabeth Ströker thus emphasizes "that the lifeworld as a ground of sense for science simply cannot be present outside of a specific act of questioning in transcendental phenomenology.... 'Ground of sense,' 'origin of sense,' 'fundament of sense' all are lacking in any mundane meaning." "Geschichte und Lebenswelt als Sinnesfundament der Wissenschaften in Husserls Spätwerk," in *Lebenswelt und Wissenschaft in der Philosophie Edmund Husserls,* ed. Elisabeth Ströker, 117.

66. Oriented to finding oneself in a pregiven world, this *being-pre-given,* as Husserl states, becomes the "title ... of a properly new science" (*Krisis,* 149), which for him as phenomenology is the "science of the universal how of the pre-givenness of the world, thus of that which constitutes the universal ground-being for any objectivity" (ibid.).

67. Ibid., 16. On the "method of inquiry" see Paul Ricoeur, "Rückfrage und Reduktion der Idealitäten in Husserls 'Krisis'" und Marx's 'Deutsche Ideologie.'" In *Phänomenologie und Marxismus* (Frankfurt: Suhrkamp, 1978), ed. Bernhard Waldenfels, Jan M. Broekmann, and Ante Pazanin 3:201–239.

68. See Waldenfels, "Die Abgründigkeit des Sinnes. Kritik an Husserls Idee der Grundlegung," in *In den Netzen der Lebenswelt,* 16; see also Waldenfels, *Einführung in die Phänomenologie*(Munich: Fink, 1992), 36.

69. Waldenfels, "Die Abgründung des Sinnes," 16.

discerns in the *one* lifeworld gained from out of phenomenological insight the presupposition for the manifoldness of all historically separate worlds, which remain merely and relativistically pluralities without this presupposition, according to Husserl. The lifeworld, in this sense for Husserl, as a "philosophical universal problem,"[70] has, to speak with Waldenfels's distinction based on Husserl, "a *ground function,* a *guiding function,* and a *unifying function.*"[71]

In order to be able to become phenomenologically thematic in these ways the lifeworld as such must somehow always already be pregiven, even if implicitly, and in fact is pregiven, as we have seen, in that which Husserl calls "natural life."[72] Reflected philosophically, he calls it the *natural attitude* and as is well known, he determines the content more precisely as "naively living straightforwardly in the world, the world which as a universal horizon is ever there for consciousness in a certain way, yet is not thereby thematic."[73] As a universal horizon of this kind, the world determines itself constitutively from out of the *correlation with the ego in the natural attitude.* It is here that the world gains "beforehand the sense [as] all of the 'actual' entities of the real realities that have their reality for us."[74] However, according to Husserl, the ego of the natural attitude is not explicitly conscious of itself therein as the subject of this correlation.[75] Rather, it takes place in the manner of "a simple living in the world"[76] as, according to its being carried out, a complete distributedness to the mundane, given, lifeworldly objects, among which Husserl counts even human beings in their social entanglement. The object relation remains framed as a whole

70. Husserl, *Krisis,* 135.

71. Waldenfels, "Die Abgründung des Sinnes," 16 (emphasis added). With regard to the transcendental function of the ground-metaphor in its historical sense, see also Ströker, "Geschichte und Lebenswelt," 107–123.

72. Husserl, *Krisis*-Lecture, 327.

73. Ibid. See also ibid., 468–472.

74. Husserl, *Krisis,* 148. It will be necessary in what follows to go into more detail on the problem of the connection between the world as universal horizon and the world as the totality of entities. Here, it is significant to note the determination of "lifeworld" formulated by Landgrebe: "'lifeworld' is thus nothing other than the designation for that correlate of the 'natural attitude' conceived in its full concretion" ("Lebenswelt und Geschichtlichkeit," 27).

75. "This manifold subjectivity runs constantly through natural-normal living in the world, yet it remains constantly and necessarily concealed therein" (Husserl, *Krisis,* 149).

76. Ibid.

therein by the unthematic validation of the being of the world accepted in the natural belief in the world.[77]

Seen from this perspective, the natural "I" holds itself with regard to its possibility of comprehension in a sort of latent condition, which is first broken up where it succeeds in revealing "functioning-performing subjectivity,"[78] precisely in normal everyday living in the world, by means of a philosophical reflection. Klaus Held accordingly defines the natural attitude by means of a second essential feature alongside belief in the world, "the self-forgottenness of its subject."[79] As much as the "constraint in this forgottenness"[80] is symptomatic for it in the execution of the natural attitude, its coinscribed essential move, as constitutive for it, still appropriates its in-principle-possible "sublatedness" at the same time.[81] This proves itself simply in the fact that natural life can be spoken of conceptually as the natural attitude.

That means, however, that the revocability of the subject's self-forgetting in the natural attitude characterizes that condition of possibility from out of which something in the way of philosophical reflection (as, for instance, the question of ontological or transcendental structures of life, world, and "I") first finds its purchase.

§ 22. On Husserl's Transcendental Self-Grounding of Philosophy with a View to the Question of the World

In view of the question concerning the motivation to leave the mundane in favor of the philosophical attitude, regarded from some shiftings of emphasis, as Held stresses, Husserl gives "no substantially new answer"[82] vis-à-vis the tradition of transcendental philosophy. Thus for Husserl as well— and one might add with a view to his sense of his mission,[83] for Husserl in a certain measure—the possibility is given entirely traditionally through

77. On this point see ibid., 146–149, 153, 160 ff, 179.
78. Ibid., 149.
79. *"Husserls Begriff der Lebenswelt,"* 81.
80. Ibid., 84.
81. Ibid.
82. Ibid., 83.
83. See for example, *Krisis*, 140, where regarding the rational insight to be won out of the 'total phenomenological attitude' for humans in the degree of the personal transformation that they are thereby able to achieve, Husserl attests that more than any religious conversion,

the philosophical (i.e., transcendental-phenomenological) attitude "to shape his whole personal life on the level of universal self-consideration and self-responsibility toward the synthetic unity of a life in universal self-responsibility,"[84] in order "to remain identical with himself as a rational I."[85] But this is possible only from out of the insight into the "all-encompassing unity of the ultimately functioning-performing subjectivity"[86]

---

it "harbors within itself the meaning of the greatest existentiell transformation given over to humanity as such."

84. Ibid., 272.

85. Ibid. How far Husserl is committed to this ideal is made evident in the early passages of the *Krisis* where, amidst the established crisis of modern science and with recourse to its Greek beginnings, he propagates "the 'philosophical' Daseinsform: the free giving to itself, throughout its whole life, its principle out of pure reason, out of philosophy" (*Krisis*, 5). For "theoretical philosophy is the first thing. . . . Philosophy as theory does not merely set free the inquirer; it sets free every philosophically educated individual" (ibid., 5), since, as Husserl assures us with his characteristic pathos, philosophy is "*the historical movement of the revelation of universal reason, 'innate' in humanity as such*" (ibid., 13).

In the model of this teleology of reason, in which Ricoeur ("Husserl und der Sinn der Geschichte," in *Husserl*, ed. Hermann Noack [Darmstadt: Wissenschaftliche Buchgesellschaft, 1973], 231–276) discerned a type of "philosophy of revelation," we can see the Husserlian fundamental requirement of resisting what he sees as the danger of "individualization and relativity" (*Krisis*, 11), in order "to establish, as a human potentiality, rational sense in its individual and general Dasein" (ibid.). And yet the gesture of a telos of reason that is for the most part sovereignly put forward in his work is nevertheless frequently accompanied by undertones that, in numerous personal letters where he adopts distinctly skeptical tones regarding the meaning and success of his undertaking, testify to an existentiell self-doubt that is visible first and foremost in reference to his own powers.

Franz Joseph Wetz (*Edmund Husserl* [Frankfurt: Campus, 1995]) attempts to capitalize on this Husserlian complexity, evident since the publication of his collected letters, in order to find a key to Husserl's work from these self-testimonies in view of a nonpsychological, but rather philosophically disclosed, background of Husserl's personality and the life he lived in resistance to a reductive naturalism or relativism. In doing so, Wetz's own intentions are directed, as in *Lebenswelt und Weltall*, following Hans Blumenberg, toward destroying the idealistic standpoint of an absolute "I" and to make fruitful, in taking up the results of the modern natural sciences—in particular, evolutionary biology and cosmology—the "view from the universe" (ibid., 162) in the mode of a cosmological realism, as it were, for the self-descriptions and self-interpretations of the human lifeworld.

86. Ibid., 149. In relation to his own programmatic approach, Husserl thereby links up with the modified—yet in its general direction nonetheless linear—progression of tradition that from Descartes onward, as we have seen, imposed self-consciousness as a guiding paradigm upon the problem of knowledge. Husserl himself famously speaks in his Paris lectures of his own conception as a "new Cartesianism" (*Cartesianische Meditationen*, 3). More precisely, this means for Husserl that the decisive, and after Kant the basic philosophical question as such—"What is the human?" (*Logik* [Berlin: De Gruyter, 1923], 25)—can only be answered in the determination of its essence as transcendental subjectivity.

For Husserl as well, the "*statement 'I am' [is] the true principle of all principles*" ("*Erste Philosophie. Zweiter Teil: Theorie der phänomenologischen Reduktion,*" in *Husserliana*, ed.

from which the answer to the 'philosophical universal problem' of the 'how of the pre-givenness of the world' issues. From this point, Landgrebe refers to a displacement of accent distinctive for Husserl, according to which the first task of philosophy can no longer consist of a priority in positing the transcendental philosophical question concerning the conditions of the possibility of scientific knowledge in the traditional manner. Rather, what urgently poses itself now is "the question concerning the transcendental functions of consciousness, on the ground of which it always already 'has' its world before all science."[87]

The primary philosophical question in Husserl's phenomenology, concerning the being of the world determined as knowledge of the world, transforms itself, as Eugen Fink clear-sightedly stresses, into the "question concerning the essence of transcendental subjectivity, for which

---

Rudolf Böhm [The Hague: Nijhoff, 1959], 8:42), yet not in such a way that by the "evidence of the 'I am'" (*Krisis*, 11) the "making oneself true" (ibid.) is thereby at the same time achieved for the human. This, as an ideal end for Husserl, is "a task of *episteme*, of 'reason'" (ibid.) and thus of philosophy as rigorous science. Even when—as Ströker (*Husserls transzendentale Phänomenologie* [Frankfurt:Klostermann, 1987], 239) has indicated—the aspect of presuppositionlessness vehemently bound up from the start with 'rigorous science' steps into the background for Husserl from the 1920s onward in his thematization of the history of philosophy with a view to the 'inner history' of phenomenology, and now in contrast the concept of 'justification' stands in the center, the claim thus posited, of a final grounding for phenomenology as rigorous science in the sense of a first philosophy, with the intended demonstration of its historically conditioned self-grounding, had in no way been dropped.

In opposition, Stephan Strasser ("Das Gottesproblem in der Spätphilosophie Edmund Husserls," in *Philosophisches Jahrbuch* [1959], 67:132), and Hubert Hohl (*Lebenswelt und Geschichte: Grundzüge der Spätphilosophie E. Husserls* [Freiburg: Alber, 1962], 78), among others, maintained that it was possible to note in Husserl, especially with respect to the *Krisis*, an abandonment of philosophy as rigorous science. Also, Wilhelm Szilasi, in his afterword to Husserl's "Philosophie als strenge Wissenschaft," with his thesis on Husserl's late resignation, supports Hohl (see *Lebenswelt*, 101), in particular by way of a remark made by Husserl: "*Philosophy as a science, as a serious, rigorous, indeed apodictically rigorous science—the dream has been dreamt out*" (*Krisis*, 508). Yet Hohl, like Szilasi or Strasser, or Landgrebe himself ("Husserls Abschied vom Cartesiansismus," 187), is mistaken in that Husserl intends here to designate the general mood of the time—*not*, however, his own position. This point becomes particularly evident in a July 10, 1935 letter to Roman Ingarden (*Briefwechsel* 3:300–303). On the correct way of reading, see among others Herbert Spiegelberg, *The Phenomenological Movement* (The Hague: Nijhoff, 1981), 1:77; Gadamer, *Die phänomenologische Bewegung*, 129; Biemel, "Doxa und Episteme in der 'Krisis,'" 22; and in direct exchange with Hohl, Paul Janssen, *Geschichte und Lebenswelt: Ein Beitrag zur Diskussion von Husserls Spätwerk* (The Hague: Nijhoff, 1970), xx, 142.

87. Landgrebe, "Lebenswelt und Geschichtlichkeit," 23. Husserl himself formulates this context in the form of a question: "How is it possible to bring the naive *self-evidence* of the certainty of the world in which we live—both the certainty of the *everyday* world and the *theoretical constructions* acquired on the basis of this everyday world—to *intelligibility*?" (*Krisis*, 99).

the 'world' ultimately is validated, and in whose life, forming a unity of a universal apperception, world-belief with its sense of being is a world in constant occurrence."[88] If Husserl thereby transposes the problem of the being of the world into that, as Welter calls it, "relater, 'pre-givenness *for a subject*,'"[89] this world is withdrawn thereby in the reduction to a subject-independent being-in-itself insofar as it is verified beforehand on the ground of the intentional constitution of consciousness, to apply as a pure phenomenon immanent to consciousness. Seen more precisely, "neither the world on the one side, nor a transcendental subjectivity posited in opposition to it, on the other side, [manifests itself as the] true theme of phenomenology, but rather the *becoming of the world in the constitution of transcendental subjectivity*."[90] In other words, Husserl's central problem is not the fundamental metaphysical relation *that* the entity [*Seiendes*] in general is. What occupies him much more is that question *how* the entity becomes world for us.[91]

88. Fink, "Husserl in der gegenwärtigen Kritik," 120. From here, Fink declares as a basic principle that the "hypothesis of Husserl's phenomenology lies in the assignment of intentionally understood originary consciousness as the true access to being. The problem of being unfolds into an intentional analytic; phenomenology becomes a science of consciousness" (Fink, "Das Problem der Phänomenologie Edmund Husserls," in *Studien zur Phänomenologie*, 201).

89. Welter, *Der Begriff der Lebenswelt*, 57.

90. Fink, "Husserl in der gegenwärtigen Kritik," 139. Husserl clarifies this basic relation in a particularly revealing manner in his essay "Kant und die Idee der Transzendentalphilosophie" (1924), in *Erste Philosophie I*, 271.

91. Welter, *Der Begriff der Lebenswelt*, 57. In Husserl's own words: "We regard thus *the world as an accomplishment*—the world for me as my accomplishment, accomplishment out of my intentional activity, on the ground of my passivity" (Husserl, *Phänomenologie der Intersubjektivität*, ed. Iso Kern [The Hague: Nijhoff 1973], 149). Therewith is posed at the same time the task of a radical critique of experience, "to whose sense it belongs to hold the existing world in question, instead of presupposing it, and to make this universal experience, at bottom constituting claimed being, into a theme. Only thereby can *subjectivity as an experiencing*—and through experience bringing an abiding worldly being in itself to validity—become a theme; yet in a way in which it can possibly be taken as in the world, and thus as humanly being" (*Erste Philosophie II*, 262). With a view to the *metaphysical* 'doctrine of the factum' that Welter (*Der Begriff der Lebenswelt*, 57 f) sets his sights on in the context of his own question of the how of the consciousness of the world (a doctrine that Husserl himself did not work out further, and which was to have demonstrated the constitution of the that of the world, while it is the theme of the *scientific* phenomenological analysis in its how), it seems convincing when Welter assumes not only that the traditional epistemological question of the existence of the external world proves to be, as is well-known, senseless on the basis of the intentional constitution of consciousness, but equally senseless—as Iso Kern stresses (*Husserl und Kant:. Eine Untersuchung über Husserls Verhältnis zu Kant und zum Neukantianismus* [The Hague: Nijhoff 1964], 188)—is the metaphysical problem of beginning in its classical form as the question why in general there is something and not nothing.

Against the background of this Husserlian "transcendental subjectivism,"[92] it finally becomes unambiguously clear with regard to the terminological strictness, manifold and lacking in proper denotation, in his use of the lifeworld concept—to which Held, among others, has alluded—that the title 'lifeworld' in the ground proposition signifies nothing other than the present world concept already worked out according to Husserl's fundamental determinations, which is from this point on extended in the outcome and the view to the critique of science carried out in the "Krisis."[93] Seen from this position, the "Krisis," as Gadamer underscores, finally gives "the same old answer,"[94] and thus the theme of the lifeworld, to speak with Orth, designates "not a change of Husserlian phenomenology in the sense of a farewell to complex transcendental phenomenological analyses. It is much more itself a roundabout surgically extracted theorem,"[95] which indeed "ex[hibits] the internal concept of simple and elementary forms of orientation, [that is,] a concrete and insurmountable ground of self-evidences, which one must make oneself expressly conscious of in order to

---

Now, insofar as for the late Husserl, the basic metaphysical impulse—metaphysically grasped "as absolute science of factical reality" (*Vorlesungen über Ethik und Wertlehre (1908–1914)*, in *Husserliana*, vol. 28, ed. Ulrich Melle [Dordrecht: Kluwer, 1988], 182)—is not simply to be abandoned, the ultimate question of meaning can possess validity only when, phenomenologically transformed, it asks "why everything (from an 'achieving' subjectivity thus created in a constitutional history proceeding in such a way) is constituted the way that it is" (Rüdiger Welter, *Der Begriff der Lebenswelt*, 57). To question the 'that of our world' for Husserl means consequently to want to investigate the final, i.e., the originary ground of the possibility of its constitution.

But to want now to see in this phenomenological transformation of the metaphysical question of the sense of meaning a variant of the 'ontological difference' thematized by Heidegger, as Welter does, is not acceptable. And this is not the case insofar as Husserl's question concerning the how of the givenness of objects is not thought from out of the ontological difference between being and beings, which he himself finds indicated in the question constitutive for the ontological difference of the sense of being of the I am, which for the first time allows an ontological difference of the modes of being to be worked out. Nonetheless, even the phenomenological modification of the question of the sense of being indicates a difference, and precisely the insight indicated within it into the *intentional difference,* according to which the world is nothing in itself, but rather is given as world in the representation of world, thus in subjective-relative relation to the subject representing it. In order, however, not to succumb to the danger of a relativism threatening Husserl, he seeks to grasp the subject as 'humanity' and thereby to formulate a generality that is thought from the founding transcendental sphere of subjectivity.

92. Waldenfels, "Die verachtete Doxa," 41.
93. See Held, *"Husserls Begriff der Lebenswelt,"* 80.
94. Gadamer, *Wissenschaft von der Lebenswelt*, 155.
95. Orth, "Phänomenologie der Vernunft," 80.

grasp better the functioning of intentional subjectivity and to determine it more precisely."[96]

In this respect, for Husserl, "the real world [reduces itself] to a universe of intentional correlates of real and possible intentional experiences of my transcendental ego, and is inseparable from these as a correlate."[97] Seen from this perspective, the subject for him is "always with itself, that is, in a closed circle of its own transcendental subjectivity"[98] without knowing it, that is, latently within the natural attitude "when it experiences the world and is devoted to it as a child of the world [*Weltkind*]."[99] In contrast, explicit access to the transcendental sphere of subjectivity demands that the human knows the manner of being of the world and conceives itself as a living being in the world. This means that the human, as Janssen stresses, attains "transcendental insight into the subjective ground of the sense of being of the world."[100] For that, it is necessary that the consciousness that knows the world knows itself in its constituting achievement as an extra-mundane transcendental subjectivity.[101] But this is possible only as the mundane "I" living in the world, which is yet first constituted in transcendental consciousness.[102]

This "paradox"[103] addressed by Husserl is not only not solvable, but rather must be known in its factical necessity as a presupposition for transcendental self-comprehension, insofar as naively carried out life-in-the-world (*Weltleben*) in the natural attitude is an unavoidable departure point

96. Ibid., 80.

97. Husserl, *Erste Philosophie II*, 180.

98. Ibid.

99. Ibid.

100. Paul Janssen, *Edmund Husserl*, 144.

101. See Husserl, *Erste Philosophie II*, 473: "Thus *the most rigorous science would require that in the beginning nothing of the world, and 'not even' the being of the world as such . . . would be presupposed. The beginning must thus be nothing—nothing worldly.* What remains? Naturally, *the subjective itself*, which always already . . . pre-gives itself as a being in the world."

102. See Husserl, *Krisis*, 188. "However, do I not say 'I' at both times, whether I experience myself worldly in natural life, or in the philosophical attitude I inquire, of the world or of myself as a human, after the manifolds of constituting 'appearances,' beliefs, modes of consciousness, and so on, and precisely in the way that I take everything objective purely as a 'phenomenon,' as an intentionally constituted unity, I now find myself as a transcendental ego? . . . How is it to be understood that the 'ego' ought to have constituted in itself its own entire essence at the same time as 'its soul,' objectivated psychophysically in connection to 'its' bodily corporeality and thus as interwoven in the spatial nature constituted in it as ego?" (*Formale und transzendentale Logik*, 245).

103. Husserl, *Phänomenologie der Intersubjektivität*, 3:483.

for all transcendental reflection. To that belongs the fact that the human being itself can represent the world in which it exists as itself a lifeworldly object in the mundane attitude—and therein lies the transcendental reflexive achievement in distinction from a merely empirical observation—that "as a phenomenological observer [it] catches sight of that on which the manner of being of worldly entities and [itself] rests."[104] From this point, Husserl (with a view to the question of the [pre]givenness of the world in elementary preference for his approach) takes the factual condition for his point of departure to the fact that the lifeworldly objects are primarily communicated in sensible experience to human beings as psychophysical unities and in this sense, bodily subjects of experience. That means that it is my body with its organs that is, according to Husserl, "the center of orientation for every experience."[105] From this point, he familiarly finds the originary way in which the human being knows itself as consciousness functioning in the body, in which consciousness to him the world in its lifeworldly objects is familiar. It is important thereby that the kinesthesia immanent to consciousness is inserted as "a complete system of kinestheses available from consciousness."[106]

As we have seen, the phenomenological perspective inhibits the general thesis of the natural attitude, and thus what, as the mundane lifeworld, comprises the "universal field of all actual and possible praxis,"[107] so that in the exposition of the performance of phenomenological analysis, the world and I now become visible in their transcendentally grounded structure.[108] In a positive approach to the above-mentioned paradox, the mundane at-

104. Janssen, *Edmund Husserl*, 146. Husserl himself emphasizes the role of the spectator in *Zur Phänomenologie der Intersubjektivität III*, 24. Welter also refers to the fact that with the adoption of the transcendental perspective "the natural attitude [is] primarily ruptured and [that means that it] enters into view only as summoned, in the 'bracketing' of its validity, as a mere *structure* of a process, not as world-forming movement itself" (*Der Begriff der Lebenswelt*, 59).

105. Landgrebe, "Die Welt als phänomenologisches Problem," in *Der Weg der Phänomenologie*, 48.

106. von Herrmann, *Subjekt und Dasein*, 51. Seen in this way, as von Herrmann notes, Husserl gives "an essential extension to the traditional concept of sensibility through the inclusion of the kinaesthetic layer of consciousness" (51; see 48–52). Karl-Heinz Lembeck (*Einführung in die phänomenologische Philosophie* [Darmstadt: Wissenschaftliche Buchgesellschaft, 1994], 58) also speaks in this sense of the fact that the transcendental aesthetic now unfolds phenomenologically as the transcendental kinesthetic.

107. Husserl, *Krisis*, 145.

108. See ibid., 155.

titude proves itself for Husserl from this point, as already indicated—even though in a status of latency—as a form of extramundane transcendental subjectivity. This functions familiarly as the original accomplishing power and at the same time makes possible therein the separation already indicated between the mundane "I" and the ultimately functioning transcendental ego. But that means that Husserl in this sense joins in the classical transcendental philosophical game of doubling the subject, whose specific phenomenological rules are fixed in the methodological concepts of 'epoché' and 'reduction.' Even if the lack of a precisely determined difference running through Husserl's work between these two concepts has frequently been critically remarked,[109] it seems at least that a measure of clarity is obtained for the "Krisis" with regard to their relation when Husserl terms[110] the "accomplishment made possible through the epoché . . . a 'transcendental reduction.'"[111]

The first step, methodologically designated by Husserl as the "first necessary epoché,"[112] means, as is repeatedly emphasized, the abstention "regarding the whole of objective theoretical interests, the entirety of aims and activities that are proper to us as objective scientists or even only as those eager to know."[113] Decisive in this is that for those exercising the *epoché* the sciences and the scientists do not disappear. To be sure, "in our [phenomenological] vocational activities (in the carrying out of our work)"[114] they are methodologically removed from validity, but they remain preserved further as "facts in the unified context of the pregiven lifeworld."[115] Seen thus, the lifeworld is experienced in the mundane life-in-the-world, as Orth highlights, "as the first, most elementary form of factual subjective-intentional orientation . . . a cultural and anthropological

---

109. See among others, Suzanne Cunningham, *Language and the Phenomenological Reductions of Edmund Husserl* (The Hague: Springer, 1976), 7; Janssen, *Edmund Husserl*, 66; Elisabeth Ströker, *Husserls transzendentale Phenomenologie*, 70; Welter, *Der Begriff der Lebenswelt*, 60.

110. Michael Theunissen refers to the fact that here "the positive aspect of the reduction gathers itself in a narrower sense upon the reduction in a comprehensive understanding and the negative aspect determines the ἐποχή, whereby indeed thanks to the positive-negative double-aspect of the *entire* movement the ἐποχή takes part in positivity and the reduction differentiated from it takes part in negativity" (Theunissen, *Der Andere: Studien zur Sozialontologie der Gegenwart* [Berlin: De Gruyter, 1977], 27).

111. Husserl, *Krisis*, 155.

112. Ibid., 138.

113. Ibid., 138.

114. Ibid., 139.

115. Ibid.

factuality."[116] More precisely, it designates what Husserl grasps as the "concrete lifeworld"[117] and indeed "in the real concrete universality,"[118] which conceives therein "all praxis, whether theoretical or extratheoretical,"[119] in itself, and thus the human purposive formations that organize themselves in thematic lifeworldly relations with respect to their manifoldness, mobility, and relativity for which Husserl reserves the conceptual coinage 'special worlds' [*Sonderwelten*].[120]

Before the task of the lifeworld's thematization in the next step—which poses itself from out of the concrete lifeworld, according to Husserl—should be drawn more precisely into observation in the form of a lifeworldly ontology with the consequences issuing from out of itself, it may be appropriate to sketch out in a few strokes the background that bears and imprints Husserl's lifeworld phenomenology as *transcendental egology*. This is necessary because according to Husserl, the *epoché* first addressed, in whose carrying out the world is reduced to the prescientifically applying lifeworld, does not yet disclose the desired transcendental sphere of pure subjectivity in its ultimately grounding foundational claim, insofar as the world in its objective sense of being always remains valid as one for everyone with the lifeworld.

From this point, Husserl himself resolves to radicalize the *epoché* to the effect that in a further restriction the implications proper to the lifeworld in particular are inhibited by means of the "primordial reduction to the world as my world of experience."[121] This, as "my perceptually given present world,"[122] plays a decisive role for the imposition of an ontology of the lifeworld, as will be seen, yet has here the particular sense "that I posit

116. Orth, "Phänomenologie der Vernunft," 81.
117. Husserl, *Krisis*, 136.
118. Ibid.
119. Ibid., 145.
120. See ibid., 460; see also Werner Marx, *Lebenswelt und Lebenswelten*, 65–68.
121. Husserl, *Phänomenologie der Intersubjektivität III*, 125 (emphasis deleted). See *Cartesianische Meditationen*, §§ 44–48; Iso Kern refers to the fact that in Husserl's reflections on the primordial sphere "two concepts [are] mixed up with one another that actually stem systematically from out of different contexts [whereby] both characterize a sphere of the I that is determined negatively through the exclusion of everything alien, every alien consciousness" (Rudolf Bernet, Iso Kern, and Eduard Marbach, *Edmund Husserl: Darstellung seines Denkens* (Hamburg: Meiner, 1989), 146).
122. Husserl, *Phänomenologie der Intersubjektivität III*, 125 (emphasis deleted).

as valid only my own actual presentations, as well as all of my appercep-tions, that I can realize as my own presentations."[123]

The "best originality that could be thought,"[124] gained abstractly in the primordial structural form, is not yet the final step of reduction from Hus-serl's viewpoint, the essence of which itself thereby determines "that the universal correlation, thus the ego, becomes the final theme. . . . It required an epoché with respect to the ultimate validation of the world."[125] With and in this transcendental-phenomenological reduction—also termed a "'transcendental' epoché,"[126]—to the ego-pole [*Ichpol*], the ultimately functioning transcendental subjectivity first succeeds in bringing itself purely into view. It can rightly be designated as the *"solipsistic sphere,"*[127] insofar as Husserl himself speaks of the fact that a transcendental phenom-enology is only possible "as *transcendental egology*."[128] Accordingly, Hus-serl's confession runs thus: "As a phenomenologist I am necessarily a so-lipsist, though not in the usual ludicrous sense that is rooted in the natural attitude, but rather precisely in that of the transcendental."[129]

With transcendental egology Husserl has discovered that ground first to be certified as originary from out of which the whole problematic of self- and world constitution is to be illuminated. "First of all, and prior to all conceivability, *I am*. This '*I am*' is for me . . . the *intentional ur-ground for my world,* whereby it may not be overlooked that even the 'objective' world, the 'world for us all,' is, in being valid for me in this sense, 'my' world."[130] By the 'world for us all' Husserl is appealing, as is well known, to the tran-scendental communalization of the ego, in which I experience myself as constituted by others. However, this being-constituted pertains to me as a communalized "I," and not the pure transcendental "I"—referred to in the passage through the phenomenological reduction—that is marked out as a *"solus ipse"*[131] through "a singular philosophical solitude that is a fun-damental methodological requirement for a truly radical philosophy."[132]

123. Ibid.
124. Ibid., 10.
125. Ibid., 530; see ibid., 535, 6–12; see also *Cartesianische Meditationen,* 125.
126. Husserl, *Krisis,* 153.
127. Bernet, Kern, and Marbach, *Edmund Husserl,* 147.
128. Husserl, *Erste Philosophie II,* 174.
129. Ibid.
130. Edmund Husserl, Formale und transzendentale Logik, 243.
131. Husserl, *Cartesianische Meditationen,* 12.
132. Husserl, *Krisis,* 187.

This solitude is not really broken up, not even where Husserl intends, in the outline of his theory of intersubjectivity at the end of the fifth *Cartesian Meditation,* to have resolved the appearance of solipsism, "although the proposition preserves the fundamental validity that everything that is for me can create the sense of its being exclusively from out of myself, from out of my sphere of consciousness."[133] In Husserl's restriction, which is not assessed here, it finally proves to be the case that in the conception of his idealistic monadology—even if therein the others and thus, the objective world are referred to as transcendental phenomena of my sphere of ownness—the transcendental solipsism of his systematic egology cannot be overridden.[134]

133. Husserl, *Cartesianische Meditationen,* 176. On the question of intersubjectivity in relation to Husserl's solipsistic approach, see Theunissen, *Der Andere,* 151–155; Gadamer, Die Wissenschaft von der Lebenswelt; David Carr, "The 'Fifth Meditation' and Husserl's Cartesianism," *Philosophy and Phenomenological Research,* (1973–1974), 43:14–35.

134. Husserl saw this difficulty himself, and his confession of a 'unique solitude' as the basic stance of radical philosophizing, which he also explicitly pushes into proximity with Descartes in the *Krisis* (188), can be connected with the designation of his egology as "a solipsistic phenomenology" (Husserl, *Erste Philosophie II,* 176; see also *Formale und transzendentale Logik,* 276). Already in 1928, in his study *Der phänomenologische Idealismus Husserls* (New York: Peter Lang, 1979), Theodor Celms, promoted in part by Husserl to the function of second examiner in 1923, and working on the foundation of the Ideas and the lecture manuscripts left to him, referred to the fact, regarding the problem of intersubjectivity (ibid., 387–405), that Husserl, even though in his thinking subjectivity only realizes itself in intersubjectivity, cannot actually avoid solipsism, and that he establishes, rather, as a model a "pluralistic solipsism" (ibid., 404) within a community of monads.

The apparent proximity to Leibniz in Husserl's model of monads carries with it, particularly with reference to this fundamental Leibnizean thought, the fact that in the multitude of given simple substances a similar idea is posed with this plurality regarding differing worlds, which themselves are nevertheless nothing other than 'perspectival points of view of individuals.' This means, however, that this perspectival approach—perspectivalism in itself—perspectivally eliminates the point of view of something that is merely 'perspectivally multiplied' (see Gottfried Wilhelm Leibniz, Monadologie, § 57, in *Philosophische Schriften,* ed. Hans-Heinz Holz (Darmstadt: Wissenschaftliche Buchgesellschaft, 1985, 1:438.) in accordance with its respective observational insight, and is thus not undertaken in a Nietzschean sense. This would not be possible, according to Leibniz, insofar as there is one ontologically founded primary order in the sense of a preestablished harmony.

Such an order unbound from experience is no longer acceptable after Kant, for Husserl, on account of which by means of the thought of the transcendental community of monads, he seeks to make plausible how subjects persist and behave towards one another in what is for them an objective and thus an identical world. This, however, is synonymous with the fact that, as Udo Tietz emphasizes, "a symmetrical relationship between ego and alter ego" must be capable of being demonstrated "with phenomenological means" (Tietz, "Vernunft und Lebenswelt: Bermerkungen zum Spätwerk von Edmund Husserl," in *Praxis-Vernunft-Gemeinschaft. Auf der Suche nach einer anderen Vernunft,* ed. Volker Caysa and Klaus-Dieter Eichler [Weinheim: Beltz, 1994], 230).

In the "search for lost certainty" (as Leszek Kolakowski, alluding to Proust, titles his reflections on Husserl's philosophical path),[135] Husserl communicated, amid the crisis of his time—which appeared distinctly to him through the dangers of naturalism and relativism—this Cartesian certainty in the conception of a transcendental egology that undertakes to shed light upon the question of the human being in the world from the approach of transcendental consciousness. Confronting this egology with the claims of the concrete mundane lifeworld is not to decide at last on the success or failure of the Husserlian program. Husserl himself seeks the solution in the project of a lifeworldly ontology, which is to be illuminated further in what follows.

§ 23. Husserl's Application of the Task of a Lifeworldly Ontology

If one attends to the "concrete lifeworld,"[136] which encompasses the entire sociocultural everyday world, as the mundane meaning of the concept of the lifeworld, the environment of life, it does not always remain the same. To be sure, this straightforward living a day at a time is always a "being-directed to this or that, directed as to an end or means, as relevant or ir-relevant, to something interesting or indifferent, to private or public, to

---

Husserl had familiarly tried this in the thought of an assimilating apperception of the other, and yet had to fail, because in a reversal of roles posited in this way and decided among possibilities of analogy "the phenomenological approach [still ultimately compels], with the privileging of an antecedent ur-ego [thus of a 'preintersubjective self-consciousness as a ground of law'], a gap, i.e., an asymmetry between me and the respective other that can no longer be worked off by phenomenological means" (Tietz, "Vernunft und Lebenswelt," ibid., 231). (See the fundamental critique of Alfred Schütz, "Das Problem der transzendentalen Intersubjek-tivität bei Husserl." *Philosophische Rundschau*, (1957) 5: 81–107). Seen thus, the exchange of perspectives to be established from ego to alter ego in Husserl's analyses contains, only to this extent, a certain symmetry when the 'singular philosophical solitude' universalizes itself to the solitude of and within a transcendental community of monads. Consequently, Husserl's path leads to the "grounding of a solipsistic-transcendental community of monads, but not to a world of intersubjective experience" (Tietz, "Vernunft und Lebenswelt," 229).

In a related sense, Theunissen already emphasizes, as the result of his investigations of Husserl, the fact that by transcendental phenomenology's culminating "in the theory of transcendental intersubjectivity, [it] confirms and reinforces this [grasped not as existentiell, but rather as epistemological] solitude, on whose ground transcendental philosophy stands" (Theunissen, *Der Andere*, 155).

135. Leslek Kolakowski, *Die Suche nach der verlorenen Gewißheit. Denk-Wege mit Edmund Husserl* (Munich: Piper, 1986).

136. Husserl, *Krisis*, 136; see ibid., 134.

an everyday necessity or to the irruption of something new."[137] Yet all of this is informed at the level of living environmental enactment through a given historically conditioned, and thereby itself a history forming, attitude. Husserl sees this as well and conceives it in turn as a "habitually fixed style of willing life in predesignated directions of willing or interests . . . The respectively determined life proceeds in this persisting style as a normal form. It changes the concrete contents of culture into a relatively closed historicity. Humanity always lives in some sort of attitude (a closed community like a nation, a clan, etc.) in its historical situation. Its life always has a normal style and a persistent historicity or development within this style."[138]

The "I"'s factical being-held [*Einbehaltensein*] in the world proves itself to be something that carries itself out in the concrete environment of life, which takes shape relatively within historical and cultural horizons. Seen in this way, the concrete lifeworld as a whole accordingly connotes a high degree of *variability*—on the one side diachronically in the sense of the historical levels of development, and on the other synchronically. This does not merely demonstrate the ethnologically interesting cultural manifold of forms of life. Rather, it shows itself already in view of one's own execution of life, which is determined synchronically by a manifoldness of special worldly concrete formations of order that in correspondingly segmenting description are usually spoken of as the 'world' of family, the sciences, the profession, art, sports, etc. To speak with Waldenfels, the concrete lifeworld manifests itself from this point as a "lifeworld *in the plural*."[139]

To remain within philosophical reflection, that is, to take the concrete historical-cultural manifoldness in a type of 'ground-validation' as something final or, rather, primary, thereby means for Husserl to move into the position of an unstable relativism. In order to escape this, for Husserl the *epoché* and reduction to the natural lifeworld—in the sense of his objective, which, like a good Cartesian, is to establish a foundational structure determined by certainty from absolute evidence—necessarily includes as a further step the reduction to the abstractly achieved world of perception.

---

137. Husserl, *Krisis*-Lecture, 327.

138. Ibid., 326.

139. Bernhard Waldenfels, "Lebenswelt zwischen Alltäglichem und Unalltäglichem," in *Phänomenologie im Widerstreit. Zum 50. Todestag Edmund Husserls*, ed. Cristoph Jamme and Otto Pöggeler (Frankfurt: Suhrkamp, 1989), 112.

In this reduction Husserl identifies the *basic layer of the lifeworld*,[140] insofar as lifewordly objects are given to the bodily subject of experience primarily in the field of perception, and thus are brought to consciousness primarily in sensuous, immediately given intuition. Seen in this way, *perception*, familiarly oriented to the paradigm of thing-experience, is for Husserl the "ur-mode of *intuition*[141] and thus the knowledge in which what is therein given in self-presence presents itself in "ur-originality"[142] and determines itself primarily as the spatiotemporal world. This assumption suggests a total common—and in intentional analyses of perception, an accessible—founding layer of experience that conveys in eidetic variation that which comprises that "formal-universal, [thus] what remains invariant in the lifeworld through all changes of what is relative,"[143] which as such provides the "idea of a universal pure lifeworldly *apriori*."[144]

In the philosophical discourse of the lifeworld in Husserl it is necessary to distinguish between the living environmental forms of appearance and their invariant givenness, discovered in eidetic variations, with their own constant structures,[145] which in the how of their pregivenness is for-

---

140. See Husserl, *Phänomenologie der Intersubjektivität III*, 120.

141. Husserl, *Krisis*, 107. See Friedrich-Wilhelm von Herrmann, *Subjekt und Dasein*, 48–53.

142. Husserl, *Krisis*, 107.

143. Ibid., 145. In the "free variations and traversals of the lifeworldly conceivabilities there emerges in apodictic evidence a universal essential existence that runs through all variants, of which we can convince ourselves truly in an apodictic certainty" (ibid., 383).

144. Ibid., 143.

145. Landgrebe also emphasizes this distinction, which is significant for a clarification of the Husserlian employment of the concept of the lifeworld: "The lifeworlds change under socio-historical conditions. But on the other hand, the 'lifeworld' is according to Husserl the apriori of history, and that means the invariant that is common to all respective individual lifeworlds and that lies at the ground of all of their modifications" (Landgrebe, "Lebenswelt und Geschichtlichkeit," 20). Regarding the multivocity in the way that the concept of the lifeworld is employed, which J. N. Mohanty ("'Lifeworld' and 'Apriori' in Husserl's Later Thought," in *The Phenomenological Realism of the Possible Worlds*, ed. Anna-Teresa Tymieniecka (Dordrecht: Springer 1974), 46–65) attempts to solve through the indices of 'lifeworld$_1$' and 'lifeworld$_2$,' Welter for his part attempts to clarify terminologically by means of the distinction inspired by Husserl of the 'environment(s)' and 'lifeworld' (Welter, *Der Begriff der Lebenswelt*, 83–87).

Held ("*Husserls Begriff der Lebenswelt*," 107) rejects this attempt at a solution and prefers a linguistic regulation that, in direct connection to Husserl and against all endeavors toward an internal terminological differentiation, adheres to the concept of 'lifeworld' as the appropriate term for the double sense indicated of the 'ground of intution' and 'concrete historical lifeworld as the horizon of praxis.' The tension between these, according to Held, is precisely expressed as self-complementary, a tension that, in their belonging together, can all too easily fall out of view through a terminological distinction.

matted by the a priori "world-form of spatiotemporality."[146] The world of experience, reduced to its intuitively given spatiotemporal corporeality, thereby becomes for Husserl that stable universal foundation, constant in sense, upon which all cultural, historical, variable achievements of sense rest.

With regard to the how of pregivenness, an "essential typology,"[147] maintaining itself through all change of the relativity related to subjectivity, thereby shows itself. To unlock this is, according to Husserl, the task of a "lifeworldly ontology."[148] It works out that general structure, which as a particular lifeworldly spatiality, temporality, and so on manifests itself a priori as the same in relativity and change of natural experiences. Thus with respect to its "actually concrete universality,"[149] the concrete lifeworld clears up the fact that it relates this "to an abstract core of the world to be surgically extracted: the world of simple intersubjective experiences."[150] These are determined in the direction to their claim to founding and universality through "the communalization of simple perception."[151] According to Husserl, it is this that comprises "the truth about objects valid unconditionally for all subjects, in which normal Europeans, Hindus, Chinese, and so on, with all relativity, agree, emerging from that which yet makes general lifeworldly objects identifiable for them and for us, although in different conceptions, as form of space, movement, sensible qualities, and the like."[152]

146. Husserl, *Krisis*, 145.
147. Ibid., 176.
148. Ibid.
149. Ibid., 136.
150. Ibid.
151. Ibid., 166.
152. Ibid., 142. The invocation of normality here intended, yet not explained further, as the internal schema for an ideation operating comparatively on the basis of sensuous experience, is that which Husserl attempted to detail a bit more exactly in a second revised edition of the Cartesian Meditations drafted in 1931 (in *Zur Phänomenologie der Intersubjektivität*, 3:227–236). It is of interest for the given connection here that Husserl takes the approach for his phenomenological determination of the normal from the fact that a "human community, in which each experiences every other as a cosubject of the same world of experience in the sense that this cosubject has direct or indirect access in its own experiences to all realities of this world, [is] a normal community" (230). "In this sense, a people is comprised of 'primitive humans' in relation to their world, which is pregiven to them, and attuning normally in reciprocally taking over experiences" (ibid.).

Husserl's historically self-developing—and thereby thoroughly relative—concept of normality includes in interesting ways the circumstance that not all communities stand on the same level; for example the 'primitive human' as the "human of a primitive homeworld [is]

Seen thus, the world is "given *to me* as something that is given *to all*,"[153] and therefore for Husserl the *"ontological world-form* [is] *that of the world*

---

not normal in the same sense" (ibid., 233) as the one belonging to the European homeworld. However, in order not to finally have to conceive the world as merely a "progressive synthesis of historical finitudes" (ibid.), Husserl specifically emphasizes the notion that "a certain structure" (235) always already belongs to the essential form of every homeworld. And this means, above all, "the formal structure of fulfilled spatiotemporality" (236), and thus the "core structure of bare nature" (ibid.), i.e., "sensuous, normally experienced nature" (ibid.), through which, in the point of departure of perception as the ur-mode of knowledge, decisive weight is lent precisely to this aspect of normality.

With a view to the sensible experience functioning in this way Husserl speaks of a second normality as the relatively constant "concurrent [essential] typical character" (231) within the former sensible experience. For its positive comprehension Husserl contrasts it with possible deviations, whether of the transient sort like those conditioned through illness (sub- or supernormal states) or lasting, irresolvable abnormalities, such as color blindness or even idiocy (230). In accordance with this invocation, normality constitutes—corresponding to, among other things, "the typicality of age as a stage of development" the manifoldly specific "averageness, in which the sensuous world is seen, heard, etc., taken as an average in such and such a manner" (231). Thereby the normal suggests itself on a natural basis as an anthropological constant able to be extracted, as it were, and precisely in direct disregard of the cultural and historical relative normality, which Husserl also sees, yet which he seeks to supersede, i.e., to ground physiologically.

Normality as 'natural disposition,' whose consequences—if, under this presupposition, one applies it to normality as an internal schema of attribution of self- and alien behavior, as can be shown in the long tradition of Plato and Aristotle, and measures its function in this manner—lead to abandoning a binding measure in regard to concrete, intentional practical directives. Just because the grid of normality as a social category is oriented in the formation of its standards to behaviors as respectively concrete criteria of order, it appears to be problematically expressed if normality, at least as Husserl suggests it to be, is invoked in its function of schematizing human modes of behavior primarily in the degree of a human "natural endowment" to be specified as normal.

Where this is nevertheless propagated, it binds itself at most to an ideologically fixed narrowness, as the history of discrimination shows, with fatal consequences. In this narrowed perspective, all self-expression (among other things) contrary to the sense of convention as a self-indebted structure of rules of normality in the formation of a sensus communis—which is simply not possible to justify in the putative anticipation of a successful rationality regarding ideal structures of communication, but rather must be conceived, with revisions in mind, out of the insight into the contingent condition of existence—becomes a source of distrust insofar as it limits, or rather shuts off, the principal testability and refutability of claims to normality through the assertion of its naturalness.

In contrast, normality has always been formed, precisely in its normative control function, in the context of sociohistorical processes of development, so that normality itself proves thus to be a historically changing, even invertable schema of the concrete lifeworld, which intuitively actualizes itself—as the history of sexual morality, among others, teaches us—in the dimension of everyday consciousness and behavior. With regard to the problem of the sociohistorical formation of normality, Michel Foucault's 1961 study *Wahnsinn und Gesellschaft: Eine Geschichte des Wahns im Zeitalter der Vernunft* (Frankfurt: Suhrkamp, 1993), despite possible criticisms, is still philosophically instructive in its details with regard to this present context.

153. Husserl, *Krisis*, 469.

for all."[154] An ontology of the lifeworld to be formulated in this respect, under the presupposition of intuition as the ur-mode of knowledge, has its point of departure and theme for Husserl purely in the world of experience as "the unified and consequently unanimously intuitable world in actual and possible experiential intuition."[155] It is thus charged to the account in advance in the intention of a 'theory of general structures,' that is, it deals with an *ontology of unity* and not with an ontology that differentially thinks the manifold as such in its particularity.

In the universal a prioristic unity determined in this way, Husserl sees the twofold grounding function of the lifeworld redeemed. For it seems to succeed from here at once in exposing, on the one hand, the ontological foundation for the manifold of the concrete living environments with the world of perception in the structural sameness "of the spatiotemporal *'onta'*"[156] (which registers the lifeworldly ontology as "concrete universal doctrine of essence of these *onta*"[157]) and on the other, in conceiving the lifeworld transcendentally, as we have seen, as the universal horizon in relation to the manifoldness of the environmentally given concrete formations of sense, and that means taking them as "being in a singularity, for which the plural is senseless."[158]

154. Ibid.

155. Ibid., 176.

156. Ibid., 145.

157. Ibid.

158. Ibid., 146. Landgrebe ("Lebenswelt und Geschichtlichkeit," 31) notes that Husserl bogs himself down in an aporia in this twofold determination with regard to the understanding of the world lying within it. That is to say, insofar as the lifeworldly ontology is the 'concrete universal doctrine of the essence of onta,' Husserl determines the world ontologically as the "universe of things" (*Krisis*, 145) and in this way the possibility opens up of clearing the way, in structural analysis of the "unanimity in the total perception of the world" (ibid., 166), to that fundamental ground upon which arise empirically, as it were, the different variable sociohistorical constructions of meaning. In natural living-in-the-world these are precisely the things we initially encounter, and in this way they offer as onta a point of departure for their ontological analysis and thereby show themselves in the abovementioned sense as founded phenomena.

As already indicated, therefore, the analysis, in the combination of eidetic variation (cf. ibid., 383) and the "primordial reduction to the world as my world of experience" (*Zur Phänomenologie der Intersubjektivität III*, 125), is assigned the task, according to Husserl, of disclosing the universally invariant ontological essential types of the lifeworld, in which the regional categories of the lifeworld belonging to regional ontologies corresponding to their conditions of being must still be grounded. Accordingly, the world as the internal concept of beings in Husserl is taken into account in this sense as an ontological concept, and yet, without Husserl being able to solve this aporia, it comes into conflict with the determination of the lifeworld as a world horizon, which, as seen, can simply no longer be grasped ontologically, but rather only transcendentally. Ulrich Claesges thus emphasizes the fact that the "concept of the lifeworld in

The 'singularity of the lifeworld' intended by Husserl, which for him guarantees the a priori singular qua formal-universal world as a universal horizon, is thereby constitutively bound with the task of a functioning "transcendental 'empiriography,'" in the sense of a transcendental aesthetic, "that projects an experiential structure and an experiential world-structure of all humankind, which has to serve any form of humanity as a norm for critiquing the relatively harmonious worlds of experience and opinion."[159] From this point, the concrete universality to be demonstrated proves itself, as Landgrebe stresses, to be synonymous with the Husserlian "universe that is in principle intuitable."[160]

In the rational "goal of a truth valid unconditionally for all subjects"[161] pursued by Husserl, the lifeworld, as perception, in all its relativities, achieves "its *general structure,* to which all relative entities are bound."[162] It is itself no longer relative and thereby bindingly establishes the order of the world as spatiotemporal. Seen thus, the manifoldness of the lifeworld is, as Waldenfels remarks, "held in check through a *first principle* of given experiences, and a *final principle* of universal regulative structures."[163] And from here, for Husserl the lifeworld, irrespective of all concretely manifested sociocultural differences, manifests itself as *one and the same* for *all* humans. That means, with the categorical order of space and time, to take his own example, it provides a common denominator of having a world, as much for the Chinese farmer as for the Hindu or the European.

While Husserl marginalizes the spectrum of historical cultural differences in this way, he yet asks what should still be called concrete in the universal thus gained. The difficulty indicated here does not even resolve itself through the fact that in the context of elucidating his reflections toward the ontology of the lifeworld, Husserl alludes to the fact that "a spatiotem-

---

Husserl [is] from the outset an ontological-transcendental hybrid-concept" ("Zweideutigkeiten in Husserls Lebensweltbegriff," 97).

159. Husserl, *Zur Phänomenologie der Intersubjektivität III*, 235.

160. See Landgrebe, "Lebenswelt und Geschichtlichkeit," 34f.

161. Husserl, *Krisis*, 142

162. Ibid.

163. Waldenfels, "Lebenswelt zwischen Alltäglichem und Unalltäglichem," 113. Cf. his "Die Abgründigkeit des Sinnes," 17. Decisive here, as Waldenfels stresses, is the balance between the two. For if the lifeworld were "merely something initially given, in the sense of simple data, we would then get ourselves into dangerous empirical waters; if it were an ultimately regulating principle that was not welded to the ground of experience, rationalism would gain the upper hand. In that Husserl grounds reason from out of experience, he avoids both pitfalls; he does this otherwise than Kant, yet in a thoroughly comparable form" (ibid.; see also ibid., 22).

porality (the 'living,' not the logical-mathematical)"[164] belongs to its own sense of being. If one is oneself ready to determine concrete universality in the sense of intuitability with a view to the living spatiotemporality beyond kinaesthetic-corporeal functions,[165] this determination of the living remains quite formal, because in the theoretical "attitude to the world of perception,"[166] as is characteristic for the lifeworldly ontology, concrete experience seems in contrast reduced in advance to natural living in the world, and indeed reduced to that which Husserl himself in the abstractive extraction names the kernel of the world. So it is to agree with Waldenfels [to say] that yet in Husserl, in opposition to the claim raised thus by him, "the 'categorial of the lifeworld' fatally resembles Cartesian nature."[167]

What Husserl has in mind in his approach to this thoroughly mundanely applied, indeed not empirically descriptive but rather abstractly procedural, reduction to a priori spatio-temporality as ontological basic form (in which each and all have a world, intended transcendentally-empiriographically), has on closer inspection little to do with a comprehension of the concrete lifeworld. But the human being finds himself in it and has to understand himself therein as a self, that is, a relation to himself that, to prefigure, constitutes ways of existence between birth and death in interminable dynamic processes, which form *constellations of the self* in the field of tension of the historically individualized or individualized historical facticity.

These can no longer be related back to an ego-pole subject, but rather are to be grasped in the sense of a matrix of progressive, transformative, and transgressive processes of subjectification that, observed existentially-hermeneutically, constitute themselves in the sensescape of projection and thrownness. In contrast, Husserl's aim is to show the lifeworld qua world of perception as founding ground, to be at the same time bound correlatively with the structural demonstration of the universality of the forms of intuition in order to find guaranteed the unity that has to structurally explicate the lifeworld ontology in view of the founding perception.

However, the ontology of the lifeworld thus brought into consideration with its orientation to a 'kernel of the world' has a great deficiency

---

164. Husserl, *Krisis*, 171.
165. As Landgrebe does in "Lebenswelt und Geschichtlichkeit," 36.
166. Husserl, *Krisis*, 171.
167. Waldenfels, "Die Abgründigkeit des Sinnes," in In den Netzen der Lebenswelt (Frankfurt: Suhrkamp, 1985), 19; as further confirmation see Husserl, *Krisis*, 142.

insofar as this kernel of the world is the result of an abstraction and thus cannot be experienced in a lifeworldly, concrete manner. For the fact that a perceived thing is also always a spatiotemporally situated object does not mean that it is primarily grasped by the perceiver as a space-time body upon which the different higher-level strata of meaning are built. With the abstractive abbreviation of the problematic of the lifeworld there obtrudes the notion that the manifoldness of cultural-historical and social worlds is situated like "shells . . . around the kernel of the single lifeworld,"[168] by which Waldenfels rightly indicates that such a "kernel, which is 'extracted abstractly,' [reminds one] more of chemical or pharmaceutical laboratories than of lived experiences."[169] With a certain emphasis it can therefore be said that in Husserl "perception . . . is pruned in such a way that it is *suited* for a universal foundation."[170]

In exchange for the allegedly achieved universalization, Husserl pays the price of letting the concept of experience, like the concrete world of perception, remain underdetermined.[171] For in the Husserlian schema and model of superimposed strata, the possibility disappears not merely

168. Waldenfels, "Lebenswelt zwischen Alltäglichem und Unalltäglichem," 113.

169. Ibid. Thus it is hardly surprising that from out of a sense for the philosophical significance of lived experiences, a clear critique of Husserl's conception has come from the side of phenomenologically schooled thinkers like Max Scheler and Maurice Merleau-Ponty. Just as sustained and consequential, this critique was formulated by Heidegger in particular, to the effect that even a natural, spatiotemporally situated thing like a pencil in my hand nonetheless is not encountered by me primarily as a space-time body, with the "demand inscribed within it," as it were, that can be clarified in its essence only from out of an analysis of a founding perception. Rather, the pencil shows itself to be an environmental thing of the sort that must be determined for the conception of its mode of being primarily from its use, its serviceability.

This critique of Husserl's primacy of a founding perception, proposed phenomenologically by Heidegger, also leads, as will be seen, to a new formulation of the concept of the lifeworld. What is decisive thereby is that this conception of the lifeworld is not projected, as in Husserl, from out of an epistemological perspective. But that means that the lifeworld assumed as pretheoretical by Husserl is equally extracted in Heidegger from its theoreticist confines; that is, it forms itself in the framework of the unfolding of the lifeworld qua living-in-the-world in the carrying out of existence—in the carrying out of the existentiell understanding of being and of the receptive, equiprimordial understanding of the different modes of being of nonhuman beings.

170. Waldenfels, "Die Abgründigkeit des Sinnes," 20. Behind this stands the above-mentioned implementation of perception as the "ur-mode of intuition" (Husserl, *Krisis*, 107), which exhibits "with Ur-originality, that is, in the mode of self-presence" (ibid.), and thereby for Husserl supports the assumption that to every human being the same things are given intuitively, i.e., as sensuously experienceable in space-time corporeality, if also in different modes and perspectives (see ibid., 107, 163).

171. See Waldenfels, "Die Abgründigkeit des Sinnes," 20–23, 25.

of seeing empirical variables in the emergence of differing things, which may be new in a given case, but as well of seeing them in their potential novelty. This means that observed from the Husserlian approach, it is not known that experiences of differing things can be grasped as competing formations of sense and structure, in comparison to the directly given. But only as such are they to be discovered in view of the concrete lifeworld in its productive possibility of transcending and restructuring the internal frame of reference that has been handed down.[172]

In this sense, the bond between founding and founded, so important for Husserl, can be problematized with regard to the question of its relational character, to the effect that this is no longer simply conceived as a derivative relation. As Merleau-Ponty shows, this relation can also be determined in contrast to a reciprocal explication of its relata, by which it then maintains the "coefficient of facticity."[173]

172. Waldenfels indicates the significance of his point in his rather sketchy defense of "a more concrete theory of perception" (ibid., 25), for instance where he refers to the fact that precisely the spatiotemporal bodily world—which Husserl intends to divest of relativity in what is for him the paradigmatic experience of things, if one thinks, for example, of the modes of appearance of animism—loses its ostensively secure foundation insofar as, for instance, its assumption of the constancy of things is not in play in the question of the differentiation of the 'lifeless' and the 'living.' Even the experience of the body is set "in a network of differing interpretations" (ibid.), the demonstration of which the history of medicine or art, among others, deliver vivid examples.

In view of the investigations of Kurt Goldstein, Merleau-Ponty, and Erving Goffman, Waldenfels refers to the fact that even the human experience of space is not based upon a univocal supposition of constancy, but rather shows itself to be dependent upon concrete spatial orientations, or whether it has to do with open or closed spaces, or shows spatial mastery in artistic expression, or even how social orders are mirrored in formations of spatial order (e.g., seating arrangements). A similarly varying spectrum exists with regard to the experience of time, which beats in differing rhythms like phases of eating, sleeping, and work, yet which also emerges in fundamentally different ways in the assumption of linear and cyclical models of time.

173. Maurice Merleau-Ponty, *Phänomenologie der Wahrnehmung* (Berlin: De Gruyter, 1966), 448. Merleau-Ponty clarifies this with reference to Euclidean geometry, which as a rational truth appears in its validity claims like a factual truth, yet after all shows itself in the transparency of history as an epoch-specific solution to a problem, meaning "that humans were able for a time to take a homogeneous three-dimensional space for the 'ground' of their thinking and to appropriate without question that which science, raised to a greater generality, will consider to be a merely contingent specification of space" (ibid.).

Consequently, the alleged factual truths prove themselves to be relational to a given rational system in their interpretation, which means for Merleau-Ponty, in light of the abovementioned problem of founding, that in the relation between the founding and the founded, that which founds—for instance, the fact or the perception—only distinguishes itself antecedently as what is first, in that it is what is determined and explicated through what is founded. Thereby

In that which the concept of facticity here indicates, a realm opens that can truly be called 'a wide field' and that establishes what essentially can no longer be a fixed ground in the sense of a '*fundamentum inconcussum,*' nor ever will be, and yet is that dimension in which the human being alone experiences himself as finite self-relation, in which he finds himself, invents and interprets himself in the interplay of constellations, and in which he takes care of himself. The philosophical task of the formation of a *hermeneutics of facticity as a hermeneutics of the self* thereby indicated stands at the center of the next section of our study. And only here does what Husserl appeals to in the formations of sense in the concrete lifeworld as the historical-social-cultural world—yet which is not properly grasped in its fundamental validity—become visible in its full scope as something relevant to human self-understanding.

Only by taking leave of the narrowed Husserlian approach to the theory of perception, with the conception of phenomenology as original science of life, as we find it in early Heidegger, does the lifeworld in its everydayness first become visible according to its true meaning. In all of this it is necessary to strip away the semblance of the lifeworld as a mere preliminary in regard to the transcendental sphere of reason. Thereby the task of an ontology of the lifeworld is determined anew, no longer conceived as that doctrine of being that aims at investigating the cultural-historical lifeworld in view of fundamental natural structures.

Husserl does not in fact dispute such a critique of his idea of a lifeworldly ontology, yet this ontology of the lifeworld, which he never brought to realization, is not his central concern insofar as it remained for him "on the natural ground, and thus outside of the transcendental horizon of interest."[174] Thus even the mundane attention to the "relativity of

---

it is ruled out "that it ever exhausts and nullifies this, while that which founds is yet not the first in an empirical sense and that which is founded by it does not simply derive from it, since only through what is founded does what founds manifest itself" (ibid., 449).

174. Husserl, *Krisis*, 176; ibid., 145. Husserl emphatically stresses that the lifeworld "can become, without any transcendental interest and therefore in the 'natural attitude' (spoken in the language of transcendental philosophy: naively, prior to the epoché), the theme of its own science—an ontology of the lifeworld purely as the world of experience (i.e., as the world unitarily and harmoniously intuitable in actual and potential experiencing intuition)" (ibid., 176). Seen thus, as Hans Jonas critically observes, Husserl's pure consciousness can tell "of a 'lifeworld' . . . but only as a datum 'for' it, constituted within it or construed by it: it is itself not a part thereof, not dependently interwoven with it" (Jonas, *Philosophische Untersuchungen und metaphysische Vermutungen* [Frankfurt: Insel, 1992], 250).

the living environment of certain humans, peoples, or times,"[175] on which it is here first insisted critically in attacks on Husserl, means merely to pursue a "world survey" for him.[176] Yet, it may be the business of the historian and not a task for the philosopher, insofar as in conducting such a survey the world is still "not converted into the universe of the purely subjective, as its own universal nexus, which now concerns us,"[177] to the extent that the "postulate [is to be correlated with] that innovative universal science of the subjectivity through which the world is pregiven."[178]

To achieve the pregivenness of the lifeworld as universal theme, according to Husserl, means to comprehend the world "purely and exclusively *as that* and *thus how* it possesses sense and existential validation in our life-consciousness."[179] However, this means transforming the lifeworld into a "mere transcendental 'phenomenon.'"[180] Of course, it remains in its essence what it was, only it can now manifest itself "as mere 'component' in concrete transcendental subjectivity and accordingly its apriori as a 'stratum' in the universal apriori of the transcendental,"[181] within which, first of all, the ultimately valid clarification of the sense of being of the lifeworld can be achieved in its constitutive relatedness to subjectivity.

Requisite here, as Husserl never tires of stressing, is "a *total* reorientation, a *wholly unique universal epoché*."[182] Only in the transcendental *epoché* and reduction does "universally accomplishing life [become visible], in which the world, constantly existing for us in fluctuating awhileness, continually comes into being for us as 'pregiven.'"[183] Only in the transcendental-phenomenological attitude, according to Husserl, do we discover "that and how the world, as the correlate of an explorable universality of synthetically bound operations, gains the sense of its being and its ontic

---

175. Husserl, *Krisis*, 150.
176. Ibid.
177. Ibid.
178. Ibid.
179. Ibid., 151. The way to transcendental, world-constituting subjectivity proceeds, according to Husserl, in two levels of reflection: "1. In the retrogression from the pregiven world with all of its sedimentations of meaning, with its science and scientific determination, to the original lifeworld; 2. In the inquiring back from the lifeworld to the subjective accomplishments from which it itself springs forth" (Husserl, Erfahrung und Urteil, 49).
180. Husserl, *Krisis*, 177.
181. Ibid.
182. Ibid., 151.
183. Ibid., 148.

validity in the totality of its ontic structures."[184] Husserl's fundamental-ism, which manifests itself therein, opens for him the possibility in which the human being "becomes a surveyor of the world [and that means first and foremost] a philosopher."[185] However, this transcendental-phenomenological position offers an irresolvable aporia from the outset, in Waldenfels's pointed formulation: "insofar as the lifeworld is concretely historical, it is no universal foundation; and to the effect that it is such, it is not concretely historical."[186]

§ 24. The Function of History in Husserl's Transcendental-Phenomenological Conception

However, the suppression of the concrete factical historical moment, which in its problematic had shown itself at the point of the perception-theoretical reduction to the spatiotemporal bodily world (observed as a hermeneutic of facticity) as a loss of the living plenitude of the concrete lifeworld, in no way means that the phenomenon of history is left out of consideration for the transcendental-philosophical conception of the 'Krisis.' Even though—as Karl-Heinz Lembeck emphasizes—Husserl's "own phenomenological theory of historical knowing is nowhere formulated,"[187] within the Husserlian conception the phenomenon retains its own specific systematic position for history—under the presupposition, however, as one may put it in looking ahead and following that which was carried out in the perception-theoretical approach, that Husserl "prunes" history in such a way that it suits his intentions.

With the historico-philosophical conception constructed in accordance with his own requirements, Husserl nevertheless entangles himself in an aporia that dangerously approaches a vicious circle and that in a certain sense submits his transcendental-phenomenological approach as a whole to a litmus—indeed, an acid—test. A decisive ground for this lies in the fact that Husserl places both the starting point and the approach to his thematization of history under the demand that the transcendental

---

184. Ibid.

185. Husserl, Krisis-Lecture, 331.

186. Bernhard Waldenfels, "Lebenswelt zwischen Alltäglichem und Unalltäglichem," 114.

187. Karl-Heinz Lembeck, *Gegenstand Geschichte: Geschichtswissenschaftstheorie in Husserls Phänomenologie* (Dordrecht: D. Reidel, 1988), 33.

phenomenology that he conceives (in the sense of the universal science to be grounded ultimately in self-evidence within the modes of appearance of European culture) is "the functioning brain"[188] that in the reflexive act of its self-determination already demands in itself the distinction between "philosophy as the historical fact of a given time and philosophy as an idea."[189] Thus for Husserl the "historically given actual philosophy [is] the more or less successful attempt to realize the guiding idea of infinity [the phenomenological task in the sense of its self-determination as the universal telos of reason] and thereby to realize the totality of truths,"[190] which is for him synonymous with the "secret yearning of modern philosophy as a whole."[191]

This means that even where Husserl sees it as necessary, in the sense of affording a self-legitimation, to illuminate the path to the transcendental reduction in the outline of historical positions, for him the history of these individual stations in their historicity as such is not at issue. For him, it is solely about demonstrating the historic-genetic progress in the emergent transcendental life of consciousness, because for Husserl the only way out of the crisis that he has diagnosed as the "spiritual necessity of our time"[192] lies in this finally grounded demonstration, which, degenerated into naturalism and historicism in a battle of worldviews, threatens "to transform all life into an unintelligible idealess mass of 'facts'"[193] This means, however, to illuminate the history of philosophy in the light of the telos of a transcendental grounding of philosophy through transcendental phenomenology as a *prehistory* that shows itself therefore also to be an ideal-typical

188. Husserl, *Krisis*-Lecture, 338.

189. Ibid.

190. Ibid. At another point, Husserl puts it: "Science, however, seeks truths that are, and remain, valid once and for all and for everyone, and accordingly seeks innovative and thoroughly implemented forms of verification" (*Cartesianische Meditationen*, 52). This manner of ultimate verification calls for a founding instance that creates, in accordance with the universal scientific claim to validity in evidence, in good Cartesian form, "the highest dignity of apodicticity" (ibid., 56) in the phenomenological recourse to the principles of knowledge, whereby at the same time it also binds the self-justification of the scientific nature of phenomenology, as it had already been stressed in his LOGOS essay. Seen in this way, Husserl's thematization of history is, as Lembeck emphasizes, stamped from the outset by the "relation of the historico-philosophical to the scientific-critical claim of phenomenology" (*Gegenstand Geschichte*, 34). See Husserl, *Formale und transzendentale Logik*, 10; *Krisis*, 398.

191. Husserl, *Ideen I*, 133.

192. Husserl, *Philosophie als strenge Wissenschaft*, 65.

193. Ibid., 66.

reconstruction, since it is attained in its end in Husserl's own project of a transcendental phenomenology.

Seen thus, for Husserl "the history of the European spirit [is] not as much a history of facts as a history of sense—i.e., history of the original sense task [*Aufgabensinnes*] of all philosophy."[194] From this perspective, it must be noted that according to Husserl all "facticities . . . have a root in the essential state of the generally human, in which a teleological reason penetrating through the entire historicity shows itself. Thereby a proper problematic is revealed, which relates to the totality of history and the total sense ultimately giving it unity."[195]

History thereby becomes a *terrain of teleological self-discovery* for phenomenology. This means the history of philosophy in Husserl stakes out the material space of possibility within which 'philosophy itself' qua transcendental phenomenology can discover itself with the demonstration of the phenomenological as the 'true method of philosophy.'[196] With a view to the diverse historical investigations of this form of phenomenological analysis, it can be established, following Gadamer, that the "result [cannot] here be otherwise upon any of the other paths of Husserlian thought: to make convincing transcendental phenomenology as the sense-giving final establishment of all history of philosophy and its 'ultimate grounding' in the transcendental ego."[197] For precisely thereby "begins a philosophy of the most profound and universal self-understanding of the philosophizing ego as bearer of absolute reason coming to itself,"[198] which in the course of history and in particular since Descartes exhibits the ground of

194. Lembeck, *Gegenstand Geschichte*, 36.

195. Husserl, *Krisis*, 386.

196. See ibid., 445. At another point in the *Krisis* it runs: "Such a mode of enlightenment of history in recourse to the originary institution of ends . . . is nothing other than the proper self-reflection of the philosopher upon that at which he actually wills, what in him is the will, from out of the will and as the will of his spiritual forefathers. That is, to revitalize the sedimented conceptuality that as self-evidence is the ground of its private and unhistorical work, in its hidden historical meaning" (ibid., 72f.). It is in this thoroughly voluntaristic sense that the first two parts of *Krisis*, as well as the *Kritische Ideengeschichte* of *Erste Philosophie I*, are to be read, yet it is, as Max Scheler once vividly formulated it, the "cone of interests, which, likened to the cone of light from a lighthouse, shines on a part of the past, . . . that is always a work of the historical present, in the first place of future tasks envisioned by the spirit and the will, that will of a new [as he says in an echo of Ernst Troeltsch] 'cultural synthesis'" (Max Scheler, *Die Wissensformen und die Gesellschaft* [Bern: Franke Verlag, 1960], 98).

197. Gadamer, "Wissenschaft von der Lebenswelt," 157.

198. Husserl, *Krisis*, 275.

being sought in transcendental subjectivity from out of the "fundamental demand of apodicticity"[199] in the phenomenologically transformed reception of Cartesian discovery. Committing oneself to this task means, according to Husserl, discovering the "final foundation surrendered to the historical process,"[200] from out of a self-determination that at once must continue the self-reflection of the tradition as insight into the *teleological beginning*"[201] carrying itself out for him with the original foundation that took place with the Greeks.

For Husserl, the exchange with history accordingly means, in an emphatic sense, for one to historically legitimate the final telos of absolute reason for the breakthrough attained in phenomenology and at the same time thereby to profile its historical configurations, which of themselves press on to their final clarification in phenomenology.[202]

199. Ibid., 274.

200. Ibid., 73.

201. Ibid., 72.

202. What thus applies for philosophy—that the endowed sense of origin shifts historically in its aims, which are to be tested phenomenologically in a critical inspection of their articulated final clarification—has, as Lembeck remarks in view of "the sense-historical strategy, concrete scientific-theoretical value" (*Gegenstand Geschichte*, 38), which Husserl himself exemplarily demonstrates in the famous third appendix of the *Krisis*, published by Eugen Fink in 1939 under the title "Die Frage nach dem Ursprung der Geometrie als intentionalhistorisches Problem." See also Derrida's commentary *Husserls Weg in die Geschichte am Leitfaden der Geometrie* (Munich: Fink, 1987).

In the strict sense, Derrida's essay does not actually enact a commentary, but rather in the exchange with Husserl and thereby with the history of philosophy, marks out, in a rigorous manner, the contours of a profile for the notion of philosophy's textuality, which Rudolf Bernet highlights in his foreword to that essay as a basic concern early on in Husserl's work that anticipates Derrida's subsequent writings. Derrida's essay was motivated not least by the fact that it conceives itself to be an introduction to a Husserlian fragment, belonging as an appendix to overlapping contexts, that focuses on the problem of the constitution of ideal objects.

In accordance with his own cognitive intentions, yet nonetheless in a thoroughgoing connection to Husserl, Derrida insistently pursues the question of their linguisticality and historicity. In doing so, Derrida's analyses undertake to push the Husserlian approach of an ideal truth that contemporizes itself within the tradition—along with the idea of infinite scientific rational progress that it implies—so far that for him it knots the Husserlian idea of the historicality of science with the question of the language of its thematization, that is, the language of phenomenology. Derrida discusses it in a detailed investigation by reference to the "possibility of writing" ("Husserls Weg," 116), and is here already on the track of his own central themes (regarding the situating of the "Introduction" in the course of his thinking, see Stephan Strasser, "Von einer Husserl-Interpretation zu einer Husserl-Kritik: Nachdenkliches zu Jacques Derridas Denkweg," in *Studien zur neueren französischen Phänomenologie*: Ricoeur, Foucault, Derrida, ed. Ernst Wolfgang Orth (Freiburg: Meiner, 1986), 130–169; Katharina Mai, *Die Phänomenologie und ihre Überschreitungen: Husserls reduktives Philosophieren und Derridas Spur der Andersheit* (Stuttgart: Metzler, 1996), 185–230).

Husserl explicitly emphasizes that these preforms cannot simply be ignored when he states that "reflection on the original sense . . . *from the beginning onward* in all its deferrals of sense and wayward self-interpretations has been *and still is* of decisive significance for the becoming and being of the modern positive sciences, and likewise of modern philosophy—indeed, even of the spirit of modern European humanity in general."[203] Yet Husserl thereby sees himself "in a kind of *circle*,"[204] insofar as the "understanding of beginnings [is] to be gained only from the given science in its present form, in the look back to its development. But with an understanding of *beginnings* this development as a *development of sense* is silent."[205] For

----

The question of writing, or rather textuality, is also a subject of reflection for Husserl precisely (as he elsewhere vividly puts it) as a "linguistic corporeality . . . that is, as it were, a spiritual corporeality" (Formale und transzendentale Logik, 25) wherein in its function, "communication that has become virtual [that is,] in continuous possibility, capable of being experienced intersubjectively in community" (*Krisis*, 371), achieves above all the constitution, in the sense of a "continuing-to-be" (ibid.), of ideal objects in their objectivity, since it is (to borrow a distinction from Erfahrung und Urteil), in opposition to 'bound idealities,' as 'free ideality,' "encompassing all space and time, which concern its possible reactivation" (Erfahrung und Urteil, 321; see also 317–325).

According to Derrida writing creates "a kind of autonomous transcendental field out of which every actual subject can disappear" (Derrida, "Husserls Weg," 117). The virtuality conceived by Husserl is for Derrida profoundly "ambivalent: it enables at the same time the passivity, forgetting, and all further crisis-phenomena" (ibid.) that he underscores with references, for example, to the "silence of prehistoric arcana and lost civilizations [or] the illegibility of inscriptions in stone" (ibid., 118), so that for Derrida, as Bernet emphasizes, in the anonymous independence of writing debit and credit ultimately cancel each other out in the accounting of his analysis (see Rudolf Bernet, "Differenz und Anwesenheit: Derridas und Husserls Phänomenologie der Sprache, der Zeit, der Geschichte, der wissenschaftlichen Rationalität," in *Studien zur neueren französischen Phänomenologie*, ed. Ernst Wolfgang Orth (Freiburg: Alber, 1986) 51–112, esp. 83–99).

In the elaboration of the constitutive belonging-together of the appearance of ideal truth with the factical possibility of its disappearance—which is therein bound to the factically inseparable context of what Husserl grasps as 'spiritual corporeality' in distinction from 'material bodies of language'—the thesis for Derrida of an independent, self-contained—that is, a purely spiritual—essence of language becomes implausble. At the same time, the claim posed by Husserl of being able to free himself from the intrinsically contingent realm of historical facticity by means of transcendental phenomenology proves to have foundered. Seen in this way the Husserlian conception ultimately proves "how foreign the author of the Krisis was to history, incapable as he was of really taking it seriously—and the degree to which he attempted at the same time to respect the originary meaning and possibility of historicity, in order to penetrate it deeply in truth" ("Husserls Weg," 124).

203. Husserl, *Krisis*, 59 (emphasis added).

204. Ibid.

205. Ibid.

Husserl this means that nothing else remains than "going back and forth in a 'zigzag'; in the interplay, one must help the other."[206]

A closer look at this zigzag finds Husserl entangled in a problem that is not insurmountable. For insofar as the end goal of historical development in his thinking finds its realization solely in transcendental phenomenology, at the same time the entire course of development of the history of thought is thereby of itself teleologically legitimated in its motivation of sense and must refer back precisely to this development in its concrete course for the demonstration of the phenomenological position that culminates in the final meaning of philosophical thought's possibility of self-grounding.

As a *historical* event, the contemplation of this course of development falls into the scope of duties of philosophical historiography, which as a discipline is itself to be situated in turn within 'scientific history' and, as Husserl stresses, transformed by it first and foremost to the effect that this creates "the timeless present of all the philosophers and philosophies of all scientifically disclosed times to be made present again and so ever again made available through the scientific history of each age and for every philosopher."[207] Lembeck refers to the fact that for Husserl, seen in this way, "critical reflection on the history of philosophy . . . accordingly [has] historical-scientific preparatory work as its condition."[208] Therefore, it can be said that his "attempt at a historically-philosophically motivated self-reflection upon the law and task of fundamental phenomenological philosophy [is caught] in a kind of scientific-philosophical petitio principii."[209]

Husserl's recourse to the historically factical course of development does not allow the historical facticities to speak for themselves in their respective historical validity. Rather, they are already disciplined in advance in the appearance of their claims to validity, so that they appear teleologically justified as historical stages in virtue of their immanent tendency to refer to phenomenology. In a fundamental proposition of Husserl, "History is in advance nothing other than the living movement of the with-one-another and the in-one-another of the original formation and sedimentation of sense."[210]

---

206. Ibid.
207. Ibid., 444.
208. Lembeck, *Gegenstand und Geschichte*, 40.
209. Ibid.
210. Husserl, *Krisis*, 380.

From this point, it can be asked whether "the 'Krisis'-manuscript authentically [delivers] actual *historical* reflection or, rather, something entirely different."[211] To be sure, all possible problems and insights, Husserl stresses, are of a historical nature because each lives his life for himself in the concrete "horizon of humanity,"[212] which is itself "for us perpetually, vitally conscious, and indeed implicated as a temporal horizon in our particular present horizon."[213] Thus, corresponding essentially to the one humanity as the environment of life in which we live is the cultural world "in its modes of being, which in every historical time and humanity is the particular tradition."[214] Although in the historical horizon determined in this way everything is itself historical, for Husserl this is not in the sense of an ultimate to which all change and transformation laid out therein are referred, insofar as this can be checked through an as yet undiscovered originary sense.

Now, if the horizon itself can indeed be reconstructed historically in its particular order in the demonstration of its factical conditions, its originary sense (if one were ready to accept such a sense) observed hermeneutically necessarily remains withdrawn, as a consequence of the temporal distance or even the presupposed contingency of its observational standpoint, so that ultimately all talk of an originary sense proves to be problematic in the highest degree, if not wholly questionable. All the same, Husserl, as we have seen, raises the claim of being able to unveil the "essential structure"[215] of the historical horizon in methodological questioning, and thus of being able to return by means of his phenomenological method "to the ur-materials of the first formation of meaning, to the ur-premises,"[216] in order thus to lay bare the structurally determined universality in the experiential present factum of its *"inner structure of sense."*[217] This also designates "the concrete historical apriori that [encompasses] all entities in

211. Lembeck, *Gegenstand Geschichte*, 41.
212. Husserl, *Krisis*, 378.
213. Ibid.
214. Ibid.
215. Ibid.
216. Ibid.
217. Ibid., 380. "Only the uncovering of the essential general structure lying as such in every past or future historical present, and, in totality, only in the uncovering of the concrete historical time in which we live—in which our universal humanity lives, with regard to its total essential general structure—only this uncovering can really make possible, perspicuously, an understanding history that is scientific in the authentic sense" (ibid.).

historical having-become and becoming or in its essential being as tradition and being handed down."[218]

As research into the apriori, Husserlian phenomenology, in its claim to truth, arrives at just this inner structure of sense. And therefore the historically relational facticities are also only significant to it with regard to strategic sense when they can be valued in view of the insight sought into the finally grounding principles and possess a disclosive function in relation to absolute reason as the agent of history.

In reference to this selective approach, Lembeck employs the concept of 'historical reduction' with the aim of terminological precision.[219] To be sure, the term does not turn up in Husserl, but rather suggests itself thoroughly from out of the issue at hand insofar as it is actually signified through a "reduction in the double sense of 'to lead back' and 'to restrict.'"[220] Leading back means, for one thing, a "leading back of spiritual formations of sense to their historical origins in the retrospective pursuit of relevant traditions of sense"[221] as "grounded legitimation of scientific intentionality."[222] For another, this reduction also conducts a leading back of the Husserlian position to its historical origins and thus, as we have seen, to its self-legitimation, which as a 'historical reduction' means the "restriction of history itself to its ostensive irrelative rational structure—

218. Ibid. In another place Husserl explicates this context more closely, in that he speaks of "the 'true' traditionality as traditionality of the truth which lies only in willing. [Therein] the will [is] in an 'authentic' sense a resolve for the absolute goal as something thoroughly known in its logicized form. . . . Therein all finite will is given up once and for all or sublated into its mere functionality in infinity" (Husserl, *Zur Phänomenologie der Intersubjektivität* vol. 3, 379), by which is intended in its immanent teleology "transcendental universal subjectivity" (ibid., 380).

219. See Lembeck, *Gegenstand Geschichte*, 162. In the sense of the meaning of a "return to historically unfolding consciousness, to historical reason aimed toward truth" (ibid.), see also Gerhard Funke, *Phänomenologie—Metaphysik oder Methode?* (Bonn: Bonvier Verlag Herbert Grundmann, 1972), 149. With regard to the second meaning of the "disregard of the merely factical-relative validity of traditionally conveyed philosophical prejudices as judgments not gained in originary evidence" advanced by Lembeck (*Gegenstand Geschichte*, 162), see David Carr, *Phenomenology and the Problem of History. A Study of Husserl's Transcendental Philosophy* (Evanston, IL: Northwestern University Press, 1974), 100, 178.

220. Lembeck, *Gegenstand Geschichte*, 162. See further Rudolf Böhm, *Vom Gesichtspunkt der Phänomenologie: Husserl-Studien*. (The Hague: Springer, 1968), 249.

221. Lembeck, *Gegenstand Geschichte*, 163.

222. Ibid. Appendix III of the *Krisis* demonstrates this in the context of geometry in an exemplary fashion.

without taking into account contingent circumstances and 'merely external' inessential factuality."[223]

Husserl's demonstration of the a priori lifeworld as that "new path of transcendental reduction," upon which he seeks to establish our contemporary historical lifeworldly relatedness as secondary, and thus to neutralize it,[224] nonetheless remains caught within its own historical situation. That is to say, the sought-after "'inner structure' presupposes, to begin with, a knowledge of this factual history, as much as its being kept continually in view."[225] In a certain degree this applies as well precisely to the philosophical discussion of one's own time, which shows itself exemplarily in Husserl's references, positioned within his own program, to Scheler and Heidegger,[226] although his way of looking upon the present is directed by the fact that he ultimately seeks to repudiate their critique. Consequently, a self-reflection capable of dialogue ceases, which, effective-historical, posits itself as conscious of the interconnection of his thinking in the meshwork of contemporary ways of posing the problem. For Husserl, rather, it is solely a matter of the possibility of promoting, by means of the transcendental *epoché* as the 'total conversion of the I,' a "*new will to life, the will to come to know himself in his whole prior and future predetermined being*: over and against wanting to come to know myself in the customary sense of *I as a human person* who has the horizon of the world, taken as the existing valid world, as a ground, stands *the coming to know the transcendental me, me, the ultimate and truly concrete ego*."[227]

223. Lembeck, *Gegenstand Geschichte*, 163.

224. See for example *Krisis*, 385: "As much as the scientist's activity of thought is called upon in his thinking of anything 'bound to time,' i.e., something bound to that which is merely factical in his present, or something valid to him as mere factical tradition, its form would likewise have a merely time-bound sense of being."

225. Lembeck, *Gegenstand Geschichte*, 163.

226. See Husserl, *Krisis*, 439.

227. Ibid., 472. As in Fichte, despite all differences in execution, the "I," as transcendental ego, thus becomes the irreducible beginning of philosophical reflection upon the possibility of apodictically certain self- and world knowledge. Herein, as has already been variously shown, Husserl's approach, just as much as that of idealism, proves to be constitutively bound to Descartes's thinking, insofar as the apodictic self-certainty of subjectivity precedes that of the true knowledge of the world, as an Archimedean point. See Husserl, *Erste Philosophie II*, 473: "The beginning must thus be nothing—nothing worldly. What remains left over? Naturally, the subjective itself, in which the world, in each case, already presents itself as existent in the form of these or those realities and horizons."

In this teleological aim, Husserl definitively takes leave of any serious possibility of a deliberation reflecting itself *as historical* on its own situation[228] in favor of reaching a possible posited "sensible, final harmony"[229] in transcendental phenomenology. For, even when he stresses "that we as philosophers, in accordance with the objective that the word 'philosophy' indicates, . . . are the *heirs* of the past,"[230] the historical reflection thus demanded remains for him determined systematically in detail "under *critical* consideration of that which manifests, in the objective and method, that ultimate originary authenticity, which, once glimpsed, *apodictically subjugates* the will."[231] And these are not the historical facticities, but rather the ideal sense of validity of the idea of transcendental subjectivity.[232]

As is self-evident, Husserl maintains the sense of validity of the idea of transcendental subjectivity in the tradition of the unity of consciousness and reason as a motive with the meaning of eternity, although temporally-historically his own historical situation yet determines itself through the radical placing into question of just this tradition, at least since Nietzsche and Freud. Husserl's dismissal of his own effective-historically determined situatedness means, at the same time, overlooking the fundamental fact

228. This becomes particularly clear in the *Krisis*, § 15.

229. Ibid, 74. "But whenever we are taught, through historical research, no matter how precisely, about such [philosophical] 'self-interpretations' (and even about those of an entire chain of philosophers), we yet experience nothing about that to which 'it' finally would will toward in the concealed unity of intentional inwardness, which alone forms the unity of history, in all these philosophers" (ibid.).

230. Ibid., 16.

231. Ibid. At another point: "The self-constitution of transcendental subjectivity as being directed into infinity to 'completeness,' to true self-preservation. . . . In addition: necessity of self-reflection in ever-higher levels, thus of a process of development of self-reflection up to transcendental self-reflection and its own systematic development" (Husserl, *Zur Phänomenologie der Intersubjektivität III*, 378).

232. Transcendentally founded subjectivity, in which the belief in the world constitutes itself, may not, as Gadamer emphasizes, be taken for that "I" "that is the self-constituted I encountered in the world, with all of its experiences of the world, the world of dreams, the world of children, the world of animals, the historical worlds, the problems of birth and death, the problem of sexes. The 'ego' is not intended as 'an I' alongside others, as existing in the world, but rather is the mere founding and ultimately founding ego in its absolute apodicticity" (Gadamer, "Wissenschaft von der Lebenswelt," 155). In view of this separation, or rather Husserl's intention standing behind it, Lembeck diagnoses an aporia precisely in relation to Husserl's mention of being an heir, since "the philosopher is not only as a philosopher a 'historical being,' but also as a personal subject. As such, however, it stands under the horizon-intentional founding causality of motivation. . . . Accordingly, even the philosopher requires a particular motivation, as a 'historical creature,' precisely to be a philosopher (Lembeck, *Gegenstand Geschichte*, 166).

that even his position, with all of its validity claims, is in advance already inscribed in a completely determined vein of tradition, one that as such requires *historical* qualification. In wanting to claim its due, as Husserl continually does, in its validity in the face of the present, it seems possible and necessary only when, in its supposed original function of directing knowledge and activity in relation to the professed sense-generative continuity of its development, it no longer possesses this very continuity, but rather records massive sites of fracture, and in this sense plunges into a crisis.

Husserl takes it upon himself to combat this crisis, wherein in the midst of contemporary condemnations, historically considered, he draws out a traditionalistic perspective, in which he attests to an ahistorical universal validity. Thereby, however, the contingency of his own situatedness disappears, which means its historicity and perspectivism as conditions of his own validity claims disappear as well from out of the level of reflection in favor of an alleged final establishment of the sense of the origin, a sense that lies in the meaning of the task of philosophy, in phenomenology. From it he expects the possibility of spelling out its sensible content invariantly—that is, ahistorically and transcendentally—in the mode of an assumed telos of reason, without thereby seeing that the final goal he assumes is itself only the result of a specifiable historical process. Seen thus, it confirms the suspicion expressed by Lembeck "whether the historical reduction [to an invariant rational structure] does not eliminate, in a certain way, its own presuppositions,"[233] insofar as this reduction itself is a "function of historical consciousness"[234] and can find its illumination only in an effective-historically reflected historical experience.

Husserl takes notice of this historical experience only insofar as he ultimately battles restoratively against it in the hypostatization of his own position as the sole possible answer to the present crisis of science and philosophy. The task, as a philosopher, of unfolding in his time just this time as reality in its ontological structures so that the situation of philosophy he perceives as a crisis is recovered from out of the *historicity of thinking* itself and as such in phenomenological reflection, is not a task that he poses.

---

233. Lembeck, *Gegenstand Geschichte*, 166.

234. Ibid. "It is historical consciousness not merely as the transcendental fixed point of historical knowledge—it is above all historically situated consciousness, which is to say: It is historically motivated consciousness" (ibid.). Therefore, however, it is shown that the historical reduction is "a philosophical process which has as its own condition that which it is to abandon as inessential" (ibid., 167).

The break that he experiences with regard to the idealistic inheritance of philosophy motivates him much more to a "reflecting reappropriation and an ideational restoration of the philosophical tradition."[235] And yet—how else can the crisis of philosophy and the sciences, indeed of European humanity, as the original lecture title of the 'Krisis' read, be grasped diagnostically, if not in exact regard to just the historical facticities, and thus the ontically real factical situation in its manifold entanglement in the concrete, historical environment of life?

But insofar as Husserl bypasses the factically concrete lifeworld in its historicity in favor of an intended final sense by means of the transcendental *epoché* and reduction, he not only takes the sting out of his diagnosis, but at the same time he endorses the possibility of a therapy, that is to say, the possibility of the demonstration of a practicable way out of the crisis. For this manifests itself only in the access to the concrete situationally bound experience of reality and its real store of problems, and this only when humanity's involvement in the crisis is illuminated as existentiell historical experience by means of an existentially founded material analysis.

Only thus can the 'inheritor of the past' to whom Husserl appeals be fathomed and critically appropriated. This is possible only in the sense of a proper present horizon in its contingent constitution as a reflective *hermeneutics of facticity* that came to be historically and is equally open to the future. It already contains within itself as such a renunciation of any teleological and, in general, historically overarching pattern of thinking uninterrupted in sense that would constantly run the de facto risk of perceiving history in its past facticity in the function of a mere illustration of its self-legitimation.

Out of Husserl's philosophical presuppositions, which in relation to history assume a "sense of truth that 'lives' within it [that is], exists in its hidden transcendental universal will,"[236] such a letting oneself in is, however, without relevance to facticity.[237] Bound therein, the *unity of reason*,[238]

---

235. Ibid., 165.

236. Husserl, *Zur Phänomenologie der Intersubjektivität III*, 379.

237. "Every conception of . . . every opinion about 'the' world, has its ground in the pregiven world. Precisely from this ground have I freed myself through the epoché; I stand above the world that has become for me, in a completely unique sense, the phenomenon" (Husserl, *Krisis*, 155).

238. Husserl grasps this unity so narrowly that "reason admits no distinction between 'theoretical,' 'practical,' 'aesthetic,' and whatever else" (ibid., 275). This telos of unity, grasped "as self-understanding in the form of philosophy" (ibid., 276), is, according to Wolfgang Wel-

constituting itself in the extramundane transcendental subjectivity and motivating it correspondingly in its claims, stands beyond any question. As its functionary, he sees the philosopher acting in the sense of the "heroism of reason"[239] that he propagates.

sch, "historically a blatant regression to the time before Kant" (*Vernunft: Die zeitgenössische Vernunftkritik und das Konzept der transversalen Vernunft* [Frankfurt: Suhrkamp, 1995], 68), since Kant's differentiation of modes of reason is here already rejected in the formulation of its possibilities. Reason is for Husserl precisely the "title for ideas and ideals valid as 'absolute,' 'eternal,' 'supratemporal,' 'unconditioned'" (Husserl, *Krisis*, 7), and thus Husserl's conception of a 'universal science of reason' is integrated with "the most ancient hopes for total knowledge and the modern aspirations of a mathesis universalis" (Welsch, *Vernunft*, 69). Welsch thus characterizes Husserl's proposed solution, unfolded in the *Krisis*, as a way out of the crisis as "a progress by means of regress" (ibid., 62).

239. Husserl, *Krisis*-Lecture, 348. This "ethical-existentiell mission of phenomenology" (Welter, *Der Begriff der Lebenswelt*, 43), unifying itself in the highest "claim to authority and the most rigorous duty to service" (Karl Schuhmann, "Lebenswelt als Unterlage der Phänomenologie," in *Lebenswelt und Wissenschaft in der Philosophie Edmund Husserls*, ed. Elisabeth Ströker [Frankfurt: Klostermann, 1979], 87), finds in the gesture of a "visionary enthusiasm" (ibid., 88) its concise expression when Husserl preaches: "We are . . . in our philosophizing functionaries of humanity. The entire personal responsibility for our own true being as philosophers in our intrapersonal vocation bears at the same time within it the responsibility for the true being of humanity, which only as being is directed to a telos and, if at all, can only come to realization through philosophy—through us, if we are philosophers in earnest" (*Krisis*, 15).

With reason thus posited as a teleological model for human history, not only is an explicitly Eurocentric picture of development assumed (see also the *Krisis*-Lecture, 319; Biemel, "Doxa und Episteme," 10; on this complex of questions in general, see Walter Bröcker, "Europäologie," Allgemeine Zeitschrift für Philosophie, (1978), 3:1–22). Moreover, as Lembeck points out, here the profile "of an ethical voluntarism bound to a metaphysics of reason" (*Gegenstand Geschichte*, 169; cf. Husserl's confirmation of this, among other places, in the relevant discussions in *Zur Phänomenologie der Intersubjektivität III*, 379, 668) is discernible, which makes clear in its programmatic postulates that for Husserl it was philosophy itself that, in neglecting its self-development as 'rigorous science,' is culpable for the general crisis of rationalism and its resulting aberration in skepticism and objectivism.

For Husserl, only the self-renewal of philosophy as a 'philosophia perennis' in the form of transcendental phenomenology can lead out of this aberration, which, however, thereby at the same time takes on the inheritance of metaphysics as prima philosophia. See Elisabeth Ströker, "Edmund Husserls Phänomenologie: Philosophia Perennis in der Krise der europäischen Kultur," in *Profile der Phänomenologie: Zum 50. Todestag Edmund Husserls*, ed. Ernst Wolfgang Orth (Freiburg: Alber, 1989) 11–38. That these rationalist metaphysical intentions, as they are particularly graspable throughout the late work of Husserl, are not the sole fruits of his last productive phase can be seen in the early testimony of the lecture—closely tied to the LOGOS essay—of the 1910/11 winter semester, titled "Logik als Theorie der Erkenntnis" (in Guy van Kerckhoven, "Die Grundansätze von Husserls Konfrontation mit Dilthey im Licht der geschichtlichen Selbstzeugnisse," in Dilthey und der Wandel des Philosophiebegriffs seit dem 19. Jahrhundert: Studien zu Dilthey und Brentano, Mach, Nietzsche, Twardowski, Husserl, Heidegger, ed. Ernst Wolfgang Orth, 159.

The transcendental "I" and humanity are thereby equated as the "subjectivity intentionally effecting the achievement of world-validity in community."[240] Husserl's conception of reason determined in this sense surpasses and drowns out for him every defense as erroneous that wants to bind the leading voice of reason intramundanely in the chorus of reflection to existentiell factical contingent experiences in which, as will be shown, in contemplation upon them, rationality disperses itself plurally and relationally.

But if the way is pointed in this direction, any project of a telos of a final grounding of the absolute *single* reason, formulated as much monologically as monolithically, becomes questionable, and at the same time reveals itself as an illusion of the singularity of the lifeworld claimed by Husserl in opposition to a plurality of lifeworlds, which extracts that phenomenal horizon of experience from finite human existence within which the irresolvable processes of self-understanding carry themselves out in always new refractions and facets. Seen in this way, to borrow from Welsch, "Husserl's traditionalistic rational strategy . . . halts before the threshold of reality."[241]

To conceive this reality, this 'concrete lifeworld' in its plural and heterogeneous structure in thinking, means no longer thinking the existentiell, experienced, factical totality of my carrying out my life with regard to the unifying achievement for itself as a universal synthesis.[242] The

240. Husserl, *Krisis*, 178.
241. Welsch, *Vernunft*, 70.
242. In the face of being interwoven in this vertically and horizontally variable lifeworldly multiplicity, the task demanded of the individual nonetheless remains—self-dictated for the most part—of knotting into a whole the heterogeneous, and sometimes thoroughly disparate, in an act of integration. Thereby life lived in the 'abiding style of the normal form' has for the most part, with regard to its self-description, the tendency of wanting to let the wholeness appear for itself as a unity in the midst of the multiplicity of different relations as well as chronological stages. Fully knowing that it cannot be autarchical, it stages itself not least by means of a self-choosing of its ends determined by reason as the 'one way of life' with suspicion of the effective and valid projection from Aristotle beyond Descartes up until Husserl of an autonomously projected, successful life, so that on the stage of a life threatened by diverse failures and determined through contingency, the vision of a θεωρία, of a successful life in theoretical knowledge as science, remains preserved in its function, considered in terms of unity, as the ideal of authenticity.

Apart from this diversely problematic vision there is, however, indeed a phenomenal region of human experience of wholeness. In fact, my life becomes experienceable to me in totality and as a whole as ontic-existentiell in a distinct manner in my life of feeling. This makes human affectivity into a privileged candidate for the hermeneutical question of self-relation, that is to say, of self-understanding, and is thus unfolded by Heidegger in the context of his

unification as in the above-mentioned Heideggerian sense of reflecting self-comprehension carries itself out rather, to speak with Waldenfels, "in processes of *transformation* and *translation,* through which the grounding differences are in no way sublated."[243] Seen in this way "the *one* lifeworld [transforms itself] into *a network and a chain of separate worlds.*"[244] It is thereby essential to attend to the fact that its relations, like the modes of its being related to one another, are to be grasped neither pervasively in the sense of a hierarchy, nor as a founding and authenticating order in the direction of a teleology toward an order founding and authenticating an encompassing unity.

This decentering is not to be equated with that relativism so feared by Husserl and others, perhaps in the variant 'anything goes.' Rather, it is a matter, as Waldenfels stresses, of a "network of heterogeneous, yet manifoldly interwoven, not only excluding but also intersecting, fields of rationality, discourses, forms of life, lifeworlds,"[245] to which we will return in detail in the further course of this investigation. They have "many knots, points of transition, possibilities of translation, even zones of conflict, yet no unitary middle or endpoints."[246] At one stroke the thought of a totality of reason must be given up; that is, it develops "in fields of meaning, in rationalities—reason as a *teleological whole* unravels into lines of development."[247]

For the self-relation carried out in disclosures of sense as self-understanding, this means that, as we have pointed out in the hermeneutic analyses of part 1 with a view to understanding oneself in reading and writing, a *fundamental opacity* is proper to it. The orientation in the lifeworld as an achievement of understanding that is grounded by an understanding of oneself therein accordingly never attains to an actual transparency nor to

---

existential ontology as the equiprimordial connection of understanding and state of mind [Befindlichkeit]. That is, the fact that the human as a complex being lives in a complex world finds a possibility, in the question of the accessibility to itself in the manner of a holistic self-givenness in Heidegger's approach, of answering this in the inclusion of the fundamental achievement of knowledge of the feelings as self- and world disclosure, without having to alter the sense-strategic paths of the delineated tradition.

243. Waldenfels, "Die Abgründigkeit des Sinnes," 27.

244. Ibid. See also Werner Marx, "Lebenswelt und Lebenswelten," in *Vernunft und Welt,* 63–77.

245. Bernhard Waldenfels, "Rationalisierung der Lebenswelt—ein Projekt," in *In den Netzen der Lebenswelt,* 117.

246. Ibid.

247. Waldenfels, "Die Abgründigkeit des Sinnes," 27.

a self-certainty, which is the dream of a philosophy of the subject and of consciousness from Descartes up to Husserl.

The lifeworld, which no longer possesses a unifying center, no endpoint, is marked by a "simultaneity of incompossibles,"[248] as Waldenfels puts it following Merleau-Ponty. That is, our experiences reach further than the cultural-social orders of our experience, which as Foucault for example has shown in reflection upon their conditions and structures, are determined as orders of reason through contingency and refer, precisely in their contingency, to the connection between reason and history. That means that reason is itself determined historically in its order and as such structures the everyday space of experience.

For this basis of everyday lifeworldly experiences, it is shown with regard to the hermeneutical exposure of the dimension of the self that at no point in its disclosure does a central perspective arise from which the human relation to self and world can be homogeneously combined into a unity. To this extent the ground of the natural lifeworld, with the experiences of contingency encountered everywhere and at each moment, remains a significant, indeed a necessary corrective against intellectual flights of thinking. As Plato had already shown in the *Symposium*, the *eros* of philosophy is a *daimon*, begotten by Poros and Penia, roaming about out of doors on the streets, sleeping in doorways, and nonetheless ever striving after insight.[249]

---

248. Waldenfels, "Lebenswelt zwischen Alltäglichem und Unalltäglichem," 115. See also Waldenfels, *Ordnung im Zwielicht* (Frankfurt: Suhrkamp, 1987).
249. See Plato, *Symposium*, 203 d–e.

PART THREE

SELF-UNDERSTANDING AND THE HISTORICAL WORLD: BASIC TRAITS OF A HERMENEUTICAL ONTOLOGY OF FACTICITY

We are all connected in such a motley and informal way out of nothing but patches and tatters that every cloth plays its own game at each moment. And there is just as much difference between us and ourselves as between us and others.

Michel de Montaigne

My soul is a hidden orchestra; I don't know which instruments, violins and harps, tympani and trumpets, it plays and roars within me. I know myself only as a symphony.

Fernando Pessoa

CHAPTER ONE

THE HERMENEUTICAL TURN:

HEIDEGGER'S CRITICAL DIALOGUE WITH

HUSSERLIAN PHENOMENOLOGY

§ 25. Husserl versus Heidegger. On Situating their Disagreement

The lifeworld as the pretheoretical world in which we live—with a view
to the question of human self-relations, how are we to make it adequately
accessible to a philosophical thematization? This question is all the more
urgent insofar as the critical objections that have arisen in the course of
the discussion of Husserl's last great transcendental meditation are taken
as valid. That the objection against the Husserlian conception shows itself
to be more than a facile detection of mistakes is something of a triviality in
the face of the circumstance that here the high road of modern philosophy
has doubtless reached a climax once more.

In the vision initiated by Descartes of a grounding of knowledge
upon a complete absence of presuppositions, Husserl brackets the (life)
world, as we have seen, with the end of "absolute, final truth transcending
all relativity."[1] That means that the path leads in the Cartesian sense of
the "pre-given world to the *world-experiencing subjectivity,* and thus to the
subjectivity of consciousness in general,"[2] which in turn for Husserl leads
in phenomenological analysis to a demonstration of transcendentally reduced consciousness, for which, in the transcendental solitude of the ego,

---

1. Edmund Husserl, "Phänomenologie und Anthropologie," in *Aufsätze und Vorträge*
(*1922–1937*), *Husserliana,* ed. Thomas Nenon and Hans Rainer Sepp (Dordrecht: Kluwer, 1989,
27:166.
2. Ibid., 167.

the bracketed world is now only a mere "validity-phenomenon of the flow of experience, of consciousness in general."[3]

If Husserl emphatically demands "putting the thumbscrews to consciousness, or rather, to the transcendental ego, so that it betrays to us its secrets,"[4] it is no surprise when, in the forced confession of an a priori and universal world-knowledge, which he celebrates as phenomenological insight into *"the pure ratio of the world,"*[5] the pressure marks are still clearly discernible. As much as Husserl struggles to justify the "consequent renunciation of the world in the transcendental reduction"[6] as the necessary path "to a true, final world-knowledge,"[7] he does not succeed in silencing the critique that, behind all of his attempts at a finally grounded knowledge, he lets the phrase '*factical life,*' as if written in invisible ink, come to appearance, and this becomes visible for all when the 'hermeneutical reagent' flows into the handling of the problem of human self- and world-understanding.

The conflict bound up with this and jarring to the foundations of its understanding of philosophy emerges quite intuitively in Husserl's Berlin lecture, which he later called "Phenomenology and Anthropology."[8] Here he unfolds with programmatic weight his own transcendental approach in opposition to the rapidly growing inclinations toward a philosophical anthropology that he perceived even within the so-called phenomenological movement.[9] Although he named only Dilthey and Scheler in connection with this tendency in his lecture, for Husserl, the actual addressee in this philosophical rivalry is Martin Heidegger.[10]

3. Ibid., 171.

4. Ibid., 177.

5. Ibid., 166.

6. Ibid., 173.

7. Ibid.

8. Presented to the *Kant-Gesellschaften* first on June 1, 1931 in Frankfurt, then again in Berlin on June 10, 1931, and in Halle on June 16, 1931. On the detailed circumstances of Husserl's only lecture tour in Germany, see the "Editor's Introduction," ibid, 21ff.

9. See ibid., 164.

10. Even when Husserl did not present himself in the manner of a teacher openly at odds with his former prized pupil, but rather propounded his program with the sober objectivity of a pathos proper to him, the object at issue, which it was necessary for him to resist, was nonetheless the Heideggerian one. And Heidegger, even after decades, still received this lecture in the sense of a *mea res agitur* as Husserl's reckoning with him (see "SPIEGEL-Gespräch mit Martin Heidegger," in *Martin Heidegger im Gespräch*, ed. Günter Neske and Emil Kettering [Pfullingen: Neske, 1988], 89; see also Karl Schuhmann, "Zu Heideggers Spiegel-Gespräch über Husserl," in *Zeitschrift für philosophische Forschung* [1978], 32:591–612). If Heidegger empha-

At one point in the lecture this implicit exchange with Heidegger comes to light in a particularly striking manner. After Husserl has once more referred to the fact that the possibility of phenomenological research depends upon "the discovery of a method of correlation research, a method of inquiring back into intentional objectivity in a concretely revealing way,"[11] he stresses that a genuine analysis of consciousness would thus be

sizes that Husserl's personal reasons for this reckoning remained obscure to him, some of the Husserlian motives can be made plausible with a look at the current state of the text.

First of all, it is to be recalled that Husserl's disappointment over Heidegger's development and the philosophical break with him, carried out internally at least, two years earlier, may have ultimately become manifest in the summer months of 1929 when Husserl disputed *Sein und Zeit* in detail (see "Randbemerkungen zu Heideggers 'Sein und Zeit' und 'Kant und das Problem der Metaphysik'" ed. Roland Breeur and Steven Spileers, *Husserl Studies* [1994], 11:3–63). Against the background of the insights into the fundamental distinctness of the Heideggerian phenomenological approach that he gained thereby, Husserl could no longer maintain any further illusions about the continuance of his work through Heidegger, and moreover he believed he had to count Heidegger in the camp of those opponents whom, already in the LOGOS essay ["Philosophie als strenge Wissenschaft," *LOGOS* 1 (1910), 3:289–341], he had found guilty of nonscientificity in their thinking. And now, scarcely two years after the decisive summer lecture, in June of 1931 at the University of Berlin (where Heidegger, having enjoyed a good year prior to that, had obtained an honorable reputation at the urging of the Prussian minister of culture and student of Husserl, Adolf Grimme), he 'took to the field [against] the anthropological deviation and softening' of phenomenology; he would thus have certainly presupposed that one could call a spade a spade here without finding it necessary, *expressis verbis*, to speak out against his successor, whom he had himself recommended, to the Freiburg *Lehrstuhl*.

The extent to which Husserl took himself to be affected and stung by Heidegger's attitude can be gathered vividly from a whole series of letters, e.g., his letter to Alexander Pfänder on January 6, 1931, in *Briefwechsel*, 2:181 and Dietrich Mahnke on January 8, 1931 in *Briefwechsel* (Dordrecht: Springer, 1994), 3:473. A further testimony in the series of documents of the break with Heidegger is the 1930 afterword to *Ideen I*, published in the *Jahrbuch*—where *Sein und Zeit* was first published—that repudiated approaches on the part of the "new anthropology, its philosophy of 'existence'" ("Nachwort zu meinen Ideen zu einer reinen Phänomenologie und phänomenologischen Philosophie," in *Ideen III*, ed. Marly Biemel [The Hague: Martinus Nijhoff, 1971], 138), by which he meant Heidegger, directed against Husserl's *lebensphilosophie*.

In a clarity that leaves nothing to be desired and thus directly calls for a more extensive citation, Husserl emphasizes that he "can in no way give warrant to all of the objections raised in these pages . . . of the general and fundamental inability to arrive at originary-concrete, practical-active subjectivity and at the problem of so-called existence. They are all based upon misunderstandings and ultimately upon . . . the fact that one has not understood the fundamental innovation of the 'phenomenological reduction' and thus the ascent from mundane subjectivity (of the human) to 'transcendental subjectivity'; that one is thus stuck in an anthropology, whether it be empirical or *a priori*, which according to my teachings has in no way reached the specifically philosophical ground, and that means for philosophy a lapse into 'transcendental anthropologism,' or rather, 'psychologism'" (ibid., 140).

11. Husserl, *Phänomenologie und Anthropologie*, 177.

that of a "*hermeneutics of conscious life,* as it were,"[12] which he determines more closely in the sense of "an incessant intending of entities (the identical), intentionally constituting the entities in themselves in manifolds of consciousness essentially belonging to them."[13]

This 'so-called hermeneutics' captures in a word the *central concept* of the *phenomenological turn* carried out by Heidegger, yet not in order to follow it, but rather in order to formulate—to demonstrate already in taking it up—the rebuttal that in the realm of phenomenology even a hermeneutics at its core must drive transcendental analyses of consciousness, insofar as it does not want to abandon the claim to genuine, that is, phenomenologically secured, scientificity. It is precisely this (in his view) theoreticist narrowing that Heidegger's new approach to phenomenology opposes most decisively. As will be seen, its reformulation in the sense of a hermeneutical phenomenology—or rather, phenomenological hermeneutics[14]—that preserves a programmatic shape (most likely with Husserl in mind)[15] in the famous seventh section of *Sein und Zeit* clearly dates back to before the revision phase of Heidegger's principal work, to the start of his duties as a lecturer in the war emergency semester of 1919.

With a view to these early years, Hannah Arendt speaks in a turn of phrase that has become famous about the fact that due to the transcripts of his lecture courses circulating, Heidegger's name travelled "throughout all Germany like a rumor of the secret king."[16] This was confirmed—and yet remained up to the 1980s little more than rumor—above all through the personal testimonies of those who were then on hand to hear Heidegger and who, like Oskar Becker, Hans Jonas, Ludwig Landgrebe, Karl Löwith and Joachim Ritter, to name a few, themselves acquired prestige and influence within philosophical circles. In particular, it was Hans-Georg Gadamer who referred time and again back to the early Heidegger, and it was Heidegger who thereby played an important role in the working out of

12. Ibid. (emphasis added)

13. Ibid.

14. Heidegger first employs the term 'phenomenological hermeneutics' in the lecture of the 1919 summer semester, "Phänomenologie und transzendentale Wertphilosophie," in Heidegger, *Zur Bestimmung der Philosophie,* ed. Bernd Heimbüchel (Frankfurt: Klostermann, 1999), *GA* 56–57:126.

15. See Friedrich-Wilhelm von Herrmann, *Der Begriff der Phänomenologie bei Heidegger und Husserl* (Frankfurt: Klostermann, 1981).

16. Hannah Arendt, "Martin Heidegger ist achtzig Jahre alt," in *Antwort: Martin Heidegger im Gespräch,* 232–246, ed. Günter Neske and Emil Kettering (Pfullingen: Neske, 1988).

Gadamer's own hermeneutics.[17] Since 1985, in the framework of the *Gesamtausgabe*, which was begun with the publication of the lectures from his years as a *Dozent*, each volume has been able to confirm, as much impressively as emphatically, the judgment of his students from that time. It is thus now evident that with Heidegger's philosophical approach in the war emergency semester of 1919 new ground was broken, which can rightly be characterized as the *breakthrough in hermeneutical phenomenology, that is, phenomenological hermeneutics*,[18] and which has kindled, precisely in the exchange with Husserl, one of "the most provocative dialogues in our century on the issue of philosophy."[19]

§ 26. The Hermeneutical Stance on a Second View

To take what is proper to Heidegger's transmutation of phenomenology more closely into view—as the working out of a general, consequential conception for hermeneutics as such—stands at the center of the following analyses. However, instead of going into it in medias res it is necessary to engage in a few intermediate thoughts pertaining to the method as well as the content. These seem advisable in order once more to call to memory

17. On the impact Heidegger had upon Gadamer in the early 1920s, see Jean Grondin, "Gadamer vor Heidegger," *Internationale Zeitschrift für Philosophie* (1996), 222–226. In addition to those listed above, this illustrious circle of Heidegger's students in the early years includes Walter Bröcker, Max Horkheimer, Wilhelm Kamlah, Fritz Kaufmann, Gottfried Martin, and Hans Reiner. It would in many ways be a worthwhile task, in light of the effective history of Heideggerian philosophy, to add a further chapter that investigates possible stimuli on the part of early Heideggerian thinking on such scholars, to which one could add Eugen Fink, Herbert Marcuse and Max Müller. In concert with the well-documented connecting strands between Heidegger, Arendt, and Gadamer, in the intersecting areas of appropriation and renunciation, contact and breakage, one could develop, moreover, a piece of philosophical historiography that aids in clarifying the contours of the profile of the philosophical landscape as it took shape after the Second World War. Eric Jakob's study, *Martin Heidegger und Hans Jonas: Die Metaphysik der Subjektivität und die Krise der technologischen Zivilisation* (Tübingen: Francke, 1996), makes progress in just this direction.

18. Cf. Theodor Kisiel, "Das Kriegsnotsemester 1919: Heideggers Durchbruch zur hermeneutischen Phänomenologie," *Philosophisches Jahrbuch* (1992), 99:105–122.

19. Manfred Riedel, *Hören auf die Sprache: Die akroamatische Dimension der Hermeneutik* (Frankfurt: Suhrkamp, 1990), 76. On the cultural-historical background of this dialogue, see Otto Pöggeler's study, "'Eine Epoche gewaltigen Werdens': Die Freiburger Phänomenologie in ihrer Zeit," in *Die Freiburger Phänomenologie* ed. Ernst Wolfgang Orth, (Freiburg: Alber, 1996), 9–32; see also Pöggeler's *Neue Wege mit Heidegger* (Freiburg: Alber, 1992), 184–201.

what is at issue in the present investigation with regard to Heidegger, and what can and cannot be expected in what follows.

First of all, it is to be established that with the publication of the early lecture courses a lacuna, extremely significant for Heidegger studies, is filled. Since the mid-1970s, with the inauguration of the *Gesamtausgabe*, once the immediate prehistory and the history of working out *Sein und Zeit* as it is portrayed in the Marburg lectures had become discernible,[20] the first span of that phase of Heideggerian thinking had come to light in the publication of his *Dozenten-Vorlesungen*—a phase that had remained for decades in the darkness of his nearly twelve-year publishing silence, a silence that was followed the release of his 1916 *Habilitationsschrift, Duns Scotus' Doctrine of Categories and Meaning.*[21]

20. Heidegger's expansive exchange with Husserl, which has become accessible in the lecture volumes of the Marburg years, initiated in its wake a new interpretive attention to Heidegger's relation to Husserl, primarily in light of *Sein und Zeit*, its prehistory and context. See, among others, Franco Volpi, "Heidegger in Marburg: Die Auseinandersetzung mit Husserl," *Philosophischer Literaturanzeiger* (1984), 37:48–69; Rainer Thurnher, "Husserls 'Ideen' und Heideggers 'Sein und Zeit,'" in *Gelehrtenrepublik—Lebenswelt: Edmund Husserl und Alfred Schütz in der Krisis der phänomenologischen Bewegung*, ed. Angelika Bäumer and Michael Benedikt (Vienna: Passagen, 1993), 145–168; Burt C. Hopkins, *Intentionality in Husserl and Heidegger: The Problem of the Original Method and Phenomenon of Phenomenology* (Dordrecht: Springer,1993); Daniel O. Dahlstrom, "Heidegger's Critique of Husserl," in *Reading Heidegger from the Start: Essays in His Earliest Thought*, ed. Theodore Kisiel and John van Buren (New York: SUNY Press, 1994), 231–244; Jacques Taminiaux, "The Husserlian Heritage in Heidegger's Notion of the Self," *Reading Heidegger from the Start*, 269–290; Walter Biemel, "Heideggers Stellung zur Phänomenologie in der Marburger Zeit," in *Gesammelte Schriften* (Stuttgart: Frommann-Holzboog, 1996), 1:265–333.

21. The door into this "hidden chamber" opened a crack in 1973 when Heidegger's "Anmerkungen zu Karl Jaspers 'Psychologie der Weltanschauungen'" (*Wegmarken, GA*, ed. Friedrich-Wilhelm von Herrmann [Frankfurt: Klostermann, 1976], 9:1–44) was published. Over a period of twelve years the *Anmerkungen* offered the only significant insight into the thinking of these early years. Nonetheless, they received an astonishingly meager amount of attention. It is possible that the general distance from Heidegger of those years was on the whole not very conducive to a larger resonance; yet perhaps more decisive for the broad lack of attention could have been that the text attracted little attention even within the restricted circle of Heidegger interpreters. Only in Otto Pöggeler's *Der Denkweg Martin Heideggers* (3rd ed., Pfullingen: Neske, 1990), which was the authoritative cicerone for Heidegger's oeuvre prior to the publication of the *Gesamtausgabe*, is there a reference, in passing, to the admission of the immense significance that Jaspers' writings had for the young Heidegger (169; a self-revision of this estimation has since been carried out: see Pöggeler, *Neue Wege mit Heidegger*, 186).

Exceptions to this trend (which seem to prove the rule) include the noteworthy references by Ernst Tugendhat in *Selbstbewußtsein und Selbstbestimmung: Sprachanalytische Interpretationen* (Frankfurt: Suhrkamp, 1979), 36, and prior to that the detailed account by David Krell, "Toward *Sein und Zeit*: Heidegger's Early Review (1919–1921) of Jaspers' *Psychologie der Weltanschauungen*," *Journal of the British Society for Phenomenology* (1975), 6:147–156. Since the

The question how 'Martin Heidegger's path of thinking' can be discerned on the basis of the study of his own texts can now be led to a sufficient step-by-step answer. In this sense, Heidegger scholarship on the changed place of his texts has to this point also accepted to a great extent that the question of the history of influence, which investigates Heidegger's explicit and implicit references, marks a significant field of work.[22] As exciting, as justified, and necessary as this genealogical posing of the question is, the reconstructive evolutionist exhibition of Heidegger's immanent history of thinking is *not* actually either a theme nor the goal of the present study.[23] Yet the boundaries are fluid. For the course of investigation is naturally connected already from the beginning in the selection of its singular stages with a grounding interest in *how Heidegger became what he is to us*—and bound up with the question *what he can be for us today.*

With this type of formula, the place of departure of the present work can be designated as much as the direction pursued in the following re-

---

beginning of the publication of the early lectures and in particular since the appearance of the *Briefwechsel 1920–1963* (ed. Walter Biemel and Hans Saner [Frankfurt: Klostermann, 1990]) between Heidegger and Jaspers, a turn [*Wende*] in the reception of this text can be noted, a text which for Hermann Schmitz constitutes a "cornerstone in the history of the construction of Heidegger's philosophy" (*Husserl und Heidegger* [Bonn: Bouvier, 1996], 173).

22. In addition to the monographs by Claudius Strube, Theodor Kisiel, and John van Buren mentioned in § 2, note 20, there are also investigations that pursue these intentions more closely: the *Dilthey-Jahrbuch*, vol. 4 (1986–1987), ed. Frithjof Rodi, in which are assembled the contributions to a symposium on the early Heidegger, contributions that constitute the first substantial document of a more extensive engagement. Since, however, the interpretational theses of that time were by and large worked out on the basis of postscripts to his lectures, these interpretations require—insofar as they are supported by the postscripts—a probing counterreading based upon lecture volumes of the *Gesamtausgabe* that have been published in the intervening years. Further references can be found in these collections: *Reading Heidegger from the Start*; *Heidegger 1919–1929: De l'herméneutique de la facticité à la métaphysique du Dasein*, Jean-François Courtine, ed. (Paris: Vrin, 1996). In addition, Martin Gessman offers insights of a more restricted scope in "Die Entdeckung des frühen Heidegger: Neuere Literatur zur Dezennie vor 'Sein und Zeit,'" *Philosophische Rundschau* (1996), 43:215–232. In the way of more recent, more or less detailed portraits of the whole of Heideggerian thought, wherein this genetic aspect plays a significant role in reference to Heidegger's early work, see Thomas Rentsch, *Martin Heidegger—Das Sein und der Tod: Eine kritische Einführung* (Munich: Piper, 1989); Dieter Thomä, *Die Zeit des Selbst und die Zeit danach: Zur Kritik der Textgeschichte Martin Heideggers 1910–1976* (Frankfurt: Suhrkamp, 1990); Günter Figal, *Heidegger zur Einführung* (Hamburg: Junius, 1992); Carl Friedrich Gethmann, *Dasein: Erkennen und Handeln: Heidegger im phänomenologischen Kontext* (Berlin: De Gruyter, 1993); Jean Greisch, *Ontologie et temporalité: Esquisse d'une interprétation intégrale de "Sein und Zeit"* (Paris: Presses Universitaires de France, 1994); Hermann Schmitz, *Husserl und Heidegger* (Bonn: Bouvier, 1986).

23. On the 'evolutionistic interpretation,' see the condensed portrait in Gethmann, *Dasein: Erkennen und Handeln*, 248–251.

flections. For the problem of human self-experience in the form of the question concerning the *self-relation as world-relation* in its historical disposition recurs in the approach of Heidegger's posing of the question to a concept of experience, as it can first be formulated in this form in the wake of the ontological turn [*Wende*] to hermeneutics he initiated. Hence the situation of the author in view of his own critical self-understanding as author of this study and the philosophical problems posing themselves to him in connection with its working out prove themselves in advance to be inspired and accompanied by the leading voice of a thinking that communicates itself uniquely in the angle of refraction of the lectures of his texts as the objectivations relevant to interpretation for us. *These texts are today—and that hermeneutically designates their effective-historical status— always already and alone perceivable to us only in the canon of the commentaries accompanying them, so that each of Heidegger's readings manifests itself as a reading of Heidegger's reading.*

The concept of 'commentary' that we appeal to here is so broad that interpretations of Heidegger's life and work are to be grasped not only in the narrower sense, but also in the historical fullness of reactions to this thinking that has left behind its traces in the contour of the present. The present, as is proved still more precisely in the course of the investigation, is always *my or our lifeworldly present* and therefore means more than only a manifoldness of spatial and temporal positing fixable as here and now. It designates that field of relation in which a life is situated in its being carried out and whose spatial and temporal dimensions must be grasped in a sense specific to existence, which is to say, as always already historical.[24] In its subject-relative, or rather existence-relative, ontological structure, the present as a phenomenon, in the face of the concrete surrender to the ontical present appearing therein, nevertheless remains at most unexpressed, but as a horizon for the present itself is always the facilitation of its appearing.[25]

---

24. Merleau-Ponty investigates how, for example, objectively considered representations of space show themselves to be historically determined (*Phänomenologie der Wahrnehmung*, 448); in this context, see § 23, note 175. On the ontological structure of an existence-specific spatiality, see *Sein und Zeit*, §§ 22–24, 102–113.

25. On this posing of the question, see the conceptually rich study by Gerd Haeffner, *In der Gegenwart Leben: Auf der Spur eines Urphänomens* (Stuttgart: Kohlhammer, 1996). In setting out from the consideration that no one can decide the age in which he lives, Haeffner inquires into this issue, wherein he connects historical investigations on the thematization of the present in Pascal, Kierkegaard, Bloch, Buber, and Weil with his own systematic concerns at exhibit-

In its relation to the subject, the present as such becomes thematic and it must be so even where it concerns, as in the given connection, structurally opening to oneself, by means of hermeneutical reflection, one's own situation as interpreter for the tasks of interpretation posited here and now in its presuppositions. Seen thus, the exchange with Heidegger is always already enmeshed within the effective history of his thinking; it updates this history as its part and it is no longer possible to step outside of it. For even Heidegger's texts, which in their reception have first and foremost triggered this effect, have become in the meantime such an integral part of their effective history that they cannot be disengaged from it; that is, attending to them is only possible in and as *a movement into this effective history.* The question of Heideggerian thinking's actualization in effective-historical consciousness does not, taken hermeneutically, decide its efficacy per se, yet it does determine the treatment of this thinking in that it qualifies the method of interpretation that, with all of its intentions and its conscious and unconscious presuppositions at a given time, threads in this way or that through the broad trail of effective history.

In accordance with these observations it is hardly surprising—and on account of its significance for the following investigations it is to be highlighted once again—that in the thematization of the historical connection of our self- and world relation, the use of Heideggerian texts from the early period is interwoven from the start with the echo that Heidegger's thinking has already engendered over such a long period of time. It resonates unmistakably even in reading his early writings, for although (with the exception of the great Jaspers review, which, however, maintains itself on the same level of reflection) in these texts from 1919 to 1923, his writings concern lectures that were originally thought prior to and on the way to *Sein und Zeit* on the basis of their publication date, they can be read only within the horizon of a perspective already affected by *Sein und Zeit*, in which today the knowledge of the so-called turn [*Kehre*] is present.

This is now, *hermeneutically treated,* of no slight relevance; the interpreting consciousness discloses the insight in a difference holding sway constitutively between itself and the texts, as much as within the texts

---

ing the present as an ur-phenomenon that poses for us, in the depth of its essence, the demand of living in the present "first, because this corresponds to our particular performative interests and duties; second, because this corresponds to our will to life, which is supported through the imperative of self-development . . .; third, because this corresponds to a behest that issues from the present of the present itself" (165).

in the angle of refraction of its mutually related possibilities of reception through this interpreting consciousness in relation to its interpretive activity and its conditions of being carried out. In order to grasp them structurally, one can speak, with regard to the interpreting contact with these texts, of a *'hermeneutics, or rather, a hermeneutical comportment of the second view,'* if one conceives of the 'first view' as that which holds itself "outside" effective history, as it were, in an originary expanse of time of the text's emergence and which, seen hermeneutically, in relation to this originariness therefore cannot even be reproduced in an interpretation, but rather is to be made present only in the differential status of its evasiveness.[26]

For the concrete labor of interpretation, this *comportment of the second view* does not mean that therein the trail was prepared of an as it were doxic arbitrariness—this would also be poisonous for the handling of the texts. If the interpreting consciousness thus individuates itself as effective-historical consciousness in the hermeneutical comportment of the second view, this means first that its 'natural' point of departure distinguishes itself through a genuine *distance from the text*. In this distance, also always historical, which Gadamer grasps terminologically as "temporal distance"[27] in its meaning for the contribution of understanding, the unbridgeable difference between reader and author—and thus also between the reader and the text—is established. Insofar as this, as the reflections of the first section showed, is retained in the authorially irretrievable meshwork of a tradition and thus always already surpasses the intentions of its author, this points to an inherent *excess of sense* constitutive for the text. This excess forms itself as well on the side of the reader, insofar as the reader is likewise entangled in a network of experience not masterable by the author and only within this meshwork does a reader actualize a text in reading and thereby motivate the interminable process of historical understanding at the same time.

26. Bearing in mind the discussions in the first section, it is necessary to hold to the fact that neither the external to which we are appealing nor the originariness bound to it intend anything extratemporal in any sense of an ahistorical "ur-creation." The text, whose interpretation—in light of the hermeneutical situation—reasonably manifests this effective-historical, classifying mode of speaking, is itself also, from the perspective of the 'first view,' always already—and only—constituted as part of an occurrence of tradition, which, as effective history, realizes itself in the potential of its possibilities in a given text, whereby with the interpretative reference to the historical, the author himself also acts in a multitude of ways in the operative mode of the 'second view.'

27. Gadamer, *Wahrheit und Methode*, 301.

It follows that each age has undertaken either to integrate (in its own manner) an inherited text in an illuminating way in its own process of sense-comprehension, or to let it descend (in a mode of becoming strange) into the latency of a forgetting, if the constellation of constitutive presuppositions and structural moments of historical knowledge—knowledge relating to the space of possibilities in which the text preserves its meaning—changes accordingly. In either case it was as a result of a rather naive misjudgment of the productivity of this temporal distance when, in the field of historicism, the aim was directed to fully leveling out this distance in order to hit upon the objectivity supposedly necessary for historical knowledge. In opposition, however, the familiar formula of "understanding a text better than its author understood it," proffered by Schleiermacher and Dilthey, indicated at the very least a hermeneutical feel for the aforementioned excess of sense.[28]

While authors such as Karl-Otto Apel[29] or O. F. Bollnow[30] engage positively in the possibility of such understanding-better, Gadamer voices reservations about the productive use of interpretative self-understanding bound up with it; for him the gesture of superiority expressed or at least suggested therein appears both suspect and inappropriate in the matter, insofar as, distinct from historical particularity, all understanding of sense, at least according to this gesture in understanding-better, does not exclude the possibility of intending a final interpretation.

28. See Schleiermacher, "Über den Begriff der Hermeneutik mit Bezug auf F. A. Wolfs Andeutungen und Asts Lehrbuch," in *Hermeneutik und Kritik*, 325; Dilthey, *Die Entstehung der Hermeneutik*, in *GS* 5:335. If, with regard to this formula, Gadamer (see *Wahrheit und Methode*, 187, note 301) refers to the Enlightenment thinker Chladenius (*Einleitung zur richtigen Auslegung vernünftiger Reden und Schriften* [1742] (Dusseldorf: Stern-Verlag Jannsen, 1969), to whom he takes himself to be related in the latter's disposition to the hermeneutics of the romantics, as an even earlier testimony for this moment of better understanding—without already being able to formulate a methodological principle—then in this sense further and more significant sources for this mode of thought in the threads of Enlightenment thinking would include Kant and Fichte, as well as Rousseau (see Johann Gottlob Fichte, "Einige Vorlesungen über die Bestimmung des Gelehrten," in *Werke*, ed. Fritz Medicus (Leipzig: Fritz Eckardt, 1911), 1:265), who in relation to Plato (see Kant's *Kritik der reinen Vernunft*, B 370) claim the necessity of better understanding.

29. Karl-Otto Apel, *Das Apriori der Kommunikationsgemeinschaft*, vol. 2 of *Transformation der Philosophie* (Frankfurt: Suhrkamp 1988), 387.

30. Otto Friedrich Bollnow, "Was heißt einen Schriftsteller besser verstehen, als er sich selber verstanden hat?" In *Zur Philosophie der Geisteswissenschaften*, vol. 1 of *Studien zur Hermeneutik* (Freiburg: Alber, 1982), 48–72.

Out of the unbridgeable difference, conditioned by temporal distance, Gadamer grasps understanding, in opposition to understanding-better, from out of his own hermeneutical presuppositions in the famous terse thesis: "It suffices to say that one understands *differently, if one understands in general.*"[31] For on the basis of the options of sense mediating themselves historically in the range of possibility of the text, its intelligible articulation already qualifies historical knowing in itself as this understanding-differently in its particular actualization through the predesignated, perspective view of the interpreter. The otherness filtering itself in temporal distance is itself to be conceived as a process of occurrence that, according to Gadamer, gives us a possibility "of making solvable the actually critical question of hermeneutics, namely, of separating the *true* prejudices under which we *understand* from the *false,* under which we *misunderstand.*"[32]

Insofar as the reader's presumptions of sense in the concrete work of interpretation are guided by the maxim of opening up the options of sense of the text as authentically as possible, that means diminishing the position of the external through approximation to the text; without devoting false hopes thereby, and admittedly neither with regard to a complete overcoming of the distance, nor with regard to the idea of a final answer exhausting the manifold of interpretations. The task of understanding lies consequently, as Gadamer has formulated it, "in expanding the unity of the understood sense in concentric circles."[33] That suffices only if one can work out the connection and order of the text's course of sense. In relation to the text, this as it were *mimetic moment of reading,* which aspires to unlock the immanent structure of sense—under the condition that a first and final sense is not to be had genealogically or teleologically[34]—may not be confounded with the above named 'first view.' The mimetic moment belongs much more to the comportment of the second view, insofar as the mimetic reading also never reproduces the 'sense of the text in itself' but

---

31. Gadamer, *Wahrheit und Methode,* 302.

32. Ibid., 304. The experience of otherness, developing productively in this sense, unfolds itself as such just as little as distantiation is effective only through temporal distance. Rather, the *distance* in general, which is always present, e.g., in the encounter with someone or in conversation between people and thus in the present shared between them, is of its own accord already a hermeneutically productive structural moment of the process of understanding. Gadamer himself later revised this notion after his slightly one-sided accentuation in favor of temporal distance in *Wahrheit und Methode.* See *Zwischen Phänomenologie und Dialektik: Versuch einer Selbstkritik* (Tubingen: Mohr Siebeck, 1986), in *GW* 2:8.

33. Gadamer, *Wahrheit und Methode,* 296.

34. See § 8; see also Figal, *Der Sinn des Verstehens,* 11–31.

rather only produces, in the consciousness of the difference of reader-I and text, what predetermines imagistically the directional sense of its act of approximation from out of its forehaving, foresight, and foreconception. The place of reading does not confound itself in this sense with that of the text, and thus the *space of critique* appropriate to it also opens itself at the same time with the disclosure of its authentic sense structure in the text. According to the original sense of the term, it sets out the text's imma-nent unity of sense to a judgment that, in reflection upon one's own stand-point—codetermined by transcendental expectations of sense—must take its starting point from and coimplicate the disposition therein that the interpreter's expectations of sense can be justified through this reveal-ing reading of the text.

With regard to the difference that is not to be harmonically leveled out with the text, as the unique internally coconfirmed yet never finally con-firmed or groundable situation of departure for the interpretation, a series of further points for clarification, seen in contact with hermeneutics, are to be formulated. In the preunderstanding constitutive for every interpreta-tion, there is always also coenacted the fact that the interpretation is based on predecisions of the interpreter; thus for hermeneutics, for the herme-neutical process as a whole, there are to be noticed *decisionistic structural moments* that prove themselves on their side as related to context. There-fore, in the methodological sense, it is vital for the transparency of the hermeneutical situation that the foreopinions are also uncovered in their decisive character as far as possible. A suitable means for this on the side of the interpreters is the enlightenment of their own site of interests with the options resulting from that for concrete interpretation, which approaches a fundamental, performative feature of hermeneutics, seen structurally.

For the present study, with regard to the question concerning the turn to Heidegger's early texts this means clarifying why going into them ap-pears meaningful in the context of the question concerning the self, and clarifying further how this is accomplished. This can only take place at present in a more formally indicative orientation, especially since it lies in the essence of phenomenological investigations how it can be said with Heidegger "that they cannot be referred in shortened form, but rather [also just in view of the texts to be interpreted] must be newly repeated and worked through in each given case."[35]

---

35. Heidegger, *Prolegomena zur Geschichte des Zeitbegriffs*. (Summer Semester 1925), ed. Petra Jaeger. (Frankfurt: Klostermann, 1994) *GA* 20, 32.

In the course of the hermeneutical discussions up to this point, which are sparked by the question concerning the self-relation of human beings in the midst of a world determined by history, it has come to light that the human being in his self-constitution can no longer position himself today in the style of Descartes in a dualistic sense in opposition to the world. Instead of this substance-ontologically grounded vis-à-vis, the human determines his situation through the experience of a manifold, equally horizontal and vertical, synchronic as well as diachronic entangledness and interwovenness in innerworldly referential contexts. Thereby it is indeed of decisive significance from a phenomenological perspective that in the mode of this interweaving one must necessarily attend to the gradations and differences constituting it; indeed, it shows that this being entangled itself is structured through a *fundamental difference*. It concerns the being given, on the one hand, of the innerworldly entities, and on the other hand, of prefinding oneself in this relation to entities as the self-givenness of the human being for himself.

This means: the relation to innerworldly things in the broad sense is so irrevocable that I experience myself only in the midst of the world—and that means in the midst of time and history, so this relatedness always already implicates the self-constituting experience of difference in its ontological presupposition. The self-relation generates and determines itself accordingly through and as difference, yet does not split in the Cartesian sense, but rather in that I experience myself qua difference as essentially open to the world; the self always already transcends itself beyond me to the understanding possible for me as historical horizon.

Transcendence and *difference,* as constituents of the innermost finite self-relation, at the same time indicate that it is constituted at least problematically with the identity of the subject in the sense of the traditional concept of self-consciousness. In order to be able to recover the sketched matter of fact reflexively, I must indeed leave the natural comportment in which I customarily move, and move into the philosophical attitude. This reflexive transposition, in unity with the phenomenological *epoché* as the essential component of the phenomenological method, according to Husserl, familiarly accomplishes the *phenomenological reduction,*[36] of which

---

36. Cf. Husserl, *Ideen I,* §§ 30–33.

Merleau-Ponty, in agreement with Fink, emphasizes that it is "the 'wonder' in the face of a world."[37]

In this type of formulation of the phenomenological reduction, the Gordian knot of phenomenology is tied, and its unraveling is decisive for the beginning of the concept of phenomenology in question. Even if it is generally conceded that only by means of an *epoché* is the sketched structural difference visible in the givenness of the relation to self and world, the natural attitude—"the attitude of the mundanized subjectivity [as] the natural being of the human in and toward the world"[38]—thus is necessarily to be closed off in order to make this difference visible, so the problems of the interwovenness mentioned above are not thereby solved, but they now stand out in accentuated form and make clear the difference between Husserl and Heidegger.[39]

With a view to the problematic of the lifeworld so virulent today, Heidegger's early lectures offer an additional accretion, not to be undervalued, of knowledge beyond what had been achieved up to this point. For Heidegger grasps phenomenology, as will be seen, in a countermove to Husserl as *ur-science or originary science of life* [*Ur- bzw. Ursprungswissenschaft des Lebens*]. In so doing he unfolds the main features of an *ontology of facticity,* which assumes the form of a *hermeneutics of the self* in the thematization of human relation to the pretheoretical world, which from 1919 onward he speaks of conceptually as "lifeworld." The possibility thereby emerges of introducing a significant "new" conception oriented to problem solving in the present widely varied hermeneutic debate on the human relation to self and world—influenced by the readoption of the motive of philosophy of life and existence—a debate that can itself be grasped in the view of the present investigation with a phrase of Foucault as the task of a "historical ontology of ourselves."[40]

37. Merleau-Ponty, *Phänomenologie der Wahrnehmung,* 10.

38. Fink, "Vergegenwärtigung und Bild," in *Studien zur Phänomenologie,* 21:11.

39. As an approach to the difference between the Husserlian and Heideggerian conceptions of phenomenology, the theme of the phenomenological reduction, inspired by the Marburg Lectures (see also note 20) in the context of *Sein und Zeit* and in recent years investigated in French scholarship in particular, has garnered increased attention once more. See Jean-Luc Marion, *Réduction et donation: Recherches sur Husserl, Heidegger et la phenomenologie* (Paris: Presses Universitaires de France, 1989); Jean-François Courtine, *Heidegger et la phenomenologie* (Paris: Vrin, 1990); Rudolf Bernet, "Phenomenological Reduction and the Double Life of the Subject," in *Reading Heidegger from the Start,* 245–267.

40. Foucault, "Was ist Aufklärung?" 48.

It would be a task sui generis (which in the framework of this study is illuminated only with a few highlights, that is to say, in differing degrees) to bring the Heideggerian conception of the self productively into conversation beyond its working out—admittedly in the sense of a synthesizing analysis as a basic feature of interpretation in general—with positions, such as those of Gadamer, Ricoeur, and Foucault, that locate themselves in the discourse on the self precisely in the effective-historical current of Heideggerian thinking, but for their own investigations could not themselves already have recourse to the early texts. In tracing the horizon of interpretation requisite for this as the indicated direction of the present analysis, it follows for the further path of investigation that, for example, the historical background of Heideggerian interpretations is illuminated only in as detailed a fashion as can be used innovatively for the present hermeneutical discussion.

Such a fading in and out, considered for itself as a fact for the time being, may not appear unproblematic; however, the particular concrete posing of the question alone finally adjudicates its suitability in the situation of analysis in question. In order to give an example, reference should be made to the fact that the Heideggerian treatment of the self from the neo-Kantian position, which has played a decisive role in the academic philosophical socialization of Heidegger in the macroclimate, as it were, of spiritual-historical situation alongside phenomenology and *Lebensphilosophie,* and consequently is of considerable significance with regard to a possible history of influence,[41] will only be touched on in the present investigations. For regardless of contemporary tendencies toward a partial reactualization of neo-Kantianism, as a historical position its influ-

---

41. On this point see Claudius Strube, *Zur Vorgeschichte der hermeneutischen Phänomenologie;* Christoph von Wolzogen, "'Es gibt.' Heidegger und Natorps 'Praktische Philosophie,'" in *Heidegger und die praktische Philosophie,* ed. Annemarie Gethmann-Siefert and Otto Pöggeler (Frankfurt: Suhrkamp, 1988), 313–337; von Wolzogen, "'Den Gegner stark machen': Heidegger und der Ausgang des Neukantianismus am Beispiel Natorps," in *Neukantianismus: Perspektiven und Probleme,* ed. Ernst Wolfgang Orth and Helmut Holzhey (Würzburg: Königshausen & Neumann, 1994), 397–417; George Kovacs, "Philosophy as Primordial Science in Heidegger's Courses of 1919," in *Reading Heidegger from the Start,* 91–107; Jürgen Stolzenberg, *Ursprung und System: Probleme der Begründung systematischer Philosophie in Werk Hermann Cohens, Paul Natorps und beim frühen Heidegger* (Göttingen: Vandenhoeck & Ruprecht, 1995), 259–294; Markus Joachim Brach, *Heidegger—Platon: Vom Neukantianismus zur existenziellen Interpretation des "Sophistes"* (Würzburg: Königshausen & Ruprecht, 1996), part 1.

ence upon the development of hermeneutics was not far-reaching and had a marginal effect, mediated only through hermeneutical methods.[42]

42. Such a connection is to be found in the fact that Max Weber's project of an interpretive or understanding [*verstehenden*] sociology (see *Gesammelte Aufsätze zur Wissenschaftslehre*, ed. Johannes Winckelmann [Tübingen: Mohr Siebeck, 1988]), even if one cannot call it hermeneutical, links up in decisive conceptual and methodological viewpoints with Heinrich Rickert's doctrine of method (see *Die Grenzen der naturwissenschaftlichen Begriffsbildung: Eine logische Einleitung in die historische Wissenschaft*, vol. 2 [Tübingen: Mohr, 1929]; *Kulturwissenschaft und Naturwissenschaft* [Stuttgart: Reclam, 1986]), which relied on Windelband's famous distinction between scientific thinking in nomothetically proceeding sciences of law and the science of events determined ideographically by its methods (see "Geschichte und Naturwissenschaft," in *Präludien: Aufsätze und Reden zur Philosophie und ihrer Geschichte*, vol. 2 [Tübingen: Mohr, 1919], 145). For Rickert these refer in theoretically valid reflection to a founding philosophy of value, grounded first and foremost by means of the objectivity of cultural-scientific knowledge in relation to absolutely valid values (see *Kulturwissenschaft*, 168, 110).

While Rickert believes that by means of this 'value-relation' he is able to state the timelessly valid conditions of the possibility of understanding historical forms of sense—which for him, in agreement with Mill and Dilthey, span even the societal dimension of social action—it is precisely this epistemological relation to the absolute validity of a transcendent realm of values that no longer plays a substantial role for the originally Weberian question, taken over by Rickert, of the value-relation within social action. See Henrich, *Die Einheit der Wissenschaftlehre Max Webers* (Tübingen: Mohr, 1952), 16–35, 51. On the other hand, the concept of a generalizing and individualizing conceptual formation as the methodological center of Rickert's science of logic remains an ongoing significant point of crystallization for the Weberian starting point. See Rainer Prewo, *Max Webers Wissenschaftsprogramm: Versuch einer methodischen Neuerschließung* (Frankfurt: Suhrkamp, 1979), 26–46; Peter-Ulrich Merz, *Max Weber und Heinrich Rickert: Die erkenntniskritischen Grundlagen der verstehenden Soziologie* (Würzburg: Königshausen & Neumann, 1990); as a supplement to the latter, see Franco Bianco's study ("Vita active und Vita contemplative: Zur Auseinandersetzung Heinrich Rickerts mit Max Weber," in *Neukantianismus*, ed. Ernst Wolfgang Orth and Helmut Holzhey [Würzburg: Königshausen & Neumann, 1994], 296–308), which investigates Rickert from the standpoint of the latter's own reading of Weber's relation to him by means of later sources on Weber.

With a view to the early Heidegger an interesting aspect emerges: in 1919–1920, thus at the time of his intensive debate with neo-Kantianism, he thematizes the distinctiveness of the Weberian conception with regard to the methodological question of interpretive understanding in a phenomenological context. This source has only recently been published in the appendix of the lecture course *Grundprobleme der Phänomenologie* ("Blatt 7: Phänomenologie und Leben—interpetatives Verstehen—Idealtypus" (GA 58, ed. Hans-Helmuth Gander [Frankfurt: Klostermann, 1993), 189–196).

If one inquires about Weber beyond Rickert's possible influence on the more recent concept of the social sciences, one can find, without being obliged to engage in overestimations, something in the way of Alfred Schütz's work (*Theorie der Lebensformen: Frühe Manuskripte aus der Bergson-Periode*, ed. Ilja Srubar [Frankfurt: Suhrkamp, 1981]; see Fred R. Dallmayr, "Phenomenology and Social Science: An Overview and Appraisal," in *Explorations in Phenomenology: Papers of the Society for Phenomenology and Existential Philosophy*, ed. David Carr and Edward S. Casey [The Hague: Springer, 1973], 133–166). And further, in Niklas Luhmann's concept of the system, as Rudiger Bubner has shown ("*Wissenschaftstheorie und Systembegriff: Zur Position von N. Luhmann und deren Herkunft*," in *Dialektik und Wissenschaft*, [Frankfurt: Suhrkamp, 1974], 112–128), there is an echo of Rickertian thinking. Yet irrespective of these

In contrast, the equally virulent *Lebensphilosophie* of the early writings—in particular in the hermeneutical unfolding of Wilhelm Dilthey, as well as those figures receiving their impulse from Kierkegaard and Nietzsche (as can be found in Jaspers and Simmel, among others)—is of significance for the development of Heideggerian hermeneutics, on account of which the questions and motives of *Lebensphilosophie* will find even stronger attention within the interpretive framework here chosen. In order to profile Heidegger's own perspective more clearly in what follows, it seems obvious next to secure the differential positing of what phenomenology, understood on the surface as a methodological concept, supposedly unites and for which in the general understanding enters into the famous and oft-cited formula 'to the things themselves.'

§ 27. The "Blind Spot" in the Phenomenological Eye: Heidegger's Critique of Husserl with a View to the Structure of Care

a) Phenomenological Maxims of Research and Cognitive Intention

The difference between Husserl's and Heidegger's understanding of phenomenology that we have addressed can, in short, also establish that Husserl's transcendental-phenomenological conception of reduction, insofar as it has its philosophical center and telos in the idea of absolute subjectiv-

---

aftereffects, the epistemologically determined neo-Kantian approaches to cultural sciences, as predominantly developed in the *Südwestdeutsche Schule*, remain rather meager in terms of their hermeneutical relevance.

In contrast, the *kulturphilosophie* of Ernst Cassirer achieves, nearly on its own, an outline in this direction, a philosophy that refers back not to scientific but rather to everyday experience in its method, and in which, as is realized in the medium of symbolic forms of expression, it undertakes, as Hans Blumenberg emphasizes, an "attempt at ascending out of neo-Kantianism" ("Ernst Cassirers gedenkend bei der Entgegennahme des Kuno-Fischer-Preises der Universität Heidelberg 1974," in *Wirklichkeiten in denen wir leben: Aufsätze und eine Rede*, 163–172 [Stuttgart: Reclam, 1981], 168). See also Heidegger's detailed discussion of the second volume of Cassirer's *Philosophie der symbolischen Formen* ("Das mythische Denken"), which first appeared in 1927 under the title "Zur Geschichte des philosophischen Lehrstuhles seit 1866," now reprinted as a supplement to *Kant und das Problem der Metaphysik*, ed. Friedrich-Wilhelm von Herrmann, in *GA* (Frankfurt: Klostermann, 1991), 3:255–270; here, (*GA* 3:304–311), can be found a brief characterization by Heidegger on the emergence, advancement, and reshaping of neo-Kantianism, published in 1927 in the *Festschrift* dedicated to the quatercentenary celebration of Marburg University.

ity, carries out a "*division*"[43] in its beginning in the natural "I" as "I-Human Being, as 'child of the world'"[44] and the transcendental "I," which is not really split off, but is in natural living in the world "for itself absolutely *anonymous*."[45] For Husserl, this means: "I, who I am, live a life that is hidden but always thematically to be opened, an absolute life, a life as stream of consciousness-of . . . But in this consciousness-of . . . I only have in the phenomenological reflection [and] reduction an absolute . . . as its theme . . . that is, only where I 'set out of play' natural positings of the objective, instead of carrying them out simply, reflect on them, and only make them thematic as consciousness, only there *have* I grasped pure consciousness, I have the pure, absolute being and life of absolute subjectivity."[46] This is the egological subjectivity of the "I" carrying out the phenomenological reduction, which first of all becomes phenomenological through its carrying out: thus, as Eugen Fink stresses, it "comes to self-conception henceforth through a universally fixed resolution of the will."[47]

Through this "act of violence of the phenomenological reduction,"[48] the transcendental observer becomes conscious of himself as transcendental "I," but at the same time the mundane "I" carrying out the *epoché* is also bracketed with the ontic world taken in the *epoché*.[49] Fink thus

43. Husserl, *Erste Philosophie (1923–1924): Zweiter Teil: Theorie der phänomenologischen Reduktion, Husserliana,* ed. Rudolf Boehm (The Hague: Martinus Nijhoff, 1959), 8:427.

44. Ibid., 417. In the *Pariser Vorträgen* (in *Cartesianische Meditationen, GW* 1:16) this means: "Thus the phenomenological reduction carries out a kind of fissuring of the I: the transcendental observer posits himself beyond himself, watches himself, and thus finds in himself as *cogitatum* himself as a human and finds in the cogitations belonging to him [the] transcendental life and being that constitute the worldly as a whole."

45. Husserl, *Erste Philosophie II, GW* 8:417.

46. Ibid., 427 (emphasis deleted). In this sense, Heidegger gets to the point of the concept of consciousness that Husserl strives after in his winter lecture course of 1923/24 when he states: "*Consciousness, as absolute being,* signifies that being in which every other possible being manifests itself, which has the possibility in consciousness of showing itself in itself" (Heidegger, *Einführung in die phänomenologische Forschung,* ed. Friedrich-Wilhelm von Herrmann, in *GA* (Frankfurt: Klostermann, 1994), 17:262).

47. Fink, "Vergegenwärtigung und Bild," 11.

48. Ibid., 12.

49. The fact that the suspension of judgment undertaken in the *epoché* brackets not only the naive belief in existence executed in the natural attitude, but also first and foremost permits this belief as such to be thematized with regard to its implicit claims to validity, counts thus among the constitutive achievements of the phenomenological reduction. See Fink, *Edmund Husserl in der gegenwärtigen Kritik,* esp. 105–129; Fink, "Reflexionen zu Husserls phänomenologischer Reflexion," in *Nähe und Distanz: Phänomenologische Vorträge und Aufsätze,* ed. Franz A. Schwartz (Freiburg: Alber, 1976), 299–322. On Fink's critique of the concept of the phenomenological reduction, illustrated primarily by means of notes from his unpublished *Nachlass*

speaks of a "dehumanizing" as the innermost intention and primary sense of the phenomenological reduction,[50] which in its transcendental version is synonymous, according to Stephan Strasser, with the disappearance of the "drama and tragedy of human Dasein and human history."[51] As the investigations of the foregoing chapter have shown, with the reduction to pure consciousness as transcendental origin of absolute being, the insight into the potential constituting our self-experience of the (in itself heterogeneous) interwovenness in the pretheoretical world is obstructed, insofar as the mundane situation—itself the still "indisputable structural moment of the phenomenological reduction"[52]—is leapt over in its relation to the *facticity* and *contingency* of the one undertaking it, which is to say, is not comprehended sufficiently 'from the thing itself.'[53]

---

that bring to light his own position within the difference that he thematizes between Husserl and the Heidegger of *Sein und Zeit*, see Ronald Bruzina's essay "Gegensätzlicher Einfluß—Intergrierter Einfluß: Die Stellung Heideggers in der Entwicklung der Phänomenologie," in *Zur philosophischen Aktualität Heideggers,* ed. Dietrich Papenfuss and Otto Pöggeler (Frankfurt: Klostermann, 1990), 2:142–160.

50. Fink, "*Vergegenwärtigung und Bild*," 13. The manner in which Husserl undertakes this ascent in the sphere of transcendental subjectivity and the lengths to which he pursues it can be seen, among other places, in a text from the summer of 1936, wherein Husserl occupies himself with the question of the anthropological world and in particular goes into the phenomenon of death. At first, in a provocative tone, he mocks Heidegger's analysis of death, and erects over and against it his own "genuine" phenomenological reflection on death, dying, and their relation to the life of transcendental consciousness, which finally climaxes in the declaration: "The human necessarily dies. The human has no worldly pre-existence, in the spatio-temporal world he was nothing before, and afterward he will be nothing. But transcendental, primeval life . . . and its ultimate I cannot come to be out of nothing and pass over into nothing; *it is 'immortal'* [and now comes the striking 'rationale'] *because dying has no sense for it*" (*Die Krisis der europäischen Wissenschaften und die transzendentale Phänomenologie: Ergänzungsband; Texte aus dem Nachlaß (1934–1937)*, ed. Reinhold N. Smid, in *Husserliana* (Dordrecht: Kluwer, 1993), 29:338) (emphasis added). This aptly illustrates, however, what Heidegger summarized eleven years earlier in the far-reaching dispute with Husserl in the Summer Semester of 1925, where he shows how in Husserl's method of the transcendental-phenomenological reduction "the ground is cut from under one's feet" (*Prolegomena zur Geschichte des Zeitbegriffs, GA* 20, 150) in the pursuit of an adequate ascertainment of the "real consciousness of the factically existing human" (ibid.).

51. Stephan Strasser, "Der Begriff der Welt in der phänomenologischen Philosophie," in *Phänomenologie und Praxis,* ed. Ernst Wolfgang Orth (Freiburg: Meiner, 1976), 176.

52. Fink, "Vergegenwärtigung und Bild," 14.

53. In this blockade the pretheoretical world, as has been shown above, is nonetheless not overlooked by Husserl in its significance, insofar as the apodictic presumption of the world remains in force and the world as the universal horizon of validity is the universal horizon of all mundane horizons. As such, it allows for no transcendence and advances, as we have seen in the concept of the lifeworld explicated in a *bewusstseins*-phenomenological sense, to become one of the central themes of recent philosophy. Considered from this angle, it was essential for the

What this means in its specifics can be illuminated with reference to Heidegger's critique of the Husserlian installation of the maxim of phenomenological research, "To the things themselves!" which Heidegger brings to speech in the framework of his first Marburg lecture (winter semester 1923/24). The decisive entry point of this critique consists in the fact that Husserl connects his understanding of phenomenology methodologically in advance to a representation or standard of evidence, which according to Heidegger prescribes "*an empty and thereby phantasmatic idea of certainty.*"[54] This self-connection is motivated by the "*care for* a determined *absolute knowledge*, taken purely as idea,"[55] which, however—according to the Husserlian demand for a grounding from absolute presuppositionlessness in the established factual field of a science of consciousness—harbors within itself the danger of a persistent dogmatism insofar as Husserl adopts, without further argument, the Cartesian *cogito sum* in the beginning of the transcendental and eidetic reduction from out of the demand for certainty bound up with it.[56] In an insightful expression, Heidegger speaks of the fact that in the sense of this tradition, Husserl's care fixes itself as "*care for known knowledge*,"[57] which itself cares for the "*securing of knowledge* on the path of the knowing of knowledge,"[58] and thereby aims at the "*securing and grounding of an absolute scientificity.*"[59]

With regard to the intention to known knowledge, the goal of knowledge thus formulated by Heidegger corresponds thoroughly to the claim of the Husserlian concept of phenomenology as rigorous science. But insofar as this *intention of knowledge as care* is spoken of, a way of seeing that differentiates itself from Husserl—that is, a specifically Heideggerian perspective—already expresses itself therein. For in the approach of care, it

---

hermeneutical question of the *self-relation as world relation* to grapple with Husserl's phenomenology of the lifeworld. However, this coming to terms took place from *today's* standpoint—that is, wholly in the sense of the effective-historical difference as the hermeneutical comportment of the second view—out of a situation that has itself already gone through the critique of Husserl's transcendental-phenomenological appropriation of the problematic of the lifeworld, a critique that has itself become historical in the meantime.

54. Heidegger, *GA* 17, 43.

55. Ibid.

56. See Friedrich-Wilhelm von Herrmann, "Husserl—Heidegger und die 'Sachen selbst,'" in *Inmitten der Zeit: Beiträge zur europäischen Gegenwartsphilosophie,* ed. Thomas Grethlein and Heinrich Leitner (Würzburg: Königshausen & Neumann, 1996), 277–289.

57. Heidegger, *Einführung in die phänomenologische Forschung, GA* 17, 61; see ibid., 100–103.

58. Ibid., 72.

59. Ibid.

circumvents that self-conception—as it is developed in the wake of scientific philosophy in the Cartesian sense in phenomenology, with its methodological orientation to a formulation of the "*mathesis* of experiences"[60]—in the orientation to the scientificity of the quantitative sciences, which under the standard of the idea of truth qua certainty can be determined as a connection grounding true propositions.[61] In contrast, Heidegger opens in advance, with the concept of care, a view to the notion that sciences should be posited as *knowing comportments of human beings*.

That sciences are pursued by scientists and that a science is known only for the scientificity of its results, seems rather trivial—one could object—in an objective-theoretical or epistemological sense. But for Heidegger this is not the point; just as little is he concerned to resolve the question of knowledge psychologistically in a description of experience. Rather, the issue for him when he addresses the sciences as comportments within the care structure is first and foremost the placing into question of the unquestioned general bond to a measure of knowledge selected *pars pro toto*. And from out of this ground he undertakes a shift in emphasis, away from the ontic reification occurring in the traditional theoretical scientific attitude and toward the incorporation of the scientific intention of knowledge into the activity that constitutes it as a mode of existence or rather a form of life, which—and this is significant—in its lifeworldly complexity can be adequately determined only from out of the phenomenally appropriate demonstration of the human mode of being. To afford such a demonstration is the task of philosophy.

Seen thus, for Heidegger, the thematization of science at the level of the desired scientificity of its results in a given context is not the primary issue. It is relevant only to the extent that it paradigmatically encroaches on philosophy's self-conception. Thus, the sharp edge of his critique of Husserl, initiated by the introduction of the structure of care, is directed first and foremost to Husserl's self-linkage to the idea of certainty as the methodological ideal of phenomenology as rigorous science—which, according to Heidegger, along with the claim to a self-evident lack of all presuppositions, precisely blocks phenomenological access to the question of human knowing as a specific mode of its being in the world. Taking this into account means, in connection with the previous discussion, that

<hr>

60. Ibid., 274.
61. See Heidegger, *Sein und Zeit*, GA 2, § 4.

the immanence of that appropriate characterization of Husserlian self-understanding (as Heidegger conveys it in a statement to the effect that it discusses his knowledge-intention in reference back to care as a cognitive comportment) is already broken open in Heidegger's approach. For Heidegger's thoroughly appropriate characterization of Husserl for this demonstration includes, together with the explicit ideas guiding it, the unexpressed effective background beliefs within them as their implicit presuppositional horizon. Heidegger's interpretation can only achieve this in that it has already transcended Husserl's perspective in the method of his presentation. In and out of the difference, the critical acuity is thus first gained for the problematic of the Husserlian conception, according to which a predominance of the idea of certainty and evidence is established *"prior to every proper qualification of the ability to encounter the proper things of philosophy."*[62]

b) The "Proper Things of Philosophy": The Being of the Human

What, then, are the 'proper things of philosophy' for Heidegger if they are no longer grasped as experiences of consciousness that are taken through the primacy of the theoretical attitude by means of the transcendental and eidetic reduction in the 'care for known knowledge'? In the delimitation of the Husserlian conception, this shows itself clearly in the first Marburg lecture course, where Heidegger determines the *being of care* more exactly. In 1923, care already indicates, as a concept, in its intention the constitution of the being of the human that has become famous since the publication of *Sein und Zeit*, a constitution which Heidegger appeals to conceptually in this lecture course with regard to its philosophical thematization as *Dasein*. However, it is necessary to see at the same time in this terminological consonance alongside this anticipatory moment the persisting objective distinctions that highlight, in view of the familiar later position qua effective history, the inherent significance of the first Heideggerian phase of development.

In *Sein und Zeit* Heidegger famously determines care as the existential–a priori structural whole of human being.[63] It cannot therefore be de-

---

62. Heidegger, *Einführung in die phänomenologische Forschung*, GA 17, 43.
63. See Heidegger, *Sein und Zeit*, GA 2, §§ 41, 42.

rived from ontic, factical comportments such as self-concern or self-care. These phenomena are themselves grounded much more for Heidegger in care, which is thereby the ontological condition of the possibility for something like the 'care of life.' Nonetheless the posited "transcendental 'universality' of the phenomenon of care and all fundamental existentials . . . has that breadth through which the ground is pregiven on which *every* ontic-worldview interpretation of Dasein moves, whether it understands Dasein as 'care of life' and necessity or the opposite."[64] Yet it remains decisive that, as Heidegger always stresses in the context of his explication of the a priori–ontological care structure in *Sein und Zeit*, care as existential concept is determined programmatically through the intention of his fundamental question concerning the sense of being. But that means that the existential–a priori care structure together with the existential-ontological necessity of an analytic of Dasein bound up with it does "*not* [aim] at an ontological grounding of anthropology" in the framework of fundamental ontology.[65]

What is thus definitive for the program of *Sein und Zeit*, however, may not simply be transferred or projected as a claim of fundamental ontological philosophy into the temporally earlier thought. Without further argumentation, one can of course concede that the first Marburg lecture shows itself in more than a mere handful of echoes to be on the way to the first main work, and this even not only tentatively and haltingly, but rather with a thoroughly valid grasp, as in the critique of Husserl, for the later work. This lecture text is not a proto–*Sein und Zeit*, as one might reasonably maintain, at least in wide parts of the lecture from the Summer Semester of 1925.[66] Although in general since 1923 the direction toward *Sein und Zeit* proves to be increasingly clearer and the use of his own conceptual language is already evident, there nonetheless remains much that emerged in the beginning of the 1920s in new, yet familiar (since the reception of *Sein und Zeit*) terms that was still in substance in close connection with insights worked out by Heidegger in earlier years and texts, insights that in comparison with *Sein und Zeit* remain determined by a number of differences.[67] One such notional difference, which concerns the problematic

---

64. Ibid., 265.

65. Ibid. (emphasis added).

66. Heidegger, *Prolegomena zur Geschichte des Zeitbegriffs, GA 20.*

67. This peculiar intermediate position or rather transition point is undervalued by such a renowned expert on '*déciennie phénomènologique*' as Jean Greisch, who, motivated by the

of grounding in the basic approach to care in *Sein und Zeit* as mentioned above, turns up at the end of the lecture course at issue. Beyond this text it marks the entire early phase from 1919 onward; it is thus so significant because in the context of the reflections on the structure of care, it designates more precisely the concept of *ontology* represented in the early work, which is crucial for what is to come in the present study.[68]

If one looks more closely, this concluding passage of the lecture course wherein Heidegger ties together the conceptual threads into an overarching network, it is for him precisely a matter of a "more originary context of being,"[69] although this context is not yet determined by the fundamental question concerning the meaning of being as the whence of the understanding of being in general and of all modes of being. Here, the context of being means much more that which relates human knowing and acting in its directedness towards an end, back to the effective ground within it as comportments—that is, first and last, "the being of the human,"[70] whose questioning, as Kant famously notes, composes "the field of philosophy."[71] For that reason, Heidegger stresses that one can also designate ontology as it is taken into account here "as *anthropology*."[72] The concept of anthropology brought thus into position should not be misinterpreted in a traditional fashion. For the anthropology intended here belongs in its approach, that is, already from taking leave of the rational primacy of reason, to that dimension which, with a view to an adequate interpretation, is determined by the programmatic claim of an as yet to be worked out *hermeneutics of facticity* that is formally indicating in the demonstration of the ontological structures of human being.

For Heidegger, facticity is not 'mere Dasein,' not a naked indeterminacy or pure factuality in the sense in which it is still used as the concept

---

critique of Husserl that has in fact not lost its validity, exclusively (and in my opinion too one-sidedly) emphasizes that the lecture course "opens the period of the editing of *Sein und Zeit*" (Greisch, "'La tapisserie de la vie': Le phénomène de la vie et ses interprétations dans les 'Grundprobleme der Phänomenologie (1919/20)' de Martin Heidegger," in Jean-François Courtine, ed. *Heidegger 1919–1929* (Paris: Vrin, 1996), 131–152, 134.

68. Cf. § 29 below on this complex of problems.

69. Heidegger, *Einführung in die phänomenologische Forschung*, GA 17, 279.

70. Ibid. (emphasis added).

71. Kant, *Logik*, 25. If Kant gathers as the fundamental questions of philosophy—what I can know, do, and hope for—into a fourth and final "What is the human?" (ibid.), this means for this concept of philosophy that for Kant the questions of metaphysics, morals, and religion in principle "can be ascribed to anthropology" (ibid.).

72. Heidegger, *GA* 17, 279 (emphasis added).

of the givenness of the contingent and the accidental in distinction from logicity in the neo-Kantian use of the word, and that in its negative connotation denotes that which lies, in a rigorous sense, outside of the field of philosophical labor.[73] As pretheoretical life in the positive indication of its contingency, its accidental aspect and individuality, Heidegger grasps facticity from the beginning as the existentiell situation of the individual, that is, as one's own concrete, particular context of life, which he speaks of prior to 1922 mostly as 'life' and 'factical life.'

At the beginning of the lecture course from the summer of 1923 Heidegger thus also maintains: "*Facticity* is the designation for the character of being of 'our' 'own' Dasein."[74] He determines it more precisely as "this *respective* Dasein . . ., insofar as it is ontologically, in its character of being, 'there.'"[75] This 'ontological being-there' means that for him Dasein is "not, and never primarily, [an] *object* of intuition and intuitive determination, the mere information and knowledge of it, but rather Dasein is itself *there* in the how of its ownmost being."[76] The 'how of being' accordingly opens up the manner in which I am my life in that it outlines and sketches in, in its limits, "the possible 'there' in a given case."[77] In a transitive sense, be-

---

73. Helmut Fahrenbach, for his article "*Faktizität*" (in *Historisches Wörterbuch der Philosophie*, ed. Joachim Ritter, vol. 2 (Basel 1972), 886), determines that this aspect of exclusion leads back the positive use of the term, in the sense of a philosophical concept, to Heidegger. Ludwig Landgrebe (*Faktizität und Individuation: Studien zu den Grundfragen der Phänomenologie*, [Hamburg: Meiner, 1982], 109) also expresses himself in this—at minimum easily misunderstood—sense of the first time of its emergence in the philosophical linguistic usage, even as *Eislers Handwörterbuch der Philosophie*, by Rudolf Eisler (Berlin: Mittler, 1922, 12) renders 'facticity' as a catchword in the neo-Kantian sense of "givenness, factuality."

The concept that emerges here and there even in Husserl (see *Ideen I*, 125) is thus no new creation of Heidegger's, yet only in Heidegger does it contain that systematic, penetrating gravity that it also possesses within the scope of the present investigation. In Dilthey, the word 'facticity' possesses an occasionally positive connotation, if without terminological rigor, when for example in the context of the religious experience of "vital originary reality" he sees this reality determined by "will, facticity, [and] history" (*Einleitung in die Geisteswissenschaften*, in *GS* 1:141). If one takes into account the usage of 'factical life,' there emerge possible connections with Max Scheler, as Pöggeler ("Heideggers Begegnung mit Dilthey," in *Dilthey-Jahrbuch*, [1986–1987], 4:138), Christoph Jamme (*Heideggers frühe Begründung der Hermeneutik*, *Dilthey-Jahrbuch* 4:76) and Mark Michalski (*Fremdwahrnehmung und Mitsein: Zur Grundlegung der Sozialphilosophie im Denken Max Schelers und Martin Heideggers* [Bonn: Bouvier, 1997], 158) emphasize. See also Theodor Kisiel, "Das Entstehen des Begriffsfeldes 'Faktizität' im Frühwerk Heideggers," in *Dilthey-Jahrbuch* [1986–1987], 4:91–120.

74. Heidegger, *Ontologie*, GA 63, 7.

75. Ibid.

76. Ibid.

77. Ibid.

ing thus signifies: "being factical life!"[78] At another point Heidegger puts together the equation: "Life = Dasein, 'being' in and through life."[79] That Heidegger's characterization of the ontology of the thing, grasped as *anthropology*, must be thought in this sense factically-hermeneutically is thus easily apparent and is confirmed through the connection of ontology and hermeneutics of facticity, as he reveals in the introduction to the summer 1923 lecture course. Here Heidegger gives such a tentative meaning with regard to content to the title of *ontology*, in relation to his own use of this term and in a conscious displacement of the tradition, that his use merely indicates "whatever thematic way the being [of humans determined by facticity strives] toward an investigation"[80]—on account of which ontology must be determined as hermeneutics of facticity and all of this 'ontologically' as a procedural designation then concerns the "positings of the question, explications, concepts, categories, which have grown or rather not grown from out of a look to the entities as being."[81]

In this sense, Heidegger also explicitly distinguishes his ontological-anthropological conception from "Dilthey's historically exhibited analysis,"[82] to which Heidegger attributes the "fundamental flaw that he did not develop any categories, any unified, precise form of questioning,"[83] with the result that Dilthey "attempted to reproduce [that which he was able to discern] through an aesthetic-artistic manner of presentation."[84]

78. Ibid. According to Heidegger, life is thus itself "a manner of 'being'" (ibid.) and 'factical life' therefore signifies "our own Dasein as 'there' in any ontological expression of its character of being" (ibid.).

79. Heidegger, *Phänomenologische Interpretationen zu Aristoteles*, GA 61, 85.

80. Heidegger, *Ontologie*, GA 63, 1.

81. Ibid., 3.

82. Heidegger, *Einführung in die phänomenologische Forschung*, GA 17, 279.

83. Ibid., 321.

84. Ibid. It is well known that Dilthey had ongoing difficulties throughout his life with the systematic design of his conception of a foundation of philosophy and as a result continually ended in fragments, or rather, abandoned his course of thinking in its outlining stage. However, recently published volumes from his *Nachlass* (esp. *GS*, vols. 19–21) exhibit an inexhaustible systematic endeavor in their outlines and as well a rigor of Diltheyan thought, for which reason one should be much more careful in judging supposed 'systematic weaknesses' than Heidegger, admittedly with different assumptions, does here.

Moreover, in the testimony from the winter semester of 1923/24 there is certainly still an echo of that impression elicited within Heidegger by the intensive reading of Dilthey's correspondence with Paul Graf Yorck von Wartenburg that had appeared in 1923 (see Heidegger's letter to Erich Rothacker from January 4, 1924, in Joachim Wolfgang Storck and Theodor Kisiel, "Martin Heidegger und die Anfänge der 'Deutschen Vierteljahresschrift für Literaturwissenschaft und Geistesgeschichte': Eine Dokumentation," in *Dilthey-Jahrbuch* (1992–1993),

By contrast, anthropology, as Heidegger understands it, should be understood as as an investigation that "is in principle assigned to categorical contexts."[85] That means concretely that it is a matter of "questioning Dasein with regard to its categories of being,"[86] with the methodologically directed intention of taking the *"evidence of omission* [as he sees it in, among

8:181–224, 202; see also Gadamer's report, *Errinerungen an Heideggers Anfänge,* in *GW* 10:8). Heidegger's esteem for Yorck, which emerges subsequently from this correspondence, along with his simultaneous devaluation of Dilthey (see *Sein und Zeit, GA* 2, 525–533), amounts, to a certain extent, to a self-correction. For this reason, the manifoldly discernible proximity to Dilthey's lebensphilosophical positions in Heidegger's early texts—positions that, however, never added up to a congruence—was qualified and subsequently undermined by the developing new systematic understanding of (fundamental) ontology that brought forth more strongly their points of divergence.

This delimitation finds its culmination in *Sein und Zeit,* where Heidegger stresses the philosophic relevance of Diltheyan research as the being-on-the-way to the question of life, and sees in the work the "rightly-understood tendency of all . . . '*lebensphilosophie*' [as] implicitly the tendency to an understanding of the being of Dasein" (*Sein und Zeit, GA* 2, 62), yet which, burdened in advance by a fundamental flaw, thinks "that 'life' itself, as a mode of being, does not become an ontological problem" (ibid.). To flash back from this judgment, which from this point on would remain valid for Heidegger's estimation of Dilthey, to the situation in the winter semester of 1923/24 will have afforded its contribution to the well-documented return to Aristotle in his early writings in the interim, in view of the indicated revaluation of Dilthey, which in relation to the systematic frequency of the development of his thinking left Dilthey's own endeavors in this respect rather faded.

With all of this in mind, Heidegger's judgment from 1923–1924 nonetheless—Helen Weiß's note, in which the citation is to be found affixed as a supplement to the final session of the lecture, reproduces the correct wording—proves to be highly questionable and to be a function of its time with regard to one point. To characterize Dilthey's manner of exhibition as 'aesthetic-artistic' and to diminish its importance in relation to the systematic train of his thought follows, without any further ado, a widespread opinion that was pushed not least by the great success of Dilthey's later publication *Das Erlebnis und die Dichtung* (appearing in 1905 and already in its twelfth edition by 1921). In view of Heidegger's other dispute with Dilthey (see his ten lectures in Kassel, "Wilhelm Diltheys Forschungsarbeit und der gegenwärtige Kampf um eine historische Weltanschauung," ed. Frithjof Rodi, in *Dilthey-Jahrbuch* (1992–1993), 8:143–180; see also *Phänomenologie der Anschauung und des Ausdrucks, GA* 59, 149–174; *Prolegomena zur Geschichte des Zeitbegriffs, GA* 20, 163 ff.), his readiness to adopt such a judgment—typical of its time and even then hardly competent—must appear surprising. In *Sein und Zeit* even he himself aptly brands such judgments as superficial.

85. Heidegger, *Einführung in die phänomenologische Forschung, GA* 17, 279.

86. Ibid. He notes, in this respect, at another point: "The categories are not fictions, nor are they a community of logical schemata for themselves, a 'latticework,' but rather they are in an originary manner *alive in life itself* . . . They have their own mode of access . . . that is precisely distinguished as that in which *life comes to itself*" (*Phänomenologische Interpretationen zu Aristoteles, GA* 61, 88). In the progession of precisely this development—with the intention of being adequate to phenomena—of the categories of human being out of the ontological insight into the difference of modes of being, what Heidegger here calls categories of being he will establish terminologically in the famous concept of transcendentally functioning existentialia [*Existenzialien*].

others, the Husserlian approach to care in known knowledge] *as a demonstration of Dasein itself according to its fundamental determinations.*"[87]

In view of this positive demonstration, care is grasped in the first Marburg lecture course as "the how of Dasein,"[88] or "Dasein's mode of being,"[89] which distinguishes itself concretely in its particular singular character. Therefore, Husserl's care for knowing as a "mode of being of the care for certainty"[90] also forms only *one* mode of human comportment, and admittedly that of a particular theoretical attitude, which as knowing aims at the truth in what is known. In it, human Dasein certainly interprets itself as knowing, yet according to Heidegger it does so in such a way that its being-known appears as a "flight before oneself"[91] in a kind of interpretation determined by the demand for certainty. This flight does not spring simply from a personally incurred misunderstanding, caused by something like a deficient attention to the analysis of the occurrence of self-interpretation, but rather in this mistaking itself in the grasp of itself, in which Heidegger discerns a "*distance from being,* as much from the *being of the world* as above all from the *being of Dasein as such,*"[92] in which the force of the Cartesian-inspired tradition functions historically. Thus regarded, the care for knowledge determined by certainty is also simply not to be dismissed as false. Rather, it is appropriate to expose this care to

---

Seen thus, what emerges with regard to the descriptive apprehension within the scope of a fundamental-ontologically motivated analytic of Dasein under the title of *Existenzial* is not, however, thereby stringently determined otherwise than as a phenomenon for itself when it is still understood—within the frame of the task of recognizing the originary context of being described above—without incorporating Heidegger's fundamental ontology, within his sense of anthropology qua hermeneutical ontology of facticity, into the program and referred to as categories of being and of life, respectively (cf. also *Ontologie,* GA 63, 31).

87. Ibid. This process, characteristic for Heidegger, of revealing an access to the positive content of phenomena in the destruction of occlusions and dissemblances, distinguishes that method which he terms '*phenomenological destruction.*' See § 33.

88. *Ontologie,* GA 63, 279.

89. Ibid., 277.

90. Ibid., 285.

91. Ibid.

92. Ibid., 282. Heidegger speaks of a distance from being because, in the care of certainty, "that whereof something is valid [depends] primarily upon *validity* and *bindingness,* yet the existent itself does not primarily come into view. . . . At the same time, however, the being of cognition in itself is never inquired as to its being and is not unsettled in its being" (ibid., 281). Elsewhere he puts it thus: "The being of cognition as care of certainty abides in a peculiar distance from being, i.e., in a position where cognition so characterized cannot approach the being of itself [as a mode of being of human comportment], but rather each existent inquires about its character of a possible being-certain" (ibid., 285).

that which, according to Heidegger, conceals itself in it or is disguised by the postulate of certainty of the theoretical attitude, and masks itself in this sense up to the self-sedation of a possession of truth hidden by the idea of certainty about itself as *res cogitans* or transcendental ego[93]—and yet in all of this, that dimension is not to be excluded out of which all living out of existence supports itself, as it were.

Heidegger characterizes such dissembling, seen more closely, by the fact that the care for certainty itself cares for the validity of binding propositions and therefore "as care for validity thus determined and the bindingness of the proposition takes its abode in the development of science,"[94] which posits all entities in advance "as a particular universe of possible regions, encounterable by a multiplicity of sciences"[95] and thereby "encounterable by valid propositions."[96] With this *"levelling of being"*[97] carried out by the idea of phenomenology as rigorous science, the care for certainty in itself becomes, according to Heidegger, *"needless* . . . in the sense that it does not at all question its appropriateness with that with which it works (with the whole foundation of the old ontology) and its origin."[98] In this relation to tradition, unproblematic for itself and stamped by oversight and finally an inability to see any longer, a nontransparent power of care is thereby conceded to this tradition over itself, with fatal consequences.

For the inclination of tradition leaves out—that is lacks the knowledge of—the past of the present, and thereby the historical situation of the care for certainty is neglected, which means "that the being of knowing itself is not transparent about its own possibilities of being."[99] But according to Heidegger, thereby *"the historical Dasein entirely degrades.*[100] This includes the fact that in the analysis of human knowing the *"temporality of Dasein*

---

93. The *'eversio opiniorum'* determined in this way for Descartes is for Heidegger thus only the "apparent unsettling of all possibilities of knowledge, [for they] are carried out upon the ground of the *pre-assurance* of the fact that the *certum esse* is secured as *bonum"* (ibid., 281).

94. Ibid., 283.

95. Ibid.

96. Ibid.

97. Ibid. By analogy one must except what Fink notes, in view of the phenomenological reduction found in the *Critique*, in a post-1929 remark: "But the innermost essence of the phenomenological reduction consists not in the thematization of being as such in the regression to subjectivity, but is rather precisely a de-being [*Ent-seinung*]" (cited by R. Bruzina, "Gegensätzlicher Einfluß—Integrierter Einfluß," 149).

98. Heidegger, *Einführung in die Phänomenologische Forschung*, GA 17, 282.

99. Ibid., 286.

100. Ibid., 93.

fails to appear"[101] and thus in the care for known knowledge human being is not thematized in the temporal dimension existentially constitutive for it from birth to death. Temporality and historicity of human being, and thus human being itself, are therefore not only not seen by the care of certainty as the care for certainty, according to Heidegger, but also as such they are taken care of precisely in their failing to appear and are in this sense disguised. Seen thus, the care for certainty, in particular in the context of the care for science, is explicitly given the chance that "the being of Dasein [could] be encountered in its own possibility *before* this primary association with regard to being."[102]

For the connection to care that we have in view, the self-connection to the idea of certainty, this "*care for absolute bindingness*"[103] means that therein "that which itself stands in care—the objective bindingness, which is to be gained—is alive in the concrete *being* of care itself, of the type that all that which comes in the field of sight of care, is determined more closely by *this* object of concern."[104] Heidegger designates this phenomenon terminologically as a *receipt* (*Rückschein*)[105] "that everything having to do with care [objective-theoretically] hangs upon the object of concern,"[106] and in just such a way that it knows nothing of itself, so that in what is unexpressed as "care for that which concerns it, [it] *lapses*."[107] In this receipt qua lapse Heidegger demonstrates, as a character of being of caring Dasein, that which he calls entanglement (*Verfängnis*), wherein care increasingly "*becomes caught up* [in the object of concern] *itself*."[108] Yet this itself again implies, thought as a phenomenon of being, a *neglect* that corresponds to

101. Ibid., 282.

102. Ibid., 283.

103. Ibid., 83.

104. Ibid.

105. Ibid. "The receipt [Heidegger critically argues] extends so far that the possibility of a concrete ethicality [*Sittlichkeit*] is made dependent upon the presence-at-hand of an ethics as the absolutely binding science" (85). This is directed at Husserl, about whom Heidegger reports in a letter to Jaspers on July 14, 1923, that he had written a plan for a "mathematics of ethics" (Heidegger and Jaspers, *Briefwechsel*, 43).

106. Heidegger, *Einführung in die Phänomenologische Forschung*, GA 17, 84.

107. Ibid. The phenomenon of the receipt serves as a prelude for the ontological reflection, well known from *Sein und Zeit*, of the understanding of the world upon the interpretation of Dasein (*Sein und Zeit*, GA 2, 21) and belongs thereby to the existential structure of falling, which Heidegger, in the context of his early Aristotle lecture course (*Phänomenologische Interpretationen zu Aristoteles*, GA 61), had already discussed in the concept of falling into ruin, where he thematizes as relucency (ibid., 119) what is here called receipt.

108. Heidegger, *Einführung in die phänomenologische Forschung*, GA 17, 85.

the flight before oneself that we have already encountered and illuminated in its threefold character, wherein care "in the manner of the flight before Dasein, is concerned with the burying of Dasein itself, the impossibilities of its encounter."[109]

In order to give this complex state of affairs the requisite transparency of its structural presuppositions, Heidegger expressly points to the fact that for the adequate interpretation of care as the how of Dasein it is necessary to uncover that "fundamental connection . . . between the being of care itself and the object of concern of this care, [that is,] that *which actually stands in care, Dasein as such*."[110] What is reminiscent in the first part of this formal indication of the connection of care is the discovery of the intentionality of consciousness constituting the ur-fact of *a priori correlation,* which Husserl also does not give up in carrying out his transcendental turn [*Wende*], so that the transcendentality in itself is determined relationally. Insofar as the transcendentality according to Husserl already holds within itself all mundane being as a phenomenon of consciousness, it would be a misunderstanding to expect a mediating force between the transcendental and the mundane in such relationality, as it would also be erroneous to assume that thereby the unity of reason authenticated for Husserl in the sphere of absolute subjectivity falls into doubt. In other words, within the conscious intentional exchange relation [*Bezugsverhältnisses*], the intended mundane correlate remains given uniquely as a phenomenon whose rational knowledge is attained under the standard of the idea of certainty through the contributions of the *epoché* and the reduction.[111]

Seen thus, according to Heidegger, the phenomenological principle no longer experiences a phenomenological indication through Husserl, be-

109. Ibid., 284. "What care flees is Dasein in the possibility of its being-known and its mode of interpretation" (285).

110. Ibid., 277 (emphasis added).

111. These achievements are not abrogated, or rather, revoked, even when the phenomenologically tuned "I" returns to the natural attitude, since in the sense of the abovementioned 'division of the I,' the phenomenologist, according to Husserl, is aware of the enworlding [*Verweltlichung*] of transcendental subjectivity as such, and thus no longer has to share in the naiveté of the original natural attitude. The problem of enworlding is treated in detail in Fink's *VI. Cartesiansichen Meditation: Husserliana Dokumente,* vol. 2, ed. with commentary by Hans Eberling, Jann Holl, and Guy van Kerckhoven (Dordrecht: Springer, 1988). Hans Rainer Sepp's essay ("Praktische Transzendalität oder transzendentale Praxis? Zum Problem der Verweltlichung transzendentalphänomenologischer Erkenntnisse," in *Gelehrenrepublik—Lebenswelt,* ed. Angelika Bäumer and Michael Benedikt [Vienna: Passagen, 1993], 189–207) deals with the question of the role and function of praxis in the context of the theoretical sense of the task of transcendental phenomenology raised by the problem of enworlding.

cause here 'to the things themselves' means turning toward them, insofar as they can be a theme of a science of consciousness. Therefore, Heidegger speaks of a characteristic deformation of intentionality, which shows itself intuitively in the fact that usually intentionality is translated as meaning in the sense of theoretical meaning. And insofar as this surrenders the foundation for every intentional analysis, the entity in its immediate givenness for analysis is taken in advance in the perspective of the theoretically reified view.

The 'something' (*Etwas*) as the 'whereof' (*Worauf*) of the intentional relation is thus already objectivated in the method of this theorizing; that is to say, it appears only in the subject-object relation reflected into itself as the correlate of a theoretical meaning through which "every judgment, every willing, every loving is founded upon a *representing* that specifies what can be willed, what can be hated and loved."[112] Upon this objectivation Heidegger sparks his fundamental critique, which he formulates positively in the demonstration of the structure of care with a view to intentionality. For as we have seen, this structure of care, determined as comportment precisely in this caring comportment-to, is always already concerned with its object and at the same time—and this is decisive—with the being of human Dasein. This means that the actual relation in which all objective knowing in its ground resonates is accordingly care itself. In its theoretical development it is, as we have seen, thus only *one* modification of the pretheoretical comportment of the human yet to be determined more thoroughly that proves itself to be the "fundamental being-in-motion of Dasein,"[113] which, as *"visible being-in-a-world,"*[114] is cooriginarily a relation to oneself as to the world and conversely relates to itself in its concern for the world.

As it takes shape here, Heidegger's critique of Husserl is thus as a whole already governed by this founding and at most implicit *orientation to oneself.* The basic feature of care in all of its modes is precisely the "apprehending being-out for something."[115] And in this concern for something it is concerned for its own Dasein, and it is so precisely when caring, in the mode of being of the care for certainty, holds itself qua burial [*Verschüttung*] in the flight before a self-knowing. As a result, when Heidegger speaks—in a kind

---

112. Heidegger, *Einführung in die phänomenologische Forschung*, GA 17, 272.
113. Ibid., 284 (emphasis deleted).
114. Ibid., 285.
115. Ibid.

of phenomenological credo—in 1923 of the fact that his sights were set on Husserl,[116] these eyes discover, in their orientation to Husserl, the latter's *blind spot*. As Guy van Kerckhoven stresses, it is a matter of that which "in viewing the εἴδη, the pure essences of a phenomenological consciousness, cannot be seen,"[117] yet nonetheless these essences, as enabling forces at the ground of consciousness, work as *factical life*, which only properly becomes a theme with the hermeneutical metamorphosis of phenomenology. In it the task is posed of "understanding *life itself in its actual being* and answering the *question concerning its character of being.*"[118]

§ 28. *The Metamorphosis of Phenomenology into the Hermeneutical*

a) *In connection with the Tendencies of Lebensphilosophie*

To seek the approach of phenomenological questioning in *pretheoretical life*, as Heidegger calls for in 1923 in his critique of Husserl's theoreticism, does not date, however, originally from this moment. Rather, this insight, as the tonic note, forms a kind of pedal point that determines the Heideggerian conception from at least 1919—that is, since the first lecture course held in the war emergency semester. In these beginning years, Husserl emerges less obviously in the role of the criticized; although in a determi-

116. Ibid., 5.

117. Guy van Kerckhoven, "Die Konstruktion der Phänomene des absoluten Bewußtseins: Martin Heideggers Auseinandersetzung met dem Denken Edmund Husserls," in *Zur philosophischen Aktualität Heideggers,* ed. Dietrich Papenfuss and Otto Pöggeler (Frankfurt: Klostermann, 1990), 2:56.

118. Heidegger, *Einführung in die phänomenologische Forschung,* GA 17, 275. For Heidegger, the *"expression 'life'* [is] a fundamental phenomenological category, meaning a fundamental phenomenon. If the expression, indicated with specifiable justification as a fundamental phenomenon, may be appealed to, then there is the possibility of drawing out the directions of sense given in a fundamental phenomenon, and this in an exemplary mode" (*Phänomenologische Interpretationen zu Aristoteles, GA* 61, 80). Nonetheless, Heidegger recognizes that a "remarkable vagueness" (ibid., 81) appertains to this expression in linguistic usage as well as an ambiguity. However, according to Heidegger, "the confusing ambiguity of the word 'life' and its usage [may] not become the occasion to simply dismiss it. . . . For philosophy the insecurity of meaning can only be the occasion for removing it, or rather, if it is necessary to ground it in its object, making it into something explicitly appropriated and transparent" ("Phänomenologische Interpretationen zu Aristoteles," 240). In order to display the sense-structure of the expression 'life,' Heidegger proceeds, as usual, from the verbal meaning—in which, as we shall see (§ 31), a given concrete experience is realized—to excavate it with respect to its sense, which is the task of the hermeneutical-phenomenological analysis.

nate sense he even functions as a type of compurgator or character witness, Heidegger was nonetheless at no point 'a pure-blooded Husserlian phenomenologist.' For his productive appropriation of phenomenology is carried out from the beginning in the sense of its *metamorphosis into the hermeneutical* and is to be recognized as such where he raises conceptually the claim for his own work to rework phenomenology toward a 'pretheoretical ur-science' (war emergency semester 1919), that is to say, to sketch out an 'originary science of life in itself' (winter semester 1919/20).

With the *primacy of pretheoretical life* implied by such a programmatic method, Heidegger appears initially to align himself with *Lebensphilosophie,* which at this time operated at the margins of the academic world in Germany, still dominated by neo-Kantianism; yet since the first decade of the twentieth century, outside the universities, *Lebensphilosophie* had begun to broadly influence wide swathes of public opinion—similar to postmodernism in the 1980s.[119] Yet Heidegger marks himself off constantly and with success from the virulent irrational motivating strands of *Lebensphilosophie* on all sides as well as from their neovitalistic and biologistic traits, in which he discerns a self-misunderstanding of their actual tendencies.[120] First of all, it is the hermeneutical form of *Lebensphilosophie,*[121] oriented to Dilthey, that sharpens for him the critical view, for the starting-point in life, upon the predominantly neo-Kantian "deeply ingrained bias toward the theoretical."[122] Accordingly, that Heidegger makes the value-theoretical criticism, as typified by the Southwest German school, into a particular

119. On this background, see Gadamer, "Erinnerungen an Heideggers Anfänge," in *Dilthey-Jahrbuch* 4 (1986–1987), 3–13 (Göttingen: Vandenhoeck & Ruprecht). Otto Friedrich Bollnow's study *Die Lebensphilosophie* (Berlin: Springer, 1958) offers an overview of this movement from the point of a thinker who was himself both biographically and philosophically bound up with it in a direct way. Further, see Karl Albert's rather cursory portrait, *Lebensphilosophie: Von den Anfängen bei Nietzsche bis zu ihrer Kritik bei Lukács* (Freiburg: Alber, 1995). On the questions raised systematically out of the context of lebensphilosophie, see also Ferdinand Fellman, *Lebensphilosophie: Elemente einer Theorie der Selbsterfahrung* (Reinbek bei Hamburg: Rowohlt, 1993).

120. See Heidegger, *Wegmarken GA* 9, 14–18; also *Phänomenologische Interpretationen zu Aristoteles, GA* 61, 79–83; see further *Phänomenologie der Anschauung und des Ausdrucks. Theorie der philosophischen Begriffsbildung,* in *GA,* ed. Claudius Strube (Frankfurt: Klostermann, 1993), 59:12–18.

121. See Heidegger, *Wegmarken GA* 9, 14; *Phänomenologie der Anschauung und des Ausdrucks, GA* 59, 153.

122. Heidegger, *Zur Bestimmung der Philosophie, GA* 56–57, 88. "*Lebensphilosophie* is for us a necessary stage on the path of philosophy, in opposition to empty, formal transcendental philosophy" (*GA* 59, 154); see also *GA* 61, 80.

theme in ever-new attempts and then dismantles it in a sustained manner in his profound analyses.[123] For Heidegger it is in no way a matter of dis-

123. See also Heidegger, *Phänomenologie und transzendentale Wertphilosophie*, in GA 56–57, 121–203. While one can certainly see a "first parricide" (as Jean Greisch suspects of this former student of Rickert) in the manner of the Heideggerian dispute with philosophy of value, (Griesch, *Hermeneutik und Metaphysik*, 180), a more important source of motivation for Heidegger could be the fact that in the face of the experiences of slaughter in the First World War, the theory of value revealed itself to be part of the declining Old European order, and thus is unsuitable as an impulse for the new beginning ahead. Insofar as it has not of itself given up its place in academic life, however, it must, according to Heidegger, be fought precisely with the means of philosophical analysis (see *Phänomenologie und transzendentale Wertphilosophie*, GA 56–57, 180). And this must be done not less, but rather more when, as Rickert had done (*Die Philosophie des Lebens: Darstellung und Kritik der lebensphilosophischen Modeströmungen unserer Zeit* [Tübingen: Mohr, 1922]), the attempt is undertaken to demonstrate, against the fiercely attacked chief representatives of *Lebensphilosophie* (Nietzsche, Bergson, Simmel, and Dilthey), that in relation to the theme of 'life' philosophy has its task in "conceptually mastering and fortifying life" (ibid., 155).

Grasped positively, this means that "the basis of *Lebensphilosophie*, correctly understood" (*Die Philosophie des Lebens*, 193), lies in values. "A system of a philosophy of life can only be constructed on the ground of a system of values" (ibid.). In the values of life, as we read in the second edition of 1922, wherein Rickert translates, so to speak, more strongly than two years prior, the concern of a philosophy of life into his own positing of the question—and thus in certain limits also accepts—there exists the "extra-logical basis of all theory" (ibid., xi), whereby, however, the problem of value remains the central question of philosophy. Against this Heidegger turns with all decisiveness since it is necessary to "destroy as phantoms the ideality of values and their like, which have been turned into something timeless and exaltedly enthroned as eternally valid" (*Phänomenologische Interpretationen zu Aristoteles*, GA 61, 111; see also ibid., 80). Heidegger's frequently imploring tone, his gesture of a radical, as it had already become characteristic of his lectures in these years immediately following the war, and which can be perceived also in his correspondence during that period (see particularly the Jaspers correspondence), consistently has something of that pathos of emergence typical of the age, without ever being wholly absorbed in it. This pathos lent Heidegger a powerful voice through the popular success of Oswald Spengler's *The Decline of the West*, among others, at that time (in the fashion of the coming cultural morphology), though Spengler remained for Heidegger "always predominantly an irritant, yet nonetheless a fascinating one" (Frithjof, Rodi, *Erkenntnis des Erkannten: Zur Hermeneutik des 19. und 20. Jahrhunderts* [Frankfurt: Suhrkamp, 1990], 116). In Heidegger, see esp. *Grundprobleme der Phänomenologie*, GA 58, 3, 15, 252; *Ontologie*, GA 63, 37, 55.

For Heidegger himself the necessity of a fundamental new consideration [*Neubesinnung*] is decidedly serious, and accordingly he seeks to initiate such a new beginning concretely, out of his own lifeworldly situation, wherein he, the twenty-nine-year-old *Privatdozent*, confidently takes a public stand in his 1919 summer lecture course *Über das Wesen der Universität und des akademischen Studiums* (in GA 56–57, 205–214), on the extent to which it illuminates the handed-down fragments of the tradition by means of an unfolding, from out of the experience of life, of the concept of the situation. Decisive here, as also in relation to the critique of value philosophy, is the fact that Heidegger continually and constitutively ties his analyses to the task of offering a comprehensively new determination of the idea of philosophy. Only when philosophy, in its proper essence, is newly founded out of the relation to concrete factical life

carding theory in general in favor of something like any type of immediately practical moral engagement. Philosophy generates theoretical knowledge, yet—as will be shown in the thematization of the formal character of indication of the hermeneutical facticity of knowledge—in such a way as to be *sui generis*.[124] It thus does not also belong in the governing field of epistemology. For this seeks, as Heidegger formulates it, to solve the problem of theoretical knowledge, in which it explains "*the theory through the theory,*"[125] that is, ultimately establishes "logic as the theory of theory."[126] But thereby for it the broad field of philosophy is locked up within the narrowness of "logicism."[127]

But now, in order to give the proper answer to the question "*What is the theoretical and its possible achievement?*"[128] Heidegger breaks open this circle of theoretical knowledge, in that he explicitly directs his view to the *origin* of the theoretical, in whose exhibition he outlines the task of phi-

---

can a metamorphosis in the varying modes of human comportment to itself and to the world be expected that is no longer obliged to seek a foothold in traditional epistemological and value-theoretic answers. This is the foundation for the claim out of which Heidegger starts on his path in phenomenology as a step in the metamorphosis of its traditional forms.

124. "Research on the differing levels of theorization, research on their contexts of motivation, is a significant concern of philosophy" (Heidegger, *Zur Bestimmung der Philosophie, GA* 56–57, 90). In this sense, the early Heidegger emphasizes the *scientific character* of his phenomenological method (e.g. *Phänomenologische Interpretationen zu Aristoteles, GA* 61, 45–48; *Phänomenologie der Anschauung und des Ausdrucks, GA*59, 153). It involves, however, a certain sui generis, and thus requires a clearer demarcation in order to avoid any misunderstanding. He thus rejects, among other things, the ever obtruding, common rationalistic scientific understanding that takes shape in methodology and in philosophy of science as an ultimately unreflective and mistaken faith in science, to which Husserl was still subject. For Heidegger, in opposition, it is a matter of the fact that "science [as a knowing comportment] becomes again a *form of life*" (*Grundprobleme der Phänomenologie, GA* 58, 20 [emphasis added]; see also *Phänomenologische Interpretationen zu Aristoteles, GA* 61, 43, 54). And the later Heidegger continued to assert of phenomenology that it is a "more scientific science . . . if one takes science in the sense of more originary knowledge in the sense of the Sanskrit word '*wit*' (to see)" (*Zollikoner Seminare,* ed. Medard Boss [Frankfurt: Klostermann, 1987], 265).

125. Heidegger, *Zur Bestimmung der Philosophie, GA* 56–57, 96.

126. Ibid.

127. Ibid., 110. At another point, this means: "The true philosophical bearing is never that of a logical tyrant, who frightens life with his stare" (*Grundprobleme der Phänomenologie, GA* 58, 263). The reproach of logicism concerns not merely the problematic of the neo-Kantians treated in detail in these lectures, but is perceived by Heidegger with a view to the theory of judgment given preference therein as the basic tendency of scientific philosophy of his time; see on this, among others, his review article, "Neuere Forschungen über Logik," in *Frühe Schrifte,* ed. Friedrich-Wilhelm von Herrmann, *GA* 1 (Frankfurt: Klostermann, 1978), 17–43.

128. Heidegger, *Zur Bestimmung der Philosophie, GA* 56–57, 88.

losophy conceived as *ur-science.* The origin of the theoretical may thereby not be taken on the level of a supreme principle out of which theoretical knowledge could be deduced according to a logical schema; as well, "origin" here does not point back evolutionarily to a historical first beginning whose "pedigree" could be spelled out genealogically. And further, origin is not even synonymous in this connection with what the discourse on 'presuppositions' means, insofar as this holds itself entirely in "the weave of *theoretical* positings and *theoretical* judgments."[129] Origin, as it becomes a theme for Heidegger in the "genuine *ur*-science,"[130] is that dimension from which all theorizing springs as a sphere of pretheoretical life, without being able to resolve this in theory.[131] The dimension of origin accordingly characterizes the primary human self- and world relation, which is antecedent to all theoretical knowledge as existentiell experience.[132]

129. Ibid., 97.

130. Ibid., 96; see ibid., 3, 12, 15.

131. "This science of the origin is of such a kind that not only does it not *need* to make any *presuppositions,* but it *cannot* make them, because it is not a theory [in the conventional sense]. It lies *before* or beyond the sphere in which talk of presupposition in general has sense. *This* sense springs-from [*ent-springt*] only the origin [*Ursprung*]" (ibid., 96).

132. Insofar as this experiencing is to be grasped as comportment to oneself as well as to the world, an antecedent *dimension of praxis* opens up therein as a fundamental region. This phenomenal basic comportment, characteristic of Heidegger's method as a whole, has stimulated research on a series of investigations of the function of praxis in Heidegger's thinking. They turn primarily upon the question of the possibility of an ethical approach in Heidegger to be unfolded from this point of departure (see Jean Grondin, "Das junghegelianische und ethische Motiv in Heideggers Hermeneutik der Faktizität," in *Wege und Irrwege des neuren Umganges mit Heideggers Werk,* ed. István M. Fehér [Berlin: Duncker & Humblot, 1991, 141–150]; Gerold Prauss, "Heidegger und die Praktische Philosophie," in *Heidegger und die praktische Philosophie,* ed. Annemarie Gethmann-Siefert and Otto Pöggeler [Frankfurt: Suhrkamp, 1988], 177–190; Manfred Riedel, "Heidegger und der hermeneutische Weg zur praktischen Philosophie," in *Für eine zweite Philosophie: Vorträge und Abhandlungen* [Frankfurt: Suhrkamp, 1988], 171–196).

The question is also asked about his contact with other potential contexts or lines of connection regarding pragmatic approaches (see Carl Friedrich Gethmann, *Dasein,* esp. 272–277, 281–321; Richard Rorty, "Heidegger, Contingency, and Pragmatism," in *Essays on Heidegger and Others: Philosophical Papers,* vol. 2 [Cambridge: Cambridge University Press, 1995], 27–49), especially the varying remarks on William James by Heidegger himself, which refer to deepened knowledge of practical conceptions. The research is in agreement that Heidegger came into contact with pragmatism through Emil Lask.

In view of Heidegger's hermeneutical approach, it is, however, necessary to take note of the fact that praxis, as it is taken into account here in pretheoretical comportment, is to be explained hermeneutically-phenomenologically in its pretheoretical sense-structure for a sufficient categorial interpretive understanding; that is to say, that it is not to be theorized again in the sense of 'ordered factual positings,' as this is characteristic of pragmatism as a theory of praxis (see *GA* 61, 135). On the critique of the pragmatist reading of Heidegger, in particular

Heidegger thereby maintains himself in noticeable proximity to the hermeneutical position of Dilthey, for whom famously life, beyond which the intellect cannot venture, does not explain, but rather can only be understood from out of its modes of self-interpretation from experience.[133] It is this Diltheyan "tendency to *Lebensphilosophie*"[134] that according to Heidegger is to be grasped in the positive sense as "the breakthrough of a more radical tendency of philosophizing."[135] Insofar as he critically compelled himself from the beginning to this tendency, he holds himself in advance in a very tense opposition not only to the methodologically extraordinary, differentiated reflections and abstractions of neo-Kantianism, but also in his approach to Husserl's consciousness-theoretical concept. As we have seen, this distantiated view already gains an incisive expression in the critique of the care structure that we have discussed.

b) The Hermeneutical Approach in Pretheoretical Life

With his approach to pretheoretical life, Heidegger positions himself explicitly on the ground of phenomenology. This shows itself in the fact that his concept of experience is in no way a mere approximation,[136] as in Dil-

---

in relation to the fundamental approach of *Sein und Zeit,* see William D. Blattner, "Existential Temporality in *Being and Time* (Why Heidegger is not a Pragmatist)," in *Heidegger: A Critical Reader,* ed. Hubert L. Dreyfus and Harrison Hall (Oxford: Blackwell 1992), 99–129; Marylou Sena, "The Phenomenal Basis of Entities and the Manifestation of Being According to Sections 15–17 of *Being and Time*: On the Pragmatist Misunderstanding," *Heidegger Studies* (1995), 11:11–31.

133. Dilthey emphasizes, in varying contexts, that it is "the governing impulse in my philosophical thinking to wish to understand life from out of itself" (*Vorrede,* in *GS,* vol. 5; see *Rede zum 70 Geburtstag, GS* 5:7; see also, *Breslauer Ausarbeitung,* in *GS* 19:58–173, esp. 153).

134. Heidegger,*Ontologie GA 63, Die Geschichte des Seyns, GA 69;* see also *Phänomenologische Interpretationen zu Aristoteles, GA 61,* 80; *Phänomenologie der Anschauung und des Ausdrucks, GA 59,* 152–168.

135. *GA 63, 69.* In this proximity to Dilthey—which Heidegger confesses he cultivated "when it was still unseemly to mention him in a philosophical seminar" ("Metaphysische Anfangsgründe der Logik im Ausgang von Leibniz," in *GA 26,* ed. Klaus Held [Frankfurt: Klostermann, 1978], 178)—he nonetheless remains a decisive critic of that Dilthey who, in "a portentous restriction of his position" (*Ontologie, GA 63,* 14; see also *Phänomenologische Interpretationen zu Aristoteles, GA 61,* 7) proposed a foundation for the human sciences by means of a hermeneutical science that in connection with the tradition of a Schleiermacher would be formed as a methodology in the sense of an *"aesthetics of interpretation of written monuments"* (Dilthey, *Die Entstehung der Hermeneutik, GS* 5, 320).

136. See Gander, *Positivismus als Metaphysik,* 168–174.

they's transcendental-psychological functional determination, but rather is revealed precisely from out of the insight into intentionality as the fundamental structure of human comportment, which, as we have seen, he makes explicit in the concept of care. Paradigmatically, Heidegger unfolds the originary dimension, which is just as immemorial as underivable and therein constitutive, in an analysis of environmental experience. This will be discussed more precisely in approach and execution (§ 32), not least because for Heidegger Husserl's mistake, namely to take the thing world for the environment, shows itself to be overcome. For the present the concern is to see that by ur-science, Heidegger does not have in mind a 'supertheory,' but rather a "pretheoretical or supratheoretical, or in any case, a nontheoretical science."[137]

Pre-, supra-, nontheoretical it is and must be, not because life itself is irrational and diffuse, but rather because according to Heidegger the requisite (ur-)science can prescribe no understanding of theory through the phenomenal measuring of its theme, the dimension of origin of pretheoretical life for its structural knowledge, which intends to form a grounding connection of true propositions aimed at methodologically secured rule following.[138] For Heidegger already sees therein a reification that from an external standpoint explains life in functional determinations. In opposition, he states: "Life is not an object and can never become an object; it is nothing objectlike."[139] From here, the question arises concerning the specific *character of (pre-)givenness' of life* in general. In an anticipatory delimitation, for Heidegger, it can be said that he fundamentally grasps

137. Heidegger, *Zur Bestimmung der Philosophie,* GA 56–57, 96.

138. For interpretation it is important to be clear about the fact that Heidegger, when he polemicizes against 'philosophy as theory' in the early lectures, understands by "theory" primarily epistemology (or value theory) in the neo-Kantian sense, and thus means a concept of theory that in his eyes conflicts with a hermeneutical-phenomenological understanding of philosophy. That for Heidegger the task of a 'theory of philosophical concept-formation' is in no way abandoned, but rather a hermeneutically-phenomenologically articulated conceptual language arising out of the new founding of the idea of philosophy is virtually demanded, is constantly shown by the concrete endeavors undertaken in his early lectures in the specific region of a semantics of philosophical terms; see, e.g., the efforts at explication of the 'idea in principle of the definition of the concept of philosophy' in *Phänomenologische Interpretationen zu Aristoteles,* GA 61, 32, 60, 79, 160, especially the 1920 Summer Semester lecture, "Phänomenologie der Anschauung und des Ausdrucks: Theorie der philosophischen Begriffsbildung," GA 59.

139. Heidegger, *Grundprobleme der Phänomenologie,* GA 58, 236. He emphasizes: "Recognizing this is our main goal" (ibid.).

life as something "to which we have no distance at all to see it in its 'in general,'"[140] so that this having cannot also be spoken of in the Husserlian sense of conscious having. We do not have this distance to life precisely "because we are ourselves it, and we see ourselves only from life itself, in its own directions, which we are, which is us (accusative case), in its own directions."[141] That means that we can only assure ourselves of life in its meaning in concrete particular *acting.*

In every having—as Heidegger stresses in a view to the philosophically relevant problem of the thematization of the how of having—there is somehow at the same time talk of the 'object' itself, that is, the "particular genuine having can now demand in itself an express discourse,"[142] and thus pose the task "of bringing 'discourse' expressly in the how of having to the what of the object."[143] This task emerges for Heidegger within and from out of the mode of having of life itself in a situation of the factical experience of carrying out, wherein for him there lies at the same time the 'origin of phenomenological investigation of categories,'[144] grasped as existentiell. By 'category' Heidegger refers to "what in principle interprets a phenomenon according to its sense in a direction of sense in a determinate way, and brings the phenomenon as what is interpreted to understanding."[145] In this sense, categories are *interpreting*, "and [are precisely] factical life, appropriated in existentiell concern,"[146] as it is called in the early formulation, which later is called 'care.' Seen thus, the categories of life are contained in life itself, and are thus *modes of life*, on account of which their determination must carry itself out in explicit demonstration of the modes of life, manifesting itself as its explication, which, determined as interpretation, designates the philosophical attitude of the hermeneut of life.

As activities, the essentially self-related modes of life are always already familiar, that is, understood, the understanding of which Heidegger had famously unfolded in *Sein und Zeit* (§ 31) as 'being-able-to-be' (*Seinkön-*

---

140. Ibid., 29.

141. Ibid.

142. Heidegger, *Phänomenologische Interpretationen zu Aristoteles*, GA 61, 18. Cf. § 32.

143. GA 61, 19.

144. See ibid., 19, 86–89.

145. Ibid., 86.

146. Ibid., 87. What is here called "concern" is the matter of the context of care, understood factically-hermeneutically, to be explicated more closely at another point.

nen). Life, which is so implicitly familiar in being carried out for us, must be first conceived in its categorial structural content and context in the concrete interpretation of its constitutive and directly historical relations of sense, so that human life, which is always already historical, thus in itself necessitates for the sake of transparency a hermeneutics that, as the next chapter will detail more closely, is a hermeneutics of historical factical life.[147] Accordingly, in Heidegger's words, "the interpretative and [life's] context of being-moved . . . are factically and essentially the same . . . different categorial modes of determination of a being whose sense of being determines itself as facticity."[148] The identity refers to the *existentiell prior wherefrom* [*Woraus*], which, thought as original life in itself for its categorial interpretation insofar as it is itself a mode of life-activity,[149] demands a methodological distancing that, as difference of the phenomenological explication necessarily reflected into itself, indicates itself semantically in the structure of knowledge in the *hermeneutical 'as'* [*Als*].[150]

Insofar as the human is enmeshed in factical life in such a way that the self as activity constitutes itself in the lifeworld, the meaning of the expression "life" is known through and in a hermeneutically interpreting active *knowing* of the having [*der Habe*] of life itself. Heidegger thus formulates as a basic insight that the "idea of determining, the logic of apprehending the

147. "It could be that phenomena of life, according to their own fundamental meaning, are 'historical,' themselves only become 'historically' accessible, whereby the question must be decided . . . whether the problem of an originary historical existential interpretation as a method does not impose itself in a seamless context of sense with the problematic of existence" (*Wegmarken*, GA 9, 38).

148. Heidegger, GA 61, 135.

149. "Philosophy is a fundamental 'how' [*Grundwie*] of life itself" (ibid., 80).

150. This structure of difference of hermeneutical interpretation is connected in Heidegger's thinking with the problem of the *formal indication* (see "Einleitung in die Phänomenologie der Religion," ed. Matthias Jung, Thomas Regehly, and Claudius Strube, in GA 60 [Frankfurt: Klostermann, 1995], 62–65). In addition, it may be noted only now that with this, Heidegger indicates a specific mode of hermeneutically structuring formalization, in opposition to generalization, as the preferred path to the solution of fundamental philosophical problems, such as that of human self-understanding in the world. On the difference between formalization, which works out in analysis the preceding categorial and logical forms of knowledge, and generalization, which in contrast ascends from the singular to the general, see Husserl, *Ideen I*, 31. The significance of this difference in the preference for the development of philosophy bound up with the paradigm shift from consciousness to language, or how it as such can be made fruitful in completely different ways in the dispute with Husserl, is shown by Ernst Tugendhat's attempt at a linguistic renewal of traditional guiding philosophical concepts, prefaced in his work, dedicated to Heidegger, *Vorlesungen zur Einführung in die sprachanalytische Philosophie* (Frankfurt: Suhrkamp, 1979), 39–51.

object, the conceptuality of the object in a given definitional determinacy [must] be created out of the manner of *how the object originally becomes accessible.*"[151] C. F. Gethmann, drawing support from Wittgenstein's theory of meaning as use, speaks in the context of his meditations on the Heideggerian theory of the concept of a "*performance theory of meaning.*"[152] By means of this Heidegger, regarding the task of defining philosophical concepts, not only staunchly protects himself against their conventional arbitrary employment, but also, according to Gethmann, proves himself to be a phenomenologist—since he isolates himself as much from a semantic realism as from a semantic conventionalism, both of which assume an independent, conceptless reality.[153] In contrast, in a performance-theoretical manner and with a view to knowing comportment, Heidegger emphasizes as philosophical the object of knowledge as object in the determining that apprehends the how of its having: "The idea of definition [as the definition of philosophical objects] is nothing other than the *formal interpretation of the full sense of knowledge.*"[154] Heidegger conceives the formal sense of this definition in a rather circuitous manner as the "determining appropriate to situation and anticipation that takes hold from out of the basic experience to be gained and that corresponds to the object in its what-how-being."[155]

That 'life in itself' (thought as performance in the how of having) is in this sense always my own life is highlighted by Heidegger (as we will see in § 34) through the notion that the explication of his concept of world as lifeworld constitutively undergoes its intensification toward the *self-world* [*Selbstwelt*]—which here is not, however, to be taken concretely as a particular biography but rather lets the question concerning the self become thematic in formal indication, that is, what it means to be the self or a self. For the answer to the question of the knowledge of life posing itself in this connection, according to Heidegger, neither a psychological nor a natural scientific—particularly a biological—explanation can appear adequate, nor does the more metaphysical endeavor to uncover an originary power or drive of life promise a sufficient prospect of success. Rather, for its phenomenal clarification, this question refers to the hermeneutic dimension of self-experience, in which life is there for us in every situation. Heidegger

---

151. Heidegger, *Phänomenologische Interpretationen zu Aristoteles, GA* 61, 20.
152. Gethmann, *Dasein,* 265.
153. See ibid., 265.
154. Heidegger, *GA* 61, 54 (emphasis added).
155. Ibid., 19 (emphasis deleted).

thus poses himself the task of uncovering "*fundamental situations* in which the totality of life expresses itself,"[156] so that he views it as his chief problem "to discover the original form of the apprehending of life itself."[157] This search for the "fundamental sense of the method in which life conceives itself, in living, as life,"[158] is carried out in the phenomenological "leading back to the fundamental experience of factical life from itself."[159] Therein it is shown that every factical experience of life is always lived out in a 'world,' that is, in a 'lifeworld,' which, as already indicated, is centered in the self-world in "phenomenological comportment (to oneself)"[160]; this is more than merely a formal comportment and does not emerge in an objective knowledge, but rather brings hermeneutically to interpretation that sphere of processes of understanding sense in its modes of evidence, modes in which I experience myself.

c) The New Hermeneutical Accentuation of Phenomenology

By setting out from factical life, Heidegger carries out a decisive new accentuation in contrast to Husserl's approach to phenomenology. For Heidegger interprets Husserl's foundational and widely known 'principle of principles'[161] as a nontheoretical "ur-intention of true life"[162] and in this sense as "the ur-attitude of experience and life as such, absolute sympathy for life [*Lebenssympathie*] that is identical with experience itself."[163] His orientation has this "*Urhabitus*,"[164] yet no longer in the demonstration of a pure consciousness as is distinctive for Husserl's approach, which burdens

156. Heidegger, *Grundprobleme der Phänomenologie*, GA 58, 231.
157. Ibid., 248.
158. Ibid.
159. Ibid.
160. Ibid., 250. In this context Heidegger stresses emphatically that the way beyond the self-world has nothing to do with psychology (see ibid., 248). We will return to this in the context of the self-world analysis.
161. "On the principle of all principles: that every originary intuition is a source of law for knowledge, that everything that . . . presents itself to us in originary 'intuition' is simply to be accepted as what it purports to be, yet only within the limits in which it presents itself, can lead no conceivable theory into error for us" (Husserl, *Ideen I*, 52).
162. Heidegger, GA 56–57, 110.
163. Ibid.
164. Ibid.

itself, according to Heidegger, with the legacy of transcendental idealism insofar as he, as we have seen, avails himself epistemologically in the wake of Descartes and Kant of the subject-object schema and thus works "in a corrupt tradition."[165] Thus, according to Heidegger it is not epistemological reflection that apprehends "the experience of taking-oneself-along in experience."[166] This occurs rather in what he, in a terse sketch during the last hours of his lecture course, calls the "understanding, the *hermeneutic intuition*."[167, 168]

165. Heidegger, *GA 63*, 73; cf. *GA 58*, 23. As seen in the previous chapter, Husserl's concept of the pure "I," which, in its formality, 'accompanies all representations,' proves itself to be—and this is the issue for Heidegger—scarcely serviceable for the concrete apprehension of phenomena, since the pure "I" is not "encounterable" in concrete factical experience in the concrete lifeworld and thus contributes nothing to the hermeneutical understanding of the factical.

166. Heidegger, *GA 56–57*, 117.

167. Ibid. At this point Heidegger uses the concept of the 'hermeneutical' for the first time, insofar as the present state of his texts allows us to say. To this extent, Heidegger's memory deceives him when, in the 1950s, he dates his first usage of the term back to the summer of 1923 (see "Aus einem Gespräch über die Sprache," *GA 12*, 90). As Manfred Riedel, in a justifiable avoidance of an entirely trivial erroneous finding, states in reference to the title of the 1920 Summer Semester lecture course (which Heidegger likewise did not quite remember correctly), Heidegger thinks *anamnestically* (see his *Hören auf die Sprache*, 75), and thus, the use of the title 'hermeneutic' is already bound for Heidegger in the trace of memory to the programmatic grasp on the problematic of facticity (which the famous remark at the end of § 15 of *Sein und Zeit* also confirms). However, as has now been shown, this is rooted in its origins in the critical transformation of Husserlian phenomenological intuition, which, in the hermeneutical radicalization carried out therein as intuition, is "so hermeneutical that it can hardly be called [in this sense] 'intuition' as Husserl intended it" (Jean Grondin, "Die hermeneutische Intuition zwischen Husserl und Heidegger," in *Inmitten der Zeit: Beiträge zur europäischen Gegenwartsphilosophie*, ed. Thomas Grethlein and Heinrich Leitner [Wurzburg: Königshausen & Neumann, 1996], 274).

In light of this fitting characterization it is surprising when, in the conception of his essay, Grondin emphasizes shortly thereafter that Husserl had made a special contribution to hermeneutics, which lies precisely in "his version of intuition, which he understood factically as hermeneutic or that which Heidegger understood when he named it 'hermeneutical intuition'" (ibid., 275). The connection with Heidegger produced by the copulative 'or,' a connection that very nearly brings one to the concept that Husserl already intended, is justified by the fact that Grondin conceives Heidegger's hermeneutical turn "originally not as a critique of Husserl, but rather as an adoption of the latter's insights" (ibid.). This strict separation of either adoption or critique is not sustained by Heidegger's style of interpretation, whether it treats of Aristotle or Kant, Hölderlin or whomever else, and in particular fails to recognize that Heidegger's adoption of Husserl, as we have seen, is from the start already carried out as a critique (see note 200).

Decisive for Grondin's rendering—posed in more detailed form in his study "Husserl's Silent Contribution to Hermeneutics" (in *Sources of Hermeneutics* [New York: SUNY Press, 1995], 35–46)—is that he loads Husserl's usage of the terms 'intuition' and 'intention' conceptually-historically with an implicit hermeneutical intention that expresses itself implicitly therein. Thus, when he attempts to see the "essential solidarity between the young Heidegger and Husserl" ("Die hermeneutische Intuition," 276) in that silent hermeneutical bond, he fails to take into consideration the new, in fact revolutionary, quality of the early Heideggerian position. And while Grondin, in other texts, insists emphatically upon this novelty in Heidegger (e.g., "Die Hermeneutik der Faktizität als ontologische Destruktion und Ideologiekritik: Zur philosophischen Aktualität Heideggers," in *Zur philosophischen Aktualität Heideggers,* ed. Dietrich Papenfuss and Otto Pöggeler, vol. 2 [Frankfurt: Kostermann, 1992], 163–178), it is here dulled in his argumentation.

Even when one grants that in fact concepts like 'intuition' or 'intention' possess hermeneutical implications in other and, in accordance with the sense of the term, more originary contexts, this does not therefore mean that these other contextual ties with Husserl can simply be applied.

In no way is the value of conceptual-historical investigations to be doubted here. For a conceptual-historical concern [*Sorgfalt*] aids the philosopher in evading a free-floating act of definition that language thereby unduly instrumentalizes. The question remains, however, whether and to what extent conceptual-historical arguments are always appropriate for lending the requisite incisiveness to a thematic state of affairs. In other words, when conceptual-historical references such as those taking place in this text gain a compelling argumentative function for the interpretation of the terms 'intuition' and 'intention,' a hermeneutic interpretation must be led, regarding their efficacy, by a view to the implementation of the concept in the context of its usage. That means that one could establish the usage of original hermeneutical terms in Husserl, or criticize them, as the case may be, without thereby having to ascribe anything cryptohermeneutical or protohermeneutical to the Husserlian approach itself. Therein would lie, to cite Riedel, the task of "philosophy as a critical interpretation of concepts," in contrast to which the role of the history of concepts would be determined as the "connecting link between philosophy, history of science, and pre-philosophical interpretation of concepts" (Riedel, *Norm und Werturteil:Grundprobleme der Ethik* [Stuttgart: Reclam, 1979], 125).

168. With regard to Heidegger's mode of proceeding, it should be pointed out here that in the last hours of the lecture course it often takes on the character of a conglomeration in which the horizontal lines on the foundation of what has hitherto been reached are, in a kind of summary, at times extracted programmatically in the direction of an onward-leading course of thought. Since this is frequently done spontaneously in his lectures, i.e., diverging from the manuscript he had worked out, these concluding remarks often appear only in transcripts that are, with respect to the course of his thinking, trustworthy for the most part; yet, as my own editorial experience has taught me, they seldom reach the degree of nuance and incisiveness distinctive in a composed lecture.

Therefore should one also be on guard against dramatizing these concluding hours of the course, as if only here the train of his thought had reached its proper goal, as Theodor Kisiel suggests, at least tendentially, in various publications (see especially *The Genesis of Heidegger's Being and Time*) with regard to what he calls the war emergency semester-schema of the lecture course *Die Idee der Philosophie und das Weltanschauungsproblem.* Due, in my opinion, to overly puristic editorial principles, this schema, because it was only present in the transcripts, was not even initially edited as an appendix within the framework of *GA* 56–57, offering Kisiel the occasion for all sorts of conjectures (see "Edition und Übersetzung: Unterwegs von Tatsachen zu Gedanken, von Werken zu Wegen," in *Zur philosophischen Aktualität Heideggers,* vol. 3, ed. Dietrich Papenfuss and Otto Pöggeler [Frankfurt: Klostermann, 1992], 89–107; for clarification, see Parvis Emad, "Zu Fragen der Interpretation und Entzifferung der Grundlagen der Gesamtausgabe Martin Heideggers," *Heidegger Studies* (1993), 9:161–171). In the interim the schema has been published by Claudius Strube (see Heidegger, "Die Idee der Philosophie und

Heidegger determines it as a "comportment to something [*Verhalten zu etwas*],"[168] a comportment that is intuitively at home with itself. The 'something' [*Etwas*] is not, however, an object or thing [*Objekt oder Gegenstand*], nor is it a thing given form through "the most sublime theorizing,"[169] which for Heidegger is synonymous with a "theoretical fixing and neutralization of something capable of being experienced"[170] as the result of the "absolute disconnectedness of a relation to life."[171] In contrast, Heidegger conceives the sense of this 'something' as "*that which is capable of being experienced in general*,"[172] and thereby designates the "index for the highest potentiality of life."[173] Thus, the experienceable intended here as such is, in this comportment-to, always a possible something that, however, indicates life itself as an ur-something [*Ur-etwas*] in the formal "relatedness" of factical experience to life .

The sense of the experienceable in general, determined in the character of its potentiality, rests precisely in life as a whole yet rests indifferently over against its possible worldliness, and thus yet without a genuinely worldly and object-specific form. Heidegger distinguishes this easily misunderstood '*not yet*' as the "essentially *preworldly*."[174] As the "not yet having broken out into a genuine life,"[175] the preworldly something is that "essential moment of life in and for itself"[176] that is constitutively intertwined with what Heidegger calls the "appropriative character [*Ereignischarakter*]

das Weltanschauungsproblem (Auszug aus der Nachschrift Brecht)," ed. Claudius Strube, in *Heidegger Studies* (1996), 12: 9–14), and can be found as well in the reissue of *GA* 56–57 (1999). In the process the schema proves, *sine ira et studio*, to be a useful addendum, without, however, warranting any hypostatizations.

169. Heidegger, *GA* 56–57, 112.

170. Ibid., 115.

171. Ibid.

172. Ibid.

173. Ibid.

174. Ibid. For Kisiel this step of Heidegger's is "at once simple and brilliant" ("Das Kriegsnotsemester," 119). For with this "non-objective formalization" (ibid.) the rift between object and knowledge is eliminated. That is, insofar as Heidegger determines the something as "comportment as such" (ibid.), this comportment is in general "no ob-ject [*Gegen-stand*], but rather the moment of out-towards (*Auf-zu*) . . ., off of which intentional structures of life can be read" (ibid.).

175. Heidegger, *GA* 56–57, 115. As a concept, this 'essentially preworldly' is easily misunderstood since the thought of a transcendence is liable to slip in, wherein the immanence of the world as such is skipped over in favor of a kind of "spiritual preexistence" conceived Platonically rather than hermeneutically.

176. Ibid.

177. Ibid., 116.

of experience as such.”[177] Considered in this way “the formally objective *something of knowability*”[178] is subsequently first motivated out of this ‘pre-worldly something of life.’ For in the meaning of something conceived as experienceable there lies, constitutively, “the moment of the ‘out-towards,’ the ‘direction-towards,’ of the ‘*Into* a (determinate) world.’”[179]

Grasping life from out of itself, bound up with the task of hermeneutic intuition with an eye towards these complex facts and circumstances, thus demands ἔρως as a basic philosophical attitude, on the other hand, as Heidegger puts it at the end of the 1919/20 Winter-Spring lecture course. Heidegger defines it as “a releasing of oneself into the ultimate tendencies of life and a return into its ultimate motives.”[180] This letting oneself go into factical life is not synonymous for him with a drifting into its colorful surface or a simply immediate approach to objects in their concrete forms. This is not to say that hermeneutic philosophy, understood as ur-science, would remain without relation to the concrete; on the contrary, for Heidegger in philosophy it is decisively a matter of concretion, and this not in some sort of supplementary applied case, but because it bears within itself the reference to concretion, precisely in the fact “that *understanding . . .* according to its own sense of performativity and temporalization, *leads into concretion.*”[181] Since, however, this concretion does not readily yield anything, it poses in its philosophical indication “a task of its own sort, that is, a task for a carrying out of its own condition,”[182] formulated as “existentiell categorial interpretation.”[183] As we have already seen, formulated therein is the fact that what is called ‘concrete,’ as Heidegger puts it, is concrete in a respective having. This means, carried out theoretically, in view of life, that this having is in life respectively in such a way “that it apprehends its determinacies fully and in their full contexts of construction and concentration, that is, actually apprehends the (ultimate) structural sense . . . in the fullness of its what-how-determinacies.”[184]

<hr>

178. Ibid.
179. Ibid.
180. Ibid., 115.
181. Heidegger, *GA* 58, 263.
182. Heidegger, *GA* 61, 31.
183. Ibid., 32.
184. Ibid., 88.
185. Ibid., 28.

The letting oneself go into factical life in this sense as a "basic attitude . . . of the vital going-along-with [*Mitgehen*] the genuine sense of life, of understanding assimilation"[185] thus serves a "deepening of the self in its originariness."[186] Therewith is formulated the immanent *telos* of what for Heidegger lies concluded in the idea of originary science as an attitude in the sense of a "placing oneself into the living motivations and tendencies of the spirit"[187] and thus represents the early conception of phenomenology in its beginnings as a *hermeneutics of the self*. Heidegger very clearly and programmatically formulates this in the context of his Jaspers review when he emphasizes that "the possibility of radical understanding and of the proper adoption of the philosophical meaning of the phenomenological tendency [depends upon] . . . the fact that full experience in its actual factical context of performance is seen in the *historically existing self, the self with which it is in some way involved, ultimately, in philosophy*."[188]

The conceptual formation adequate to *hermeneutical intuition* as the "semantic index"[189] of the hermeneutical transformation of phenomenology thus does not have, in its particular linguistic expression, to be "simply meant theoretically or in any way specific to an object, but is rather originally experiential,"[190] so that "universality of the meaning of words"[191] for Heidegger primarily signifies something originary, namely the "worldliness of lived-through experience [*erlebten Erlebens*]."[192] Thereby the old dualistic separation of concept and object advocated in Kantian and neo-Kantian epistemology becomes obsolete in favor of a philosophizing immediately out of life. This signifies that in Heidegger the 'preworldly' as well as the 'worldly' functions of meaning as accompanying life are in the condition to express its "event-character [*Ereignischarakter*],"[193] thus going along with experience in life, and precisely in such a way that "in going along . . . they are at the same time approaching, and carrying within

186. Heidegger, *GA* 58, 23.
187. Ibid., 263.
188. Ibid., 24. What, as the ur-something, is otherwise referred to as life and here as spirit, he also calls in this context élan vital, "yet in a sense other than the mystically nebulous one found in Bergson" (ibid.).
189. Heidegger, *GA* 9, 35 (editor's emphasis).
190. Greisch, *Hermeneutik und Metaphysik*, 180.
191. Heidegger, *GA* 56–57, 117.
192. Ibid.
193. Ibid.
194. Ibid.

themselves, the origin."[194] In this way, Heidegger determines hermeneutical intuition more closely as an "originary, phenomenological formation of recourse and anticipation, out of which every theoretical-objectivating, indeed transcendent, positing falls away."[195] Anticipation is to be read here in the sense of the grasping tendency lying within it, which is at one and the same time also a recourse to the motivation, to be thought in a more deeply penetrating manner, in the factical something of life [*Lebensetwas*] whereby this something proves itself, with regard to its sense, "as the *motivat* of an entire process of motivations."[196] In view of the 'I experience something,' Heidegger stresses that the motive to be discerned cannot therefore mean "searching for the causes of existence, the reifying conditions, the things that explain experience as thing and reified, that is, posit in a factual connection."[197] In contrast, it is proper that "we are to understand the pure motive of sense of pure experience."[198]

It is important to see that in this stress the hermeneutical understanding of meaningful sense is already formulated in a critical resistance to the Husserlian phenomenological stance of seeing or intuition. For motives, as Heidegger understands them, cannot be beheld eidetically, but rather are apprehended hermeneutically solely in their character of meaning in the mode in which they express themselves in and as a connection of sense reference.[199] In this sense, the meaningful for Heidegger is "originarily expe-

195. Ibid.
196. Ibid.
197. Ibid., 68.
198. Ibid., 66.
199. Ibid.
200. That related traces of this can be found as well in Husserl, especially in his early work, does not speak against what we have discussed above (see note 167), insofar as the traces do certainly point in this direction yet on the whole have little hermeneutical effect and are dissolved again in the concept of his Cartesian-inspired idealism. Notably, one hits upon this above all in the *Logische Untersuchungen*, particularly in the first section, "Ausdruck und Bedeutung" (see Paul Ricoeur, "Phénoménologie et herméneutique: en venant de Husserl," in *Du texte à l'action: Essais d'herméneutique II* [Paris: Éditions du Seuil, 1986], 39–73, esp. 62–73).

From this vantage, light is also cast upon a possible motive for Heidegger's persistent high regard for the *Logische Untersuchungen*, which he does not really explain, but which in the context of the hermeneutical restructuring of phenomenology nonetheless holds some plausibility when he emphasizes that the *Logische Untersuchungen* is 'the basic text of all future scientific philosophy,' although—and this qualification can well be read with an eye on the hermeneutical grasping tendency—Husserl himself "was never fully reflectively clear on his own discoveries, i.e., their full sense and the entirety of their scope" (*GA* 58, 14), insofar as he did not succeed in "clearly working out the driving motive in its tendency" (ibid.). On Heidegger's relationship to the *Logische Untersuchungen*, see Françoise Dastur's study "Heidegger und

riencing, *preworldly or rather worldly*,"[200] and in this way the understanding has in view the particular factical itself as expression of experience, that is, the factical in the particular concrete expression of the experienced.[201]

If one holds this in view, the solicited 'purity' of the sense motive and its experiences will not be confused with the a priori character of the transcendentally purified experience of consciousness. 'Pure' [*rein*] means, rather, precisely the pure [*Pure*] of the factical in the sense of the originary of pretheoretical life, whose enlightenment Heidegger himself hopes to achieve in the course of a "return to the phenomenon of motivation,"[202] which as such in itself has to illuminate equally the historical spiritual-historical [*historisch geistesgeschichtliche*] sphere of motivation and also the problem-oriented systematic. However—and on this basis Heidegger rightly places the greatest value and determines thereby at the same time an *essentially hermeneutical thinking*—both strands of the task signify nothing different from the matter in question. That means the usual separation of philosophy into 'systematic' and 'historical' research is at bottom spurious. For in the sense of the return to the original motivation, a genuine, thus true, phenomenally adequate historical understanding already has to take the systematic problematic into view. And conversely, a genuine systematic treatment will not be able to shut out the historical depth of the problem, so that with regard to these fields of tasks, the "phenomenological-historical exchange [phenomenologically exhibits] an identical-unified, originary method"[203] of hermeneutical research.

If one takes all of this into consideration, an exceedingly significant turn is thereby carried out for the fundamental phenomenological stance, which Manfred Riedel, in light of the task of exposing the acroamatic dimension of hermeneutics, regards as a shift "from the reflective view of conscious experiences to 'sounding out' their *motivation*: how the experience of one's own 'I' is experienced and thereby *appropriates* itself, that is, how the intelligible *occurrence* is at once the 'I' of an overlapping *connection*

---

die 'Logische Untersuchungen,'" in *Heidegger Studies* (1991), 7:37–51, which, however, treats not the hermeneutical but rather the ontological and methodological problematic, whereas in Heidegger all three aspects are ultimately related to one another.

201. Heidegger, *GA* 56–57, 117.

202. In this sense, it means, as Heidegger elsewhere puts it: "In phenomenological understanding life itself has its origin in sense-genetic expression" (*GA* 58, 185).

203. Heidegger, *GA* 56–57, 121.

204. Ibid., 125.

of sense."[204] According to Riedel, this shows that and how the step "to hermeneutically turned phenomenology . . . opens up, with the working out of the program of a *phenomenological hermeneutics* . . . hidden dimensions of a linguistic phenomenology in the background."[205] But that means that in the beginning, Heidegger's path of thinking is always already codetermined by a constitutive belonging-together of life and language. For the above-mentioned sense connection refers "in its ground to the spoken-heard language, in which the 'I' is thereby 'historical' (proper to oneself, particular) in timely 'appropriation' of the experience of the question and the environment."[206] The task laid out therein, of conceiving and illuminating historical life in advance as a connection, on the hither side of all 'fragmentation into essential elements,'"[207] makes the "intuitive, inductive phenomenology, philosophical ur-science [into] an intelligible science."[208] The phenomenological criterion hereby decisive is the "intelligible evidence and the evident understanding of experiences, of life in and for itself in the *eidos* [to be understood phenomenologically]."[209]

The "reorientation in sensibility for the absoluteness of originary evidences"[210] thereby required means taking leave of the (for Heidegger) illusory task of wanting to present and designate the given experience reflexively in a final grounding as conscious experience in the transcendental consciousness of the eidetically beheld ur-"I," with a view to the constitution of sense. But this is nothing other than a fundamental critique of Husserl's ideal of a philosophy as rigorous science with the radical presuppositionlessness intended therein.[211] To Heidegger, this evidences a meth-

---

205. Riedel, *Hören auf die Sprache*, 78. In this context Riedel recalls that motive signifies not only ground of action [*Beweggrund*], but also "the dominant, recurring 'movement' [*Satz*] in a tonal sequence of music" (ibid., 80. See Heidegger, GA 56–57, 67, 126.

206. Riedel, *Hören auf die Sprache*, 74.

207. Ibid., 78.

208. Heidegger, GA 56–57, 117.

209. Ibid., 208.

210. Ibid., 126. Klaus Held's study, "Heidegger und das Prinzip der Phänomenologie," investigates the extent to which Heidegger's thinking phenomenologically radicalizes the principle of evidence as the original idea of phenomenology.

211. Heidegger, GA 56–57, 126.

212. Presuppositionlessness as the ideal of epistemic certainty results, as has become visible in the last few paragraphs, from an uncritical absolutizing of the idea of science, and thus through a restriction of transcendental questions to the "constitution-form 'science' and the viewing of all regions of life under this banner" (GA 58, 23).

odological "naiveté,"[212] which in the "return to 'the things themselves,' as it is often declared in the radicalism of phenomenology,"[213] means being able to rid oneself of all traditional relations as if one could "set out into philosophy today, or at any point, from scratch."[214] In this naiveté, which is precisely what Husserl's care for certainty inspires and still influences the later phenomenology of the lifeworld, as we have seen, there is expressed this "ahistoricality" with which Heidegger reproaches phenomenology.[215]

It expresses itself in the notion that—formulated pointedly—"the thing is to be won through any desired perspective whatever in *naive evidence.*"[216] However, insofar as history in this sense as a phenomenological issue is not actually known, as in Husserl, the question of how and what life factically is and how it can be understood from out of itself cannot be answered. For "*life is historical,*"[217] insists Heidegger, and thus demands a hermeneutical transformation of a *phenomenology of life,* which in its approach already foreswears the transparent possibility of a final grounding for the ahistorical ideal, because for it "the understanding of spiritual-historical motives [is] *a genuine piece of the preparation and setting to work of phenomenological critique.*"[218]

If Heidegger presents his own method emphatically as phenomenological, despite this—that is, for him certainly in compliance with the criterion of evidence-formulated critique[219]—this is so particularly because for him phenomenology signifies, to begin with and primarily, a method of a "*how of research* that makes objects intuitively present and only critiques

213. Heidegger, *GA* 59, 29.

214. Ibid., 30.

215. Ibid., 29.

216. Heidegger, *GA* 63, 75.

217. Ibid.

218. Heidegger, *GA* 56–57, 117 (emphasis added). On Husserl's relationship to history, see § 24.

219. Ibid., 131.

220. Heidegger describes the essence of the phenomenological critique by saying that it is not to be understood as refutation or providing counterevidence, "but rather the principle [in the sense of a thesis] to be critiqued is to be understood with reference to *whence* it, according to its meaning, comes. Critique is the positive sounding out of proper motivations" (*GA* 56–57, 126). Thereby the business of critique proves itself to be from the outset an exposure of the inherent structures of sense and at the same time the historical abolition of occlusions. In other words, phenomenological critique is here already that which Heidegger later calls *destruktion,* what Grondin grasps as the "actual contribution of hermeneutics to phenomenology" ("*Die Hermeneutik der Faktizität als ontologische Destruktion und Ideologiekritik,*" 174).

them insofar as they [indeed in the sense of the hermeneutical intuition] are there in intuition."[220] Seen thus, life in the how of its givenness is nei-

---

221. Heidegger, *GA* 63, 72. This avowal of Husserl's method of phenomenological research can be found throughout Heidegger's work (*GA* 56–57, 110; *GA* 58, 139, 233; *GA* 59, 30 ff.; *GA* 60, 75 f.; *GA* 61, 187 f.; *GA* 63, 74 f.), but it maintains itself, as can be easily seen from the ground we have covered, in a *critical break* that shows itself not least in Heidegger's stressing the "urgent task, for the present position of phenomenology, of properly clarifying its philosophical sense" (*GA* 9, 36), insofar as, according to Heidegger, "the most originary and ultimate fundamental problem of phenomenology [is] that of *itself* for itself" (*GA* 58, 1). Heidegger's gesture, thinking *with* Husserl *against* him, thus characterizes from the beginning his interpretive method and thereby delivers at the same time the proof for the perspectival structure of understanding as it is brought to bear, among other places, in the hermeneutical attitude of the second view.

With respect to the distance always implied therein—without seeking at present to carry it out in more intimate detail—it is to be noted, as these details themselves point to the fact, that in the famous concluding chapter (drafted only for publication) of his *Habilitationsschrift* on Duns Scotus's doctrines of categories and meaning (whose original authorship, however, Martin Grabmann proved circa 1920 to be the work of Thomas of Erfurt [translators' note: actually, just the doctrine of meaning, for the material on the doctrine of categories was genuinely that of Duns Scotus], through primary sources [see Hermann Köstler, "Heidegger schreibt an Grabmann," in *Philosophisches Jahrbuch* (1980), 87:96–109]) Heidegger anchors, in relation to the category as the approach to the problem of the "most general determination of the object" (*GA* 1, 403), the notion that object and objectivity only have sense "as such *for* a subject" (ibid.).

This insight, clearly inspired by Husserl, shows a "*merely* objective-logical treatment of the problem of the category as one-sided" (ibid., 407). Thus, the determination of the function and the structure of the subject itself become a pressing part of the problem to be solved. In relation to this, a closer inspection shows that the "depth-dimension" (ibid.) of the problem of the category reached beyond the intentional structure of action cannot be sufficiently clarified in the determination and assessment of consciousness as an "epistemological subject" (ibid.), as is characteristic for neo-Kantianism and for Husserl as well. Against this, Heidegger defines it through and as a "sensible and sense-effecting living deed" (ibid., 406), whereby here his later explicit transformation of the intentional structure into the pretheoretical praxis of human relating-to is already apparent *in nuce*.

The emphasis on 'sense-effecting' and 'living' reads like a prelude to that which a few years later, in the context of the hermeneutical transformation of phenomenology into a pretheoretical ur-science of life, hardens into his critique of Husserl. Already in 1916, however, Heidegger undertakes the decisive and groundbreaking step toward the solution of the problem, wherein he now determines, in distinction to the epistemological approach, the subjectivity of the subject through the constitutive integration of *history*, or rather, *historicity*, which for him becomes, in view of the problem of the categories, a "*meaning-determining element*" (*GA* 1, 408). Thereby, however, he already distances himself clearly in his *Habilitationsschrift* from Husserl, in whose program of 'philosophy as rigorous science,' as is well known, history possesses no constructive place of value.

Heidegger works out his own philosophical approach to the solution, including the historicity of subjectivity, in the context of the problem of the categories through a return to Hegel, insofar as Hegel's historical determination of philosophizing signifies for him the decisive and liberating renunciation of "a theory detached from life" (ibid.) In this sense Heidegger strengthens Hegel's concept of living spirit insofar as in it the "singularity, individuality of acts is incorporated with the universality, the independent existence of *sense*, into the living unity" (ibid., 410), and thus binds the universality of the experience of sense constitutively to the

ther solicited in a reifying manner as an object, nor is it on a trajectory, in an epistemological sense, toward a transcendental "I"; rather it is hermeneutically interpreted in the how of its meaningfulness as an expressive context of sense in a historically and temporally situated field of experience, that is, lived experience [*Erfahrungs- bzw. Erlebnisfeld*]. Put concretely, this how of research method has to do with the interpretation of the sense of being of factical life in regard to its fundamental categorial structures, and that means that it has to do with that manner in which "factical life yields itself and in yielding [*zeitigt und zeitigend*], speaks with itself."[221]

concrete individual carrying out of the act as a historically determined condition of access. (On the role and function of the *Habilitationsschrift* in the context of Heidegger's path of thought, see, in differing accentuations among others, Karl Lehmann, "Transzendentalphilosophie und die Phänomenologie in den ersten Schriften Martin Heideggers (1912–1916)," *Philosophisches Jahrbuch* (1963–1964), 71: 331–357; Strube, *Zur Vorgeschichte der hermeneutischen Phänomenologie*, 85–91; Günter Figal, *Heidegger zur Einführung*, 11–22. For Thomä's critical approach, see *Die Zeit des Selbst*, 60–78).

The relation to Hegel's concept of *Geist*, which connotes the absolute—here also taken up by Heidegger thoroughly positively—would later recede again, but even into the 1950s Heidegger adheres under a different aspect to the insights achieved in his *Habilitationsschrift* and their significance for the development of his thinking, when he indicates that the scholastic doctrine of categories, with its general determination of the objectivity of objects, thus has to do with the being of beings and is, in this sense, ontology; while in the doctrine of meaning qua *grammatica speculativa* language is the theme and thus the constellation of being and language in approach is already to be found at the beginning of Heidegger's path of thinking (see "*Aus einem Gespräch von der Sprache*," in GA 12, 87).

222. Heidegger, *Phänomenologische Interpretationen zu Aristoteles*, 246. This long-famous, so-called Natorp Report—only rediscovered at the end of the 1980s in Josef König's *Nachlass* from 1922—does not only contain a comprehensive draft of an as-yet-unedited book on Aristotle. It offers as well, precisely in its first (and for our present study exceedingly significant) part, in the "Anzeige," taken as an introduction, a sort of manifesto in which Figal perceives "the nucleus of *Sein und Zeit*" (*Heidegger zur Einführung*, 24), yet which at the same time also—and this is of special import for us here—furnishes guiding threads and sketches for a phenomenological-hermeneutical anthropology. On the background, history, and function of the Natorp Report, see Gadamer, "Heideggers 'theologische Frühschrift,'" in *Dilthey-Jahrbuch* (1989), 6:228–234; see also Theodor Kisiel, "The Missing Link in the Early Heidegger," in *Hermeneutic Phenomenology: Lectures and Essays*, ed. Joseph J. Kockelmans (Lanham, MD: University Press of America, 1988), 1–40.

From yet another perspective, Jürgen Stolzenberg calls attention to the meaning of the Natorp Report. In the context of his investigation of Heidegger's relation to Natorp as it is portrayed in the early lectures, Stolzenberg refers to a certain parallel between the two, which for him culminates in the notion that in these early texts Heidegger "anticipates, in accordance with the later work of Natorp, the overturning and dissolution of the neo-Kantianism propounded by the Marburg school and—like the later Natorp himself—turns critically against its beginnings" (*Ursprung und System*, 261). This is shown concretely as well in the concept of understanding as Natorp implements it in *Philosophische Systematik* (Hamburg: Meiner, 1958), whereby he takes recourse to Dilthey for precisely this purpose. If this is to be read as a source

Accordingly, if "the being of factical life in a given how of being-addressed and being-interpreted"[222] is the theme of philosophy, this means for Heidegger that philosophy as "the ontology of facticity [is] at the same time the categorial interpretation of address and interpretation, that is to say, logic."[223] Heidegger can thus say in conclusion: "Ontology and logic are to be taken back into the unitary origin of the problematic of facticity, and to be understood as the projections of fundamental research, which can be characterized as the *phenomenological hermeneutics of facticity.*"[224]

What Heidegger formulates in this programmatic statement, which points the way for his early work, at the same time thereby extracts horizon lines within which the present investigation moves in its interpretive resumption. Heidegger famously conceived his own thinking, as it is described in notes for the no-longer-published foreword to the *Gesamtausgabe* of his work, as "a being-underway in the pathfield of the ambiguous being-question's self-transforming questioning,"[225] which offered for his part "multiple occasions for self-examination,"[226] as is not least strikingly attested to in the range and diversity of his posthumous writings. Such a self-examination underlay the beginning and the conception of his understanding of ontology as well. Precisely because the aspect of the question to be thematized regarding the human self- and world relation is made possible and decisive in the development of the preunderstanding of ontology, it is of not inconsiderable significance for the present observations to outline still more clearly the contours of the differences in the Heideggerian concept of ontology.

---

for the above-mentioned parallel, it provides a further, immediate relation between Natorp and Heidegger, precisely by way of the Natorp Report, which according to Stolzenberg is to be seen as a direct source of inspiration for Natorp's own efforts for a 'correct starting-point,' so that he "has bound together Heidegger's remarks on an original understanding with his own systematic intentions in a productive manner for him" (*Ursprung und System*, 266). Natorp's letters to Husserl, especially that of November 9, 1922, strikingly reflect the extent to which he saw himself addressed through Heidegger's text (in E. Husserl, *Briefwechsel*, 5:162).

223. Heidegger, *Phänomenologische Interpretationen zu Aristoteles*, 246f.

224. Ibid., 247.

225. Ibid.

226. Heidegger, *GA* 1, 437 (emphasis deleted).

227. Ibid., 438 (emphasis deleted).

§ 29. The Function and Relation of the Hermeneutical Ontology of Facticity, Fundamental Ontology, and Metontology

The requisite clarification of Heidegger's use of the concept of ontology does not follow here in the sense of a genetic-historical questioning that undertakes to illuminate the particular guiding understanding of ontology in the course of Heidegger's work in its presuppositions and objectives. Instead, the present study maintains its aim to profile the basic traits, developed in his early work, of a hermeneutics of the self in the relation of tension between facticity and historicity as a distinct and systematic contribution capable of providing a distinctive and ground-breaking impulse to the recently revitalized interest in anthropological questions.

That the question concerning the human being in its world-relation as self-relation poses itself today under the conditions of what has become a widely effective de(con)struction of the traditional concept of the subject lends to the hermeneutics of facticity an estimable actuality, which certainly neither ostensibly lives to its fullest in modish trends, nor—in light of its temporal origin—emerges with the nostalgic charm of a remake. Rather, its actuality is grounded in the fact that in the midst of a historical world characterized by historical transitions and breaks in continuity, many of its pressing questions for an appropriate analysis can be reflected in a manner oriented toward problem solving with a prospect of success if the situation is apprehended with regard to the perspectives of sense in a hermeneutical consciousness that forms its knowledge critically at the outset of the being-historical of all experiences of an entity, experiences which are reflexively mediated therein in the historically critical exchange with tradition, as the last three chapters have shown. The fact that in the sense of effective-historical consciousness this turn, on the one hand, testifies in advance—independent of any connection or break—to the effect of the history of tradition, and on the other, is only possible as a selection of perspectives manifoldly determined by given presuppositions in the midst and as part of a mesh of traditions, was already worked out in the first section as a constituent of every interpretation, and thus offers nothing new in this respect.

It is nonetheless reasonable in terms of interpretive strategy to become conscious once more of this accompanying coknowing (*Mitwissen*) in order to reflexively situate, within the hermeneutical situation of interpretation, its efforts at objectivation in the relational field of its various motivations and hidden designs and thereby to clarify and to activate, in light of the basis of their claims, the thematized region of phenomena in the perspectivally delineated potential of the guiding discourse. Corresponding to this determinacy, hermeneutics works out its conception in the phenomenological exhibition of the ontological structure of human being in the world, in a way that historically determines the lifeworldly meshed possibilities of self-experience in the midst of an actuality determined by manifold connotations, particularity, and contingency, and that thinks from out of its relational enmeshing and thereby attributes to hermeneutics the task of a "historical ontology of our selves."[227]

It would be a fatal error, however, simply to link Heidegger's name with the task and concept of such an ontology without further elaboration, as if one could assume that there were some sort of a tacit agreement to be reached on the issue. As has been often mentioned, the "oldest" hermeneutics of facticity, according to its genesis, regarding the history of the effects and reception of Heideggerian thinking, is a "younger" offshoot. Focusing our view through this renewed consideration means, then, to become attentive to the circumstance that in light of the anthropologically significant arrangement of the early work, the concept of ontology (meant here in a broadly related, that is, looser terminological sense) distinguishes itself considerably from the widely acknowledged understanding of it laid out in *Sein und Zeit*. However, insofar as that received understanding corresponding to effective-historical consciousness cannot be simply excluded or ignored, an interpretation that proceeds hermeneutically must bring these differences and nuances to light, in order to profile the non-simultaneous phenomenological hermeneutics of facticity—regarded in the transparency of reception—to the point of recognition, in light of its relevance to the present in the potential of an ontology of actuality.

To stress this properly seems appropriate, because with good reason it points to the fact that, in the face of such a request, Heidegger himself after all made more and more precise this "tentative" use of the concept 'ontology' on the path to *Sein und Zeit*. And in the framework of fundamental ontology the concept as much as the task of an ontology, which has to determine the being of human beings, has found in the form of the analytic of Dasein its famously valid form, from which the early disconnectedness of the concept of ontology could be identified as a type of preformative

228. Foucault, "Was ist Aufklärung?" 48.

state of the being-question. The task to be formulated from this perspective of reconstructively demonstrating the addressed course in its singular steps of thinking, as we have mentioned, makes the present study not entirely proper in this case—insofar as it was thereby operating on the view that Heidegger implicitly intends something which the text (still) does not make explicit—and poses the problem whether the authorial intentions are to be rehabilitated again in the sense of classical hermeneutics as the instance of the final testing of sense, which in the first section of the present work was taken leave of with a view to the beginning of this study's own hermeneutics.

Apart from this question, however, there are yet further grounds to strengthen the early concept of ontology in its own right, wherein the being-question poses itself as the question concerning human being, that is, positions itself in the direction of a *hermeneutics of the self.* Along with this it is to be borne in mind, as an important distinguishing feature, that in the context of fundamental ontology the analysis of human being possesses no "autotelic character." Rather, Heidegger's analytic of Dasein remains within the self-chosen and necessarily drawn limits determined in advance by the task of working out the fundamental question concerning the sense of being. Seen thus, the analytic of Dasein "is not intended to give a complete ontology of Dasein that must be certainly constructed, but is to stand, something like a 'philosophical' anthropology, on a philosophically sufficient basis."[228] In this rather formal indication there is a hidden claim that the fundamental ontology unfolded in *Sein und Zeit* is the condition for the possibility that something in the way of a regional ontology of Dasein can be successfully worked out. For only out of a fundamental-ontological clarification of the sense of being—as the whence of the understanding of being in general and of all of its modes of being—that carries itself out in the existential-ontological demonstration of the human understanding of being can the multiplicity of the modes of being become thematic in relation to the diverse regions of entities worked out as fundamental-ontologically-based regional ontologies.

229. Heidegger, *GA* 2, 23. This comes to light with the desired clarity in the 1960s when, in conversation with doctors and psychotherapists, Heidegger works out this drawing of the limit in the tasks set by the analytic of Dasein and the analysis of Dasein. See Heidegger, *Zollikoner Seminare,* 159–164.

Beyond this more formal suggestion, Heidegger characterizes the place at which a sufficiently founded anthropology must be settled philosophically more precisely where it appears to him necessary—within the framework of his exchange with the Leibnizian metaphysics of subjectivity—to bring a renewed clarification to the idea and function of fundamental ontology.[229] This stands in the context of the new approach to the question of being of metaphysics, which in the years immediately following *Sein und Zeit* did not yet connote for Heidegger a deteriorating form to be overcome, as it did subsequently when the question concerning the sense of being turned [*kehrt*] in the direction of the question of the truth of being.[230] It is necessary to reappropriate metaphysics in the light of the radically posed fundamental-ontological question of being, as Heidegger emphasizes, insofar as the basic problem of metaphysics is "in its radicalization and universalization an interpretation of Dasein with regard to temporality, from out of which the inner possibility of the understanding

230. See Heidegger, *GA* 26, 196–202.

231. After Heidegger had stressed, in the concluding section of his *Habilitationsschrift*, that "*Philosophy* [cannot], *in the long run, do without metaphysics, its own optics*" (*GA* 1, 406), he avoided more and more the concept of 'metaphysics,' but he continued to treat its problems and inner concerns with a great deal of engagement. This "conceptual *epoché*" was motivated, to begin with, by the renunciation of Hegel as a positive inspiration in the above-mentioned conclusion and the turn toward the somewhat metaphysicocritical existential and *Lebensphilosophie* in the sense of Nietzsche, Dilthey, and Kierkegaard, whereby, aside from the wholly particularized and intensive collaboration with Husserl, his metaphysical-skeptical perspective may well have been sharpened. On the other hand, it certainly contributed temporarily to avoiding the concept that the "attempt at a resuscitation" of metaphysics in the writings of Peter Wust or those of Nicolai Hartmann, which, as the opening sentences of *Sein und Zeit* reflect, was suspect for Heidegger.

Thus it had to appear as a sensation of sorts in the Freiburg of Husserl that Heidegger delivered his public inaugural lecture under the title of "Was ist Metaphysik?" even if here, as the final Marburg lecture (*GA* 26) already demonstrates, the concept of 'metaphysics' is thought in a decisively transformed way in opposition to the tradition. Evidence for this can also be found in the Summer Semester lecture course of 1929, roughly contemporaneous with the inaugural lecture (*Der Deutsche Idealismus [Fichte, Schelling, Hegel] und die philosophische Problemlage der Gegenwart*, ed. Claudius Strube, in *GA*, vol. 28 [Frankfurt: Klostermann, 1997], esp. part 1), to an extent in the later book on Kant (*GA* 3), and particularly impressively in the long lecture course of Winter 1929/30 (*Die Grundbegriffe der Metaphysik. Welt—Endlichkeit—Einsamkeit*, ed. Friedrich-Wilhelm von Herrmann, in *GA* 29–30 [Frankfurt: Klostermann, 1983]). The conjecture that this recent positive connotation of the concept of metaphysics has roots in Heidegger's engagement with Max Scheler finds confirmation in accordance with references provided by Otto Pöggeler (*Schritte zu einer hermeneutischen Philosophie*, [Freiburg: Alber, 1994], 207) in the enlightening study by Mark Michalski, *Fremdwahrnehmung und Mitsein*, which treats this encounter in detail (13–32).

of being and thus of ontology is to be illuminated."[231] However, the concept of metaphysics in no way emerges from that of fundamental ontology. For it is formed only in the unity of fundamental ontology and a metontology to be designated more closely—in which unity Heidegger discerns the "transformation of the one basic problem of philosophy itself,"[232] which, as the question of being, is to be explained for him in the "ur-phenomenon of human existence"[233] as the given "concretion of ontological difference,"[234] that is, the "concretion of the performance of the understanding of being."[235]

Seen thus, the question that Heidegger himself poses at the end of *Sein und Zeit*—"can ontology be grounded *ontologically* or does it require an *ontic* foundation, and if so, *which* entity must take on the function of founding?"[236]—can be answered positively in favor of an ontic founding in the human distinguished by the understanding of being. For "in the horizon of the radically posed problem of being it is shown that everything is only visible and can be understood as being *when a possible totality of beings is already there.*"[237] To this extent, for Heidegger "thinking being as the being of entities and grasping radically and universally the problem of being [means] at the same time making the entity into a theme in the light of ontology in its totality."[238] But an entity as a whole cannot only become a theme with regard to its regional structure from out of the above-discussed prior understanding of being, and so, according to Heidegger, "the possibility that there is being in the understanding [has] for its presupposition the factical existence of Dasein."[239] This means that ontology as the fundamental form of metaphysics returns to its source. The inner necessity for this reversion, recognized by Heidegger in the essence of ontology, formulates in itself the task of a development of that which he designates,

232. Heidegger, *GA 26*, 201. Beyond the posing of the question only sketched out here, Friedrich-Wilhelm von Herrmann discusses its context in light of the inner architectonic of Heidegger's work in "Das Ereignis und die Fragen nach dem Wesen der Technik, Politik und Kunst," in *Wege ins Ereignis*. (Frankfurt: Klostermann, 1994), 85–107.

233. Heidegger, *GA 26*, 202.

234. Ibid., 199.

235. Ibid., 202.

236. Ibid. See also *GA 28*, 42–45, 274–279.

237. Heidegger, *GA 2*, 576.

238. Heidegger, *GA 26*, 199—(emphasis added).

239. Ibid., 200.

240. Ibid., 199.

in harmony with its transformation, its μεταβολή, as *metontology*, that is to say, *metaphysical ontics.*

For the answer to the question of an ontologically appropriate situating of a philosophical, that is, existential anthropology (which interests us in the following) it is, according to Heidegger, a matter of developing it "in the region of a metontological-existentiell questioning"[240] as a metontology, or rather a "metaphysics of existence"[241] that—in distinction from *Sein und Zeit,* where "only a few, if not inessential 'pieces'"[242] are worked out—would have to be heeded in now demonstrating the existence structures thoroughly to completion and must run through the existentiell phenomena in all their shadings from "the work on factical possibilities."[243]

In the concentration of analyses designated therein to the human being in its ontic givenness, it is decisive for an adequate understanding of the Heideggerian conception of metontology that it is "not [understood as] a summary ontics in the sense of a universal science that empirically collects the results of the individual sciences into a so-called world image in order to then derive from it a *Weltanschauung* and life intuition."[244] Metontology pursues no ontification in the sense of scientific empiricism, but rather as *metaphysics of existence* is always already and constantly related in being carried out, in its "metaphysical ontics,"[245] as Heidegger calls it, to the fundamental ontology that founds it, in whose perspective it thus preserves itself continuously. For as it has thus now shown itself, "precisely the radicalization of fundamental ontology grows out of what we have called the transformation of ontology itself."[246]

In observation of the investigations still to come, as a facet of these excursive reflections it follows that in the framework of the approach of fundamental ontology, the question concerning the possibility of a philosophical anthropology finds its answer in the form to be worked out of a metontology of existence founded as fundamental ontology.[247] And

241. Ibid.
242. Ibid.
243. Heidegger, *GA* 2, 23.
244. Heidegger, *GA* 26, 198.
245. Ibid., 199.
246. Ibid., 201.
247. Ibid., 200.
248. Heidegger speaks in this context of the notion that the question of ethics can be posed here first and foremost. Hence, in reference to Heidegger's concept of metontology, the reproach frequently aimed at *Sein und Zeit* of the deficit regarding an ethics can be rebutted,

insofar as its analyses are always "on the ground and in the perspective of the radical [fundamental-] ontological problematic and are only possible in being united with it,"[248] this means that existential anthropology as metontology and the regional ontology of Dasein, respectively, cannot simply be equated with anthropology or ontology qua the hermeneutics of facticity.[249]

---

insofar as within Heideggerian thinking in the compass of his first major work one can certainly mark the point from which an ethics is to be developed (see also his extremely significant discussion of Kant's concept of *personalitas moralis* in GA 24, 185–201).

249. Heidegger, GA 26, 200.

250. In order to avoid possible misunderstandings, it is to be indicated at the outset that nothing is intended by this insight like that which William J. Richardson (*Heidegger: Through Phenomenology to Thought* [The Hague: Martinus Nijhoff, 1963]) introduced, regarding the much-discussed notion of *Kehre,* into the secondary literature (and which was authorized on the basis of Heidegger's expressed—if hesitant—consent in the letter that serves as the book's preface), i.e., the utterly hypostatized schema of a 'Heidegger I' and 'Heidegger II,' with the result that one might now add to these a further station pertaining to his early work.

The characteristic rigidity of such schematization is easily seen—without intending to deepen any further this problem of *Kehre,* which would take us far afield of the investigation at hand—when, instead of conceiving *Kehre* as a conversion or a reversal, one discerns in it, as with von Herrmann, Pöggeler, and others, a 'turn away' [*Wegkehre*]. One may then indeed speak, in harmony with Heidegger's self-interpretation, of a totality of his course of thought that nonetheless "lies outside of the idea of a pre-planned path that ensues in traversing a course and that is maintained when that course describes an arc" (Friedrich-Wilhelm von Herrmann, *Die Selbstinterpretation Martin Heideggers* [Meisenheim: Hain, 1964], 277). In the sense of such a change in the same totality of thought, Gadamer speaks of the 'one path' as the fundamental movement of Heideggerian thinking (see "Der eine Weg Martin Heideggers," in *GW,* 3:417–430).

In consideration of the string of texts that has come to light through publication in the scope of the *Gesamtausgabe* it is further confirmed that Heidegger's work is stamped in its intellectually related basis by an astounding yet simple uniformity that eludes schematization, a uniformity that yet in no way produces within itself monotony, but rather multiplicity, and thereby knows as many gradations in nuance as weight displacements of accent. Otto Pöggeler has this specific form of wholeness in view when, against his own earlier position, he sharply emphasizes, "Heidegger's path of thought is a plurality of paths that made possible the perspectives upon one and the same issue, yet perspectives which are not to be brought into alignment with each other" (*Der Denkweg Martin Heideggers,* 353).

It is necessary for the sake of this plurality not to answer the manifoldness of approaches to a solution implied therein on the part of the interpreter with the gesture of a compulsory schematization or a unification. And this even less because this thinking meanders considerably in the region that is the source of Heideggerian philosophizing. Therefore the flow of Heidegger's thinking is not commensurate with the canal that has been realigned through interpretation, but rather the branches and tributaries also belong to it, streams that Heidegger, in his later self-interpretations, frequently redirected back into the main current in light of the points he had reached, so that the task of interpretation can precisely consist in strengthening, *with* Heidegger *against* himself, the question of a given philosophic relevancy from out of its *original contexts* and *subterranean constellations.*

How can this difference be fixed? And how can a preference for the early conception be secured if one grants, with a view to the conceptually formidable architectonic, that the success of *Sein und Zeit* together with its perpetuation in the metontological conception possesses a great pull in the direction of a further differentiation as the task of the analysis of phenomena following it in its coexecution and reenactment. The density of the Heideggerian course of thinking doubtless has something captivating in its *coherence*, by means of which Heidegger sets himself explicitly against an interpretation of the philosophy placed by him on a new ground as a system whose basic discipline would then be fundamental ontology.[250] Certainly if one understands by "system" something like the positions of an idealistic system of speculation or thinks of the image of the tree from Descartes's letter to Picot, it is easy to agree with Heidegger that his conception does not conform to those philosophically intended concluding indications. But if one takes "system" in a formally broad sense, which pretends to a thoroughly *dynamic open order* in itself, whose textual character marks itself out through an inner coherence of the referential relations

---

This does not occur, however, in order to play the early off against the late, but rather in order to make visible once again, in this *archaeological forensics*, as it were, the manifoldness of those approaches to the problem that were immanent for Heidegger himself in the path of his thinking and that could well be considered to have overcome his own perspective (see GA 12, 121, where he dismisses his early lectures as 'youthful leaps'), approaches that, as paths taken individually, nevertheless preserve, in the potential of what has been dismissed, debatable and revealing answers to questions that may well be exigent in the present, much like the way in which this comes into consideration upon viewing Foucault's question of the self-constitution of the subject. And was it not Heidegger himself who, with an eye toward the accomplishments of his thinking, entitled the *Gesamtausgabe* with the maxim "Ways—not Works"?

That he was to the last unclear on whether the early lecture courses in general were to make their way into the *Gesamtausgabe* must in no way amount to a self-devaluation of this part of his oeuvre, but instead could well have to do with a sense, from his later vantage point, of the somewhat oppositional, yet no less *creative disquiet of the early work*, which simply continues to elude Heidegger's later self-definitions. All of this belongs to the authenticity of his thinking.

For the setting of the task of his interpretation it is, seen hermeneutically, essentially a matter of giving a precise account, as an interpreter, of *whether and to what extent one brings a text's content to language or whether one thinks through problems with a text*. This self-clarification, which engenders transparency on the part of the interpreter in the question of the treatment of a text, is vital for a methodologically sound assessment of one's own work of, and aims in, interpretation, although ultimately as a basic move of philosophizing both modes—in the consciousness of a differentially reflected belonging-together—are interlaced with each other, since the presence of a text always actualizes it in its reading from out of the horizon of the understanding of sense that interprets, an understanding that thereby ineluctably becomes a feature of the presence of the text itself.

251. See Heidegger, *GA* 26, 200.

forming it and possesses thereby a strong *tendency to ultimate evidence,* then the closure of the Heideggerian fundamental ontological thought project can still be grasped as a type of system.[251]

But what is gained by such a designation? In any event, an attentiveness intended with this special "systematic" perspective of fundamental ontology, a feature of sighting, if you will, is established immanently and constitutively for the question of its discursivity, which posits in advance, with a view to theory and praxis of the analysis of phenomena, the claims to validity of the intended knowledge under the condition of its possibility and capability of integration in the fundamental ontological concept. In other words, the claim to truth of the metaphysics brought into play by Heidegger—as the unity of fundamental ontology and metontology (and this is decisive) through the fundamental insight into the finitude of human existence—is never absolute and still equally universal and in this sense total. That this totalization in Heidegger does not revert to or open into a totalization is conditioned on the *finitude of human being,* which does not exhaust itself in the fact of corporeal mortality, but rather must be methodologically recovered in thinking as the structure of thinking.

In an innovative way for hermeneutics, Heidegger achieves this, as already seen, when he reconsiders the character of enactment in view of the structures constituting philosophical knowledge. Nevertheless, the self-securing of one's own finitude in no way restricts the universal claim to validity of the knowledge aimed at in the analytic of Dasein within Heidegger's fundamental ontological position, so that its ability to be criticized from the fundamental ontological perspective restricts itself to a possible internal revision. This is motivated primarily by an immanent 'not-yet-enough,' a not-yet-concretized given provisionality [*Vorläufigkeit*] that, in running out ahead [*Vorlaufen*], outstrips itself; taken strictly, opens itself up—and not metacritically—to an understanding otherwise.

252. The use of the concept 'system' here has a solely heuristic function. To this extent it holds no relation to the lively conducted debate over systematic starting points for thought as it has been developed, among other places, in the evolutionary epistemology of Humberto R. Maturana and Francisco J. Varela, for example, with their conception of *autopoiesis*. In his recent cognitive scientific work (e.g., *Kognitionswissenschaft—Kognitionstechnik: Eine Skizze aktueller Perspektiven.* [Frankfurt: Suhrkamp, 1990]), Varela seeks to incorporate particular conceptions of phenomenology, principally those of Merleau-Ponty and Husserl, to whom Niklas Luhmann (see, e.g., *Soziale Systeme: Grundriß einer allgemeinen Theorie* [Frankfurt: Suhrkamp, 1996], esp. 153, 201, 356) also makes reference within the scope of his presently well-received systems theory.

This *understanding otherwise* is, however, as we have shown, the inner driving force of an approach that reflects *finitude as a fundamental hermeneutical experience* and hence integrates the anthropologically determined contingency into the capacity for grounding a hermeneutics as an indispensable regulative principle for understanding-claims. This also appears necessary because each hermeneutical situation is in itself always already constituted, through an antecedent fullness of referential relations, as an effective-historically profiled meshwork that in the horizon of possibilities of experience, is just as interminable as it is polyphonic, synchronically as well as diachronically; for this reason, Heidegger's own view initially also appears as only *one* possible perspective for a reading of this plurality in hermeneutical reflection.[252]

Yet does this not simply amount to putting the case for a kind of relativism? Our investigation will show in detail that this characterization does not apply. Moreover, it is worth considering whether the strong emphasis on the proper weight of Heidegger's early thinking does not necessarily signify a marginalization, or rather a dismissal, of insights that Heidegger had only later achieved. Even here the suspicion that it aims at a rigid separation is misplaced. As the discussion of the hermeneutical comportment of the second view has shown, this is simply not possible, insofar as in the admitted clearly accentuated focus of the early work the reading can extricate itself from the effective-historical conditionedness of its own situation as little as can the explicating interpretation.[253]

§ 30. Aspects of a Contemporary Philosophical Situating of the Discourse on Facticity

How will we get around this emanation of the fundamental-ontological analysis of phenomena if the approach of the hermeneutics of facticity is preferred and divergences thereby emerge, as in the question of the Heideggerian version of the concepts of ontology and anthropology? This cir-

---

253. Pöggeler (*Der Denkweg Martin Heideggers*, 353) also emphasizes the fact that in light of the "continuous nature of experience" Heidegger's thinking must be interpretively related to "a polyphonic situation . . . in which Heidegger has only *one* voice."

254. As Gadamer also shows (*Wahrheit und Methode*, 381), we cannot step out of the historical conditionedness in which we find ourselves and from out of which we carry out our understanding.

cumvention takes place while *the epoché is exercised in a hermeneutical way.* This means that with regard to the analysis of phenomena unfolded in the analytic of Dasein its conception of sense can become thematic, while at the same time validity claims, as fundamental-ontological truth claims, are bracketed. With this temporary suspension, the discourse on the human self-relation as world relation opens itself to hermeneutic questioning and understanding in such a way that other voices can become audible at the same time along with Heidegger's own in an equally weighted multiplicity. For on the condition of the possibility of truth that is now held in abeyance they cannot merely be heard in their experiences with respect to their degree of integration or distanciation. In the understanding that makes use of the *epoché* they as well, with their respective factual views, work their way into the hermeneutical analysis of a phenomenon to whose hermeneutical illumination belongs the testing out (by turns) of possibilities that no longer appear qualified from the outset, through a truth claim that the being of the human fixes fundamentally-ontologically and thus refers the concrete ontic [*Ontik*] back to itself.

This opening of hermeneutical discourse occurs in harmony with the position of the early Heidegger, and is thus covered by the approach of the hermeneutical understanding of ontology in its facticity. That is to say, for Heidegger the central problem consists in knowing "the being of facticial life"[254] and revealing it in its structures. Seen thus, being here means *factical life.* And since "the possible radical problematic of the being of life"[255] is centered in facticity, the task of its philosophical interpretation is that of an "ontology of facticity,"[256] which for him is at the same time *"ontology in principle."*[257] As such, it stands in strict opposition to the widespread opinion that philosophy is an "invented activity only shadowing life with whatever 'generalities' and arbitrarily posited principles."[258] In contrast, philosophy determines itself as knowing such that—as Heidegger already comes close to saying in anticipation of the famous formula of existence from *Sein und Zeit*—it is "the genuinely explicit implementation of the tendency to interpretation [*Auslegungstendenz*] of the basic mobility [*Grund-*

255. Heidegger, *Phänomenologische Interpretationen zu Aristoteles*, 246.
256. Ibid.
257. Ibid.
258. Ibid.
259. Ibid.

bewegtheit] of life in which it is a matter of this itself and its being."[259] In this sense, to make factical life with respect to its facticity into an actual theme of philosophy means, in consideration of the task bound to it, "positing factical life of itself from out of its own factical possibilities toward itself."[260]

The imperative of explication issuing from this will not be implemented in what follows by means of concrete descriptive analyses of individual phenomena, but instead will be approached in the form of *hermeneutic reflection*. It fulfills its task as phenomenologically motivated ontology in such a way that it directs its primary intention beyond the factical 'what' as the 'that' [*Daß*] of life toward the structural context as the 'how' of its givenness,[261] which in the ontic-existentiell implementation cannot immediately be taken up empirically, but rather comes first to formal indication in the reflexive attitude, where here it is not to be understood formally in the sense of Kant or Husserl. Nonetheless, in the ontology of facticity it is also a matter of an apriori that is not a formal, but rather a *historical apriori,* as can be said with Foucault.[262]

This difference becomes more comprehensible when it is recalled that for Husserl, among others in the wake of Kant, the empirical human in its true cognitions realizes in itself the universal ahistorical (and therein no longer contingent) transcendental absolute reason—even if the human is not capable of sustaining it, in a Kantian sense, on the basis of the human's essential sensible-intelligible constitution as the form of existence for his earthly duration. Motivated by this ineluctable contingency of conditions of reflection in life-historical factical finitude, the question becomes, as in Dilthey's program of a 'critique of historical reason,' an actual problem—without being able to solve it satisfyingly—whether transcendental reflection, given its results, is really independent from such finitude and

260. Ibid.

261. Ibid.

262. Structure and structural context are not to be grasped as ahistorical invariants, but on the contrary are in themselves essentially historicized as classifying concepts for phenomenal states of affairs. The nonetheless functional coherence and stability indicated in a structural context resembles somewhat Marcel Mauss's picture of a spiderweb in which the knotting of individual moments is determined in its supporting capacity through an elastic webbing of threads that run in and out of each other.

263. See Foucault, *Archäologie des Wissens,* 183–187. We will explore this notion in more detail in the context of the hermeneutical concept of experience (§ 31).

contingency.[263] In taking up this doubt positively the self-apprehension of humanity as a rational animal can no longer authenticate ahistorical principles of reason. Against Husserl and Kant, and in a step beyond the positive tendency recognized in Dilthey by Heidegger, human self-determination thereby becomes dependent upon the historically mutable conditions of its factical life.

Reason, as well as language, consciousness, ego, and so on—none of these will possess, in the sense of ontological hermeneutical explication, the constancy of ahistorical invariance, as is characteristic for the method of Husserlian phenomenology of transcendental subjectivity. Yet through this insight into the *historicity* of the knowledge of the knowledge of human being in the world, which can be structurally determined as *relationality*, the dimension of concrete reality of life—neglected, or rather bypassed, in the transcendental method as the "purely empirical"—opens itself positively in all of its contingency for philosophical investigation as the actual horizon from out of which a hermeneutically explicative discourse on facticity is motivated and formulated as the hermeneutical task of an unclosable and ultimately ungroundable dialogue on historical factical life.

Admittedly, the concept of *postmodernity* has by now become so inflationary and in large part devoid of content—if it was not already so from the first[264]—that it is hardly of any use to designate precisely the issue involved. This has led to the fact that even its protagonists like Lyotard have long since distanced themselves from the concept.[265] Nevertheless, one must grant that such a vagueness with regard to the concept of the modern corresponds to the justly criticized haziness of this concept, regarded more precisely, to which it is conventionally opposed. When Jür-

264. Herbert Schnädelbach (*Reflexion und Diskurs: Fragen einer Logik der Philosophie* [Frankfurt: Suhrkamp, 1977], 373) also emphasizes the fact that in the turn from transcendental to hermeneutical reflection a decisive point is reached, when he sees, in reference to Karl-Otto Apel's method, the turn therein of transcendental philosophy to transcendental hermeneutics qua transcendental pragmatics.

265. For reference, the concept of the postmodern first appears in the German language in 1917 in Rudolf Pannwitz's *Die Krisis der europäischen Kultur* (Nuremberg: Carl, 1917), 64, which was modeled in use of tragic language, style and diagnosis, even to the point of paraphrasing, on Nietzsche.

266. See, e.g., Jean-François Lyotard, "Die Moderne redigieren," in *Wege aus der Moderne: Schlüsseltexte der Postmoderne-Diskussion*, ed. Wolfgang Welsch (Weinheim: Akademie Verlag, 1988), 204–214; on the question of the form and character of so-called postmodernism, see Welsch (still something of an accepted cicerone in his own way), *Unsere postmoderne Moderne* (Weinheim: Akadamie, 1987).

gen Habermas,[266] as their spokesperson, conceives the 'project of the moderns' as the program of the Enlightenment, in spite of its suggestion of univocity, one can ultimately expect, as Peter Koslowski stresses, "little gain in knowledge, because the equivocal concept of modernity is equated with the equivocal concept of the Enlightenment"[267] from this determination. That the waning fashion of the concept of postmodernity in recent philosophical discussion cannot make the concept of modernity obsolete in equal measure (and thus at least could backhandedly suggest a recovery of the proponents of the discourse of modernity) certainly has something to do with the fact that for long stretches "the modern as the proper name of an epoch [was] curiously confounded with modernity as a concept for a property or an attribute."[268] Thus, as Koslowski underscores, the "project of the moderns [profits in a parasitical way] from the suggestive talk of the most advanced state of consciousness that is precisely modern consciousness—or the consciousness of the moderns."[269]

Intuitively, the dilemma, perhaps just as unavoidable as fundamental, shows itself in this state of affairs, which must register for itself an ultimately interpretive conceptual epochal ascription motivated by classification—whether it now has to do with the modern or classical or whichever historical age—when it seeks to bind together the manifold historical (and therein frequently untimely and yet contemporaneous) relations into a unity. Grasped all too well, thereby, according to the style of the 'lowest common denominator,' this then functions as a signature of epochs and converts the originally operative access into a quasi-objective statement of fact, as it were self-forgotten, in this methodologically motivated description.[270]

267. See Jürgen Habermas, "Die Moderne—Ein unvollendetes Projekt," in *Kleine politische Schriften* (Frankfurt: Surhkamp, 1981); *Der philosophische Diskurs der Moderne: Zwölf Vorlesungen* (Frankfurt: Suhrkamp, 1988).

268. Peter Koslowski, "Die Baustellen der Postmoderne—Wider den Vollendungszwang der Moderne," in *Moderne oder Postmoderne? Zur Signatur des gegenwärtigen Zeitalters*, ed. Peter Koslowski, Robert Spaemann, and Reinhard Löw (Weinheim: VCH, 1986), 4.

269. Ibid.

270. Ibid., 5.

271. If one looks to the central texts of the postmodern debate, like those documented in the aforementioned collections by Welsch and Koslowski, it becomes clear, among other things, that a certain skepticism is requisite against the epochal sectioning that is overhastily connoted by the prefix in the typical understanding of talk about the postmodern. For in fact the so-called postmodern also programmatically represents concerns that have been hit upon

as typical of the moderns or late moderns arising out of the ideology of the Enlightenment, whereby constitutive moments of sense have been, however, as much sustained in decisively modified ways as also transcended. Thus, for example, principled and universalistic models of justification are abandoned without having to give up the sensible content of reason as a regulative force, while yet in reflection upon the pervasive post-Nietzschean critique of reason in the twentieth century the classical ideas of reason were in need of a fundamental transformation.

Wolfgang Welsch delivers such a model in his concept of a 'transversal reason' (see *Vernunft: Die zeitgenössische Vernunftkritik und das Konzept der transversalen Vernunft* [Frankfurt: Suhrkamp, 1995]) that human sovereignty formulates in its validity claims and strives to prove under the signs of pluralization, transformation, and relativity, and which demonstrates at the same time "that the field of rationality as a whole is determined through interrelations—which then can become starting-points for the interventions of reason" (ibid., 450; see also ibid., 442, 433). Seen in this way, it can also be said, following Welsch: "The postmodern is in actual fact . . . not anti-modern, but rather radically modern. And its thinking is no exotic narcotic, but instead—quite possibly—the philosophy of this world" (Welsch, "Die Postmoderne in Kunst und Philosophie und ihr Verhältnis zu technologischen Zeitalter," in *Technologisches Zeitalter oder Postmoderne,* ed. Walther Zimmerli [Munich: Fink, 1988], 56).

On this claim of wanting to be the philosophy of its age, there belongs to the diagnostic sense of what can be achieved by so-called postmodern, in-itself historicized thinking a sensibility for the historical processes within factical contexts of life-experience, indeed as much at the level of individual enactments of life as at that of social reality. Now this, however, implies at the same time, as a *reflexive comportment,* an *openness* for the interpretation of reality as it is presented on the part, for example, of the social sciences, which aid in sharpening a reflexive view of reality in the results of their own inquiries as critical interlocutors, and reciprocally can clarify the more empirically oriented analyses in the diagnostic approach to categorial problems with the help of philosophical reflection.

To give an example, contemporary sociologists like Ulrich Beck and Anthony Giddens, in avoidance of the odium of the arbitrariness adhering to the concept of postmodernism, speak nonetheless in the sense, conceived by Welsch, of a 'radical modernism'—in light of the collapse of the world-order at the end of the 1980s and the catchphrase of globalization bound up with it—that carries with it, complementarily, an appreciation of the regional and local, that is, of an emergent historical formation of social relations, a *'reflexive modernization'* (see Ulrich Beck, Anthony Giddens, and Scott Lash, *Reflexive Modernisierung: Eine Kontroverse* [Frankfurt: Suhrkamp, 1996]). It signifies the modernization, i.e., self-transformation, of late-industrial modern societies. These transformations show themselves vividly, among other places, in the mode in which the old, hitherto consensus-sheltering foundations are to be renegotiated—for instance, the debate over the task of a nation-state's claims to sovereignty such as monetary law, or even the discussion of the renovation of the structural foundations of the welfare state (cf. Giddens, *Jenseits von Links und Rechts: Die Zukunft radikaler Demokratie* [Frankfurt: Suhrkamp, 1997], 186–266).

For Beck and Giddens, a certain program inscribes itself in the processes of reflexive modernization—which can no longer be conceived within the semantics of traditional models of rationality and control—namely, the program of a breaking out into a *'second modernity,'* which, on the presupposition of "internalized democracy" (Ulrich Beck, "Kinder der Freiheit: Wider das Lamento über den Werteverfall," in *Kinder der Freiheit,* ed. Ulrich Beck [Frankfurt: Suhrkamp, 1997], 11), supersedes the lost 'world of traditional security' as precisely a second modernity "if it goes well—the democratic culture of a properly sanctioned individualism for all" (ibid.), in a new radical-modern confrontation to be ignited with the "source of sense

The battle of the 1980s over postmodernism is not to be restaged once again in the present investigation. It only finds mention in the given context because in opposition to the postmoderns and their "forefathers" Nietzsche and Heidegger the objection is still always raised that with the abandonment of the unity of reason, they at the same time surrendered the standard of rationality [*Rationalität*] together with the morally binding claims of rationality [*Vernünftigkeit*]. But must the abandonment of the unity of reason and thus its dispersal into the manifold of discourse necessarily already jettison all rationality, as Habermas presumes? Is irrationalism the necessary consequence? Does holding and finding oneself in a plural lifeworld—as cogiven manifold participation in the multiplicity of forms of life and knowing—mean that there can no longer be talk of rational self-determination?

Finding answers to these questions, answers that are not formulated haphazardly or in a simplified manner, means allowing oneself, as an interpreter in a given context, to sketch out their phenomenological orientation through the space of concepts opened up in their texts with the hermeneutics of facticity. This space of understanding can only be opened up productively, however, when it is taken into consideration that this opening up must be carried out against the time in which these texts appeared, under the changed and thus nonsimultaneous conditions of life and thought. In this hermeneutically reflexive, clarified sense, the text constitutes, as Günter Figal stresses, the "free space of its interpretation and in this way, as free space, the freedom of the interpreter,"[271] whereby "this freedom of the interpreter [is] actually the freedom of the text,"[272] insofar as its space of play always already prestructures its possibilities of understand-

---

[settled in the center of Modernity] that is at once age-old and thoroughly current: political freedom" (ibid., 10; see also "Utopie als Ursprung: Politische Freiheit als Sinnquelle der Moderne" *Kinder der Freiheit*, 382–401).

It can be said, following Rorty, that such a culture would "catch sight of its most important goal not in truth, but rather in freedom" (Richard Rorty, *Eine Kultur ohne Zentrum: Vier philosophische Essays* [Stuttgart: Reclam, 1993], 11). Such a projective vision, which at the same time does not deny the classical motivations of morality, justice, solidarity, and sense, is based, however one might be disposed toward it, on a concept of the individual in the endview of societal conditionedness, considered philosophically, which can no longer be displaced back behind Nietzsche, Freud, or Heidegger, and which for Beck is also not capable of being consistently formulated without the "father figures" of Kant and Tocqueville (see Beck, "Väter der Freiheit," *Kinder der Freiheit*, 333–381).

272. Figal, *Der Sinn des Verstehens*, 18.

273. Ibid.

ing. If the hermeneutic situation of texts, to which every interpretation is relative,[273] is now included as such in the motivation of interpretation, the turn to texts does not thus follow primarily in the strict sense as historical investigation.

Texts are interrogated, rather, with the inclusion of other positions as partners in the dialogue of interpretation, with an eye to the potential that the experiences through which they are formulated possesses today, in the change of questions, for a clarification of the historical existence of the human. This change in questioning, which should not be confused with a linear progression, refers within philosophical research ideally to the *configuration of basic concepts,* as they take shape in a given time as *central concepts* for their theoretical projects. As capable of change in a sense that is significant for our present investigation, however, these concepts prove to be the *potential for their transgression* insofar as they already carry in themselves historical limits of experience that figure them in and out of the context of their world.

This transgression is made possible and demanded whenever in the historical course of time the conditions of human self- and world relations change such that contemporarily pressing problems necessarily can enable new perspectives of sense. Seen thus, the transformation at the basis of an age establishes itself as a transgression of that which takes shape within the historical constellation, breaking open into experience, and which now forces itself out in new structures of experience that concretely and situationally challenge human historical existence. And in the process, what comes to appear in new theoretical configurations remains constitutively inscribed within a relation to the voices of the tradition, which counts as inevitably posing a challenge in itself to the tasks of a hermeneutics of the processes of self-understanding.

Insofar as these voices can be textually interrogated in historical testimonies, that is, in given cases, which themselves constitute historically at the same time the experiential scope of history, this means being able to comport oneself historically toward history, to understandingly open up in texts a so to speak "materialized memory."[274] In the sense of a herme-

---

274. "A given hermeneutics of the situation must develop its transparency and bring it, as hermeneutic, into the method of interpretation" (Heidegger, *Phänomenologische Interpretationen zu Aristoteles,* 237).

275. Figal, *Der Sinn des Verstehens,* 18. See §§ 6, 8, 10.

neutical condition of access, this holds that the "past . . . only opens itself in accordance with the resoluteness and force of the capacity for opening, over which a present holds sway."[275]

Whether the tradition is able to maintain its validity claims once more, so that it gains anew that power of conviction in which it shows its knowledge as still effective-historical in its productive progress—this is not already settled in advance with the given necessity of exchange in the hermeneutical process of self-understanding. It could, as in Descartes or Husserl, in view of the understanding of the present situation, have to do with diagnostically indispensable and in large part still inspiring insights that under the sign of historical change nonetheless, to put a twist on a famous saying from Beauvoir, at each step of their renovation appear to be "ceremonies of farewell." As with every farewell, the departed nonetheless remains there in a transformed way, and because it is a matter of a work of thought and not mortal persons, the continuity in the stream of tradition in no way excludes a programmatic return (always modified) in the sense of a newly recognized challenge. The decision about this falls on the presentness of what is present and thus with a view to what Heidegger calls the "original unity of the problematic of facticity."[276] A necessity for such a return will be found just as little as a lawfulness. And thus, against Hegel's decree that in regard to history, philosophical investigation should have "no other intention than to eliminate chance,"[277] one should—on hermeneutical presuppositions, that is, under the conditions of finite knowledge—rather be disposed to confer plausibility upon Nietzsche's dehybridizing dice cup of chance.[278]

276. Heidegger, *Phänomenologische Interpretationen zu Aristoteles*, 237.
277. Ibid., 247.
278. Hegel, *Vorlesungen über die Philosophie der Weltgeschichte*, ed. Johannes Hoffmeister (Hamburg: Meiner, 1970), 1:29 (emphasis deleted).
279. See Nietzsche, *Morgenröthe* 2:130, in *KGW*, 5:1, 120.

CHAPTER TWO

THE EXPERIENTIAL STRUCTURE OF THE SELF: TOWARD A HERMENEUTICS OF FACTICAL HISTORICAL LIFE

*§ 31. The Leap into the World. On Outlining the
Factical-Hermeneutical Concept of Experience*

To gain the philosophical attitude that appears necessary from out of the hermeneutical turn of phenomenology for an analysis of determinate human life as facticity means, to begin with, as Pöggeler puts it, "to break away from or shut off the machinery of Husserl's phenomenological reductions."[1] Instead of wanting to penetrate into a deep layer of the immutable ideal "I" on the path of reductions, phenomenological hermeneutics forms its approach by recurring to *pretheoretical experiences,* from which it works on its ontological analysis of structure by means of the interpretation of concrete appearances. In the context of discussions of the lifeworld, it has been shown that for its hermeneutically appropriate ontological determination the factical historical experiential reality of the human, as the in-itself-plural-structured fabric of situations, may not be overlooked. The concept of experience functions thereby in a notable manner as the basis of hermeneutical philosophizing and marks at the same time in this function,

---

1. Pöggeler, "Eine Epoche gewaltigen Werdens," 26. Heidegger himself speaks of the fact that he had "only to divest [himself] of the fetters" (*Grundprobleme der Phänomenologie,* GA 58, 151) of the phenomenological reduction in order, with regard to factical life, to be able to capture the positively accentuated bearing of immediate co-participation in, or rather, accompanying of, experience (see also ibid., 162, 254).

as has already shown itself many times in various connections, the line of division to transcendental phenomenology. Seen thus, the categories of understanding take shape in the observation of our own being, as also with regard to the world, and both of these in the cultural and historically factical situation comprehending subject and object alike. Observed systematically, this functions, spoken in harmony with Foucault,[2] as the *experiential structure of the self.*

In order to bring out still more clearly the contours of the hermeneutically posited concept of experience, one can cite for critical consideration Kant's ur-dictum that "all of our knowledge begins with experience; of that there is no doubt."[3] Nevertheless, experience here is famously synonymous with sense perception, and Kant then also explains that to let our knowledge begin with experience does not already mean that all knowledge springs from out of experience, that is, intuition. "For it could well be that our knowledge of experience itself may be simply a composite of what we receive through impressions and what our own faculty of knowledge (merely occasioned through sensible impressions) produces out of itself."[4] The investigation of this state of affairs, pursued as the business of a transcendental critique of reason, determined the transcendental concept of experience established as categorial and in itself as objective and necessary, universally valid authenticated experience.

With regard to this essential feature, the concept of experience, as it functions in its approach as the ground of the hermeneutics of facticity, now signifies something decidedly different. For this experience is just not objective in the sense of universal validity and necessity. Rather, experience here is subjective and thus contingently and individually determined. In the context of the hermeneutically transformed phenomenology of historically factical life, it is the *existentiell experience* that Heidegger also addresses in clear dependence on the philosophy of life in the early lectures as 'experience of life.' In the framework of traditional transcendental philosophy, which essentially concerns the demonstration of the universal conditions of *experience in general,* this cannot properly be grasped.[5] 'Con-

<hr>

2. See, for example, Foucault, *Wahnsinn und Gesellschaft;* Hans Herbert Kögler, *Michel Foucault* (Stuttgart: Metzler, 1994), 37.

3. Kant, *Kritik der reinen Vernunft* B 1.

4. Ibid.

5. See Annemarie Pieper's study "Erfahrung in der Existenzphilosophie," in *Der Begriff der Erfahrung in der Philosophie des 20. Jahrhunderts,* ed. Jürg Freudiger, Andreas Graeser, and

tingent' and 'individual' mean that with these existentiell experiences the matter concerns ontic, concrete occurrences of an individual human being, which mark themselves out in appropriating life situations such that they neither confront the respective experiencing "I" as an object nor appear in the rank of mere accidents, as is suggested in view of the order of pure reason as the philosophically conscious transcendental standpoint, which aspires to separate out from itself everything merely empirical. Therefore, the existentiell experiences are determined by the fact *that I do not merely have them, but I am them.*

Seen in this way, with Heidegger, the "I" can be denoted as the *"situational I."*[6] In this sense, experiences are always already—whether explicitly or not—*self-experiences,* in which I comport myself toward myself without possessing the possibility in this existential–a priori connection of exempting myself from them.[7] That means that existentiell experiences are neither objectifiable in an actual sense, nor simply neutral.[8]

Klaus Petrus [Munich: Beck, 1996], 153–177). In relation to Jaspers, Sartre, Camus, and the Heidegger of the "Letter on Humanism," Pieper sees the concept of experience rooted in an originary dimension "that is indicated by *'existere'*" (ibid., 153) and as such is not to be grasped from the tradition of a philosophy of consciousness; for the latter "is only capable of being reflected formally-scientifically in a priori constructions of reality" (ibid.).

6. Heidegger, *Zur Bestimmung der Philosophie,* GA 56/57, 206 (emphasis added).

7. "Every situation is an 'event' [*Ereignis*] and not a 'process' [*Vorgang*]. That which has happened has a relation to me; it stands within my own I" (ibid.). Heidegger connects the term *'Vorgang'* with the theoretical attitude, whereas *'Ereignischarakter'* signifies situational experience [*Situationserlebnis*]. It is in this sense that Heidegger emphasizes: "Appropriative events 'happen to me' [*passieren mir*]" (ibid., 205).

8. This is evident, for example, in the fact that in reflexively pursuing a situational analysis wherein I again bring to mind events that have befallen me, I relate them from out of this remove back to myself as the one presently thinking them, in whose recollection that which is recollected shows itself selectively and in the mode of presently being recollected situationally, and thus as always already perspectivally refracted. As a further structurally unsublatable moment for this notion that what is made present is not given "neutrally or objectively" in the sense of material data, it has been shown that the modes of making present in such self-interpreting observation, like the situation made present therein in all the reflexively demanded cognitive acts of analysis, is always already a *matter of attunement,* as the famous Heideggerian investigations on the equiprimordial interplay of understanding and state of mind in *Sein und Zeit* have shown.

Thus, what is at issue in the self-incitement to rational elaboration implicated in the framework of a situational analysis in place of an emotional residual feeling is consequently a *displacement of preference* in the access to self, one that in no case can mean a dispensing of all understanding equiprimordially with constituting states of mind, insofar as the structures [*Dispositiv*] of the attaining of knowledge in rational analysis are always already grounded by an attunement. This is evident in the fact that I assess realized situations in corresponding affective scales of experience, for example, as agreeable or disagreeable, yet also as advantageous

The concept of experience that in this sense fundamentally refers to *self-relation* at the basis of human existence is always already situationally related or bound in its performance-structure. Consequently, I make experiences only in situational connections, and situations create in themselves possibilities of experience for me, designated by a "relative closure,"[9] whereby the situation is characterized in the rule by a "disengagement [*Unabgehobenheit*] of the I."[10]

To underscore this as a *fundamental thesis of the hermeneutics of facticity* seems at first glance to be hardly original. Yet it is not a question here of originality in the sense of some kind of constant "spirit of invention." In view of the conspicuous accentuation here on the situational character, from the view of the natural attitude it might in addition have the appearance of scraping up hard against the borders of alleged triviality. Yet the allegedly trivial has often enough proved itself to philosophers upon closer inspection to not be as banal as commonly assumed—and not only since the age of Socrates. And precisely the reflection on that which seems self-evident—how we live in situational relations—transforms it therein into a thematic field, which in illuminating its synchronic and diachronic, ex-

---

or impairing, and so on. And it is precisely there, where events in current experience or in subsequent reflection may appear rather meaningless or indifferent, that this assessment is not to be confused with value-neutral objective scientific sense. For even the indifference in the face of humans and things is a bearing in which—outside of or within my relatedness to the world—my relation to my self-experience plays itself out in terms of attunement in just this way.

If one keeps this in view, it is thus shown, however, that the *view-at-a-distance* at one's own experiences acting in such a situational analysis is itself nothing other than an *existentiell experience*. As such, it has nothing to do with distanciation in the sense of objectification, insofar as the realization of a situation at a reflective distance as the refraction of a respective engaged and situatively conditioned being-involved does not in principle override the relation to self-experience: it is and remains *my* situation that I am here considering. This is also the case whenever the conditions of this reflection are subject to distortion, whether it be through temporary restriction due, for example, to intoxication, or through longer-term disturbances as in the case of mental illnesses.

Bearing these possibilities in mind, it becomes still clearer—beyond the factical 'that' [*Daß*] I am in a particular condition—*how* I am in the place of opening up in reflexive access to my situation in its dispositional interweavings, with regard to which an elevated meaning is assigned to the formative capacity of my self-relation as world-relation. The proverbial lesson that I draw from the experience hangs together with it and is motivated essentially from out of this capacity that traditionally accompanies the concept of the force of judgment [*Urteilskraft*]. With Heidegger, one can therefore determine the situational I as "a function of 'life experience' [*Lebenserfahrung*]" (GA 56/57, 208); such life experience, for its part, means a "constantly changing nexus of situations of motivational possibilities" (ibid.).

9. Ibid., 206.

10. Ibid. See also §36 in this context.

plicit and implicit effective presuppositions, swiftly loses its semblance of mere self-evidence.

In this sense, as the insight of an initial step along the path toward phenomenological-hermeneutical differentiation, we must retain the notion that in the approach to the analysis of situation envisaged here the structure of self-relation comes to appearance in light of the *existential dimension*. At the same time, concerning a further clarification of the scope of the subjects in question, all formal questions of self-relation, as one might find them problematized in semantics or metamathematics, for example, remain excluded from the outset. That means that our approach concerns the present hermeneutical discussion of the problem of self-relation, observed at its core in the questions and possibilities of the human *relation of self-understanding*. Here too in no way can the role of the "originator" be ascribed to Heidegger, but he can be regarded distinctly as one who opened and illuminated perspectives for the thematization of the basic existential self-relation of human beings, which lend the question of self-relation a new transparency through the existentially constitutive basic comportment of human situatedness.[11]

11. From out of the perspective thus gained, a tradition could be newly reintroduced or brought into discussion in an alternate hermeneutical way, wherein a historical sequence of theoretical outlines for human self-relations are referred back to someone like Kant, who in his practical philosophy construes the practical as self-relation in his treatment of the will, as Gerold Prauss shows (see his *Kant über Freiheit als Autonomie* [Frankfurt: Klostermann, 1983], 123–126). As an example from another strand of tradition, one could invoke the Stoic doctrine of *oikeosis* (cf. Maximilian Forschner, "Glück als personale Identität: Die stoische Theorie des Endziels," in *Über das Glück des Menschen: Aristoteles, Epikur, Stoa, Thomas von Aquin, Kant* [Darmstadt: Wissenschaftliche Buchgesellschaft, 1993], 45–79). And it would be natural to refer in addition to Kierkegaard in the given context in a prominent position, for in his approach to his philosophy of existence, he thinks being able to be oneself is sufficient for the ethically founding self-comportment to God.

With regard to the subject of self-relation qua discourses of self-understanding, we can also include as a significant representative the *tradition of grand self-inquiry* (*Tradition der großen Selbsterkundungen*), which begins with Augustine's *Confessions,*and which brings together under the question of the justification of one's own self (in fact, precisely with an eye to situative relations within which the self is formed) such diverse literary formulations as Montaigne's *Essais*, Rousseau's *Confessions*, Nietzsche's *Ecce Homo*, and Walter Benjamin's *Berliner Kindheit*.

Furthermore, the *diary* occupies a preeminent place in the field of self-inquiry, particularly when it concerns viewing a person's work through other, supplementary means, as in those of Kierkegaard or Camus. The famous image of "lining and skirt," with which Kassner characterizes Rilke's letters in relation to his works, likewise finds a fitting usage here, including the observation that the value of lining material can often tempt one to wear one's skirt with the lining turned to the outside.

This situative relatedness is vividly underscored by a characteristic of the self that Heidegger, in a letter from August 1921 to his former student Karl Löwith, formulates as follows: "I work concretely, factically from my 'I am'—from out of my general spiritual factical origin—milieu—life connections, from that which is accessible to me as living experience, wherein I live. This facticity is as existentiell no mere 'blind Dasein'; it lies together in existence, which means, however, that I live it—that 'I must,' of which one does not speak. With this *facticity of being-thus*, the historical, existence rages."[12] The pointed, expressive style of correspondence gives one immediately to know that Heidegger conceives his own philosophizing as a *form of life* bound up with facticity.[13]

While it would seem at first glance easy to exclude such self-conceptions from consideration, the question nonetheless arises whether, from a methodological perspective, this insight becomes de facto relevant when it concerns the determination of Heidegger's own personal opinion. A simple *yes* or *no* will not provide a sufficient answer here. For insofar as there looms behind the question the assumption that one can indeed distinguish between the subjective (personal, private) and the objective (universally authoritative, true), the question shows itself to be misguided from the outset. For this assumption conceals in itself, as an unclarified presupposition, a tacit orientation to the scientific yardstick of one's cognitive capacity for insight. But with a view to a given connection, not only is an implicit shift of context carried out, but this assumption also burdens itself in its scientific division with a murky metaphysical "legacy," insofar

---

Should one bring to mind the wide field of interpreting self-reference even if only in these excerpts, that means for the following analysis to pose and investigate the question of what is visible of new perspectives through the approach of the Heideggerian hermeneutics of facticity in the philosophical demonstration of the existentiell basic structure of human situational being-in-the-world. And this in turn means making oneself sensitive, in the reflexive look at the self-relation, to that in the moment holding sway of manifold withdrawal into it.

12. Heidegger, "Drei Briefe Martin Heideggers an Karl Löwith," ed. Hartmut Tietjen, in *Zur philosophischen Aktualität Heideggers*, ed. Dietrich Papenfuss and Otto Pöggeler (Frankfurt: Klostermann, 1990), 2:29.

13. Guided by this insight into philosophy as a *Lebensform*, characterized thus not only by Heidegger but also in his own way by Wittgenstein, Thomas Rentsch develops his systematic comparison of both thinkers for the sake of a 'logical propaedeutic to anthropology,' which he sketches out as an 'existential grammar' (Rentsch, *Heidegger und Wittgenstein: Existential- und Sprachanalysen zu den Grundlagen philosophischer Anthropologie* [Stuttgart: Klett-Cotta, 1985], 254–321). Rentsch offers a further development of this line of thinking in the direction of an analysis of fundamental practical situations in *Die Konstitution der Moralität: Transzendentale Anthropologie und praktische Philosophie* (Frankfurt: Suhrkamp, 1990).

as 'objective/subjective' shows itself to be a transformation of the metaphysical opposition 'absolute/relative.'[14]

Against this, it is of no small significance for the considerations ahead that—and how—the possibility for insight in making this division remains unconsidered, namely the insight that the situation in which humans ineluctably comport themselves possesses in its experience-formative character an *identity-founding function (identitätsstiftende Funktion)*. This becomes evident when we observe that the self-understanding exhibited in Heidegger's letter is concretely conditioned in its very possibility through a (life-)situation that, taken as a specific context of self-experience in the sense exemplified above (and in precisely this same respect), situationally produces and structures—in the immediate present—the existential possibility of this individual and contingent form of self-understanding. What thus announces itself in *the situatedness of the human* is therefore not the proclamation of a self-understanding speaking out of some definite individual, substantially conceived interiority residing within an exteriority that can be differentiated from it.

The self-interpretation that shows itself in Heidegger's letter is, on the contrary, constituted solely in and through the concrete situation as the *selfhood*[15] of the author. Seen thus, the situation pertains specifically to a sense-endowing creature that—since we live in no other way than situationally—*is* selfhood in accordance with its structure and function.[16] Sense-endowing should not be misunderstood, however, by attributing to it a kind of power of determination. Nor is it a matter of some sort of causal relation that has always already taken effect in the region of existential experience. Rather, situational meaning endowing coalesces with

14. Cf. Picht, *Geschichte und Gegenwart*, 84.

15. The concept of selfhood employed here follows Paul Ricoeur's distinction between two kinds of identity, namely self-sameness (*Selbigkeit, mêmeté, idem*) and selfhood (*Selbstheit, ipséité, ipse*). Self-sameness carries the sense of an "I" persisting throughout changes in space and time as an identical *idem*, while selfhood means that an "I" comports itself to itself as *ipse*, whereby this *ipséité* takes place in *idem*, yet is not to be identified therein as precisely the same throughout a flux of circumstances. See Paul Ricoeur, *Das Selbst als ein Anderer* (Munich: Fink, 1996), 144, 150–152.

16. The concepts of structure and function are here distinct from those prominent in the discourses of structuralism, as seen for example in the work of Claude Lévi-Strauss (see *Strukturale Anthropologie I* [Frankfurt: Suhrkamp, 1977], 111, 301), in the sense of a general theory of relationships conceived as more or less atemporal invariants; rather, Heidegger thinks these as hermeneutical concepts; that is, he thinks structure and function as dynamically historicized, as we will see in greater detail below.

the cultural, historically preformed space of projection (*Entwurfsraum*), with its respective options for developing meaning; insofar as the human experiences situatedness in the openness to the future, these latter options locate the meaning-endowing power of the situation in the relation of tension between past and future from the outset.

Viewed in this way, this also does not mean that in order to philosophically thematize the present question of the structure of self-relation, the chosen investigative approach exhausts itself for existentiell experience in the descriptive account of ontic possibilities of formation as possibilities of expression. However, to thus include its colorful roundelay of motives in hermeneutical reflection—so that the existentiell experience in them becomes the content of the point of relation for the hermeneutical view in its ever-particular individual formation, without one's thinking simply being narratively overplayed—does not appear without methodological difficulty, if at the same time the claim to a structural analysis of the relations of conditionedness and function remains in play. This difficulty resolves itself without therefore having to neglect or shut off the ontic, concrete, existentiell basis of experience, in that the interpretive representation of Heidegger's confessional letter brings this personal experience to hermeneutical formal indication in an *exemplary function,* so that the concrete existentiell experience methodologically abets the insight into a fundamental structure of factical situatedness of human being-in-the-world.[17]

17. While I can only offer a basic sketch here, a concrete possibility for such exemplary meditations on self-interpretation as it relates to the comportment to oneself in the medium of letter-writing would—following Gerhart Baumann's outline of a phenomenology of the letter (see Baumann, "Der Brief: Mitteilung und Selbstzeugnis," in *Sprache und Selbstbegegnung* [Munich: Fink, 1981], 98–112)—have to take note of the fact that letters, admittedly drawn up in a concrete situation and from out of a given occasion, are nonetheless not exhausted in their documentary content. As the lines to Löwith indicate, letters quite often attain, as *messages,* the status of personal testimonials in which writers, under the protection of confidentiality, entrust thoughts to their addressee that show them to be in pursuit of themselves, or even occasionally lead them first and foremost to a kind of self-discovery. Letters thereby unfold within the peculiar temporal field of an essentially deferred play of address and reply as excerpts of an ongoing conversation.

The way in which such epistolary conversations can be carried out broadens itself into a spectrum that spans the informal 'you' of the address in a barely certifying monologue of someone like Kafka or Kleist, on the one hand, all the way to the respective otherness of the addressee in a receptive, corresponding, self-differentiating response that is highly distinctive of a writer like Goethe. In figures such as Kierkegaard, Nietzsche, Rilke, or Valéry, it is at times difficult, sometimes impossible to always and carefully distinguish personal correspondence from poetic or intellectual works from one another. And on occasion, as in Seneca, Pascal, or Leibniz, the work itself assumes the form of letters.

Does the status of the exemplary, however, inevitably attach itself to a universalization in the horizontal and a transcendentalization in the vertical? And how is this to be related to the manifoldly expressed skepticism in the face of the generalization to which it is bound? And likewise to individuality and contingency, which we have made clear are constitutive structural moments of existentiell experience? These questions will be taken up again in a next step and, with an eye to Heidegger's programmatic intention of a hermeneutic of the self, will be given a more exact determination. In order to succeed in gaining a necessary, if only provisional, clarity in our initial approach, we must refer once more to the letter we have just cited.

With a view to the existentiell fundamental sense of his philosophizing, Heidegger here explains the facticity of being-thus, by means of an appositional determination, as *the historical.* This has its form of expression, on the one hand, in being-thus as the respective concrete life-connection with which the individual life-historical moment of facticity is accentuated as existentiell. On the other, the "'intellectual-historical' historical consciousness ['*geistesgeschichtliche' historische Bewußtsein*]"[18] is also bound up for Heidegger with the aforementioned facticity of being-thus as historical, which as such locates one's own being-thus reflexively beyond the situational in the precedence of the historical nexus of the effect, which as such does not emerge in the order of the life situation, but rather simply co-forms its conditions.

The letters and personal correspondence of Heidegger that have come to light in recent years cannot be established with the same degree of decisiveness; nonetheless, they enjoy, almost universally, a certain closeness with respect to his work, and experience their influence from this proximity. See in particular his correspondence with Elisabeth Blochmann (*Briefwechsel 1918–1969*, ed. J. W. Storck [Marbach: Deutsche Schillergesellschaft, 1989]; cf. Günter Seubold, "Dienstbar der Sache des Denkens," *Heidegger Studies* [1991], 7:149–155) with Karl Jaspers (Heidegger and Jaspers, *Briefwechsel 1920–1963*); cf. Walter Biemel, "Zum Briefwechsel Jaspers/Heidegger," in *Zur philosophischen Aktualität Heideggers*, vol. 2, ed. Dietrich Papenfuss and Otto Pöggeler [Frankfurt: Klostermann, 1990], 71–86) with Erhart Kästner (Heidegger and Kästner, *Briefwechsel 1953–1974*, ed. Heinrich Wiegand Petzet (Frankfurt: Insel, 1986); cf. Gander, "Martin Heidegger und Erhart Kästner. Anmerkungen zu einem Gespräch im Wegfeld von Dichten und Denken," *Heidegger Studies* 1987–1988], 3–4:75–88) with Ludwig von Ficker (in Heidegger and Ficker, *Briefwechsel, Vol. 4: 1940–1967*, ed. Martin Alber (Innsbruck: Haymon, 1996) and with Imma von Bodmershof (Heidegger and von Bodmershof, *Briefwechsel 1959–1976*, ed. Bruno Pieger (Stuttgart: Klett-Cotta, 2000). For the reader, throughout all of this a Heidegger becomes visible who, in the characteristic tension of self-assertion and self-surrender, offers such an abundance of testimonials of the stream of the transformations in his thinking throughout the decades that the continuity of the existentiell claim is manifest, under which his thinking is reported so vividly in the letter to Löwith cited above.

18. Heidegger, *Erster Brief an Löwith*, 29.

As the principle of effective history made explicit in connection with Gadamer, this connection had already become the theme of the interpretation in the first section. And in fact, a structural commonality takes shape at this point between the hermeneutics of facticity now in view and that which issued in the earlier discussions with regard to a hermeneutics of the text related to facticity, insofar as the sense-connection articulated in the textual weave evidences itself as constitutively intertwined or contained in a plural event of sense that in the network of strands of tradition discloses the ontic existentiell space of the project again and again within the historical lifeworld.

In this sense, our biography represents history, and thus the thesis can be posited with Georg Picht that "our opinions about history [determine] our relation to ourselves"[19]—with the consequence that then, if we understand history inadequately or falsely, we necessarily also misunderstand ourselves. Life is, Heidegger stresses, historical and as such "not fragmentation into essential elements, but rather connection [*Zusammenhang*]."[20] Therefore, the question of historical understanding is of fundamental significance for the concepts of self-understanding taking shape in the existential–a priori self-relation of human being.

The fact of human being-thus in its twofold performative structure has accordingly a kind of apriori in the dimension of the historical. Insofar as this a priori is determined constitutively in its content of expression and structure through historicity, it can be spoken of, as with Foucault, as a *historical apriori*.[21] It would be a misunderstanding indeed "to conceive this historical *apriori* as a formal *apriori* that would be provided with a history beyond it."[22] In contrast, it is to be maintained that "the formal *apriori* and the historical *apriori* do not stand on the same level, nor are they of the same nature."[23] That is to say, the formal apriori expresses the conditions

---

19. Picht, *Geschichte und Gegenwart*, 5.

20. Heidegger, *Zur Bestimmung der Philosophie*, GA 56/57, 117.

21. See Foucault, *Archäologie des Wissens*, 183–187. One of the most compelling objections against the long-standing inclination to assign Foucault to the so-called structuralist camp is found in the conception of the historical a priori. See also Hubert L. Dreyfus and Paul Rabinow, *Michel Foucault*, 81. According to Wilhelm Schmid, the "attempt to disclose this *a priori*, which is something historical, [comprises] the clasp that comprehends Foucault's entire work." Schmid, *Auf der Suche nach einer neuen Lebenskunst: Die Frage nach dem Grund und die Neubegründung der Ethik bei Foucault* (Frankfurt: Suhrkamp, 1992), 49.

22. Foucault, *Archäologie des Wissens*, 186.

23. Ibid.

of the possibility of a given experience in its universal, transhistorical conditions of validity from out of transcendental subjectivity, so that according to Kant's 'sovereign principle'—which maintains its validity beyond Fichte and Hegel up to the idealistic approach of Husserlian transcendental phenomenology—precisely these formal a priori conditions are "at the same time conditions of the *possibility of the objects of experience.*"[24]

Seen thus, however, everything empirical is dependent upon the transcendental power of cognition possessed by the subject of consciousness that grounds it, a power that is also, in its constituting capacity, the proper object of transcendental analysis. In contrast, with regard to the historical apriori, it is a matter of the historical conditions in which the organizing schemata that form experience themselves take shape, schemata that prove to be "a transformable group"[25] insofar as the historical a priori makes clear that "discourse does not only possess a meaning or a truth, but a history, a specific history, that cannot refer discourse back to the laws of an obscure process of becoming."[26] In this light, the historical a priori appears not as a transcendental but as a "purely empirical figure."[27] Yet as a "condition of reality for statements"[28] it must, on the other hand (to the extent that it encompasses the capacity for rules that structure discursive practice) "be able to account for the fact that, at a given point in time, a certain discourse can take up or utilize this or that formal structure, or on the contrary exclude, forget, or misconstrue it."[29]

Having recourse to Foucault in the given context is not due solely, or even primarily, to the circumstance that the proper concept of the historical apriori is, as it were, "borrowed" from him in order to lay out the actual situation—to be distinguished in greater detail—of the historically

---

24. Kant, *Kritik der reinen Vernunft*, B 197.
25. Foucault, *Archäologie des Wissens*, 185.
26. Ibid., 184.
27. Ibid., 185.
28. Ibid., 184. Cf. § 7 on the approach to problems of statements.
29. Foucault, *Archäologie des Wissens*, 185. It would nonetheless be a mistake, as Foucault points out, to assume that the approach of a historical a priori would be able to explain a formal apriori in something like a cultural or psychological genesis. Yet it permits us "to understand how the formal *aprioris* can have in history points of linkage, of insertion, of irruption or of emergence, areas and occasions of application; and to understand how this history can not be absolutely external to contingency, not be a necessity of form deploying its own dialectic, but instead a specific orderliness" (ibid., 185 f.).

constituted facticity of being-thus.[30] The relation in force here is already a great deal more stable, insofar as a methodologically and textually given analogy with what Foucault's concepts describe comes into view in hermeneutically demonstrating the a priori structure of the historical. This is to say, in both cases it is a matter of revealing the *knowledge-constituting function of experience,* which itself provides—not transcendentally, but rather ontically and concretely—the scope of its epistemological reach in the contingent modes and possibilities of a historical consciousness. This clarification, indispensable for a methodological approach to epistemolo-

30. Even if the points of contact with hermeneutical thinking regarding proximity and distance in the approach of the Foucauldian analyses vary considerably in their details as well as over the course of his larger thought (generally partitioned into phases through *Archäologie des Wissens, Genealogie der Macht,* and *Ethik als Ästhetik der Existenz*), constructive possibilities for dialogue from a hermeneutic point of view nonetheless open up—for example, in the discursive-analytic style that has thoroughly transformed the history of ideas through its new concepts. In addition, Foucault's insistence upon the finitude of knowledge (see, e.g., the "Analytik der Endlichkeit" in *Ordnung der Dinge,* 377–384) and his famous destruction of subject-centered approaches can be drawn upon in order to generate hermeneutically productive readings (see Dieter Teichert, "Zwischen Wissenschaftskritik und Hermeneutik: Foucaults Humanwissenschaften," *Zeitschrift für philosophische Forschung* [1993], 47:204–222).

In his later work, notably in his *Konzeption der Selbstsorge,* Foucault himself takes up a decidedly hermeneutical position that is of particular interest for what follows. It is also distinctive for this affinity to the hermeneutical, taken in a broad sense, that all phases of his thought are marked by traces of Heidegger, who—although at most only tacitly, yet in any case as a starting-point—is a lasting source of inspiration for him, along with Nietzsche and Kant. In his final interview, appearing in "Les nouvelles littéraires" three days after his death, Foucault highlighted, almost as a kind of confession, Heidegger's significance for his own thought: "Heidegger has always been for me the essential philosopher. . . . My entire philosophical development was determined by my reading of Heidegger. I admit, however, that it was Nietzsche with whom my development was carried through. Heidegger [and now comes a gesture of evasiveness, typical for Foucault, with which he intends to thwart any attempts to pin him down] I know only insufficiently; actually, I know neither *Sein und Zeit* nor the recently published works. My knowledge of Nietzsche is quite a bit better than that of Heidegger. Despite this fact, it remains the case that both were fundamental experiences for me. It is very possible that had I not read Nietzsche, I would not have read Heidegger. I had tried to read Nietzsche in the 1950s, yet Nietzsche on his own didn't speak to me at all! Whereas Nietzsche and Heidegger, that was the philosophical shock. Yet I have never written anything on Heidegger, and on Nietzsche only a very small article; nonetheless, it is these two authors whom I have read the most [and whoever is familiar with Foucault's work knows what an enormous reader he was, which means that the qualification noted above in his evasiveness is itself qualified again, or rather, rescinded]; I believe it is important to have a small number of authors with whom one thinks, with whom one works, but on which one does not write. Perhaps I will one day write on them, but then they would no longer be for me *instruments of thinking*" (emphasis added). "Die Rückkehr der Moral: Ein Interview mit Michel Foucault [29. 5. 1984]," in *Ethos der Moderne,* ed. Eva Erdmann, Rainer Forst, and Axel Honneth (Frankfurt: Campus, 1990), 140; Foucault, *Dits et écrits 1954–1988,* ed. Daniel Defert and François Ewald (Paris: Gallimard, 1994,. 4:703).

gy, at the same time brings to light the questions that, as we become aware of the necessity for demonstrating the fundamental structures of human factical situatedness, are so pressing in relation to what we have called the exemplary function of existentiell experience.

What on first impression appeared perhaps to be a tacit repetition of transcendental-qua-universal validity claims has in fact been brought to light, with the demonstration of the structure of the historical apriori, with regard to a sufficient understanding of this meshwork of fundamental relations. Decisive here is that the individual character of existentiell experience, upon which the structural clarification of the question of the self as self-relation is based, shows itself to be founded in a historically preconditioned—and thus limited and variable—horizon of experience. Inscribed within this latter, as a historical, factical network of lifeworlds in the sense of the actuality of living out individual experience, hermeneutical reflection qua effective-historical consciousness discovers the ground of the possibility of existentiell experiences and, in tandem with it, their own basis of knowledge.

What effective historical reflection achieves in this sense is to expose the question concerning the self-relation as the task of a "hermeneutics of the situation [*Lage*]."[31] Bound to this is the notion that "interpretation . . . in the present [applies] in a certain average intelligibility, out of which philosophy lives and in which it *responds*."[32] This relation of situation, thought in the historical apriori, means uncovering the *conditions of constitution* of a particular concrete ground of experience in the nexus of effective history. Thus, if a central task for the hermeneutics of facticity as phenomenology of factical historical life also consists in pursuing the analysis of constitution in view of self-experience, this is done in such a way *that the conditions of the possibility of knowledge prove themselves now as historical.*[33] Methodologically, demonstration and analysis are carried out in phenomenological *destruktion,* which will be observed in more detail at a further point. For the present, the concern is seeing that the constitutional conditions that prestructure knowledge in the sense of the historical apriori are of the sort that take shape *in* the ontic, existentially experienced cultural and

31. Heidegger, *Ontologie, GA* 63, 29.

32. Ibid., 17. Heidegger notes, in addition: "Dasein as historical, its present. Being in the world, being lived from the world; present-everyday" (ibid., 29).

33. Foucault himself operates from out of this presupposition from *Wahnsinn und Gesellschaft* through the volumes of *Sexualität und Wahrheit.*

historical lifeworld, and thus, as predetermining the conditions of knowledge for our objective experience, belong to that historical lifeworld whose objects structure it in their concrete capacity for being experienced.

§ 32. Analysis of Environmental Experience

For the task of phenomenologically-hermeneutically illuminating this issue, Heidegger's analysis of the experience of the environment, written in the *Kriegsnotsemester,* offers an incisive point of access. For the "experience of the environment is no matter of contingency, but rather lies in the essence of life in and for itself"[34] and, in positively demonstrating environmental experience, outlines with precision human situational being in the world. It is in this sense that Manfred Riedel emphasizes the notion that the experience of the environment possesses nothing less than an "exemplary function for reformulating phenomenological philosophy from its origin as pretheoretical science."[35] Heidegger underlines this intention not least in the formation of his terminology, which in his approach to this analysis consciously shapes its concepts in harmony with phenomenology and *Lebensphilosophie*—in a manner that one might call '*lebensphenomenological*,' in opposition to object-theoretic positions. With a sense for the dramatic, Heidegger speaks of a "methodological crossroads that will be decisive for the life or death of philosophy in general"[36] with respect to the idea of an ur-science and an anticipated ur-scientific methodology in connection with this pending analysis of the structure of experience.

In order to punctuate this decisive situation as philosophy's situation of self-discovery, Heidegger cites the images of the 'tree of life' and the 'tree of knowledge of good and evil'[37] from the book of Genesis as an analogy, with which, in the Fall, the constitution of factical human life is thenceforth mortally and historically determined in its possibility for knowledge. In this context, however, Heidegger heightens the dramatic a bit more, to the effect that here, with the decision in favor of knowledge (read: epistemology), access to the tree of life (phenomenology as the ur-

---

34. Heidegger, *Zur Bestimmung der Philosophie,* GA 56/57, 88.
35. Riedel, *Hören auf die Sprache,* 82.
36. Heidegger, *Zur Bestimmung der Philosophie,* GA 56/57, 63.
37. Ibid., 65.

science of life) is misplaced, which brings with it, articulated in images, death (philosophy) insofar as the fateful path taken leads into the absolute objectivity of the epistemological position, which he characterizes, in its "deeply entrenched obstinacy for the theoretical,"[38] as nothing (*Nichts*). Philosophy threatens to be mired in this obstinacy if it cannot succeed in its "leap into *another world*, or more precisely, into the world as such."[39] This leap must be conceived in that which it originally makes accessible, in the sense of the activity of factical experience outlined above (§ 28). For Heidegger therefore—and here the change in his phenomenological approach reveals itself—"instead of always *knowing* things [it is a matter of] understanding intuitively and intuiting understandingly."[40] With an eye to the relatedness to the world as self-relatedness, the hermeneutically significant moment of such intuiting lies decidedly in the fact that in such immediate intuiting I do *not* find anything like that 'I' at which Husserl's eidetic intuition, with its intention towards the ur-I, aims.

What I find instead is only, as it were, "a 'living-through [*Er-leben*] of something,' a 'living towards something.'"[41] Of note here is that "the 'something' [*das Etwas*] signifies . . . 'what is experienceable in general' [*Erlebbares überhaupt*]."[42] This comportment-to is not of the sort that simply appends *das Etwas*; that is, "experiencing and what is experienced are not as such set together as if they were existent objects."[43] I live instead as a his-

38. Ibid., 88. As discussed above (§ 28), for Heidegger this obstinacy means not the simple dismissal of the theoretical per se, but rather the absolutizing of its epistemological validity claims, i.e., the "general reign of the theoretical" (ibid., 87). This becomes particularly clear in what he sees as the absurdly conducted traditional discussion of epistemological problems of the reality of the external world (see ibid., 77–84, 91–94). The only person who was, in his view, able thus far to outline positively the problem of the possibility and capacity for real contributions was Emil Lask, to whom he paid respect throughout his life (cf. *Zur Bestimmung der Philosophie*, GA 56/57, 88, 180; Heidegger, "Mein Weg in die Phänomenologie," in *Zur Sache des Denkens* [Tübingen: Niemeyer, 1976], 83). On Heidegger's relation to Lask and the latter's influence on his own intellectual approach, see Markus Joachim Brach, *Heidegger—Platon*, 115–146; Georg Imdahl, *Das Leben verstehen*, 69–90.

39. Heidegger, *Zur Bestimmung der Philosophie*, GA 56/57, 63

40. Ibid., 65.

41. Ibid., 68. According to Rolf Buchholz (*Was heißt Intentionalität?*, 54) the new understanding of intentionality shows itself here in writing for the first time, and understanding that Heidegger led "out of the shadows of Husserl."

42. Heidegger, *Zur Bestimmung der Philosophie*, GA 56/57, 115. "Whatever is experienceable in general is a possible something, regardless of its genuine world-character" (ibid., 115).

43. Ibid., 70. According to Heidegger, behind this conception stands a theoretical, reified statement of the environmental in its givenness as thingliness, wherein as a thing, i.e., an object, it is "simply there as such, which is to say it is real, it exists" (ibid., 89). In this sense, how-

torical I[44] toward the worldly [*das Welthafte*] in each case, which is to say that human experience—borrowing from Heidegger's formulation for basic modes of comportment as a priori–experiential—is first and foremost always already an environmental experience.[45] Accordingly, environmental experience signifies not that objects first confront me—objects that are grasped in a particular meaning—but rather that the environment is experienced in such a way that the meaningful [*das Bedeutsame*] is given to me immediately as what is primary "without a conceptual detour through a grasping of subject-matter."[46]

Heidegger clarifies this—in what Riedel fittingly characterizes as his "seasoned art of thinking out of closeness"[47]—by means of the example of glimpsing the lectern on entering a lecture hall. His initial question is "What do 'I' see?"[48] Heidegger rejects the notion of a fundamental connection, explicable in terms of traditional theories of perception, as an answer. It is not "as if I first see brown, intersecting surfaces that then present themselves to me as box, then as console, further as an academic lectern, so that I am lecternly, as it were, affixing to the box like a label."[49] For Heidegger, such a notion involves a misguided interpretation, that is, "turning from pure looking into the experience [which he now determines as] I see the lectern in a stroke, as it were; I see it as not only isolated, I see the console as placed too high for me . . . I see the lectern in an orientation, a certain lighting, a background."[50]

---

ever, reality is "not an environmental characterization, but something that lies in the essence of thingliness, something specifically theoretical" (ibid.). With the prefix 'ent-,' intended here as privative, Heidegger indicates the process structure constitutive of the theoretical attitude: "What bears meaning [*das Bedeutungshafte*] is de-signified [*ent-deutet*], except for this residue: being-real. Experiencing the environment [*Umwelt-erleben*] is de-lived [*ent-lebt*], except for the residue: knowing a 'real' as such. The historical I is de-historicized [*ent-geschichtlicht*], except for a residue of specific I-ness as the correlate of thing-ness" (ibid.). This means, in sum: "Experience of an object is indeed experience [*Erlebnis*], but from its origin out of the experience of the world it is already de-living [*Ent-lebnis*]" (ibid., 90). The fact that experiencing the environment is passed over in favor of the experience of things is for Heidegger the scandal to which his debate with transcendental phenomenology is repeatedly drawn back.

44. This self-distinction is here already determined in the full sense by that which is conceived more exactly in his letter to Löwith above as the facticity of being-thus.

45. Cf. Heidegger, *Zur Bestimmung der Philosophie*, GA 56/57, 74, 88.

46. Ibid., 73.

47. Riedel, *Hören auf die Sprache*, 83.

48. Heidegger, *Zur Bestimmung der Philosophie*, GA 56/57, 71.

49. Ibid.

50. Ibid.

We can easily see that this example clearly serves as a prelude, in structure and content, to the famous analysis of environmentality in *Sein und Zeit*. That is, it makes clear that the environmental is not presented to me for itself, but rather is presented solely in its meaningfulness for me. "Experience does not pass before me as if it were something that I arrange, like an object, but instead I en-own [*er-eigne*] it to myself, and it en-owns itself in accordance with its essence."[51] If experiences are in this sense events [*Ereignisse*], they are such according to Heidegger "insofar as they live thus only out of life and living that which is one's own [*dem Eigenen*]."[52] In seeing the lectern I am, as he emphasizes, "involved with my entire I."[53] With this event-character Heidegger underscores the idea that the environmental has its "genuine self-demonstration within itself"[54] in relation to its experience, wherein its meaningful character reveals itself to me immediately and 'as if in one stroke' in experience. "Living in an environment means to me everywhere and always, it is all worldly, '*it worlds*,'"[55] where the "'it worlds' [is] not established theoretically, but experienced 'as worlding.'"[56]

51. Ibid., 75.

52. Ibid., "En-owning also does not signify my ap-propriating [*an-eignen*] to myself the lived experience [*Er-lebnis*] from outside or from anywhere; 'outer' and 'inner' have as little sense as 'physical' and 'psychical'" (ibid.).

53. Ibid.

54. Ibid., 91.

55. Ibid., 73.

56. Ibid., 94. If one considers the example of seeing the lectern and thereupon calls to mind the analysis of environmentality in *Sein und Zeit* that we have further developed here, it thus appears problematic, indeed fallacious, when Gadamer speaks, in reference to the phrase "it worlds," of a "turn before the turn (*Kehre vor der Kehre*)" (Gadamer, *Der eine Weg Martin Heideggers*, 423). In the interim, a host of interpreters like Theodor Kisiel (*Being & Time*, 16, 457), Manfred Riedel (*Hören auf die Sprache*, 85), and John van Buren (*The Young Heidegger*, 289) have fallen in line with this catchy formulation, and occasionally also with the slightly modified form of a "return with a difference (*Rückkehr mit einer Differenz*)" (Rudolf Makkreel, "Heideggers ursprüngliche Auslegung der Faktizität des Lebens: Diahermeneutik als Aufbau und Abbau der geschichtlichen Welt," in *Zur philosophischen Aktualität Heideggers*, ed. Dietrich Papenfuss and Otto Pöggeler [Frankfurt: Klostermann, 1990], 187). For their purposes, such interpreters take this phrase, identical to the later Heidegger's famous usage, to be of one and the same meaning.

Closer inspection shows, however, that this identification quickly undermines itself. For what Heidegger has in mind is that in the impersonal aspect of the early expression 'it worlds,' neither an I nor a subject or consciousness is referred to, and it is motivated—like his use of the term 'event'—by the attempt to show that, in the context of the hermeneutic of historical-factical life, it emerges explicitly from the "new fundamental typology of experience" (*Zur Bestimmung der Philosophie*, GA 56/57, 46), in order thus to circumvent the traditional—yet phenomenologically inadequate—split into the spheres of subject and object.

In his lecture course of the following winter semester—in which he thematizes the factical context of experience in a related manner—Heidegger characterizes the 'as' appealed to in the example of seeing the lectern as "the 'as' of meaningfulness."[57] More precisely, it is determined by the fact that this wholly distinctive 'as' is "necessarily always growing out of a situation, is historical."[58] We must therefore take note—as will be demonstrated in the following paragraphs—of the fact that for Heidegger the factical "I" indeed experiences itself in the factical activities of life, yet it does so precisely not in the 'as' of itself.[59] In this light, much the way we find it in the glimpsing of the lectern, the 'as' already designates nothing other than that famous hermeneutical 'as,' which—in opposition to the apophantic 'as' in *Sein und Zeit*, which is a constituent of the fundamental pretheoretical mode of being of interpretation in which the human constantly moves—is here demonstrated.

It is decisive thereby that any pre-predicative simple seeing of ready-to-hand equipment is itself "always already understanding-interpreting. It conceals in itself the explicitness of referential relations (of the in-order-to), which belong to the totality of relevance [*Bewandtnisganzheit*], from which simple encountering is understood."[60] Interpretation, as already seen (§ 3), stands under the conditions of implementing the tripartite forestructure (forehaving, foresight, foregrasping), which together form the particular leading preunderstanding. Seen thus, every interpretation that articulates understanding has already understood that which is to be interpreted. That in which this intelligibility of something holds itself is what Heidegger calls *sense*. Sense is therefore for him nothing that could be determined as a property of entities. That means there is sense only in the understanding articulated through the forestructure. Accordingly sense

---

In this connection it should also not be overlooked that Heidegger had already engaged the question of impersonal judgments in his dissertation, in the debate with Theodor Lipps, precisely in the context of the problem of an 'undetermined subject' (see Heidegger, "Die Lehre vom Urteil im Psychologismus," in *GA* 1, 138, 186). One must therefore regard the purported structural similarity or proximity between the early use of this concept and the thinking of a return (as the latter is developed in the transition from the fundamental-ontological to the being-historical approach to the question of being) as an unsustainable construction that, further, stands in danger of minimizing that which is one's own [*das Eigene*] in the first phase to the level of a mere preliminary.

57. Heidegger, *Grundprobleme der Phänomenologie, GA* 58, 114.

58. Ibid.

59. "My self stands unnoticed in the ongoing character of the factically lived context of meaningfulness" (ibid.; see also ibid., 94).

60. Heidegger, *Sein und Zeit, GA* 2, 198.

is that which "is articulable in understanding disclosure."[61] Thus, "sense" refers to the mode of being of the human, and thus is itself an existential. "Only Dasein can therefore be full of sense or senseless. That means: its own being and the entity disclosed with this being can be appropriated in understanding or be denied in failing to understand."[62]

That which at this point proves to be, in the context of pretheoretical environmental experience in the sense of the approach outlined above (§ 29), possibly a direct reference to *Sein und Zeit* therein discloses at the same time options of understanding for further remarks that Heidegger makes in reference to the example of the lectern.[63] What is to be interpreted must be preunderstood in its referential relations by the interpreter, in order to disclose itself in its serviceability; Heidegger details this more precisely, manifesting the environmentally experiencing "I" now in its interpreting understanding first and foremost in its constitutive possibilities, by means of an artfully presented and strategically well-placed self-objection.

Having analyzed the experience of one's environment in the form of 'seeing the lectern' in such a way that this analysis rejects the foundational context of traditional perceptual theory, Heidegger poses the question whether this 'grasping of the lectern in a stroke' is not solely determined by the presupposition of being a participant in his own academic form of life, for which reason the choice of seeing a lectern as the example of experiencing the environment in general—and consequently the step from individual experience to universally applicable statements—must appear as precarious, at the very least.

Heidegger himself supports this objection by referring to a Black Forest farmer, who could enter the lecture hall without knowing that this is a lectern or rather is called a lectern. Heidegger sharpens this objection still further when he associates himself with a Senegalese person who, suddenly removed from his hut, faces a lectern in complete unfamiliarity with its utility.[64] With these examples, the point for Heidegger is that the

---

61. Ibid., 201.

62. Ibid. (emphasis deleted).

63. The function of the examples, which are numerous not only in the lectures of the early years, and which are drawn from the environment determined as the concrete lifeworld, have never had the task of merely illustrating, in a vivid manner, abstract or complex states of affairs. It is the outcome, already expressed, of pretheoretical experience as the actual basis of philosophy that makes this retreat back into environmental experience inescapable for Heidegger, both phenomenologically and hermeneutically.

64. Cf. Heidegger, *Zur Bestimmung der Philosophie*, GA 56/57, 71f.

unfamiliarity with the context of scientific and academic life does *not* lead to the notion that accordingly now in the sense-disclosive qua meaning-disclosive experiences of this environmental encountering, only unique complexes of colors and surfaces are seen in place of the lectern. For even the Black Forest farmer unfamiliar with the rules of science sees the thing found before him with a meaning determining it; that is, he sees "'the place for the teacher.'"[65] And Heidegger's still colonially impregnated speech, in the coloration typical of the time, uses the example of the exotic alien— cited here as the "unscientific (not: cultureless) Senegalese negro" to whom the referential connection in the use of the lectern is fundamentally excluded in the wherein of its intelligibility, and who sees the lectern corresponding to a priori existential interpretation not as a mere something, but rather in all probability "as a something 'with which he does not know how to begin.'"[66] But that means that however individual and possibly fundamentally distinct seeing a lectern (for example) can even turn out to be, a "significant moment"[67] is still proper to environmental experience per se—which, as structural, can be demonstrated in a universally valid way, insofar as it is not conceived as a supplementary meaning-character in addition to the initially given object.

From this point Heidegger formulates the fundamental insight according to which "what is significant [*Bedeutungshafte*] in 'equipmental foreignness' and the significance 'lectern' [are] at bottom absolutely identical."[68] This kind of identical significance has its essential core in the potential of its environmental-constituting meaningfulness, which, since it is always that of a significance for this or that, appears in relation to the one experiencing the environment as either accessible or inaccessible. This means, however, that something is first and foremost understood by me only when I prove to be guided in my seeing it as something by an antecedent understanding of the context of reference to which it belongs, a context which, as a totality of references, sets out that lifeworldly horizon in which I comport myself understandingly and interpretively to it.

This comportment to . . . refers to the antecedent sense-disclosing understanding of the lifeworldly situation, out of which I experience it as

---

65. Ibid.

66. Ibid., 72.

67. Ibid. At another point, it reads: "Characterization of experience as ap-propriative event [*Er-eignis*]—what is significant [*Bedeutungshaftes*], not thinglike [*sach-artig*]" (ibid., 69).

68. Ibid.

worlding. The worldliness of the environmental and accordingly the genuine self-identification [*Selbstausweisung*] spoken of are thereby constitutively bound in just this significance of the "I" experiencing it in the way that the possibility of sense-disclosure of the a-priori-significant something is disclosed as significant for me, if I can identify the something as belonging to my concrete lifeworldly situation, out of which my possibilities of understanding presignify themselves for me. It must be held in view in advance that the aforementioned life relations already must be conceived on the one side in Heidegger's approach as cultural historical phenomena; on the other side it must be noted that the "practical-historical I [is] necessarily *social* in nature,"[69] insofar as it is constitutively linked with others from out of its particular concrete life connection.

In a first pass, the phenomenal state of affairs will thereby be brought to indicate that Heidegger's concept of *lifeworld* as a '*context of interpenetrations,*' as it is later called, exhibits what he later differentiates more precisely and outlines as *environment, with-world,* and *self-world* [*Umwelt, Mitwelt, und Selbstwelt*]. Without jumping ahead of ourselves in our investigation, the tendency still to be detailed becomes observable already from the environmental experience of 'seeing the lectern,' which can let a constitutive intensification be known in this interpenetrating connection to his notion of self-world. Heidegger discussed it in the demonstration of the structural moments of the lifeworld in the winter semester 1919/20 lecture course as a fundamental problem of phenomenology, that is, the original science of 'life in and for itself.'

In the context of the lecture course of summer 1919, the turn toward the "I," as the starting-point that was yet to be clarified in his analysis, had become thematic in the investigation of the experience of the question, "Is there something at all?"[70] This question appears, however, in the theoretical attitude in which it is taken up, to have bracketed out from itself precisely the worldliness of its relatedness to an "I." And yet there remains a "relatedness to an I [*Ichbezogenheit*] reduced to a minimum of experience,"[71] insofar as in the possibility of being posed this question refers to a questioning, comporting subject who is always already involved at the same time in the situating, and thus in the hermeneutical situation.

69. Ibid., 210.
70. See ibid., 63–70.
71. Ibid., 74.

With regard to the clarification of the question concerning the questioner, it thus points from the outset to a hermeneutical analysis to the extent that it can demonstrate *lebensphenomenologically* the multiplicity of referential connections with the I-situation, which will be the theme of the next step of the investigation in what we have called the self-differentiation of the lifeworld.

§ 33. Remarks on the Problematic of the Alien

In laying out the moment of significance proper to all experience of the environment as the product of his analysis, Heidegger not only contradicts those foundational and universal claims of Husserl that we have looked at in detail above (in the latter's attempt to avoid the concretely experience-able plurality of the lifeworld by recourse to the conception of a "communalization of the simply perceptible [*schlicht Wahrnehmungsmäßigen*]"[72]); he also, in the analysis of environmental experience, punctuates the crucial emphasis in the context of this paragraph, on situational relatedness in hermeneutical experience, in such a way that it is suited to trace out subcutaneous lines of connection, as it were, beyond the context of the early Heideggerian hermeneutics of facticity with a contemporary phenomenological and hermeneutical discussion called up by such terms as "interculturality," "multiculturality," and "transculturality," "the alien," or even "normality and normalization"[73] However, we cannot hope to venture,within the scope of the present inquiry, any detailed—or even abbreviated—account of this widely ramified debate that has developed in the intervening years.[74]

---

72. Husserl, *Krisis*, 166. See above, § 23.

73. See Bernhard Waldenfels, *Der Stachel des Fremden* (Frankfurt: Suhrkamp, 1990); see also his four-volume *Studien zur Phänomenologie des Fremden* (*Topographie des Fremden*, [Frankfurt: Suhrkamp, 1997]; *Grenzen der Normalisierung*, [Frankfurt: Suhrkamp, 1998]; *Sinnesschwellen*, [Frankfurt: Suhrkamp, 1999]; and *Vielstimmigkeit der Rede*, [Frankfurt: Suhrkamp, 1999]). For more, see Hinrich Fink-Eitel, *Die Philosophie und die Wilden: Über die Bedeutung des Fremden für die europäische Geistesgeschichte* (Hamburg: Junius, 1994); Ram Adhar Mall, *Philosophie im Vergleich der Kulturen: Interkulturelle Philosophie—Eine neue Orientierung* (Darmstadt: Wissenschaftliche Buchgesellschaft, 1995); Mario Ruggenini, "Phänomenologie und Alterität," in *Phänomenologie in Italien*, ed. Renato Cristin (Würzburg: Königshausen & Neumann 1995), 137–168.

74. For such purposes it would be necessary to thematize the far-reaching debate issuing from Husserl's characterization of alterity as "accessibility to one's own inaccessibility, in

On the other hand, in the present connection a few references can be usefully ventured that might lead us, in the context of our reflections, to the point at which we can sketch out the possibility for integrating different factical-hermeneutical analyses. Moreover, these references may also assist, in connection with Derrida, in rebutting the widely held preconception that the hermeneutically central task of the clarification of self-understanding must necessarily result in the disappearance of the alien as alien. For the most part, in doing so one overlooks the fact that the space in which the alien is confronted, in becoming a phenomenon of the hermeneutical as-relation [*Als-Bezuges*], is itself precisely constituted relationally to me in a given case, yet the alien per se is not thereby appropriated in the sense of a disposing power.

The bearing of the problem is positively pregiven through the way that Heidegger outlines the situation of the observer with regard to the environmental experiencing act of seeing the lectern. It is, as we have noted, its constitutive inclusion in the lifeworldly situational referential connection in the sense of an experiential dispositive or historical a priori that enables the sense-disclosing understanding in environmental experience,

---

the mode of incomprehensibility" (Husserl, *Zur Phänomenologie der Intersubjektivität* vol. 3, 631; cf. *Cartesianische Meditationen*, 144) extensively, at the very least in its principal voices of Merleau-Ponty, Levinas, Derrida, and Waldenfels. In addition, such a debate would also require a view into the historical influences at work within it, where further figures such as Freud, Nietzsche, Husserl, or Dilthey are invoked, and these figures would require discussion in turn in the backlight, as it were, of a Foucauldian reading. Among the varying perspectives on the current state of the discussion are Iris Därmann, "Der Fremde zwischen den Fronten von Ethnologie und Philosophie," *Philosophische Rundschau* (1996), 43:46–63; *Philosophische Grundlagen der Interkulturalität*, ed. Ram Adhar Mall and Dieter Lohmar (Amsterdam: Rodopi, 1993). For emphasis on social-scientific questions, see *Furcht und Faszination: Facetten der Fremdheit*, ed. Herfried Münkler (Berlin: Akademie, 1997); Franz Wimmer, "Fremde," in *Vom Menschen: Handbuch Historische Anthropologie*, ed. Cristoph Wulff (Weinheim: Beltz 1997), 1066–1078. With direct reference to Heidegger (yet with his early work for the most part omitted), see *Europa und die Philosophie*, ed. Hans-Helmuth Gander (Frankfurt: Klostermann, 1993), containing Gadamer's "Europa und die Oikoumene" (67–86), Klaus Held's "Europa und die interkulturelle Verständigung" (87–103), and Ka Kyung Cho's "Der Abstieg über den Humanismus: West-Östliche Wege im Denken Heideggers," 143–174); On those taking steps along the path of an intercultural dialogue to be led with Heidegger, see Elmar Weinmayr, *Entstellung: Die Metaphysik im Denken Martin Heideggers; Mit einem Blick nach Japan* (Munich: Fink, 1991); Okonda Okolo, "Afrikanische Heidegger-Rezeption und -Kritik," *Im Spiegel der Welt: Sprache, Übersetzung, Auseinandersetzung*, vol. 3 of *Zur philosophischen Aktualität Heideggers*, ed. Dietrich Papenfuss and Otto Pöggeler (Frankfurt: Klostermann, 1992), 264–272; Reena Sen, "Heidegger und die indische Perspektive: Heidegger und Sri Aurobindo," *Im Spiegel der Welt*, 273–291).

so that it can be said that the self- and world relation are interlocked in a self-alternating, founding texture of conditions.

It is decisive for our reference to the debate regarding the alien that, by means of the Black Forest farmer—and still more clearly in the figure of the African—in this chosen example, in reference to the moment of significance as the formal structure of all environmental experience the *difference of significance as a difference of worlds* comes into effect in a cognitively foundational manner. As previously discussed, the lifeworld (and life reality) is in itself always already grasped as both plural and contingent at one and the same time, and is historically determined at its core as this cultural multiplicity of relations of significance. As such, then, it is a respective concrete lifeworld that constitutes, in its significance, the disclosiveness of meaning in a respective experience of one's environment. This is clear with reference to the example that Heidegger employs. The Senegalese, characterized in terms of his concrete lifeworldly situatedness—and only in this specific respect is he thematic in the sense of this example—makes possible, from out of his own nonscientifically-shaped historical horizon of experience that for its own part forms his own categories of interpretation, a grasping of the lectern otherwise than as a lectern. At the level of the current example, in its contexts of meaningfulness the scientific lifeworld remains for him undiscovered, and in this sense—in its inaccessibility—foreign.[75]

75. The *discoverability* to which we refer in this example characterizes the qualitative difference in the condition of the Senegalese and the farmer from the Black Forest at the same time. The latter's individual lifewordly relation of experience is also unscientific, yet he nonetheless remains enlisted, as it were, in the cultural-historical horizon that exceeds him as an individual, a horizon that opens to him the possibility of unveiling, in glimpsing the lectern and grasping it as the 'place for the teacher,' this moment of significance as a relation of meaning. Thus, the relation of arrangement between the stand and benches could remind him of the classroom from his own time in school, or even perhaps the same could be said of visits to Sunday service, where that which is taught comes to the listeners from the pulpit, et cetera.

In the sense of the spectrum of differences in the experience of alterity as put forward by Waldenfels (see *Topographie des Fremden*, 16), one can speak here accordingly of a 'relative other.' To this extent it is necessary, in order to see the point of Heidegger's example here, to conceive the Senegalese only in the situative context sketched out by Heidegger and accordingly not to burden the example with additional aspects. For naturally this example would be skewed this way or that if one were to insert added associations like that of a Senegalese who belongs to a missionary school, for example, that might for its part integrate a 'place for the teacher' into its own horizon of experience. And of course there would obviously be no further difficulties in seeing the lectern once the meaning of 'lectern' has been explained to him.

The experience of alterity in Heidegger's example is bound, in an emphatic sense, to displacement.[76] It retains its *lebensphenomenological* weight through the notion that displacement must be interpreted *as an experience of limits*. In so doing, the concept of experience brought into play, which is no longer restricted to the givenness of empirically gathered data, allows us to conceive, as Dilthey puts it, that process "through which something real rises to consciousness."[77] In accordance with its structure, it is an *open occurrence*. And one certainly speaks of the fact that 'having experience' presupposes that one makes or, put more precisely, gathers experience. Only in this way can experience teach us something, and what it teaches is the recognition of the real in the factical 'that' [*Daß*] of its 'how' [*Wie*]. Taken hermeneutically, it is a matter of the recognition of the manifest plurality appropriating itself within interpretively and understandingly experienced differences of significance, a plurality of fundamentally varied lifeworldly contexts as interpenetrating in what Heidegger has called worlds of care,[78] whereby experience refers to the openness within the always already differential being of life and world in itself.[79]

Against the background of this complex ontological structural relation, the hermeneutical basic insight emerges that the "knowledge, which is . . . the actual result of all experience, [is] as that of all desiring to know in

76. Within the scope of reflections on the linguistic difference between the words 'alien' and 'alterity' and taking into account varying languages, Waldenfels establishes (*Topographie des Fremden*, 20–23) three respects in which this distinction is tied to the difference from what is one's own: 1. in relation to place, what is alien is "what occurs outside of one's own region" (ibid., 20); 2. with regard to ownership, what is alien is "what belongs to another" (ibid.); 3. in relation to a type [*Art*], what is alien is "what is of a foreign kind and what counts as alien" (ibid.). Most remarkably, the aspect of place is consistently predominant in the lifewordly connotation of the use of this concept (ibid.).

77. Wilhelm Dilthey, *Philosophie der Erfahrung: Empirie, nicht Empirismus*, in *GS*, 19:23. "This real thing can be an external thing, an external process, or a fact of physical life."

78. See Heidegger, *Phänomenologische Interpretationen zu Aristoteles*, GA 61, 94.

79. That the differential of the world is not merely a phenomenon of ontic diversity, but instead signals its ontological structure and thereby overturns the traditional concept of world as the totality of beings, is to be attributed to the decisive insights of Heideggerian analyses of the experience of the environment. Indeed, Heidegger himself had emphasized its applicability for the analyses of worldliness of *Sein und Zeit* at the end of its fifteenth section. This is also confirmed by the investigations of Mario Ruggenini ("Phänomenologie und Alterität," 160–164), which take up the "experience of the difference of the world" (ibid., 163)—with an eye to Heidegger's famous analysis of angst—wherein "the world reveals itself as nothing, as difference over and against every being, yet therefore as the enabling of the manifold, innerworldly determinacies that occur on the basis and for human existence" (ibid., emphasis deleted).

general."[80] However, the universal of experience, so to speak, thus gained is not, as Aristotle teaches, synonymous with the universal validity of the concept.[81] And insofar as experience always occurs only actually in the active carrying out of experience, it is therefore also not derivable in general in whatever way from a presently known or knowable universality. Bound positively to the structural actuality, as Gadamer shows, is "the fundamental openness of experience for new experience—not only in the general sense that errors can be rectified,"[82] errors which certainly—and as the fundamental nature of things also emphasizes—nothing can undo. What is more, experience in its openness for new experience "depends, in accordance with its essence, on perpetual acknowledgment and is thus necessarily itself an other when such acknowledgment is absent."[83]

With the moment of 'acknowledgment/disappointment' qualitatively fulfilling the intentional relation of experience, experience proves itself antecedently structured in its ontological openness by a guiding preunderstanding grounded in facticity and constitutive therein, which was demonstrated by Heidegger in the analysis of environmental experience as always living-toward in the significant moment of perception. At the level of the significant, therefore, experience lacking confirmation through the fact that sense disclosure of the significant does not succeed for me becomes in no way nothing or meaningless. For when the experienced *possibility of the refusal of sense* is actually carried out, the refusal is experienced as in and for itself from out of the openness of the world relation; the withdrawal thereby positively inscribes itself in the contextual relation of experience and therein also modifies the self-relation with the environmental experience at the same time, without which the foreign would itself lose the manifest foreignness from itself in its sense closure.

In this regard, the Heideggerian example clarifies the fact that the shift in place is completely necessary but by itself not yet sufficient for opening the lifewordly horizon—in and out of which the interpretive categories are prestructured—to the meaningfulness arising out of another lifeworldly context. In order to avoid any misunderstanding, the horizon referred to here is in no way thought as something in itself inflexible or closed, win-

---

80. Gadamer, *Wahrheit und Methode*, 363.

81. See Aristotle, *Zweite Analytiken*, ed. Horst Seidl (Würzburg: Rodopi, 1984), book 2, ch. 19; see also Hans-Georg Gadamer, "Wie weit schreibt Sprache das Denken vor?" in *GW*, 2:200.

82. Gadamer, *Wahrheit und Methode*, 357.

83. Ibid.

dowless, as it were, like a monad. Rather, the lifeworldly horizon, as it is conceived here hermeneutically, is to be thought as always already dynamic and as historicized in its situationality. This means, in the example before us, that the hermeneutical interpretation of the experience of alterity for the Senegalese must be revised in the clarification of the horizon as the conditions of (put in a Husserlian way) 'inaccessability in the mode of incomprehensibility,' as much in its historical aspects as in the present alterity of the immediate encounter, now in the sense of gradual differences.

Given that each person carries their lifeworldly horizon with them a priori and for the most part preconsciously, it is the encounter with a different culture that makes the limits of their categories visible to them in a distinctive way, precisely in the break and fragility of hitherto sovereign understanding. This break, however, does not highlight a lack, but rather outlines the finitude of human capacities for understanding and at the same time promotes (along with the fragility of what is considered self-evident) one's consciousness of *contingency*. According to Blumenberg, the phenomenological method provides a paradigmatic disclosure of contingency, insofar as the "last and most concealed modes of self-understanding are still to be put in question [which is] precisely what phenomenology claims as its program."[84] The capacity-to-also-be-otherwise appealed to therein, the evaluation of the real on the basis of the possible, allows contingency in this sense to be conceived at the same time as "the stimulant to becoming conscious of the demiurgic power of humanity."[85] That is, insofar as "the sphere of natural facts no longer transmits a higher justification

84. Blumenberg, "Lebenswelt und Technisierung unter Aspekten der Phänomenologie," in *Wirklichkeiten in denen wir leben*, 48. What becomes clearer, however, in the sense of our present considerations of the pluralization of the lifeworld with structural emphasis on its character of contingency, is developed by Blumenberg himself, in the scope of his reflections, precisely in opposition to a phenomenology of the lifeworld. Yet these reflections reveal, in their unfolding, only an apparent conflict. For according to Blumenberg, it has to do with a contestation of the Husserlian conception, in which he charges Husserl with making the lifeworld the object of a theoretical description, which would mean "not a preservation of this sphere, but rather in disclosing it thus, bringing with it the inevitable destruction of its essential attributes of self-comprehensibility" (ibid., 48), insofar as—as we have seen above—Husserl's conception depends in principle on an 'ahistorical world-nucleus that must be extracted abstractively' as the idea of the originary lifeworld. Thereby, however, the plurality, contingency, and historicity of the phenomenal (and not abstractively abbreviated) concrete reality of experience are overlooked, a reality whose determination, on the other hand, in fact draws upon the Blumenbergian remarks on contingency.

85. Ibid., 47.

and sanction"[86]—and that means one's own respective lifeworld happens to appear only as a segment in the plurality of possible worlds and in accordance with its status—"does the facticity of the world become a gnawing impetus, . . . to fill the merely factical through the realization of the possible, through the exhaustion of the scope of invention and construction with an eye to a cultural world that is consistent in itself and which is of necessity self-justifying."[87] Its consistency and necessity are made possible in and through contingency, that is, borne by a fortuitousness that experiences that which could also be otherwise, as changeable in and through human designs.

Indeed, this 'demiurgic power' in the sense of the *condition humaine* remains determined in itself (as Odo Marquard can say, borrowing from Kierkegaard) through a chance resistant to negation, yet through "'that which could also be otherwise' and is simply not—or only a little—changeable by us,"[88] such as birth, gender, family, historical age, geographical region, culture—in short that which Marquard calls *"chance-fate."*[89] Both these types of contingency are grasped as existential a priori structures of experience, which can describe the *ontological place of the human in the world* as that of a *between*.

More approximately, what is meant thereby becomes clearer once one takes note of the fact that it belongs to the positivity of the experience of limits that the encounter with the alien, as what is incomprehensible, opens up a *distance to oneself*. For in the backlight of the alien, which proves itself to be one's own capacity for understanding precisely as its withdrawal, what is one's own [*das Eigene*] is referred to itself through a difference, never fully recovered, and first appears to its own understanding from outside, as it were.[90] What is thereby opened up is precisely this

<hr>

86. Ibid.

87. Ibid. Blumenberg's study, *Schiffbruch mit Zuschauer: Paradigma einer Daseinsmetapher* (Frankfurt: Suhrkamp, 1979)—which investigates nautical metaphors of existence that have become increasingly significant in the history of descriptions of human placement in the world—provides a constructively expanded view of innovation as the setting and marking of limits of human habitation.

88. Odo Marquard, "Apologie des Zufälligen: Philosophische Überlegungen zum Menschen," In *Apologie des Züfalligen: Philosophische Studien* (Stuttgart: Reclam, 1986), 128.

89. Ibid.

90. Heidegger also emphasizes that "precisely in experiential encounters that appear strange and unprecedented, [I] experience . . . how I always in fact am. In the sense of the alien lies precisely that self-conscious, immediately reflected familiarity" (*Grundprobleme der Phänomenologie GA* 58, 157f.). That the alien is thus always understood and appealed to in one's

'between strangeness and familiarity' that Gadamer finds to be *"the true site of hermeneutics."*[91] At the same time, this is a reference to the fact that the experience of limits in the larger course of experience as such already constitutes a transgression in which I see myself, as if mirrored from a certain focal point, referred back to my own place—the focal point of a site from which I am absent, directed towards me and thereby catching sight of me myself as I could otherwise never do.[92] Thus is Gadamer moved to suppose that we perhaps "never know so much about our own historical being as when the breeze of wholly other historical worlds blows by us."[93]

own language further makes the problem of translation into a distinctive phenomenon for a thematization of the limit behavior between other and oneself. See Figal, *Der Sinn des Verstehens,* 101–111.

91. Gadamer, *Wahrheit und Methode,* 300.

92. Taken in a Foucauldian sense, this mirror would not only be a 'space of the external,' a 'heterotopia,' but one could say, rather, that the plurally experienced lifeworld is in itself heterotopically structured. On the problematic of the heterotopic, see Foucault, "Andere Räume," *Zeitmitschrift: Journal für Ästhetik und Politik* (1990), 1:4–15.

93. Gadamer, *Das Problem der Geschichte in der neueren deutschen Philosophie,* in *GW* 2:35. For the phenomenally adequate hermeneutical thematization of the *culturally foreign,* it is thereby inadmissible, in particular, to consider the leading differences developed in the newer ethnology. They have developed themselves as a consequence of a *paradigm change* carried out above all in North American ethnology, which has departed from the prevailing direction of Lévi-Strauss and the structuralist conceptions developed in his followers, on the one hand, and the methodology of the natural sciences determined scientifically by neo-evolutionary and functionalistic models on the other.

The new paradigm, initiated essentially also through impulses external to the field, particularly philosophical impulses, developed itself on the side of cultural anthropology in the project of an interpretative anthropology, which possesses its programmatic text in Clifford Geertz, "Thick Description: Toward an Interpretative Theory of Culture" (orig. 1973), dt. 1983, now in: *Dichte Beschreibung: Beiträge zum Verstehen kultureller Systeme.* (Frankfurt/M.: Suhrkamp, 1995), 7–43. It therefore brought explicitly into play what today is referred to as the *hermeneutical turn* [*Wende*] of ethnology, which indeed itself has already run through at least two stages (Irmtraud Stellrecht, "Interpretative Ethnologie: eine Orientierung," in *Handbuch der Ethnologie,* ed. Thomas Schweizer and Ulla Johansen (Berlin: Reimer, 1993), 29–78; Karl-Heinz Kohl: *Ethnologie: die Wissenschaft vom kulturell Fremden: Eine Einführung* (München: Beck, 1993), 165).

It was decisive that this turn saw through the status of ethnographically elevated data as facts in their positivistic character in a self-reflexive revision of its approach and worked out its interpretative structure over against it. In the accentuation of this approach it is a positive inclusion in the 1970s to register indeed in parts a clear borrowing (for example Geertz, "Thick Description," 28) of Ricoeur's influential model of textual interpretation, particularly as developed in his fecund essay *"Der Text als Modell: Hermeneutisches Verstehen"* (in *Die Hermeneutik und die Wissenschaften,* ed. Hans-Georg Gadamer and Gottfried Boehm [Frankfurt: Suhrkamp, 1978], 83–117) with regard to the two main questions: "1. How far can we regard the concept of the text as a good paradigm for the so-called object of the social sciences? 2. How far can we use

In this sense, "the experience of the alien [brings] the limits between one's own and other into movement,"[94] and for this reason—following a famous phrase from Hölderlin—"one must learn oneself as well as the other."[95] At the same time self and other refer in their tension to a further phenomenon, namely the alterity within oneself. Even the question of the

---

the methodology of the interpretation of texts as a paradigm of the interpretation of the region of the human sciences in general?" (ibid., 83).

In opposition to the approaches imprinted hermeneutically or holistically for the most part in the first phase, in the postmodern-colored 1980s with the question of the interpretative, the *perspectivism* problematized by Nietzsche rose ever more strongly to the moment. Thereby the *aspect of power*—eminently significant for ethnology—moves into view as relevant to discourse, indeed as the determining element of the problematization of ethnographical observation and description. Beyond the reception above all of Foucault, the question of power finds its sudden and sustained entry into the discussion. Bound up with that, therefore, is at the same time a newly strengthened critique of all the structuralist tendencies stemming from the 1950s and 1960s, which aim at the development of culturally determined universals, roughly as intended in Lévi-Strauss's structural anthropology. And decisively co-conceived in this critique is also the contrasting relational determination of the foreign from the proper or what is one's own, as is proposed by Lévi-Strauss, among others, in the framework of his 'theory of wild [or savage] thinking' (*Das wilde Denken* [Frankfurt: Suhrkamp, 1994]), whereby this early critique may be inspired by phenomenological positions and approaches, in particular on the part of Merleau-Ponty (see "Von Mauss zu Claude Lévi-Strauss," 13–28; see also Lévi-Strauss's remarks in "Begegnungen mit Merleau-Ponty," *Leibhaftige Vernunft*, 29–36).

The philosophical impulse, which presently gains an increasingly stronger influence from the phenomenological view for the discussion concerning the foreign or the foreigners, emerges indeed from the thinking of Emmanuel Levinas. His thinking of the other opens the possibility of bursting the order of the same, i.e., of grasping the relation of the proper and the foreign from irreducible otherness (see Derrida, "Gewalt und Metaphysik. Essay über das Denken Emmanuel Levinas," in *Die Schrift und die Differenz*, 121–235 on the question of otherness). In the point of departure of an irreducible otherness, the demand is raised as a claim in the encounter with the foreign, thus to emerge at the foreign, that it disappears therein, not in and through appropriation. This intention connects itself to the phenomenological side in particular also in Waldenfels's concept of a 'responsive rationality' (see Waldenfels, *Antwortregister*, particularly part 3), which at the same time conceals the theoretical frame of reference of the studies on the phenomenology of the foreign that he first conducted. It would be a thoroughly praiseworthy attempt to bring his theory of responsive rationality into conversation—in consideration of the conceptions of foreignness of the indicated interpretative ethnology inspired above all in the exchanges with Husserl, Merleau-Ponty, and Levinas—with that hermeneutical approach that no longer emerges in terms of a hermeneutics of facticity from the possibility of an originary instance of sense, but rather pluralizes, historicizes, and discontinuously experiences occurrences of sense on the ground of a contingently grasped reason as from out of itself.

94. Waldenfels, *Topographie des Fremden*, 44; see "Heimat in der Fremde" in *In den Netzen der Lebenswelt*, 194–211. See also Michael Makropoulos, *Modernität und Kontingenz* (Munich: Fink, 1997), 136–145.

95. Hölderlin to Casimir Ulrich Böhlendorff, December 4, 1801, in *Briefe*, ed. Adolf Beck in *Sämtliche Werke*, vol. 6/1 (Stuttgart: Kohlhammer, 1954), 426. The relation between self and other is not only a leitmotif of Hölderlin's poetry, but also belongs to the most important aspects of Heidegger's exchange with the poet, in which it is always a matter, in different ways, of

existence of the alien in oneself is itself initiated to a certain degree by the existential experience of the suspension of limits between other and oneself, insofar as out of the increased attention to and preparedness for self-distanciation in the sense of the external perspective named above, the distance (difference) that alterity is, is also in itself obscured, and thereby refers to the existential plurality in the identity of the self.[96] In a later context, this phenomenal region, which can truly be called a 'broad field,' recurs anew, when it thus has to do with returning to question the plurality of lifeworlds in the constitution of the inherently pluralized human experience of self. In the given context it is to be noted that the encounter with the other, in the example of the experience of the environment, brings to light hermeneutically, in the experience of contingency, the historicity of one's own lifeworld.

The *leap into the world* of which Heidegger speaks, as we can now easily see, does not essentially disclose the world taken as a totality. Rather, this leap carries out the insertion into the inherently plural happening of different levels of reality and strands of tradition, a happening that in the manifoldness of cultural effective histories ties together the network of inherently diverse lifeworlds, or rather life realities [*Lebenswirklichkeiten*]. It is these lifeworlds in which humans find themselves without ever being able, in factical life—oscillating as it does between opacity and transparency and compelled of itself toward self-interpretation—to achieve full self-possession.

In other words, there is a lifeworld only in the form of mutually displacing lifeworlds, out of whose respectively individuated order the environmental, in the immediate concretion of lifeworldly understanding and interpreting experience, discloses itself to me in its situational significance. The lifeworld, as this context of orientation in self-relation—manifoldly differentiated through varied situative constellations (family, vocation, asylum, exile, and so on)—antecedently structures, for the most part implicitly, the manner of one's capacities of perception. We see what in this sense our individual historicocultural horizon makes it possible for us to know; that is, we never entirely see, but rather do so only

---

the self-instruction of thought. See among others Heidegger, "Hölderlins Hymne 'Andenken,'" in *GA* 52, ed. Curd Ochwadt (Frankfurt: Klostermann, 1982), esp. 123–155.

96. See Julia Kristeva's rich historical study—inspired by Freud, and taken up as the 'phenomenology of lifewordly experience of otherness'—*Fremde sind wir uns selbst* (Frankfurt: Suhrkamp, 1990).

ever in perspectival shadings. Behind this thesis stands the hermeneutical insight—transmitted from Schleiermacher by way of Dilthey, Nietzsche, and Heidegger, up through Ricoeur, Gadamer, and even Foucault—into the preunderstanding. Tied to this, to emphasize once more, is not only the decisive renunciation of the theoretical assumption of a bare seeing, but along with it the intentional approach of seeing-something in accordance with its full determinacy; this proves to be sufficiently grasped only when this seeing, like all understandingly interpretive comportments, is understood in its pretheoretical, hermeneutical 'as-relation' [*Als-Bezug*].[97]

To sum up, in a concrete hermeneutical situation like seeing the lectern, the 'as-relation' proves to be beyond an immediate objective context in its lifeworldly relation, predetermined through a historicocultural constellation, which in itself includes the conditions that form it. In other words, the environmental in environmental experience appears meaningfully accessible to me only out of a respective lifeworld-horizon that I have discovered (or that is discoverable by me), a horizon that in its synchronic and diachronic orders holds me open myself in my possibilities for understanding the world. We are, as we have established earlier, hermeneutic as ourselves; always already antecedently interpreted, precisely through our cultural, historical belongingness to a constellative context of effects, which (pre)structures interpretation understandingly, as it were.

Self-relation implies understanding the world, and accessibility to the world takes place only as accessibility to oneself—realized and realizable within the heterogeneous spaces of possibility in the ordering of facticity opened up in comprehending, interpretive comportment. This a priori, situationally constituted source of the self[98] is, as can now be easily seen, not synonymous with a centering upon the traditionally defined "I" qua self-consciousness, which functions as the founding subject of an ordering of the

---

97. In the wake of Wittgenstein's famous example in the *Philosophische Untersuchungen* of seeing a duck/rabbit, Hans Lenk (*Interpretation und Realität: Vorlesung über Realismus in der Philosophie der Interpretationskonstrukte* [Frankfurt: Suhrkamp 1995], 109–119) criticizes the notion of a 'pure, bare seeing' as an 'empty analytical abstraction.' In conversation with positions in gestalt psychology, he comes to the comparable result of a situationally related 'seeing as something,' which he grasps as 'interpretively impregnated seeing'; see Lenk's clarifying discussions of 'interpretation' and 'impregnation' in *Schemaspiele: Über Schemainterpretationen und Interpretationskonstrukte* (Frankfurt: Suhrkamp 1995), 43–46.

98. "Only in the sounding-with of one's own respective I does it experience something environmental, does it world, and wherever and whenever it worlds for me, precisely there *I* somehow am" (Heidegger, *Die Idee der Philosophie*, GA 56/57, 73).

universal—an ordering that a priori guarantees, through the universality of the language of reason, my participation and that of an 'alter ego' in humanity as transcendentally purified subjectivity, whereby real differences are taken only as empirically given, graduated nuances that the principle of generality cannot circumvent.[99] Against this, the phenomenological-hermeneutic insistence on the plurality of lifeworlds promotes—over and above the demonstration (which is not to be neglected) of the variety of its orders and the experiences of limits belonging to it as the experience of limits—the dissolution of the standard idea of a wholly active ahistorical subject. And with this hermeneutically driven decentralization, the concept of the self is ontically established in that phenomenally demonstrable experience that there is not just one (life)world in which the individual can, in carrying out its enownment, make itself at home.

We live, reads Foucault's diagnosis, "within a mélange of relations that define positions which cannot be referred to each other and which are not to be united with each other."[100] The thread of unity is severed, the thread which in the end promised to lead harmlessly from out of the labyrinth of concrete life threatened by irrationality and unreason—as it flares up in childhood, madness, dream, passions as experiences of foreignness—and into the freedom of the self-possession of a sovereign reason that erects its mastery on the ground of an originary world constituted through transcendental subjectivity. The experience of not being master in one's own house, the unity of consciousness having been demolished with Freud,[101] has exposed the fragility of the ground of self-certainty and thereby made visible the outward rift in the façade of the sovereign "I."

Yet this insight is no longer new enough to still be able to subvert or ward off, like a seismic shock under the pillars of the tradition, attention to the dominant idea of the human qua subject. As with every tectonic fault, new spaces in the landscape open themselves over the old. In the wakefulness of the self, they create and created for themselves new relative or relational stabilities from out of the experience of the differentiation of living realities, in accordance with their validity claims, upon the 'there is' ['*es gibt*'] of new orders of facticity. In this sense, a philosophical observation

---

99. This is not least a reason for the fact that, as Waldenfels states, the "alien (ξένον) [does not constitute] a basic concept of classical philosophy" (*Topographie des Fremden*, 16).

100. Foucault, "Andere Räume," 8.

101. Sigmund Freud, "Vorlesung zur Einführung in die Psychoanalyse," in *Studienausgabe* (Frankfurt: Fischer, 1989), 1:284.

of the question of self-relation—which as hermeneutical seeks and must seek its self-understanding as a situating in the present in the exchange with the meshwork and maze of the tradition—is obliged to carry out the discursive view back from out of the present with its impulses to a survey and projection into the future.

As a hermeneutical demonstration in this sense, proceeding *retroperspectively* means not simply setting aside the severed threads of the unity of reason, but rather taking up again these many ends in their scattered states. And that means tying these to each other as varieties of reason in everyday life—reason here conceived as wisdom, in which, on the basis of a pluralized experience, can be heard the voice of Aristotelian φρόνησις. Yet this tying together should be undertaken in such a way that these knots form a weave, a latticework of plural possibilities for relations of meaning, in which—to transmute a phrase from Maurice Blanchot—difference is always setting itself into work. As a result, not only is the self illuminated from out of being-other, but in one's very self that synchronically and diachronically prevalent unavailability becomes discernible, which refers for its structural analysis to the Heideggerian context of the interpenetration of worlds of care [*Sorgenswelten*].

§ 34. *The Self-World as the Center of Life-Relations*

It has come to light that with the analysis of the experience of the environment, whose task proceeds on the basis of the pretheoretical situational experience of life, the hermeneutics of facticity that Heidegger brings into play in his initial creative phase takes the form of a *phenomenology of the lifeworld*. At a point in his Winter 1921/22 lecture course,[102] the world is defined, in formal indication from out of the relation to life, in such a way that the concept of 'world' fixes that 'something' which, in the concrete realization of the decisive (for Heidegger) intransitive verbal meaning of 'life,' indicates the "manifold relatedness to 'life,'"[103] insofar as 'life' as such is always already a 'living in (out, for, with, against, from out of) something,' or rather, 'living toward something.' Seen thus, factical life is not a process for itself in opposition to the world, but rather the world is in life, that is,

---

102. See Heidegger, *Phänomenologische Interpretationen zu Aristoteles, GA* 61, 85–89.
103. Ibid., 85.

at the same time always there for it.[104] Accordingly, it remains decisive for Heidegger's hermeneutical thematization as a basic experience that "life [is] *not* an object."[105] This in no way means, however, that his philosophical ascertainment can simply be determined in the subject "through egoic modes of reflection."[106] For Heidegger, subjectivation and objectivation alike are forms of a theorizing, that is, conceptually hypostatized modes of knowing, that, over and against factical life, have "severed, through their immanent tendency, all bridges to it."[107]

Thereby a problem is raised anew, a problem that has already become a theme for us at the end of § 28, when the *basic phenomenological hermeneutic attitude* of a "living going-along-with [was exposed] with the genuine sense of life,"[108] which as such implicitly guides the further investigative view in the steps of analysis to follow, as a historical enactment.[109] If this

104. Cf. § 28 on this point.

105. Heidegger, *Grundprobleme der Phänomenologie*, GA 58, 145; see also ibid, 236. If this is referred to the positions of the text in *GA* 58 with clearly higher page numbers next to those first-cited, in addition, as in the further course of the interpretation of this lecture in comparable cases, this signifies as a rule no further "genuine" parallel positions. Rather it concerns cross-references to such passages in the text that correspond to the transcript of Oskar Becker shown in print in the attached appendix and with the corresponding high page numbers (223–263), to which we will always return on grounds of the fragmentary character of the Heideggerian manuscript, which offers the thematically significant concluding part of the lecture in the given connection only in a convoluted set of notes.

The decisive degree of authenticity, which this transcript possesses and by which it qualifies unproblematically as a textual foundation of an interpretation, shows itself easily through the comparison with the Heideggerian notes and is consequently therefore also not bound up in my or the editor's assurance of its worth. The admonitory evidence given above (§ 28, n. 168) as a caution about dealing with transcripts not editorially authorized certainly remains unaffected. It finds confirmation in the context of the following discussion of Heidegger's thought of the diahermeneutic, insofar as already in 1989, and thus before the publication of *GA* 58, a first interpretation was proposed by Rudolf A. Makkreel ("Heideggers ursprüngliche Auslegung der Faktizität des Lebens: Diahermeneutik als Aufbau und Abbau der geschichtlichen Welt," in *Zur philosophischen Aktualität Heideggers*, vol. 2, ed. Dietrich Papenfuss and Otto Pöggeler [Frankfurt: Klostermann, 1990], 179–188), which is based on one of the lecture manuscripts [*Vorlesungsmitschrift*] also available for my edition, whose formulation of this problem is not as a whole false, but in the degree of its deviation does not offer the precision requisite for a precisely accurate interpretation.

106. Heidegger, *Grundprobleme der Phänomenologie*, GA 58, 145.

107. Ibid., 144; see also ibid., 236: "life [always determined in relations of meaning as my own] is no object and never becomes an object; it is not object-like at all. Our primary aim is to understand that.—But as well, a return to life premised upon a *subject* (in an epistemological or a psychological sense) is impossible."

108. Ibid., 23.

109. In the coming discussions, a series of thoughts, themes, and analyses that were objects of inquiry in §§ 28, 31, and 32 must be taken up again. It is certainly not a matter of simple

basic attitude recurs as a problem at a given point in time, this is so because only with the explicit demonstration of its structure—and with regard to the tendency toward a *hermeneutic of the self* inscribed within it—can the position of a hermeneutical phenomenology of the lifeworld be fully clarified. For this reason it is necessary to realize that Heidegger sets down a clear distinction between the existential everyday process of factical life (which he appeals to in the Winter 1919/20 lecture course as 'life in itself'), and his philosophical thematization, which, as we have already seen, is to mobilize as hermeneutical phenomenology an 'originary science of life in itself.'[110] Heidegger appeals to its sphere of objects, the ur- or originary sphere accessible above all in the phenomenological-hermeneutic method, also as 'life in and for itself.'[111]

The 'for itself' Heidegger here sets into play in his investigation can be understood in such a way that factical life becomes, out of the continuum of its immediate performative 'in itself,'[112] a phenomenologically reflected

repetitions, but rather of a nuancing, a shading-in, or a resetting. That is to say, an individual case might find an echo hermeneutically that shows itself to be a *pervasive formative principle* of a Heideggerian hermeneutics of facticity. For Heidegger, as is well known, argumentation construed for striking probative force does not guarantee the requisite phenomenological material insight into the human self- and world relation. Rather, this is achieved only in the interpretively indispensable 'going-along-with in factical life' as the intuitively inductive phenomenological habitus, as it were, which as such necessarily mirrors the animatedness of life in interpretive contexts of exhibiting what is experienced, insofar "*as* [it] is determined by particular courses of motivation of living oneself [*Selbstlebens*]" (*Grundprobleme der Phänomenologie*, GA 58, 68) and is thus structured as "a tangle of strivings and retrievals of tendencies" (ibid., 69).

Heidegger clarifies the developing textile character, in harmony with the context of life experience, within the connecting themes of his strands of thought in an aside wherein he makes use of Stefan George's image of a "'tapestry' of life" (ibid.). See also Jean Greisch, who makes reference to the programmatically accentuated position of value of this Georgian employment for Heidegger, and thus entitles his own discussion with this poetic term ("La 'Tapesserie' de la vie," 146). As well, Pöggeler (*Schritte zu einer hermeneutischen Philosophie*, 15, 146) has pointed out that Heidegger's occasional use of the term 'vital impetus' [*Lebensschwungkraft*] can be traced back to George's translation of Bergson's '*élan vital*,' which in distinction from Heidegger is, however, grasped as a characteristic metaphysical intuition.

110. Cf. Heidegger, *Grundprobleme der Phänomenologie*, GA 58, 55, and further, ibid., 78. On the idea of an ur-science: "'originary-science' [*Ursprungs-Wissenschaft*] is not at all a science in the typical sense; it is just—philosophy" (ibid., 230).

111. Cf. on this point, see ibid., 27, 62, 184, 203. Imdahl correctly characterizes Heidegger's distinction here as "a subtle, yet significant achievement of this lecture course" (*Das Leben verstehen*, 110).

112. "The more unbroken, the more effusive, the less concerned with reflection, each momentary phase of factical life is lived, the livelier the concurrent context of experience" (Heidegger, *Grundprobleme der Phänomenologie*, GA 58, 117).

'for itself' in the mode of a hermeneutically reflexive appropriation; it is this appropriation that, as a reflexive having [*Haben*] in the sense of a hermeneutical interpenetration, determines factical life, by means of philosophical concepts, in the dimension of its relations of sense, that is, in the "'as' of [formal] characterization."[113]

For Heidegger, philosophical concepts, as they are taken into account here, share with all concepts "the *formal function of determining*."[114] Nevertheless, he differentiates them clearly from concepts of objects and order, like those in the sciences, through the fact that philosophical concepts are determined not through generalizing ordering schemes but rather as *expressions* of sense.[115] The phenomenal adequacy of such philosophical concepts proves itself through "the proximity of its forms of expression to their origin."[116]

Yet this origin, insofar as life is essentially characterized through the tension between possible transparency and inevitable opacity, shows itself as such in mediated fashion. Rather, it must be expressly disclosed as meaning [*Sinn*]—whereby it becomes clear at the same time, however, that the phenomenon 'life' can never be fully clarified through the understanding of expressive discourse. Nor does "origin" mean a real- or ideal-

113. Ibid., 114.

114. Ibid., 262. On the function of determination, see Heidegger, "Einleitung in die Phänomenologie der Religion," ed. Matthias Jung and Thomas Regehly in *GA* 60 (Frankfurt: Klostermann, 1995), 60 on the question of the function of determination [or definition, *Bestimmungsfunktion*].

115. Cf. Heidegger, *Grundprobleme der Phänomenologie*, GA 58, 236. Heidegger grounds his resistance to ordering relationships on the fact that for him the old philosophical problem of the appearance of individuation remains in force, where the factical in one's own life is abbreviated in an objectivizing manner to a fact, which is subsumed under a species and genus, or is otherwise conceived as a particular case of a universally valid law. In this way, "the fundamental problem of the relation between *fact and sense*" (ibid., 256), is overlooked, which can only first be determined in any measure when one understands the factical in its forms or levels of manifestation (see ibid., §§ 10, 12) as an *expression*, whereby having-oneself (*Sich-Selbst-Haben*), as will be shown in the next section, proves to be the "expression of originary life" (ibid., 257).

If one holds this in view, one will then, as Pöggeler does ("Heideggers Begegnung mit Dilthey," 125), be forced to see Heidegger's late self-disclosure to his Japanese interlocutor as inaccurate (see GA 12, 121; cf. § 28, n. 167), which suggests that he had already used the concept 'expression' in 1920 in his critical defense. Rather, for the early Heidegger a *hermeneutics of life* is also required, since the experience of life can have an expression that is to be interpreted structurally for its significance. See GA 58, §§ 15–17 among other places.

116. GA 58, 262.

transcendent source of being or meaning; instead, it constitutes factical life in its lifeworldly context of experience, insofar as it is referred to in its basic function by means of hermeneutical reflection. Considered ontically, the origin is nothing other than the factical context of life itself, and it functions ontologically in the immanence of life as its hermeneutically reflexive transcendence.

This means, however, that "adequation of expression"[117] determines itself under the recognition of the primacy of life in itself solely through "the originariness of the motives that are living in presentation."[118] As a

117. Ibid., 263.

118. Ibid.; see ibid., 227. With this determination, Heidegger avoids a *difficulty or ambiguity,* which burdens the employment of 'adequation' and in the broad sense 'expression' as well, insofar as they suggest the thought of the traditional *concept of the correspondence theory of truth,* according to which expression or interpreting [*Auslegen*] implies a depictive apprehension of knowledge of reality. It is not necessary, first of all, to call to mind the famous idea of the theory of knowledge in circulation at the time, but rather—and this comes forth in Heidegger's fascinating context—correspondence-theoretical considerations and approaches are to be found within the hermeneutical tradition, from Johann Konrad Dannauer and Georg Ast up to Friedrich Schleiermacher, August Boeckh, and Johann Gustav Droysen, who offer motivations and justifications alike for a hermeneutics as a technical, i.e., rule-based theory of interpretation, that then increasingly took the form of a methodology with scientific claims to validity. And it is precisely against this technical methodological aspect that Heidegger defends himself in view of his own hermeneutical approach as much as in his followers, particularly Gadamer (see "*Wahrheit und Methode:* Der Anfang der Urfassung (ca. 1956)," in *Dilthey-Jahrbuch* [1992–1993], 8:132).

The basis of this resistance is in Heidegger from the beginning of the positive link to *Lebensphilosophie,* in particular to Dilthey, Georg Simmel, and Nietzsche, according to whose famed word "of the world yet again infinitely becoming," which therefore "contains within itself infinite interpretations" (Nietzsche, *Fröhliche Wissenschaft, KGW* 5/2:309; cf. § 11), and thus can let an approach to the interpretation of the theory of correspondence melt into nothing in advance. This context is to be borne in mind in order not to lead into error through the avowedly easy misunderstanding of Heidegger's formulations. When he speaks of the fact that the "adequation of the expression [can] have no contact with that which is first seen" (*Grundprobleme der Phänomenologie, GA* 58, 263), then an operative uncertainty is not meant, which could be removed in the process through gradual approximation in order to achieve an '*adaequatio intellectus* (*qua iudicii*) *ad rem*'—unaffected by the constitutional reduction, with respect to the human power of knowledge, of its de facto impossible implementation, which, on the basis of a stable assumption of reality, certainly does not challenge the in-principle-possible transcendence of factical difference.

Moreover, as little as talk of a 'relation of uncertainty' (such as that found in Heisenberg) intends or must carry with it an uncertain mode of discourse or expression, just as little does insight into the interpretive character of world relations imply, or rather initiate, a free-floating description; rather, from out of the much-professed phenomenological attitude it indeed finds its way to an "adequation of expression." This means nothing other than a phenomenal appositeness of understanding, which, in Gadamer's words, preserves its "sense from the manner of its motivation" (*Begriffsgeschichte als Philosophie,* in *GW,* 2:82), whereby the "sensible, genuine

form of expression in the sense of understanding the meaning of life activity in the betweenness of disclosedness and closedness, Heidegger thus conceives this as a mode of dialectical movement in philosophy, a movement in which for him the original meaning of διαλέγειν can still be heard. It is thereby also not determined "in the sense of a synthetic assortment of concepts."[119] In the relation of the originary understanding of life as "the question concerning the *new basic experience of life in and for itself*"[120] in the sense of the task of phenomenological understanding—of which he speaks in a certain sharpened formulation—it is "nothing other than an intuitive going-along-with, proceeding-alongside to the sense [to be thought in the plural]"[121]—dialectic for Heidegger in this sense is that which he grasps as *diahermeneutics*.[122]

If Heidegger did not go on to use this term further, the *lebensphänomenological* differentiation gained from this circumstance remains intact with regard to its methodological relevance for the exposition of the task of a hermeneutics of facticity. The 'new basic experience' thereby appealed to does not objectivate life by means of an ordering schema, but rather brings it to demonstration diahermeneutically as a context of expression qua context of a relation of sense, so that the philosophical task therein consists in "discovering the original form of the apprehension of life."[123] And Heidegger seeks this in "*basic situations*, in which the totality of life is expressed."[124] What is meant here by 'basic situations' is not necessarily limit situations or extreme situations, insofar as—and this is decisive—life is "entirely there in every situation."[125] Rather, it is a matter of a given

---

motive of a problem" (Heidegger, *Zur Bestimmung der Philosophie*, GA 56/57, 128) is not, from the first, for Heidegger to be sounded out otherwise than in the horizon of history, which is the "guiding thread, or better, the *guiding experience* for phenomenological research" (*Grundprobleme der Phänomenologie*, GA 58, 252).

In sum, this means that insight into the historicity of life and of the world is counted, along with the ontologization of understanding which forms its *phenomenology of life as the hermeneutics of facticity,* for the *initial insights* of Heidegger, which therefore in spite of occasional fluctuations in expression, have already from the start taken leave from a constitution of truth in the sense of a classical relation in the correspondence theory of truth between thinking and being.

119. Ibid., 262.
120. Ibid., 227.
121. Ibid., 262.
122. Cf. ibid., 262.
123. Ibid., 248.
124. Ibid., 231.
125. Ibid.

concrete *"situation of decision . . . that is not to be achieved by some sort of leap, but instead in the constant motion of a strict access."*[126] According to Heidegger, it modifies itself insofar as it has to do with philosophical research into a *"situation of evidence,"*[127] precisely in the sense of the hermeneutically explicative demonstration of the desired originary sphere of life in and for itself. Seen in this way, it is now a matter of revealing, in consideration of factical life, its unexpressed relations and tracing them in their ramifications and modifications,[128] in order to conceive in turn the "basic meaning of the sphere of objects so experienced."[129]

What is achieved hermeneutically on this level is the *lebensphänomenological* analysis of factical experience, or rather the context of experience, guided by a performative theory. Hermeneutics is the interpretation of factically situated life, which thereby modifies the concrete execution of a change of attitude and makes explicit at the same time in the ensuing structuring "a connection that factical life itself does not know, for which it has no organ at all [in the mode of the natural attitude]."[130] "'Practical life,'"[131] as Heidegger calls it, in its average everydayness, in which—here, as later in *Sein und Zeit*—the philosophical analysis of human being-in-the-world is to be put into play, also has no need of such an organ, because its *"basic aspect* [is] *'self-sufficiency.'"*[132]

With this term, Heidegger structurally fixes the procedural forms of life in itself, insofar as for the fulfillment of its own tendencies and motivations it must not withdraw itself from its circle. As a *"structural character of life, which it places on itself,"*[133] the sense of self-sufficiency lies in the fact "that it is itself an 'in itself.'"[134] Seen thus, it therefore addresses itself

---

126. Heidegger, *Phänomenologische Interpretationen zu Aristoteles, GA* 61, 157.

127. Ibid., 35. It is the "situation of the ur-decision of the practice of philosophizing" (ibid.).

128. Thus the aim of hermeneutical analysis, as it is put elsewhere, formulates itself in "discovering, from out of 'life in itself,' the ur-region of *'life in and for itself'"* (*Grundprobleme der Phänomenologie, GA* 58, 203). This comment should not be overvalued, as Hegelian as the tone in this distinction rings. Cf. Greisch, "La 'Tapisserie' de la vie," 149.

129. Heidegger, *Grundprobleme der Phänomenologie, GA* 58, 250.

130. Ibid., 118. (emphasis deleted).

131. Ibid., 203.

132. Ibid., 27; see also ibid., 30., 41.

133. Ibid., 42. Self-sufficiency is, along with significance and character of expression, the third 'situation-condition' of factical life (see ibid., 137).

134. Ibid. (emphasis deleted).

"only ever in its own 'language'"[135] and does not see that and how it could be spoken otherwise, that is, out of the transcendence of its own perspective. In other words, facticity as the ontological character of factical life in all its possibilities, in which it interprets itself particularly and is therein at the same time always already also interpreted, attains to knowledge *as such* first in the phenomenological interpretation, which as its own possibility of being in the sense of methodological opening of access refers to that second decisive discovery of phenomenology, next to intentionality, for Heidegger: *categorial intuition*.[136] It means, in opposition to the immediate, self-sufficient carrying out of life, a *distance taking,* in that it takes it in a kind of *epoché.* Certainly, concrete life is not overcome thereby in its life-worldly experiential connection, but rather, observed methodologically, is visible in the *hermeneutical difference* posited therein first and foremost as a structural totality experienced as such, though never factically, together with its articulability in the moments of structural comportment.

As the last paragraph has shown, environmental experience offers a point of departure for hermeneutical analysis, for, so reads Heidegger's basic assumption, "our life exists only *as life,* insofar as it lives in a world."[137] The world is thus there for it as a 'basic category of life,'[138] yet not primarily in the mode of an epistemological or traditionally ontological observation. Rather it yields itself as reality in the concrete movement of carrying out life qua movement of life. In other words, the Dasein of the world as a point of departure for the hermeneutical thematization of factical life is only what it is insofar as it grows out of a determinate mode of experience. As directed movement of life, Heidegger designates it in its basic sense as care and stresses that in directed, "caring 'being-out-for-something' . . . the for what of care of life [is] the particular world."[139]

---

135. Ibid., 31; see also ibid., 250. "Factical life takes itself and concerns for itself not only as a significant occurrence and as the importance of the world, but it also speaks the *language* of the world, as often as it speaks with itself" (Heidegger, *Phänomenologische Interpretationen zu Aristoteles,* 243).

136. See Heidegger, "Diltheys Forschungsarbeit," 160. In this connection, Heidegger's particular estimation of Husserl's "VI. *Logische Untersuchung*" explains itself, which concentrated his focus on the question of categorial intuition.

137. Heidegger, *Grundprobleme der Phänomenologie,* GA 58, 34; see ibid., 96.

138. See Heidegger, *Phänomenologische Interpretationen zu Aristoteles,* GA 61, 85–89; cf. 242.

139. *Phänomenologische Interpretationen zu Aristoteles,* GA 61, 240; see § 27. "The world, worldly objects are there in the *basic mode of the relation to life:* care. [. . .] Encountering objects, and care is an experience of objects in their respective encounter. *Encounter [Begegnis]* characterizes the basic mode of the existence [*Dasein*] of worldly objects. *Experience [Erfah-*

In this 'caring being-out-for-something,' Heidegger formulates his *new approach to the phenomenological basic insight in intentionality as 'self-relation-to-something.'* He specifies it in detail in the lecture of winter semester 1921/22, according to which the care of the *sense of relation* of life is that which, insofar as it is addressed in its how, comprises the *sense of its enactment* [*Vollzugssinn*].[140] Since the meaning of its enactment, as we have seen, only ever produces [*zeitigt*] itself situationally and thus historically, it belongs together intimately with what Heidegger calls the sense of temporalization [*Zeitigungssinn*].[141] In caring being-out-for-something, this something is consequently, as the world, that "which is lived, by which life is maintained, on which it holds itself."[142] In this sense, the world is designated by Heidegger in the formal indication of intentionality as the *content-sense* that in care assumes the already indicated character of *significance.*[143]

As always already taken in this sense in some way in care, the lifeworld articulates itself, as indicated above, with respect to its possible "direc-

---

rung] characterizes the basic mode of approaching them, of confronting them. Experience here not understood in a theoretical sense, empirical perception over against rational thinking or the like; the expression is to be taken as broadly as the relational sense of care: it characterizes this only in accord with a . . . real mode of its execution, insofar as its knowledge-character, the attention given through care, dominates in a particular manner" (Heidegger, *Phänomenologische Interpretationen zu Aristoteles*, GA 61, 90, stress added, except for the second use of "experience").

140. See Heidegger, *Phänomenologische Interpretationen zu Aristoteles*, GA 61, 90. "Caring [*Sorgen*] is the fundamental sense of the relation of life [it] has in itself a direction [*Weisung*] that life itself gives, which it experiences: in-struction [*Unter-Weisung*]. The full sense of *intentionality* in the original! Theoretical attitude fading away" (ibid., 98); see also *Grundprobleme der Phänomenologie*, GA 58, 260. Hereby, however, Heidegger no longer poses the problem of intentionality at the theoretical level of the experience of consciousness, but rather at the underlying level of everyday comportment. Seen thus, Heidegger's hermeneutical ontology of facticity—in the sense of its existential-formal attitude—proves itself to be philosophically, from the outset, *eminently "practical,"* which also not least underscores its self-understanding and self-clarification alike in his analysis of Aristotle, particularly in book 6 of the *Nicomachean Ethics* (see *Phänomenologische Interpretationen zu Aristoteles*, 255–261; also Manfred Riedel, "Heidegger und der hermeneutische Weg zur praktischen Philosophie," in *Für eine zweite Philosophie*, 171–196; Franco Volpi, "La question du λόγος dans l'articulation de la facticité chez le jeune Heidegger, lecteur d'Aristotle," in *Heidegger 1919–1929*, ed. Jean-François Courtine, 33–65; Walter Brogan, "The Place of Aristotle in the Development of Heidegger's Phenomenology," in *Reading Heidegger from the Start*, ed. Theodor Kisiel and John van Buren, esp. 214–220; Ted Sadler, *Heidegger and Aristotle: The Question of Being* (London: Athlone, 1996, 141–150).

141. See Heidegger, *Phänomenologische Interpretationen zu Aristoteles*, GA 61, 53, 98, 247.

142. Ibid., 86.

143. See ibid., 93–99; see also *Grundprobleme der Phänomenologie*, GA 58, 102–110.

tions of care"[144] in "*worlds of care*"[145] in the *environment, with-world,* and *self-world* [*Umwelt, Mitwelt, und Selbstwelt*] as "relief-like forms of life in themselves,"[146] which, for the most part indifferently, determine their everydayness. With these three characters of relief, the point is not the three ontologically distinct regions of reality. Rather, this methodological difference gains its sense "from the form (the character of possibility and temporalization) of the mode of care that can itself be motivated differently."[147] In the interpenetration of *environment, with-world, and self-world as the phenomenal mode of givenness* the connection of significance lived thus factically does not abstract out what is proper to itself. Only through a methodologically guided change of perspectives does the factical connection of life, which does not distinguish itself in its enactment, become explicit and visible in categorial determination or intuition of the environment, with-world, and self-world in and as structural form of the lifeworld in the sense of human self-living as an achievement of a science—the originary science that is hermeneutically transformed phenomenology.

For such an ur-science, everything hinges upon understanding life from out of its peculiar, phenomenologically accessed origin, which demands first and foremost securing itself in the right mode of origin. Corresponding to the distinction between life 'in itself' and life 'for itself,' the sought-after subject matter of phenomenology cannot be apprehended immediately with an eye to factical life and its lifeworlds, nor can it be laid hold of mediately in the questioning of world contents regarding the determinations of its 'what' [*Wasbestimmtheiten*], which, investigating in the theoretical attitude, as is generally known, delimits the field of tasks of the individual sciences. It thereby becomes obvious at the same time that the philosophical attitude sought by Heidegger cannot be found in the orientation to scientific comportments. Nonetheless, factical life enacting itself in the lifeworlds leaves that which alone can motivate and disclose access to the originary realm sought. Thus, in recourse to the lifeworlds spoken of

---

144. Heidegger, *Phänomenologische Interpretationen zu Aristoteles*, 240.

145. Ibid., 94.

146. Heidegger, *Grundprobleme der Phänomenologie*, GA 58, 39.

147. Heidegger, *Phänomenologische Interpretationen zu Aristoteles*, GA 61, 94; cf. *Grundprobleme der Phänomenologie*, GA 58, 38 f., 98, 171; *Phänomenologie der Anschauung*, GA 59, 173.

by Heidegger almost constantly in the plural here, a "survey in factical life" becomes necessary.[148]

This survey certainly maintains an equal distance from universal theories on life and personal worldviews or metaphysical standpoints, and thus makes itself into an as it were neutral "observer of factical life."[149] If this requirement allows the phenomenological pathos of objectivity [*Sachlichkeit*] in the sense of a maxim of research to become audible in its undertones, Heidegger himself raises an important objection against this methodological fiction: insofar as we always stand in a particular *epoché* of intellectual history, this means that—unseen by the intended comportment of a pure objectivity—the what-content that is aimed at itself is not given otherwise than relatively, under certain presuppositions and with corresponding implications. Recall in particular the discussion of the first section or the critical consideration of Descartes and Husserl; it appears highly problematic in general to attempt to edit relationality and perspectivity out of the consideration of a matter.

For Heidegger, such relativity constitutes no direct objection, but rather guides one's own attention to what is necessary for the demonstration of the originary region, admittedly in a necessary factical sense. For the circumstance that the content of nontheoretical life as much as the what-content of theoretical observation does not prove itself to be ahistorically invariant means, seen positively, that they "always portray themselves in a particular manner, in a 'how,'"[150] and considered thus, "a concentratedness [*Zugespitztheit*] on factical self-living [is to be encountered] individually, for many, or for entire generations in life."[151] What Heidegger here means by 'concentratedness' is itself in turn not a 'what-content,' but rather "a how-content [*Wiegehalt*] in which each differing 'what-content' can

148. Heidegger, *Grundprobleme der Phänomenologie*, GA 58, 83. "The philosophical experience of life itself is motivated for philosophy from out of life itself" (ibid., 253).

149. Ibid., 83.

150. Ibid., 84. This insight into the relationality of even (and precisely) scientific forms of knowledge finds confirmation in other terms—without therefore being permitted to overextend it—in Thomas S. Kuhn's investigations of the history of science, which have dominated the fields of the philosophy of science and the history of science under the catchphrase *paradigms* since the 1960s. See Kuhn, *Die Struktur wissenschaftlicher Revolutionen*, 2nd ed., and the postscript to the 1969 edition, which is included in the second edition (Frankfurt: Suhrkamp, 1976). From another orientation Kurt Hübner formulates the interesting thesis that the historical situation decides over scientific facts and principles and not the reverse (*Kritik der wissenschaftlichen Vernunft* [Freiburg: Alber, 1986], 193–199).

151. Heidegger, *Grundprobleme der Phänomenologie*, GA 58, 85.

stand."[152] With this 'how-content' the question concerning the original region corresponding to the requisite survey into *the factical*, in the sense of a hermeneutical intuition on the hither side of all theoretical abstraction, gains its approach performatively-historically as a point of departure, insofar as the particular what-content always shows itself in the form of the how as the particular "factical *mode[s]*, in which experiences factically come to pass."[153] This takes place precisely within respective self-living in a "functional rhythmics, which gives shape to factical life itself,"[154] and refers to the historicization of its how-content qua parameters, as it were, as a dynamic structure in formal indication. Heidegger calls this the "'to'-(there)concentration ['*Zu*'-(*Hin*)*gespitztheit*] upon factical self-worlds and *their factical constitution*."[155]

The centering on the self-world that ensues from the phenomenological perspective on the relational, dynamical 'how' of historical individual life means, observed in methodological terms, that in exposing this pointing that ground of experience that is nothing other than the originary realm sought is uncovered with the self-worlds. *Seen thus, formal phenomenology determined as 'originary science of life' [is] therefore in thematic con-*

---

152. Ibid.
153. Ibid.
154. Ibid.
155. Ibid. Heidegger makes clear that factical life is "lived, experienced [in a] concentratedness on the self-world," (ibid., 59) and, in accordance with this 'functional stress [*Betontheit*] on the self-world,' "can also, to that effect, be understood historically" (ibid.), through the fact that he introduces "for the remarkable process of the displacement of the emphasis on factical life and the lifeworld in the self-world" (ibid., 61), as the hitherto "deepest historical paradigm" (ibid.), the emergence of Christianity and the life of the ur-Christian community, with their guiding ideas on the world of inner experience. Therein Heidegger discerns the "great revolution against ancient science, above all Aristotle" (ibid.), which in the wake of its thousand-plus-year triumph has even rewritten the history of metaphysics. To overcome this process now, i.e., to get away from it radically, is for him "*one* of the innermost tendencies of phenomenology" (ibid.).

While this proves itself to be a fundamental critique of metaphysics, the process itself also appears to have developed in this way because it "is ever being interrupted by claims to genuine ur-Christian positions" (ibid.); among them, as is shown by phenomenological analysis, that Augustine saw the self-world much more deeply than Descartes (see ibid., 205). From this point, the path toward the thematization of religious life opens itself out of *phenomenological* motivations for Heidegger, as attested by the lecture courses of Winter 1920/21 (*Einleitung in die Phänomenologie der Religion*) and Summer 1921 (*Augustinus und der Neuplatonismus*) in GA 60. See Theodor Kisiel, *The Genesis of* Being and Time, 69–115, 149–219; Thomas Sheehan, "Heidegger's 'Introduction to the Phenomenology of Religion,'" in *A Companion to Martin Heidegger's* Being and Time, ed. Joseph Kockelmans (Washington, DC: University Press of America, 1986), 40–62; Gerhard Ruff, *Am Ursprung der Zeit*.

cretion the 'science of the self-world.' Thus, what we have appealed to above now takes a much clearer, recognizable shape as the proper tendency of the phenomenology of lifeworlds to a hermeneutics of the self.

However, there is still a further need for clarification with respect to the complexity of the matter of fact, at least in one respect. Discourse on the self-world has not been limited simply to the context of an originary realm. Heidegger himself indicates this when he recalls "pretheoretical experiences of the self-world,"[156] which he makes into a theme[157] in ever-new attempts in the situational manifestation of their motives and tendencies in these early lectures. Even without having been treated in detail in individual cases in the present investigation, these experiences were already indicated in their function in formal ways when we spoke of the environment, with-world, and self-worlds in the sense of the pretheoretical relief-characters of factical life articulated into worlds of care.[158]

What Heidegger promotes from out of the numerous examples he provides as hermeneutical insight is that the "*lifeworld*, the environment, with-world, and self-world [are] lived in a situation of the self,"[159] such that the lifeworlds manifest themselves in and for a particular situation of the self-world; this also therefore shows in the manifest layer of the everyday en-

---

156. Heidegger, *Grundprobleme der Phänomenologie*, GA 58, 86.

157. Descriptively, there are choice examples, rich in number, particularly ibid., §§ 7, 10, 24—*pars pro toto* Heidegger's depiction of his way back home: "After the lecture, I come out of the university building: over there I see an acquaintance greeting me; I return the greeting; I hear music as I pass by the coliseum; it occurs to me that I want to go to the theater tonight, that I still want to settle this and that, that I should not come too late; in the meantime it comes to me that in one place in the lecture, I did not generate a formulation in such a way as to adequately convey what is seen; in going on, I live in what I still want to settle; in so doing, I see people and enter a cigar shop on the street-corner, buy Swiss cigars, hear the proprietor behind the counter speaking animatedly about the last football match; what he has to say doesn't interest me; what interests me is how he tells it; while I pack up, I see only how he grows more animated and enthusiastic about the brilliant performance of a player" (ibid., 103).

The depiction of these everyday moments and trivialities of concrete contexts of life-experience allows Heidegger to clarify that the manifoldness of tendencies and motivations of factical life must be understood as significant in their relation to self-worldly experienced reality, for one thing; for another, it bears in itself the fulfillment of the tendencies and motives fully as self-sufficiently determined in their fundamental directedness.

158. See ibid., 33: "our environment [*Umwelt*]—countrysides, districts, cities and wilder-nesses; our with-world [*Mitwelt*]—parents, siblings, friends, the elderly, teachers, students, officials, strangers, the man with the crutches, the woman over there with the elegant hat, the little girl here with the doll; our *self-world*—insofar as that directly engages me so and so and lends to my life precisely this, my personal rhythm," among others.

159. Ibid., 62.

actment of life, if at most unexpressly, that factical life is in itself centered on the self-world. In its basic function, the self-world in no way provides an unshakable foundation of absolute certainty; rather it is lived and experienced as a "labile state."[160] The self-world, as it is taken into account here, as a "center of life-relations,"[161] is thereby first a phenomenon in the sense of the "manifest character created from out of the intuition"[162] of factical self-sufficent life.

This "situational character of the self-world"[163] in the sense of self-living centered in it as a form of expression can become the theme of a science, not unlike those examples of historical-biographical research[164] or psychology[165] chosen by Heidegger, which as a manifest or express connection is determined formally by Heidegger as "the *concrete logic* of a subject area lifted out of one of the grounds of experience."[166] This field, revealed with an eye to self-world situations, sketches out the approach as much as the structure of formation of concepts and just as much as the strategies of grounding in which the particular states of affairs of the relevant subject area identify, so that in this way, it suffices "to apprehend factical life and

160. Ibid., 59. It is of decisive significance for hermeneutical analysis that the aforementioned designation of the self-world does not mean the negation of the environment [*Umwelt*] and in particular the with-world [*Mitwelt*]. Rather, it is the case that precisely and above all by means of the demonstration of the self-world's distinction does "its appropriation [*Aneignung*] of the with-world and environment, determined in its sense by it" (*Phänomenologische Interpretationen zu Aristoteles*, GA 61, 95) become possible in a way adequate to the matter, insofar as the "entire with-world [is] a context of self-worlds, determinately articulated and capable of being experienced in a determinate manner" (ibid., 86). This does not mean that Heidegger thereby privatizes everything—and thus also philosophy—where intersubjective validity-claims would be abandoned. Heidegger insists, against "fanaticism" (ibid., GA 61, 36), on an *inter-existentiell validity-claim*. For "the communication of philosophy to another, the demand that one places to another with this indicating target . . . must have a sort of understandability that produces a with-worldly decision in a determinate situation. Then it must, however . . . ultimately be radical and rigorous in its intelligibility and demonstrability and in the manner of its appearance" (ibid.), and that means self-developing in "methodological reflection [*Besinnung*]" (ibid., 157) as "an essential part of its own enactment" (ibid.), which therein refers, on the basis of human existential relations and thus even relations of knowledge, to the factical constitution of intensity toward the self-world.

161. Heidegger, *Grundprobleme der Phänomenologie*, GA 58, 87.

162. Ibid., 50.

163. Ibid., 62.

164. See ibid., 56–59.

165. See ibid., 87–100, 241–246.

166. Ibid., 72; see Buchholz, *Was heißt Intentionalität?* 77–84.

its worlds and world-content according to its what-determinacies and their contexts."[167]

However, in order to be able to speak in this sense about the ongoing forms of factical life, the constitution of the sciences as concrete logics and about their categorical, universal structural forms it is necessary, with regard to the senses of relation and enactment, to carry out in advance a shift in situations, that is, occupying the philosophical attitude. As such, this shift does not thereby come into conflict with the individual sciences; it "does not get into their business,"[168] insofar as within *all* the modes of knowing as modes of enacting a common referential framework of life in itself from out of the hermeneutical difference, it "lives in *another* tendency in opposition to life and its lifeworlds,"[169] in the sense of the reflected 'for itself,' namely in the "tendency of the understanding of life *from out of* its origin,"[170] which, as seen, has shown itself as the self-world.

Self-world in this context, as a concept, is now no longer merely the pretheoretical relief character in the connection of interpenetration of the lifeworld; nor is it the theoretical, scientifically disclosed field of inquiry. Rather, motivated in the phenomenological observation of the factical experience of life, the self-world unfolds its basic sense in its manifold sense relation, in that the phenomenological analysis of the categorical dependencies of life, in the sense of an existentiell "genealogy of the realms and concepts of being,"[171] considered qua facticity in existence, discovers in them those formal ontological structures that interweave the different concrete structural forms as they appropriate particular manifest relations as connections of significance.[172]

The concept of being appraised here by Heidegger does not think being traditionally as essence qua essential, but rather construes being in

---

167. Heidegger, *Grundprobleme der Phänomenologie, GA* 58, 81.

168. Ibid.

169. Ibid.

170. Ibid.

171. Heidegger, *Phänomenologie der Anschauung, GA* 59, 37.

172. With this, Heidegger at the same time refutes, in the form of a self-objection in the sense of an *"argumentation out of the factical"* (Heidegger, *Grundprobleme der Phänomenologie, GA* 58, 80), any declared doubt as to the possibility of a *science* of the self-world (see ibid., 78–81) to the extent that, as is clear from what we have examined, in the project of a phenomenology as 'originary science of life in itself,' in accordance with its own claim, it is *not* a matter of descriptively grasping or prescriptively forming, in an objectivating tendency, factical life as a whole in the wealth of all of its facets, which in the sense of the objection would also in fact be just as unfeasible as nonsensical and even ultimately superfluous.

terms of a hermeneutics of facticity, as we have already seen, as the being of factical life in the historically enacting orientation of how-content. The centering on the self-world bound up with it is that which Heidegger accentuates in a twofold manner according to its own genuine tendencies as "self-*world*,"[173] insofar as the motivations of the "facticity of experience"[174] grow from it as horizons of sense, which at the same time therein recur (back) to "the *self*-world and its particular ready to be fulfilled situations, which are the 'factical' of factical life."[175] Within such ready-to-be-fulfilled situations, it is a matter of producing one's own, that is, philosophical, contribution of understanding, precisely in the sense of a "fundamental experience of self-world,"[176] that as a "*particular style* of experience"[177] in

173. Ibid., 63.
174. Ibid., 107.
175. Ibid., 63.
176. Ibid., 101.
177. Ibid. For Heidegger, the individual manner of world-experience discloses itself through its *style* thus as the foundation of all understanding, so that style counts as self-living's "formative mode of being-expressed [*Gestaltart des Ausdrucksseins*]" (*Ontologie, GA 63*, 52) and thus, as Heidegger suggests, allows philosophizing to be grasped in its historical world-relation as a phenomenon of style. The question of style—since the ancients' form of expression of the psyche (see Wolfgang G. Müller, *Topik des Stilbegriffs: Zur Geschichte des Stilverständnisses von der Antike bis zur Gegenwart* (Darmstadt: Wissenschaftliche Buchgesellschaft, 1981)—has already been a hermeneutical theme since Schleiermacher, who, with a view to the goal of knowledge in the context of psychological interpretation, grasps this goal as the "*complete understanding of style*" (*Hermeneutik und Kritik*, 168; see also "Über den Styl" in *Jugendschriften 1787–1796*, ed. Günter Meckenstock [Berlin: De Gruyter, 1984]). If one keeps in sight the fact that Heidegger brings the question of style to language in the context of the achievement of existentiell understanding disclosing possibilities of self-living bound up with facticity, there appears, in view of this fundamental aspect of self-formation, a proximity lying in the imposition of style to the mode in which the question of style as bearing, as ethos of the 'practices of the self,' is discussed as Foucault places style in the center of his ethics, i.e., as mode and way, "how one is supposed to constitute oneself as a moral subject" (*Sexualität und Wahrheit*, vol. 2 of *Der Gebrauch der Lüste* [Frankfurt: Suhrkamp, 1990], 37).

Within the scope of his own project of a theory of self-experience whose lebensphilosophical and hermeneutical strands of tradition are bound up with Wittgensteinian insights, Ferdinand Fellmann (*Lebensphilosophie*, 217–228) thematizes the problem of style in the context of his reflections on the linguistic aspect of life, precisely as the point of intersection of 'life and language' and 'pragmatics and semantics.' In addition, the problem of style has received more attention in various forms since the postmodern debate about the critique of reason, particularly through the controversial discussion of literary forms of philosophy and of the boundary line between philosophy and literature. In Germany, this debate gained its profile and direction first and foremost through Habermas's critique of the purported 'levelling of categorical differences,' of which he accused Derrida in particular (see Derrida's equally central and destructive work in this context, *Dissemination* [Wien: Passagen, 1995]), who, as Habermas saw it, moved in Heidegger's line of succession, whereby the poeticization of thinking steps forward as a reproach of Heidegger's later philosophy as a whole, without regard yet to the strict Heidegge-

self-enacting abstraction qua understanding, discloses *"the mode of the experience of the self-world, its own sense, the tendencies and possibilities decided therein."*[178]

The mode of disclosure enacts itself, in view of the "primacy of concrete life as an [ontological functional analysis] fulfilled in its sense," as a hermeneutical structural analysis of the situated and situating 'how' of human being, and oriented "in each of its stages."[179] That means that it now comes down to uncovering the constitutive relation of human life experience on its own in phenomenological *destruktion,* which relation as caring being-out-for refers to the lifeworlds, that is, worlds of care, corresponding to intentional determinacy and corresponding demands following critically the directives issuing from out of this relation "in the basic bearing of research into life."[180] From this point—suggested by the analysis of environmental experience—the Heideggerian basic insight emerges: "What is experienced expresses me myself somehow. In the factical experience of life, I live in a fragmentary circuit in which I have and find myself and become intelligible to myself.[181] Seen thus, with respect to this basic comportment in the center of the hermeneutical, phenomenological analysis, there stands the question concerning the sense "1. Of *having* myself therein; 2. Of the *self* that is thereby had."[182]

---

rian distinction between poetry and thinking in that period. See Habermas, *Der philosophische Diskurs der Moderne,* 219–247; "Philosophie und Wissenschaft als Literatur?" in *Nachmetaphysisches Denken: Philosophische Aufsätze* (Frankfurt: Suhrkamp, 1988), 242–263.

The hermeneutical and linguistic modes of vision combined in Manfred Frank's study, *Stil in der Philosophie* (Stuttgart: Reclam, 1992), offer a differentiated project of a philosophy of style in opposition to this mostly polemical discussion. With regard to the debate in question, his study advances the insight that while a differentiation between philosophy and literature, as perspectives of access to the world, can certainly be discerned, determining this differentiability in its essence as a categorical difference bound up with a dividing line for a capacity for truth must be cast into doubt. According to Frank, one cannot "tear open an unbridgeable abyss between 'world-disclosure/literature' on the one side, and 'truth-bound argumentation/philosophy,' on the other" (ibid., 84), since, for one, in connection to Novalis and the early Romantics, art continually insists on claims to truth in its 'aesthetic imperatives,' and for another, since Wittgenstein the literariness of thinking can be shown through its linguistic nature.

178. Heidegger, *Grundprobleme der Phänomenologie,* GA 58, 101.

179. Ibid., 150.

180. Ibid., 160.

181. Ibid., 161.

182. Ibid. Heidegger makes clear that I find myself expressed in experience, wherein he discerns the "fundamental character of factical life" (ibid., 252), by means of the phenomenon of memory. For in the recollection of something experienced I can "pursue, much more immediately than in that earlier experience itself, that which is enacted in the manner of having-

§ 35. *The Having-of-Oneself within the Field of Tension between Winning and Losing Oneself*

In order to advance to the phenomenally appropriate insight into *having oneself,* for the most part undiscovered in factical experience, Heidegger rejects from the start any possible misinterpretations of the character of having in the sense of the methodological task of *destruktion.* Thus, in having, it is *not* about an "explicit closure to myself as an 'I,' which belongs in general to the order of the 'I,'"[183] and admittedly without regard to whether the discourse is about the "I" as an 'empty point of relation' or as the 'concrete manifoldness of determinations of the object,'[184] because in this case as well, the concrete "I" does not appear otherwise than "in the ordering tendency of objectification."[185] Further, having also is not gained for Heidegger by a "deduction from a fact of experience to a person experiencing, which the experiences must *logically* have . . . *to* which something like experience precedes as its property,"[186] which supported the assumption of an "I" that in the claim to an ultimately valid knowledge would be more originary than self-living or self-having. Heidegger then refutes the further misconception that in having myself, the "I"-consciousness, because it is not phenomenally present, grasps (as a product of an inductive observation), marshaling together the individual experiences of life, from which it then springs in the style of a "passing result."[187]

Heidegger makes use of all of these differing modes of objectivation in which the meaning of the object is fixed in the "I" as aids in determining a positive sense of having, to the effect that, as a mode of enactment

---

experienced, how what is recollected has its wholly specific character in which it is familiar to me" (ibid.) insofar as I myself am that which finds myself, as it were, in what is recollected, that "I myself occur to myself in a particular *form* [*Gestalt*]" (ibid., 158) and seen thus, this form expresses me myself as such.

183. Ibid., 257.

184. See ibid., 164.

185. Ibid., 257.

186. Ibid., 165.

187. Ibid., 258 (emphasis deleted). Heidegger discusses the problem of how the "I" has itself on the basis of the hermeneutical self-understanding aimed at in the winter semester 1919/20 lecture course, beyond his own phenomenological position revised in the Summer Semester of 1920 (*Phänomenologie der Anschauung*, GA 59, §§ 13–14), in the framework of an intensive exchange with Paul Natorp, whose general psychology he subjects to a critical destruction by means of his interpretation of Natorp's *Allgemeine Psychologie nach kritischer Methode* (Tübingen: Mohr Siebeck, 1912). See Stolzenberg, *Ursprung und System,* 267–294.

of human self-relation, it is not some isolatable thing, but rather a *process,* namely "of the winning and losing of familiarity with concretely lived life itself."[188] In the rhythm of having-onself there thus also resonate modes of self-withdrawal, yet not in the sense of a simple bipolar tendency, as it were, of alternating ticks of a pendulum. Insofar as having oneself, in essence, never amounts to a univocally assured self-possession, the modes of having oneself always already hold themselves—and never otherwise—in that interminable polyvocal play of proximity and distance to oneself, so that in every being-possible [*Möglichsein*] a possible other-being [*Anderssein*] is always constitutively realized, like a shadow of oneself, along with one's critical self-appraisal. As a structural relation, this became clear even in the first section of the present work, inspired already in terms of a hermeneutics of facticity by means of the comportment to the text in the relation of reading and writing. Therefore, having oneself, which, grasped primarily as a self-experience, is consequently also not to be determined voluntarily, always already actualizes itself as a *difference* in the ineluctable tension of winning and losing oneself, by which, in anticipation, an absolute consciousness identical with itself is undermined as a unifying ground of the self.

The structure of gain and loss distinguished in self-having is not necessarily to be seen as something dramatic. Rather, this winning and losing reveals itself in the alternating play of familiar life; for example in the everyday tension between forgetting and remembering in which we ourselves, with considerable effort, are never able to call to mind the whole of the previous day, but instead only parts, moments that are ever subject to reconfiguration under alternating perspectives. Regarded more closely, in Heidegger's diction, this having is "the *leaning-forward coming from life*

188. Heidegger, *Grundprobleme der Phänomenologie, GA* 58, 165; see also ibid., 258. Analyses that probably count among Heidegger's most famous philosophemes thematize precisely this characteristic of being-torn-hither-and-yon [*Hin- und Hergerissenheit*] in self-experience, under the existential headings of the they-self [*des Man*]—authenticity and inauthenticity. When Heidegger thereby emphasizes that authentic being-oneself is part of "an existentiell modification of the they-self" (*Sein und Zeit, GA* 2, 173), this means that in losing oneself in the surrender to the they-self, the self does not simply disappear. In a related sense, Rudolf Bernet, in his study "Den Anderen wie Dich selbst" (in *Fragmente: Schriftenreihe zur Psychoanalyse* 39–40 (1992):173–188) has indicated that—with a view to the "divided modes of existence" (178) according to which Dasein experiences itself tossed hither and yon between "the concern for one's own self and the refuge in an anonymous self of a well-functioning busyness [*Beschäftigt-Sein*]" (ibid.)—conscience is then not least "a fundamental form of self-experience, since it relates the two forms of existence to one another, without suspending their differences" (ibid.).

experiences into new, living, proximal horizons, a coming and leaning toward in which living *I am intelligible to me,* and where what is experienced may itself present the most difficult puzzle to my existence."[189] Doubtless, the existentiell experience of knowing *that* I am counts as the most difficult task without being able to know always with the same certainty *who* I am. Seen thus, *a distance to itself* is always already constitutively appropriate to all having-oneself.

This distance is nothing to be overcome, but rather is itself a function constituting knowledge. Too close to an object, one seeing it may not know what it is; too near to a text, dependent upon one's preconceptions, no interpretation succeeds. As the explications of the hermeneutical comportment of the second view have shown, knowledge is only possible from out of a distance. What applies to the work of interpretation in the operative sense exhibited earlier (see § 26 above), however, refers beyond 'being toward the text,' as Gadamer once put it,[190] to a capacity, conditioned by existence, for forming and taking a distance to itself—which observed according to its innermost motive is grounded in the constitution of the human being as mortal and reflectively composes itself in the philosophical consciousness of finitude.[191] With a view to the basic movement of factical life, this connection of self-knowledge and the distance implied to itself therein is brought to formulation by Heidegger in the summer of 1923: "Dasein is *itself* only in it. It *is*, but as the *being-underway* of itself to *it!*"[192]

With this being-underway, a constitutive how of the being of factical life is addressed—*the being-possible,* which as an ontological character of factical human Dasein signifies for Heidegger the task-character of life, which he terminologically fixes more closely in the concept of existence.[193]

---

189. Bernet, "Den Anderen," 165 (emphasis added).

190. Gadamer, *Text und Intepretation, GW,* 2:335.

191. From Plato (see *Phaidon,* 64 a–c, in *Werke,* vol. 3, ed. Gunther Eigler. [Darmstadt: Wissenschaftliche Buchgesellschaft, 1974]) up through Heidegger's famous analysis of human being-towards-death, a far-reaching philosophical tradition has taken shape in relation to this ur-distance, as it were, in which consciousness of living reflects in consciousness that this life is finite. Death, the "exit out of time," as Georg Picht calls it (Picht, "Philosophie oder vom Wesen und rechten Gebrauch der Vernunft," in *Hier und Jetzt: Philosophieren nach Auschwitz und Hiroshima* (Stuttgart: Klett-Cotta, 1980, 1:13), "since the anticipation of death at the same time distances us from the time that we are in" (ibid.), thereby proves to be the existentiell motive in the creation of distance in human knowledge.

192. Heidegger, *Ontologie, GA* 63, 17.

193. "Facticity and existence do not imply the same thing, and the factical being-character of life is not determined by existence; this is only a possibility that brings itself about in the being

As Heidegger formally indicated in an original reformulation of Jaspers's, stressed in connection with the concept formed in Kierkegaard, to grasp *existence* as "a determinate mode of being, as a determinate 'is'-sense, which essentially (I) 'am'—'is' sense."[194] The 'is' addressed here may not be grasped in the sense of an "'is'-like objectifying attention."[195] How this becomes evident according to what has been demonstrated is to be gained here genuinely from the "basic experience of the concerned having of itself,"[196] in contrast to the sense of existence here to be explained, and thus solely in the enactment of the 'am' as the basic experience of having itself, "in which I encounter myself as [the concrete historical-factical] self, so that I, living in this experience, corresponding to *its* sense can question the sense of my 'I am' [still to be designated more closely]."[197]

The *being-underway surrendered in experience as basic movement of factical life* to itself does not have the fixed path of a consciously aimed destination before it such that in this enacting movement human Dasein itself is on its track. Talk of being underway or on track, which already plays a ma-

of life, which is designated as factical. This means, however: the possible radical problematic of being [*Seinsproblematik*] of life is centered in facticity" (Heidegger, *Phänomenologische Interpretationen zu Aristoteles*, 245).

194. Heidegger, *Wegmarken*, GA 9, 29. On the philosophical relationship between Heidegger and Jaspers, whose most significant document is Heidegger's critical review of Jaspers's *Psychologie der Weltanschauungen* (Berlin: Springer, 1954), see, among others: Richard Wisser, "Aneignung und Unterscheidung: Existenzphilosophie im Kampf um die Existenz der Philosophie; Karl Jaspers und Martin Heidegger," In *Philosophische Wegweisung: Versionen und Perspektiven* (Würzburg: Königshausen & Neumann, 1996), 277–300; Reiner Wiehl, "Die Frage nach dem Menschen: Zur Auseinandersetzung zwischen Jaspers und Heidegger," in *Inmitten der Zeit*, ed. Thomas Grethlein and Heinrich Leitner (Wurzburg: Königshausen & Neumann, 1996), 335–353. While both of these studies take Heidegger's philosophical quarrel with the Jasperian conception as their theme, appealed to in a direct manner, the investigations of Schmitz (*Husserl und Heidegger*, 184–187) show that and how—at numerous points marked out by Heidegger—the critique is neither simply nor primarily aimed at Jaspers as the proper addressee, but instead has in fact the Husserlian position in its sights.

195. Heidegger, *Wegmarken*, GA 9, 30.

196. Ibid. What is spoken of here by means of concern [*Bekümmern*], Heidegger discusses in another place as follows: "*Bekümmerung* does not mean a mood with a doleful [*kummervoll*] countenance, but rather a factical being-decisive [*Entschiedensein*], the apprehension of *existence* [i.e., that being of itself accessible for itself in factical life] as that for which one must be concerned [*besorgenden*]. If one takes 'care' [*Sorgen*] as a *vox media* (which in itself has its origin, as a category of meaning, in the appeal to facticity), then *Bekümmerung* is care for existence" (*Phänomenologische Interpretationen zu Aristoteles*, 243).

197. Heidegger, *Wegmarken*, GA 9, 29.

jor role in Freud and more recently in particular in Levinas and Derrida,[198] is in the context of the hermeneutics of facticity not as a mere metaphor, or even a concept defined in a narrow sense, but rather it designates a conception[199] that grasps being in the world in the sense of the enactment of self-finding and self-orientation in the world.

In the *trace* [*Spur*] understood in this way, the proper alternating play of presence and absence constitutes itself. For the trace of something is not yet the thing itself. 'To come upon the trace of someone' means 'to establish something,' 'to discover in its identity.' 'To be or remain on their trace' means 'to pursue them,' 'investigate them,' 'track them down.' Whoever is on the trace is, however, not free from surprises, has still not guaranteed the way out, because the origin has already withdrawn from them. Traces are laid in order to throw someone off, but they can also unintentionally be left behind and lead unexpectedly thus to the right tracks. They are fresh, but little by little they fade away. They indicate and in fact must do so in order to be a sign in this sense, to be read as such, but this means that they can indeed be read. Whoever can read traces interprets what shows itself, but does not thus show itself immediately and yet is with it there in that which is other than the present situation, which itself always already holds itself in a predesignated interpretedness. It determines the course of factical life with its world in such a way that in these enacting paths, "factical life does not so much blunder into something on the customary path as it expressly dedicates itself to it. . . . The interpretedness of the world is factically that in which life itself stands"[200] and understands itself.

This being-self-understood, in which—with the enmeshment within culturally and historically determined lifeworlds—all of the exhibited hermeneutical structures of the preunderstanding (or, to use Gadamer's concept, the prejudice-ladenness [*Vorurteilshaftigkeit*] of understanding determined as the human mode of being) are to be thought togeth-

---

198. See Hans-Jürgen Gawoll, "Spur: Gedächtnis und Andersheit; Teil 1," in *Archiv für Begriffsgeschichte*, (1986–1987), 30:44–69; Teil 2, in *Archiv für Begriffsgeschichte* (1989), 32:269–296; see also Pöggeler, "Das Gedicht als Spur," in *Neue Wege mit Heidegger*, 315–358.

199. Pöggeler has undertaken to determine the philosophical discourse of the trace as a conception, and with recourse to Hans Lipps (*Die Verbindlichkeit der Sprache: Arbeiten zur Sprachphilosophie und Logik* [Frankfurt: Klostermann, 1977], 103) illustrates, by means of the promise of fidelity: "when I pledge to be true, I cannot specify in full what that promise means; I have only a bare sketch of that which must find, in varying situations, its unanticipated fulfillment" (Pöggeler, "Das Gedicht als Spur," 340).

200. Heidegger, *Phänomenologische Interpretationen zu Aristoteles*, 241.

er, is what Heidegger conceives—and labels the *"original articulation* of life"[201]—as something that is not synonymous with self-certainty or full self-transparecy, but is instead, as the phenomenon of the other within the analytical scope of environmental experience shows, an *intimacy,* holding itself within a peculiar fragile tension, *with itself and with the lived world, experienced in its contexts of meaningfulness.*[202]

From the start and in carrying out the hermeneutical intuition—and thus without obstructing tendencies toward objectification—this self-sufficent comprehensibility first and foremost becomes hermeneutically-reflexively explicable when that "motive point"[203] comes to manifestation in the factical reality of life (*Lebenswirklichkeit*) by which out of the thematic grasp of the relations of life, these relations themselves can be appealed to from out of life itself. To anticipate, this motive for Heidegger is *history,* but not in the sense of a domesticated, empirical reality in individualized conceptual formation via historical science. As the sought motive, history always opens itself in the sense of an experiential dispositive "into a connection of *expression* of life seen by a particular present living"[204] and is therefore also the "actual *organon of life-understanding,*"[205] insofar as, observed hermeneutically, all self-understanding in the sense of having itself always already enacts itself in the field of tension of tradition. I am enmeshed in it through strands of tradition transforming me, which themselves on their side modify themselves through the ways that I, corresponding to the historically opened conditions of possibility, inscribe myself in the enactment of my self- and world relation in them.[206]

§ 36. The Structure of the Self as a Function of Life-Experience

In proceeding to the next step, the question arises as to what, in this having, the 'had self' is. Yet this question poses itself in this form only within that philosophical perspective that undertakes to exhibit the self-sufficient having-oneself of factical life in its ontological structures, namely when-

201. Heidegger, *Grundprobleme der Phänomenologie,* GA 58, 158.
202. See ibid., 157, 251.
203. Ibid., 159.
204. Ibid., 162.
205. Ibid., 256.
206. See §§ 6–11.

ever one considers the Heideggerian formulations regarding the defense strategies implicit therein, among them the hermeneutically and methodologically clarified presupposition, for phenomenological understanding, that now with the self an evolutionary or transcendental-logical first cause or a supreme condition for having-oneself is not to be found. And just as little as it is possible to point to the 'self' in a locative sense, as one would with an object, is there to be uncovered through introspection a meaning of 'self' in consciousness, so to speak, from out of the existential transformation of the traditional concept of spirit [*Geistbegriff*].

As Carl FriedrichGethmann emphasizes, Heidegger breaks with positions of the 'mentalism of meaning,' as they were known to him from Brentano or Husserl.[207] Rather, the problem in view for Heidegger formulates itself as a genetics of sense in the hermeneutical question concerning the '*as*,' in which the self is given or better, is there, in the having itself thought as a process. Thus, it is asked of the "form of expression of the self *in* having myself [*Michselbsthaben*]."[208] The sense of the expression 'self' develops in and as the mode of comportment. The focus is directed in Heidegger to the fact that I encounter myself in the lifeworld from out of those relations in which I for the most part live unexpressly. Sharing it coexistentially with others as a rule, I thereby concern myself in those relations with what is to be attended to in a given situation. Seen thus, I encounter myself primarily in my environment or my with-world—thus in a world that gains its characteristic meaningfulness from myself. This significance 'of myself' that is

---

207. See Gethmann, *Dasein: Erkennen und Handeln*, 272. In the frame of a discussion on the theory of meaning, as Gethmann has in view, it is shown to him that Heidegger occupies the position of an "extreme intentionalist" (ibid., 274), insofar as from out of his determination of the concept of sense [*Sinn*] the meaning of an expression proves to be "only a moment of sense, 'sense-relation' [*Bezugssinn*]" (ibid.), that is to say that "the relation . . . of the expression [is] intentionality in its enactment" (ibid.). If one calls to mind (in order not so much to relativize as to situate the position that Gethmann establishes regarding context) that even according to Husserl, as is well known, the object for the phenomenological interpretative sense [*Auffassungssinn*] is only accessible in the 'how' of its givenness, it shows itself generally, as a basic trait of hermeneutical-phenomenological thinking—as it is of interest in the given context—that the awareness of referential objects of linguistic expression in general is mediated through a particular sense, and the referential objects can thus be identified by it under the appropriate circumstances. Seen thus, the act of cognition presupposes an antecedent knowing bound up with the intention of linguistic expression, a knowing that—in the sense of average everydayness that Heidegger opts for at the outset of his phenomenological analysis—both takes shape descriptively within the cultural-lifeworldly adopted standards of normalcy and is acquired in concrete interaction.

208. Heidegger *Grundprobleme der Phänomenologie*, GA 58, 166.

to be grasped structurally makes itself present for Heidegger, however, not first by means of a reflexive act, but rather because our world-relation is constituted as self-relation before all reflection and consequently *our self-relation is originally world-relation.*[209]

The answer that Heidegger therefore gives to the question of the sense of the self in the factical enactment of life reads concisely: "The self's form of expression is its situation. 'I have myself' means: *the living situation becomes intelligible.*"[210] The phenomenon of the self formulated without objectification, in opposition to the tradition of the 'I,' articulates "only the rhythm of experience itself."[211] That means that the self is only "present [in the] expression of the *situation.*"[212] In this sense, the historically factical self is neither a ὑποκείμενον in the traditional sense, nor *substantia,* nor subject as ego-like essential core, but rather a *"function of 'life-experience.'"*[213] Its concretion is just the self-worldly "*situation* without objectification,"[214] on account of which Heidegger, as we have seen, also addresses this self as "the I of the situation [*Situations-Ich*]."[215]

With the positing of the *self as a function of life-experience,* the idea of the "I"—this "category of complicated formation"[216]—is decentered, as it were. It is thereby once more clarified, with emphasis, that the Heideggerian demonstration of experiential centering on the self-world that has been explained cannot be based somehow in traditional understanding (for example, in egoistic consciousness in the Husserlian sense)—insofar,

209. Cf. Heidegger, *Phänomenologische Interpretationen zu Aristoteles,* GA 61, 95.

210. Heidegger, *Grundprobleme der Phänomenologie,* GA 58, 166.

211. Ibid., 258.

212. Ibid. "I am concrete to myself in a certain experience of life, I am in a *situation*" (ibid.).

213. Heidegger, *Zur Bestimmung der Philosophie,* GA 56/57, 208 (emphasis added).

214. Heidegger, *Grundprobleme der Phänomenologie,* GA 58, 258.

215. Heidegger, *Zur Bestimmung der Philosophie,* GA 56/57, 206. Heidegger elucidates this to the effect that the context of life-experience is "a context of situations that interpenetrate" (ibid., 210), whereby the basic character of life-experience is given "through the necessary relation to *corporeality*" (ibid.), which thus constitutes a 'basic stratum within the course of life' and which knows, in the "function of eliciting certain contexts of modification" (ibid., 211), the most diverse formations that fuse together, as it were, in the sense of experience. Heidegger does not explain further the suggestion that 'significance' [*Sinnlichkeit*] is thus—whether in Plato or in German idealism—life-experience. Nonetheless, these remarks show where, in the wake of the hermeneutical positing of the self as a function of life-experience, the thematization of corporeality—which famously gained its status as an object of phenomenological research in particular through Merleau-Ponty—can be systematically located within early hermeneutical phenomenology of life.

216. Heidegger, *Phänomenologische Interpretationen zu Aristoteles,* GA 61, 94.

that is, as factical life, in the decentering of the "I," constitutes itself as a particular self-being [*Selbstsein*] in accordance with its sense of enactment in the function of plural lifeworldly situational contexts that intersect one another in the diachrony of history or histories.

The phenomenon of the situation has already become a theme in the present investigation, as the situational being of the human was explained in the context of the phenomenology of lifeworlds, governed by a hermeneutics of facticity. It suffices therefore to refer at this point to the insights gained there, which, with Heidegger, can be grasped succinctly: "*The self lives in ever-new and newly self-penetrating situations that cannot be lost for those that follow.*"[217] Such a self-world situation is therefore "not a configuration determined in its order by thing-elements, but rather a phenomenon, a life form, a context of life."[218]

The proximity to Dilthey's basic hermeneutical concept of life-context is palpable here, and underscores Heidegger's positive evaluation of the tendency of Dilthey's *Lebensphilosophie* as a necessary station on the path to philosophy for him.[219] This positive assessment of Dilthey has, more-

217. Heidegger, *Grundprobleme der Phänomenologie*, GA 58, 62. Heidegger elucidates this when he maintains that "the *lifeworld* [*Lebenswelt*], the environment [*Umwelt*], the with-world and self-world [*Mit-* und *Selbstwelt*] [are] lived in a situation of the self. The encounters in the lifeworld always encounter a situation of the self. The lifeworld makes itself known in these or those ways in and for a given situation of the self-world" (ibid.). Situation, he writes at another point, "is just *that peculiar character in which I have myself*, and not the content of what is experienced" (ibid., 260 [emphasis added]).

218. Ibid., 165.

219. See Heidegger, *Phänomenologie der Anschauung*, GA 59, 155. Now, in Dilthey one must take note of a peculiar double sense in the use of the concept 'context of life' [*Lebenszusammenhang*]—thought as "structure of the self" (Dilthey, *Leben und Erkennen*, GS, 19:349), that is, insofar as 'context of life' points, for one, to a totality that is as such only constituted in retrospect. Looked at more closely, life is found here de facto as a context, in the sense of a life-history, in the character of wholeness only in a recollective final view, which is to say that it is authenticated only at the moment of death.

This notion of wholeness—in the sense of a successful life—has been passed down since the time of the ancients, in particular in the idea that no one can be called εὐδαίμον prior to death. Even Kierkegaard—to whom Heidegger on his side refers explicitly in the context of the hermeneutical determination of existence as being-possible (see *Ontologie*, GA 63, 16)—among others, follows this insight when he notes, for example, that "life . . . can be explained first when it is lived through, the way that Christ, too [in allusion to Luke:24, 27] only began to interpret the writings and to show how they taught about him—when he was resurrected" (Kierkegaard, *Tagebücher*, [Düsseldorf: Diederichs, 1975], 1:103).

If one shifts this understanding of the context of life into the center of hermeneutical inquiry, its capacity to be a whole, considered from the point of the enactment of life, can be thematized as an ontological structure only through the perspective of a thinking anticipation

over, confirmed itself permanently in the interim by the texts published from Dilthey's *Nachlaß* that were available yet admittedly still unknown to Heidegger at the time.[220] These texts indirectly support the Heideggerian interpretation, insofar as the thematization of individuality and facticity implied therein appears in Dilthey's turn to life as the dominant reading.[221]

Notwithstanding this proximity to Dilthey,[222] Heidegger's independent act of transformation, upon which it depends, steps into view at the

---

of wholeness that is possible only in outline. As Liebsch emphasizes in the sketch of his 'hermeneutics of biography'—which seeks, in the exhibition of the structure of a passing life from the point of view of another, "to come upon the trace of a corporeal responsivity in relation even to an anonymous other" (*Geschichte im Zeichen des Abschieds* [Munich: Fink, 1996], 12)—life futurizes itself for its success to the effect that the temporality of life shows itself to be "the subtlest presence of death in life" (ibid., 149). Seen in this way, the "hermeneutics of life [is] a hermeneutics of the dead" (ibid., 150).

This thought of being able to be a whole, which has the parameters of its thinkability in the "co-onset [*Mitansatz*] of death and of 'having death'" (Heidegger, *Phänomenologische Interpretationen zu Aristoteles*, 244) as a "purely constitutive ontological problematic" (ibid.), achieves in Heidegger an increase in significance, albeit in a qualitatively different, radicalized way (i.e., through the ontological foundation of history in historicity as a phenomenon of temporality)—to begin with, in outline in the "Natorp-Bericht" and then sweepingly in *Sein und Zeit*, in the analyses of being-towards-death. These analyses differentiate themselves from Dilthey in that, to use one example, they do not construe wholeness at the level of within-time-ness [*Innerzeitigkeit*] beyond recollection as a futurized preliminary reminder [*Vorerinnerung*] (see Heidegger, *Diltheys Forschungsarbeit*, 165–171).

Apart from this first aspect, 'context of life' means for Dilthey (and in large part also predominantly) that in the enactment of life itself there is given "a context of life and of history in which each part has a meaning" (Dilthey, "Zusätze zu den Studien zur Grundlegung der Geisteswissenschaft," *GS* 7:291). The context does not therefore come to its wholeness only in the course of time, but also forms as a structural context, "in itself a solid system of relationships of its parts" (Dilthey, "Zusätze zum Aufbau der geschichtlichen Welt," *GA* 7:324); that is, the "entire course of life is a structural context . . . articulated from within and bound into a unity" (ibid., 325). It is, however, decisive for the concept of a context of life in Dilthey that both aspects mesh and as such only form the context of life. For the "flow of life, in which everything falls victim to the past, is overturned through recollection and the contingency of the occurrence through the context of what has been thought [in the concept of the structure exhibited and in this sense]" (ibid., 329).

220. See, e.g. Dilthey, *Leben und Erkennen*, *GS* 19:331–388, esp. 348–356.

221. See also Fehér, "Phenomenology, Hermeneutics, *Lebensphilosophie*: Heidegger's Confrontation with Husserl, Dilthey, and Jaspers," in *Reading Heidegger from the Start*, 73–89.

222. Pöggeler refers to a point in a message from Gerda Walther to Alexander Pfänder from June 20, 1919, according to which Heidegger pointed out to Husserl in conversation that "whenever he speaks of a transcendental ego, this would have to be grasped historically; the pure I emerges through a repression of historicity" ("Heideggers logische Untersuchungen," in *Martin Heidegger: Innen- und Außenansichten*, ed. Forum für Philosophie Bad Hamburg [Frankfurt: Suhrkamp, 1989], 83). Reflected indirectly in this critique—in light of the abovementioned controversy surrounding the LOGOS article—is Heidegger's taking sides with the Diltheyean position (see chap. 2, sec. 2, note 12).

same time, insofar as it is articulated for him in the situation as an explicit phenomenon of the *ontological character of the self*. According to Heidegger, Dilthey mistakes this also just by the fact that for him the self qua solidarity, establishing the unity of the 'forces of the soul,' acts only as a structural context in the role "of the impulse for the development"[223] of the context of life. On the basis of his failure to attend to the ontological structure of the self, Dilthey's turn to the reality of life remains, in the sense of the "relations of life in which this self finds itself,"[224] in a properly indifferent state, with the result that in neglecting the question concerning the sense of being in factical life, he has no answer to the question concerning the being-historical [*Geschichtlichsein*] of human life.[225]

In Heidegger's radicalization of Diltheyean lebensphilosophical tendencies—tendencies that were, according to Heidegger, undetermined in view of their sense-constituting achievements—from the outset it is a matter precisely of this exposition of the *historicity of factical life*. Decisive for the shaping of the direction taken by Heidegger himself, the understanding of intentionality newly gained in the exchange with Husserl, which methodologically discloses the access to life and thereby the concept of *Lebensphilosophie* handed down, advances into a *phenomenology of life*.[226] That this, according to its essence, must be unfolded as a hermeneutics of the self can be easily seen from the present state of the investigation, if one realizes that against the background of the question concerning the basic sense of the being-moved of life in the sense of care, the new Heideggerian positing of intentionality qua comportment—i.e. comporting *oneself*-to-something—uncovered, as a result of the analysis, the centering of the self-relation, with-relation, and environmental relation of life in the self-world; it thereby placed the question concerning having-oneself at center stage.

According to Heidegger, the decisive point lies thus in the fact "that I *have myself*, the basic experience in which I encounter myself as a self, so that I, living in this experiencing [that is, in one's own historical, concrete

---

223. Heidegger, *Phänomenologie der Anschauung*, GA 59, 167.

224. Dilthey, *Leben und Erkennen*, 349.

225. See Heidegger, "Diltheys Forschungsarbeit," 161.

226. At another point, Heidegger emphasizes, with programmatic intent: "*full intentionality* (being-related to, the 'to which' of relation as such, the enactment of self-relating, the temporalization of enactment, the safekeeping of temporalization) is nothing other than that of the object of the being-character of factical life" (*Phänomenologische Interpretationen zu Aristoteles*, 247)

experience], corresponding to *its* sense, can question the sense of my 'I am.'"[227] Insofar as not the what-content, but rather the how-content guides the orientation in the thematizing view of this emphasis on self-living, as we have noted, Heidegger thereby binds himself formally to the basic tendency of phenomenology. This occurs, however, in such a way that for him the presupposition as a possibility of an understanding of the phenomenological approach depends on the fact that "the full experience in its actual factical enacting context is seen in the *historically existing self, the self with which philosophy ultimately, in some way or another, is concerned.*"[228] It is thus a matter of understanding the "fully concrete, historical-factical self,"[229] which proves itself therefore in a transforming approach to intentionality in hermeneutically modified categorial intuition, to be the oft-cited 'thing itself' around which things revolve in the hermeneutics of facticity.

A decisive step in the direction of the "original attitude [*Urhaltung*] of experience and of life as such"[230] bound up with such a hermeneutics consists in the fact that Heidegger develops the situation as the articulation of life in the three 'guiding directions of sense' [*Sinnführungen*]—which interpretatively circumscribe its self-sufficient constitution—as the *original structure of factical life* in accordance with the senses of relation, enactment, and content.[231] It is thereby of fundamental significance that the relation of access [*Zugangsbeziehung*], that is, the sense of relation, is not as such to be conceived between two objects, but rather is "itself already

227. Heidegger, *Wegmarken, GA* 9, 29.

228. Ibid., 35 (emphasis added). Prefigured in the marking out of the self, as Kierkegaard had outlined it, is the notion that the 'self,' within the context of the Heideggerian critique of Jaspers, does not function from the outset as a concept of reflection, as it does in Hegel, but rather is precisely a *historical self* and is therefore central to the present analytic of factical life. For Kierkegaard, the self is distinguished in its basic structure as existent subjectivity that is determined in its individuality, which as such can no longer ground itself from out of itself with ultimate assurance. See Kierkegaard, *Die Krankheit zum Tode,* trans. and ed. Hans Rochol (Hamburg: Meiner, 1995) and in the given context in particular the famous opening passage, where he states that the self is a relation "that relates itself to itself" (9), and more precisely is "that in the relation that the relation relates itself to itself" (ibid.). In this sense, "a person can not divest himself of the relation himself, as little as [he can be free of] himself, which is, moreover, one and the same" (30).

229. Heidegger, *Wegmarken, GA* 9, 30.

230. Heidegger, *Zur Bestimmung der Philosophie, GA* 56/57, 110. It is significant here that Heidegger sees this "original intention of genuine life" (ibid.) as being kept free as much from any logicism as from any philosophy of feelings.

231. See Heidegger, *Grundprobleme der Phänomenologie, GA* 58, 261.

the sense of an enactment, of the self's 'being-there-with' [*Dabeisein*]."[232] In the sense of what has been detailed about having-oneself, it necessarily remains open "how near to or far from the sense of relation the self is, whether the sense of relation is lived on the surface or in the depths of the self,"[233] which self, in its relation to its own content-sense, is ontically kept in a particular self-world situation determined by worldly care in its contours.

In the variable constellation of the three elements of the guiding directions of sense that formally describe the ontological structure of the situation, it is, in view of the enactment of the relation-sense, the *"basic sense of the self's enactment in its life"*[234] explained above whose sufficient understanding is interpretively decisive in the approach and viability of Heidegger's hermeneutical phenomenology of the self. Concretely tied to this is the insight that in the factic-hermeneutically reshaped intentionality of Heidegger's approach to the historical, factical self, that which one is traditionally used to grasping conceptually in and as 'I' is interpreted in in its own way, without thereby simply reformulating the traditional 'I'-sense.[235]

232. Ibid., 260.

233. Ibid.

234. Ibid., 261 (emphasis added). See also § 28 above.

235. In distinction to the position given preference here in the context of the 'I am,' it appears, on the contrary, nonetheless natural to some interpreters—such as Ludwig Landgrebe (*Phänomenologie und Metaphysik* [Hamburg: Schröder, 1949], 99) or Ernst Tugendhat (*Der Wahrheitsbegriff bei Husserl und Heidegger* [Berlin: De Gruyter, 1970], 263), among others—on the basis in particular of the Heideggerian link to the problematic of intentionality or even that of reduction, to pose the question of whether, with respect to the question after the capacity of self-being, the Husserlian 'I' bound up with it is not to be situated as a kind of starting-point. In doing so, however, they refer first and foremost to the setting of *Sein und Zeit*. Insofar as their considerations lie outside of the focus of our present study, but since they consistently, and almost seamlessly, include the early Heidegger within the scope of their theses, it seems sensible in all brevity to refer at the least to this approach.

Walter Biemel, to name yet another prominent exponent, has attempted in his study "Husserls Encyclopedia-Brittanica Artikel und Heideggers Anmerkungen dazu" (*Gesammelte Schriften* 1:173–207) to work out a particular agreement between Husserl and Heidegger that pertains to the present point, an agreement understood however not as a congruence, but rather as a kind of parallelism that he develops from the outset on the presupposition—which constitutes their difference—that the question of being in Heidegger's philosophical approach, in the fundamental-ontological form established in *Sein und Zeit*, was already guiding from the beginning of his path of thinking—something that Heidegger himself suggests frequently in his later texts (see *Mein Weg in die Phänomenologie* or the foreword to his *Frühe Schriften*). Outside of the difficulty, which produces this imbalance, of bringing the frame of reference belonging to *Sein und Zeit*'s transcendental context into connection with problems that are set

What is at issue in this transformation shows itself clearly in that Heidegger grasps the concept of philosophy explicitly as 'phenomenological ontology,' or rather, ontological phenomenology, and defines it more precisely as an *"in principle, knowing comportment to an entity as being (sense of being), so that in this comportment and for it it comes down, decisively, to the respective being (sense of being) of the having of comportment."*[236] One can conceive this step as an *ontologizing of phenomenology,* yet one must bear clearly in mind that here a concept of ontology finds an application that does not already anticipate the idea of fundamental ontology. 'Ontology' and 'ontological' are, as already explained, grasped by Heidegger much more in enactment and sense-determinacy as phenomenological hermeneutics of facticity, in which being means explicitly the being-sense of human life in its historical factical temporality as the manner of the self's enactment.[237]

If one so chooses, in view of this ontologizing one could speak of a hermeneutically motivated *lebensphenomenological* or *hermeneutic-existential question of being.*[238] With respect to content, this is determined through the fact that Heidegger can reformulate, in synonymous terms, the ontological problematic of the sense of being of factical life, and thus of a particular individual concrete life, in the "question concerning the meaning of the 'I am.'"[239] In so doing, it is decisive that from the outset Heidegger

forth in the early hermeneutics of the self, the transformation of the I-sense into being-sense is in fact for Heidegger a decisive problem, indeed completely in reference to Husserl, although not in agreement but in critical debate with him (see § 27).

236. Heidegger, *Phänomenologische Interpretationen zu Aristoteles, GA* 61, 60.

237. See Heidegger, *Ontologie, GA* 63, 3; also *Phänomenologische Interpretationen zu Aristoteles,* 247.

238. This, however, Heidegger himself had spoken of in a rather "weak emphasis," in view of his determination, given in the *Jaspers-Critique,* of existence (which terminologically contains the 'I am') as "a determinate mode of being" ("Anmerkungen zu Karl Jaspers," *Wegmarken, GA* 9, 29), to the effect that this characterization "actually emerges as a misconstruing digression in the face of the meaning of existence" (ibid.).

239. Heidegger, *Phänomenologische Interpretationen zu Aristoteles, GA* 61, 172. From an ultimately genealogical, reconstructive viewpoint in all breadth of variation, in this question concerning the sense of the being of the 'I am' one can perceive a harmony with the fundamental-ontological question of being, as in Friedrich Hogemann ("Heideggers Konzeption der Phänomenologie in den Vorlesungen aus dem Wintersemester 1919/20 und dem Sommersemester 1920." in *Dilthey-Jahrbuch* [1986–1987] 4:64); or as in Dieter Thomä (*Die Zeit des Selbst,* 139), one can recognize therein a discrete intermediary step from self to Dasein under the exclusion of the ontological as a hermeneutical problematic; or even, as in Fehér ("Identität und Wandlung der Seinsfrage: Eine hermeneutische Annäherung," In *Mesotes: Supplementband Martin Heidegger,* ed. Maria Fürst and Thomas Hübel [Vienna: Braumüller, 1991], 108), in recogni-

situates the hermeneutical question of being, in distinction from the traditional concept of ontology, within the context of the understanding of factical life. Here the enactment of understanding is originally grasped in its ontological connotation at the level of everyday self-comportment, which in the sense of the fundamental hermeneutical 'as-relation' (as the experience of the environment has shown) always already means an interpreting and thus, with the concomitant universalization, famously reveals understanding as the fundamental human mode of being.

The ontological turn to hermeneutics bound up with it, which, under the influence of Kierkegaard's critique of idealism, returns to life with Dilthey behind transcendental consciousness as the immemorial of human existence and therein, as seen, initiates a hermeneutical turn in phenomenology, establishes itself concretely in the ontological radicalization of the concept of understanding, as it is carried out in Dilthey's work in particular.[240] One can say with Gadamer—whose own philosophical approach to

---

tion of its particular position, yet with attention directed to *Sein und Zeit*, linking it with the question of "whether Heidegger would not have even become Heidegger through the fact that he bound the problem of the 'I am' to the question concerning being" (ibid., 109). Who would contest this effective-historical fact?

And in fact in the years that followed from this juncture the decisive course is set in the direction of working out the question of being in regard to the analytic of Dasein, which more and more gains its contours, above all in the Marburg years, as the question of time and temporality, among others, is introduced—in its famously prominent function for the conception of fundamental ontology—into the discussion of human self-relation through analyses that are, in the face of the tradition, as far-reaching as they are subtle (see Heidegger's lecture *Der Begriff der Zeit*, ed. Hartmut Tietjen. [Tübingen: Niemeyer, 1989] as an early document). In this way, therefore, a relevantly oriented tracking [*Spurensuche*] of initial impetuses and manifestations, as Theodor Kisiel in particular pursues them, could indeed make a find in the early Freiburg texts. Numerous resonances in the sense of prior indications to be seen in the direction of the analytic of Dasein are to be found, and confirm the richness of the early conception of hermeneutics, which is why, even in a given context of an investigation operating with different preferences, no rigid separation from the later conception should be maintained.

Nonetheless, it is not unproblematic to qualify the proper value of this ontological form of the 'I am' solely or primarily in the mode of a preliminary stage of the question of being as it is traditionally linked to Heidegger. For the view of the fundamental-ontological question of being, anchored in the analytic of Dasein, is muddied, as is easily seen according to what has already been said—in that the setting of the 'I am'-question in the concept of the early hermeneutic of the self in the thematization of the being of the self now to be explained more closely shifts the basic experience of having-oneself in its structurally thought situatedness (that is to say, the lifeworldly factical historical tie to reality with an anthropological preference, as it were) into view.

240. Driven from the question of the interpretation of individual expressions of life (see W. Dilthey, *Die Entstehung der Hermeneutik*, in *GS* 5:318) in Dilthey is, famously, the association with the factical context of life itself fixed in turn through an antecedent epistemological set-

the "construction of a historical hermeneutics"[241] opens the door—that with the hermeneutics of facticity Heidegger reaches the point "at which the instrumental sense of method of the hermeneutic phenomenon must turn back into the ontological. 'Understanding' no longer means one comportment of human thinking among others, which methodologically disciplines itself and develops into a scientific procedure, but rather constitutes the fundamental movement of human Dasein."[242] Factical life is thereby opened up at the same time, as we have seen, for philosophical self-reflection [*Selbstbesinnung*] as the center and original theme of factical life, which in the breakthrough of the tendencies of *Lebensphilosophie* since their radicalization is the stated goal for the early Heidegger.

If one looks again at the Heideggerian definition of philosophy from this point, it shows that the fundamental problematic of the sense of the being of factical life—as the genuine directional sense in view of the determinacy of the sense of the self—implies that the concept of philosophy as a knowing comportment structures the mode of being my respective self, philosophically, and does so in such a way that philosophy takes shape as itself a mode of being qua mode of enactment of factical life.[243] In other words, the hermeneutics of facticity, as a factical historical enactment of life, is the attempt to interpret self-sufficient life in the exhibition of the basic categories that structure it and therein articulate and identify it. As the interpreted exhibited in this sense, they prove themselves again as ways of the factical enactment of life, so that for example the concept of ruinance formulated by Heidegger in his analysis of factical life only gains its

---

ting of an objective according to which, as a scientific-theoretical task, it is a matter of how "a manageable degree of objectivity" (ibid., 319) in the understanding of individual expressions of life is to be attained. That means, however, that for Dilthey hermeneutics is established as a theory of understanding and of interpretation, considered according to its systematic positioning, in the context of the methodological doctrine of the human sciences, logic, and epistemology as an "important connecting link between philosophy and the historical sciences" (ibid., 331), and in this sense is a "primary component in the foundation of the human sciences" (ibid.), which as a fundamental concern of Dilthey's requires nothing other than developing hermeneutics into the true philosophy of the human sciences. With regard to its epistemological status and in relation to the role of psychology in Dilthey, the still peculiarly fluctuating position of hermeneutics within philosophy as a whole is only ultimately overcome, i.e., mastered, in the ontologizing and existentializing of understanding, which the conventional hermeneutics therein turns, as it were, into a philosophical hermeneutics that becomes hermeneutical philosophy.

241. Gadamer, *Wahrheit und Methode*, 267.

242. Gadamer, *Klassische und philosophische Hermeneutik*, in *GW* 2:103.

243. "The authentic having . . . of a comportment qua comportment is a 'how' of its enactment. What is decisive is thus *the being of enactment* (temporalization, the historical)" (Heidegger, *Phänomenologische Interpretationen zu Aristoteles*, GA 61, 60).

distinctive meaning as a basic category insofar as ruinance itself can be identified as a mode of being of factical life.[244] That means, however, that categories are for Heidegger "something that, in accordance with its sense, interprets, in principle [and this constitutes its status], a phenomenon in a direction of sense in a determinate way, something that brings the phenomenon as *interpretat,* to understanding."[245] Seen thus, *every category* is *interpreting,* and what it interprets is factical life, "appropriated in existential concern [*Bekümmerung*]."[246]

In this sense, for Heidegger the "interpretative and the context of movement [are] factically and actually the same . . . different categorial modes of determination of an entity, whose sense of being determines itself as facticity."[247] According to Gethmann, the "difference between enactment and the concept of enactment is included in enactment."[248] For Gethmann, the idea of philosophy conceived by Heidegger shows itself therein, which can be grasped as *"the philosophy of the identity of life [Identitätsphilosophie des Lebens]."*[249] By the latter he intends a historical parallel to Fichte's conception of the self-explication of knowing capable of being known according to the 1804 *Wissenschaftslehre.* The point of this analogy, according to Gethmann's insight, consists in the suggestion (to be construed as an epistemocritical exhortation) that with the suspension of the difference "between the knowing of the philosopher and the knowing that he thematically investigates"[250] philosophy becomes *"immediate,* although it incurs the danger of being *incommunicable [unvermittelbar]."*[251] For "the more strongly philosophizing coalesces with the factical enactment of life,

---

244. See ibid., *GA* 61, 131–155. Aside from the explication of all of the basic categories (among them relucence, prestruction) that we cannot pursue further at present, the 'basic sense of the enactment of the self' is further clarified in the 1921/22 winter semester lecture course—and only this is of interest in the present context—as the approach of the theoretical comportment. It is to be noted, however, that the basic categories for the most part offer no immediate description, but must rather be understood 'structural-conceptually' and as such can correspondingly return transformed in a fundamental-ontological manner in a newly modified specification gained within the analytic of Dasein from *Sein und Zeit*—and in the case of ruinance, for instance, as an existential structure of falling (see Hartmut Tietjen, "Philosophie und Faktizität: Zur Vorbildung des existenzial-ontologischen Ansatzes in einer frühen Freiburger Vorlesung Martin Heideggers," *Heidegger Studies* [1986], 2:11–40).

245. Heidegger, *Phänomenologische Interpretationen zu Aristoteles, GA* 61, 86.

246. Ibid., 87.

247. Ibid., 135.

248. Gethmann, *Dasein: Erkennen und Handeln,* 269.

249. Ibid.

250. Ibid.

251. Ibid.

the more it loses its intersubjective claim to validity, and the more private and therefore the more irrelevant the utterances of philosophy become."[252]

Granted, such danger, as given in the situation thus sketched, is incontestable. Yet when Heidegger shows that the *interpretation* of the facticity marked out as the ontological character of human Dasein is itself a *mode of enactment of facticity,* with which the constitutive preference of the sense of enactment is bound up, does he dissolve the addressed difference in the concept of the hermeneutics of facticity so simply into factical life? To be sure, hermeneutics and facticity in the present sense are tied to each other in a unity, so that each—qua self-living—always already understands life sensibly in enactment, and what is more, prior to any philosophical reflection, as is easily recalled from our analysis of the experience of the environment (see § 32). Yet for just this reason philosophical reflection is not impossible. It is instead secured above all phenomenally by Heidegger in its concrete fundamental claim; that is to say, the validity claims, as they mark out precisely the idealist philosophy of identity[253]—insofar as this philosophy thinks the indifference of subjective and objective (constitutive for it) as absolute reason—are robbed of their force.

Philosophical reflection is thus "only a mode of self-*apprehension,* but not the primary manner of self-disclosure."[254] As reflection it is, in the optical sense of the word, "a self-showing of something in reverberation [*Widerschein*],"[255] whereby this 'something' is nothing other than factical, world-related life. That means that life, in the Heideggerian understanding, signifies neither a metaphysical ur-substance, nor a metaphysical principle in a Bergsonian sense,[256] but rather, taken hermeneutically, the *fundamental-ontological reference-point of understanding* without which a full and conclusive sensible interpretation could never be possible.

In this sense, what indicates at the same time the limits of knowing as the posing of a task refers back to a *finitude* that must constitutionally be thought in a factical way, and therein grounds the fact that life is es-

252. Ibid., 270.

253. See Friedrich Wilhelm Joseph Schelling, *Darstellung meines Systems der Philosophie,* in *Ausgewählte Werke: Schriften von 1801–1804* (Darmstadt: Wissenschaftliche Buchgesellschaft, 1976), 1–108.

254. Heidegger, *Grundprobleme der Phänomenologie* (SS1927), GA 24, 226.

255. Ibid.

256. See Henri Bergson, *L'évolution creatrice,* in *Oeuvres* (Paris: Presses Universitaires de France, 1991), 569–578.

sentially characterized through *opacity*—what Heidegger refers to in the 1921/22 winter semester lecture course as "haziness" [*Diesigkeit*].[257] As an opaqueness "due to life itself,"[258] it grounds only facticity's need of interpretation [*Auslegungsbedürftigkeit*] in general. As such, it is regarded as making it visible; that is, appropriating itself in understanding qua philosophical reflection, yet not in order to overcome it. Rather, it is a matter of gradually illuminating this facticity-constituting opacity in an analysis of its structures without being able to fully clear it up, since it is, and remains, the blind spot, as it were, for hemeneutical-phenomenological eyes.

When we bear this in mind, Gethmann's surmised danger of a coalescence—within the indicated primacy of the enactment-sense—of philosophical reflection into the concrete enactment of life does not apply to Heidegger's approach. What is more, it is, in contrast, even constitutive for his hermeneutics of facticity that it makes the self-explication of its difference from the *phenomenological approach* into its hermeneutical method and then fixes it in the concept of formal indication.[259] In other words, this difference forms in itself the starting-point for the concept of the formal indication, which, as the "methodological moment of the phenomenological explication,"[260] belongs to the act of interpretation and thus structures the enactment-character of hermeneutical phenomenology. It should be noted that for Heidegger the formal is not determined in opposition to the material, nor does it mean the eidetic, nor even that form whose content would be the indication. Rather, 'formal' signifies here "the 'approach-character' [*Ansatzcharakter*] to the enactment of the temporalizing of the original

257. Heidegger, *Phänomenologische Interpretationen zu Aristoteles, GA 61,* 88.

258. Ibid.

259. On the basis of the changed status of the text due to the appearance of the early lectures, the problem of the formal indication encounters an increasingly broad interest in the secondary literature; see among others, Theodorus C. W. Oudemans, "Heideggers 'logische Untersuchungen,'" *Heidegger Studies,* (1990), 6:85–105; Georg Imdahl, "'Formale Anzeige' bei Heidegger," *Archiv für Begriffsgeschichte* (1994), 37:306–332. In substance, it was already reflexively recovered when Heidegger methodologically implemented the above-thematized distinction between 'in itself' and 'for itself' with an eye to factical life, and thereby clarified that, in accordance with its concept, philosophy is indeed enactment, yet not that enactment which conceives as such. Heidegger's approach to the formal indication, discussed explicitly in precisely this function in *Phänomenologische Interpretationen zu Aristoteles, GA 61,* 32–35, is also appealed to thematically in Gethmann's study (see *Dasein: Erkennen und Handeln,* 270), yet not in such a way that he departs from his subject of "self-endangerment," which on my assessment in any case comes to nothing in the concept of the formal indication.

260. Heidegger, *Phänomenologie des religiösen Lebens, GA 60,* 63.

fulfillment of what is indicated."[261] As a result, the formal is "something relational [*Bezugsmäßiges*],"[262] while the indication is to "indicate before-hand the phenomenon's relation."[263] In the indication, however, the "phenomenon's relation and enactment [is] *not* determined in advance [and objectivated in this way]; it is held in abeyance"[264]—that is, apprehended enactment-historically in the 'how' of its being-given in awhileness [*Jeweiligkeit*], as it appears phenomenally in and as the structured and structuring lifeworldly situation.

If the formal indication for Heidegger has "the meaning of *positing* the *phenomenological explication*,"[265] this implies, as a task or capacity of the formal indication, that the one philosophizing hermeneutically must become clear about the mode of phenomenological contemplation as enactment-like corresponding to its own concrete experience of the structure of its apprehending in the revealed basic experience of having-oneself. For phenomenological interpretation in the sense of hermeneutics thinks "out of the direction-sense of its enactment."[266] Thus, a "methodological reflection [*Besinnung*]"[267] directed to itself belongs constitutively to a hermeneutical and phenomenological explication, a reflection about which Heidegger emphasizes that it is "an essential part of its own enactment, something which interpretation itself forms."[268]

In light of the exhibited situational determinacy of the performances of understanding, the traditional "demand for a standpoint-free

<hr>

261. Heidegger, *Phänomenologische Interpretationen zu Aristoteles, GA* 61, 33.

262. Heidegger, *Phänomenologie des religiösen Lebens, GA* 60, 63. "The 'formal' is never independent, but only a worldly projection and support" (*Ontologie, GA* 63, 18), whereby it is to be noted that there is thus also not "an 'in general' of hermeneutical understanding above and beyond the formal" (ibid.).

263. Heidegger, *Phänomenologie des religiösen Lebens, GA* 60, 63.

264. Ibid., 64.

265. Ibid.

266. Heidegger, *Phänomenologische Interpretationen zu Aristoteles, GA* 61, 174.

267. Ibid., 157.

268. Ibid. The *self-referential tendency of philosophical thinking* appealed to here is not as such consigned simply, or primarily, in its range of tasks to methodology. Rather, this tendency characterizes a basic trait in the self-understanding of the modern, whereby 'modern' signifies less an epoch than a specific comportment of modernity, which as *hermeneutical* consciousness takes shape in connection with Nietzsche's foundational insight that all knowledge is interpretation. Out of the constitutive experience of distance that arises with it, it has since consistently expected, by means of philosophy, to look over its shoulder, so to speak. See the discussion of the second glance's hermeneutical comportment (§ 26) on this point.

contemplation"[269] reveals itself to be untenable, even disastrous, as Heidegger emphasizes, insofar as behind the semblance of an "apparent highest idea of scientificity and objectivity,"[270] in truth "the lack of a criterion is elevated into a principle."[271] For Heidegger, the hermeneutics of facticity confronts the "general dispensing with critical questioning"[272] tied to it, wherein it is revealed that even the unprejudiced seeing from a standpoint at which one might aim is itself carried out, as Heidegger states, from out of a *viewpoint* [*Blickstand*]: *"freedom from a standpoint* is—if that phrase means anything at all—nothing other than an explicit *adoption of a point of view."*[273] For him what matters according to its inner constitution is that it is always already "something historical, i.e. no supratemporal, chimerical Dasein apprehended in itself (responsibility for how Dasein stands toward itself)."[274]

In the critically implemented adoption of a point of view, it turns out for the hermeneutics of facticity as the interpretation of the self—the self which is always already maintaining itself factically in having-been-interpreted—that the concept of the self, as it is here applied as a function of life-experience, cannot be simply grasped in the traditional understanding of an ego-pole [*Ichpol*] or of a center of acts [*Aktzentrum*]. In view of a categorial interpretation of factical life—in which "life [is] to be brought to light"[275] from out of its enactment, which as factical, as we have seen, only is or lives in its lifeworld, that is, encounters itself enactment-historically as world, or rather as worldly—this means that in the thematization of the ontological character of the 'I am' it is not thereby a matter of the 'I' qua consciousness, as all egoistic idealism wrongly understands it from Descartes up through Husserl.[276] Rather, from the outset the 'am' of the 'I am'

269. Heidegger, *Ontologie*, GA 63, 82 (emphasis deleted).
270. Ibid.
271. Ibid.
272. Ibid.
273. Ibid., 83. At another point, he puts it thus: "a respective hermeneutics of the situation has to cultivate its own transparency and to bring it as hermeneutical into the approach of interpretation" (*Phänomenologische Interpretationen zu Aristoteles*, 237).
274. Heidegger, *Ontologie*, GA 63, 83. Cf. the corresponding discussions in §§ 5, 6, 10, 11, 26, and 31 on this problematic.
275. Heidegger, *Phänomenologische Interpretationen zu Aristoteles*, GA 61, 174.
276. In *Phänomenologische Interpretationen zu Aristoteles*, GA 61 Heidegger enlists Descartes, as an *"illustration from history"* (ibid. 173 [emphasis added]), in order to show "that for him the 'sum' . . . in no way becomes problematic, but instead the meaning of the word 'sum' was intended in an indifferent, formal, objective, uncritical, and unclear sense not genuinely

stands at the center of Heidegger's ontological interests, whereby—and
this is decisive—the 'I' according to Heidegger is to be read "solely in the
sense of pointing to my concrete factical life in its concrete world, in its
condition and situational possibility in the history of ideas"[277] as the manner of *how* I am, my being thus having to be. But that means that in the
sense of early phenomenological hermeneutics, it is thus not seen as still
sensibly possible to speak of a being of the "I" that is independent of how
it is given.

Thus, it is not the case that Heidegger is here offering us new wine in
old bottles, as it were. For his conception of the factical-historical self cannot be grasped either in the traditional concept of the empirical subject
or "as the source and agent of a determinately grasped transcendental-
relative or absolute-idealistic problematic of constitution."[278] Rather in a
given instance it is determined, in the situational sense that we have identified, historically and concretely in the enactment-historical function of the
context of life-experience within the factical "'how' of the self's distressed
self-appropriation."[279] In view of a "concentration of enactment (of the
sense of relation)"[280] escalating in differing degrees, this process achieves
its highest qualitative concretion, in terms of a "domination of the enactment-sense,"[281] for Heidegger in the "full *spontaneity* of the self."[282]

related to the ego" (ibid.). As indisputable as Descartes' preeminent meaning is for Heidegger
throughout this problematic (see Jean-Luc Marion, "L'ego et le Dasein," in *Réduction et Donation: Recherches sur Husserl, Heidegger, et la phénoménologie* [Paris: Presses Universitaires de
France, 1989], 119–161), it yet means, on my view, a not inconsiderable abridgement in opposition to Husserl's role in particular for the Heideggerian self-discovery when one assumes, as
Griesch does, "that Heidegger's first ontological discussions at the time of the working out of
the hermeneutics of facticity actually [had] only one main conversation partner" (*Hermeneutik
und Metaphysik*, 190), namely, Descartes.
  277. Griesch, *Hermeneutik und Metaphysik*,174.
  278. Heidegger, *Phänomenologische Interpretationen zu Aristoteles*, GA 61, 173.
  279. Heidegger, *Wegmarken*, GA 9, 35 (emphasis deleted).
  280. Heidegger, *Grundprobleme der Phänomenologie*, GA 58, 260.
  281. Ibid., 261 (emphasis deleted).
  282. Ibid., 260. In this concept of spontaneity, as Heidegger brings it into play here without a
closer relation to the tradition, one should be wary of assuming, in the face of the given explications, an immediate recourse to the fundamental Kantian concept. That spontaneity is used
here without its complementary concept of receptivity is also not neo-Kantian, and therefore
not motivated by Natorp's attempt to insert receptivity, as it were, into that constructive thinking which he grasped as spontaneity (see *Philosophie: Ihr Problem und ihre Probleme; Einführung in den kritischen Idealismus* [Göttingen: Vandenhoeck & Ruprecht, 1929], 46). Closer to
Heidegger's version of spontaneity, if one is on the lookout for a relation to the tradition, lies
Henri Bergson's thesis of spontaneity as the structure of freedom (see *Essai sur les donnés im-*

If, as we have seen, the self as a function of life-experience is only present in the situation, the situation thus undergoes, in the spontaneity characterized by the dominant sense of enactment, "a modification of its content-sense: it comes down to a creative *formation* of the lifeworld,"[283] whereby at the same time modes of self-formation are brought into being.[284] Seen thus, the 'spontaneity of the living self' is the last, or rather first, phenomenon out of which "the basic sense of 'existence'"[285] is to be constructed, insofar as spontaneity, this "basic sense of the enactment of the self in its life [gives] to the sense of 'existence' its original meaning,"[286] as the "being of its self accessible for it in factical life,"[287] which can only be "interpreted" in its sense "in the facticity seized and relative to this,"[288] in order thus "to be and to become *understanding* for itself."[289] Heidegger's hermeneutical phenomenology of the self has thereby identified and hermeneutically fixed that point from which "each sense-structure of the theoretical [as well as practical] comportment [has just as much to take] its ultimate origin"[290] as well as that point from which "the sense of *reality* in all strata of life"[291] becomes understandable.

My life, self-worldly centered and careworldly articulated, thus proves to be in sum, as Heidegger formulates it in seemingly circumlocutionary diction, "something that 'is' in the mode of having the tendency to 'be' in the enactment-sense of the *having 'itself'*. . . . Whereby the 'itself' does not express a specifically abstract 'egoic' direction of the sense of relation

---

médiates de la conscience, ch. 3, in *Oeuvres* [Paris: Presses Universitaires de France, 1991], esp. 143–156), which for him finds its metaphysical basis and development in the *élan vital*. Stripped of its neovitalist coloring already in Heidegger, Bergson's notion echoes, in a related way, throughout the Husserl-Heidegger break—and further still in Jean-Paul Sartre's work, when the latter emphasizes that the "attachment of the ego to its condition," is not to be confused, as an "unintelligible spontaneity," with the spontaneity of consciousness (see Sartre, "Die Transzendenz des Ego," in *Die Transzendenz des Ego: Philosophische Essays 1931–1939* [Reinbek bei Hamburg: Rowohlt, 1982], 73).

283. Heidegger, *Grundprobleme der Phänomenologie*, GA 58, 261.

284. In this formative moment, considered according to its hermeneutical function, a structure of the sense of being [*Seinssinnstruktur*] is indicated that allows us, in the concept of spontaneity according to its ontological form, to recognize a prior reference to the project-character of Dasein that is developed existential-ontologically in *Sein und Zeit*.

285. Heidegger, *Grundprobleme der Phänomenologie*, GA 58, 261 (emphasis deleted)

286. Ibid. (emphasis deleted)

287. Heidegger, *Phänomenologische Interpretationen zu Aristoteles*, 245.

288. Ibid. (emphasis deleted)

289. Heidegger, *Ontologie*, GA 63, 15.

290. Heidegger, *Grundprobleme der Phänomenologie*, GA 58, 261.

291. Ibid.

of this having and is not to be understood itself as something like self-observation and reflectedness, but rather *determines self-having and being precisely according to its sense from out of the concrete situation, that is, the lived lifeworld*."[292]

What Heidegger brings to language, in this dense manner, as a basic trait of his phenomenological hermeneutics opens up the possibility in the present interpretation, in view of its approach as it is identified in the concept of the ontological turn, of manifesting with additional nuance those determinative presuppositions that the hermeneutics of facticity has to formulate as the hermeneutics of the self. As Heidegger constitutively links up hermeneutics as the interpretation of factical life with the question of the 'I am'—that is to say, distinguishing *understanding as the fundamental human mode of being*—this means that his hermeneutical conception no longer finds its primary orientation, as was the case with Dilthey, in understanding foreign individuality and the content of their expressions. Over against this, the intentionally directed understanding of other persons, like all objectivations of life seen structurally, is carried out only in and as the *unity of self-understanding*. However, self-understanding is as such always already *understanding oneself in a lifeworld,* and thus in a concrete factical historical situation. If, in other words, all objectively directed knowing precedes self-understanding as a 'situational lifeworldly having-oneself and having-being,' this means nothing other for Heideggerian hermeneutics than, as Paul Ricoeur puts it: "*La question* monde *prend la place de la question* autrui."[293]

"World," as the lifeworld disclosed in the how of its being-experienced, thus situationally, proves to be that prior referential connection that, as the transsubjective dimension, opens the play space of possibility of human self-understanding in which (self-)understanding, observed functionally, seeks situative orientation through which, in the sensibly enacting first element of understanding, the subject-object distance is subverted in favor of the *being-involved in situative contexts of relation.* With a view to the Husserlian conception discussed in the second part of the present investigation,

---

292. Heidegger, *Phänomenologische Interpretationen zu Aristoteles*, GA 61, 171 (emphasis added).

293. Ricoeur, "La tâche de l'herméneutique: en venant de Schleiermacher et de Dilthey," in *Du texte à l'action. Essais d'herméneutique II* (Paris: Éditions du Seuil, 1986), 91. And bound up with it, this means at the same time: "*En mondanisant ainsi le comprendre, Heidegger le dépsychologise*" (ibid.).

this means that "world" is now no longer grasped as a constitutional product of subjectivity, but rather as a *dimension of disclosure* factically *inaccessible* [*unverfügbare*] for human beings in their constitutive openness for the world, in which they always already find themselves factically displaced. With an eye to the hermeneutical approach to the self, that means that in the hermeneutically grounding demonstration of the self, this can no longer be presupposed subjectivistically in the Cartesian-Husserlian manner, but rather gains its ontological identity for itself in a prior experienceability in a (life-)world.[294]

Considered thus, what in the early Heidegger forms the self- as world relation refers structurally in its content of explication to the basic condition of human being, as it has been determined existentially-ontologically as being-in-the-world in *Sein und Zeit* and its milieu. What does this mean in relation to the claim to autonomy raised as a thesis for the hermeneutics of facticity in the scope of this study? Are the differences, which can undoubtedly still be found present in the reading, nevertheless not ultimately marginal to fundamental ontology? Are there internal differences thus within a mainly coherent concept of ontology, which shifts the early writings to the rank of a preliminary level? In order to attain an answer appropriate to the matter that does not overhastily set motivation and tendency into a harmonious coincidence, but rather makes the ontological turn to hermeneutics transparent in its manifold layers, it is necessary on the part of the interpreter to secure more exactly still the hermeneutical basis of the problem, as well as the basis of its starting-point, with a differentiating view.

§ 37. On the Status of a Hermeneutics of Facticity as Ontological Hermeneutics

By means of the demonstration of understanding carried out as the original mode of human being, Heidegger succeeds in the traditional task of hermeneutics in the phenomenological orientation to human life: philosophically thinking together the understanding of structures of sense implied in the objectivations of life and the facticity that signifies the "on-

---

294. "The comprehensible context is life itself, and therein I have myself" (Heidegger, *Grundprobleme der Phänomenologie, GA 58*, 165).

tological character of 'our' 'own' Dasein,"[295] in which each finds himself involuntarily displaced and must correspond in projecting appropriation understanding-interpreting as enactment of life in the tracks of his own particular finite existentiell possibilities. This existential approach of understanding as a whole remains as obligatory as it is fundamental for Heidegger's path of thinking and can be grasped, as Gadamer puts it, thus: "Understanding is not something that Dasein occasionally does when it encounters something sensible, but rather understanding is that which defines it as Dasein. The human being is something that wants to understand and that must understand itself."[296] As we can better see at this point, Heidegger has thereby overcome not only the traditional epistemological confines of the problematic of understanding, but what is more, with the demonstration of the ontological basis of his hermeneutics he has broken up the traditional Cartesian-Husserlian approach in self-consciousness and established as a *new determination of the essence of the human the self-understanding involved in concrete enactments of life.*

If one registers this, then phenomenological hermeneutics is always already *ontological hermeneutics* in the course of the development of the hermeneutics of the twentieth century after Heidegger—and thus in the passage through the ontological turn. As such, however—in order to clarify the tasks resulting therefrom by means of a terminological differentiation—it is for that reason not necessarily hermeneutical ontology, since it is explicitly characterized as ontology for the approach of the analytic of Dasein in *Sein und Zeit,* whose level of explication directed to the concrete is, as we have seen, metontology (see § 27). Over and against this more narrow, explicit ontology there is to be noted—along with the ontologically radicalized concept of understanding as the human mode of being in the hermeneutics of factical life achieved in Heidegger's early work—an ontological hermeneutics in a broader sense. It is ontological, insofar as in the sense of the hermeneutically existentiell (or as one could also say anthropologically intended) question of the sense of being, it focuses the problematic of philosophy on the being of concrete, historically factical life, that is, on the particular how of its interpretedness. But insofar as factical life is always already determined as a lifeworldly sense of enactment,

---

295. Heidegger, *Ontologie, GA* 63, 7 (emphasis deleted).
296. Gadamer, *Die deutsche Philosophie zwischen den beiden Weltkriegen,* in *GW* 10: 366.

that means that 'ontological hermeneutics in the broad sense' can therefore be called a *lifeworldly hermeneutics.*

Seen thus, the ontological turn to hermeneutics as hermeneutical radicalization of phenomenology enacts a turn to the lifeworld articulated in terms of care (see § 32). In other words, this means that an interpreting acting in concrete factical-historical, phenomenal relations enacts itself as philosophical lifeworldly hermeneutics. This occurs in an (at the least) implicit reference back to ontological presuppositions and preliminary decisions. What is to be stressed here in particular is the formulation of understanding in its self- and world opening function as an existential structure of enactment, through which it delimits itself against the earlier, primarily methodologically determined hermeneutics.

Depending on whether one now extends the interpretive perspective's thematic emphasis more in the direction of the broader 'lifeworldly hermeneutics' or shifts the accent toward 'hermeneutical ontology,' in light of the ontological turn on the part of interpretation, differing possibilities are produced that reveal the Heideggerian transformation of traditional philosophical hermeneutics with and by itself. If one remains operationally on the level of the transformation of lifeworldly contributions of understanding and thereby in the field of view of the *philosophy of the historically factical situation* aimed at in the early work, Heidegger's hermeneutics in just this tendency would be—as István Fehér grasps it, yet without working out the metahermeneutical differentiations pursued here, which first and foremost protect its characteristics from misunderstanding—"in essential points nothing other than ontologically radicalized or ontologically turned humanistic [*geisteswissenschaftliche*] hermeneutics."[297]

In order to situate these theses properly in their approach, it must be added that the concept of the human sciences here, in the Diltheyean sense, analogous to the 'moral sciences' sketched out by John Stuart Mill, is to be grasped to the extent that it also determines in itself the systematic sciences of action. Observed hermeneutically, therefore, the historical human sciences [*Handlungswissenschaften*], also called 'humanities' or '*lettres*,' are distinguished through the fact that in them a historical knowing appears articulated as modes of the enactment of the understanding. In hermeneutical reflection on the determinacy of sense of the human sci-

---

297. Fehér, "Gibt es 'die' Hermeneutik? Zur Selbstreflexion und Aktualität der Hermeneutik Gadamerscher Prägung," *Internationale Zeitschrift für Philosophie,* (1996) 2:242.

ences, one can identify therein, as a constitutive trait, a survival, or rather an inheritance of practical philosophy, and more precisely of practical knowledge (φρόνησις), whereby the transmission of this inheritance is itself always already modified (cf. above, § 8). In this respect, it becomes apparent that, with a view to hermeneutics, its formerly stronger disciplinary theoretical orientation opens itself in a more forceful displacement of accent to the practical, so that with regard to the mode of enactment of the historical human sciences one may feel oneself reminded of a certain correspondence to the famous sentence of Erasmus, 'lectio transit in mores.' According to Riedel, the demand of the present is virtually to form a "hermeneutics with a practical intention,"[298] and this in particular therefore because, as Gadamer stresses, "understanding and coming to an understanding [*Verstehen und Verständigung*] are not primarily and originally a methodologically schooled comportment to texts, but rather the form of enacting human social life . . . which [is] in the final formalization a community of conversation [*Gesprächsgemeinschaft*]."[299]

As a humanistic hermeneutics ontologically radicalized in this sense, which aims at a philosophy of factical-historical situations, it is, in the ontological justification of the critique of historical objectivism to be ventured here, to speak with Gadamer, "a historicism of the second degree, so to speak, which not only opposes the historical relativity of all knowledge to the absolute claim to truth, but thinks its ground, and therefore can no longer regard the historicity of the knowing subject as a limitation of truth."[300] Furthermore it can be read, according to a proposal of Ernst Wolfgang Orth, in lifeworldly concretion as a contribution to a philosophy of culture.[301]

298. Riedel, *Für eine zweite Philosophie*, 7.

299. Gadamer, *Replik zu "Hermeneutik und Ideologiekritik," GW* 2:255. The speech community functions as such, among others, according to the patterns of acquired rule-bound speech acts, which the speech community itself generates in part to begin with. In terms of enactment in everyday speech they are all at most only implicitly guiding our comportment, yet could nonetheless both be revealed in methodological reflection specifically as regulative structures of communicative modes of comportment, as well as deliver such a productive contribution to the hermeneutical analyses of the situation of the speech community.

300. Gadamer, *Hermeneutik und Historismus, GW* 2:411.

301. Ernst Wolfgang Orth, "Heidegger und Husserl: Kultur als Horizont des Erscheinens," in *Heidegger—neu gelesen,* ed. Markus Happel (Würzburg: Königshausen & Neumann, 1997), 54–74, esp. 64–74.

One can also pursue this suggestion in phenomenal identification in such a way that the hermeneutics of facticity shows itself to be standing in the traditional line of 'philosophy's concept of the world.' It proves to be indebted to a self-constitution of thinking that since Kant formulates philosophy not merely as scholastic concept [*Schulbegriff*] but also always as a *world-concept*, in precisely such a way that this, as Kant puts it, "has lain at the basis [of it] at each time."[302] In the world-concept Kant thinks philosophical "science from the relation of all knowing about the essential ends of human reason."[303] Consequently he distinguishes "that which concerns what interests every person"[304] and philosophy, as it is meant in his "Reflections," "as really nothing other than a practical human knowing,"[305] thus "the science of the adequacy of all cognitions with the determination of humans,"[306] through which the bridge in Kant out of the *world- qua lifeworld-motif* stretches toward the anthropology famously aimed at with pragmatic intent. Seen thus, Kant was able, beyond the scholastic consideration[307] that he himself preferred (namely, the task of a comprehensive critique of reason), to recognize the actuality of the question of time as a substantial philosophical matter and, on the presupposition of his conception of reason, to elaborate it from out of the claim of the situation, as illustrated in pieces like *"Zum ewigen Frieden"* and *"Was ist Aufklärung?"*[308]

302. Kant, *Kritik der reinen Vernunft*, B 866.

303. Ibid. In his *Logik*, Kant emphasizes: "Philosophy is thus the system of philosophical cognitions or of cognitions of reason from concepts. That is the *scholastic concept* of this science. According to the *world-concept* it is the science of the ultimate ends of human reason. This elevated concept gives philosophy dignity, i.e. an absolute value" (*Logik*, ed. Tillmann Pinder [Hamburg: Meiner, 1997], 23), on account of which Kant can call it *"a science of the highest maxims of the employment of our reason . . .* insofar as one understands by maxims the inner principle of choice among differing ends" (ibid., 24).

304. Kant, *Kritik der reinen Vernunft*, B 868.

305. Kant, *Reflexionen zur Metaphysik*, No. 4927. In *Kants Gesammelte Schriften* (Berlin and Leipzig: Preußischen Akademie der Wissenschaften, 1928), 18:30.

306. Ibid., *No. 4970*, 18:44.

307. See ibid., *No. 5031* 18:67.

308. In his reading of this essay, Foucault refers to the fact that the text "is located at the crossroads of critical and historical reflection" (Foucault, "Was ist Aufklärung?" 41). That is to say that in this kind of text Kant "connects, from within, the meaning of his work, regarding knowledge, with a historical reflection and with a particular analysis of that unique moment in which and on account of which he writes" (ibid.). Even if Foucault does not at any point thematize it, precisely thereby is that difference retained that sets itself forth in the scholastic and worldly concepts of philosophy and which, without equating them, strives in the Kantian project toward a unity that can be grasped in the manner that Foucault describes above. Foucault himself, as his further remarks show, thoroughly incorporates within his concerns a "historical

Regarding that which the above-mentioned line of tradition of the 'world-concept of philosophy' and the present discussion involves, this reference to Kant possesses no merely illustrative function. For to have recourse to Kant makes sense, in the sense of the echo-chamber of effective history relevant to a hermeneutics of facticity, since he famously represents, in his conceptual distinction between scholastic and worldly concepts, both dimensions of philosophy in their essential belonging-together in a possible unity that, as such in its divisibility as well as in its belonging-together, would be shown in detail precisely in Heidegger, when one thinks, for example, of the relation of fundamental ontology and metontology being rehearsed or reactivated in a hermeneutically and phenomenologically transformed way.

That this, taking into consideration the critical discussion of possible objections (see § 29), can be grasped as a constructive contribution to the status of contemporary philosophy in the discourse of knowledge, is clear when one briefly brings to mind the historical course of the development of the scholastic and worldly concepts of philosophy. Their belonging-together, as the unity of philosophy, was famously broken apart after the end of German Idealism. Scholastic philosophy, which had come under the pressure of empiricism through the rise of the natural sciences, survives by its scientific and epistemological transformation into positivism and in particular into neo-Kantianism, and here experiences a new blossoming in which, up through the formation of phenomenology and analytic philosophy, as Wolfgang Wieland emphasizes, "the perpetuation of good traditions, together with the maintenance and advancement of that culture which is indispensable to a proper intercourse with the world of the concept,"[309] is upheld.

Within scholastic philosophy as we have been considering it, however, the perspective of the 'world-concept of philosophy' increasingly closes

---

ontology of ourselves" (ibid., 48) into the modern tradition—that is, having passed through the destruction of metaphysics—of the world-concept of philosophy. See also Gander, "'Ich weiß nicht, ob wir jemals mündig werden'—Anmerkungen zu Foucaults Aufklärungskritik," in *Das 18. Jahrhundert*, ed. Monika Fludernik and Ruth Nestvold (Trier: WVT Wissenschaftlicher Verlag, 1998), 199–213.

309. Wolfgang Wieland, "Philosophie nach ihrem Weltbegriff," in *Georg Picht—Philosophie der Verantwortung*, ed. Constanze Eisenbart (Stuttgart: Klett-Cotta, 1985), 92. According to Michael Dummett (*Ursprünge der analytischen Philosophie* [Frankfurt: Suhrkamp, 1988], not insubstantial points of contact with the phenomenological tradition can be found in the original area of analytic philosophy.

itself off; that is, direct philosophical answers are no longer produced to address current historicosocial problems. In these matters its capacity for offering solutions wanders, as it were, out into the newly forming humanities and social sciences, which at this point are removing themselves from philosophy's jurisdiction. The former philosophical world-conceptual questions come to be appropriated—Auguste Comte is a prominent example—into questions of sociology qua social physics.

This does not mean, however, that the world-conceptual questions have completely vanished from philosophy's field of vision. Rather, they have since found a new home within the destructions—formulated as counterprojects—of the idealistic programmatic philosophy to which Marx, Kierkegaard, and Nietzsche, to name only a few of the most influential, lent their voices and their weight. Their (and also tangentially Freud's) conceptions, which together continue to have their effects in differing aspects and accents on the development of *lebensphilosophie* and existential philosophy, compose—as 'exercises in doubt' (after Ricoeur's phrase) over and against metaphysical speculative systems—a 'hermeneutics of suspicion,'[310] coconstructed on that horizon within which the scope of functions (qua phenomenological hermeneutics) of both dimensions of philosophy converge in a new manner. This is carried out, as Heidegger's involvement with phenomenology and neo-Kantianism shows, in the early period—with, however, a preference with regard to an implicit yet clearly accentuated adjustment of the world-concept—without its thereby blurring the rigorous concept of philosophy in contemporary lebensphilosophical haziness. On the contrary, the concept of philosophy is, as we have seen, newly determined precisely in a hermeneutical-phenomenological manner.

In order to avoid an unnecessary misunderstanding, we should make reference to the fact that in moving out of this line of tradition it is not to be maintained that the world-concept first entered the arena of philosophy with Kant. In agreement with Kant's own views,[311] it can be discerned well prior in older, even the oldest, traditions, namely—as Georg Picht has shown[312]—always already enacted implicitly in reflection [*Besinnung*]

---

310. See Ricoeur, *Die Interpretation: Ein Versuch über Freud* (Frankfurt: Suhrkamp, 1993), 45–49.

311. See Kant, *Reflexionen zur Metaphysik*, Nr. 5065–5066, 77.

312. See Picht, "Philosophie oder vom Wesen und rechten Gebrauch der Vernunft," in *Hier und Jetzt*, 1:11–17. In this connection it is sensible to refer to Picht's work (see also *Von der Zeit*

on humans' role in the world, where they experience, in an ineluctability of the existentiell questions pertaining to their self-relation, their openness to the world as a closing off of their connectedness to instinct. The loss of security associated with this ontologically determined distanciation is picked up by humans and compensated for in part by the formation of social systems that, in their regulating and normalizing power, are not rigid but flexible and dynamic in themselves, and for the sake of their functionality virtually effect their (self-)transcendence in a historical manner. These regulative systems offer and require, in carrying out their self-having, a constantly changing, never fully observable variability of adjustment (think, for example, of the adaptive achievements involved in the experience of the environment, in which there is always contained a form of self-understanding; thus does "the lability of its historical orders"[313] declare itself, according to Picht, out of the manifoldness of modes of human behavior created by lifeworldly demands, a lability that is both historical and genetic at once.

This lability refers to the multiple structural moments of *contingency*, which we have addressed above, in lifeworldly orders that both synchronically and diachronically constitute the human self- as world relation. In the medium of its plural constitution the task for interpretation thereby takes shape; the task of reconstruing, in the disclosure of their hermeneutic conditions, the varying orders from out of their respective horizons of sense. A guiding fundamental idea remains in the gesture of the radical dismissal of any final revelations of meaning, the insight belonging to the hermeneutical 'world-concept of philosophy' that, over and against historical immanence, there is not, nor can there be, any transcendent idea of a substantial human being, however this may be defined in its particulars. The *consciousness of relationality* tied to it, as a structure that founds and limits knowledge in like measure, belongs therefore as an integral component in the reflexive approach of a historical hermeneutics.

Regardless of whether all the aforementioned classifications are felicitously selected or not, a *tendency to utilization* constitutive for its methodological status as a consequence of the lifeworldly turn clarifies itself

---

[Stuttgart: Klett-Cotta, 1999], esp. 21–60), because his philosophical life's work, also inspired by Heidegger, can be conceived as a kind of renewal of the world-concept of philosophy. See Wieland, "Philosophie nach ihrem Weltbegriff," 89–108.

313. Picht, "Philosophie oder vom Wesen," 12.

thereby as a decisive moment of the clarification here sought. In the framework of the methodological scope of formal indication, the contribution sensible in enactment of understanding and interpretation demands the identification of the structural moment of a *hermeneutical application* with a view to the phenomenological explication to be taken up here as an integral function of the hermeneutical occurrence.

CHAPTER THREE

APPLICATION—*DESTRUKTION*—HISTORY:

HERMENEUTICAL SKETCHES OF A

PHILOSOPHY OF THE SITUATION

§ 38. *Hermeneutical Application*

As a hermeneutical problem of utilization [*Anwendung*], the application [*Applikation*] forms its own ontological sense of contribution of historical hermeneutics. Hans-Georg Gadamer in particular has stressed this with a view to the task of textual interpretation in this sense and he has exemplarily developed it in regard to its function in legal hermeneutics.[1] In the given context, to introduce this application structure in the discussion of the hermeneutics of facticity does not mean simply wanting to interpret Heidegger by way of Gadamer. Rather, as we shall see, a structural comportment is explicated, which, even though it is not made explicit through hermeneutic reflection at the level of an autonomous conceptual formation, yet belongs to the sense of enactment of Heideggerian hermeneutics.

---

1. See Gadamer, *Wahrheit und Methode*, 314 ff. An exemplary discussion of the problematic of application relevant for legal hermeneutics, which is essentially not metahermeneutical but rather concretely oriented (and admittedly, with reference to the object-field of art, virtually paradigmatic for modern hermeneutics), is offered in the multilayered consideration of the so-called Mephisto Case (the suit brought by the heirs of Gustaf Gründgens against the dissemination of Klaus Mann's novel *Mephisto*), as documented in the contributions of Wolfhart Pannenberg, Martin Kriele, Karl Oettinger, Anselm Haverkamp, Detlef Liebs, Jürgen Schläger, and Dieter Nörr to *Text und Applikation: Theologie, Jurisprudenz und Literaturwissenschaft im hermeneutischen Gespräch*, ed. Manfred Fuhrmann, Hans Robert Jauss, and Wolfhart Pannenberg [Munich: Fink, 1981], 129–246, 599–635).

Incidentally, therewith a further piece of evidence hitherto unnoticed is worked out as a possibility for Gadamer's often-stressed, yet at best vaguely held, self-connection to the conception of the hermeneutics of facticity, on the structure of the historicity of understanding. It finds its basis in the notion that the hermeneutics of facticity is determined by Heidegger in the existentialization of understanding over the turn to the lifeworld.[2] Herein Gadamer's conception, if only implicit and with quite significant modifications, follows on Heidegger and makes it possible to identify the *application as an integral structural moment of a hermeneutics of facticity*, even though, on the other hand, its explicit conceptual development and definition—lacking in Heidegger—is not, as will be seen, without its consequences.

Decisive for a sufficient understanding of a structure of application is seeing from the beginning that it does not mean the subsequent application of a sense-content either already worked out beforehand in interpretation or pregiven in it.[3] Further, as Gadamer emphasizes, it would be mis-

2. Seen in this way, the lifeworldly turn in hermeneutics is not primarily, as Ting-Kuo Chang (*Geschichte, Verstehen und Praxis: Eine Untersuchung zur philosophischen Hermeneutik Hans-Georg Gadamers unter besonderer Berücksichtigung ihrer Annäherung an die Tradition der praktischen Philosophie* [Marburg: Tectum, 1994], 114) holds, carried out via Gadamer. Just as little can it be maintained, as Otto Friedrich Bollnow ("Festrede zu Wilhelm Diltheys 150. Geburtstag," 28–50, in *Dilthey-Jahrbuch* [1984], 2:49) obliquely suggests, that it is already in effect in Dilthey's approach.

3. With application, what is familiar from the traditional theological hermeneutics as '*subtilitas applicandi*' should not as a consequence be simply revitalized. Gadamer's brief reference (*Wahrheit und Methode*, 312) in this connection to Johann Jacob Rambach's pietistic '*institutiones hermeneuticae sacrae*,' in view of the thematic prehistory, can be complemented more precisely in terms of the source material by reference to Johann Salomon Semler. He is of significance for the development of historicocritical biblical exegesis, and therewith for hermeneutics as methodology, insofar as he skeptically circumvents a simple equation of the Holy Scriptures with the word of God (see Gottfried Hornig, "Über Semlers theologische Hermeneutik," in *Unzeitgemäße Hermeneutik: Verstehen und Interpretation im Denken der Aufklärung*, ed. Axel Bühler [Frankfurt: Klostermann, 1994], 192–222) and thereby at the same time attests to the authorship—significant for the present context—for the differentiation of 'historical interpretation' and the edifying, that is, "the current real application for teaching our Christians from out of the correctly explained positions" (Johann Salomon Semler, *Lebenbeschreibung von ihm selbst agbefaßt* [Halle: n.p., 1781], 1:208, cited in Hornig, 198).

All in all, the question of application within the hermeneutics of the Enlightenment hangs closely together with the famously constitutive demand of thinking for oneself, which is connected with an attitude characterized (particularly in the early Enlightenment) as *eclecticism* and demands, in critical examination from out of the tradition, independently and with respect to rational application, a choice—whereby in hermeneutical distinction from Gadamer or Heidegger, and with an eye to implementation, it is not so much the self-worldly oriented process of understanding that occupies the center, but rather the authorial intention, to be conveyed

guided to assume that hermeneutic praxes "were guided in each case by a consciousness of application and an intention of application."[4] Instead, application proves to be "an implicit moment of all understanding,"[5] insofar as it is the task of hermeneutics "to adapt the meaning of a text to the concrete situation in which it speaks."[6] This does not mean that whenever the interpreter faces a text in the above-mentioned sense of adaptation this application primarily characterizes "the relation of something general [in this case the text] that would be pregiven, to a particular situation."[7] In adaptation as we are considering it, it should also not be overhastily reported—as is often done in deconstructivist critiques of hermeneutics—that an exclusive tendency can be seen that in a given case the other of a text transforms into one's own thinking and thus ultimately lapses into the famous Derridean verdict of a metaphysics of presence.

Bearing in mind the introductory discussions of the first part of the present investigation, the fundamental experience of hermeneutics shows itself to be, in contrast, a constitutive tension of belongingness and distance. It is thus determined by that differential play between alterity and familiarity, that the in between comprises the 'true site of hermeneutics,' and that, in the Gadamerian basic principle according to which understanding is always 'understanding otherwise,' finds its expression against teleological or identity-logical tendencies to totalization,[8] without the hermeneutical anticipation of meaning [*Sinnvermutung*] coming to noth-

---

from behind the text's meaning. Therefore we find already laid out in embryo that which is discussed in Schleiermacher's hermeneutics as a principle of psychological understanding. At the same time, questions within the scope of application thus determined, questions like those of possible critieria, methodological approaches, and so on, become pressing objects of reflection, which as a consequence places hermeneutical preference upon elaborations of rule-bound theories of interpretation and accordingly gauges application by the degree of rule-following.

4. Gadamer, *Replik zu "Hermeneutik und Ideologiekritik,"* 261. The refutation enunciated here is aimed against Karl-Otto Apel's rendering of a structure of application (in *Transformation der Philosophie* 2:96–127, esp. 116–120).

5. Gadamer, *Replik*, 260; see also *Wahrheit und Methode*, 313, 346, 407.

6. Gadamer, *Wahrheit und Methode*, 313. Paul Ricoeur speaks analogously of application, which he also designates as *appropriation*, when he speaks of a "hermeneutic bow [that arises] out of life, goes through the literary work, and returns to life" (*Die erzählte Zeit*, 254; see "Appropriation," in *Hermeneutics and the Human Sciences: Essays on Language, Action and Interpretation*, ed. John B. Thompson. [Cambridge: Cambridge University Press, 1993], 182–193).

7. Gadamer, *Wahrheit und Methode*, 329.

8. See ibid., 300. The emphasis of this vacillating play of familiarity and strangeness, which in its function of constituting understanding identifies the strange and the familiar as only relative to each other, belongs, for its function in the principles of understanding, to the fundamentals of hermeneutics as we already find them in Schleiermacher (see "Über den Begriff der

ing, and thus in the end being left with the iterability of signs as a basic structure in the Derridean sense. According to Gadamer, the interpreter wants rather to understand the text in its sense and meaning in this historically enacted, opened between; that is, understand listening to what and how the tradition speaks. For such understanding interpreters cannot disregard themselves and thereby the concrete hermeneutical situation in which they holds themselves. Rather, they must relate the text—in the sense of Ricoeurean appropriation—to its own self-worldly-centered situation, insofar as they want to understand in general.[9]

What is determined structurally in this sense as application, or rather, appropriation, holds not only in the narrower sense of the understanding of texts. In the programmatic outline of the "Natorp-Report," Heidegger grasps the conditions for understanding and interpreting in a phenomenally broader, yet thoroughly structurally congruent and thus applicative sense when, for the "material content of every interpretation, which is the thematic object in the 'how' of its being-interpreted,"[10] he maintains that "it is only then [able] to adequately speak for itself when the particular hermeneutical situation, to which every interpretation is relative, is made available as clearly distinguished."[11] Seen thus, in the mode of a maxim of interpretation, it can thematically claim "to develop the transparency of the respective hermeneutics of the situation . . . and to bring it as hermeneutical within the approach to interpretation."[12] This means, however,

---

Hermeneutik mit Bezug auf F. A. Wolfs Andeutungen und Asts Lehrbuch," in *Hermeneutik und Kritik*, 313) and Dilthey (see *Die Entstehung der Hermeneutik*, 333).

9. While in Gadamer's hermeneutic discourse regarding the problem of application the vertical relation of text (present) and tradition stands in the center of his analytical interest, the necessity of situational applicative connection of acts of understanding within the linguistic event can also easily be indicated horizontally—e.g., within the scope of questions of translation, when, with an eye to an adequate carrying over [*Übertragung*], the level of pure literality does not suffice for a transmission of sense. Thus, to give a simple example, the German "striking a compromise" [*einen Kompromiß schließen*] is translated into French as "*couper la poire en deux*," and when someone is "dead serious" [*todernst*] in German, in French it goes by "*il est serieux comme un pape.*"

10. Heidegger, *Phänomenologische Interpretationen zu Aristoteles*, 237.

11. Ibid.

12. Ibid. For this purpose Heidegger names, as hermeneutical conditions of enactment that—in other words, i.e., in harmony with the phenomenological preference for visualizing concept formation—make up the famous pre-understanding: 1. their more or less expressly assigned and solidified *viewpoint*; 2. a *direction of vision* motivated therefrom, in which the 'as something' ['*als was*'] is determined, in which the object of interpretation is taken preconceptually and the 'whereupon' ['*woraufhin*'] from which it is to be interpreted; 3. a *range of visibil-*

nothing other than that the *"interpreter, who has to do with tradition,* [seeks] *to apply this same thing."*[13]

With this, "application" within the Gadamerian conception refers to the already discussed hermeneutical structure of the fusion of horizons (§ 8), which means that the relation to tradition, which identifies itself as historical consciousness, is thought from out of the sense of enactment of situational understanding as an existential mode of being in the sense of the function of life experience explained above.[14] For a historical consciousness always also reflects its own present, and does so in such a way that it knows "itself as well as the historical other in the correct relations."[15] The relation of tension between tradition and the past produced in historical consciousness from out of the encounter with tradition therefore applies "not in covering over in naive assimilation, but rather in consciously unfolding it."[16] With a view to Gadamer's approach to the hermeneutical contribution to application, that means that this hermeneutics does not level out the historical difference of sense horizons just in favor of a merely affirmative traditional relation, as is more often maintained in literature, seduced by its devoted but not always sharply contoured diction.[17] In this affirmation, solely a determinate and largely uncritical mode of historical consciousness imprints itself, on account of which it also is not suitable for describing in general the structural principle of that continuity that is linearly datable within time but is not yet thoroughly unconditioned by a sense horizon. Therefore, the applicative task of historical understanding consists in communicating the impact of history in an effective-historical consciousness.

---

ity, isolated with viewpoint and visual direction, within which a given claim to objectivity of interpretation operates" (ibid.).

13. Gadamer, *Wahrheit und Methode,* 329. Emphasis added.

14. "Historical Dasein always has a situation, a perspective and a horizon. It is like in painting: perspective, the ordering of things according to 'nearer' and 'farther,' includes a visual point that one must adopt. Likewise, one steps into a relation of being [*Seinsverhältnis*] to things and belongs to their order, wherein one refers oneself to them" (Gadamer, *Das Problem der Geschichte,* in *GW,* 2:35).

15. Gadamer, *Wahrheit und Methode,* 310.

16. Ibid., 311. "The situation of interpretation, as the understanding appropriation of the past, is always such a living present" (Heidegger, *Phänomenologische Interpretationen zu Aristoteles,* 237)

17. See, e.g., Dietrich Böhler, "Philosophische Hermeneutik und hermeneutische Methode," in *Text und Applikation,* 502; Habermas, *Theorie des kommunikativen Handelns* 1:195.

Effective-historical consciousness, as has already become visible earlier under other perspectives, is designated by a peculiar ambiguity. For it is both a consciousness effected and determined in the course of history by history itself and "a consciousness of this being-effected and determined itself."[18] In the sense of the character of the task of application, the latter opens up the possibility of now uncovering, in reflexive recourse to the hermeneutical situation, the being-effected as the historicity of factical enactments of life in their concrete structures and along with it, as well as sounding out the limits of understanding within the space of its lifeworldly possibilities (cf. §§ 31–32). Put summarily, understanding proves to be "a mode of effecting and knows itself as such an effect,"[19] and thus the application is determined reflexively as a decisive structure of the self-understanding sense of enactment of factical life in a lifeworldly context of significance. The application is thereby one (to speak with Heidegger's famous term of formal indication, *equiprimordial*) with the self-interpretation, whereby the one alternately demands the other. For that reason, one can also speak of a structural coincidence in understanding and application.

Therefore the application is in the view of its task of communication *always presentist*, yet not such that the word is related to a historical realization that would conjure up an omnipresence in which historical difference would be equalized. In an addendum to *Wahrheit und Methode*, Gadamer refers to Kierkegaard's concept of *simultaneity*—in defense against Hegel's intended thoughts of total mediation directed to a closed system—for the clarification of his effective-historical mediating function of application.[20] According to this notion, as Gadamer elsewhere explains, historical truth is not just "the shining-through of an idea," in the Hegelian sense, "but rather the binding character of an irretrievable decision."[21] For a hermeneutically initiated connection to Kierkegaardian simultaneity, it is decisive as a structural moment that it must as such and above all be accomplished.[22] That means, seen formally, dialogically relating interpreter and

18. Hans-Georg Gadamer, *Wahrheit und Methode, Vorwort zur 2. Auflage*, in *GW*, 2:444.

19. Gadamer, *Wahrheit und Methode*, 346.

20. See Gadamer, *Wahrheit und Methode, Nachwort zur 3. Auflage (1972)* in *GW*, 2:471. The connection to Kierkegaard's presentist ideas can already be discerned early on, in the 1930 treatise *Praktisches Wissen* (*GW* 5:243).

21. Gadamer, *Das Problem der Geschichte*, 35.

22. See Gadamer, *Nachwort zur 3. Auflage*, 471.

interpreted to one another in the space of the established being-simultaneous [*Zugleichsein*] so that therein the discontinuity of the horizons of sense remains preserved for mediating understanding in it, which itself is already indicated phenomenally in it, so that the understanding always already *modifies* what is to be understood in the enactment of understanding from out of its situational binding.

With regard to the named aspect of presentism, it can be structurally recognized therein qua methodological instruction what Gadamer thinks as the "controlled enactment of the horizonal fusion," in which he sees "the wakefulness of effective-historical consciousness" formulated as a hermeneutical contribution of reflection.[23] In Heidegger's approach to the hermeneutics of facticity, that means the "past opens itself only according to the measure of resoluteness and the force of being able to disclose, about which a present decrees."[24] Seen thus, for Heidegger the effective power [*Wirkungsmacht*] of the past is based upon its future, "in the ever-achieved and concretely developed originariness of questioning [*Frageursprünglichkeit*] through which it can become a model awakening constantly a new present as a problem."[25]

If one realizes at this point that which is explicated in the factic-hermeneutical turn to a phenomenology of the lifeworld and, at one with it, in the approach to a hermeneutics of the self, then the phenomenon of application—thus, the question of concrete implementation—proves to be a central problem of hermeneutical reflection, insofar as this is not caught in the cogital immanence of a transcendental reflection based in absolute subjectivity, a reflection in which ultimately, despite all tendencies toward self-immunization, "a little tag end of the world"[26]—or however it may be defined, whether as life, history, or even body—in some way might yet intensify the problem. This means, on the positive side, that hermeneutical reflection circumvents the approach of a transmundane sovereignty of the subject of the concretely factical, and as one with it thereby also limits its validity claims, wherein it discovers the boundaries of knowability.[27] Her-

23. Gadamer, *Wahrheit und Methode*, 312.
24. Heidegger, *Phänomenologische Interpretationen zu Aristoteles*, 237.
25. Ibid., 238.
26. Husserl, *Cartesianische Meditationen*, 63 (emphasis deleted).
27. It is at this point that the traditional claim to autonomy, raised out of the sovereignty of subjectivity, as Käte Meyer-Drawe (*Illusionen von Autonomie: Diesseits von Ohnmacht und Allmacht des Ich* [Munich: Kirchheim, 1990]) shows in a multifaceted way, proves to be problem-

meneutical reflection consciously develops its historicity in the midst of and from out of the concrete lifeworldly historical manifold of relations of sense in particular contexts of life-experience. In other words, application as task includes within itself a concretization. It produces in such a way that, in the sense of phenomenological explication, whose philosophical setting carries out the *formal indication,* self-understanding discovers itself hermeneutically in the process of self-having as a *situational "I,"* and does so in the historically enacting belongingness to the sociocultural life environment, in and from out of which the self understands itself and at the same time applies in understanding as a function of life experience.[28]

Therefore its sociologization, psychologization, and the like are not to be spoken of in relation to philosophy tendentially.[29] Rather, over against

---

atic, insofar as through the demonstration of being involved experientially and dispositively in lifeworldly and historical constellations the oppositive settings of 'I/world,' 'inner/outer,' 'subject/object,' 'own/other,' etc., come to light in the questionability of their phenomenal capacity for determination. In the process, it is not to be said that heteronomy simply steps into the place of autonomy, that the human is thus nothing but completely dependent, or rather determined, by this or that set of circumstances. Rather, this proves to be, in philosophical reflection on the ontological position of the self in the fabric of the world, as we have seen—in the capacity for self-determination—that which Heidegger identifies in the counterplay of facticity and existence and determines in its most famous form as 'thrown projection' [*geworfenen Entwurf*].

As such, human life is woven into sociohistorical configurations in which—borrowing from Foucault, who describes therein the field of activity of his late thinking—"the forms and modalities of relations to onself . . . through which the individual constitutes and recognizes itself as a subject" (*Der Gebrauch der Lüste,* vol. 2 of *Sexualität und Wahrheit,* [Frankfurt: Suhrkamp, 1990], 12), take shape. And this in such a way that the modes of self-formation can and must always be responded to by an individual, which, appealed to in a Nietzschean manner as a *'dividuum,'* can no longer recur to an undivided, autonomous substance, but rather experiences itself antecedently, relationally in its play space of possibilities as limited, and precisely through vital, biographically and culturally historical irreducibilities.

28. Only insofar as application, thus considered, is an integral structural moment of existentially identified understanding can the question of application, in the sense of a τέχνη, come into play, guiding action, as a concrete solution to the problem. At this point the structurally constitutive proximity of hermeneutics to practical philosophy unfolds, which the early Heidegger, as much as Gadamer, regardless of significant differences, develops in the interpretively shaped turn to Aristotelian φρόνησις. On this relation in Gadamer, see Günter Figal, "Verstehen als geschichtliche Phronesis," *Internationale Zeitschrift für Philosophie* (1992), 1:24–37; also Chang, *Geschichte, Verstehen und Praxis,* 119–123. On the conceptual difference between Heidegger and Gadamer emerging in the thematization of Aristotelian φρόνησις, which is particularly evident in Heidegger's virtual disregard of the ethical virtues extraordinarily significant for Aristotle, see Figal, *Der Sinn des Verstehens,* 35–38.

29. That hermeneutics, in adopting the problem of application *as philosophy,* in no way loses its resonance, or rather, its relevance, within the social sciences, can be seen via the comparison

that, application, or rather appropriation, as a structural moment of interpretation considered in terms of its existential determination qua mode of enactment of understanding, is motivated in regard to the functional ontological structure of situationality in its adaptive force and related to philosophical hermeneutics, which in *formal indication* as its *form of enactment* possesses the manner in which philosophy works in the "'how' of now-being [*Jetztseins*]"[30] and in this sense becomes situative.

If one associates praxis in a broad sense with *situative being*, the philosophical task of determining the structures of factical life in formally indicating concepts thus distinguishes the hermeneutical situation, or rather philosophy's becoming situative, in its respective development and implementation. Taken from a traditional perspective, that means *the praxis of philosophy is its enactment as theory*—philosophy is reflective action. The innovative moment of the Heideggerian conception of formal indication is thereby certainly not grasped descriptively in any adequate sense. This becomes apparent only when in relation to the formal indication, as Heidegger names it in another place, its *"character of hermeneutical indication"*[31] is seen.

In this function, the specific aspect of situative becoming in the present context becomes visible, an aspect that neither ends in a mere actionism nor shuts itself up in the bearing of reflection, in order, after a Hegelian fashion, to see the enactment in the being-with [*Bei-sich*] of the concept. What formal indication as a methodological "basic sense of all philosophical concepts and conceptual contexts"[32] can achieve according to its own essence with regard to the posing of the tasks of a lifeworldly hermeneutics, in contrast, is to indicate "the possible understanding and the possible conceivability of the structures of Dasein accessible in such an understanding."[33] With this, by means of the formal indication, a hermeneutics of facticity avoids "an uncritical lapse into a determinate concep-

---

presented by Alan How (*The Habermas-Gadamer Debate and the Nature of the Social* [Aldershot: Averbury, 1995], 63–67) of the thematization of the structure of application in Gadamer and Peter Winch, whose influence on sociology is famously based on his work *The Idea of a Social Science and Its Relation to Philosophy* (Frankfurt: Suhrkamp, 1974).

30. Heidegger, *Ontologie*, GA 63, 18.

31. Heidegger, *Logik: Die Frage nach der Wahrheit,* ed. Walter Biemel, GA 21 (Frankfurt: Klostermann, 1976), 410 (emphasis added).

32. Heidegger, *Wegmarken*, GA 9, 10.

33. Heidegger, GA 21, 410.

tion of existence like Kierkegaard's or Nietzsche's . . . in order to win the possibility of pursuing a genuine sense of the phenomena of existence and to explicate this pursuit."[34]

Insofar as the specific philosophical thematization of factical life does not aim at its object-character from without, this means for Heidegger that the "fixing of the basic historical bearing of interpretation [in the sense of concrete application] grows out of the explication of the sense of philosophical research that opens its space of possibility"[35] as the 'upon which' [*Worauf*] of the hermeneutical relational attitude.[36] This is, as was already shown, the explicit enactment of a "fundamental movement of factical life,"[37] within which it maintains itself constantly as "a fundamental 'how' of life itself."[38] Seen in this way, the formal indication of philosophy is not merely an antecedent and purely abstractive mode of explication over and against the concrete. Rather, it itself belongs to phenomenological explication, in the sense of the possibility to be gained as a methodological structural moment of a hermeneutics of facticity itself, insofar as it, even if indifferent to content, nonetheless, in pointing ahead, ought to "indicate in advance the relation to the phenomenon."[39] This takes place in such a way that the pregiven phenomena of factical life experience, from out of their tendency to reification by means of formal indication, attained to a mode of experience in which "the relation and enactment of the phenomenon [are] *not* determined in advance [but rather] held in abeyance"[40] for an explication of the phenomenological totality of sense (the sense of content, relation, and enactment) that is not prejudiced, but is instead open in its enactment character for what is experienced particularly in experience. But that means that philosophical investigation for Heidegger is not first cotemporalized in subsequent application, but rather "in its enactment cotemporalizes the particular concrete being of life in itself."[41]

In what Heidegger speaks of conceptually as *cotemporalization* [*Mitzeitigung*], that applicative structure constitutive for understanding evinces

---

34. Heidegger, *GA* 9, 11.

35. Heidegger, *Phänomenologische Interpretationen zu Aristoteles*, 239.

36. See Heidegger, *GA* 60, 59–62.

37. Heidegger, *Phänomenologische Interpretationen zu Aristoteles*, 239.

38. Heidegger, *GA* 61, 80.

39. Heidegger, *GA* 60, 63.

40. Ibid., 64. "The specification of the sense of 'method' is to be held open in formally indicated meaning for actual concrete determinations" (Heidegger, *Wegmarken*, *GA* 9, 9).

41. Heidegger, *Phänomenologische Interpretationen zu Aristoteles*, 239.

itself, insofar as the "upon which of the care of life"[42] has always already adapted itself in view of the exhibited motion of care of factical life—with its intentional directed sense of enactment qua 'being-out-for-something' as the 'with which' of caring access, that is, the particular historical factical lifeworld encountered in the character of significance—and in the manifoldness of its environmental, with-worldly, and self-worldly modes as the possible directions of care of having oneself. The situational relation constitutively exhibited for application is conceptually grasped by Heidegger in the summer of 1923 in the framework of the hermeneutics of facticity as the *awhileness of temporal particularity* [*die Jeweiligkeit*], that, as a starting point of the self-interpretation of facticity is, according to its determinacy, '*the today*' [*das Heute*]—which as "the ever-tarrying [Je-Ver-weilen] in the present, which is ever its own"[43] thus itself becomes the appropriative determination of human Dasein.[44]

However, as this ever one's own, human factical life is thus *always already historical* as concrete Dasein. Thought historically in this way, human Dasein is, as Heidegger already puts it after Marburg on the threshold of his departure, "being-in-the-world,"[45] yet such that being-in-the-world is as "being lived from the world,"[46] and admittedly in view of "everyday presence."[47] Therefore, the interpretive approach of a hermeneutics of facticity finds itself always already referred from a thematically given object to a today concretely determined from out of the awhileness of everyday presence, which is determined by Heidegger ontologically as the structure

42. Ibid., 240.

43. Heidegger, *Ontologie, GA 63*, 29.

44. This means, for one, that "factical Dasein is what it is always only as its own, not the Dasein-in-general of some kind of general humanity, to care for which is merely a dreamed task" (Heidegger, *Phänomenologische Interpretationen zu Aristoteles*, 239; see also *Ontologie, GA 63*, 18). And for another, each is as such always only and already a present, a contemporary self, which is why it is only something dreamt to imagine that one belongs, for example, to another time and epoch in accordance with its supposed character. For the temporal distance and thus the discontinuity of historical horizons of sense can as little be bridged as contemporaneity can be betrayed, and at most it can be critically illuminated in historical reflection. Another such form of wishcasting in relation to one's own person, differently placed in time and history, that one can find clearly and consistently expressed in the stylizing of personal forms of life is evidenced—in the factical unfeasibility of an exit out of one's own time—by an immediate applicative relation to the present situation, yet now in the mode of a perceived and chosen distance as a possible self-denial in the face of contemporary tendencies and demands.

45. Heidegger, *Ontologie, GA 63*, 29.

46. Ibid.

47. Ibid.

of the how of facticity as *'our time.'* Its explication demands a *hermeneutics of the situation,* according to its philosophical claim, as can be easily seen according to what has been said above. Seen thus, the tasks of a lifeworldly hermeneutics are also to be formulated in the demonstration of the concrete structures of the historical world.

§ 39. *The Critical Sense: On the Task of Phenomenological Destruktion*

The interpretedness [*Ausgelegtheit*] of today becomes, in the perspective of effective-historical consciousness in the applicative sense, a thematic focal point of hermeneutical analysis. Heidegger thereby aims, in the 'presence of the proximal' [*Gegenwart des Zunächst*], at its basic phenomena of 'everydayness' and 'publicness,' primarily with an eye to the situation-character of *das Man* marked out conceptually and thematically in the "Natorp-Report," which, seen applicatively, concerns factical life as much in its circumspection as in its self-interpretation. Thus, a phenomenological hermeneutics of facticity finds itself positioned before the task "of breaking up the traditional and prevalent interpretedness according to its hidden motives, inexplicit tendencies and interpretive paths, and to press forward into the retrenching regression to the original motive sources of explication."[48] This dismantling of masks and dissimulations is the task of what Heidegger famously calls *phenomenological Destruktion.* It has already been thematized in a different manner and has—in methodological implementation with regard to the present investigation—from the beginning found its mode of enactment expressed as historical hermeneutics.

Heidegger concisely formulates his methodological credo in the thesis: "*Hermeneutics effects its task only on the path of Destruktion.*"[49] It is decisive that *Destruktion,* as this regression, is always a *"directed* dismantling,"[50] since, in accordance with the hermeneutical prestructure of understanding, it is as such essentially nothing other than "*anticipatory* . . . and therewith [cannot be] *ultimately original* [or] *ultimately decisive.*"[51] This marking

48. Heidegger, *Phänomenologische Interpretationen zu Aristoteles,* 249.
49. Ibid.
50. Heidegger, *Phänomenologie der Anschauung, GA* 59, 35 (emphasis supplied).
51. Ibid. (emphasis supplied).

of a limit regarding the capacity of achieving *Destruktion* is can be validly fixed as an insight in order not to misinterpret the discourse, consistently co-led by Heidegger in the context of 'regression' and 'dismantling,' of what is originary therein in the sense of an ultimate grounding.

The restriction of the philosophically thematizing look in anticipation is not to be construed in a narrow sense. Rather, it refers, as the motivating and structuring 'preaspect' of understanding in the sense of destruction— "as a basic component of phenomenological philosophizing"[52]—to the "phenomenon of the 'preliminary sketch,'"[53] which is to be grasped in the broader sense of the hermeneutical situation. Formulated as a task, it has to do with demonstrating "how sense-manifoldness and sense-unity are cocharacterized through the preliminary sketch."[54] In the process, manifoldness and unity of sense are intelligible and understood only "as explicated from out of existence,"[55] an existence towards which *Destruktion* thus possesses its sense of direction. In the sense of this explicative function, determined in preliminary sketching and in anticipation as "'pursuance in an understanding that provokes vigilance,'"[56] phenomenological *Destruktion* as a method contrasts, according to Heidegger, with "the *inductive* (thing-object inducing) epagogical method"[57] and its guiding idea of ascending from individuals (qua particulars) to the general. Seen thus, the hermeneutical sense of *Destruktion* is fulfilled precisely in its explicative function.

In the determinacy of *Destruktion,* as already seen in another context, philosophical investigation for Heidegger is "in a radical sense '*historical*' [*historisches*] knowing,"[58] "insofar as it [understands] the mode of objectivity and the mode of being of its thematic 'upon which,'"[59] that is, the facticity of life, or rather, "the objectivity of the human, [namely] factical life . . . in historical-historic [*historisch-geschichtlichen*] concretion."[60] Tied to this is the notion that for philosophical investigation qua *Destruktion* the debate with its own history belongs to the essential existence of a her-

52. Ibid.
53. Ibid.
54. Ibid.
55. Ibid.
56. Ibid.
57. Ibid.
58. Heidegger, *Phänomenologische Interpretationen zu Aristoteles,* 249.
59. Heidegger, *GA* 61, 172.
60. Heidegger, *Phänomenologische Interpretationen zu Aristoteles,* 249.

meneutically applied phenomenological approach. The factically pregiven philosophical positions in accordance with the appropriative determination of the point of departure of a hermeneutics of facticity are always already thematized by Heidegger, in a destructive relation, with regard to the originariness of this hermeneutics' own particular relation to existence.[61]

When Heidegger speaks of the notion that the enactment of *Destruktion* in its function regarding pregiven philosophy thoroughly recognizes the "continuity of the history of ideas,"[62] that thus reflects the insight that hermeneutic philosophy itself cannot be isolated over and against content, relation, and enactment of factical connections of life experience. Rather, philosophy is always "an element of *factical life experience*,"[63] and in such a way that "philosophical concepts, principles, and modes of observation [intermingle], more or less extensively, with factical life experience"[64]— *intermingle with [durchsetzen]*, not compose [*zusammensetzen*]. The same applies mutatis mutandis for science, art, and religion. In addition, methodological consciousness protects the approach of *Destruktion* from "playing the fool on one's own"[65] and naively thinking that "one could begin from the outset in philosophy today or at any point and be so radical that one can do without all so-called tradition."[66]

Seen in this way, the oft-cited phenomenological view to the 'things themselves' in the context of the hermeneutics of facticity means, for Heidegger, nothing other than "always to enact more originarily one's own factical situation and in this enactment to prepare for genuineness."[67] In so doing, the recognition of tradition that we have mentioned is as little determined for Heidegger through affirmation as it is for Gadamer. On the contrary, in tracing the *destruktive* debate of philosophical contexts of tradition back to their sources, tradition is being dismantled in order to make transparent the respective effective-historical motivating contexts in their having-become [*Gewordensein*]. For Heidegger, this laying-open return is, considered philosophically in terms of its form of enactment, "fundamen-

<hr>

61. See Heidegger, *Phänomenologie der Anschauung*, GA 59, 37.
62. Heidegger, GA 59, 29.
63. Ibid., 36.
64. Ibid., 37.
65. Gadamer, *Wahrheit und Methode*, 2.
66. Heidegger, GA 59, 29. See §§ 3, 26.
67. Heidegger, GA 59, 30. On Heidegger's approach to the 'things themselves,' see § 27.

tally *historical critique*."[68] The destructive-critical recognition of tradition is, so conceived, "the proper path on which the present must encounter its own basic movement, and encounter it in such a way that the constant question emanates, from out of history, of how far it (the present) itself is concerned with appropriations of radical basic possibilities of experience and their interpretations."[69]

68. Heidegger, *GA* 59, 30.

69. Heidegger, *Phänomenologische Interpretationen zu Aristoteles*, 249 (emphasis supplied). At times, however, this possibility is virtually concealed by Heidegger's own accomplishments. Heidegger's sustained, far-reaching ignoring of Roman-Latin antiquity at all stages of his path of thinking offers a particularly marked example of this. His famously intensive and early turn to Augustine, in its uncontested eminent meaning (see Jean Grondin, "Hermeneutische Wahrheit: Heidegger und Augustinus," in *Die Frage nach der Wahrheit*, ed. Ewald Richter [Frankfurt: Klostermann, 1997], 165–177), is considered rather the exception that proves the rule from this perspective.

Seen more exactly, it is also in Heidegger no neutralizing disregard, but rather by and large a constant devaluation—to be taken heuristically in *singulare tantum* [an uncountable noun or word referring to a unique object]—of the Roman in favor of a thoroughgoing valorization of the Greek beginning of Western European thinking, which famously composes, at the other end with Nietzsche later on, the clasp of his outline of a history of metaphysics. It would be a worthwhile task to investigate more precisely what Heidegger's lumping together of Roman-Latin thinking—which, with a view to the Greeks, is not simply deprivation but also essentially constructive transformation—thus leaves out of consideration in the way of possibilities and impulses for the formation of his own thinker's position (See Franco Chiereghin, "Der griechische Anfang Europas und die Frage der Romanitas: Der Weg Heideggers zu einem anderen Anfang," in *Europa und die Philosophie*, ed. Hans-Helmuth Gander (Frankfurt: Klostermann, 1993) 197–223).

However it may be determined in its details, in the given context, the circumstance of lasting significance for this critical reference is that for the *time-diagnostic function* constitutively bound to application and destruction, it is to be noticed that the relevant fields of explication here, namely culture, history, politics, economics, and others taken effective-historically in their mutual influencing, are multivalent and, seen historically in the perspective of possible ancient roots or analogies, prove for the most part to have been passed down materially from Greek *and* Roman sources. Instead of this, when in the excavation of Greek origins of interpretations of life Heidegger neglects the effective power of the Romans in its relation to the present—one need only think of the sphere of jurisprudence—historical consciousness thus distorts itself therein for such contexts and developments. Reflected in this path of vision is the tendency discernible in Heidegger's philosophical attitude to evade (or rather, to step behind it toward its origins) the factically constitutive, formative *rationality* within the relation to the present, whose mode of givenness, however, is mediated in no other way than effective-historically.

The price for eschewing an effective-historically precise genealogy of the forces forming the situation is that—in the sense of hermeneutical application—a *concrete* philosophical discussion of present questions, as can be found for example in Ricoeur or Gadamer, is de facto not provided by Heidegger. Untouched by this, however, remains the circumstance that the approach of the hermeneutics of facticity in itself—and thus Heidegger overplaying his own concrete achievements to some extent—grounds this possibility qua formal indication in a

Human existence, maintaining and enacting itself in lifeworldly contexts of experience, formulates itself particularly as its *being-in-history*, and this because the human is thought from the beginning as a historical creature [*Wesen*]. The *entanglement of history and the present*, as Heidegger takes it here, grounds itself, as already discussed, in the fact that it lies in the idea of facticity that the exit out of one's own time makes this, as the today of the awhileness of temporal particularity, into the actual object of philosophical investigation. As has since been shown, the ownness of one's self is being-in-the-world as environmental, with-worldly, and self-worldly experience centered in the present horizon of respective referential connections, whose character of significance motivates a given direction of questioning after the self.

The world qua lifeworld has formed itself historically. To this extent, a hermeneutics of facticity must thematize the self- as world-understanding enactment of factical Dasein under the perspective of its historicity, wherein historicity is also coimplemented in the interpretation of interpretations, that is, in hermeneutics itself. The basic finitude of human knowing indicated therein approaches Nietzsche's insight, properly understood, into the "interpretive character of all events."[70] At the same time, this state of affairs codetermines the fact that in the wake of the lifeworld—never to be finally sensibly illuminated through manifold strands of tradition interwoven with one another—the hermeneutics of facticity has to implement its phenomenological enlightenment as a 'hermeneutics of the case' [*Hermeneutik der Lage*] and therein brings history into account conceptually as a "*history of concealment* [*Verdeckungsgeschichte*]."[71]

Heidegger develops the primary methodological arsenal of a hermeneutics of facticity in *Destruktion* as a historical critique in this sense, about which Jean Grondin stresses that as "historical *Destruktion* [it is] the actual contribution of hermeneutics to phenomenology,[72] namely, as a critical removal of concealments in the interpretedness of factical life determined through strands of tradition. And for the ontology of facticity as hermeneutics of the self, insofar as the basis of its interpretation is the

---

philosophical manner such that the relation to the situation is placed on a *qualitatively new hermeneutical basis*, which sees Heidegger's ontology of facticity, as already indicated, according to the view of the 'world-concept of philosophy' in line with Kant and Hegel.

70. Nietzsche, *Nachgelassene Fragmente—Herbst 1885 bis Herbst 1887*, in *KGW*, 8:1, 34. See § 11.
71. Heidegger, *GA* 63, 75 (emphasis supplied).
72. Grondin, "Hermeneutik der Faktizität," 174.

respective today [*das jeweilige Heute*], it expresses itself as a *hermeneutics of the situation,* as has become evident in the present discussion.

Dasein's becoming-accessible as being-open for the ownness of a free self-relation, which occurs in the enactment of *Destruktion,* must be critically extracted, in the sense of a having-of-oneself (see § 35), from a tendency to self-alienation, to be grasped ontologically. Seen thus, self-alienation is not something that can be totally removed. It belongs constitutively to the reality of human Dasein within which above all the possibility forms "of becoming and being *understanding* for oneself"[73] as what has been called "Dasein's *vigilance* for itself"[74]—which, however, will never lead to an ultimately meaningful transparency of myself for myself.[75]

Therefore, Heidegger's early hermeneutics, as Grondin has insightfully worked out, strikes "throughout the tone of an *Ideologiekritik,* which in regard to the proper vigilance to be cultivated rebels against the self-alienation of Dasein."[76] Seen thus, the "critique already springing forth through

73. Heidegger, *GA* 63, 15.

74. Ibid.

75. A simple look at life-historical relations shows that I will never be able to fully secure myself in the transparency of how and who I have been. The memory of the preceding day is already, in its perspectival segments, also always the finding (invention) of my active imagination. And the initial phase of life, so eminently significant for the development of one's own personality, guarantees to me as knowing only over the evidence of a third, which itself in turn can only convey itself to me in the refraction of a temporal distance, as for example of a personally and functionally disposed attitudinal aspect in the system of the family (father, mother, siblings, etc.). And when Heidegger further speaks of the "mask of public interpretedness" (*Ontologie, GA* 63, 32) in which I confront myself and accordingly formulate my questions and claims within a predisposition that I hermeneutically open—a predisposition that is destructive for the "vigilant view for oneself"—but can never eliminate, there thus shows itself therein, as an appearance, that basic comportment that is unfolded in *Sein und Zeit*'s fundamental existential structure of falling [*Verfallen*] as the falling away [*Abfallen*] of the originally forming possibility of a self-determination. See also Heidegger, *Ontologie, GA* 63, 32, 35–47.

76. Grondin, "Hermeneutik der Faktizität," 171; see also Grondin, "Das junghegelianische und ethische Motiv in Heideggers Hermeneutik der Faktizität," in *Wege und Irrwege des neueren Umganges mit Heideggers Werk,* ed. István M. Fehér [Berlin: Duncker & Humblot, 1991] 141–150. The critical ideological turn against the forms of self-alienation for the sake of an autonomous self-determination strived for through *Destruktion* harbors within it that potential in which, in addition to Grondin, authors such as Manfred Riedel (see *Hören auf die Sprache,* 131–162) have recognized a genuinely ethical approach to questioning. In his hermeneutics of facticity Heidegger does not expand it into a materially developed ethics, yet it nonetheless becomes so through the fact that in the place of an ahistorical subjectivity, historical Dasein provides, in the praxis of its care, the starting-point of philosophical questioning, and in maintaining its care for its own existence, thought in such a way, the *human* rediscovers itself *as a being of the ought,* with which Heidegger on his side has jointly cleared the path toward the rehabilitation of practical philosophy in the twentieth century.

the concrete enactment of *Destruktion* [does not apply to] the fact *that* in general we stand within a tradition, but rather at *how* we do,"[77] which as an intentional relation dynamic in itself proves to be at the same time history qua tradition as a constituent of facticity.

For human being-in-the-world as essentially historical—that is, for the 'how' of its standing within tradition—it remains thoroughly open in detail whether the relation to tradition forms itself in a way that is concretely factically affirmative, negative, or simply self-forgetting. In any case, it is impossible to get around the fact that the today functions as a temporal field of crystallization for this relation, namely as a point of intersection of diverse strands of tradition, which regulate self-understanding and world-understanding in its antecedent interpretedness. For that reason, the *Destruktion* of tradition is as "*critique of history . . . always only critique of the present.*"[78] This means that the *Destruktion* of tradition as a critique of history always stands under the applicative foregrasping of an *illumination of the present.* To this extent, phenomenological destruction in its interpretation as hermeneutical understanding also never reaches tradition as itself—that is, what has been handed down in a historical in-itself—but rather always only in relation to its function as that which is passed down in a tradition for present life. On the other side, the present—coconstituted essentially through contexts of tradition—cannot simply be deduced from out of tradition either.

As Heidegger emphasizes, philosophical investigation (and that now means hermeneutical-historical investigation) is according to its ownmost determination something that "a 'time'—insofar as it is not merely concerned about it in terms of development—can never borrow from another; but also something that—having understood itself and its possible sense of achievement in human Dasein—never seeks to come forth with the claim of the right and ability to relieve the burden and distress of radical questioning for coming ages."[79] There is thus only meaning within history

---

77. Heidegger, *Phänomenologische Interpretationen zu Aristoteles*, 249 f.

78. Ibid., 239 (emphasis supplied).

79. Ibid., 238. In his demonstration of the present as an ur-phenomenon of human life in view of the concrete factical enactments of existence, Gerd Haeffner links what can be read here as an affirmation of the demand to live in the present and to take on its challenges, to the enabling conditions for one appropriate approach to living in the present, namely 'letting the past be' (see Haeffner, *In der Gegenwart leben*, 159–162) and at one with this, 'letting the future be' (163). In this 'letting-be' there is as much a negative as a positive connotation in both directions. For to 'letting-be' there belongs "on the one side a letting-go that does not deny to what

insofar as contexts can be clarified structurally in their referential relations in view of Dasein's self-worldly possibilities of experience. Consequently, one cannot speak of a general sense of history. Seen thus, it is decisive for Heidegger's approach that the originary realm of everything historical is centered in human existence, and this for the reason that existence is in its essence historical.

§ 40. History as the Organon of Understanding Life

The taking up of human existence as the originary realm of the historical, *existentiell historicity,* is the relation on which the criterion must be established, which in the sense of its relevance for Dasein allows just as much for an adequate positing of the question of history, or more precisely of its forms of appearance in factical life, as for the question concerning the philosophical possibilities of thematization. It is thereby clear from the start that history is in no way to be hypostatized into a historical subject.[80]

is let go its being what it is, thus a release from the attempt to change something. And on the other side, a positive admission belongs to it that is not a making, but beyond a merely negative release, is yet an active letting-arrive" (ibid., 159).

From another perspective, the question concerning the ethos of the present in view of an art of living to be designed, Foucault speaks of the fact that a "period that is not ours . . . possesses no exemplary value . . . nothing to which one can return" (Foucault, "Zur Genealogie der Ethik: Ein Überblick über laufende Arbeiten," in Hubert L. Dreyfus and Paul Rabinow, *Michel Foucault: Jenseits von Strukturalismus und Hermeneutik* [Weinheim: Beltz, 1994], 271), which however in Foucault releases one just as little as in Heidegger or Haeffner, in the passage through the insight into the historicity of human life, from engagement with the past as from openness to the future in the sense of the creative constitution of the present.

80. Considered historically, history arrives at this subject-function (relevant for a philosophy of history) first from the time of the Enlightenment, in which the collective singular was developed and broadened among the Germans around 1780. This movement stands in connection with the detachment, produced historically therein over a long period of time, away from history grasped in its course as an occurrence of salvation [*Heilgeschehen*] and, in support of Augustine's *De civitate Dei*, from theological history, which in Jacques Bénigne Bossuet's *Discours sur l'histoire universelle* in 1681 once more constituted a powerful apotheosis. The aforementioned disengagement from theological "fetters" took place under the sign of the Enlightenment by means of a conception that recognized in natural reason a notion of history dwelling within it. With this step emancipating history from its theological connection to divine providence, the presuppositions for a philosophy of history were created, presuppositions that found a first testimony in Voltaire's 1753 *Essai sur les moeurs et l'esprit des nations et sur le principaux faits de l'histoire depuis Charlemagne jusqu'à Louis XIII*, which he later published as an introduction, and thereby added the concept forming the 1765 essay, *La philosophie de l'histoire*. See Karl Löwith, *Weltgeschichte und Heilsgeschehen*, esp. 114–125, 150–158; Rüdiger

Rather, history is to be conceived as a *process* that, as Dieter Henrich formulates it, is to be determined as *"sui-sufficient"*[81] [*suisuffizient*] and in this formally structural sense appears, according to its status, not dissimilar to Spinoza's understanding of substance. This means that history as an occurrence determined by unavailability is to be conceived through itself and also only through itself, without therefore, to borrow a phrase from Lyotard, having to promote it at the level of a "grand narrative."[82]

In the manner of this processual character, according to which history appears as a dispositive of our possibilities for self-understanding in the sense of a historical apriori—Heidegger speaks of an "organon of understanding life"[83]—it is of decisive significance for hermeneutical explication to remain aware that this process-character does not in itself already imply that "sui-sufficiency [must] be interpreted as the self-revelation of the rationality of self-being [*Selbstsein*].[84] Within a processual notion of history, such teleological approaches take shape on the presupposition that the in-itself of the process of history, as the factically contingent realm of enactment in human life, in truth ultimately implies, beyond this medial, if you will (in the sense of the elementary and alimentary), that human history is always at the same time also 'history *for* humans.'

Such a *teleological 'for'* lives out of the assumption of a sense of finality or origin that can be seen at least in principle, and can differently realize itself properly in individual cases. Thus, it can incarnate itself theologically as in Augustine in the transcendently guaranteed occurrence of salvation. A final sense in history can, however, also be explicated philosophically, as in the best-known case, Hegel, where in the gradation of the self-revelation of absolute spirit, the historical stages in the modes of appearance of philosophy, art, religion, and so on manifest "the spirit of the age."[85] Taken up as tradition, this creates "not an unmoved stone sculpture,"[86] but rather "a

Bubner, *Geschichtsprozesse und Handlungsnormen: Untersuchungen zur praktischen Philosophie* (Frankfurt: Suhrkamp, 1984), 72–92; Hans Blumenberg, *Lebenszeit und Weltzeit*, 218–248.

81. Dieter Henrich, "Selbsterhaltung und Geschichtlichkeit," in *Subjektivität und Selbsterhaltung. Beiträge zur Diagnose der Moderne*, ed. Hans Ebeling, (Frankfurt: Suhrkamp, 1996), 312.

82. Cf. Jean-François Lyotard, *Das postmoderne Wissen: Ein Bericht* (Graz: Böhlau, 1986), esp. 96–111.

83. Heidegger, *Grundprobleme der Phänomenologie*, GA 58, 256. See above, § 35.

84. Henrich, "Selbsterhaltung und Geschichtlichkeit," 313.

85. Hegel, *Vorlesungen über die Geschichte der Philosophie I*, in *Werke*,18:74.

86. Ibid., 21.

powerful current"[87] on Hegel's thinking, and for him his life is the deed that allows him to know the exhibition of our becoming in the manifestations of the course of history, in the final sense of science that he has grounded.[88] This allows in pure thinking, which withdraws from everything other, for *Geist* to "be free in an absolute manner"[89] and thus proves the "highest, absolute goal"[90] of history to be "spirit's being-with-itself [*Beisichsein*], this coming-to-itself [*Zusichselbstkommen*]."[91] This teleological process unfolded by Heidegger in a dialectics of the concept, however, does not end in a final stasis; it is instead—and only thus is referred to Hegel in the form of this fleeting suggestion—held in its course through the motivation of the historical subject for the knowledge of itself.

In consideration of the notion of history thereby applied, however, there exists a serious difference between the Hegelian tendency to self-knowledge and hermeneutical self-understanding. It has been established by Hegel that his critical conception of history, on the one hand, emerges from the fact that knowing historical events [*Ereignisse*] depends on the subjective conditions of apprehension, and thus, as Herbert Schnädelbach stresses in Hegelian diction, "the conditions of the systematizability of the *res gestae* [are to be sought] in the realm of the *rerum gestarum memoria*."[92] On the other hand, to ward off the specter of relativism, Hegel bases his conception on an objectively valid teleology that secures, or rather founds, in the concept of 'reason in history,' the generally pervasive context of historical occurrences by means of familiar philosophical theory.

In the summer of 1920, in a broadly conceived phenomenological-critical *Destruktion* of the problem of the apriori, Heidegger thematizes the question concerning the function and mode of appearance of history in factical life, which issues from the approach of the hermeneutics of facticity opposing this idea of the philosophy of history. As such, that is to say, he designates the traditional philosophical standpoint, that is, "the transhistorical question of the oppositional relations of final ideas and goals to be achieved, the question of the system *of* values and of the apriori system-

87. Ibid.
88. See ibid., 22.
89. Ibid., 42.
90. Ibid., 41.
91. Ibid. This coming-to-itself as the fundamental teleological structure still signifies the history of consciousness in Husserl's project (see § 24).
92. Schnädelbach, *Geschichtsphilosophie nach Hegel*, 15.

atics *of* reason."[93] Thus, choosing the approach in the sense of the tradition is motivated by the fact, among others, that the 'tendency to the apriori' indeed without seeing the varied points of entry and changing methods, aims epistemologically at the intrinsic preservation of a standpoint transcending all history. Beyond this, its role and determinacy of sense in this tendency are to be referred at the same time to the empirical and historical, so that they appear—if one thinks, for example, of Rickert—normalized from out of the apriori.[94]

Heidegger conceives these moments of the apriori, whether now weighted constitutively or ancillarily, as determining the concept of philosophy as "the transcending of the historical, in empirical terms, or rather the supravalidity over it and at the same the *validity placed* [*Hingeltung*] upon it."[95] By validating [*Hingeltung*], he means the *applicability* of a priori concepts of value to historical reality. It is a matter of "winning, with the apriori ... the norms and ends with regard to *human* life,"[96] and it thus only succeeds when history is assigned a conceptually leading part—through which, however, the "problematic of the apriori, in its ownmost tendency, runs counter to itself,"[97] insofar as according to its approach, history is set over against the ahistorical-qua-transhistorical apriori. In other words, that which is meant by history emerges in the consideration of the apriori merely as the "correlate of a theoretically idealized and abstracted determination that disregards any concrete present."[98]

What history, historical life in its concrete factical sense of enactment, means is not to be apprehended by this approach, according to Heidegger. Consequently, access to a context of a sense of history must, as a subject of hermeneutical explication on the path of *phenomenological-critical destruction,* be opened up in another way. Heidegger chooses such access in setting out on a descriptive outline of the use of the term 'history' [*Geschichte*]. In doing so, he differentiates six ways in which the human as a being who has history can apply this *having of history.* What Heidegger vividly argues in

93. Heidegger, *Phänomenologie der Anschauung*, GA 59, 20. "The relativity and non-recurring singularity of every historical formation of culture stands over against the absoluteness and transhistorical 'universality' of the idea, of values and of the principle of reason; against the factical contingency of history stands the transhistorical necessity of the valid" (ibid.).

94. See ibid, 68.

95. Ibid., 67.

96. Ibid., 73.

97. Ibid.

98. Ibid., 72.

an extensive discussion[99] of its differing facets can be summarized with regard to the modes of access to how and as what history is experience, in view of the six central aspects, by reference to the schema
  'a (= example)—b (= philosophical inference)'—thus:

I: (*a*) "My friend studies history."[100] (*b*) History qua the science of history functions here "as a theoretical context of attitude [*Einstellungszusammenhang*], as the concretizing logic of a field of study."[101]

II: (*a*) In the treatment of a philosophical problem, there is the advice: "Just orient yourself within history!"[102] (*b*) History appears here as "what has passed, what has occurred in its totality; a whole of being as what has become, within its [totality], the historical in a narrower sense, particularly according to the what: the human as individual and standing in a community in systems of achievement with its objectivated achievements in becoming and having become."[103]

III: (*a*) In a Eurocentrically directed look thoroughly typical of the time herein for Heidegger, unproblematic modes of discourse are still not to be disputed by "'historyless' tribes and peoples [*Stämmen und Völkern*]";[104] even they are the "product of previous factuality."[105] Heidegger means that "they have no tradition,"[106] although today this is no longer to be held as a thesis from out of a cultural anthropological view.(*b*) History is determined in this third meaning in a negative way as the "correlate of the preserving and continually renewing taking-with: tradition."[107]

IV: (*a*) One speaks of history as "the great teacher of life, for example for politics."[108] (*b*) History appears here as "not one's own, but

99. See ibid., §§ 6, 7.
100. Ibid., 43.
101. Ibid., 59.
102. Ibid., 43.
103. Ibid., 59.
104. Ibid., 43.
105. Ibid.
106. Ibid. (emphasis deleted).
107. Ibid., 59.
108. Ibid., 43. (emphasis deleted).

directed through current, nonspecific, self-worldly tendencies
of Dasein [as] a past accentuated as the correlate of an
intimacy that serves as a guide."[109]

V: (a) Another mode of historical experience signifies: "This person
has a sad history."[110] (b) Here history is understood as "one's
ownmost past as the correlate of a 'having' motivated in only
self-worldly-directed tendencies."[111]

VI: (a) Further, it can be said: "A very unpleasant history has come
to pass for me."[112] (b) Here history is an "occurrence in the
appropriative event-character of factical life related to the
factical self-world, with-world, and environment."[113]

By means of a critical *Destruktion*, Heidegger analyzes the meanings
of the word "history" in everyday modes of discourse in their references as
explications of contexts of sense, namely, as the constitutive sense direction of the sense of relation thus grasped terminologically for the hermeneutics of facticity, as we have seen (§ 34). It is, "depending upon the level
of immanence on which it necessarily inserts itself according to its sense in
a concrete Dasein, a gauge of the level and form of what is meant by history
for this concrete Dasein itself."[114] Since the relation itself is only as had in
an enactment, it refers from out of itself to the *sense of enactment* that, in
accordance with the distinction shown for the hermeneutics of facticity,
elevates history to the rank to which Heidegger refers in the context of
having-oneself as the *"organon of understanding life."*[115]

For the explication of the original contexts of sense and, bound to
them, the articulation of the directions of sense constitutive for them as
the 'ur-structure of factical life,' in the understanding of what he characterizes as the "ultimate end[s] of the phenomenological task"[116] regarding
the context of sense of history, Heidegger accentuates yet another methodological aspect that helps to bring into sharper focus a phenomenologi-

---

109. Ibid., 59.
110. Ibid., 44.
111. Ibid., 59.
112. Ibid., 44.
113. Ibid., 59.
114. Ibid., 66.
115. Heidegger, *Grundprobleme der Phänomenologie*, GA 58, 256. See § 35 on this point.
116. Heidegger, *Phänomenologie der Anschauung*, GA 59, 74.

cally adequate understanding of history. Tied to the genuineness to be disclosed in the critical *Destruktion* of history's 'what-content' "in order for it to correspond to such *Destruktion*"[117] is what Heidegger identifies as 'phenomenological diiudication.' As an integral component of the phenomenological method, it signifies—and this concerns the context of sense of history—the "decision about the genealogical position that, seen from the point of its origin, corresponds to the context of sense."[118] Origin, in the sense of the historically enacting function of the context of life-experience, is thereby to be grasped as the basic sense of existence (see above, § 36), whose philosophical thematization hermeneutical phenomenology assigns to the originary science of life.

Diiudication requires a *criterion*, which can be found in the formal indication of it, whether the enactment of the having of history is respectively originary or not. As such, it cannot—according to the enactment-theoretical approach—stem from outside. This means that it must, according to Heidegger, "co-reveal itself out of the ultimate tendencies of the phenomenological problematic."[119] These ultimate tendencies refer, as seen (§ 36) in the concentration of the sense of relation as sense of enactment, to the spontaneity of the self, which can be unfolded in the direction of the originary existent life in its ontological structure in the self-worldly centering of the careworldly articulated life. This means that in the context of the sense of history, the criteriological perspective required for a *destruktive* and *diiudicative* understanding of origin is *self-worldliness*. In the sense of a more exact distinction, this means that with a view to the characteristic of enactment as a criterion of the originariness of historical experience, a *"co-directed relation that is at least genuinely self-worldly"*[120] and the demand for an *"always current renewal in a new self-worldly Dasein"*[121] must be fulfilled, and just so that the demanded renewal *"co-forms [the] self-worldly existence."*[122]

---

117. Ibid.
118. Ibid.
119. Ibid., 75.
120. Ibid.
121. Ibid.
122. Ibid. Heidegger provides the phenomenological evidence for the *experience of history indicated by the self-world* where, in a consideration of the sense of enactment, he once more shines a light criteriologically through the above-mentioned six modes of having history under the (henceforth) *diiudicative* aspects (ibid., 75–86). In so doing, it is shown that the self-worldly relation to the current enactment of Dasein in cases III, IV, V, and VI in the respectively

In the context of the philosophical question concerning the structure and context of self-understanding and lifeworld, this investigation into the hermeneutical relation of an understanding having-oneself to the occurrence of tradition was of great significance from the beginning. In the third case of historical experience Heidegger thematizes this question, under the catchphrase 'tradition,' in the sense of that horizon in which and from out of which we come to an understanding about ourselves. This means, more exactly, that the self-worldly relation to tradition is conceived as such a "new preserving taking-with [*Mitnehmen*] of its own past in one's own current Dasein."[123] In this sense it pervades the self-worldly enactment of life, motivates it, occasionally even to the point of determining its course. A tradition, imposed in this narrower sense of self-relation, requires for its own part ongoing current renewal, insofar as it preserves itself and unfolds itself solely in being handed down [*Tradieren*].

What seems to be discerned as a fulfillment of the criterion in question, seen in this way above, pertains in truth only insofar as a renewal is indeed demanded in the enactment being passed down, but in the sense of mere preserving onward, it is not, according to Heidegger, for its part carried out in such a way that it originarily co-forms the self-worldly existence. That is, the past qua tradition, in spite of its constitutive connection to particular Dasein as a relation, is "not purely (immanently) related to the self-world,"[124] insofar as it is shaped by adopting, for example, forms of life that are not self-formed or self-caused in the narrower sense. For this reason, according to Heidegger, in this relation to tradition it is primarily a matter of "a preserving of the formed environment, the determined with-world, and the forms of living in the with-world and having the with-world,"[125] that is, seen more closely, "a preserving of the objectivated achievements of life in its relation to the self-world."[126] In its lifeworldly "situational (hori-

---

varying weighting of both partial aspects of the criterion is more originary than in cases I and II, without cancelling them completely here. It appears in its depersonalized tendency to the objectivation of history, rather than at the level of something derivative.

123. Ibid., 80. Elsewhere Heidegger characterizes this relation in more detail as "a preservation taken along and, in becoming, a new preserving of the past and what has come to pass in becoming, namely one's own past, so that one lives, as it were, in one's own tradition that Dasein itself provides" (ibid., 57).

124. Ibid., 80.

125. Ibid., 57.

126. Ibid.

zonal) sphere,"[127] tradition takes shape and is maintained in the sense of a "secondary coconstituent of current Dasein."[128] Seen thus, it is similar, in its significance for the human within its factical world of experience, to the character of (pre)givenness of the environmental-worldly and with-worldly. Over and against this, the human exists experientially-histori-cally within the constitutive occurrence of tradition of having-itself as its horizon *in an originary way* for Heidegger only insofar as the "factical *sig-nificance* of life [is] intensified to a dominant [i.e. dominant in enactment] mode of significance."[129] This is directed to the self-world and determined qua mode of significance by Heidegger in view of the phenomenological hermeneutic procedure, therefore as a 'constant impetus [*Anstoß*]' to "self-worldly-directed *Destruktion*"[130] and in this sense also *diiudication*.

For a *diiudicative* understanding of historical origins, the historical ex-perience, inserted as case V in Heidegger, plays the decisive role in func-tional-ontological terms. In the case of "this man has a sad history," the having is carried out so that here only one's own past sheds that dominant environmental character in which self-worldly significances are constantly under the threat of falling back. Regardless of the intention that connects itself to the expression of the proposition—for example, whether one would like to effect sympathy or indulgence for the person concerned—and irrespective also of that which may here seem "sad" with regard to its content, that which is to be grasped in formal indication as "sad" for Hei-degger in his approach is always already related "to history, insofar as it is the ownmost of human beings."[131] This means that what is concerned is "*the becoming of the self-world and its tendencies to itself and for itself.*"[132]

In this sense, with regard to self-worldly significance, the realization of being sad is for Heidegger also neither a performance of empathy in earlier situations nor a simulation of a past to a present. Rather, the sad being-attuned [*Gestimmtsein*][133] recurs, Heidegger emphasizes, as if for

127. Ibid., 83.
128. Ibid., 81.
129. Ibid., 82.
130. Ibid.
131. Ibid., 58.
132. Ibid. (emphasis added).
133. This link between history and phenomena of being-attuned already foreshadows, with-out, however, being explicated more precisely, Heidegger's fundamental insight—worked out in *Sein und Zeit* and always maintained later on in his path of thought—into the self- and world disclosing force of attunements.

the first time; that is, "my own past seizes me, so that it is ever again had for the first time, and I myself am always newly affected by myself, and, in a renewed enactment, 'am.'"[134] The existential déjà vu, present within the enactment-sense, of the 'as if for the first time' does not consume itself in its recurrence; instead the being-affected becomes intensified in renewed enactment. That means that "self-affectivity 'grows' in a certain sense, and each 'as if for the first time' is characterized as a precursor."[135] Seen thus, 'having' does not here signify an 'approaching' [*Zukommen*], but rather "'having one's own past' is grounded in the innermost self-worldly-directed tendencies and takes the past as what is earlier [*das Frühere*], yet with what is vital in one's own previous actual self tendencies."[136]

In the accomplishment of this characteristic of enactment, once both criteria are fulfilled—the self-worldly relation and the demand for renewal in this relation—it has the appearance of being "unmistakably and finally the *diiudication* to originality."[137] Against this, Heidegger emphasizes, in view of the sense of enactment, the notion that the self-worldly having of history as one's ownmost past—which therein possesses at the same time both an environmental and a with-worldly character—is in itself constantly threatened by the "*decline* of a pure, self-worldly-directed significance at the environmental, waning level of that which is for the most part carried along as secondary,"[138] in which everything that Heidegger exhibits as ruinance [*Ruinanz*], or rather falling [*Verfallen*], can also be seen. There can thus be, in terms of fulfilling the criteria, no *pure* and (in this sense) isolatable self-worldly significance. As a result, the self—identified as a function of the context of life-experience—seen from the perspective of significance (that is, of the encounter-character [*Begegnischarakter*] of the world) as care and concern, is consequently, constitutionally enmeshed in the web of referential contexts of environment, with-world, and self-world, in which it, as we have seen (§ 34 ff.), acts factically in the alternating play of nearness and distance to itself.

---

134. Ibid., 84.

135. Ibid. What is formulated in the approach to a historical hermeneutics of self-understanding in this originary, immediate and ever-new capacity to be affected is "*the renunciation of any trace of finality*" (ibid.). In the understanding of the origin of history it is excluded from the exposed self-world relation in its history on no side and, despite any possible displacement, does not ultimately close any of its chapters for us.

136. Ibid., 58.

137. Ibid., 84.

138. Ibid.

In spite of this hermeneutically generated demonstration of the impossibility of a pure self-worldly significance of historical experience, the self-positing appearance of an ultimate primordiality is to be taken quite seriously according to Heidegger. For just "this appearance of formally indicating observation, finality, and universal applicability fools philosophy in such a way that in its opinion it is to be found in abstract, systematic conceiving itself and its task, which is in itself requisite and therefore so difficult to discover and confirm."[139] In the background of this noteworthy reference to the self-induced erring of philosophical claims, possible addressees in situating what was contemporary for Heidegger seem to be not only the neo-Kantianism of a Windelband or Rickert, but just as much the transcendental phenomenology of Husserl. It is not difficult to discern here a proximity, if only at a distance, from the lebensphilosophical hermeneutics of Dilthey, especially when Heidegger confesses a little later that that to which it all comes down is "the human being in his concrete, individual historical Dasein."[140]

It would be a mistake to seek to deduce a possible counterposition to the meaningful application of formally indicating analyses from the Heideggerian critique of the philosophical claims in question, because it was Heidegger himself who referred, within the philosophy of the formal indication, to its "inevitable significance."[141] Looked at more precisely, his critique applies exclusively to a hypostatization of the formal indication, which it raises autotelically to the sole "end and object of philosophical observation,"[142] instead of recognizing that the formal indication itself only "stands in a concretely determined manner in service to the task of philosophy: *bringing to awareness originary understanding [Ursprungverstehen].*"[143] This interpretive understanding gains its motivation from what is historically concrete and factical, without thereby collapsing the formal indication itself into the factical.

Above and beyond Heidegger, the ontologically intrinsic linkage of hermeneutics with the situatedness of its questioning in the present confronts hermeneutics, on the basis of its constitutive structure of application, with the task of a *diagnosis of the age.* It can only fulfill this task by

139. Ibid., 85.
140. Ibid., 86.
141. Ibid., 85.
142. Ibid.
143. Ibid. (emphasis added).

illuminating today's ontic space of experience from within in the sense of a functional-ontological structural analysis and thus with respect to the particular concrete factical hermeneutical modes of appropriation, historical and systematic, with a view to the connection of self-understanding and lifeworld in recursive dialogue with all of the sociohistorical discourses co-constitutive of the hermeneutic situation, whether they be philosophic, scientific, economic, artistic, or whatever other sort. Hermeneutics fulfills this task, according to Heidegger, in the sense of "a *radical phenomenological anthropology*"[144] that cannot be confused, however, on the basis of its constitution as a hermeneutics of facticity, with traditional anthropological conceptions.[145]

This confession, notable for Heidegger, regarding research that takes the *historical as anthropological*, or rather the *anthropological as historical*, is not isolated, but rather belongs as a task of concrete historical interpretation to the context of an applicative, diagnostic inspection of the "decisive, constitutive effective forces of the ontological character of the present-day situation."[146] Heidegger substantiates this mode of access as the relation to the problematic of facticity when (to name just one instance) he discusses the primacy of the enactment-sense of ontological hermeneutics that had by then been established. Here he speaks of the fact that the relation as a 'mode of coming-to-experience,' or rather 'coming-to-be-had' for the 'actual philosophical observation' centers on the enactment of the 'factical' or 'anthropological' subject, which means the "enactment in its factical concretion on the side of the concretion in its now, here, and thus."[147] In this context Heidegger refers to the notion that the philosophy of consciousness, with its preference for the "sphere of theoretical acts and enactments"[148] in the fight against the anthropological, at the same time

---

144. Heidegger, *Phänomenologische Interpretationen zu Aristoteles*, 251.

145. It is thus not a matter of placing the early work under a rubric in the sense of a disciplinary codification, nor is the work to be pigeonholed by a history of philosophy as, and attributed to, a determinate intellectual history trend of the twentieth century. That trend is invoked by mention of figures like Max Scheler, Helmuth Plessner, and later Arnold Gehlen as well, who, emerging in the wake of a metaphysical critique carried out by Nietzsche, had posed the question of a philosophical anthropology as the order of the day and the core problem of philosophy. On the situating of the positions in the anthropological discourse of the twentieth century, see Wolfgang Pleger, *Differenz und Identität: Die Transformation der philosophischen Anthropologie im 20. Jahrhundert* (Berlin: Duncker & Humblot, 1988).

146. Ibid., 250.

147. Heidegger, *Phänomenologie der Anschauung*, GA 59, 63.

148. Ibid.

expels all existential problems from philosophy itself. And therewith the historical dimension, as well as the lifeworldly, would recede from philosophy.

Yet lifeworld and history are, as the course of our investigation has shown, as much thematic horizons as they are conditions of the possibility (that is, motivating grounds) of the self-constitution of philosophy as the phenomenological hermeneutics of facticity. That it always already at the same time also articulates itself in theoretical enactment as *historical* is easily visible from the exhibited hermeneutical approach, and first makes it possible in general in the displacement of the traditional conception of the "I" to express and to hermeneutically profile the problem of the self[149] from out of the "engulfment of the decisive constitutive effective forces of the ontological character of the contemporary situation."[150]

In the conversation about the multifaceted interweaving of discourses—as the historical factically and as such always only perspectivally and relationally opened reality of the self—the hermeneutic leading voice [*Stimmführung*] can, qua the function of life-experience, be brought in as a "*philosophy of the contemporary situation*"[151] without thereby "intending to carry over an evidentiary ideal or anything as overstated as an 'essential in-

---

149. *Phänomenologie der Anschauung*, 250.

150. From this vantage, new paths of reflexive self-ascertainment can be disclosed, particularly in the discourse of *historical anthropology*, in light of its philosophical location. With the displacement of the classical positions of an anthropology oriented to the ahistorical nature and naturalness of human beings, it appears, in view of the historicity of the phenomena of human life in historical anthropology, that a *new paradigm* is taking shape within the historical, social, and cultural sciences (see Gunter Gebauer, Dietmar Kamper, and others, *Historische Anthropologie: Zum Problem der Humanwissenschaften heute oder der Versuch einer Neubegründung* [Reinbek: Rowohlt 1989]).

As Jochen Martin emphasizes, insofar as "the object of a historical anthropology [is always] codetermined through philosophical anthropology" ("Der Wandel des Beständigen. Überlegungen zu einer historischen Anthropologie," in *Freiburger Universitätsblätter*, [1994], 126:40), a hermeneutics of facticity, with its phenomenologically-hermeneutically guided structural exhibition of human being-in-the-world, offers that reflexive dispositive out of which access to the interpretation of the phenomena of human enactments of life is no longer obscured by traditional interpretations of the human. This means that an examination, and in certain cases a revision, of fundamental intuitions and fundamental concepts regarding the reflexive connection to Heidegger's phenomenology of human life could conceivably be initiated.

On the other hand, historical anthropology for its part, with the material resources of its research—familial relations, for instance, or those of gender, institutions, etc.—offers that concrete field of intuition and result, which, for example, is extraordinarily fruitful for the reflexive attempt regarding a factical-hermeneutical lifeworld-phenomenological conception of a social ontology to be worked out in a 'pragmatic respect.'

151. Heidegger, *Phänomenologische Interpretationen zu Aristoteles*, 249 (emphasis added).

sight'" in relation to the applicative space of its concrete interpretations,[152] since that would be "a mistaking of what it can and may do."[153] With respect to the "with-worldly tendency of effecting"[154] that holds for all philosophizing, Heidegger thus calls for remaining "in the range of claims aimed at *bringing-one-to-attentiveness* [*Aufmerksammachens*]."[155]

In the immediate turn to the ontic concrete world of experience that marks the natural horizon of questioning of historical hermeneutics, whose retreat back into the transcendental self-claim of the fundamental ontological position of *Sein und Zeit* is lamented not only by Gadamer and Ricoeur as a kind of loss of ontic situative concretion,[156] there exists for Heidegger in consideration of each respective concrete phenomenological analysis a definite "eventuality of its miscarriage [and indeed] a fundamental one, belonging to its ownmost being,"[157] so that the "evidentiary character of its explication [is] fundamentally labile."[158] Accordingly, there is no stable, that is, finally grounded, hermeneutical knowledge.

In other words, this means that philosophy is a "mode of knowing existing in factical life itself [and thus not functioning from an external position of observation],"[159] which therefore neither begins with itself nor from out of itself. Philosophy is contingent, according to its structure of sense.[160] That is, it makes a decisionistically imposed beginning with

152. Heidegger, *Ontologie, GA* 63, 16.

153. Ibid.

154. Heidegger, *Wegmarken, GA* 9, 6.

155. Ibid.

156. On different aspects of the question, see Burkhard Liebsch, *Geschichte im Zeichen des Abschieds,* 161; Dieter Sturma, *Philosophie der Person: Die Selbstverhältnisse von Subjektivität und Moralität* (Paderborn: F. Schöningh, 1997), 127; Reiner Wiehl, *"Heideggers Verfehlung des Themas 'Metaphysik und Erfahrung,'"* in *Metaphysik und Erfahrung. Philosophische Essays* (Frankfurt: Suhrkamp, 1996), 155–202.

157. Heidegger, *GA* 63, 15 f.

158. Ibid., 16. Yet does the specter of relativism not surface at the horizon here? Heidegger himself does not appear to be concerned by this. In a letter to Löwith written in August 1921, he describes himself as "a *dogmatically* subjective relativist, i.e., I fight my 'position'—and am 'unjustly' against other [positions] in the knowledge that I am myself 'relative'" (Heidegger, "Drei Briefe an Löwith," 31). However, it is of decisive significance—and easily perceptible, according to what has been detailed—that the relativism that Heidegger here reclaims for himself does not imply an evaporation into arbitrariness, but rather only removes itself from all supratemporal validity claims; that is to say, it is reflected in finite historical standards as a *relationally conditioned and relationally grounded self.*

159. Heidegger, *Ontologie, GA* 63, 18.

160. In thoroughly material proximity to what is described here, the thought of contingency is also a dominant feature of Richard Rorty's philosophy. Proceeding from the insight that

the pregiven phenomena in it as a diagnostically structuring conception of that which is therein hermeneutically ever again the experience that its knowledge-determining and leading concepts come from out of a past. This leads these concepts along in the mode of effective-history in articulating its own self- and world-related intentions of knowledge precisely such that the past changes in relation to the present as much as all present conceiving is only from out of the particular self-modifying relation to tradition.

there can be no initial or ultimate ground of human knowledge that would be accessible to us, Rorty unfolds—in the linkage between the analytic, pragmatic, and hermeneutic strands of tradition—his own approach as a thinking of radical contingency, which he opposes decisively to any varying fundamental(ist) positions whatsoever, since for him hermeneutics is also not to be seen as a 'successor discipline' to epistemology (see Rorty, *Der Spiegel der Natur: Eine Kritik der Philosophie* [Frankfurt: Suhrkamp, 1981], 343, 347).

Reality for Rorty is thus only possible to grasp perspectivally within our respective (essentially contingent) systems of reference as "reality-under-a-certain-description" (ibid., 409). *Descriptive systems* are accordingly the element of human knowledge. In being brought forth by humans, they are from the outset contingent. And in the face of facts in a multiplicity of possible descriptive systems this means at the same time that the factical situation of human knowledge is constituted and structured through contingency and plurality.

In the progression of his philosophical reflections on the epistemological status of human knowledge—formulated, among other places, in *Kontingenz, Ironie, und Solidarität* (Frankfurt: Suhrkamp, 1991)—Rorty grounds his position in the concept of the *ironist*. He elucidates this concisely where he notes that people are called ironists "because their knowledge that everything can appear good or evil in accordance with a given description, and that they give up the attempt to formulate decisive criteria among limited vocabularies, brings them into the position that Sartre calls 'metastable': never completely able to take themselves seriously because they are always cognizant that the concepts through which they describe themselves are subject to change; always in the consciousness of the contingency and fragility of their limited vocabulary, thus also of their own self" (ibid., 128).

OPEN END

The most important thing in life and in work is to become something that one was not in the beginning.

Michel Foucault

Who of us can say, when he turns around on a path for which there is no return, that he followed it as only he had to?

Fernando Pessoa

§ 41. Retrospective Reflections on the World-Conceptual Relevance of a Hermeneutics of Facticity

With the hermeneutical demonstration that our never other than life-worldly situated self-understanding is always already historical at the origin of its self-worldly significance, the factual analysis of Heidegger's early work comes to an end, in that for one thing, it makes explicit the point of departure of phenomenological hermeneutics of factical historical life in the wealth of its structures. For another, beyond the fact of placing the starting point in life, the central question of his early work illuminates at the same time *how* "factical life-experience belongs in a wholly originary sense to the problematic of philosophy,"[1] in that the structure and task of a phenomenological 'ur-science of life' is determined more precisely as a *hermeneutics of the situation*. To sharpen the contour and profile in these ontological-functional relations was the aim of the present investigation.

---

1. Heidegger, *Phänomenologie der Anschauung und des Ausdrucks*, ed. Claudius Strube [Frankfurt: Klostermann, 1993], GA 59, 38.

If one considers the hermeneutics of the situation thus expressed according to its *material side,* one finds the claim inherent in it, as philosophy of our own time, also to work up its pressing social questions qua *concrete critique of the time* in a historical analysis oriented to the solution of problems; with Heidegger there is indeed only a comparably weak resonance, in particular, if one thinks of Kant, Herder, Humboldt, Fichte, and Hegel, of Kierkegaard and also Nietzsche in the sworn gesture of proposed diagnoses of a dawning age of European nihilism. And while from out of the circle of Heidegger's contemporaries—whether it is a matter of Scheler and Simmel, esteemed by him, or his friend Jaspers—there are found extensive defenses of current social-political questions of the present, such testimonies are found rarely in the early Heidegger, with the exception of reflections on the place of the university. In other words, this means that at the level of explication Heidegger clearly undersells the structural insights, gained in hermeneutical reflection, into the contingency and relationality of human life-relations with regard to their potential in the direction of the material working out of a philosophy of the situation.

That he almost exclusively uses the innovative impetus of this insight—aimed at re-shaping phenomenology in the direction of a hermeneutics of historical factical life—with regard to lifeworldly existential explication and application in terms of the individual enactment of everyday life, and not in a historical critique of his times, which is another possible tendency gained from this transformation, does not mean that the factical-hermeneutical position articulated in formal indication cannot accommodate such concretion.[2] In the generation of his students, that is, of Karl Löwith, Hannah Arendt, Hans Jonas, or Georg Picht, one very often encounters philosophical interventions of the type of diagnostic of the present aimed at and even inspired by Heidegger's existential analyses. Like other philosophical guides or auspices of the time, such as Sartre, Camus,

---

2. If one searches in Heidegger's work after reasons for the missing world-conceptual implementation, its absence may be connected with the fact that in the course of the generally acknowledged formation of the approach of his lifeworldly hermeneutics, precisely this historical hermeneutics of facticity as it was proposed programmatically in the summer of 1923 in the form of a lecture, appeared to be comprehended at the threshold of the shift to a hermeneutical phenomenology as the ontology of Dasein—which, as Heidegger repeatedly emphasizes in *Sein und Zeit,* since the mid-1920s follows other aims in the question of being posed therein than that of a factical-hermeneutically-initiated anthropology or social ontology. And yet where an interest for its localization within the conception of fundamental ontology does appear, its systematic place is thereby understood rather than ascribed, as we have seen (§ 29), in metontology.

or Vattimo, Heidegger's students bear witness as a whole to a not insignifi-
cant effective potential for and within the scope of duties of the *critique of
the age,* in connection with numerous other philosophical and extraphilosophical influences and stimulants even in the Heideggerian approach.

Finally, to emphasize this, if only in a set of intimations, is to this extent relevant for a critical development of thought, as it is apparent from
this point that the *world-conceptual relevance* of the Heideggerian approach
need not, at least with regard to concrete explication, be laid bare by what
he himself implements in his own investigations. If this deficit, seen as
such, contains in itself a "need for catching up," it can thus, with regard
to his concrete work of analysis, turn out all the more productively if one
bases oneself on the insights into the structure of experience of human being-in-the-world gained by the early Heidegger and communicated in corresponding conceptual explications.[3] For Heidegger, as this investigation
has shown, it is chiefly a matter of all individual experience in the face of
the formal existential structures antecedently formatting, that is, opening
up the horizon of experienceability in general, and as such constituting the
image of the self and the world alike. In the dynamically shaped functional
constancy of the self and world, the variance of the historically determined
dispositive of the interpretation of life is inscribed, and accordingly the
conditions—bound to their ontological structures—of the hermeneutical
situation (as part 1 of the present treatise has shown) are always already
historicized in themselves; consequently, the ontological character of facticity exhibited and revealed in formal indication is not to be uncoupled
from concrete factical historical hermeneutics in which philosophy itself,
as we have seen, is handed down in accordance with its conception of the
world.

In other words, it is the phenomenological working out of formally
indicating structures with and by Heidegger's successors in historical
hermeneutics that has excavated the fundamental structures of human
self- and world understanding in a way that nonetheless in its formalization does not leap over the lifeworldly dimension of the factically concrete
enactment of life in its historical experiences as its own originary level of
thematization. On this view, the fact that the hermeneutics of facticity be-

---

3. See, e.g. Hans-Helmuth Gander, "Interpretation—Situation—Vernetzung. Hermeneutische Überlegungen zum Selbst- und Weltbezug im multimedialen Zeitalter," in *Hermeneutik und Ästhetik. Die Theologie des Wortes im mulitmedialen Zeitalter,* ed. Ulrich H. J.
Körtner (Neukirchen-Vluyn: Neukirchener Verlag, 2001), 19–33.

longs to the aforementioned line of tradition proves itself not simply and solely as consistent with the grasped philosophy according to its 'concept of the world.' Further still, with the hermeneutically enacted turn to phenomenology in general, the world-concept of philosophy is determined anew; that is, it preserves a hermeneutic basis, which in itself opens the possibility of knowing the coherence of the self-relation and world-relation in the indicated self-understanding as an ontologically revealed context of wholeness.

If one keeps in view this basic state of affairs constitutive of sense for the hermeneutics of facticity, this means that, to stress it once more, the critically remarked deficiency in the Heideggerian 'world-conceptual process' does not concern the basic conception of lifeworldly hermeneutics. What is deficient, if you will, exclusively in view of the present texts is their material arrangement or the concrete explication and application of the approach of the hermeneutics of facticity. But in exactly this respect, a wide field of future tasks opens itself for an existential-phenomenological hermeneutics also applied pragmatically therein.

A situational thinking of this sort easily, habitually achieves a proximity to an understanding of philosophy that conceives theory as practice. As has been shown over the course of this investigation, Heidegger's hermeneutics of facticity forms itself *in* the experience of life, in that it governs the insertion of phenomenological explication in the concrete, factical interpretedness of life, through which it possesses a predominant orientation to the *"present of the proximal [Gegenwart des Zunächst]."*[4] As a life-experience itself in this sense, in which it opens possibilities for the "self-encounter of Dasein,"[5] this hermeneutics at the same time formulates the claim represented from the ancients onward, to conceive philosophy as a mode of life, as a "mode of knowing in which factical Dasein poses itself... unrelentingly for itself."[6]

Philosophy as a form of life is a familiar theme that was broached in multifaceted ways in ever-new chapters in the history of thinking in the twentieth century, just as much in the late Wittgenstein as under other particular philosophical auspices in the existentialism of Sartre, the skeptical humanism of Camus, or in Levinas's 'humanism of the other' and again otherwise in Foucault's late creative period in the project of a philosophy

---

4. Heidegger, *GA 63*, 30; cf. ibid., 85ff.
5. Ibid., 18.
6. Ibid.

of the art of life conceived as an aesthetics of existence. The question of philosophy as a form of life expresses itself phenomenologically-hermeneutically, in that the attentiveness or conceptual carefulness first and foremost directs itself to the mode of sight(ing) distinguished in and as coming to self-understanding, in which the natural and philosophical attitude itself draws closer to phenomena.

The fact that since the time of Thales a tripwire has existed imperiling the steadfastness of the philosopher in the nearest environment of sound human understanding leads familiarly to the fact that from the optics of the maid and the philosopher, contact with things and access to the commonly divided world seem so different. Insofar as this tension between the natural and the philosophical attitude, as we have seen, cannot be overcome, but instead virtually constitutes phenomenological-hermeneutical consciousness at the basis of the point of departure of pretheoretical experience, this itself becomes the motive for the developing of philosophy as a form of life. This basic phenomenon of the self- and world-relation of philosophical thinking proceeds before our eyes both vividly and impressively and at the same time thereby concludes this investigation in terms of a forerunning preliminary, as it were, when one recalls, in the place of a succinct closing remark as an open end, a note in which Paul Valéry—both phenomenologically in description and sharply edged in hermeneutical explication—clarifies the tension between philosophical and nonphilosophical self-understanding in relation to the lifeworld:

Does the greatest philosopher know no more than the first hack to happen along?

Perhaps it is to his advantage to know less. To know that he knows less.

Or—what comes to the same—to know that that which goes on in this hack when he is disturbed, astonished, confused—that this can be brought into play in every context, at every moment, systematically.

Philosophy is that which, at each moment, can bring things to a halt.

In this way, a certain dream unsettles the hack, the coachman, in waking to astonishment. But the philosopher transfers to the events and thoughts of the condition of wakefulness, the clearest waking—the same questions and surprises that related them only to the unambiguously alien in the dream.

Each lives in a clear, albeit diffuse world, the thinker in a darkness with a few bright spots.[7]

7. Paul Valéry, *Cahiers* [*Hefte*] vol. 2, ed. Hartmut Köhler and Jürgen Schmidt-Radefeldt [Frankfurt: Suhrkamp, 1988], 62.

Albert, Karl. *Lebensphilosophie: Von den Anfängen bei Nietzsche bis zu ihrer Kritik bei Lukács.* Freiburg: Alber, 1995.

Apel, Karl-Otto. *Transformation der Philosophie,* 2 vols. Frankfurt: Suhrkamp, 1988–1991.

———, ed. *Hermeneutik und Ideologiekritik.* Frankfurt: Suhrkamp, 1971.

Arendt, Hannah. "Martin Heidegger ist achtzig Jahre alt." In *Antwort: Martin Heidegger im Gespräch,* edited by Günter Neske and Emil Kettering, 232–246. Pfullingen: Neske, 1988.

Aristotle. *Ethica Nicomachea.* Oxford: Clarendon Press, 1991.

———. *Metaphysik.* Edited by Horst Seidl. Hamburg: Meiner, 1978.

———. *Zweite Analytiken.* Edited by Horst Seidl. Würzburg: Rodopi, 1984.

Assmann, Jan. *Das kulturelle Gedächtnis: Schrift, Erinnerungen und politische Identität in frühen Hochkulturen.* 2nd ed. Munich: C.F. Beck, 1997.

Augustine. *Confessiones* [Bekenntnisse]. Translated by Joseph Bernhart. Munich: Kösel, 1966.

———. *Vom Gottesstaat,* 2 vols. Zurich: Artemis, 1978.

———. *Über den Wortlaut der Genesis,* 2 vols. Edited by Carl Johann Perl. Paderborn, DE: Ferdinand Schöningh, 1961–1964.

Bacon, Francis. *Neues Organon.* Edited by Wolfgang Krohn. Hamburg: Meiner, 1990.

Baumann, Gerhart. "Der Brief: Mitteilung und Selbstzeugnis." In *Sprache und Selbstbegegnung,* 98–112. Munich: Fink, 1981.

Beck, Ulrich. *Die Erfindung des Politischen: Zu einer Theorie reflexiver Modernisierung.* Frankfurt: Suhrkamp, 1993.

———. "Kinder der Freiheit: Wider das Lamento über den Werteverfall." In *Kinder der Freiheit.* Edited by Ulrich Beck, 9–33. Frankfurt: Suhrkamp, 1997.

———. "Utopie als Ursprung: Politische Freiheit als Sinnquelle der Moderne." In *Kinder der Freiheit.* Edited by Ulrich Beck, 382–401. Frankfurt: Suhrkamp, 1997.

———. *Risikogesellschaft: Auf dem Weg in eine andere Moderne.* Frankfurt: Suhrkamp, 1986.

———, Anthony Giddens and Scott Lash. *Reflexive Modernisierung: Eine Kontroverse.* Frankfurt: Suhrkamp, 1996.

Beierwaltes, Werner. "Heideggers Rückgang zu den Griechen." In *Bayer Akademie der Wissenschaften; Philosophische-Historische Klasse; Sitzungsberichte,* vol. 1, 5–30. Munich: Akademie der Wissenschaften and Beck, 1995.

Benjamin, Walter. *Berliner Kindheit um Neunzehnhundert.* In *Gesammelte Schriften,* vol. 4, pt. 1, 235–304. Edited by Tillman Rexroth. Frankfurt: Suhrkamp, 1980.

Bergson, Henri. *L'évolution creatrice.* In *Oeuvres,* 487–809. Paris: Presses Universitaires de France, 1991.

———. *Essai sur les données immédiates de la conscience.* In *Oeuvres,* 3–157. Paris: Presses Universitaires de France, 1991.

Bernet, Rudolf. "Den Anderen wie Dich selbst." *Fragmente: Schriftenreihe zur Psychoanalyse* 39–40 (1992): 173–188.

———. "Differenz und Anwesenheit: Derridas und Husserls Phänomenologie der Sprache, der Zeit, der Geschichte, der wissenschaftlichen Rationalität." In *Studien zur neueren französischen Phänomenologie: Ricoeur, Foucault, Derrida*, edited by Ernst Wolfgang Orth, 51–112. Freiburg: Alber, 1986.

———. "Phenomenological Reduction and the Double Life of the Subject." In *Reading Heidegger from the Start: Essays in His Earliest Thought*, edited by Theodore Kisiel and John van Buren, 245–267. New York: SUNY Press, 1994.

Bernet, Rudolf, Iso Kern, and Eduard Marbach. *Edmund Husserl: Darstellung seines Denkens*. Hamburg: Meiner, 1989.

Berti, Enrico. "*Heideggers Auseinandersetzung mit dem platonisch-aristotelischen Wahrheitsverständnis*." In *Die Frage nach der Wahrheit*, edited by Ewald Richter, 89–105. Frankfurt: Klostermann, 1997.

Betti, Emilio. *Allgemeine Auslegungslehre als Methodik der Geisteswissenschaften*. Tübingen: Mohr Siebeck, 1967.

Bialas, Wolfgang. "*Das Geschichtsdenken der klassischen deutschen Philosophie: Hegels Geschichtsphilosophie zwischen historischem Erfahrungsraum und utopischem Erwartungshorizont*." In *Geschichtsdiskurs*. vol. 3, *Die Epoche der Historisierung*, edited by Wolfgang Küttler, Jörn Rüsen, and Ernst Schulin, 29–44. Frankfurt: Fischer, 1997.

Bianco, Franco. *Vita activa und Vita contemplative: Zur Auseinandersetzung Heinrich Rickerts mit Max Weber*. In *Neukantianismus. Perspektiven und Probleme*, edited by Ernst Wolfgang Orth and Helmut Holzhey, 296–308. Würzburg: Königshausen & Neumann, 1994.

Biemel, Walter "Heideggers Stellung zur Phänomenologie in der Marburger Zeit." In *Gesammelte Schriften*, vol. 1, 265–333. Stuttgart: Frommann-Holzboog, 1996.

———. "Husserls Encyclopaedia-Britannica Artikel und Heideggers Anmerkungen dazu." In *Gesammelte Schriften*, vol. 1, 173–207. Stuttgart: Frommann-Holzboog, 1996.

———. "Zur Bedeutung von Doxa und Episteme im Umkreis der Krisis-Thematik." In *Lebenswelt und Wissenschaft in der Philosophie Edmund Husserls*, edited by Elisabeth Ströker, 10–22. Frankfurt: Klostermann, 1979.

———. "Zum Briefwechsel Jaspers/Heidegger." In *Zur philosophischen Aktualität Heideggers*, vol. 2, *Im Gespräch der Zeit*, edited by Dietrich Papenfuss and Otto Pöggeler, 71–86. Frankfurt: Klostermann, 1990.

Blattner, William D. "Existential Temporality in *Being and Time* (Why Heidegger is not a Pragmatist)." In *Heidegger: A Critical Reader*, edited by Hubert L. Dreyfus and Harrison Hall, 99–129. Oxford: Blackwell, 1992.

Blumenberg, Hans. *Das Lachen der Thrakerin: Eine Urgeschichte der Theorie*. Frankfurt: Suhrkamp, 1987.

———. "Ernst Cassirers gedenkend bei der Entgegennahme des Kuno-Fischer-Preises der Universität Heidelberg 1974," in *Wirklichkeiten in denen wir leben: Aufsätze und eine Rede*, 163–172. Stuttgart: Reclam, 1981.

———. *Lebenszeit und Weltzeit*. Frankfurt: Suhrkamp, 1986.

———. *Die Legitimität der Neuzeit:. Erneuerte Ausgabe*. Frankfurt: Suhrkamp, 1988.

———. *Die Lesbarkeit der Welt*. Frankfurt: Suhrkamp, 1981.

———. *Schiffbruch mit Zuschauer: Paradigma einer Daseinsmetapher*. Frankfurt: Suhrkamp, 1979.

Bochenski, Joseph M. *Autorität, Freiheit, Glaube*. Munich: Philosophia, 1988.

Böhler, Dietrich. "Philosophische Hermeneutik und hermeneutische Methode." In *Text und Applikation: Theologie, Jurisprudenz und Literaturwissenschaft im hermeneutischen Gespräch*, edited by Manfred Fuhrmann, Hans Robert Jauss, and Wolfhart Pannenberg, 483–511. Munich: Fink, 1981.

Boehm, Gottfried. "Der erste Blick: Kunstwerk-Ästhetik-Philosophie." *Deutsche Zeitschrift für Philosophie* 1, no. 41 (1993): 44–53.

———. "Zur Hermeneutik der Abstraktion." In *Verstehen und Geschehen: Jahresgabe der Martin-Heidegger-Gesellschaft*, 13–25. Messkirch: Martin-Heidegger-Gesellschaft, 1990.

Böhm, Rudolf. *Vom Gesichstpunkt der Phänomenologie: Husserl-Studien*. The Hague: Springer, 1968.

Bollnow, Otto Friedrich. "Dilthey und die Phänomenologie." In *Dilthey und die Philosophie der Gegenwart*, edited by Ernst Wolfgang Orth, 31–61. Freiburg: Alber, 1985.

———. "Festrede zu Wilhelm Diltheys 150. Geburtstag." In *Dilthey-Jahrbuch*, vol. 2, 28–50. Ed. Frithjof Rodi. Göttingen: Vandenhoeck & Ruprecht, 1984.

———. *Die Lebensphilosophie*. Berlin: Springer, 1958.

———. *Studien zur Hermeneutik*, vol. 1, *Zur Philosophie der Geisteswissenschaften*. Freiburg: Alber, 1982.

———. "Was heißt einen Schriftsteller besser verstehen, als er sich selber verstanden hat?" In *Zur Philosophie der Geisteswissenschaften*, vol. 1, 48–72, of *Studien zur Hermeneutik*. Freiburg: Alber, 1982.

Bossuet, Jacques Bénigne. *Discours sur l'histoire universelle*. Paris: Garnier-Flammarion, 1966.

Brach, Markus Joachim. *Heidegger—Platon. Vom Neukantiansmus zur existentiellen Interpretation des "Sophistes."* Würzburg: Königshausen & Neumann, 1996.

Brand, Gerd. *Die Lebenswelt: Eine Philosophie des konkreten Apriori*. Berlin: De Gruyter, 1971.

Brentano, Franz. *Psychologie vom empirischen Standpunkt*. Edited by Oskar Kraus. 3 vols. Hamburg: Meiner, 1971–1974.

Bröcker, Walter. "Europäologie." *Allgemeine Zeitschrift für Philosophie* 3 (1978): 1–22.

Brogan, Walter. "The Place of Aristotle in the Development of Heidegger's Phenomenology." In *Reading Heidegger from the Start: Essays in His Earliest Thought*, edited by Theodor Kisiel and John van Buren, 213–227. New York: SUNY Press, 1994.

Bruzina, Ronald. "*Gegensätzlicher Einfluß—Integrierter Einfluß: Die Stellung Heideggers in der Entwicklung der Phänomenologie*." In *Zur philosophischen Aktualität Heideggers*. vol. 2, *Im Gespräch der Zeit*, edited by Dietrich Papenfuss and Otto Pöggeler, 142–160. Frankfurt: Klostermann, 1990.

Bubner, Rüdiger. *Geschichtsprozesse und Handlungsnormen: Untersuchungen zur praktischen Philosophie*. Frankfurt: Suhrkamp, 1984.

———. "Wissenschaftstheorie und Systembegriff: Zur Position von N. Luhmann und deren Herkunft." In *Dialektik und Wissenschaft*, 112–128. Frankfurt: Suhrkamp, 1974.

Buchholz, Rolf. *Was heißt Intentionalität? Eine Studie zum Frühwerk Martin Heideggers*. Essen: die blaue Eule, 1995.

Burckhardt, Jacob. *Weltgeschichtliche Betrachtungen*. Stuttgart: Alfred Kröner, 1978.

Camus, Albert. *Tagebücher 1935–1951*. Reinbek bei Hamburg: Rowohlt, 1989.

———. *Tagebuch 1951–1959*. Reinbek bei Hamburg: Rowohlt, 1991.

Carr, David. "The Fifth Meditation and Husserl's Cartesianism." *Philosophy and Phenomenological Research* 34 (1973–1974): 14–35.

———. *Phenomenology and the Problem of History: A Study of Husserl's Transcendental Philosophy.* Evanston, IL: Northwestern University Press, 1974.

Carrier, Martin and Jürgen Mittelstraß. *Geist, Gehirn, Verhalten: Das Leib-Seele-Problem und die Philosophie der Psychologie.* Berlin: De Gruyter, 1989.

Cassirer, Ernst. *Descartes: Lehre-Persönlichkeit-Wirkung.* Hamburg: Meiner, 1995.

———. *Philosophie der symbolischen Formen.* 3 vols. Darmstadt: Wissenschaftliche Buchgesellschaft, 1994.

———. "Vom Wesen und Werden des Naturrechts." In *Zeitschrift für Rechtsphilosophie,* vol. 6:1, 1932–1934, 1–27.

Celms, Theodor. *Der phänomenologische Idealismus Husserls.* New York: Peter Lang, 1979.

Chang, Ting-Kuo. *Geschichte, Verstehen und Praxis: Eine Untersuchung zur philosophischen Hermeneutik Hans-Georg Gadamers unter besonderer Berücksichtigung ihrer Annäherung an die Tradition der praktischen Philosophie.* Marburg: Tectum, 1994.

Chiereghin, Franco. "Der griechische Anfang Europas und die Frage der Romanitas: Der Weg Heideggers zu einem anderen Anfang." In *Europa und die Philosophie,* edited by Hans-Helmuth Gander 197–223. Frankfurt: Klostermann, 1993.

Chladenius, Johann Martin. *Einleitung zur richtigen Auslegung vernünftiger Reden und Schriften.* [1742]. Düsseldorf: Stern-Verlag Janssen, 1969.

Cho, Ka Kyung. "Der Abstieg über den Humanismus: West-Östliche Wege im Denken Heideggers." In *Europa und die Philosophie,* edited by Hans-Helmuth Gander, 143–174. Frankfurt: Klostermann, 1993.

Claesges, Ulrich. "Zweideutigkeiten in Husserls Lebensweltbegriff." In *Perspektiven transzendentalphänomenologischer Forschung,* edited by Ulrich Claesges and Klaus Held, 85–101. The Hague: Martinus Nijhoff, 1972.

Columbus, Christopher. *Das Bordbuch 1492: Leben und Fahrten des Entdeckers der Neuen Welt in Dokumenten und Aufzeichnungen,* edited by Robert Grün. Stuttgart: Marix, 1983.

Courtine, Jean-François. *Heidegger et la phénomenologie.* Paris: Vrin, 1990.

———. "Phénoménologie et/ou herméneutique." In *Comprendre et interpreter: Le paradigm herméneutique de la raison,* 151–175. Paris: Beauchesne, 1993.

———, ed. *Heidegger 1919–1929: De l'herméneutique de la facticité à la métaphysique du Dasein.* Paris: Vrin, 1996.

Cramer, Konrad. "Descartes antwortet Caterus: Gedanken zu Descartes' Neubegründung des ontologischen Gottbeweises." In *Descartes Nachgedacht,* edited by Andreas Kemmerling and Hans-Peter Schütt, 123–169. Frankfurt: Klostermann, 1996.

Cunningham, Suzanne. *Language and the Phenomenological Reductions of Edmund Husserl.* The Hague: Springer, 1976.

Därmann, Iris. "Der Fremde zwischen den Fronten von Ethnologie und Philosophie." *Philosophische Rundschau* 43 (1996): 46–63.

Dahlstrom, Daniel O. "Heidegger's Critique of Husserl." In *Reading Heidegger from the Start. Essays in His Earliest Thought,* edited by Theodore Kisiel and John van Buren, 231–244. New York: SUNY Press, 1994.

Dallmayr, Fred R. "Phenomenology and Social Science. An Overview and Appraisal." In *Explorations in Phenomenology: Papers of the Society for Phenomenology and Existential Philosophy,* edited by David Carr and Edward S. Casey, 133–166. The Hague: Springer, 1973.

Dastur, Françoise. "Heidegger und die 'Logische Untersuchungen.'" In *Heidegger Studies* 7 (1991): 37–51.

Derrida, Jacques. "Cogito und die Geschichte des Wahnsinns," in *Die Schrift und die Differenz*, 53–101. Frankfurt: Suhrkamp, 1985.

———. *Dissemination*. Vienna: Passagen, 1995.

———. "Gewalt und Metaphysik. Essay über das Denken Emmanuel Levinas," in *Die Schrift und die Differenz*, 121–235. Frankfurt: Suhrkamp, 1985.

———. *Grammatologie*. Frankfurt: Suhrkamp, 1974.

———. *Husserls Weg in die Geschichte am Leitfaden der Geometrie: Ein Kommentar zur Beilage III der* Krisis. Munich: Fink, 1987.

———. *Die Schrift und die Differenz*. Frankfurt: Suhrkamp, 1985.

Descartes, René. *Discours de la Méthode*. Edited and translated by Lüder Gäbe. Hamburg: Meiner, 1969.

———. *Meditationen über die Grundlagen der Philosophie mit den sämtlichen Einwänden und Erwiderungen*. Translated by Artur Buchenau. Hamburg: Meiner, 1972.

———. *Meditationes de Prima Philosophia*. Translated by Gerhart Schmidt. Stuttgart: Reclam, 1986.

———. *Oeuvres*. Edited by Charles Adam and Paul Tannery. Paris: Vrin, 1996.

———. *Les Passions de l'Ame*. Translated by Klaus Hammacher. Hamburg: Meiner, 1984.

———. *Die Prinzipien der Philosophie*. Translated by Artur Buchenau. Hamburg: Meiner, 1965.

———. *Regulae ad directionem ingenii*. Translated by Heinrich Springmeyer, Lüder Gäbe, and Hans Günter Zekl. Hamburg: Meiner, 1973.

Dilthey, Wilhelm. *Gesammelte Schriften*. Edited by Karlfried Gründer and Frithjof Rodi. Stuttgart/Göttingen: Vandenhoeck & Ruprecht, 1959–.

———. *Breslauer Ausarbeitung*, in *Grundlegung der Wissenschaften vom Menschen, der Gesellschaft und der Geschichte: Ausarbeitungen und Entwürfe zum zweiten Band der Einleitung in die Geisteswissenschaften (ca. 1870–1895)*. Edited by Helmut Johach and Frithjof Rodi. Göttingen: Vandenhoeck & Ruprecht, 1982.

———. *Die Abgrenzung der Geisteswissenschaften*, edited by Bernhard Groethuysen. Göttingen: Vandenhoeck & Ruprecht, 1973.

———. *Der Aufbau der geschichtlichen Welt in den Geisteswissenschaften*, edited by Bernhard Groethuysen. Göttingen: Vandenhoeck & Ruprecht, 1973.

———. *Einleitung in die Geisteswissenschaften: Versuch einer Grundlegung für das Studium der Gesellschaft und der Geschichte*, edited by Bernhard Groethuysen. Göttingen: Vandenhoeck & Ruprecht, 1914.

———. *Die Entstehung der Hermeneutik*. Göttingen: Vandenhoeck & Ruprecht, 1990.

———. *Das Erlebnis und die Dichtung: Lessing—Goethe—Novalis—Hölderlin*. Göttingen: Vandenhoeck & Ruprecht, 1985.

———. *Leben und Erkennen. Ein Entwurf zur erkenntnistheoretischen Logik und Kategorienlehre*, in *Grundlegung der Wissenschaften vom Menschen, der Gesellschaft und der Geschichte: Ausarbeitungen und Entwürfe zum zweiten Band der Einleitung in die Geisteswissenschaften (ca. 1870—1895)*, edited by Helmut Johach and Frithjof Rodi. Göttingen: Vandenhoeck & Ruprecht, 1982.

———. "Rede zum 70 Geburtstag," in *Die Geistige Welt*. Edited by Karlfried Gründer and Frithjof Rodi. Göttingen: Vandenhoeck & Ruprecht, 1990.

———. "Vorrede," in *Die Geistige Welt*. Edited by Karlfried Gründer and Frithjof Rodi. Göttingen: Vandenhoeck & Ruprecht, 1990.

———. *Weltanschauungslehre*, edited by Bernhard Groethuysen. Göttingen: Vandenhoeck & Ruprecht, 1991.

———. "Zusätze zu den Studien zur Grundlegung der Geisteswissenschaft," in *Der Aufbau der geschichtlichen Welt in den Geisteswissenschaften*, edited by Bernhard Groethuysen. Göttingen: Vandenhoeck & Ruprecht, 1973.

Dreyfus, Hubert L., and Paul Rabinow. *Michel Foucault: Jenseits von Strukturalismus und Hermeneutik*. Weinheim: Beltz, 1994.

Droysen, Johan Gustav. *Historik: Vorlesungen über Enzyklopädie und Methodologie der Geschichte*. Edited by Rudolf Hübner. Munich: Oldenbourg, 1971.

Dummett, Michael. *Ursprünge der analytischen Philosophie*. Frankfurt: Suhrkamp, 1988.

Eco, Umberto. *Das offene Kunstwerk*. Frankfurt: Suhrkamp, 1973.

Eisler, Rudolf. *Eislers Handwörterbuch der Philosophie*. Berlin: Mittler, 1922.

Emad, Parvis. "Zu Fragen der Interpretation und Entzifferung der Grundlagen der Gesamtausgabe Martin Heideggers." *Heidegger Studies* 9 (1993): 161–171.

Eucken, Rudolf. *Mensch und Welt: Eine Philosophie des Lebens*. Leipzig: Quelle & Meyer, 1920.

Fahrenbach, Helmut. "*Faktizität*." In *Historisches Wörterbuch der Philosophie*, edited by Joachim Ritter, vol. 2. Darmstadt: Wissenschaftliche Buchgesellschaft, 1972, 886.

Fehér, István M. "Gibt es 'die' Hermeneutik? Zur Selbstreflexion und Aktualität der Hermeneutik Gadamerscher Prägung." *Internationale Zeitschrift für Philosophie* 2 (1996): 236–259.

———. "Identität und Wandlung der Seinsfrage: Eine hermeneutische Annäherung." In *Mesotes: Supplementband Martin Heidegger*, edited by Maria Fürst and Thomas Hübel, 105–119. Vienna: Braumüller, 1991.

———. "Phenomenology, Hermeneutics, Lebensphilosophie: Heidegger's Confrontation with Husserl, Dilthey, and Jaspers." In *Reading Heidegger from the Start: Essays in His Earliest Thought*, edited by Theodore Kisiel and John van Buren, 73–89. New York: SUNY Press, 1994.

Fellmann, Ferdinand. *Gelebte Philosophie in Deutschland: Denkformen der Lebensweltphänomenologie und der kritischen Theorie*. Freiburg: Alber, 1983.

———. *Lebensphilosophie: Elemente einer Theorie der Selbsterfahrung*. Reinbek bei Hamburg: Rowohlt, 1993.

Fichte, Johann Gottlieb. "Einige Vorlesungen über die Bestimmung des Gelehrten." In *Fichtes Werke*, vol. 1, 217–274. Edited by Fritz Medicus. Leipzig: Fritz Eckardt, 1911.

———. "*Erste Einleitung in die Wissenschaftslehre*" ("*Versuch einer neuen Darstellung der Wissenschaftslehre*"). In *Fichtes Werke*, vol. 3, 1–33. Edited by Fritz Medicus. Leipzig: Fritz Eckardt, 1911.

Figal, Günter. *Für eine Philosophie von Freiheit und Streit: Politik—Ästhetik—Metaphysik*. Stuttgart: Metzler, 1994.

———. *Heidegger zur Einführung*. Hamburg: Junius, 1992.

———. *Martin Heidegger: Phänomenologie der Freiheit*. Weinheim: Beltz Athenäum, 2000.

———. "Philosophische Zeitkritik im Selbstverständnis der Modernität: Rousseaus 'Erster Discours' und Nietzsches 'Zweite unzeitgemäße Betrachtung.'" In *Selbstverständnisse der Moderne. Formationen der Philosophie, Politik, Theologie und Ökonomie*. Edited by Günter Figal and Rolf-Peter Sieferle, 100–132. Stuttgart: Metzler, 1991.

———. *Der Sinn des Verstehens:. Beiträge zur hermeneutischen Philosophie*. Stuttgart: Reclam, 1996.

———. "*Verstehen als geschichtliche Phronesis.*" *Internationale Zeitschrift für Philosophie* (1992) (1): 24–37.

———. "Vom Schweigen der Texte," in *Für eine Philosophie von Freiheit und Streit: Politik—Ästhetik—Metaphysik,* 7–19. Stuttgart: Metzler, 1994.

Figl, Johann. *Interpretation als philosophisches Prinzip. Friedrich Nietzsches universale Theorie der Auslegung im späten Nachlaß.* Berlin: De Gruyter, 1982.

Fink, Eugen. *VI. Cartesianische Meditation: Husserliana Dokumente,* vol. 2. Edited by Hans Ebeling, Jann Holl, and Guy van Kerckhoven. Dordrecht: Springer, 1988.

———. *Die Phänomenologische Philosophie Edmund Husserls in der gegenwärtigen Kritik.* In *Studien zur Phänomenologie 1930–1939.* The Hague: Martinus Nijhoff, 1966, 21: 79–156.

———. "*Reflexionen zu Husserls phänomenologischer Reflexion.*" In *Nähe und Distanz: Phänomenologische Vorträge und Aufsätze,* edited by Franz A. Schwarz, 299–322. Freiburg: Alber, 1976.

———. "Vergegenwärtigung und Bild." In *Studien zur Phänomenologie 1930–1939.* The Hague: Martinus Nijhoff, 1966, 21: 1–78.

Fink–Eitel, Hinrich. *Die Philosophie und die Wilden: Über die Bedeutung des Fremden für die europäische Geistesgeschichte.* Hamburg: Junius, 1994.

Forschner, Maximilian. "Glück als personale Identität: Die stoische Theorie des Endziels." In *Über das Glück des Menschen: Aristoteles, Epikur, Stoa, Thomas von Aquin, Kant,* 45–79. Darmstadt: Wissenschaftliche Buchgesellschaft, 1993.

Foucault, Michel. "Andere Räume." In *Zeitmitschrift: Journal für Ästhetik und Politik* 1990 (1): 4–15.

———. *Archäologie des Wissens.* Frankfurt: Suhrkamp, 1986.

———. *Dits et écrits 1954–1988,* 4 vols. Edited by Daniel Defert and François Ewald. Paris: Gallimard, 1994.

———. *Nietzsche, die Genealogie, die Historie.* In *Von der Subversion des Wissens.* Edited by Walter Seitter, 83–109. Munich: Hanser, 1974.

———. *Die Ordnung der Dinge: Eine Archäologie der Humanwissenschaften.* Frankfurt: Suhrkamp, 1993.

———. *Die Ordnung des Diskurses:* Frankfurt: Ullstein, 1977.

———. "Die Rückkehr der Moral: Ein Interview mit Michel Foucault (29. 5. 1984)." In *Ethos der Moderne. Foucaults Kritik der Aufklärung,* edited by Eva Erdmann, Rainer Forst, and Axel Honneth, 133–145. Frankfurt: Campus, 1990.

———. *Schriften zur Literatur,* edited by Daniel Defert and François Ewald. Frankfurt: Suhrkamp, 1988.

———. *Sexualität und Wahrheit,* vol. 2 of *Der Gebrauch der Lüste.* Frankfurt: Suhrkamp, 1990.

———. *Technologien des Selbst.* Edited by Luther H. Martin, Huck Gutman, and Patrick H. Hutton. Frankfurt: S. Fischer, 1993.

———. *Überwachen und Strafen: Die Geburt des Gefängnisses.* Frankfurt: Suhrkamp, 1976.

———. *Von der Subversion des Wissens.* Edited by Walter Seitter. Munich: Hanser, 1974.

———. *Wahnsinn und Gesellschaft: Eine Geschichte des Wahns im Zeitalter der Vernunft.* Frankfurt: Suhrkamp, 1993.

———. "Was ist Aufklärung?" In *Ethos der Moderne: Foucaults Kritik der Aufklärung,* edited by Eva Erdmann, Rainer Forst, and Axel Honneth, 35–54. Frankfurt: Campus, 1990.

———. "Was ist ein Autor?" In *Schriften zur Literatur,* 7–31, edited by Daniel Defert and François Ewald. Frankfurt: Suhrkamp, 1988.

———. "Zur Genealogie der Ethik: Ein Überblick über laufende Arbeiten." In Hubert L. Dreyfus and Paul Rabinow, *Michel Foucault: Jenseits von Strukturalismus und Hermeneutik.* Frankfurt: Beltz Athenäum, 1994, 265–292.

Frank, Manfred. *Conditio moderna: Essays, Reden, Programm.* Leipzig: Reclam, 1993.

———. *Stil in der Philosophie.* Stuttgart: Reclam, 1992.

Freud, Sigmund. "Vorlesung zur Einführung in die Psychoanalyse und Neue Folge." In *Studienausgabe*, vol. 1. Frankfurt: Fischer, 1989.

Freyer, Hans. *Theorie des Objektiven Geistes. Eine Einleitung in die Kulturphilosophie.* Darmstadt: Teubner/Wissenschaftliche Buchgesellschaft, 1966.

Fuchs, Thomas. *Die Mechanisierung des Herzens: Harvey und Descartes—Der vitale und der mechanische Aspekt des Kreislaufs.* Frankfurt: Suhrkamp, 1992.

Furhmann, Manfred, Hans Robert Jauss, and Wolfhart Pannenberg, eds. *Text und Applikation: Theologie, Jurisprudenz und Literaturwissenschaft im hermeneutischen Gespräch.* Munich: Fink, 1981.

Funke, Gerhard. *Phänomenologie—Metaphysik oder Methode?* Bonn: Bonvier Verlag Herbert Grundmann, 1972.

Gadamer, Hans-Georg. *Gesammelte Werke*, 10 vols. Tübingen: Mohr Siebeck, 1986–1995.

———. *Begriffsgeschichte als Philosophie*, in *Hermeneutik II.* Tübingen: Mohr Siebeck, 1986.

———. *Die deutsche Philosophie zwischen den beiden Weltkriegen.* Tübingen: Mohr Siebeck, 1995.

———. "Der eine Weg Martin Heideggers," in *Neuere Philosophie 1: Hegel, Husserl, Heidegger.* Tübingen: Mohr Siebeck, 1987.

———. *Erinnerungen an Heideggers Anfänge.* In *Dilthey-Jahrbuch* 4 (1986–1987): 3–43. Göttingen: Vandenhoeck & Ruprecht.

———. "Europa und die Oikoumene." In *Europa und die Philosophie,* edited by Hans-Helmuth Gander, 67–86. Frankfurt: Klostermann, 1993.

———. "Heideggers 'theologische' Frühschrift." In *Dilthey-Jahrbuch* 6 (1989): 228–234. Göttingen: Vandenhoeck & Ruprecht.

———. *Hermeneutik und Historismus*, in *Hermeneutik II.* Tübingen: Mohr Siebeck, 1986.

———. *Klassische und philosophische Hermeneutik*, in *Hermeneutik II.* Tübingen: Mohr Siebeck, 1986.

———. *Philosophische Begegnungen.* Tübingen: Mohr Siebeck, 1995.

———. *Praktisches Wissen.* Tübingen: Mohr Siebeck, 1985.

———. *Das Problem der Geschichte in der neueren Deutschen Philosophie*, in *Hermeneutik II.* Tübingen: Mohr Siebeck, 1986.

———. *Replik zu 'Hermeneutik und Ideologiekritik.* Tübingen: Mohr Siebeck, 1971.

———. *Text und Interpretation.* Tübingen: Mohr Siebeck, 1986.

———. *Wahrheit und Methode.* Tübingen: Mohr Siebeck, 1986.

———. "*Wahrheit und Methode: Der Anfang der Urfassung (ca. 1956).*" Edited by Jean Grondin and Hans-Ulrich Lessing. In *Dilthey-Jahrbuch,* 8 (1992–1993): 131–142. Göttingen: Vandenhoeck & Ruprecht.

———. *Wahrheit und Methode, Nachwort zur 3. Auflage (1972),* in *Hermeneutik II.* Tübingen: Mohr Siebeck, 1986.

———. *Wahrheit und Methode, Vorwort zur 2. Auflage,* in *Hermeneutik II.* Tübingen: Mohr Siebeck, 1986.

———. *Zwischen Phänomenologie und Dialektik,* in *Hermeneutik II.* Tübingen: Mohr Siebeck, 1986.

Gander, Hans-Helmuth. "*Die Geschichtlichkeit des Verstehens: Zu Gadamers Theorie der hermeneutischen Erfahrung.*" *Filozofia* (*Berichte der Slowakische Akademie der Wissenschaften*) 48 (1993): 274–286.

———. "'Ich weiß nicht, ob wir jemals mündig werden'—Anmerkungen zu Foucaults Aufklärungskritik." In *Das 18. Jahrhundert*, edited by Monika Fludernik and Ruth Nestvold, 199–213. Trier: WVT Wissenschaftlicher Verlag, 1998.

———. "Interpretation—Situation—Vernetzung: Hermeneutische Überlegungen zum Selbst- und Weltbezug im multimedialen Zeitalter." In *Hermeneutik und Ästhetik. Die Theologie des Wortes im multimedialen Zeitalter*, edited by Ulrich H. J. Körtner, 19–33. Neukirchen-Vluyn: Neukirchener Verlag, 2001.

———. "Martin Heidegger und Erhart Kästner: Anmerkungen zu einem Gespräch im Wegfeld von Dichten und Denken." *Heidegger Studies* 3–4 (1987–1988): 75–88.

———. *Positivismus als Metaphysik: Voraussetzungen und Grundstrukturen von Diltheys Grundlegung der Geisteswissenschaften.* Freiburg: Alber, 1988.

———, ed. *Europa und die Philosophie.* Frankfurt: Klostermann, 1993.

Gawoll, Hans-Jürgen. "Spur: Gedächtnis und Andersheit; Teil 1." *Archiv für Begriffsgeschichte* 30 (1986–1987): 44–69.

———. "Spur: Gedächtnis und Andersheit; Teil 2." *Archiv für Begriffsgeschichte* 32 (1989): 269–296.

Gebauer, Gunter, Dietmar Kamper, and others. *Historische Anthropologie: Zum Problem der Humanwissenschaften heute oder der Versuch einer Neubegründung.* Reinbek: Rowohlt, 1989.

Geertz, Clifford. *Dichte Beschreibung: Beiträge zum Verstehen kultureller Systeme.* Frankfurt: Suhrkamp, 1995.

Genette, Gérard. *Paratexte: Das Buch vom Beiwerk des Buches.* Frankfurt: Campus, 1992.

Gessmann, Martin. "Die Entdeckung des frühen Heidegger: Neuere Literatur zur Dezennie vor 'Sein und Zeit.'" *Philosophische Rundschau* 43 (1996): 215–232.

Gethmann, Carl Friedrich. *Dasein: Erkennen und Handeln; Heidegger im phänomenologischen Kontext.* Berlin: De Gruyter, 1993.

———. "Phänomenologie, Lebensphilosophie und Konstruktive Wissenschaftstheorie: Eine historische Skizze zur Vorgeschichte der Erlanger Schule." In *Lebenswelt und Wissenschaft. Studien zur Phänomenologie und Wissenschaftstheorie*, edited by Carl Friedrich Gethmann, 28–77. Bonn: Bouvier, 1991.

Gethmann-Siefert, Annemarie and Pöggeler, Otto, eds. *Heidegger und die praktische Philosophie.* Frankfurt: Suhrkamp, 1988.

Giddens, Anthony. *Jenseits von Links und Rechts: Die Zukunft radikaler Demokratie.* Frankfurt: Suhrkamp, 1997.

Gil, Thomas. *Kritik der Geschichtsphilosophie: L. von Rankes, J. Burckhardts und H. Freyers Problematisierung der klassischen Geschichtsphilosophie.* Stuttgart: M & P, 1993.

Grathoff, Richard. *Milieu und Lebenswelt: Einführung in die phänomenologische Soziologie und die sozialphänomenologische Forschung.* Frankfurt: Suhrkamp, 1989.

Greisch, Jean. *Hermeneutik und Metaphysik. Eine Problemgeschichte.* Munich: Fink, 1993.

———. *Ontologie et temporalité: Esquisse d'une interprétation intégrale de "Sein und Zeit."* Paris: Presses Universitaires de France, 1994.

———. "La 'tapisserie de la vie': Le phénomène de la vie et ses interprétations dans les 'Grundprobleme der Phänomenologie (1919/20)' de Martin Heidegger." In *Heidegger 1919–1929.*

De l'herméneutique de la facticité à la métaphysique du Dasein, 131–152, edited by Jean-François Courtine. Paris: J. Vrin, 1996.

Grondin, Jean. *Einführung in die philosophische Hermeneutik.* Darmstadt: Wissenschaftliche Buchgesellschaft, 1991.

———. "Gadamer vor Heidegger." *Internationale Zeitschrift für Philosophie* 1996, 197–226.

———. "Die Hermeneutik der Faktizität als ontologische Destruktion und Ideologiekritik: Zur Aktualität der Hermeneutik Heideggers." In *Im Gespräch der Zeit,* vol. 2, *Zur philosophischen Aktualität Heideggers,* edited by Dietrich Papenfuss and Otto Pöggeler, 163–178. Frankfurt: Klostermann, 1990.

———. "Die hermeneutische Intuition zwischen Husserl und Heidegger." In *Inmitten der Zeit: Beiträge zur europäischen Gegenwartsphilosophie,* edited by Thomas Grethlein and Heinrich Leitner, 271–276. Würzburg: Königshausen & Neumann, 1996.

———. "Hermeneutische Wahrheit. Heidegger und Augustinus." In *Die Frage nach der Wahrheit,* edited by Ewald Richter, 165–177. Frankfurt: Klostermann, 1997.

———. "Ist die Hermeneutik eine Krankheit? Antwort auf Herbert Schnädelbach." *Zeitschrift für philosophische Forschung* 45 (1991) 430–438.

———. "Das junghegelianische und ethische Motiv in Heideggers Hermeneutik der Faktizität." In *Wege und Irrwege des neueren Umganges mit Heideggers Werk,* edited by István M. Fehér, 141–150. Berlin: Duncker & Humblot, 1991.

———. "Husserl's Silent Contribution to Hermeneutics," in *Sources of Hermeneutics.* New York: SUNY Press, 1995, 35–46.

Habermas, Jürgen. "Die Moderne—eine unvollendetes Projekt." In *Kleine politische Schriften.* Frankfurt: Suhrkamp, 1981.

———. *Nachmetaphysisches Denken: Philosophische Aufsätze.* Frankfurt: Suhrkamp, 1988.

———. "Philosophie und Wissenschaft als Literatur?" in *Nachmetaphysisches Denken: Philosophische Aufsätze.* Frankfurt: Suhrkamp, 1988, 242–263.

———. *Der philosophische Diskurs der Moderne: Zwölf Vorlesungen.* Frankfurt: Suhrkamp, 1988.

———. *Theorie des kommunikativen Handelns.* 2 vols. Frankfurt: Suhrkamp, 1988.

Haeffner, Gerd. *In der Gegenwart leben: Auf der Spur eines Urphänomens.* Stuttgart: Kohlhammer, 1996.

Halbwachs, Maurice. *Das kollektive Gedächtnis.* Stuttgart: Fischer, 1967.

Hammacher, Klaus. "Einige methodische Regeln Descartes' und das erfindende Denken." In *Zeitschrift für allgemeine Wissenschaftstheorie IV,* 1973, 203–223.

Hastedt, Heiner. *Das Leib-Seele-Problem: Zwischen Naturwissenschaft des Geistes und kultureller Eindimensionalität.* Hamburg, 1989.

Haverkamp, Anselm. "Zur Interferenz juristischer und literarischer Hermeneutik in Sachen 'Kunst' (Art. 5 Abs. 3 GG)." In *Text und Applikation. Theologie, Jurisprudenze und Literaturwissenschaft im hermeneutischen Gespräch,* edited by Manfred Fuhrmann, Hans Robert Jauss, and Wolfhart Pannenberg, 199–202. Munich: Fink, 1981.

Hegel, Georg Wilhelm Friedrich. "Einleitung: Über das Wesen der philosophischen Kritik überhaupt und ihr Verhältnis zum gegenwärtigen Zustand der Philosophie insbesondere." In *Werke,* vol. 2, edited by Eva Moldenhauer and Karl Markus Michel, 171–187. Frankfurt: Suhrkamp, 1974.

———. *Vorlesungen über die Geschichte der Philosophie I–III.* In *Werke,* vols. 18–20. Frankfurt: Suhrkamp, 1974.

———. *Vorlesungen über die Philosophie der Weltgeschichte,* vol. 1. Edited by Johannes Hoffmeister. Hamburg: Meiner, 1970.

———. *Wissenschaft der Logik I.* In *Werke,* vol. 5. Frankfurt: Suhrkamp, 1974.

Heidegger, Martin. *Gesamtausgabe.* Edited by Friedrich-Wilhelm von Herrmann et al. Frankfurt: Klostermann, 1975–.

———. "Anmerkungen zu Karl Jaspers 'Psychologie der Weltanschauungen'" in *Wegmarken,* edited by Friedrich-Wilhelm von Herrmann, 1–44. Frankfurt: Klostermann, 1976.

———. *Augustinus und der Neuplatonismus (Sommersemester 1921)* in *Phänomenologie des religiösen Lebens,* edited by Matthias Jung, Thomas Regehly, and Claudius Strube. Frankfurt: Klostermann, 1995.

———. "Aus einem Gespräch über die Sprache," in *Unterwegs zur Sprache.* Edited by Friedrich-Wilhelm von Herrmann. Frankfurt: Klostermann, 1985.

———. *Der Begriff der Zeit.* Edited by Hartmut Tietjen. Tübingen: Niemeyer, 1989.

———. "Drei Briefe Martin Heideggers an Karl Löwith," edited by Hartmut Tietjen. In *Zur philosophischen Aktualität Heideggers.* vol. 2, *Im Gespräch der Zeit,* edited by Dietrich Papenfuss and Otto Pöggeler, 27–39. Frankfurt: Klostermann, 1990.

———. *Der Deutsche Idealismus [Fichte, Schelling, Hegel] und die philosophische Problemlage der Gegenwart.* Edited by Claudius Strube. Frankfurt: Klostermann, 1997.

———. *Die Grundbegriffe der Metaphysik. Welt—Endlichkeit—Einsamkeit.* Edited by Friedrich-Wilhelm von Herrmann. Frankfurt: Klostermann, 1983.

———. *Die Idee der Philosophie und das Weltanschauungsproblem (Kriegsnotsemester 1919),* in Heidegger, *Zur Bestimmung der Philosophie.* Edited by Bernd Heimbüchel. Frankfurt: Klostermann, 1999.

———. "Die Idee der Philosophie und das Weltanschauungsproblem (Auszug aus der Nachschrift Brecht)," edited by Claudius Strube. *Heidegger Studies* 12 (1996): 9–14.

———. *Einführung in die phänomenologische Forschung.* Edited by Friedrich-Wilhelm von Herrmann. Frankfurt: Klostermann, 1994.

———. *Einleitung in die Phänomenologie der Religion (Wintersemester 1920/21),* in *Phänomenologie des religiösen Lebens,* edited by Matthias Jung, Thomas Regehly, and Claudius Strube. Frankfurt: Klostermann, 1995.

———. *Grundprobleme der Phänomenologie (1919/20).* Edited by Hans-Helmuth Gander. Frankfurt: Klostermann, 1993.

———. *Die Grundprobleme der Phänomenologie (Sommersemester 1927).* Edited by Friedrich-Wilhelm von Hermann. Frankfurt: Klostermann, 1997.

———. *Hölderlins Hymne 'Andenken' (Wintersemester 1941/42).* Edited by Curd Ochwadt. Frankfurt: Klostermann, 1982.

———. *Hölderlins Hymnen "Germanien" und "Der Rhein."* Edited by Susanne Ziegler. Frankfurt: Klostermann, 1980.

———. *Die Idee der Philosophie und das Weltanschauungsproblem (Kriegsnotsemester 1919),* in Heidegger, *Zur Bestimmung der Philosophie.* Edited by Bernd Heimbüchel. Frankfurt: Klostermann, 1999.

———. "Die Lehre vom Urteil im Psychologismus," in *Frühe Schrifte.* Edited by Friedrich-Wilhelm von Herrmann. Frankfurt: Klostermann, 1978.

———. *Logik: Die Frage nach der Wahrheit,* edited by Walter Biemel. Frankfurt: Klostermann, 1976.

————. *Mein Weg in die Phänomenologie*, in *Zur Sache des Denkens (1962–1964)*, edited by Friedrich-Wilhelm von Herrmann. Frankfurt: Klostermann, 2007.

————. *Metaphysische Anfangsgründe der Logik im Ausgang von Leibniz*. Edited by Klaus Held. Frankfurt: Klostermann, 1978.

————. "Neuere Forschungen über Logik," in *Frühe Schrifte*. Edited by Friedrich-Wilhelm von Herrmann. Frankfurt: Klostermann, 1978.

————. "Nietzsches Wort 'Gott ist tot'." In *Holzwege*, edited by Friedrich-Wilhelm von Herrmann. Frankfurt: Klostermann, 1977.

————. *Ontologie (Hermeneutik der Faktizität)*. Edited by Käte Bröcker-Oltmanns. Frankfurt: Klostermann, 1995.

————. *Phänomenologie der Anschauung und des Ausdrucks:Theorie der philosophischen Begriffsbildung (Sommersemester 1920)*. Edited by Claudius Strube. Frankfurt: Klostermann, 2007.

————. *Phänomenologie und transzendentale Wertphilosophie (SommerSemester 1919)*, in Heidegger, *Zur Bestimmung der Philosophie*. Edited by Bernd Heimbüchel. Frankfurt: Klostermann, 1999.

————. "Phänomenologische Interpretationen zu Aristoteles (Anzeige der hermeneutischen Situation)," edited by Hans-Ulrich Lessing. In *Dilthey-Jahrbuch,* vol. 6, edited by Frithjof Rodi, 233–274. Göttingen: Vandenhoeck & Ruprecht, 1989.

————. *Phänomenologische Interpretationen zu Aristoteles: Einführung in die phänomenologische Forschung*. Edited by Walter von Bröcker and Käte Bröcker-Oltmanns. Frankfurt: Klostermann, 1994.

————. *Prolegomena zur Geschichte des Zeitbegriffs*. (Summer Semester 1925). Edited by Petra Jaeger. (Frankfurt: Klostermann, 1994).

————. *Sein und Zeit*. Edited by Friedrich-Wilhelm von Hermann. Frankfurt: Klostermann, 1977.

————. "SPIEGEL-Gespräch mit Martin Heidegger." In *Martin Heidegger im Gespräch*, edited by Günter Neske and Emil Kettering, 81–114. Pfullingen: Neske, 1988.

————. *Über das Wesen der Universität und des akademischen Studiums (Sommersemester 1919)*. In Heidegger, *Zur Bestimmung der Philosophie*. Edited by Bernd Heimbüchel. Frankfurt: Klostermann, 1999.

————. *Vorträge und Aufsätze*. Pfullingen: Neske, 1978.

————. *Wegmarken*. Edited by Friedrich-Wilhelm von Herrmann. Frankfurt: Klostermann, 2004.

————. "Das Wesen der Sprache." In *Unterwegs zur Sprache*, edited by Friedrich-Wilhelm von Herrmann. Frankfurt: Klostermann, 1985.

————. "Wilhelm Diltheys Forschungsarbeit und der gegenwärtige Kampf um eine historische Weltanschauung." In *Dilthey-Jahrbuch* vol. 8, edited by Frithjof Rodi, 143–180 (1992–1993). Göttingen: Vandenhoeck & Ruprecht.

————. *Zollikoner Seminare*. Edited by Medard Boss. Frankfurt: Klostermann, 1987.

————. "Zur Geschichte des philosophischen Lehrstuhles seit 1866," in *Kant und das Problem der Metaphysik*, edited by Friedrich-Wilhelm von Hermann. Frankfurt: Klostermann, 1991.

————. *Zur Sache des Denkens*. Tübingen: Niemeyer, 1976.

————, and Elisabeth Blochmann. *Briefwechsel 1918–1969*. Edited by Joachim Wolfgang Storck. Marbach: Deutsche Schillergesellschaft 1989.

————, and Imma von Bodmershof. *Briefwechsel 1959–1976*. Edited by Bruno Pieger. Stuttgart: Klett-Cotta, 2000.

————, and Ludwig von Ficker. *Briefwechsel.* In Ludwig von Ficker, *Briefwechsel,* vol. 4: *1940–1967,* edited by Martin Alber. Innsbruck: Haymon, 1996.

————, and Karl Jaspers. *Briefwechsel 1920–1963.* Edited by Walter Biemel and Hans Saner. Frankfurt: Klostermann, 1990.

————, and Erhart Kästner. *Briefwechsel 1953–1974.* Edited by Heinrich Wiegand Petzet. Frankfurt: Insel, 1986.

Held, Klaus. "Europa und die Interkulturelle Verständigung: Ein Entwurf im Anschluß an Heideggers Phänomenologie der Grundstimmungen." In *Europa und die Philosophie,* edited by Hans-Helmuth Gander, 87–103. Frankfurt: Klostermann, 1993.

————. "Grundstimmung und Zeitkritik bei Heidegger." In *Zur philosophischen Aktualität Heideggers, vol. 1: Philosophie und Politik,* edited by Dietrich Papenfuss and Otto Pöggeler, 31–56. Frankfurt: Klostermann, 1990.

————. "Heidegger und das Prinzip der Phänomenologie." In *Heidegger und die praktische Philosophie,* edited by Annemarie Gethmann-Siefert and Otto Pöggeler, 111–139. Frankfurt: Suhrkamp, 1988.

————. "Heimwelt, Fremdwelt, die eine Welt." In *Perspektiven und Probleme der Husserlischen Phänomenologie,* edited by Ernst Wolfgang Orth, 305–337. Freiburg: Alber, 1991.

————. *Heraklit, Parmenides und der Anfang von Philosophie und Wissenschaft: Eine phänomenologische Besinnung.* Berlin: De Gruyter, 1980.

————. "Husserls neue Einführung in die Philosophie: Der Begriff der Lebenswelt." In *Lebenswelt und Wissenschaft: Studien zum Verhältnis von Phänomenologie und Wissenschaftstheorie,* edited by Carl Friedrich Gethmann, 79–113. Bonn: Bouvier, 1991.

————. "Husserl und die Griechen." In *Profile der Phänomenologie: Zum 50. Todestag von Edmund Husserl,* edited by Ernst Wolfgang Orth, 137–176. Freiburg: Alber 1989.

Henrich, Dieter. *Die Einheit der Wissenschaftslehre Max Webers.* Tübingen: Mohr, 1952.

————. "Selbsterhaltung und Geschichtlichkeit." In *Subjektivität und Selbsterhaltung: Beiträge zur Diagnose der Moderne,* edited by Hans Ebeling, 97–143. Frankfurt: Suhrkamp, 1996.

Herrmann, Friedrich-Wilhelm von. *Der Begriff der Phänomenologie bei Heidegger und Husserl.* Frankfurt, 1981.

————. *Einleitung: Die Exposition der Frage nach dem Sinn von Sein.* Vol. 1 of *Hermeneutische Phänomenologie des Daseins: Eine Erläuterung von* Sein und Zeit. Frankfurt: Klostermann, 1987.

————. "Das Ereignis und die Fragen nach dem Wesen der Technik, Politik und Kunst," in *Wege ins Ereignis. Zu Heideggers "Beiträgen zur Philosophie,"* 85–107. Frankfurt: Klostermann, 1994.

————. "Husserl—Heidegger und die 'Sachen selbst.'" In *Inmitten der Zeit: Beiträge zur europäischen Gegenwartsphilosophie,* edited by Thomas Grethlein and Heinrich Leitner, 277–289. Würzburg: Königshausen & Neumann, 1996.

————. "Husserl und Descartes." In *Perspektiven der Philosophie: Neues Jahrbuch,* vol. 23 (1997), 45–72.

————. *Husserl und die Meditationen des Descartes.* Frankfurt: Klostermann, 1971.

————. *Die Selbstinterpretation Martin Heideggers.* Meisenheim: Hain, 1964.

————. *Subjekt und Dasein: Interpretationen zu "Sein und Zeit."* Frankfurt: Klostermann, 1985.

Hirsch, E.D. *Prinzipien der Interpretation.* Translated by Adelaide Anne Späth. Munich: Fink, 1972.

Hirsch, Rudolf. "Edmund Husserl und Hugo von Hofmannsthal: Eine Begegnung und ein Brief." In *Sprache und Politik*, edited by Carl Joachim Friedrich and Benno Reifenberg, 108–115. Heidelberg: Lambert Schneider, 1968.

Hölderlin, Friedrich. *Briefe*. In *Sämtliche Werke*, vol. 6 pt. 1, edited by Adolf Beck. Stuttgart: Kohlhammer, 1954.

———. Friedrich Hölderlin to Casimir Ulrich Böhlendorff, December 4, 1801. In *Briefe*, edited by Adolf Beck, *Sämtliche Werke*, vol. 6 pt. 1, 425–428. Stuttgart: Kohlhammer, 1954.

Hofmann, Johann. N. *Wahrheit, Perspektive, Interpretation: Nietzsche und die philosophische Hermeneutik*. Berlin: De Gruyter, 1994.

Hofmannsthal, Hugo von. "*Ein Brief*." In *Gesammelte Werke in Einzelausgaben: Prosa II*, edited by Herbert Steiner, 7–22. Frankfurt: S. Fischer, 1951.

———. "Tausendeine Nacht." In *Gesammelte Werke in Einzelausgaben: Prosa II*, edited by Herbert Steiner, 311–320. Frankfurt: S. Fischer, 1951.

Hogemann, Friedrich. "Heideggers Konzeption der Phänomenologie in den Vorlesungen aus dem Wintersemester 1919/20 und dem Sommersemester 1920." In *Dilthey-Jahrbuch*, vol. 4 (1986–1987), 54–71. Göttingen: Vandenhoeck & Ruprecht.

Hohl, Hubert. *Lebenswelt und Geschichte: Grundzüge der Spätphilosophie Edmund Husserls*. Freiburg: Alber, 1962.

Honneth, Axel. *Kritik der Macht: Reflexionsstufen einer kritischen Gesellschaftstheorie*. Frankfurt: Suhrkamp, 1989.

Hopkins, Burt C. *Intentionality in Husserl and Heidegger: The Problem of the Original Method and Phenomenon of Phenomenology*. Dordrecht: Springer, 1993.

Hornig, Gottfried. "Über Semlers theologische Hermeneutik." In *Unzeitgemäße Hermeneutik. Verstehen und Interpretation im Denken der Aufklärung*, edited by Axel Bühler, 192–222. Frankfurt: Klostermann, 1994.

How, Alan. *The Habermas-Gadamer Debate and the Nature of the Social: Back to Bedrock*. Aldershot, UK: Avebury, 1995.

Hübner, Kurt. *Kritik der wissenschaftlichen Vernunft*. Freiburg: Alber, 1986.

———. "Von der Intentionalität der modernen Technik." In *Sprache im technischen Zeitalter*, vol. 25 (1968), 27–48.

Husserl, Edmund. *Briefwechsel*. Edited by Karl Schuhmann. Dordrecht: Springer, 1994.

———. *Cartesianische Meditationen und Pariser Vorträge*. In *Husserliana: Edmund Husserl—Gesammelte Werke*, vol 1. Edited by Stephan Strasser. The Hague: Martinus Nijhoff, 1973.

———. *Erfahrung und Urteil: Untersuchungen zur Genealogie der Logik*. Edited by Ludwig Landgrebe. Hamburg: Claassen & Goverts, 1948.

———. *Erste Philosophie (1923–1924): Zweiter Teil: Theorie der phänomenologischen Reduktion*. In *Husserliana*, vol. 8. Edited by Rudolf Boehm. The Hague: Martinus Nijhoff, 1959.

———. *Formale und transzendentale Logik: Versuch einer Kritik der logischen Vernunft*. Edited by Paul Janssen. The Hague: Martinus Nijhoff, 1974.

———. *Ideen zu einer reinen Phänomenlogie und phänomenlogischen Philosophie. Erstes Buch: Allgemeine Einführung in die reine Phänomenologie (Ideen I/Ideas I)*. In *Husserliana*, vol. 3. Edited by Walter Biemel. The Hague: Martinus Nijhoff, 1950.

———. *Die Krisis der europäischen Wissenschaften und die transzendentale Phänomenologie*. In *Husserliana*, vol. 6, edited by Walter Biemel. The Hague: Martinus Nijhoff, 1976.

———. *Die Krisis der europaischen Wissenschaften und die transzendentale Phänomenologie. Texte aus dem Nachlass 1934–1937.* In *Husserliana*, vol. 29, edited by Reinhold N. Smid. The Hague: Kluwer, 1992.

———. *Logische Untersuchungen. Zweiter Teil. Untersuchungen zur* Edmund Husserl, "*Phänomenologie und Theorie der Erkenntnis*, edited by Ursula Panzer, Anthropologie," in *Aufsätze und Vorträge (1922–1937), Husserliana: Edmund Husserl—Gesammelte Werke.* The Hague: Martinus Nijhoff, 1984, edited by Thomas Nenon and Hans Rainer Sepp. Dordrecht: Kluwer, 1989, *GW* 27.

———. *Logische Untersuchungen. Ergänzungsband. Erster Teil.* Entwürfe zur Umarbeitung der VI. Untersuchung und zur Vorrede für die Neuafulage der Logischen Untersuchungen (Sommer 1913). In *Husserliana*, vol. 20–21, edited by Ullrich Melle. Dordrecht: Kluwer, 2002.

———. *Nachwort zu meinen Ideen zu einer reinen Phänomenologie und phänomenologischen Philosophie.* In *Ideen III*, edited by Marly Biemel. The Hague: Martinus Nijhoff, 1971.

———. "Phänomenologie und Anthropologie," Berlin: Kant-Gesellschaft, 1931.

———. *Phänomenologische Psychologie.* In *Husserliana: Edmund Husserl—Gesammelte Werke*, vol. 9, edited by Walter Biemel. The Hague: Martinus Nijhoff, 1968.

———. "Philosophie als strenge Wissenschaft," *LOGOS* 1 (1910), 3:289–341.

———. *Philosophie als strenge Wissenschaft*, edited by Wilhelm Szilasi. Frankfurt: Klostermann, 1965.

———. "Randbemerkungen zu Heideggers Sein und Zeit und Kant und das Problem der Metaphysik," edited by Roland Breeur and Steven Spileers. *Husserl Studies* 11 (1994), 3–63.

———. *Vorlesungen über Ethik und Wertlehre (1908–1914).* In *Husserliana*, vol. 28, edited by Ulrich Melle.

———. *Zur Phänomenologie der Intersubjektivität: Texte aus dem Nachlass.* Edited by Iso Kern. The Hague: Martinus Nijhoff, 1973.

Imdahl, Georg. "'Formale Anzeige' bei Heidegger." In *Archiv für Begriffsgeschichte,* 37 (1994): 306–332.

———. *Das Leben verstehen: Heideggers formal anzeigende Hermeneutik in den frühen Freiburger Vorlesungen (1919 bis 1923).* Würzburg: Königshausen & Neumann, 1997.

Ineichen, Hans. *Philosophische Hermeneutik.* Freiburg: Alber, 1991.

Iser, Wolfgang. *Der Akt des Lesens: Theorie ästhetischer Wirkung.* Munich: Fink, 1976.

———. *Die Appellstruktur der Texte: Unbestimmtheit als Wirkungsbedingung literarischer Prosa.* Konstanz: Universitätsverlag, 1970.

Jakob, Eric. *Martin Heidegger und Hans Jonas: Die Metaphysik der Subjektivität und die Krise der technologischen Zivilisation.* Tübingen: Francke, 1996.

Jamme, Christoph. "Heideggers frühe Begründung der Hermeneutik." In *Dilthey-Jahrbuch,* vol. 4 (1986–1987), 72–90. Göttingen: Vandenhoeck & Ruprecht.

Janke, Wolfgang. *Existenzphilosophie.* Berlin: De Gruyter, 1982.

Janssen, Paul. *Edmund Husserl: Einführung in seine Phänomenologie.* Freiburg: Alber, 1976.

———. *Geschichte und Lebenswelt: Ein Beitrag zur Diskussion von Husserls Spätwerk.* The Hague: Martinus Nijhoff, 1970.

Jaspers, Karl. *Psychologie der Weltanschauungen.* Berlin: Springer, 1954.

Jauss, Hans Robert. *Ästhetische Erfahrung und literarische Hermeneutik.* Frankfurt: Suhrkamp, 1991.

———. *Literaturgeschichte als Provokation.* Frankfurt: Suhrkamp, 1970.

Jonas, Hans. *Philosophische Untersuchungen und metaphysische Vermutungen*. Frankfurt: Insel, 1992.

Kant, Immanuel. *Kritik der reinen Vernunft*. Edited by Raymund Schmidt. Hamburg: Meiner, 1976.

———. *Logik*. Edited by Tillmann Pinder. Hamburg: Meiner, 1997.

———. *Reflexionen zur Metaphysik*. In *Kants Gesammelte Schriften*, vol. 18. Berlin: Preußischen Akademie der Wissenschaften, 1928.

Kerckhoven, Guy van. "Die Grundsätze von Husserls Konfrontation mit Dilthey im Lichte der geschichtlichen Selbstzeugnisse." In *Dilthey und der Wandel des Philosophiebegriffs seit dem 19. Jahrhundert: Studien zu Dilthey und Brentano, Mach, Nietzsche, Twardowski, Husserl, Heidegger*, edited by Ernst Wolfgang Orth, 134–160. Freiburg: Alber, 1984.

———. "Die Konstruktion der Phänomene das absoluten Bewußtseins: Martin Heideggers Auseinandersetzung mit dem Denken Edmund Husserls." In *Zur philosophischen Aktualität Heideggers*, vol. 2, *Im Gespräch der Zeit*, edited by Dietrich Papenfuss and Otto Pöggeler, 55–70. Frankfurt: Klostermann, 1990.

Kern, Iso. *Husserl und Kant: Eine Untersuchung über Husserls Verhältnis zu Kant und zum Neukantianismus*. The Hague: Springer, 1964.

Kierkegaard, Søren. *Die Krankheit zum Tode*. Edited by Hans Rochol. Hamburg: Meiner, 1995.

———. *Tagebücher*. 5 vols. Düsseldorf: Diederichs, 1960–1975.

Kisiel, Theodor. "Edition und Übersetzung: Unterwegs von Tatsachen zu Gedanken, von Werken zu Wegen." In *Im Spiegel der Welt: Sprache, Übersetzung, Auseinandersetzung*, vol. 3, *Zur philosophischen Aktualität Heideggers*, edited by Dietrich Papenfuss and Otto Pöggeler, 89–107. Frankfurt: Klostermann, 1992.

———. "Das Entstehen des Begriffsfeldes 'Faktizität' im Frühwerk Heideggers." In *Dilthey-Jahrbuch*, vol. 4 (1986–1987), 91–120. Göttingen: Vandenhoeck & Ruprecht.

———. *The Genesis of Heidegger's* Being and Time. Berkeley: University of California Press, 1993.

———. "Das Kriegnotsemester 1919: Heideggers Durchbruch zur hermeneutischen Phänomenologie." In *Philosophisches Jarbuch* 99 (1992): 105–122.

———. "The Missing Link in the Early Heidegger." In *Hermeneutic Phenomenology: Lectures and Essays*, edited by Joseph. J. Kockelmans, 1–40. Lanham, MD: University Press of America, 1988.

Kisiel, Theodor, and John van Buren, eds. *Reading Heidegger from the Start: Essays in His Earliest Thought*. New York: State University of New York Press, 1994.

Kober, Michael. *Gewißheit als Norm: Wittgensteins erkenntnistheoretische Untersuchungen in* Über Gewißheit. Berlin: De Gruyter, 1993.

Kögler, Hans Herbert. *Michel Foucault*. Stuttgart: Metzler, 1994.

Köstler, Hermann. "Heidegger schreibt an Grabmann." In *Philosophisches Jahrbuch* 87 (1980), 96–109.

Kohl, Karl-Heinz. *Ethnologie—die Wissenschaft vom kulturell Fremden: Eine Einführung*. Munich: Beck, 1993.

Kohlenberger, Helmut K. "Buch der Schöpfung." In *Historisches Wörterbuch der Philosophie*, 1:959f., edited by Joachim Ritter. Basel: Schwabe, 1971.

Kolakowski, Leszek. *Die Suche nach der verlorenen Gewißheit: Denk-Wege mit Edmund Husserl*. Munich: Piper, 1986.

Koslowski, Peter. "Die Baustellen der Postmoderne—Wider den Vollendungszwang der Moderne." In *Moderne oder Postmoderne? Zur Signatur des gegenwärtigen Zeitalters*, edited by Peter Koslowski, Robert Spaemann, and Reinhard Löwe, 1–16. Weinheim: VCH, 1986.

Kovacs, George. "Philosophy as Primordial Science in Heidegger's Courses of 1919." In *Reading Heidegger from the Start: Essays in His Earliest Thought*, edited by Theodor Kisiel and John van Buren, 91–107. New York: State University of New York Press, 1994.

Krell, David Farrell. "Toward *Sein und Zeit*. Heidegger's Early Review (1919–1921) of Jaspers' *Psychologie der Weltanschauungen*." *Journal of the British Society for Phenomenology* 6 (1975): 147–156.

Kriele, Martin. "Juristische Hermeneutik am Beispiel der 'Mephisto'-Entscheidung." In *Text und Applikation. Theologie, Jurisprudenz und Literaturewissenschaft im hermeneutischen Gespräch*, edited by Manfred Fuhrmann, Hans Robert Jauss, and Wolfhart Pannenberg, 149–162. Munich: Fink, 1981.

Kristeva, Julia. *Fremde sind wir uns selbst*. Frankfurt: Suhrkamp, 1990.

Kuhn, Thomas. *Die Struktur wissenschaftlicher Revolutionen*. 2d ed. Frankfurt: Suhrkamp, 1976.

Landgrebe, Ludwig. *Faktizität und Individuation: Studien zu den Grundfragen der Phänomenologie*. Hamburg: Meiner, 1982.

———. "*Lebenswelt und Geschichtlichkeit des menschlichen Daseins*." In *Phänomenologie und Marxismus*, vol. 2, edited by Bernhard Waldenfels, Jan M. Broekman, and Ante Pazanin, 13–58. Frankfurt: Suhrkamp, 1977.

———. *Phänomenologie und Metaphysik*. Hamburg: Schröder, 1949.

———. *Der Weg der Phänomenologie: Das Problem einer ursprünglichen Erfahrung*. Gütersloh: Mohn, 1963.

Lehmann, Karl. "Transzendentalphilosophie und Phänomenologie in den ersten Schriften Martin Heideggers (1912–1916)." *Philosophisches Jahrbuch* 71 (1963–1964): 331–357.

Leibniz, Gottfried Wilhelm. "Monadologie." In *Philosophische Schriften*, vol. 1, 439–483, edited by Hans Heinz Holz. Darmstadt: Wissenschaftliche Buchgesellschaft, 1985.

Lembeck, Karl-Heinz. *Einführung in die phänomenologische Philosophie*. Darmstadt: Wissenschaftliche Buchgesellschaft, 1994.

———. *Gegenstand Geschichte: Geschichtswissenschaftstheorie in Husserls Phänomenologie*. Dordrecht: Springer, 1988.

Lenk, Hans. *Interpretation und Realität: Vorlesungen über Realismus in der Philosophie der Interpretationskonstrukte*. Frankfurt: Suhrkamp, 1995.

———. *Schemaspiele: Über Schemainterpretationen und Interpretationskonstrukte*. Frankfurt: Suhrkamp, 1995.

Levinas, Emmanuel. *Die Spur des Anderen*. Freiburg: Alber, 1987.

———. *Totalität und Unendlichkeit: Versuch über die Exteriorität*. Freiburg: Alber, 1987.

Lévi-Strauss, Claude. "Begegnungen mit Merleau-Ponty." In *Leibhaftige Vernunft: Spuren von Merleau-Pontys Denken*, edited by Alexandre Métraux and Bernhard Waldenfels, 29–36. Munich: Fink, 1986.

———. *Strukturale Anthropologie*. 2 vols. Frankfurt: Suhrkamp, 1992–1997.

———. *Das wilde Denken*. Frankfurt: Suhrkamp, 1994.

Liebs, Detlef. "Zum Begriff 'Kunst' im Recht." In *Text und Applikation: Theologie, Jurisprudenz und Literaturwissenschaft im hermeneutischen Gespräch*, edited by Manfred

Fuhrmann, Hans Robert Jauss, and Wolfhart Pannenberg, 203–205. Munich: Fink, 1981.

Liebsch, Burkhard. *Geschichte im Zeichen des Abschieds.* Munich: Fink, 1996.

Lipps, Hans. *Die Verbindlichkeit der Sprache: Arbeiten zur Sprachphilosophie und Logik.* Frankfurt: Klostermann, 1977.

Löwith, Karl. *Mensch und Menschenwelt: Beiträge zur Anthropologie.* In *Sämtliche Schriften,* vol. 1, edited by Klaus Stichweh. Stuttgart: Metzler, 1981.

———. *Weltgeschichte und Heilsgeschehen: Zur Kritik der Geschichtsphilosophie.* In *Sämtliche Schriften,* vol. 2, edited by Klaus Stichweh. Stuttgart: Metzler, 1983.

Lübbe, Hermann. *Bewußtsein in Geschichten: Studien zur Phänomenologie der Subjektivität; Mach, Husserl, Schapp, Wittgenstein.* Freiburg: Rombach, 1972.

Luhmann, Niklas. *Soziale Systeme: Grundriß einer allgemeinen Theorie.* Frankfurt: Suhrkamp, 1996.

Lyotard, Jean-François. "Die Moderne redigieren." In *Wege aus der Moderne: Schlüsseltexte der Postmoderne-Diskussion,* edited by Wolfgang Welsch, 204–214. Weinheim: Akademie Verlag, 1988.

———, *Das postmoderne Wissen: Ein Bericht.* Graz: Böhlau, 1986.

Mai, Katharina. *Die Phänomenologie und ihre Überschreitungen: Husserls reduktives Philosophieren und Derridas Spur der Andersheit.* Stuttgart: Metzler, 1996.

Makkreel, Rudolf A. "Heideggers ursprüngliche Auslegung der Faktizität des Lebens: Diahermeneutik als Aufbau und Abbau der geschichtlichen Welt." In *Zur philosophischen Aktualität Heideggers,* vol. 2, edited by Dietrich Papenfuss and Otto Pöggeler, 179–188. Frankfurt: Klostermann, 1990.

Makropoulos, Michael. *Modernität und Kontingenz.* Munich: Fink, 1997.

Mall, Ram Adhar. *Philosophie im Vergleich der Kulturen: Interkulturelle Philosophie—Eine neue Orientierung.* Darmstadt: Wissenschaftliche Buchgesellschaft, 1995.

———, and Dieter Lohmar, eds. *Philosophische Grundlagen der Interkulturität.* Amsterdam: Rodopi, 1993.

Marion, Jean-Luc. "Heidegger and Descartes." In *Critical Heidegger,* edited by Christopher E. Macann, 67–96. London: Routledge, 1996.

———. *Réduction et donation: Recherches sur Husserl, Heidegger et la phénoménologie.* Paris: Presses Universitaires de France, 1989.

Marquard, Odo. *Apologie des Zufälligen: Philosophische Studien.* Stuttgart: Reclam, 1986.

Martin, Jochen. "Der Wandel des Beständigen: Überlegungen zu einer historischen Anthropologie," in *Freiburger Universitätsblätter* (1994), 126: 35–46.

Marx, Werner. *Vernunft und Welt: Zwischen Tradition und anderem Anfang.* The Hague: Martinus Nijhoff, 1970.

Maturana, Humberto R., and Francisco J. Varela. *Der Baum der Erkenntnis: Die biologischen Wurzeln des menschlichen Erkennens.* Bern: Goldmann, 1987.

Matuschek, Stefan. *Über das Staunen: Eine ideengeschichtliche Analyse.* Tübingen: Niemeyer, 1991.

Merleau-Ponty, Maurice. *Phänomenologie der Wahrnehmung.* Translated by Rudolph Boehm. Berlin: De Gruyter, 1966.

———. *Das Sichtbare und das Unsichtbare.* Edited by Claude Lefort. Munich: Fink, 1986.

———. "Von Mauss zu Claude Lévi-Strauss." In *Leibhaftige Vernunft: Spuren von Merleau-Pontys Denken,* edited by Alexandre Métraux and Bernhard Waldenfels, 13–28. Munich: Fink, 1986.

Merz, Peter-Ulrich. *Max Weber und Heinrich Rickert: Die erkenntniskritischen Grundlagen der verstehende Soziologie.* Würzburg: Königshausen & Neumann, 1990.

Meyer-Drawe, Käte. *Illusionen von Autonomie: Diesseits von Ohnmacht und Allmacht des Ich.* Munich: Kirchheim, 1990.

Michalski, Mark. *Fremdwahrnehmung und Mitsein: Zur Grundlegung der Sozialphilosophie im Denken Max Schelers und Martin Heideggers.* Bonn: Bouvier, 1997.

Mill, John Stuart. *System der deduktiven und induktiven Logik.* Translated by Theodor Gomperz (1886). In *Gesammelte Werke,* vols. 2–4. Aalen: Scientia, 1968.

Misch, Georg. "Lebensphilosophie und Phänomenologie. Eine Auseinandersetzung mit Heidegger." In *Philosophischer Anzeiger* 3 1929, 267–368.

Mittelstraß, Jürgen. "Das lebensweltliche Apriori." In *Lebenswelt und Wissenschaft: Studien zum Verhältnis von Phänomenologie und Wissenschaftstheorie,* edited by Carl Friedrich Gethmann, 114–142. Bonn: Bouvier, 1991.

Mohanty, J. N. "'Lifeworld' and 'Apriori' in Husserl's Later Thought." In *The Phenomenological Realism of the Possible Worlds,* edited by Anna-Teresa Tymieniecka, 46–65. Dordrecht: Springer, 1974.

Montaigne, Michel de. *Oeuvres complètes.* Edited by Albert Thibaudet and Maurice Rat. Paris: Gallimard, 1962.

———. *Essais.* Translated and edited by Hans Stilett. Frankfurt: Eichborn, 1998.

Müller, Max. *Erfahrung und Geschichte: Grundzüge einer Philosophie der Freiheit als transzendentale Erfahrung.* Freiburg: Alber, 1971.

Müller, Wolfgang G. *Topik des Stilbegriffs: Zur Geschichte des Stilverständnisses von der Antike bis zur Gegenwart.* Darmstadt: Wissenschaftliche Buchgesellschaft, 1981.

Münkler, Herfried. ed. *Furcht und Faszination: Facetten der Fremdheit.* Berlin: Akademie, 1997.

Natorp, Paul. *Allgemeine Psychologie nach kritischer Methode.* Tübingen: Mohr Siebeck, 1912.

———. *Philosophie: Ihr Problem und ihre Probleme: Einführung in den kritischen Idealismus.* Göttingen: Vandenhoeck & Ruprecht, 1929.

———. *Philosophische Systematik: Aus dem Nachlaß.* Hamburg: Meiner, 1958.

Niebel, Wilhelm Friedrich, Angelica Horn, and Herbert Schädelbach, eds. *Descartes im Diskurs der Neuzeit.* Frankfurt: Suhrkamp, 2000.

Nietzsche, Friedrich. *Werke: Kritische Gesamtausgabe.* Edited by Giorgio Colli and Mazzino Montinari. Berlin: De Gruyter, 1968–.

———. *Die fröhliche Wissenschaft.* In *Werke,* div. 5, pt. 2, edited by Giorgio Colli and Mazzino Montinari. Berlin: De Gruyter, 1973.

———. *Jenseits von Gut und Böse,* In *Werke,* div. 6, pt. 2, edited by Giorgio Colli and Mazzino Montinari. Berlin: De Gruyter, 1968.

———. *Morgenröthe* In *Werke,* div. 5, pt. 1, edited by Giorgio Colli and Mazzino Montinari. Berlin: De Gruyter, 2014.

———. *Nachgelassene Fragmente: Herbst 1869–Herbst 1872,* In *Werke,* div. 3, pt. 3, edited by Giorgio Colli and Mazzino Montinari. Berlin: De Gruyter, 1978.

———. *Nachgelassene Fragmente: Frühjahr–Herbst 1884,* In *Werke,* div. 7, pt. 2, edited by Giorgio Colli and Mazzino Montinari. Berlin: De Gruyter, 2015.

———. *Nachgelassene Fragmente: Herbst 1884—Herbst 1885,* In *Werke,* div. 7, pt. 3, edited by Giorgio Colli and Mazzino Montinari. Berlin: De Gruyter, 1974–.

———. *Nachgelassene Fragmente: Herbst 1885—Herbst 1887,* In *Werke,* div. 8, pt. 1, edited by Giorgio Colli and Mazzino Montinari. Berlin: De Gruyter, 1974–.

———. *Nachgelassene Fragmente: Herbst 1887–März 1888*, In *Werke*, div. 8, pt. 2, edited by Giorgio Colli and Mazzino Montinari. Berlin: De Gruyter, 1970–.

———. *Nachgelassene Fragmente: Anfang 1888–Anfang Januar 1889*, div. 8, pt. 3, edited by Giorgio Colli and Mazzino Montinari. Berlin: De Gruyter, 1972–.

———. *Über Wahrheit und Lüge im aussermoralischen Sinne*, div. 3, pt. 2, edited by Giorgio Colli and Mazzino Montinari. Berlin: De Gruyter, 1968–.

Noack, Hermann, ed. *Husserl*. Darmstadt: Wissenschaftliche Buchgesellschaft, 1973.

Nobis, Heribert Maria. "Buch der Natur." In *Historisches Wörterbuch der Philosophie*, edited by Joachim Ritter, 1:957ff. Basel: Schwabe, 1971.

Nörr, Dieter. "Triviales und Aporetisches zur juristischen Hermeneutik." In *Text und Applikation: Theologie, Jurisprudenz und Literaturwissenschaft im hermeneutischen Gespräch*, edited by Manfred Fuhrmann, Hans Robert Jauss, and Wolfhart Pannenberg, 235–246. Munich: Fink, 1981.

Oeing-Hanhoff, Ludger. "Der Mensch in der Philosophie Descartes." In *Die Frage nach dem Menschen: Aufriß einer philosophischen Anthropologie*, edited by Heinrich Rombach, 375–409. Freiburg: Alber, 1966.

Oettinger, Karl. "Kunst ist als Kunst nich justitiabel—Der Fall 'Mephisto'—Zur Begründungsmisere der Justiz in Entscheidungen zur Sache Kunst." In *Text und Applikation: Theologie, Jurisprudenz und Literaturwissenschaft im hermeneutischen Gespräch*, edited by Manfred Fuhrmann, Hans Robert Jauss, and Wolfhart Pannenberg, 163–177. Munich: Fink, 1981.

———. "Kunst ohne Schranken?—Zur juristischen Interpretation der Kunstfreiheitsgarantie des Grundgesetzes." In *Text und Applikation: Theologie, Jurisprudenz und Literaturwissenschaft im hermeneutischen Gespräch*, edited by Manfred Fuhrmann, Hans Robert Jauss, and Wolfhart Pannenberg, 179–198. Munich: Fink, 1981.

———. "Kunstverstand—Sachverstand. Zur Funktion des Gerichtsgutachters in Sachen 'Kunst.'" In *Text und Applikation: Theologie, Jurisprudenz und Literaturwissenschaft im hermeneutischen Gespräch*, edited by Manfred Fuhrmann, Hans Robert Jauss, and Wolfhart Pannenberg, 225–234. Munich: Fink, 1981.

Okolo, Okonda. "Afrikanische Heidegger-Rezeption und -Kritik." In *Zur philosophischen Aktualität Heideggers*, vol. 3, *Im Spiegel der Welt. Sprache, Übersetzung, Auseinandersetzung*, edited by Dietrich Papenfuss and Otto Pöeggeler, 264–272. Frankfurt: Klostermann, 1992.

Orth, Ernst Wolfgang *Edmund Husserls 'Krisis der europäischen Wissenschaften und die transzendentale Phänomenologie': Vernunft und Kultur*. Darmstadt: Wissenschaftliche Buchgesellschaft, 1999.

———. "Heidegger und Husserl: Kultur als Horizont des Erscheinens." In *Heidegger—neu gelesen*, edited by Markus Happel, 54–74. Würzburg: Königshausen & Neumann, 1997.

———. "Phänomenologie der Vernunft zwischen Szientismus, Lebenswelt, und Intersubjektivität." In *Profile der Phänomenologie: Zum 50. Todestag von Edmund Husserl*, edited by Ernst Wolfgang Orth, 63–87. Freiburg: Alber, 1989.

———. "Die unerfüllte Rolle Descartes' in der Phänomenologie." In *Descartes im Diskurs der Neuzeit*, edited by Wilhelm Friedrich Niebel, Angelica Horn, and Herbert Schnädelbach, 286–302. Frankfurt: Suhrkamp, 2000.

———, ed. *Perspektiven und Probleme der Husserlischen Phänomenologie*. Freiburg: Alber, 1991.

Oudemans, Theodorus C. W. "Heideggers 'logische Untersuchungen.'" *Heidegger Studies 6* (1990), 85–105.

Pannenberg, Wolfhart. "Über Menschenwürde, persönliche Freiheit und Freiheit der Kunst: Theologische Erwägungen aus Anlaß des Falles 'Mephisto.'" In *Text und Applikation: Theologie, Jurisprudenz und Literaturwissenschaft im hermeneutischen Gespräch,* edited by Manfred Fuhrmann, Hans Robert Jauss, and Wolfhart Pannenberg, 137–148. Munich: Fink, 1981.

Pannwitz, Rudolf. *Die Krisis der europäischen Kultur.* Nuremberg: Carl, 1917.

Pascal, Blaise. *Gedanken über die Religion and über einige andere Gegenstände.* Translated by E. Wasmuth. Stuttgart: Reclam, 1987.

Patzig, Günther. *Tatsachen, Normen, Sätze: Aufsätze und Vorträge.* Stuttgart: Reclam, 1980.

Perler, Dominik. "Cartesianische Emotionen." In *Descartes Nachgedacht,* edited by Andreas Kemmerling and Hans-Peter Schütt, 51–79. Frankfurt: Klostermann, 1996.

Pessoa, Fernando. *Das Buch der Unruhe des Hilfsbuchhalters Bernardo Soares.* Zurich: Ammann, 1989.

Picht, Georg. *Der Begriff der Natur und seine Geschichte.* Stuttgart: Klett-Cotta, 1990.

———. *Geschichte und Gegenwart.* Stuttgart: Klett-Cotta, 1993.

———. *Hier und Jetzt: Philosophieren nach Auschwitz und Hiroshima.* 2 vols. Stuttgart: Klett-Cotta, 1980–1981.

———. *Von der Zeit.* Stuttgart: Klett-Cotta, 1999.

Pieper, Annemarie. "Erfahrung in der Existenzphilosophie." In *Der Begriff der Erfahrung in der Philosophie des 20. Jahrhunderts,* edited by Jürg Freudiger, Andreas Graeser, and Klaus Petrus, 153–177. Munich: Beck, 1996.

Plato. *Phaidon.* In *Werke,* vol. 3, edited by Gunther Eigler. Darmstadt: Wissenschaftliche Buchgesellschaft, 1974.

———. *Phaidros.* In *Werke,* vol. 5, edited by Gunther Eigler. Darmstadt: Wissenschaftliche Buchgesellschaft, 1981.

———. *Nomoi II.* In *Werke,* vol. 8, edited by Gunther Eigler. Darmstadt: Wissenschaftliche Buchgesellschaft, 1977.

———. *Symposion.* In *Werke,* vol. 3, edited by Gunther Eigler. Darmstadt: Wissenschaftliche Buchgesellschaft, 1974.

———. *Theaitetos.* In *Werke,* vol. 6, edited by Gunther Eigler. Darmstadt: Wissenschaftliche Buchgesellschaft, 1970.

———. *Timaios.* In *Werke,* vol. 7, edited by Gunther Eigler. Darmstadt: Wissenschaftliche Buchgesellschaft, 1972.

Pleger, Wolfgang. *Differenz und Identität: Die Transformation der philosophischen Anthropologie im 20. Jahrhundert.* Berlin: Duncker & Humblot, 1988.

Pöggeler, Otto. *Der Denkweg Martin Heideggers.* Pfullingen: Neske, 1990.

———. "'Eine Epoche gewaltigen Werdens': Die Freiburger Phänomenologie in ihrer Zeit." In *Die Freiburger Phänomenologie,* edited by Ermst Wolfgang Orth, 9–32. Freiburg: Alber, 1996.

———. "Das Gedicht als Spur," in *Neue Wege mit Heidegger,* 315–358. Freiburg: Alber, 1992.

———. "Heideggers Begegnung mit Dilthey." In *Dilthey-Jahrbuch,* vol. 4 (1986–1987), 121–160. Göttingen: Vandenhoeck & Ruprecht.

———. "Heideggers logische Untersuchungen." In *Martin Heidegger: Innen- und Außenansichten,* edited by *Forum für Philosophie Bad Homburg,* 75–100. Frankfurt: Suhrkamp, 1989.

———. *Neue Wege mit Heidegger*. Freiburg: Alber, 1992.

———. *Schritte zu einer hermeneutischen Philosophie*. Freiburg: Alber, 1994.

Prauss, Gerold. "Heidegger und die praktische Philosophie." In *Heidegger und die praktische Philosophie*, edited by Annemarie Gethmann-Siefert and Otto Pöggeler, 177–190. Frankfurt: Suhrkamp, 1988.

———. *Kant über Freiheit als Autonomie*. Frankfurt: Klostermann, 1983.

Prewo, Rainer. *Max Webers Wissenschaftsprogramm: Versuch einer methodischen Neuerschließung*. Frankfurt: Suhrkamp, 1979.

Proust, Marcel. *Tage des Lesens: Drei Essays*. Frankfurt: Suhrkamp, 1995.

Rang, Bernhard. "Die bodenlose Wissenschaft: Husserls Kritik von Objektivismus und Technizismus in Mathematik und Naturwissenschaft." In *Profile der Phänomenologie: Zum 50. Todestag von Edmund Husserl*, edited by Ernst Wolfgang Orth, 88–136. Freiburg: Alber, 1989.

———. *Husserls Phänomenologie der materiellen Natur*. Frankfurt: Klostermann, 1990.

Ranke, Leopold von. *Über die Epochen der neueren Geschichte: Vorträge, dem König Maximilian II von Bayern gehalten*. Darmstadt: Wissenschaftliche Buchgesellschaft, 1965.

Rentsch, Thomas. *Heidegger und Wittgenstein: Existential- und Sprachanalysen zu den Grundlagen philosophischer Anthropologie*. Stuttgart: Klett-Cotta, 1985.

———. *Die Konstitution der Moralität: Transzendentale Anthropologie und praktische Philosophie*. Frankfurt: Suhrkamp, 1990.

———. *Martin Heidegger—Das Sein und der Tod: Eine kritische Einführung*. Munich: Piper, 1989.

Richardson, William J. *Heidegger: Through Phenomenology to Thought*. The Hague: Nijhoff, 1963.

Rickert, Heinrich. *Die Grenzen der naturwissenschaftlichen Begriffsbildung: Eine logische Einleitung in die historischen Wissenschaften*. Tübingen: Mohr, 1929.

———. *Kulturwissenschaft und Naturwissenschaft*. Stuttgart: Reclam, 1986.

———. *Die Philosophie des Lebens: Darstellung und Kritik der philosophischen Modeströmungen unserer Zeit*. Tübingen: Mohr, 1922.

Ricoeur, Paul. "Appropriation." In *Hermeneutics and the Human Sciences: Essays on Language, Action and Interpretation*, edited by John B. Thompson, 182–193. Cambridge: Cambridge University Press, 1993.

———. *Du texte à l'action: Essais d'herméneutique II*. Paris: Éditions du Seuil, 1986.

———. *Die erzählte Zeit*, vol. 3, *Zeit und Erzählung*. Munich: Fink, 1991.

———. *Hermeneutics and the Human Sciences: Essays on Language, Action and Interpretation*. Edited by John B. Thompson. Cambridge: Cambridge University Press, 1993.

———. "Husserl und der Sinn der Geschichte." In *Husserl*, edited by Hermann Noack, 231–276. Darmstadt: Wissenschaftliche Buchgesellschaft, 1973.

———. *Die Interpretation: Ein Versuch über Freud*. Frankfurt: Suhrkamp, 1993.

———. "Phénoménologie et herméneutique: en venant de Husserl," in *Du texte à l'action: Essais d'herméneutique II*. Paris: Éditions du Seuil, 1986.

———. "Rückfrage und Reduktion der Idealitäten in Husserls 'Krisis' und Marx' 'Deutscher Ideologie.'" In *Phänomenologie und Marxismus*, vol. 3, edited by Bernhard Waldenfels, Jan M. Broekmann, and Ante Pazanin, 207–239. Frankfurt: Suhrkamp, 1978.

———. *Das Selbst als ein Anderer*. Munich: Fink, 1996.

———. "La tâche de l'herméneutique: En venant de Schleiermacher et de Dilthey," in *Du texte à l'action. Essais d'herméneutique II*. Paris: Éditions du Seuil, 1986.

———. *"Der Text als Modell: Hermeneutisches Verstehen."* In *Seminar "Die Hermeneutik und die Wissenschaften,"* edited by Hans-Georg Gadamer and Gottfried Boehm, 83–117. Frankfurt: Suhrkamp, 1978.

———. *"Von einer Husserl-Interpretation zu einer Husserl-Kritik: Nachdenkliches zu Jacques Derridas Denkweg."* In *Studien zur neueren französischen Phänomenologie: Ricoeur, Foucault, Derrida,* edited by Ernst Wolfgang Orth, 130–169. Freiburg: Alber, 1986.

Riedel, Manfred. *Für eine zweite Philosophie: Vorträge und Abhandlungen.* Frankfurt: Suhrkamp, 1988.

———. "Heidegger und der hermeneutische Weg zur praktischen Philosophie," in *Für eine zweite Philosophie: Vorträge und Abhandlungen.* Frankfurt: Suhrkamp, 1988, 171–196.

———. *Hören auf die Sprache: Die akroamatische Dimension der Hermeneutik.* Frankfurt: Suhrkamp, 1990.

———. "Naturhermeneutik und Ethik im Denken Heideggers." *Heidegger Studies.* 5 (1989), 153–172.

———. *Norm und Werturteil: Grundprobleme der Ethik.* Stuttgart: Reclam, 1979.

Röd, Wolfgang. *Descartes: Die Genese des Cartesianischen Rationalismus.* Munich: Beck, 1995.

Rodi, Frithjof. *Erkenntnis des Erkannten: Zur Hermeneutik des 19. und 20. Jahrhunderts.* Frankfurt: Suhrkamp, 1990.

Rodi, Frithjof, ed. *Dilthey-Jahrbuch,* vol. 4. Göttingen: Vandenhoeck & Ruprecht, 1986–1987.

Rorty, Richard. *Eine Kultur ohne Zentrum: Vier philosophische Essays.* Stuttgart: Reclam, 1988.

———. *Essays on Heidegger and Others: Philosophical Papers,* vol. 2. Cambridge: Cambridge University Press, 1995.

———. "Heidegger, Contingency, and Pragmatism," in *Essays on Heidegger and Others: Philosophical Papers,* vol. 2. Cambridge: Cambridge University Press, 1995.

———. *Kontingenz, Ironie, und Solidarität.* Frankfurt: Suhrkamp, 1991.

———. *Objectivity, Relativism, and Truth: Philosophical Papers,* vol. 1. Cambridge: Cambridge University Press, 1995.

———. *Solidarität oder Objektivität?: Drei philosophische Essays.* Stuttgart: Reclam, 1988.

———. *Der Spiegel der Natur: Eine Kritik der Philosophie.* Frankfurt: Suhrkamp, 1981.

Rousseau, Jean-Jacques. *Die Bekentnisse.* In *Werke,* vol. 2. Munich: Winkler, 1978.

Ruckteschell, Peter von. *Die Intentionalität im frühen Denken Martin Heideggers: Von der Urwissenschaft zur Fundamentalontologie.* Freiburg: Universität Freiburg im Breisgau, 1999.

Ruff, Gerhard. *Am Ursprung der Zeit: Studie zu Martin Heideggers phänomenologischem Zugang zur christlichen Religion in den ersten "Freiburger Vorlesungen."* Berlin: Duncker and Humblot, 1997.

Ruggenini, Mario. "Phänomenologie und Alterität." In *Phänomenologie in Italien,* edited by Renato Cristin, 137–168. Würzburg: Königshausen & Neumann, 1995.

Ryle, Gilbert. *Der Begriff des Geistes.* Stuttgart: Reclam, 1969.

Sadler, Ted. *Heidegger and Aristotle: The Question of Being.* London: Athlone, 1996.

Sartre, Jean-Paul. *Die Transzendenz des Ego: Philosophische Essays 1931–1939.* Reinbek bei Hamburg: Rowohlt, 1982.

Savigny, Eike von. *Die Philosophie der normalen Sprache: Eine kritische Einführung in die "ordinary language philosophy."* Rev. ed. Frankfurt: Suhrkamp, 1993.

Schapp, Wilhelm. *In Geschichten verstrickt: Zum Sein von Mensch und Ding*. Frankfurt: Klostermann, 1985.

———. *Philosophie der Geschichten*. Frankfurt: Rautenberg, 1981.

Scheler, Max. *Die Wissensformen und die Gesellschaft*. Bern: Francke, 1960.

Schelling, Friedrich Wilhelm Joseph. *Darstellung meines Systems der Philosophie*. In *Ausgewählte Werke: Schriften von 1801–1804*, 1–108. Darmstadt: Wissenschaftliche Buchgesellschaft, 1976.

Schläger, Jürgen. "Herméneutique dans le boudoir." In *Text und Applikation: Theologie, Jurisprudenz und Literaturwissenschaft im hermeneutischen Gespräch*, edited by Manfred Fuhrmann, Hans Robert Jauss, and Wolfhart Pannenberg, 207–223. Munich: Fink, 1981.

Schleiermacher, Friedrich. "Über den Begriff der Hermeneutik mit Bezug auf F. A. Wolfs Andeutungen und Asts Lehrbuch," in *Hermeneutik und Kritik*. Edited by Manfred Frank. Frankfurt: Suhrkamp, 1977.

———. "Über den Styl." In *Jugendschriften 1787–1796*, edited by Günter Meckenstock. Berlin: De Gruyter, 1984.

Schmid, Wilhelm. *Auf der Suche nach einer neuen Lebenskunst: Die Frage nach dem Grund und die Neubegründung der Ethik bei Foucault*. Frankfurt: Suhrkamp, 1992.

Schmidt, Gerhart. *Aufklärung und Metaphysik: Die Neubegründung des Wissens durch Descartes*. Tübingen: De Gruyter, 1965.

Schmitz, Hermann. *Husserl und Heidegger*. Bonn: Bouvier, 1996.

Schnädelbach, Herbert. *Geschichtsphilosophie nach Hegel: Die Probleme des Historismus*. Freiburg: Alber, 1974.

———. *Philosophie in Deutschland 1831–1933*. Frankfurt: Suhrkamp, 1983.

———. "Morbus Hermeneuticus: Thesen Über eine Philosophische Krankheit." In *Vernunft und Geschichte: Vorträge und Abhandlungen*, 279–284. Frankfurt: Suhrkamp, 1987.

———. *Reflexion und Diskurs: Fragen einer Logik der Philosophie*. Frankfurt: Suhrkamp, 1977.

———. *Vernunft und Geschichte: Vorträge und Abhandlungen*. Frankfurt: Suhrkamp, 1987.

Scholtz, Gunter. "*Was ist und seit wann gibt es 'hermeneutische Philosophie?'*" in *Dilthey-Jahrbuch*, vol. 8 (1992–1993), 93–119. Göttingen: Vandenhoeck & Ruprecht.

Schrödter, Hermann. "Der Gottesdanke in der Metaphysik des Ich als substantia cogitans." In *Descartes im Diskurs der Neuzeit*, edited by Wilhelm Friedrich Niebel, Angelica Horn, and Herbert Schnädelbach, 103–124. Frankfurt: Suhrkamp, 2000.

Schütt, Hans-Peter. "Kant, Cartesius, und der sceptische Idealist." In *Descartes nachgedacht*, edited by Hans-Peter Schütt and Andreas Kemmerling, 170–199. Frankfurt: Klostermann, 1996.

Schütz, Alfred. "Das Problem der transzendentalen Intersubjektivität bei Husserl." *Philosophische Rundschau* 5 (1957): 81–107.

———. *Der sinnhafte Aufbau der sozialen Welt: Eine Einleitung in die verstehende Soziologie*. Frankfurt: Suhrkamp, 1993.

———. *Theorie der Lebensformen: Frühe Manuskripte aus der Bergson-Periode*. Edited by Ilja Srubar. Frankfurt: Suhrkamp, 1981.

———, and Thomas Luckmann. *Strukturen der Lebenswelt*. 2 vols. Frankfurt: Suhrkamp, 1994.

Schuhmann, Karl. "*Lebenswelt als Unterlage der Phänomenologie.*" In *Lebenswelt und Wissenschaft in der Philosophie Edmund Husserls,* edited by Elisabeth Ströker, 79–91. Frankfurt: Klostermann, 1979.

———. "Zu Heideggers Spiegel-Gespräch über Husserl." *Zeitschrift für Philosophische Forschung* 32 (1978): 591–612.

Schulz, Walter. *Der gebrochene Weltbezug: Aufsätze zur Geschichte der Philosophie und zur Analyse der Gegenwart.* Stuttgart: Neske, 1994.

———. *Ich und Welt: Philosophie der Subjektivität.* Pfullingen: Neske, 1979.

———. *Philosophie in der veränderten Welt.* Pfullingen: Neske, 1972.

———. *Subjektivität im nachmetaphysischen Zeitalter: Aufsätze.* Pfullingen: Neske, 1992.

Seebohm, Thomas. "Die Begründung der Hermeneutik Diltheys in Husserls transzendentaler Phänomenologie." In *Dilthey und die Philosophie der Gegenwart,* edited by Ernst Wolfgang Orth, 97–124. Freiburg: Alber, 1985.

Semler, Johann Salomon, *Lebenschreibung von ihm selbst agbefaßt.* Halle: n.p., 1781.

Sen, Reena. "*Heidegger und die indische Perspektive: Heidegger und Sri Aurobindo.*" In *Zur philosophischen Aktualität Heideggers* vol. 3, edited by Dietrich Papenfuss and Otto Pöggeler, 273–291. Frankfurt: Klostermann, 1992.

Sena, Marylou. "The Phenomenal Basis of Entities and the Manifestation of Being According to Sections 15–17 of *Being and Time*: On the Pragmatist Misunderstanding." *Heidegger Studies* 11 (1995): 11–31.

Sepp, Hans Rainer. "Praktische Transzendentalität oder transzendentale Praxis? Zum Problem der Verweltlichung transzendentalphänomenologischer Erkenntnisse." In *Gelehrtenrepublik—Lebenswelt. Edmund Husserl und Alfred Schütz in der Krisis der phänomenologischen Bewegung,* edited by Angelika Bäumer and Michael Benedikt, 189–207. Vienna: Passagen, 1993.

Seubold, Günter. "Dienstbar der Sache des Denkens." *Heidegger Studies* 7 (1991): 149–155.

Shakespeare, William. *Der Kaufmann von Venedig,* edited by Barbara Puschmann-Nalenz. Stuttgart: Reclam, 1998.

Sheehan, Thomas. "Heidegger's 'Introduction to the Phenomenology of Religion.'" In *A Companion to Martin Heidegger's* Being and Time, edited by Joseph Kockelmans, 40–62. Washington, D.C.: University Press of America, 1986.

Simmel, Georg. *Die Religion.* In *Gesamtausgabe,* vol. 10, edited by Otthein Rammstedt, 39–118. Frankfurt: Suhrkamp, 1995.

Sommer, Manfred. "Der Alltagsbegriff in der Phänomenologie und seine gegenwärtige Rezeption in den Sozialwissenschaften." In *Pädagogik und Alltag: Methoden und Ergebnisse alltagsorientierter Forschung in der Erziehungswissenschaft,* edited by Dieter Lenzen, 27–43. Suttgart: Klett-Cotta, 1980.

———. *Husserl und die frühe Positivismus.* Frankfurt: Klostermann, 1985.

Spaemann, Robert, and Reinhard Löw. *Die Frage Wozu? Geschichte und Wiederentdeckung des teleologischen Denkens.* Munich: Piper, 1985.

Specht, Rainer. *Commercium mentis et corporis: Über Kausalvorstellungen im Cartesianismus.* Stuttgart: Frommann-Holzboog, 1966.

Spengler, Oswald. *Der Untergang des Abendlandes: Umrisse einer Morphologie der Weltgeschichte.* Berlin: Beck, 1923.

Spiegelberg, Herbert. *The Phenomenological Movement: A Historical Introduction.* The Hague: Martinus Nijhoff, 1981.

Spinoza, Baruch. *Ethica*. Edited by Konrad Blumenstock. In *Opera*, vol. 2. Darmstadt: Wissenschaftliche Buchgesellschaft, 1980.

———. *Die Ethik nach geometrischer Methode dargestellt*. Translated by Otto Baensch. Hamburg: Meiner, 1976.

Stegmüller, Wolfgang. "Walther von der Vogelweides Lied von der Traumliebe und Quasar 3 C 273." In *Rationale Rekonstruktion von Wissenschaft und ihrem Wandel*, 27–86. Stuttgart: Reclam, 1979.

Stellrecht, Irmtraud. "Interpretative Ethnologie: eine Orientierung." In *Handbuch der Ethnologie*, edited by Thomas Schweizer and Ulla Johansen, 29–78. Berlin: Reimer, 1993.

Stolzenberg, Jürgen. *Ursprung und System: Probleme der Begründung systematischer Philosophie im Werk Hermann Cohens, Paul Natorps und beim frühen Heidegger*. Göttingen: Vandenhoeck & Ruprecht, 1995.

Storck, Joachim Wolfgang, and Theodor Kisiel. "Martin Heidegger und die Anfänge der 'Deutschen Vierteljahresschrift für Literaturwissenschaft und Geistesgeschichte': Eine Dokumentation." In *Dilthey-Jahrbuch*, 8 (1992), 181–224. Göttingen: Vandenhoeck & Ruprecht.

Strasser, Stephan. "Der Begriff der Welt in der phänomenologischen Philosophie." In *Phänomenologie und Praxis*, edited by Ernst Wolfgang Orth, 151–179. Freiburg: Meiner, 1976.

———. "Das Gottesproblem in der Spätphilosophie Edmund Husserls." *Philosophisches Jahrbuch* 67 (1959), 130–142.

———. "Von einer Husserl-Interpretation zu einer Husserl-Kritik: Nachdenkliches zu Jacques Derridas Denkweg." In *Studien zur neueren französischen Phänomenologie. Ricoeur, Foucault, Derrida*, edited by Ernst Wolfgang Orth, 130–169. Freiburg: Meiner, 1986.

Ströker, Elisabeth. "Edmund Husserls Phänomenologie: Philosophia Perennis in der Krise der europäischen Kultur." In *Profile der Phänomenologie. Zum 50. Todestag Edmund Husserls*, edited by Ernst Wolfgang Orth. Freiburg: Alber, 1989.

———. "Geschichte und Lebenswelt als Sinnesfundament der Wissenschaften in Husserls Spätwerk." In *Lebenswelt und Wissenschaft in der Philosophie Edmund Husserls*, edited by Elisabeth Ströker, 107–123. Frankfurt: Klostermann, 1979.

———. *Husserls transzendentale Phänomenologie*. Frankfurt: Klostermann, 1987.

———. *Phänomenologische Studien*. Frankfurt: Klostermann, 1987.

Strube, Claudius. *Zur Vorgeschichte der hermeneutischen Phänomenologie*. Würzburg: Königshausen & Neumann, 1993.

Sturma, Dieter. *Philosophie der Person: Die Selbstverhältnisse von Subjektivität und Moralität*. Padernborn: F. Schöningh, 1997.

Taminiaux, Jacques. "The Husserlian Heritage in Heidegger's Notion of the Self." In *Reading Heidegger from the Start: Essays in His Earliest Thought*, edited by Theodor Kisiel and John van Buren, 269–290. New York: SUNY Press, 1994.

Taylor, Charles. "Agency and the Self." In *Human Agency and Language: Philosophical Papers I*, 13–114 Cambridge: Cambridge University Press, 1985.

———. *Quellen des Selbst: Die Entstehung der neuzeitlichen Identität*. Frankfurt: Suhrkamp, 1994.

Teichert, Dieter. *Erfahrung, Erinnerung, Erkenntnis: Untersuchungen zum Wahrheitsbegriff der Hermeneutik Gadamers*. Stuttgart: J. B. Metzler, 1991.

———. "*Zwischen Wissenschaftskritik und Hermeneutik: Foucaults Humanwissenschaften.*" In *Zeitschrift für philosophische Forschung,* 47 (1993): 204–222.

Theunissen, Michael. *Der Andere: Studien zur Sozialontologie der Gegenwart.* Berlin: De Gruyter, 1977.

Thomä, Dieter. *Die Zeit des Selbst und die Zeit danach: Zur Kritik der Textgeschichte Martin Heideggers 1910–1976.* Frankfurt: Suhrkamp, 1990.

Thurnher, Rainer. "Husserls 'Ideen' und Heideggers 'Sein und Zeit.'" In *Gelehrtenrepublik—Lebenswelt: Edmund Husserl und Alfred Schütz in der Krisis der phänomenologischen Bewegung,* edited byAngelika Bäumer and Michael Benedikt, 145–168. Vienna: Passagen, 1993.

———. "Kierkegaards Zeitkritik und die Thematisierung der Existenz." In *Wissenschaft und Glaube: Vierteljahresschrift der Wiener Katholischen Akademie,* 3 (1990): 277–293.

Tietjen, Hartmut. "Philosophie und Faktizität. Zur Vorbildung des existenzial-ontologischen Ansatzes in einer frühen Freiburger Vorlesung Martin Heideggers." *Heidegger Studies* 2 (1986): 11–40.

Tietz, Udo. "Vernunft und Lebenswelt: Bemerkungen zum Spätwerk von Edmund Husserl." In *Praxis—Vernunft—Gemeinschaft: Auf der Suche nach einer anderen Vernunft,* edited by Volker Caysa and Klaus-Dieter Eichler, 216–233. Weinheim: Beltz, 1994.

Tugendhat, Ernst. *Selbstbewußtsein und Selbstbestimmung: Sprachanalytische Interpretationen.* Frankfurt: Suhrkamp, 1979.

———. *Vorlesungen zur Einführung in die sprachanalytische Philosophie.* Frankfurt: Suhrkamp, 1979.

———. *Der Wahrheitsbegriff bei Husserl und Heidegger.* Berlin: De Gruyter, 1970.

Valéry, Paul. *Cahiers* [Hefte]. 6 vols. Edited by Hartmut Köhler and Jürgen Schmidt-Radefeldt. Frankfurt: Suhrkamp, (1987–1993).

van Buren, John. *The Young Heidegger: Rumor of the Hidden King.* Bloomington: Indiana University Press, 1994.

Varela, Francisco J. *Kognitionswissenschaft—Kognitionstechnik: Eine Skizze aktueller Perspektiven.* Frankfurt: Suhrkamp, 1990.

Volpi, Franco. "Heidegger in Marburg: Die Auseinandersetzung mit Husserl." *Philosophischer Literaturanzeiger* 37 (1984): 48–69.

———. "La question du λόγος dans l'articulation de la facticité chez le jeune Heidegger, lecteur d'Aristote." In *Heidegger 1919–1929: De l'herméneutique de la facticité à la métaphysique du Dasein,* edited by Jean-François Courtine, 33–65. Paris: Vrin, 1996.

———. "Σημαίνειν, λέγειν, ἀποφαίνεσθαι, als ἑρμενεύειν: Die Ontologisierung der Sprache beim frühen Heidegger im Rückgriff auf Aristoteles." In *Sagen, was die Zeit ist: Analysen zur Zeitlichkeit der Sprache,* edited by Enno Rudolph and Heinz Wismann, 21–42. Stuttgart: Metzler, 1992.

Voltaire, François-Marie. *Essai sur les moeurs et l'esprit des nations et sur le principaux faits de l'histoire depuis Charlemagne jusqu'à Louis XIII.* 2 vols. Paris: Bordas, 1963.

———. *La philosophie de l'histoire.* Utrecht: Aux dépens de la Compagnie, 1765.

———. Vossenkuhl, Wilhelm. "Eigenes 'Ich': Ein Essay über die menschliche Identität." In *Eigenes Leben: Ausflüge in die unbekannte Gesellschaft, in der wir leben,* edited by Ulrich Beck, Wilhelm Vossenkuhl, and Ulf Erdmann Ziegler, 194–215. Munich: Beck, 1995.

Waldenfels, Bernhard. *Antwortregister.* Frankfurt: Suhrkamp, 1994.

———. *Deutsch-Französische Gedankengänge.* Frankfurt: Suhrkamp, 1995.

———. *Einführung in die Phänomenologie.* Munich: Fink, 1992.

———. *Grenzen der Normalisierung: Studien zur Phänomenologie des Fremden 2*. Frankfurt: Suhrkamp, 1998.

———. "Heimat in der Fremde," in *in den Netzen der Lebenswelt*, 194–211. Frankfurt: Suhrkamp, 1985.

———. *In den Netzen der Lebenswelt*. Frankfurt: Suhrkamp, 1985.

———. "Lebenswelt zwischen Alltäglichem und Unalltäglichem." In *Phänomenologie im Widerstreit: Zum 50. Todestag Edmund Husserls*, edited by Christoph Jamme and Otto Pöggeler, 106–118. Frankfurt: Suhrkamp, 1989.

———. "Metamorphosen des Cogito: Stichproben französischer Descartes-Lektüre." In *Descartes im Diskurs der Neuzeit*, edited by Wilhelm Friedrich Niebel, Angelica Horn, and Herbert Schnädelbach, 349–370. Frankfurt: Suhrkamp, 2000.

———. "Michel Foucault: Ordnung in Diskursen." In *Spiele der Wahrheit: Michel Foucaults Denken*, edited by François Ewald and Bernhard Waldenfels, 277–297. Frankfurt: Suhrkamp, 1991.

———. *Ordnung im Zwielicht*. Frankfurt: Suhrkamp, 1987.

———. *Der Stachel des Fremden*. Frankfurt: Suhrkamp, 1990.

———. *Sinnesschwellen: Studien zur Phänomenologie des Fremden 3*. Frankfurt: Suhrkamp, 1999

———. *Topographie des Fremden: Studien zur Phänomenologie des Fremden 1*. Frankfurt: Suhrkamp, 1997.

———. *Vielstimmigkeit der Rede: Studien zur Phänomenologie des Fremdem 4*. Frankfurt: Suhrkamp, 1999.

Weber, Max. *Gesammelte Aufsätze zur Wissenschaftslehre*. Edited by Johannes Winckelmann. Tübingen: Mohr Siebeck, 1988.

———. *Wirtschaft und Gesellschaft*. Tübingen: Mohr Siebeck, 1976.

Weinmayr, Elmar. *Entstellung: Die Metaphysik im Denken Martin Heideggers: Mit einem Blick nach Japan*. Munich: Fink, 1991.

Welsch, Wolfgang. *Aisthesis: Grunzüge und Perspektiven der Aristotelischen Sinneslehre*. Stuttgart: Klett-Cotta, 1987.

———. "Die Postmoderne in Kunst und Philosophie und ihr Verhältnis zu technologischen Zeitalter." In *Technologisches Zeitalter oder Postmoderne*, edited by Walther Zimmerli, 36–72. Munich: Fink, 1988.

———. *Unsere postmoderne Moderne*. Weinheim: Akademie Verlag, 1987.

———. *Vernunft: Die zeitgenössische Vernunftkritik und das Konzept der transversalen Vernunft*. Frankfurt: Suhrkamp, 1995.

———, ed. *Wege aus der Moderne: Schlüsseltexte der Postmoderne-Diskussion*. Weinheim: Akademie Verlag, 1988.

Welter, Rüdiger. *Der Begriff der Lebenswelt: Theorien vortheoretischer Erfahrungswelt*. Munich: Fink, 1986.

Wetz, Franz Joseph *Edmund Husserl*. Frankfurt: Campus, 1995.

———. *Lebenswelt und Weltall: Hermeneutik der unabweislichen Fragen*. Stuttgart: Klett-Cotta, 1994.

Wiehl, Reiner. "Die Frage nach dem Menschen: Zur Auseinandersetzung zwischen Jaspers und Heidegger." In *Inmitten der Zeit: Beiträge zur europäischen Gegenwartsphilosophie*, edited by Thomas Grethlein and Heinrich Leitner, 335–353. Würzburg: Königshausen & Neumann, 1996.

————. "Heideggers Verfehlung des Themas 'Metaphysik und Erfahrung.'" In *Metaphysik und Erfahrung: Philosophische Essays*, 155–202. Frankfurt: Suhrkamp, 1996.

Wieland, Wolfgang. "Philosophie nach ihrem Weltbegriff." In *Georg Picht—Philosophie der Verantwortung*, edited by Constanze Eisenbart, 89–108. Stuttgart: Klett-Cotta, 1985.

Wienbruch, Ulrich. *Das bewußte Erleben: Ein systematischer Entwurf.* Würzburg: Königshausen & Neumann, 1993.

Wimmer, Franz. "Fremde." In *Vom Menschen: Handbuch Historische Anthropologie*, edited by Christoph Wulf, 1066–1078. Weinheim: Beltz, 1997.

Winch, Peter. *Die Idee der Sozialwissenschaft und ihr Verhältnis zur Philosophie.* Frankfurt: Suhrkamp, 1974.

Windelband, Wilhelm. "Geschichte und Naturwissenschaft." In *Präludien: Aufsätze und Reden zur Philosophie und ihrer Geschichte*, vol. 2. Tübingen: Mohr, 1919.

Wisser, Richard. "Aneignung und Unterscheidung: Existenzphilosophie im Kampf um die Existenze der Philosophie; Karl Jaspers und Martin Heidegger." In *Philosophische Wegweisung: Versionen und Perspektiven*, 277–300. Würzburg: Königshausen & Neumann, 1996.

————. *Philosophische Wegweisung: Versionen und Perspektiven.* Würzburg: Königshausen & Neumann, 1996.

Wittgenstein, Ludwig. *Philosphische Untersuchungen.* In *Werkausgabe*, vol. 1. Frankfurt: Suhrkamp, 1984.

————. *Vermischte Bemerkungen.* In *Werkausgabe*, vol. 8, 445–573. Frankfurt: Suhrkamp, 1984.

Wittkau-Horgby, Annette. *Historismus: Zur Geschichte des Begriffs und des Problems.* Göttingen: Vandenhoeck & Ruprecht, 1994.

Wolzogen, Christoph von. "'Es gibt': Heidegger und Natorps 'Praktische Philosophie.'" In *Heidegger und die praktische Philosophie*, edited by Annemarie Gethmann-Siefert and Otto Pöggeler, 313–337. Frankfurt: Suhrkamp, 1988.

————. "'Den Gegner stark machen': Heidegger und der Ausgang des Neukantianismus am Beispiel Paul Natorps." In *Neukantianismus: Perspektiven und Probleme*, edited by Ernst Wolfgang Orth and Helmut Holzhey, 397–417. Würzburg: Könighausen & Neumann, 1994.

SUBJECT INDEX

Affectivity [*Affektivität*] 165n242

Anthropology, existential 232–233; factical-hermeneutical 195, 197–199; historical 359n150; interpretative 273n92; phenomenological-hermeneutical 225n222, 358; philosophical 172, 229, 232, 358n145

Application [*Applikation*] 327, 329–339, 357, 364, 366

Apriori, formal 254, 255n29; historical 142n145, 158, 159, 238, 254, 255, 257, 267, 348, 349, 350; lifeworldly 121, 123, 142, 151; methodological 79

Art [*Kunst*] 43, 79, 109n79, 293n176, 342, 348

Attitude [*Einstellung*], hermeneutical (philosophical) 211, 224, 245, 286n139, 287, 292, 367; natural 72, 83, 113n3, 117n16, 118, 123n52, 125 f., 128–129, 134–136, 138, 150n174, 185, 189n49, 202n111, 248, 284, 367; phenomenological 83, 126, 129n83, 130, 151, 282n117; theoretical (philosophical) 13, 24, 72, 83, 116–118, 367; theoretical (scientific) 72, 116–118, 193, 199, 200, 247n7, 260n43, 264, 286n139, 287

Author 15, 16, 22, 24, 28–30, 32–34, 39n50, 40, 42, 44

Autonomy 56, 319, 335, 336n27

Awhileness [*Jeweiligkeit*] 151, 314, 339, 344

Being-in-the-world [*In-der-Welt-sein*] 8, 13, 83, 92n29, 94, 97, 100n59, 250n11, 252, 319, 339, 344, 346, 359n150, 365

Being, category of/existential 197–198, 199n86, 204n118, 208n132, 211–212, 218, 224n221, 225–226, 241n271, 246, 268, 270–271, 285, 287, 292, 293–294n176, 298n195, 302, 306, 310–311, 315

Being, question of, fundamental ontological 226, 229–331, 262n56, 307n234, 308, 309n238, 364n2; hermeneutical-

existentielle 308–309; phenomenological (Husserl) 204

Body-soul dualism 101–103

Care structure 193–194, 203, 209

Care(s) 42 (of the self, Foucault), 191–195, 199, 201–203, 210–211, 285–287, 298n195, 321, 339, 345n76, 356; of/for certainty 199–201, 223; world of (see also Environment [*Umwelt*]; Self-world; With-world [*Mitwelt*]) xiv, xv, 269, 278, 287, 290, 294, 307, 317, 353

Chance [*Zufalls, Zufälligkeit*] (see also Contingency) v, 11, 36, 62, 196, 201, 244, 272

Concept-formation [*Begriffsbildung*] 210n138

Concept-interpretation [*Begriffsinterpretation*], hermeneutical 80 f.

Concern [*Bekümmerung*] (see also Care) 211, 298, 311

Consciousness [*Bewußtsein*], aesthetic 57; (in Descartes) 99–102; effective-historical (see also Effective history [*Wirkungsgeschichte*]) 12, 17, 32, 42, 48, 50, 60–63, 179 f., 257, 333, 335, 340; everyday 118n21, 144n152; hermeneutical (see also Understanding, hermeneutical) 49, 62 f., 227, 314n267; historical 162, 253, 256, 333 f., 343n69; of finitude 297; of relationality 326; transcendental/pure 134, 140, 171, 190 f., 214, 222, 309

Content-sense [*Gehaltssinn*] 286, 307, 338

Contingency 27, 158, 162, 165n242, 167, 190, 196, 228, 236, 238–239, 253, 255n29, 258, 271–272, 275, 304n218, 350n93, 360n160, 364

Corporeality [*Leiblichkeit*], (in Heidegger) 302n214; (in Husserl) 101 f., 134–135

INDEX OF NAMES

Adorno, Theodor 118n21
Albert, Karl 205n119
Apel, Karl-Otto 46n68, 56n100, 181,
    239n264, 331n4
Arendt, Hannah 174, 175n17, 364
Aristotle 1, 84, 85, 87, 116, 120n32, 144n152,
    165n242, 198n84, 201n107, 215n167,
    225n222, 270, 286n139, 289n154, 336n28
Arnaud, Antoine 102n65
Assmann, Jan 55n99
Ast, Georg 282n117
Augustine xix, 1, 13, 51n90, 249n11, 289n154,
    343n69, 347n80, 348
Avenarius, Richard 112n1

Bacon, Francis (painter) 81n4
Bacon, Francis (philosopher) 27n12
Baumann, Gerhart 252n17
Bayle, Pierre 70n136
Beauvoir, Simone de 244
Beck, Ulrich 6n13, 92n29, 241n271
Becker, Oskar 174, 279n104
Beckett, Samuel 39, 81n4
Benjamin, Walter 249n11
Bergson, Henri 55n99, 114, 187n42, 206n23,
    219n188, 280n108, 312, 316n281
Berkeley, George 100
Bernet, Rudolf 111n1, 137n121, 138n27,
    155n202, 185n39, 296n187, 297n188
Betti, Emilio 28
Bianco, Franco 187n42
Biemel, Walter 74n144, 111n1, 116n10,
    119n24, 121n38, 131n86, 164n239, 176n20,
    177n21, 253n17, 307n234, 337n31
Blanchot, Maurice 40n57, 278
Blattner, William 208n132
Bloch, Ernst 178n25
Blochmann, Elisabeth 1n1, 253n17
Blumenberg, Hans 47n72, 51–53, 71n137,
    131n85, 188n42, 271, 272n86, 348n80
Bochenski, Joseph 56n100

Bodin, Jean 70n136
Bodmershof, Imma von 253n17
Boeckh, August 282n117
Boehm, Gottfried 57n101, 109n79, 273n92
Boehm, Rudolf 125n57, 189n43
Böhler, Dietrich 333n17
Bollnow, Otto Friedrich 81n5, 116n10, 181,
    205n119, 330n2
Bossuet, Jacques Bénigne 347n80
Brach, Markus Joachim 186n41, 259n38
Brand, Gerd 112n1
Brentano, Franz 91n26, 164n239, 301
Bröcker, Walter 164n239, 175n17
Brogan, Walter 286n139
Bruzina, Ronald 190n49, 200n97
Buber, Martin 178
Bubner, Rudiger 187n42, 348n80
Buchholz, Rolf 9n20, 259n41, 291n165
Büchner, Georg 80n4
Bultmann, Rudolf 80n4
Burckhardt, Jacob 50n86
Buren, John van 9n20, 177n22, 261n56

Camus, Albert 247n5, 249n11, 364, 366
Carr, David 139n133, 159n219, 187n42
Carrier, Martin 103n67
Cassirer, Ernst 70n136, 105n71, 188n42
Celan, Paul 81n4
Celms, Theodor 139n134
Chang, Ting-Kuo 330n2, 336n28
Chiereghin, Franco 343n69
Chladenius, Johann Martin 181n28
Cho, Ka Kyung 267n73
Claesges, Ulrich 114n5, 145n158
Columbus, Christopher 85n11
Comte, Auguste 325
Courtine, Jean-François 177n22, 185n39,
    195n67, 286n139
Cramer, Konrad 101n61
Cunningham, Suzanne 136n109

Dahlstrom, Daniel 176n20
Dallmayr, Fred 187n42
Dannauer, Johann Konrad 282n117
Därmann, Iris 267n73
Dastur, Françoise, 220n200
Davidson, Donald 46n68
Derrida, Jacques 33, 40n55, 45, 46n68, 54,
    70n136, 89n20, 155n202, 267, 274n92,
    293n176, 299
Descartes, René 5, 12 f., 59, 68n134, 70n136,
    82 f., 88–95, 97–108, 116, 124, 126n63,
    130n86, 139n134, 154, 160n227, 165n242,
    167, 171, 184, 200n93, 215, 234, 244, 288,
    289n154, 315
Diderot, Denis 70n136
Dilthey, Wilhelm 3, 9, 28, 30, 46n68, 50n86,
    63n110, 75, 79, 89, 91n26, 100n59, 110,
    114–116, 164n239, 172, 181, 187n42, 188,
    196n73, 197, 198n84, 205, 209, 226n222,
    230n231, 238–239, 267, 269, 276, 282n117,
    303–305, 309, 310n239, 318, 321, 357
Dreyfus, Hubert 41n58, 209n132, 254n21,
    347n79
Droysen, Johan Gustav 3, 46n68, 282n117
Dummett, Michael 324n308
Duns Scotus 224n221

Eco, Umberto 61n106
Emad, Parvis 216n168
Erasmus von Rotterdam 322
Eucken, Rudolf 111n1

Fahrenbach, Helmut 196n73
Faulkner, William 21
Fehér, István 208n132, 304n220, 308n238, 321
Fellmann, Ferdinand 112n1, 113n3, 293n176
Feuerbach, Ludwig 70n136
Fichte, Johann Gottlieb 24, 35, 73, 160n227,
    181n28, 255, 311, 364
Ficker, Ludwig von 253n17
Figal, Günter xx, 14, 46n70, 93n31, 177n22,
    182n34, 225n221, 242, 243n275, 273n89,
    336n28
Fink, Eugen 118n20, 131, 132n88, 155n202,
    175n17, 185, 189, 190n50, 200n97, 202n111
Fink-Eitel, Hinrich 85n11, 266n72

Flaubert, Gustave 40n57, 52
Forschner, Maximilian 249n11
Foucault, Michel 11, 21, 33, 36–43, 50,
    68n134, 81n4, 144n152, 155n202, 167, 185
    f., 228n228, 234n250, 238, 246, 254–257,
    273n91, 274n92, 276–277, 293n176,
    323n307, 336n27, 347n79, 363, 366
Frank, Manfred 66, 294n176
Freud, Sigmund 46n68, 70n136, 89, 161,
    242n271, 267n73, 275n95, 277, 299, 325
Freyer, Hans 111n1
Funke, Gerhard 159n219

Gadamer, Hans-Georg xiii–xvi, xx, 1, 8, 11,
    12, 18, 26, 27n12, 28 f., 30, 32–34, 42,
    45–50, 53 f., 56–59, 61 f., 68n134, 74–75,
    80n4, 81n5, 84n10, 89, 95, 111, 125n60,
    131n86, 133, 139n133, 154, 161n232,
    174–175, 180–182, 186, 198n84, 205n119,
    225n222, 233n250, 236n254, 254, 261n56,
    267n73, 270, 273, 276, 282n117, 297, 299,
    309, 310n240, 320, 322, 329–336, 342,
    343n69, 360
Galilei, Galileo 52
Gander, Hans-Helmuth 3, 28, 59n103, 115n9,
    209n136, 253, 324n307, 365n3
Gawoll, Hans-Jürgen 299n197
Gebauer, Gunter 359n150
Geertz, Clifford 273n92
Gehlen, Arnold 358n145
Genette, Gérard 15, 17
George, Stefan 280n108
Gessmann, Martin 177n22 (misspelled in
    manuscript–please fix)
Gethmann, Carl Friedrich 112n3, 119n27,
    177n22, 208n132, 213, 301, 311, 313
Giddens, Anthony 92n29, 241n271
Gil, Thomas 50n86
Goethe, Johann Wolfgang von 45, 252
Goffman, Erving 149n172
Goldstein, Kurt 149n172
Grabmann, Martin 224n221
Grathoff, Richard 113n3
Greisch, Jean 177n22, 194n67, 206n123,
    219n190, 280n108, 284n127
Grimme, Adolf 1n1, 173n10

HANS-HELMUTH GANDER is professor of philosophy and director of the Husserl Archive at the University of Freiburg.

RYAN DRAKE is associate professor of philosophy at Fairfield University in Connecticut. He specializes in twentieth-century European philosophy and ancient philosophy.

JOSHUA RAYMAN is associate professor of philosophy at the University of South Florida. He is the author of *Kant on Sublimity and Morality*.

CPSIA information can be obtained
at www.ICGtesting.com
Printed in the USA
BVOW08*0933070917

494222BV00007B/145/P